PARIS AT WAR

Paris at War

1939–1944

DAVID DRAKE

THE BELKNAP PRESS OF HARVARD UNIVERSITY PRESS
Cambridge, Massachusetts · London, England · 2015

First printing

Library of Congress Cataloging-in-Publication Data

Drake, David, 1946–
　Paris at war, 1939–1944 / David Drake.
　　　pages cm
　Includes bibliographical references and index.
　ISBN 978-0-674-50481-3 (alk. paper)
　1. World War, 1939–1945—France—Paris.　2. France—History—German
occupation, 1940–1945.　3. Paris (France)—History—1940–1944.　I. Title.
　D762.P3D73 2015
　940.53'44361—dc23

2015011939

To Sarah

and to Kieran, Rachael, Edith, *and* Hadley

Contents

Illustrations follow Chapters 5 and 11

Paris and the department of the Seine

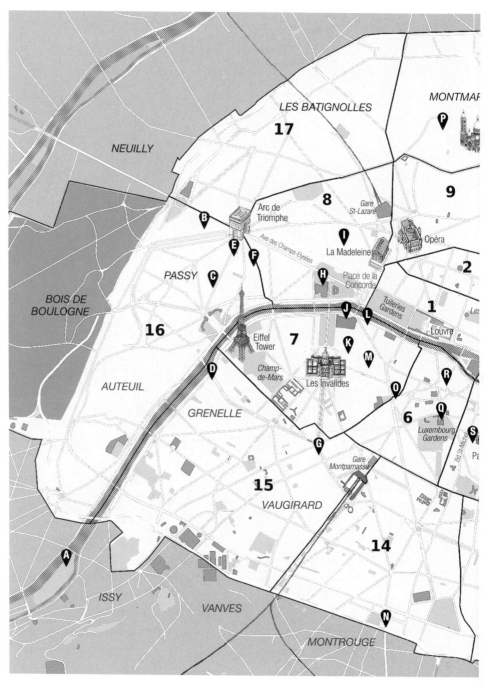

Paris locations mentioned in the text

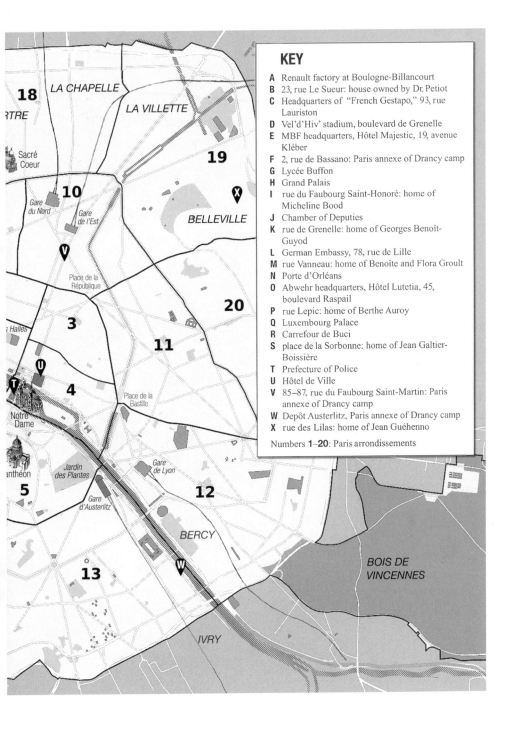

KEY

A Renault factory at Boulogne-Billancourt
B 23, rue Le Sueur: house owned by Dr. Petiot
C Headquarters of "French Gestapo," 93, rue Lauriston
D Vel'd'Hiv' stadium, boulevard de Grenelle
E MBF headquarters, Hôtel Majestic, 19, avenue Kléber
F 2, rue de Bassano: Paris annexe of Drancy camp
G Lycée Buffon
H Grand Palais
I rue du Faubourg Saint-Honoré: home of Micheline Bood
J Chamber of Deputies
K rue de Grenelle: home of Georges Benoît-Guyod
L German Embassy, 78, rue de Lille
M rue Vanneau: home of Benoîte and Flora Groult
N Porte d'Orléans
O Abwehr headquarters, Hôtel Lutetia, 45, boulevard Raspail
P rue Lepic: home of Berthe Auroy
Q Luxembourg Palace
R Carrefour de Buci
S place de la Sorbonne: home of Jean Galtier-Boissière
T Prefecture of Police
U Hôtel de Ville
V 85–87, rue du Faubourg Saint-Martin: Paris annexe of Drancy camp
W Depôt Austerlitz, Paris annexe of Drancy camp
X rue des Lilas: home of Jean Guéhenno

Numbers **1**–**20**: Paris arrondissements

PARIS AT WAR

Prologue

$\mathscr{I}$ₙ 2008, I visited a controversial exhibition of colour photographs of Paris staged in the library devoted to the history of the city. Most of the photos presented a picture of that great city, which, at first glance, was familiar to anyone who knew its quarters, its streets, its boulevards, its people. But there were deeply unsettling aspects to the exhibition: the presence, in a few of the shots, of unwanted, but apparently accepted and unthreatening, "guests" in military uniforms. These were German soldiers, usually shown mingling with the crowds. The pictures had been taken during the Occupation by French photographer André Zucca, who worked for the Wehrmacht photo-magazine *Signal*. Even more than the Teutonic presence, it was precisely Zucca's untroubled, bland depiction of the city that caused many people to take offence. There was much more to the story of occupied Paris than was revealed in Zucca's photographs, as many visitors to the exhibition realised.

I think I was first alerted to the vast difference in the British and French experience of the Second World War when, as a teenager, I spent a month in the summer of 1961 at the home of my French pen friend Pierre, near Lyons, and at Fréjus, on the Mediterranean coast. France during the Second World War has been an interest of mine ever since, and it was certainly a weighty presence when I visited the library exhibition that day.

By then I was already working on this book and had read many diaries and recollections of Parisians of all ages who had been in the city during the war. These people did not hold high office—in many cases they held no office at all—and I knew that their voices would help me to tell a richer, more complex story of what life was like for "ordinary Parisians" than the one Zucca had portrayed. I heartily agreed with a leaflet produced by the Office of the Mayor of Paris and distributed at the exhibition, which stated that Zucca failed to capture "anything, or hardly anything of the harsh realities of life experienced by most Parisians. Suffering, exclusion, and misery are generally absent."

When France went to war against Germany on September 3, 1939, it marked the third armed conflict between these two countries in less than seventy years. Parisians were still alive who could remember the Franco-Prussian War of 1870 and the 1871 siege of Paris. The people of Paris, like all French people, were haunted by the 1914–1918 conflict; most families had lost at least one member in this bloodbath, in which more than six million French soldiers were killed, wounded, taken prisoner, or reported missing (about three-quarters of the total number mobilised), about twice as many as those from Britain and its empire, and almost twenty times the number from the United States.

The five years between the start of the Second World War and the Liberation of Paris (especially the years of the German Occupation, from June 1940 to August 1944) are among the most traumatic in the history of the capital of France: even today, they remain a topic of sensitivity and controversy. That is why, in writing *Paris at War*, I wanted to delve into personal history, remembered conversations, the minutiae of routine, and fragments of memory.

I describe the atmosphere in Paris during the Phoney War that preceded the German onslaught in spring 1940, the mass exodus that followed, and the feeling of abandonment of those who remained behind. The German Occupation saw a majority of Parisians facing growing deprivation while a tiny minority lived the highlife: the collaborationists who enthusiastically aligned themselves with Nazism were mainly based in Paris, but the city also saw the birth and growth of fragmented Resistance groups that formed within months of the arrival of the Germans. The book traces the growth of armed resistance in Paris from the summer of 1941—with German soldiers being gunned down in the street—and the reactions of the population and the German au-

thorities to this dramatic development; I detail the inhumanity of the
rafles—the mass arrest and detention of thousands of Jews—and their
treatment in the camp at Drancy in the Paris suburbs from which tens
of thousands were deported to the death camps, never to return. I write
about the clandestine clubs where Zazous danced the night away to swing
music, the role of the black and grey markets, and the depravity of the
Bonny-Lafont gang (also known as the French Gestapo). There are the
curious details too—like the extraordinary case of a serial killer on
the run who passed himself off as a Resistance fighter. I conclude with
the euphoria of the Liberation of the city in August 1944 and the huge
disappointment that followed as living conditions failed to improve.

I began researching this book about ten years ago. One of the most
vibrant and important sources I found were the memoirs and diaries of
people who were in Paris during the war, many of which have not appeared in English. Among the many witnesses whose testimonies I have
drawn on are a retired schoolmistress living in Montmartre; a Russian-
born Jewish art critic and journalist, deported in 1942 who never came
back; a schoolgirl who joined in the first mass demonstration against
the Occupation in November 1940 and who went on to befriend young
German soldiers; two sisters grappling with the dilemmas and dramas
of adolescence and young womanhood during war, evacuation, and occupation. Other witnesses include a retired military officer with plenty
of time to wander about the city and record what he saw; a Catholic medical student, apolitical in the early days of the war, who took part in the
Liberation of the city; Parisian conscripts who gave insights into what
life was like at the front during the Phoney War; a female Catholic student who was thrown into Drancy for wearing a yellow star in solidarity
with the city's Jews. I have included a list of the main dramatis personae,
as well as a chronology of the period and a glossary of the names of key
organisations towards the end of the book.

My witnesses are not representative of the population of Paris in any
strict sociological sense—I am not aware of any published diaries by
factory workers, for example—whereby a sample would reflect the de-
mographic profile of the population as a whole. But I believe that collectively these testimonies—together with other contemporaneous
material such as police reports and Paris newspapers—do convey a vivid
sense of what living in that occupied city was like; my findings have
also been confirmed by what other people who lived in Paris through

this period have told me. I discovered no diary kept by an "ordinary" collaborationist—but letters denouncing Jews that were sent to the authorities provide a fruitful, albeit depressing source. The accounts of rank-and-file German soldiers in Paris give a useful view of aspects of life in the city as seen through the eyes of the occupiers.

And what about the Wehrmacht top brass, officially in charge of the Occupation, battling to keep Heinrich Himmler's secret police and Otto Abetz, Germany's ambassador to Paris, in their place? I examine those officers' attitude to the Jewish "problem"—and how some of them tried to prevent the plundering of Jewish art treasures by Abetz, Hermann Göring, and the Einsatzstab Reichsleiter Rosenberg (ERR), a shadowy Nazi organisation that began pillaging in the city from the very beginning of the Occupation.

To capture the dynamics of the period, I have opted for a chronological account. I wish to demonstrate how the Paris of the Phoney War was different from the Paris that emerged once the Germans had arrived; how everyday life in Paris changed as the war went on as most of its inhabitants became preoccupied with finding enough to eat, securing enough clothes to wear, and keeping warm. Today, more than seventy years later, we bask in the knowledge of how the Occupation, and indeed the war, ended. Back then, no one knew what history had on offer: would it be a definitive Nazi triumph, liberation, or more moral ambiguities? The testimonies reflect these uncertainties.

Crucial to my research and to identifying the evolution of Paris life were the many hours I spent in the archives of the Prefecture of Police, reading the fortnightly reports filed by members of the French Renseignements généraux, the plainclothes political police (the equivalent of the British Special Branch). These officers gathered intelligence on the mood of the city by hanging around railway stations and eavesdropping on conversations in food queues, cafés, and other public places. They also took notes at officially sanctioned political meetings, recorded Resistance activity and arrests for black-market dealings, made summaries of articles in the collaborationist press, and undertook much more besides. Their reports were available on the flimsy, almost transparent paper on which they had originally been prepared; while reading them I sometimes imagined a moustachioed Frenchman in a smoke-filled room, a black-market Gauloise dangling from the corner of his mouth, hunched over his typewriter hammering out the very words I was now scrutinising. The diaries and the police reports also make clear how Parisians reacted to international events, such as Hitler's failure to invade Britain in 1940, his fateful decision to invade the Soviet Union in June 1941, the German Occupation of the hitherto Unoccupied Zone in November 1942, and the D-Day landings of June 1944. Without dwelling on the machinations of high politics, I wanted to place my account of life in Paris in a national context. From June 1940 Paris was in the Occupied Zone and all its inhabitants were subject to German directives. But, importantly, Parisians, like everyone else in the Occupied Zone, were also subject to laws passed by Marshal Pétain's government in Vichy, located in the Unoccupied Zone, as Jews and Freemasons in Paris soon discovered. It was the French police who provided the manpower for the *rafles*, it was French gendarmes who initially policed the camp at Drancy, and it was a Vichy law that resulted in hundreds of thousands of young men from all over France (including Paris) being conscripted to work in German factories.

The German bombing of British cities was very much a part of the collective consciousness in postwar Britain. My own father had been a fireman in the London Blitz, and I was born and grew up in the shadow of the war in Exeter, a city in the southwest of England that had been damaged in 1942 during one of Hitler's "Baedecker raids." It was not until I began researching this book that I realised just how extensively Paris had been bombed—mostly by the British and the Americans—whom many Parisians viewed as would-be liberators: in a single fortnight in April 1944, for example, more than 1,500 people in Paris and its suburbs were killed in Allied bombing raids. The diarists revealed how Parisians responded to the raids and to the anti-British and anti-American propaganda campaigns waged in the collaborationist press.

My childhood in the 1950s was full of books, comics, and films about the Second World War. But it was not until that summer in 1961, which I spent with Pierre and his parents, when things began to make another kind of sense. Although the experiences of Pierre's parents took place in and around Lyons and therefore do not feature in this book, they were formational in my understanding of the profound difference between wartime Britain and France. Pierre's father was conscripted to work in Germany, but, like many other conscripts, he "missed his train," went into hiding, and joined the Resistance. With false papers he worked in a munitions factory, where he had a brief to sabotage whatever operations he could. Pierre's mother, aged seventeen in 1940, was in a small Resistance group specialising in forging identity papers. On one occasion she narrowly avoided arrest but a good friend was caught by the Nazis, doused in petrol, set alight, and burned alive. In July 1944, on the edge of a village just across the road from where Pierre and his family lived, fifty-two men aged between seventeen and forty-five, most of whom were Jews, were brought from prison in Lyons and executed by Germans soldiers who then went on their way singing, leaving the bodies where they lay.

As a child and a teenager I had seen plenty of bombsites at home in Exeter but I had never before seen gaping holes like the ones in the walls of houses near the seafront at Fréjus caused by tanks and heavy artillery during the Allied landings on August 15, 1944, that were still visible in the early 1960s. Near some rocks where Pierre and I used to go snorkelling we could clearly see an Allied landing craft rusting on the seabed, and all the locals seemed to have army shovels that the Allied soldiers abandoned when they made their way north.

Seven years after that summer I studied in Paris for a year. That was in the autumn of 1968, just a few months after the "events" of May and June—another time when the French reassessed the past—and when, incidentally, protesting students shocked many of the city's inhabitants by likening the behaviour of the Paris police to that of the German SS. Although I subsequently devoted much time to writing about French intellectuals (especially Jean-Paul Sartre) and politics, my interest in France and the Second World War persisted, featuring in courses on French politics and society that I taught at universities in London beginning in the early 1990s. In 2004, when I started teaching at the Institute of European Studies at Paris VIII University, I decided to take my interest in the Second World War further by writing this book.

Introduction: The Road to War

SEPTEMBER 1938–SEPTEMBER 1939

O N SEPTEMBER 30, 1938, huge crowds lined the road from Le Bourget airport to Paris to welcome Édouard Daladier, the head of the French government. He was just back from Munich where he had signed an agreement with German chancellor Adolf Hitler, Italian dictator Benito Mussolini, and British prime minister Neville Chamberlain. The crowds believed, or at least desperately hoped, that the Munich Agreement, allowing Hitler to annexe the Sudetenland (the German-speaking part of Czechoslovakia), meant that war had been averted. After a long wait in the sunshine they were now cheering, waving French flags and throwing flowers, as Daladier, standing upright in the back of an open-topped car sped past on his way to the French capital. The Paris press, too, believed that war had been avoided: "Victory! Victory! Victory!" declared *Le Matin*. "Peace! Peace! Peace!" echoed *Paris-Soir*.

However, not everyone was as joyous as those who turned out to greet Daladier. Léon Blum, the former head of the Popular Front government, privately confessed to feeling "cowardly relief." Ernst Erich Noth, a German writer, literary critic, and anti-Nazi refugee, watched newsreel coverage of Daladier's return in a cinema on the Champs-Élysées. He thought Daladier appeared "pre-occupied, anxious and frightened," as if he could not believe the rapturous welcome he received at the airport and on his triumphal drive to Paris.[1] Perhaps Noth was on to something, since Daladier is reported to have muttered on seeing the jubilant crowds at Le Bourget, "The imbeciles—if only they knew what they were acclaiming."[2]

Daladier recognised that by acceding to Hitler's territorial claim to much of Czechoslovakia at Munich he had colluded in its dismemberment. Unlike Chamberlain, Daladier did not believe Hitler when he protested that he had no intention of annexing any other territory; Daladier believed that, at best, France had bought some breathing space; and when he reached his home in Paris, he immediately warned his son that he would soon be packing his bags and setting off to war.[3]

On March 15, 1939, Hitler's forces again marched into Czechoslovakia, taking over Bohemia and establishing a protectorate in Slovakia. Next Hitler threatened Poland by demanding that Danzig (Gdańsk) be attached to the Third Reich. France and Britain duly issued promises to defend Polish territorial integrity against any German aggression, hoping that the prospect of a war pitting Germany against the joint forces of Britain and France would stop Hitler in his tracks.[4] This new standoff triggered an increase in international tension, raising fears in Paris—as in the rest of France—that war was once again looming. As the French Communist philosopher Henri Lefebvre wrote in a letter in April 1939: "We live in a strange intermediate state between peace and war."[5]

This fear of France being sucked into a war with Germany over Poland conjured up terrible memories of the four-year traumatic bloodbath of the First World War. The revulsion at the thought of another conflict fuelled pacifist sentiments in all social classes across the country. Marcel Déat,[6] a former government minister and socialist who had travelled from the Left to the Far Right, caught this mood in May 1939 in a controversial newspaper article in which he concluded that it was not worth French people dying to save Danzig.[7]

By the summer more and more people were coming to believe that war was not far off: an opinion poll in July revealed that 45 percent of those questioned believed that war would be declared before the year was out, compared to 37 percent only three months earlier. Although pacifist sentiments were widespread, there were still those who feared that if Britain and France did not make a stand against Hitler the whole of Europe would soon be under the Nazi jackboot. The same poll revealed that just over three-quarters of those questioned believed that France should intervene, using force if necessary, if Germany tried to seize Danzig.[8]

The Daladier government was threatening to retaliate against Germany should Hitler invade Poland while simultaneously struggling to pursue a strategy that would maintain peace in Europe. The government hoped to keep Hitler in check by very publicly assuring that war would not break out and believing, or at least hoping, that Hitler would not be foolish enough to pick a fight with France. On July 3, Parisians could read newspaper reports of a speech made in Lille the previous day by General Maxime Weygand, one of France's top military men, now retired, in which the general stated: "I believe that the French army is in a better shape than at any time in its history. It has top quality equipment, first-class fortifications, its morale is excellent and it has a remarkably talented high command. Nobody in France wants war but I can assure you that if we are forced to win another victory, win it we shall."[9] Less than a fortnight later, the Parisians had a chance to see France's fighting forces for themselves.

The annual Bastille Day parade held in Paris on July 14, 1939, marked the 150th anniversary of the storming of the Bastille prison at the beginning of the French Revolution.[10] It also provided the government with its annual opportunity to reveal to the world France's military might. On that day, according to the newspaper *Le Matin*,[11] two million people braved the blustery summer showers and lined the Champs-Élysées to watch and cheer as a cavalcade of tanks and more than 35,000 soldiers proceeded down the famous avenue. This carefully choreographed display was aimed at reassuring the French that their country was well prepared should Hitler be reckless enough to provoke a war.

Significantly, the July 14 parade included soldiers brought from the "invincible" Maginot Line,[12] the jewel in the crown of France's defences. This massive fortification, generally believed to be impenetrable, ran for 100 miles along part of the Franco-German border, starting near Basel in Switzerland and stretching to Haguenau about twenty miles north of Strasbourg. It was more than seven miles wide and any invading land force attempting to breach it would need to overcome barbed wire, pillboxes, land mines, and lines of iron anti-tank spikes set in concrete. Some sixty feet below ground lay a complex network of tunnels, barracks, hospitals and even cinemas. This "Great Wall" of France seemed to provide a cast-iron—or rather, a reinforced-concrete—guarantee that Germany would be incapable of mounting a land offensive against France. The Maginot Line did not continue farther along the border, since the French generals believed it would be impossible for Germany to mount a land invasion through the dense forests and hilly terrain of the Ardennes.

The Bastille Day parade was also a reminder that France was not alone. The newspaper *Le Journal* carried a headline (in English), "A Hearty Welcome to Our British Friends" above a colour drawing of two children waving the Union flag and the French tricolour. At the parade itself British minister of war Leslie Hore-Belisha, chief of the Imperial General Staff of the British army General John Gort—the professional head of the army—and head of the Royal Air Force (RAF) Sir Cyril Newall were among the guests of honour. They watched as troops from mainland France, the Foreign Legion, and the French Empire marched past, along with soldiers from the British Grenadiers, the Coldstream Guards, and the Scots, Irish and Welsh Guards, while planes from the RAF and the French air force roared overhead in a symbolic confirmation of the Franco-British alliance. Meanwhile, as if to reinforce the message, the Imperial Cinema was showing *Entente Cordiale*, starring Gaby Morlay as Queen Victoria and Victor Francen as Edward VII.

The detachments of marching soldiers from Algeria, Morocco, Tunisia, Senegal, and Indochina provided a reminder that, should it come to war, France would also be able to call on soldiers from the colonies of her extensive empire. The theme of the inseparable links between France and its empire was driven home that evening during a radio broadcast, when an inhabitant of Alsace, a silk manufacturer from Lyons, a metalworker, a man of Chinese descent from Annam (today Vietnam), a holy man from Senegal, and a Tunisian lawyer extolled the values of France and French civilisation.

As well as a public reminder of France's military might and global reach, the parade was also designed to impress German officials in Paris in the hope that reports to Berlin of such a show of strength would give the Führer pause for thought.

But Hitler did not look as if he was about to be deterred from his intention to invade Poland. On August 23, while he was finalising his plans, France and the wider world were shaken to the core by news of the signing of a non-aggression pact between Nazi Germany and Communist Russia.[13] If the pact caught the British and French governments by surprise, it threw the French Communist Party (PCF) into turmoil. The Soviet Union had set itself up as the world leader of the anti-fascist struggle and the Communist parties across the globe had been loyally following strategic and tactical directives laid down by Moscow and communicated through the Third International (also known as the Comintern). In France, as elsewhere in Europe, Communists had marched against fascism and battled its supporters in the streets; Communists had gone to Spain to take up arms against the fascists in the Spanish Civil War (1936–1939). For many Communists and socialists in Europe, it was as hard as it was incomprehensible to see the Soviet Union supping with the devil.

In Paris, rank-and-file PCF members, and indeed some of its leaders, were stunned. One cadre in Paris wept on hearing the news, another individual locked himself in his office for two days, while Ilya Ehrenbourg, the Russian journalist, author, and veteran of the Spanish Civil War, could neither eat nor sleep. According to Pierre-Laurent Darnar, former editor of the PCF daily newspaper *L'Humanité*, news of the pact "came crashing down like a paving stone onto the heads of the Party cadres" and provoked cries of "It isn't possible" throughout the ranks of the Party.[14] French fellow-traveller and author Romain Rolland spoke for many other Communist sympathisers when he noted in his diary on 24 August: "None of us can understand such a betrayal at a time when Hitler posed a greater threat than ever to the democracies."[15]

The signing of the non-aggression pact greatly increased the probability of war, since Hitler now had a guarantee that Russia would not intervene if he attacked Poland. As Simone de Beauvoir, then a secondary school teacher and would-be philosopher/writer noted: "What a blow! Stalin has left Hitler free to attack Europe. The chance for peace has gone forever . . . Stalin couldn't care less about the European proletariat."[16] Members of Far Right nationalist groups in Paris gathered outside the PCF headquarters, howling for Communists to be shot as traitors—a demand publicised with relish by conservative newspapers. Within a few days, "communism" had become Public Enemy Number One, with many of the French people and its government appearing to be angrier about the Soviet "betrayal" than they were about the threat posed by Hitler.[17]

In 1939 the PCF was the biggest single political party in France: it had over seventy elected parliamentary *députés*, two senators, and the

support of over a million and a half voters. Its headquarters were in
Paris; its leading members lived there, as did around a third of its rank
and file, making Paris and its suburbs by far the greatest concentration
of Communist support in the country. The Paris region was the heart
of French industrial production, most of which was located in the city's
working-class, suburban "red belt," so-called because of the number of
Communist Party members and sympathisers living there.[18]

Most ordinary Communists were bewildered, disgusted, or disillusioned by the signing of the pact. Some resigned on the spot; many
stopped being active members. A few remained loyal, stubbornly hoping
against hope that Stalin was cunningly following a new revolutionary
strategy. On 25 August the Daladier government responded to the
Communist Party's support for the non-aggression pact by seizing
L'Humanité, the party's daily and its evening paper *Ce Soir* as well. The
police raided party premises and the homes of known militants; they
seized leaflets and anyone distributing them was arrested and imprisoned.[19] Suspected foreign Communist sympathisers—above all, Spanish
Republican refugees and anti-Nazi militants, who had fled from Austria and Germany—were deported or interned in appalling conditions
in concentration camps.[20]

While the government began its offensive against the "unpatriotic" Communists, most people still clung to the hope that war might
be avoided. Less hopeful, the government, like the Prefecture of
the Seine—the administrative authority for the Seine department,
which included Paris—had already begun introducing precautionary
measures.

On August 24, the day after the pact was signed, the government instructed 350,000 French reservists to join their units, followed two days
later by more than double that number. Simone de Beauvoir described
the prevailing atmosphere in Paris at the time as "a mixture of brag-
gadocio and cowardice, hopelessness and panic."[21] Rail travel between
France and Germany was suspended and war appeared almost inevitable. Charles Braibant, a fifty-year-old archivist, wrote in his diary,
"Daladier used to put the chances of peace 3 or 4 out of 10, but since the
signature of the Hitler-Stalin Pact the chances are down to 1 in 10."[22]

Without abandoning their trust in the government, some fearful
Parisians were turning to religion and superstition. On Sunday, August 27, 20,000 Parisians made their way up to the Sacré-Coeur basilica

in Montmartre, which had been built to give thanks for the deliverance of the city from the 1871 Paris Commune. Here they listened to a stirring appeal for peace delivered by Cardinal Verdier, who reassured them that God, who had heard their prayers for peace a year earlier at the time of Munich, had a special place in his heart for France. He urged them to have faith, confidence, and hope as they once again prayed for peace.[23] Similar prayers were heard in other churches across the city, and in an address a day earlier the chief rabbi Julien Weill had declared his hope that wisdom and reason would triumph over fanaticism and violence.[24]

The following day an astrologer assured the readers of *Le Journal* that "there would be no war that summer" since Hitler's and Mussolini's horoscopes revealed "strange weaknesses." Another astrologer foresaw that 1940 would be a year of French grandeur, predicting that "Poland will crush Germany, Mussolini will be dismissed by the King of Italy, Hitler will be locked up in a lunatic asylum and the civil war that will follow his fall will be ended by French intervention."[25] Meanwhile, pessimists pointed to the number of Bohemian waxwings that had been seen that summer in Germany and in the east of France. Thought to be harbingers of catastrophe, these birds had allegedly been observed in large numbers in 1870 and 1914, the last two occasions when France and Germany went to war.[26]

On August 29 the front page of *Le Matin* carried an article on how the threat of war had transformed Paris. Shops were plunged into darkness; lighting used for advertising was extinguished; trucks in Les Halles market were requisitioned by the army and replaced by horses. In the interest of security, while private telephone subscribers could continue to call other private subscribers within the Paris area, calls to numbers outside Paris could be made only from post offices and callers had to produce proof of identity. It was forbidden to use public telephones, including those in cafés and hotels, to make phone calls within Paris during the evening, and any telegrams to be sent abroad had first to be vetted by the local head of police.[27]

At this time, France was divided into ninety *départements*, or departments—administrative areas, each one headed by a *préfet*, or prefect. Paris was in the Seine department, one of the smallest but most densely populated and its prefect, Achille Villey,[28] was the official ultimately responsible for its administration. Earlier in August he decreed that children from Paris and the suburbs, many of whom were already away from the city in summer holiday camps for youngsters *(colonies de vacances)*, should remain there with their monitors. On August 30 the evacuation of the boys and girls who were still in the city began. The following day, photos of the evacuees at the capital's main railway stations were splashed all over the Paris newspapers, while boy scouts aged fourteen and over from the city were allowed to go to the countryside and work on the land, replacing agricultural workers who had been called up. More than 16,000 evacuee children left Paris for the provinces on August 30,[29] and on September 1 *Le Matin* announced that more than 31,000 of them had been evacuated in twenty-four hours.[30]

Each of the twenty Paris arrondissements (municipal administrative areas) was linked to a particular department or city in the provinces. In the event of a general evacuation of the city, parents were to be sent to the same part of France as their children, but it did not always go according to plan. For example, the cathedral city of Chartres was expecting to welcome children from the 2nd and 3rd Paris arrondissements, but soon discovered that it had to host children from six other arrondissements as well.[31] It was not just children: as many as 500,000 Parisians left the city during the first few days of September.[32]

Things were not easy for those outside Paris, where towns and villages were filled with evacuees. The arrival of these incomers in the Yonne department, for example, placed heavy demands on an area that had already hosted a wave of refugees from the Spanish Civil War. The influx of Parisians reignited traditional tensions between city-dwellers and country folk and cases occurred of adults and children being put on trains back to Paris. Nevertheless, the exodus from Paris continued over the months ahead. It was all very well for the minister of the interior to call on towns and villages to improve facilities for the refugees, but across France local councils complained they had neither sufficient accommodation nor the resources to cope.[33]

Besides the hundreds of thousands who opted to leave Paris, many wealthy Parisians who were holidaying in their second homes decided to stay there, reasoning that if war did break out they would be safer in the provinces than in the capital. The city's treasures were also being taken out of harm's way. Thousands of precious panes of stained glass, including windows from the basilica in the northern suburb of Saint-

Denis (the final resting place of the kings and queens of France), from Notre-Dame Cathedral, from la Sainte-Chapelle, and from the churches of Saint-Eustache and Saint-Séverin, were removed and taken away from the city for safe-keeping, as were treasures from the Louvre and other museums.

During the Munich crisis a year earlier, the *Mona Lisa* had been temporarily taken to the château at Chambord on the River Loire, before being brought back to Paris once peace seemed secure. Now she was ready to make the trip again in a specially designed crate as part of a convoy of fourteen trucks.[34] Among the other art treasures that were removed from Paris were the three-ton marble statue the Victory of Samothrace, a tiny twenty-carat diamond that had belonged to Louis XIV, an extremely fragile Egyptian Book of the Dead, and Veronese's enormous *The Wedding at Cana*, measuring 7 metres high and 10 metres wide. *The Wedding at Cana*, along with other large paintings by Courbet, David, Rubens, and Géricault, was carried to safety, thanks to the administrator at the Comédie-Française theatre company, who provided large trucks that were normally used for transporting scenery. These huge vehicles crawled along, preceded by a team from the French telecommunications company (PTT), who raised any overhead cables in danger of snagging the trucks.[35]

As people and treasures were being moved to safety away from Paris, the face of the city itself was changing radically. Sandbags were stacked around national monuments, buildings, and statues, including those on the place de la Concorde, and the ones of Louis XIV in the place des Victoires and Henri IV on the pont Neuf, in the hope that this would protect them in the event of German bombing raids. Treasures within buildings that could not be moved were also given some rudimentary protection: Napoleon's tomb in Les Invalides, for example, was shielded by a wooden frame and a pyramid of sandbags. Paris was being placed on a war-footing, even if nobody would say so officially and the government continued talking about peace.

The government had been preparing for war for some time. In 1938 the street lamps of Paris were fitted with dimmers, and the lampposts were wrapped in protective sleeves, should a driver crash into one during a blackout. Earlier in 1939, the Défense passive (DP), the civil defence organisation, mounted a week-long exhibition in front of Les Invalides, where visitors could see mock-ups of air-raid shelters. Classes on civil defence had been obligatory in school since May, and the Ministries of Defence and Education publishing a joint guide to civil defence for children to take home and discuss with their parents. The head-quarters of the Paris police (the Prefecture of Police, located on the Île de la Cité, opposite Notre-Dame Cathedral) also published a booklet of its own with a slogan on the cover, "Read and keep this brochure safely. It could save your life one day." Inside it detailed what to do in the event of bombing raids or gas attacks, and set out what to do if an air-raid alert sounded.[36]

On the morning of September 1, 1939, Simone de Beauvoir was in the Dôme café in Montparnasse, feeling in a good mood for the first time in days and believing that her life was happy and balanced. She had just ordered a coffee when the waiter told her that Germany had declared war on Poland. He had heard it from a customer, who had read it in the newspaper *Paris-Midi;* shortly afterwards the German army invaded Poland. The news that Germany had declared war on Poland had broken too late for the morning papers, but the signs were not looking good as *Le Matin* carried another reminder from the govern-ment that all Parisians who had somewhere to go should leave the city as soon as possible.[37]

That afternoon a radio broadcast announced a general call-up, starting at midnight, and Paris was covered with posters publicising the decision. Crowds gathered in front of them as well as in front of posters issued by the prefect of the Seine, appealing to the inhabitants of the capital to do their duty: "Parisians, our country is in danger and with it our freedoms. . . . As always, Parisians will do their duty while re-maining cool, calm and collected. They will all enthusiastically rally to the flag and defend the same ideal. *Vive la France.*" Such words were no doubt intended to reassure and encourage a sense of solidarity, but by the end of the day, many Parisians, like de Beauvoir, were wracked with fear and uncertainty and saw the future as a huge, dangerous void: "An elusive sense of horror underpinned everything in the here and now and that lay ahead: you could not predict anything, imagine anything or relate to anything."[38]

The call-up in the city went smoothly. On his return from the Gare de l'Est, the main railway station from which conscripts were leaving Paris, Anatole de Monzie, the French minister of public works, noted with some satisfaction: "No frenzy, no dissent."[39] The German chargé d'affaires concurred, informing Berlin that "the population has greeted the call-up calmly and, according to our military attaché, it is taking place in an orderly way according to plan."[40] However, this is not how it appeared to Simone de Beauvoir, who accompanied her friend and lover Jean-Paul Sartre[41] as he reported to his designated assembly point in a square[42] near the Porte de la Chapelle. The square was deserted apart from two gendarmes, who told Sartre to come back at 5 A.M. Very early the next morning de Beauvoir and Sartre made their way in the moonlight, through almost empty streets to one of their favourite haunts, the Dôme where de Beauvoir had first heard about the German invasion of Poland. Now the café was noisy and packed with men in uniform. The couple stopped there long enough for a coffee before returning to the assembly point by taxi. The ghostly moonlit square was still empty, except for the same two gendarmes, who this time redirected Sartre to the Gare de l'Est. "It was like a novel by Kafka," de Beauvoir wrote in her diary.[43]

The Gare de l'Est was almost empty when Sartre eventually boarded his train bound for Nancy shortly before 8 A.M., but a few hours later the station was packed with men, the young and the not-so young, waiting to board the trains that would take them off to war. In all, some five million Frenchmen were mobilised, of whom almost 40 percent had fought in the 1914–1918 war but who were still considered young enough to be called up again.[44]

Some of the conscripts waiting on the platforms had arrived in Paris from the provinces, where they had bid *au revoir* to friends and family. They now stood alone, unlike those from Paris and the suburbs, who were mostly accompanied by wives or mothers or girlfriends and sometimes children. Alain Laubreaux, the anti-Semite and Far Right journalist who visited the Gare Montparnasse railway station, caught the subdued but powerful emotional dimension of the whole business. "Groups of women weeping in silence . . . I recalled when my older brother went off in 1914 in the midst of people who were wailing. This time it was nothing like that. A great sadness; an almost bovine-like submission to fate."[45]

The atmosphere was sober and subdued with the conscripts at best compliant, at worst resentful. Jean Paulhan, editor of the prestigious *La Nouvelle Revue française*, described the mood as one of "a sort of surprised resignation."[46] There was certainly none of the bravado seen in some Paris railway stations in August 1914, when Frenchmen in uniform had set off to war in high spirits, confident they would reclaim Alsace-Lorraine, beat the Hun, and be home in time for Christmas.

Sartre's recollection of his first hours as a conscript was typical: "I found myself torn away from the place where I was and from those dear to me. I was taken by train to a place where I had no desire to go, with guys who were no keener than I, who were still in civvies, as I was, and who were asking themselves, as I was, how we had ended up here like this."[47]

The conscripts may have left their loved ones in a mood of subdued resentment and resignation, but away from the railway stations it was a different story. Edmond Dubois, a Paris-based Swiss journalist, wrote of a Paris teeming with people in a high state of agitation: fathers rushing to settle wives and children in the countryside; businessmen making plans to move out; factory owners trying to cope with the mobilisation, which would deprive them of some of their best workers; those who were worried and anxious; and those claiming to be privy to inside information, who behaved as if they were acting on advice from the head of the government himself. He noted: "And then there were those who were simply scared stiff and who spread panic around them wherever they went."[48]

The morning papers of September 2 carried detailed instructions as to how victims of a bomb or gas attack on the city should be treated. They also included a drawing of a strange many-legged insect; in fact, it was Paris, the eleven "legs" of the creature being routes out of the city for motorists.[49] In addition, large boards were erected at major junctions and in squares of the city, indicating the routes, signposted with numbered arrows, that those leaving the city by road should take. Civilians who failed to follow the official routes risked getting snarled up in military traffic, including soldiers and equipment heading north to the front.

Not surprisingly parts of Paris soon became clogged with cars, crammed with people and possessions, heading for the main roads out of the city. The right-wing author Alfred Fabre-Luce wrote of "terrified families with luggage, furniture and mattresses on the roofs of their cars. They had assembled everything in haste as if the enemy planes were already there."[50] Dubois described "overladen cars burdened with human cargoes and luggage heading for the Basque coast, Normandy and secret hideaways in the provinces," adding, "The whole of France is on the move whirling around in a frantic circle with Paris at its centre."[51] At the same time almost as many cars were racing back to Paris carrying people desperate to sort out their affairs, withdraw money from banks, or hide their valuables.[52]

For those who wanted to leave the city but had neither a car nor a friend to give them a lift, there was always the train. From September 2 the prefect of the Seine had posted notices informing Parisians that for ten days the SNCF, the French state-owned railway company, would be running a special service of long-distance trains. Parisians could take any of these extra 900 trains by presenting a ticket, which they could obtain free of charge from local town halls *(mairies)* and schools. Would-be passengers were told to make sure they had their identity papers and they were advised to bring two cold meals, a blanket and, if possible, a sleeping bag. Only hand luggage would be permitted. Passengers were also informed that, before leaving home, they should switch off the gas on the landing with a special key, following instructions given in the Paris press. However, so many people responded to the government's call to leave Paris that the system virtually ground to a halt with the eight-seat compartments in the trains full to overflowing and trains running up to two days late.

On the afternoon of September 2, as conscripts were being transported to their barracks outside Paris, thousands more children were being evacuated and Parisian motorists were trying to get out of the city as fast as they could, Daladier addressed the Chambre des députés (Chamber of Deputies), the lower house of the French parliament, in its building across the Seine from the place de la Concorde. He called on his fellow parliamentarians to vote for extra military credits to "meet the obligations of the international situation"; this they duly did, with only a handful voting against and some twenty abstentions. Daladier frequently used the word "peace" in his speech, referring only sparingly to "war," but it was war that now seemed inescapable.

The government was haunted by fears of a German gas or bomb attack on the city. It believed a raid would most likely be launched at night, so the safest way to protect the Parisian population was a black-out, strictly enforced. On the evening of September 2, Georges Sadoul, a Surrealist-turned-Communist who had been conscripted, was near the Bastille preparing to join his unit in Metz. The civil defence service had turned off all the street lights and he saw all sorts of cars with their headlights off and mattresses strapped onto their roofs driving round the Bastille column as they prepared to flee the capital.[53] Soon, however, the rules concerning car headlights were relaxed a little: they had to be completely blacked out except for a narrow horizontal blue strip or they had to have blue-painted glass, making cars look, according to Simone de Beauvoir, as if they were adorned with "large precious stones."[54] If an air-raid warning sounded, drivers were to switch off their lights, abandon their vehicles, and head straight for the nearest air-raid shelter. Bicycles had to have a white strip painted on the rear mudguard, and pedestrians were urged to make themselves more visible at night by carrying a newspaper or a handkerchief.

That same evening de Beauvoir noticed that the cafés were closing at 11 P.M. and the night clubs were not opening at all; she also saw people on the avenue de l'Opéra queuing for their gas masks. In June the Paris authorities had finally announced that gas masks would be distributed, but because of years of procrastination only about a third of the number needed for the city were available. Parisians were haunted by memories—and in some cases personal experience—of the German use of mustard gas in the trenches in the 1914–1918 war; fears that Paris might be subjected to a gas attack from the air had been heightened by recent reports of Italy using gas in Ethiopia.

Paul Léautaud, an eccentric writer and literary critic, decided to collect a gas mask from his local *mairie* on the day of Germany's invasion of Poland. "It's unbearable," he wrote. "When I tried it on I had to get someone to take it off almost at once. I thought I was going to faint. And moreover, as the officials working in the gas-mask department admit, it *is* difficult to put it on; and the final straw—it is impossible to put on while wearing your glasses."[55] Edmond Dubois was similarly concerned: "A fireman tested the apparatus and concluded it was fit for purpose. I, on the other hand, had a mask that sat so badly on my face that I could breathe freely round the edges and was certain that at the slightest whiff of poisonous gas I would collapse to the ground asphyxiated."[56] The writer Georges Perec recalled the sickening smell of rubber when, as a child, in the cellar of his school, he tried on a gas mask with its huge mica-covered eyeholes.[57]

Meanwhile, thousands of Parisians rushed to join the ranks of the Défense passive (DP), keen to do their bit to protect the city and its population.[58] To be accepted by the DP they had to present their birth certificate and a health certificate; married women needed the written permission of their husbands, and everyone under twenty-one required that of their parents. The Prefecture of Police reserved the right to refuse anyone whose moral standing it considered to be questionable.[59]

For the purposes of civil defence, Paris was divided into approximately 5,000 small areas *(îlots)*, each with its own air-raid warden, who wore a distinctive yellow armband. Working under the air-raid wardens were shelter wardens *(chefs d'abri)*. They were often concierges, responsible for bomb shelters in their buildings, usually in the cellars. Buildings with a shelter had to display a notice to this effect on an outside wall and indicate how many people it could accommodate in addition to the inhabitants. The wardens had to ensure that, in anticipation of a possible gas attack from the air, all ventilation gaps and bricks were blocked up. They also had to check that pickaxes and shovels were at hand so people could dig themselves out if the building was damaged during a bombing raid. No pets were to be brought into the shelters and everyone was to take their gas mask. Tenants were to dispose of any inflammable materials that were not needed and told to use sand and not water, should the building be hit by incendiary devices, since water risked spreading any oil-based inflammable liquid.[60]

By September 3, 1939, Paris had all the trappings of a city already at war: buildings were protected, men had been mobilised, a civil defence service was up and running, and some half a million Parisians and most of the state's most precious art treasures had been moved to safety. "The weather has been marvellous ever since the terrible threat that has prevented us from taking advantage of it,"[61] Charles Braibant wryly noted in his diary, and September 3 itself was, he wrote, a lovely balmy day, which stood in stark contrast to the news that everyone was dreading.

On the same day, in Berlin, Robert Coulondre, the French ambassador, met Joachim von Ribbentrop, a former champagne salesman and now the German minister of foreign affairs. Coulondre informed Ribbentrop that, unless Germany started withdrawing troops from Poland by 5 P.M. that day, France would meet her obligations and come to Poland's aid.

"Very well," replied Ribbentrop, "France will be the aggressor."

"History will be the judge of that," retorted Coulondre.

By five o'clock no response had come from Germany and no withdrawal of German troops from Poland. For the third time in seventy years France was at war with Germany.

I

The Phoney War

SEPTEMBER 3, 1939–MAY 10, 1940

*W*HEN THE POET Paul Valéry heard the news that France was at war, he reacted by mimicking the speaking clock: "At the fourth stroke it will be the end *of the world* precisely."[1] The journalist Geneviève Tabouis was equally fatalistic: "Tomorrow all this will have disappeared; our beloved Paris will exist no more."[2] A writer and journalist, Wladimir d'Ormesson, noted in his diary, "We knew, with a regime run by a bunch of gangsters established at the heart of Europe, that war was inevitable. But now it is here we can't believe that the catastrophe is real. It is a whole civilisation, a way of life, our lives, everything which is collapsing. It is an abyss into which every one of us is falling."[3]

At a quarter to four in the morning on September 4 came the sound the Parisians had been dreading: the wail of the air-raid siren described by the writer and literary critic Paul Léautaud as "a terrible, slow, drawn-out, modulated melody, a cry of anguish and of despair. . . . They really could have found something else," he added grumpily.[4]

At the sound of the sirens, most Parisians rushed for cover, unaware that this was just the first of many, many "practice alerts." Some made for the cellars under the block of flats where they lived, others to one of the eighty or so public shelters. These included designated underground Métro stations, one of the biggest of which—at the place des Fêtes in northeastern Paris—could accommodate up to 5,000 people.[5] But sheltering in the Métro could be dangerous. During the alert on

tables with the same apéritifs in front of them."[47] Many soldiers were enraged at the contrast between the comfortable, relatively "normal" life in Paris and the dull, cold, Spartan life at the front. "What the soldiers cannot forgive about Paris is that life on the home front is the same as it used to be,"[48] wrote Sadoul, while Sartre met a French conscript who was so angered that he raged, "The Parisians deserve to be bombed twice a week."[49]

The main difference that Sadoul observed in Paris was the large number of British soldiers from the British Expeditionary Force who were out on the boulevards. He noted that they were resented because they were paid more than their French counterparts; because they were away from what would be the front line if hostilities broke out; and because (it was rumoured) they were lined up to be used as prison warders if there was any social unrest.[50]

It was a cold winter. A few days before Christmas it was markedly cold in Paris, with heavy falls of snow. For the soldiers it was often worse. At the end of December in Hirsingue, where Georges Sadoul was stationed, the temperature at dawn dropped to below minus 20°C; the troops were confined to barracks, but to stay warm Sadoul and his fellow soldiers had to steal coal from a nearby railway station. Dulled by boredom and cold, many soldiers gave up washing, shaving, getting properly undressed at night, or keeping their quarters clean and tidy.[51] In the new year, Sadoul wrote of travelling theatre groups performing for the soldiers and of games of football and tournaments of card games that were organised to try to cheer up the troops—but nothing had done the trick. "Lots of people drunk this evening," he wrote at the end of February. "As the days pass more and more people are getting drunk, and it is the same story in other units."[52]

In the early weeks of the war the Paris press had been gloating that while Germany had been forced to introduce rationing, French shops remained quite well stocked. Within a few days of the declaration of war, the government had taken steps to protect consumers. Prices were fixed to try to prevent speculation and excessive profiteering, and shopkeepers who broke the law were liable to be fined, to be imprisoned, or to have their business closed down. However, by the end of 1939 things were looking less rosy. It was increasingly difficult for Parisians to buy what they wanted in the shops. Coffee had become scarce and they were encouraged to mix it with chicory and take it with milk; oil, soap, and coal were also hard to find. Despite French government price controls, life was getting more expensive; the cost of domestic gas and water was rising as was the price of clothing, paper, and hardware.

Parisians entered 1940 in a state of confusion and worsening anxiety. The government was failing to provide leadership in promoting unity in the country. Nowhere was this clearer than in the activities of its own News and Information Commissariat (CI). An effective war propaganda service could have tried to build national unity through a clear and repeated articulation of France's war aims, while a subtle use of censorship could have been employed to boost the morale of French soldiers and civilians. However, the CI failed miserably on both counts.

Instead, it banned any film that it believed might run the slightest risk of upsetting or having a depressing effect on its audience. Any music-hall acts that made fun of the French soldier were forbidden as were any plays that presented the military in a poor light. German or Russian films in which the slightest hint of propaganda might be discerned were outlawed; by January 9, 1940, nearly eighty films had been banned, although some were later reprieved.

Nothing was to be reported about any social tensions, strikes, and social movements; nothing about secularism versus clericalism, which characterised so much of social life; nothing that might possibly revive the earlier tensions of the 1930s when it looked as if clashes between Left and Right might propel France into civil war. From January 25 the CI censored any criticism of the French parliament and outlawed the publication of all parliamentary reports. According to the deputy head of the SNCF attached to the Ministry of Armament, censorship "was universally arbitrary, incoherent and absurd, allowing in one place what it banned in another or the other way around and even going as far as censor its own communiqués."[53] On one occasion, the royalist Far Right newspaper *L'Action française* submitted an article protesting against censorship only to find the article itself was censored.[54]

Paris newspapers appeared with more and more white spaces indicating where passages or in some cases whole articles had been removed. The press was even banned from publishing weather reports on the grounds that such information could aid the enemy—as if Germany did not have its own spies, supporters, and sympathisers who could let Berlin know what the weather in Paris was like. In February 1940 the newspaper *Paris-Soir* was obliged to report that twelve people "had to be hospitalised in Paris because they had slipped on the ***** which covered the pavements."[55]

As for the "news" that *could* be published, readers were told that Hitler was so ill that Reichsmarschall Hermann Göring might replace him, and that Germans were suffering a general famine. Readers were also told, among other things, about the poor quality of German planes and the low morale of the Germans as a result of allegedly huge losses incurred during the invasion of Poland, which Giraudoux himself multiplied by five for good measure.[56] Alongside reassuring but bland reports from the military and the government, readers were fed pseudo-patriotic nonsense, such as the story of the seventy-seven-year-old veteran who dyed his hair with shoe polish in order to try to join the army, or the pygmy who, when rejected by the army, picked up his bow and arrows and allegedly told the recruitment panel that he was going to kill himself.[57]

At the front the occasional skirmish still occurred, but no serious engagement took place. Parisians were fed a steady flow of vacuous communiqués that told them nothing. Very occasionally there was good news to report. In March 1940, for example, the magazine *Match*[58] reported that the conscript Joseph Darnand, a future arch-collaborator, had been decorated for returning close to enemy lines to bring back the body of a fellow soldier killed in a brief engagement with the enemy.[59] Brave, certainly, but the fact that *Match* described this as "the most beautiful piece of armed action in this war" six months after war had been declared reveals just how strange the war was. In March, Georges Sadoul studied a page from the newspaper *Paris-Soir* itemising the events of the war so far, and he noted there was not one word about any ground conflict. There was more about diplomatic initiatives against the Soviet Union than there was about any anti-German activity at sea or in the air or even of a diplomatic nature.[60]

As well as keeping tight control over what Paris and the rest of France could read and watch, the CI also broadcast its own radio programmes designed to reassure listeners and stiffen their resolve. Parisians tuned in hoping to hear inspirational rallying calls, but all they got were intellectual musings from Jean Giraudoux. The government's choice of Giraudoux as head of the CI had been quite deliberate: it promoted the view of France—especially Paris, "the city of light"—as the very epitome of culture, civilization, and enlightenment, standing as the absolute antithesis of Nazi Germany's philistinism, barbarism, and ignorance. French "propaganda" would therefore be subtle, refined, and honest, unlike the crude, mendacious rantings of Dr. Josef Goebbels, Hitler's propaganda chief, which Giraudoux described as "spectacular advertising." As Giraudoux delicately put it in a Christmas Eve message to his staff at the Hôtel Continental, "French propaganda is a matter of style, truth, and purity."[61]

But Giraudoux's lofty, abstract offerings were wholly uninspiring. "Democracy," said Giraudoux in an October broadcast, "rather than being this vast truth that blazed above the nation, sometimes accompanied by a little smoke," had become "a sort of secret granted to the [French] soldier, to every [French] soldier."[62] In the same message he described the French soldier as "dressed in that uniform whose colour should make him invisible to the enemy but more visible to his family and the people from his hometown."[63] Giraudoux went on to refer to two opposing armies at rest. "All the soldiers are sleeping, but not the same sleep." According to Giraudoux, the angel of death who was flying above them sensed that the French army was more at ease, more confident, more serene than the German one. The angel regretted he was not the angel of life, able to favour the army over which his flight was so light and easy "but he is the angel of death and has to be impartial. He prepares to select his chosen ones in each camp."[64]

Antoine de Saint-Exupéry, the author of *Le Petit Prince*, referred scathingly to Giraudoux's "intellectual artifices, these amusing little puns, which appeal to the mind, but which have no impact at all on the heart."[65] As the French minister of public works Anatole de Monzie observed, Giraudoux versus Goebbels was like pitting a little dagger against a sword.[66] Not surprisingly, Peter de Polnay, an Anglophile Hungarian living in Paris, believed that the CI (which he referred to as the French Ministry of Information and Censorship) "seemed to be run by a pack of fatuous fools."[67]

At the end of March the government announced the result of its nationwide anticommunist crackdown: more than 2,700 elected Communist councillors had been dismissed, all Communist printing presses had been closed down, and more than 3,400 militants had been arrested, many of them interned in camps. A trial of forty-four Communist parliamentarians, which opened in March, was held in camera and all but three (who had announced their resignation from the party during the trial) were found guilty of reconstituting themselves as a parliamentary group, of requesting a parliamentary debate on peace, and of being linked to the Communist International; they all received stiff prison sentences. In April a decree made the mere possession of Communist propaganda punishable by death.

Although the Right and Far Right were delighted with this anti-communist crackdown, democrats felt that such draconian measures were a mistake. After all, France had gone to war against a dictatorship under the banner of democracy and freedom.

By March, shopping and eating out were becoming increasingly difficult. What Parisians could legally buy and when they could buy it also grew impossibly complicated: in addition to three days when meat could not be sold, the sale of apéritifs was banned on Tuesdays, Thursdays, and Saturdays; the sale of chocolate in shops and restaurants was outlawed on Tuesdays, Wednesdays, and Fridays. However, no acute shortages in the shops yet existed; so, when they could, people just bought extra quantities of the goods they needed.

In April 1940 Paul Reynaud, who had replaced Daladier as the head of the government a month earlier,[68] took to the radio to explain why the government was planning to introduce rationing. He told his listeners that with so many men in the army and away from the fields and the factories, France was producing less than before, but consumption remained at the same level or higher. Rationing, he asserted, was an equitable way of tackling rising prices and the increase in the cost of living, and it would also reduce waste and prevent stockpiling.

In May, after eight months of the "Phoney War," Parisians had left the harsh winter behind them and, as spring arrived, they felt bemused rather than afraid. Like everyone else in France they were apprehensive about what rationing would mean, confused as to why they were still at war, and wondering how much longer this odd state of affairs was going to last. They were about to find out.

2

Blitzkrieg and Exodus

MAY 10, 1940–JUNE 14, 1940

$\mathcal{I}$N MAY 1940, Michel Junot was living in Paris with his wife and baby son and hoping to secure a senior post in the French civil service. On May 10, a few hours before Winston Churchill replaced Neville Chamberlain as the British prime minister, Michel wrote in his diary: "Woken this morning at 4h 50 by sound of sirens (first alert since February). Aircraft droning overhead. Sound of ack-ack fire. Lydie puts baby Philippe in his carry-cot and goes down to the cellar with him." Michel clearly was not too bothered by the noise since he and his mother stayed looking out of the window watching "the sun rise on a glorious day."[1] Some two hours later he heard on his TSF wireless set that German soldiers had stormed into Belgium and the Netherlands. The Phoney War had ended.

Initially the French high command was not unduly bothered. It had been expecting a German offensive at some point and it was launched against Belgium and the Netherlands just where the French generals thought it would be. Extra French forces were duly moved north to engage with the enemy, in accordance with the French contingency plans. What the French military had not expected at all was a second German offensive in the region of the Ardennes, confident that an attack would be impossible through this hilly, densely wooded area.

As the French generals focused on the fighting in the Low Countries, they were completely unaware that 134,000 German soldiers,

1,222, tanks, and nearly 40,000 trucks—"the greatest traffic jam known to that date in Europe"[2]—were steadily making their way through the forested valleys of the Ardennes, pushing relentlessly towards the River Meuse in four slow-moving columns each nearly 250 miles long.

On May 12, Alexander Werth, the Paris correspondent of the *Manchester Guardian*, accused the French wireless of talking a lot of tripe: "All it says, in effect, is that the Belgians are in full retreat."[3] He noted that the radio's theme tune—the last bars from the Marseillaise—sounded horribly funereal. He resented that the strict government censorship restricted to a ridiculous degree what he, as a journalist, was allowed to file or, as a Paris resident, was allowed to know: "The censorship has caused dreadful harm to France. It has cultivated a smug complacent frame of mind, with victory taken for granted; and I doubt whether, after all this soft soap, French morale will be able to stand up to a terrific *blitzkrieg*. The papers have told us a hundred times that the Maginot Line and its 'extension' are impregnable. Never has the slightest query been allowed to appear in the Press. Well, we shall see."[4]

It was also on May 12 that the first German units reached the Meuse near Sedan, where the Germans had defeated France in 1870, and it was only there that they encountered any serious French resistance. The German High Command responded by sending in about 1,000 Stuka bombers to pound French positions around Sedan. It was one of the heaviest air assaults in military history. Waves of attacks lasting up to eight hours gave the French troops on the ground no option but to take cover or withdraw. This onslaught from the air was followed by ground offensives. By the end of the day on May 13 German troops were on the French side of the river. The French counterattack came too late and, despite fierce and courageous fighting, the French were unable to halt the German advance.

The French government was shaken to its core. Its plans for the defence and protection of Paris, such as they were, were posited on the absolute certainty that the Maginot Line made France invincible to a land invasion from the east. If an attack on Paris did come, the government reasoned, it would come from the air—hence, the importance attached to civil defence, the distribution of gas masks, and the establishment of air-raid shelters.

But the Germans, by fooling the French into thinking the main thrust of their attack would occur farther north, had launched a brilliantly successful land offensive. The protection of Paris was now revealed as ridiculously inadequate. It consisted of an 80-mile semi-circular line of ground defences running west to east to the north of the city with about 200 concrete shelters, a similar number of machine-gun nests, about 1,000 anti-tank tetrahedrons, and some eight miles of anti-tank trenches. Only after the German advance through the Ardennes and the fall of Sedan in May did it begin to be reinforced. Besides the Paris police and the Garde républicaine (the Republican Guard, deployed on state occasions), only two battalions of Senegalese soldiers, four platoons of Gardes mobiles (the state riot police), and a few tanks were available within the capital to defend it.

With the German breakthrough onto French soil, the hitherto guarded optimism of French military and political leaders evaporated. At La Ferté-sous-Jouarre in the headquarters of General Alphonse Georges, commander of the northeastern front, the atmosphere resembled that of a family in which a death had occurred. General André Beaufre described the scene: "Georges got up quickly. . . . He was terribly pale. 'Our front has been broken at Sedan. There has been a collapse. . . .' He flung himself into a chair and burst into tears."[5]

Even after this dramatic turn of events near Sedan, strict censorship ensured that French citizens remained in the dark and had to choose between the hopelessly optimistic and misleading outpourings from the French press and radio, broadcasts from the BBC in London, and triumphalist broadcasts in French from Germany's propaganda station, Radio Stuttgart.

Piecing together what they could, Parisians sensed that all was not going according to plan. Nineteen-year-old Benoîte Groult and her fifteen-year-old sister Flora were daughters of a respectable Paris fashion designer, living in the rue Vaneau in the 7th arrondissement. On May 13 Benoîte was still hoping that Belgium would act as a buffer: "Three air raid alerts yesterday. Events in Belgium mean we are taking them more seriously. We stay in our beds but we're no longer sleeping. We're thinking of these seven or eight million people who are our shield."[6]

On May 14 the Paris newspaper Le Temps told its readers that the situation in the Netherlands had "greatly improved." The next day, a mere five days after the start of the German offensive, the Netherlands surrendered. Paul Reynaud, the French head of government, telephoned Churchill. "We have been defeated," he said. These devastating developments did not reach the journalists in Paris. As Alexander Werth noted that same evening, "Wrote a very dull piece for the paper. The military won't give us any information; so it's just hopeless."[7]

Soon Radio Stuttgart was crowing with news of French and Belgian towns and French positions being taken by the rapidly advancing German army. While Paris newspapers blandly referred to the German tank advances as "commando raids," Benoîte Groult was much nearer the mark: "Bastions are falling around us," she wrote on May 14. "It's rather as if items of clothing were being torn off us one by one. We shall soon be completely naked before the enemy."[8] The next day she wrote in her diary, "People say Paris is under threat,"[9] and named friends who had left the city or were about to do so. On May 16 Alexander Werth echoed this: "No doubt about it. People are clearing out of Paris. Taxis are hard to get. There is panic in the air."[10] Thousands of Parisians who had left the city in September 1939 only to return were once again contemplating flight.

Ironically, at this time Paris was not under immediate threat, despite what many Parisians believed. After their breakthrough at Sedan, the German troops had not turned south towards Paris; nor had they turned east to attack the Maginot Line from the rear, as the soldiers on the Maginot Line, their weaponry facing east towards Germany, feared. Instead, the German forces raced westwards and northwards towards the English Channel.

On May 16, the day after Reynaud's telephone call, Churchill arrived in Paris for a meeting with French leaders. "Utter dejection was written on every face," Churchill noted. He asked General Maurice Gamelin, commander-in-chief of France's armed forces, where he proposed to attack the German flanks. Gamelin replied, " 'Inferiority of numbers, inferiority of equipment, inferiority of method'—and then a hopeless shrug of the shoulders."[11]

On the battlefield, despite having been let down by incompetent leaders whose defensive, static strategic mind-set was straight out of a 1914–1918 war manual, French soldiers fought back bravely. A German officer wrote of a Moroccan cavalry brigade, half of whom were killed in a battle near Sedan: "I have fought against many enemies in both wars. . . . Seldom has anyone fought as outstandingly."[12] At the end of a fierce tank battle in central Belgium, a German tank commander, Ernst von Jungenfeld, paid an indirect tribute to the French when he described the fighting as "hard and bloody" and wrote how "many a brave [German] *Panzermann* had to lay down his life for the Fatherland, many were wounded, and a large number of tanks was lost."[13]

As the German army swept on towards the English Channel, the French government still refused to recognise publicly the gravity of the situation. It continued to churn out its cocktail of misinformation and platitudes. The vacuum this created was soon filled by rumour, frequently printed in the Paris papers as "news." A recurrent buzz was that German parachutists (in some versions disguised as nuns) had been dropped into Paris. Percy Philip, a *New York Times* journalist, was mistaken for a parachutist and almost lynched on the place de l'Alma.[14] Other rumours claimed that certain French ministers and military leaders had died or committed suicide. Still others asserted that Hitler had been taken prisoner, that the Soviet Union had declared war on Germany, or yet again that the Germans had dropped poisoned sweets on the capital and some children had already died.[15] All this fuelled the rising sense of fear and anxiety among Parisians, who by now were increasingly asking themselves what was really going on and why they were not being told.

On May 17 Reynaud made a radio broadcast in which he finally conceded that some serious military reverses had occurred. He emphatically dismissed "the most absurd rumours that are circulating. People are saying the government wants to leave Paris. This is untrue. The government is in Paris and will remain in Paris."[16] Even if Goebbels's propaganda unit in Berlin was not necessarily the origin of the rumour that the French government planned to flee Paris, it was naturally doing its upmost to spread it, hoping to whip up fear and confusion among the Parisians and their fellow countrymen and women.

On the same day as Reynaud's radio broadcast, Goebbels ordered that everything should be done to generate an atmosphere of panic in France. On May 18 Radio Stuttgart specifically targeted Paris with broadcasts announcing that there were "tumultuous events" in the Métro, that all roads out of the capital were guarded by patrols, and that the government was on the point of leaving Paris for Canada.

Hitler feared that the German army was moving too quickly towards the English Channel, so the advance was briefly halted before Berlin gave the green light to proceed once again. On May 18 Reynaud took advantage of this short-lived pause to take over the post of minister of defence from Daladier, who became foreign minister. The same day, in an attempt to bolster the government's credibility and boost public morale, Reynaud invited Marshal Philippe Pétain, the octogenarian hero of the 1914–1918 war, to return to Paris. Pétain, who until then had been France's ambassador to General Franco's newly victorious right-wing dictatorship, joined Reynaud's government as his deputy. In a radio broadcast Reynaud hailed the marshal's return: "The victor of Verdun, thanks to whom the aggressors of 1916 did not pass, thanks to whom the French army recovered its morale and was victorious . . . is now at my side . . . placing all his wisdom and strength at the service of the country."[17]

The situation on the ground in northern France remained dire. Not that Parisians would know this from reading their newspapers. On May 18 Alexander Werth noted: "*Paris-Soir* says the French soldiers are now getting accustomed to dive bombers, and are quickly learning how to dodge the bombs and bullets." His verdict? "Tripe."[18] Parisians were fed other mendacious "news" items: *Le Figaro* reported that the enemy had stopped at Sedan and the RAF had unleashed a grand offensive, while *Le Jour-Echo de Paris* proclaimed that the German advance seemed to have stalled. *Le Matin* announced that the enemy had lost three times more planes than the Allies.[19]

On Sunday, May 19, Reynaud sacked Gamelin as commander-in-chief of the French armed forces, and he brought General Maxime Weygand out of retirement to replace him. In another public bid to rally Paris and the country, Reynaud, Pétain, and other government ministers, along with the British, American, and Canadian ambassadors, attended special Mass in Notre-Dame Cathedral. There they heard appeals to the Archangel Michael to support France in its conflict, to Saint Louis to protect the government, to Saint Rémy to give France faith, to Saint Joan of Arc to fight alongside the French soldiers, and to Saint Geneviève, the patron saint of Paris. For sceptical Parisians, the sight of so many atheists, agnostics, and Freemasons from the government's ranks trotting out religious litanies and seeking supernatural aid—in a country where state and religion had been separated since 1905—simply confirmed that things were even more desperate than they had thought.

While the government appealed to divine intervention, Werth wrote of Belgian refugees reaching the city and of more Parisians getting ready to leave. "There are lots of Belgian cars with mattresses on their roofs but—also some French cars with the same—and with *Paris* number plates. *On fout le camp*."[20]

Radio Stuttgart kept up its barrage of propaganda: on May 20 its French-language broadcasts told listeners that the government was going to Bordeaux, and two days later it asserted that half the ministers had already moved south to Clermont-Ferrand.[21] The broadcasts lambasted those who wanted to defend Paris; they encouraged demonstrations calling for peace "in order to avoid the worst," blamed the war on the Jews, and, playing on incipient Anglophobia, insisted that the French government was but a tool of *les Anglais* and had no right to speak in the name of France. One of the Germans' favourite ploys to destabilise the capital was the repeated insistence that the city harboured an enormous fifth column of German spies and sympathisers who were poised ready to spring into action. This rattled the city authorities enough for them to mobilise, starting at the end of May, twelve daily armed patrols of the Paris sewers to "provide surveillance, prevent sabotage and, if appropriate, arrest any suspects."[22]

The dribble of Belgian refugees in cars soon became a flood;[23] others were arriving en masse and on foot. There were far more refugees than the Paris authorities had anticipated and makeshift camps had to be set up in schools, stadiums, and hospitals before the refugees could be dispatched farther south by train. The authorities asked the refugees not to talk about their experiences, fearing this would have a demoralising effect on Parisians. The Belgian refugees were joined by others from the Netherlands. The fear was widespread that German spies and fifth columnists would use the flow of refugees as cover for entering the city.

On May 21 Paul Reynaud told the Senate: "The *patrie* is in danger," and, to gasps of bewilderment from the benches of the senators, he announced that the French towns of Amiens and Arras had been taken.[24] Inhabitants from the wealthier *quartiers* took this as their cue to leave the city, but, despite the bad news and these departures, most of the population stayed put—for the time being.

Alexander Werth was also contemplating leaving Paris. On May 22 he went to get some photos taken at a photo booth in the Galeries Lafayette department store.[25] He found "Queues of people who need photos for all the various travel permits. Otherwise the shop is absolutely empty. The only other very busy department is that dealing in trunks and suitcases."[26]

On May 24 Hitler once again halted the German advance in northern France. He had been assured by Hermann Göring, his deputy and the head of the Luftwaffe, that the German air force could finish off the Allied troops. Hitler also wanted to give his soldiers a break before they turned south towards Paris. This reprieve gave General Lord Gort, commander of the British Expeditionary Force (BEF), a chance to re-patriate as many as he could of the 250,000–300,000 BEF soldiers. With approval from London, these men and their materiel headed for Dunkirk, the only English Channel port not under German control. On May 26 the BEF began its retreat across the Channel. The opera-tion was made possible by an armada of small boats, which had chugged over from the south coast of England to take the British soldiers home, along with thousands of French troops, all of whom were caught be-tween the German army and the sea.

German claims that this was a rout[27] were dismissed as lies by the French government. However, official communiqués as to what was actually happening continued to be vague in the extreme. On May 28, Belgium capitulated.

By May 29 a total of 120,000 troops had been evacuated from Dunkirk, including some 6,000 French soldiers. The German troops resumed their advance, and while British and French soldiers continued to be evacuated, French soldiers bravely fought a rear-guard action to keep the Germans at bay. On June 4 the Germans finally took Dunkirk, but not before more than 300,000 troops had been evacuated.[28]

Thanks to their own government's news censorship, Parisians were unaware that plans to establish a line of defence from the Somme to the Maginot Line had been abandoned, and they did not know that the French army had failed to retake Abbeville, Amiens, Laon, and Rethel. But they saw the waves of refugees arriving in the Paris region—not just Belgians, but also ever-increasing numbers of *French* people, both military and civilian, who were fleeing south.

The refugees brought terrifying tales of "attacks by German machine-gunners flying low over the columns of escaping civilians, lost chil-dren often orphaned by these very actions, enemy agents disguised as nuns or even disguised as French officers."[29] The refugees' stories and the sight of French troops in shambolic retreat, scavenging food as they went, fuelled the Parisians' worst nightmares. More and more of them realised that the French army was on the run and the German barbar-ians were on their way.

At the same time, Parisians who remained in the city were determined to carry on as normal, as if doing so would somehow make the war go away. Sunday June 2 was a glorious sunny day and people took trains, buses, cars, and bicycles and headed for the nearby countryside. The day before, Paul Paray had conducted the orchestra at the Opéra in a performance of Berlioz's *The Damnation of Faust* in front of an almost packed house; the nightclubs were still open; the top restaurants were doing a roaring trade; Moliere's *Tartuffe* and *Les Précieuses ridicules* were being performed at the Odéon Theatre; and Parisians were queuing up outside the cinemas to see the latest box-office hits *La Mousson* and *Goodbye, Mr. Chips*. All the while, the official communiqués still failed to communicate what was really happening around Dunkirk or spell out the threat that Paris was facing.[30]

That same day Paul Reynaud and Marshal Pétain visited the city's defences on their way back from a trip to the Somme. They were appalled to see just a few men sitting around near machine guns, watching the refugees stream by. The following day, the Ministry of Labour promised to supply 100,000 workers to build up the city's defences, but this immediately met objections from the military high command, who wanted to know how they would be fed, where they would be housed, and who would supply their tools. Exasperated, Reynaud placed the extensions for the defence of Paris under civilian control, which at a stroke provoked military suspicion of both the workers and of the scheme, while simultaneously adding to the general sense of chaos and unpreparedness.

Efforts to bolster the feeble defences of Paris were complicated not only by the arrival of millions of civilian refugees, but also by the appearance of growing waves of shocked, demoralized, and angry French soldiers. As they did with the Belgian refugees, the Paris authorities tried to prevent these grimy, exhausted men, many accusing their senior officers of betrayal, from making contact with Parisians lest they provoke unrest and undermine the government. Three reception centres were set up just outside Paris at Colombes, Maisons-Laffitte, and Massy, but within days they were full to overflowing and there were not enough trucks or trains to move the troops elsewhere. Because of a shortage of weapons and of senior officers, the soldiers were ordered to set off on foot to Brittany and Lower Normandy, some two hundred miles away. Some decided to opt out altogether by pretending to be civilian refugees. Often soldiers and civilians swapped clothes: the soldiers could go home and the civilians could access food and shelter provided by the army.[31]

On Monday June 3 the first confirmation that Parisians were in danger came not from the French government but from the Germans. Schoolboy and part-time air-raid warden Igor de Schotten was having lunch at his home in the 16th arrondissement in southwestern Paris[32] when the air-raid sirens sounded. Clutching his helmet and gas mask, he put on his official armband and jumped onto his bicycle. He was off to take up his position, as he had been trained to do, at the top of a tall building on the banks of the Seine from where he was charged to report any damage caused by incendiary bombs that he could see. On arrival, he found a huge crowd trying desperately to make its way through the little door to the air-raid shelter in the cellar beneath the building. The main staircase inside was so packed he decided to break the rules and take the lift to the top of the building and then go through the door leading on to the flat roof.

"I opened it," he wrote. "Incredible . . . [German] Stukas swooping down towards me with an ear-splitting roar which gripped my guts and made me shake so much I had to lie down flat on my belly, with my hands over my ears . . . I then stood up and looked across the River Seine above the Citroën factory . . . from about the same height as the building I was in, each plane was releasing a cluster of small bombs. When they exploded, they threw masses of debris into the air in bursts of flames."[33]

He had just witnessed a daring daytime German air raid on Paris, during which more than 200 German aircraft dropped approximately 1,000 bombs in just under an hour in southwestern Paris on the Renault and the Citroën factories, which were both vital contributors to France's war effort. The bombs also damaged homes and other buildings in the largely working-class 15th arrondissement[34] as well as in the adjacent 16th arrondissement, where many well-to-do Parisians lived.

Twenty-four hours after claiming that the raid had caused "only" 200 civilian casualties, including forty-five deaths, the French government had to admit that there had been 906 casualties and 254 deaths, including those of twenty children. The ability of the German air force to carry out a bombing raid on Paris in broad daylight confirmed suspicions of the military superiority of the enemy and encouraged the view that the French government was incapable of protecting Parisians. On the day the city was bombed, the Paris press was still publishing delusional reports, such as the one in the newspaper *Le Jour* that asserted: "The enemy is winning on the map, but that is the extent of his success. His offensive is a failure."[35]

While the Paris authorities were struggling to cope with the influx of civilian and military refugees, they were also trying to reinforce the city's defences. On June 4 General Henri Dentz replaced General Lanoix as commander of the Paris region, while General Pierre Héring was made military governor of Paris itself. This division of authority gave rise to endless arguments between Dentz's and Héring's staff over questions of protocol and about who was responsible for what.

At seven o'clock in the morning of June 5, just thirty-six hours after the bombing raid, the lugubrious voice of Radio-Paris, the Paris radio station, announced that the Germans had launched a new offensive along the Somme. By June 8 the German forces had reached Forges-les-Eaux, a mere 75 miles north of Paris. Extra men had been drafted to man the Paris defences, so that by June 8 some 10,000 soldiers were in place about thirty miles north of Paris together with 200 guns and 30 assault tanks—although only ten were recent models. This effort marked an improvement, but it was scarcely sufficient to defend the capital against a full frontal assault by the German army, which by June 9 was only nineteen miles away.

Ever since the start of the German offensive, the French government had repeated its mantra that it would remain in Paris come what may. The message was meant to reassure Parisians and stand as proof that Paris was not in any immediate danger. It also meant that the converse was true: if the government left, it would mean Paris was under threat. Thus, when Parisians heard on the radio late on June 10 that the government was "obliged to leave the city" for "compelling military reasons," they took this as confirmation that Paris was in danger of becoming a war zone and of falling into German hands. Thousands upon thousands of Parisians followed the government's example and fled south.

According to Colonel Groussard, French chief of staff for the Paris region, "The government's unexpected flight created a situation which was catastrophic for the population of Paris, who were left without directives or even advice. In all classes it provoked a psychosis of panic."[36]

As if this were not bad enough, on the same day that the French government abandoned Paris, Italy declared war on France.

As the Germans advanced towards the city, the Paris newspapers and radio stations attempted to bolster anti-German sentiment and stiffen the resolve of Parisians: they described the Germans as "barbarian hordes," recalling the recent bombing of Rotterdam and Warsaw; they wrote about "German butchers" and compared Hitler to the marauding Attila the Hun. But far from encouraging Parisians to stand firm, this lurid propaganda had the opposite effect. Parisians were already in a state of shock. They felt abandoned. Now folk memories were revived of the 1914–1918 war, when the Kaiser's army was believed to have systematically raped French women, disembowelled children, castrated men, and randomly put out eyes and chopped off hands. Jubilant propaganda broadcasts on Radio Stuttgart also played a part in rattling the Parisians, especially since German news items were nearly always subsequently and grudgingly confirmed by French sources. On June 12 Parisian schoolgirl Micheline Bood wrote in her diary, "At 1:30, Verneuil was bombed. [Radio] Stuttgart had announced it and nobody wanted to believe it. But every time Stuttgart announces something, it happens."[37] By now, more and more Parisians were tuning in to Radio Stuttgart for news, especially once it began broadcasting the names of captured French soldiers.

The bombing raid on June 3, the realisation that the Germans were getting ever closer, the fear generated by German and, inadvertently, anti-German propaganda, and the hasty departure of the French government from Paris resulted in a mass exodus from the city, which swelled the ranks of the refugees already fleeing south. One French historian has written that, of all the shifts of population in May–June 1940, "the exodus of people from the Paris region was, without any doubt, the mass displacement of people that had far and away the greatest impact both topographically and psychologically."[38]

The departure of some three million people from Paris and its immediate surroundings altered the face of the city. "I left Paris," wrote the Swiss journalist Edmond Dubois, "because the face of Paris had suddenly changed."[39] He wrote of the burning of documents by French officials at the Ministry of the Interior, of the offices, theatres, cafés, bars, restaurants, and bakers' shops that had closed. He wrote about the diminishing number of cinemas still in business, with most of those that remained open playing to almost empty houses. It was impossible to telephone anyone outside the Paris area, and when you made a call within the city, no one was there to answer it. There were fewer and fewer cars and buses, and, perhaps most bizarre of all, a herd of hungry, lowing cows wandered unattended around the place de l'Alma. Familiar faces on the street had disappeared. "You cannot imagine how much the street sweeper or news vendor can stabilise confidence on the street," Dubois wrote. "When the street sweeper no longer appears or the news-stand is closed, the locals take fright."[40]

Paris was now close to the state of total panic that Goebbels had aimed to generate. Peter de Polnay dated the start of the "great exodus" from the June 3 bombing raid on the Renault and Citroën factories. "Its first impetus was given by the only blitz on Paris. Rumour and fear and an utter lack of knowing what was happening came next; but mostly fear of the Germans. The simple people believed the Germans would cut their hands off and poke out their eyes. The middle classes, the *bourgeoisie* . . . went because they feared the battle of Paris. But the majority went because their neighbours went."[41]

The exodus included retreating French soldiers joined by fleeing refugees from Belgium, the Netherlands, Luxembourg, northern France, and now Paris: in total between eight and ten million people. Many of them were women: the young and the not so young, grandmothers, mothers—often with young children—and mothers-to-be, fiancées, and adolescent girls.[42]

While Parisians of all social classes fled the city, the better off, often having planned to leave, tended to depart earlier; those who were poorer left later or not at all. A metalworker who cycled through Paris a month or so later noted: "In the rich areas there was nothing. Not a soul. All the windows were locked and bolted—especially in the 16th arrondissement. But there were people around in the popular *quartiers*."[43] As always, the affluent had more options than those who were less well off. Many wealthy Parisians had not returned to the capital after the mini-exodus of September 1939. Those who were still in Paris in May–June had both a means to leave the city (car and petrol) and a place to go, be it a second family home or a rented property in the provinces. They were also rich enough not to have to find work when they reached their destination.

Pierre Mendès France, a *député* from the Radical-Socialist Party and a member of Léon Blum's 1936 Popular Front government, wrote:

"During the early days, we saw sumptuous and fast American cars pass by, driven by chauffeurs in livery; inside were elegant ladies holding their jewellery boxes and men poring over directories or road maps. . . . Then came the older, less smart cars, driven by *petit-bourgeois*, usually accompanied by their families. One or two days later it was the turn of the most incredible contraptions. . . . Then came the cyclists."[44]

Those determined to leave had to decide what to take with them and, more painfully, what to leave behind. Ilya Ehrenbourg, a Paris-based Russian journalist and author, painted an almost surreal picture of some Parisians about to flee the capital. "Here's a man who looks a bit lost carrying an armchair on his back. A little boy clutching his wooden horse from which he did not want to be separated. An old woman who's setting off with a bird in a cage. A man wearing pince-nez with a brief-case under his arm is holding a cat which is miaowing in desperation as it tries to get away. A grandmother is being pushed in a wheelbarrow. A woman is carrying two small children in her arms. What a horrible feeling of anxiety grips my heart in this deserted city."[45] Another eye-witness described the crazy panic on the roads leading to the Porte d'Orléans in the south of the city. "Cars, bicycles, prams, wheelbarrows, filled to overflowing with mattresses, blankets, cats, bird cages, dolls, pots and pans, suitcases fit to burst, parcels of all shapes and sizes. In other words, mad panic."[46]

Conscript Georges Sadoul's unit was heading south. On the road near Longjumeau he, too, saw the aged and infirm being pushed in wheel-barrows; in particular, he noticed one little old lady, who, according to Sadoul, might have thought twice about a long walk in the Luxembourg Gardens and who was now cheerfully making her way along the road with two heavy suitcases and a yappy little dog on a lead, telling everyone she was walking to the city of Orléans, where she planned to catch a train.[47]

Even for those travelling by car it could still be difficult and upsetting having to decide what to take. On June 10 some well-placed friends of the author and historian André Maurois tipped him off that the government was planning to leave Paris, and, possibly because Maurois was Jewish, they advised him to do the same. Early the next morning he and his wife said a final farewell to the Louvre and Notre-Dame. "We went back home and, as millions of Parisians must have been doing at that moment, began to ask ourselves what we could save and take with us. I cannot think of anything more distressing than to look around one's familiar surroundings, at the books one has collected with so much care, at the cupboard full of friendly letters, and to think: 'I've only one car, I must choose and I can choose very little.'" They chose what they thought was absolutely essential or so dear to them that they could not bear to part with it. But when they had chosen, it still proved ten times too much; in any case, they did not have enough bags for all the books and letters and had to buy more.[48]

If books and letters were a priority for the Maurois couple, for others it was luxury goods. Geneviève de Séréville, the fourth wife of the actor and playwright Sacha Guitry, took dozens of bottles of nail varnish, tubes of lipstick, and jars of beauty cream. She was able to do this because she had a spacious Cadillac parked outside their grand house on the avenue Élisée-Reclus near the Eiffel Tower.[49]

In mid-May, a few days after the start of the German offensive, Benoîte and Flora Groult had been sent to stay with their grandmother on the Atlantic coast of Brittany, not far from Quimper.[50] They were still there on June 9 when their cousin Gérald arrived from Paris with his car "piled up to the roof with Sèvres porcelain, jewels, three fur coats, knick-knacks, satin cushions, objects in gold and silver and hat boxes full of men's and women's hats." Cousin Gérald's mother had left a note on the door of her Paris apartment on the exclusive avenue Victor-Hugo, near the Champs-Élysées, addressed to German officers (she assumed only officers would go to her apartment) inviting them to help themselves to food and drink and to listen to the radio but appealing to them in the name of their "good upbringing" to respect the premises and its contents.[51]

In the early days of the exodus, with the roads still relatively uncongested, it was fairly easy for drivers to buy petrol and make rapid progress. Travel proved less easy for those who left later. Soon petrol was in short supply and the main roads south of Paris were littered with abandoned cars that had run out of fuel; in some cases farm animals had been commandeered to tow vehicles. But even if those who had delayed leaving were able to find somewhere or someone still selling petrol and were able to afford the inflated prices that were usually demanded, progress was likely to be very slow, as writer Léon Werth discovered. On his first day on the road he was caught up in "an interminable caravan," crawling along at between five and ten kilometres an hour. Things were even worse on the second day: despite setting off at 4 A.M. it took him fifteen hours to cover ten miles.[52]

The constant stopping and starting put a strain on all the vehicles: gearboxes made ominous grinding noises and radiators threatened to boil over; cars were overtaken by motorcyclists, cyclists, people on strange vehicles cobbled together with planks and old bicycle tyres, and even by pedestrians, some of whom were pushing prams piled high with personal belongings. Werth even saw a man pedalling a delivery tricycle, a woman sitting in the trailer. They were followed by huge, two-wheeled carts pulled by "enormous horses" (presumably carthorses).[53]

The chaos of the exodus was made worse by constant rumours and by practical necessity: where was one supposed to buy more petrol? It was almost impossible to leave "the caravan" since the army was blocking civilian access to other roads to ensure the unimpeded movement of military supplies. "I am the prisoner of a road I have not chosen," Werth complained. "I have become a refugee without a refuge. I am sleepy."[54]

For some of the refugees, the anxiety, the shortage of food, the lack of sleep, the fatigue, and the terror incurred by enemy planes flying low overhead and sometimes opening fire proved too much and they became mentally unbalanced. Léon Werth had left Paris in his car in the morning of June 11. On a road south of Paris he saw a woman jump out of a van, shouting, "We've been sold out! We've been betrayed!" She then tried to direct the traffic. In the ensuing chaos the woman insulted a soldier and screamed for bread and petrol. Werth later met "a sort of emaciated, dishevelled female prophet, spouting abstruse words."[55] Farther on he shared a hayloft with an old woman, who, "in a voice that was both full of rage and whingeing, endlessly bombarded her son and daughter-in-law with insults and reproaches."[56]

Simone de Beauvoir also left Paris on June 11, travelling with Bianca Bienenfeld, a former pupil, in a car driven by Bianca's father.[57] In Angers, where she had arranged to be met by friends, de Beauvoir noticed among the crowd of refugees in front of the station "some mad woman wrapped in a blanket, desperately going round and round the square, pushing a pram piled high with suitcases."[58] On June 16, during a battle between French and German troops for control of the bridges at Orléans, Parisian conscript Georges Sadoul encountered a woman whose terror was such that she had become unhinged. She was so distressed that her female companions were becoming as crazy as she was. Mistaking a passing French convoy for the arrival of a German tank division, they spent the whole night chanting "Heil Hitler! Heil Hitler!"[59]

Although women were still legally inferior to men and were still de-
barred from voting in elections,[60] the crisis compelled them to assume
new responsibilities—and in the most dramatic of circumstances.
Women with husbands conscripted into the armed forces had been
thrust into the role of head of the household, making important financial decisions on their own as well as looking after their children and
the home. On the road, they found support from and solidarity with
other women, which gave them added strength and self-confidence.
Many believed that being part of a crowd meant they were less likely to
make mistakes.[61] "The women are very good, I can tell you," noted
Anne Jacques, who was part of the exodus. "I saw many of them and at
times when they were being put to the test. They are neither chatter-
boxes nor highly strung nor weak: they rely on reason, are calm, generous to one another and often heroic."[62]

Many people in the exodus had strapped one or two mattresses to
the car roof in the belief—or hope—that this would protect them from
attacks from the air. A woman de Beauvoir encountered assured her that
refugees from the north were bringing their dead hidden between mattresses on top of their bullet-ridden cars. This may not be quite as absurd as it seems, if Georgette Guillot is to be believed. In her diary she
claimed she met some people on the road who had left Paris with an
aunt of advanced age who had died on the way. Unable to find anywhere
to leave her body, they put it on top of the car, under a mattress, out of
sight of the children. While the family was resting in a barn, somebody
stole the car, along with the corpse, thus depriving the family of the
evidence required to obtain the death certificate they needed to claim
their inheritance.[63]

Eyewitness accounts of the exodus agree about the chaos of this huge
displacement of refugees, but descriptions of the mood of the exodus
vary. Werth describes it as dreary and monotonous.[64] Others paint a
more upbeat picture. One refugee described it as being like "a large
countryside party,"[65] and Sadoul writes of young women treating the
exodus as a fashion parade, adding that "the happiest of all are the
eighteen-year-old youngsters you see going by in groups, on bicycles,
boys and girls, light rucksacks on their backs, almost cheerful that they
are free to set off towards the unknown."[66]

Others had to abandon their flight. Some found they were not physically strong enough to continue; some realised too late that they were

overdressed but did not want to carry any superfluous items of clothing and refused to discard them. In the blistering mid-June sun with the heat bouncing off the tarmac of the dusty roads, which offered little shade, women wore layer upon layer of clothing, blouse on top of blouse, skirt over skirt, a jacket under a coat, plus scarves, gloves, and hats, all of which they preferred to wear rather than carry in a bag or suitcase.

It was quite common for members of family groups to become separated from their relatives. Children got lost in the crowds or sometimes desperate mothers on foot begged motorists to take their children away from the ever-present threat of attack from the skies, never to catch up with them again. It has been estimated that some 90,000 children became separated from their families during the exodus.[67] Walls were covered with heartfelt messages in chalk along the roads leading south, and people left notes in official buildings, telling relatives where they and other family members were to be found.[68]

For those who wanted to get out of Paris but did not have a car, the train was, theoretically, an option. Thousands of Parisians, along with thousands of Belgians and refugees from northern France, descended on the city's mainline railway stations, especially those serving towns and cities to the south, in the hope of finding space on a train. However, despite extra trains laid on by the SNCF, stations were soon struggling to cope with hordes of people desperate to leave.

Gabriel Danjou, a junior civil servant, was planning to go south of the Loire with other members of staff from his office. He described the scene at the Gare Montparnasse, a mainline railway station in the south of the city. "In the entrance hall, designed to allow for the coming and going of 10,000 people, there were 50,000. On the central reservation providing access to the platforms which was built for 20,000 people there were 100,000. How to describe this delirious multitude? . . . In the middle of a chaotic heap of bags and luggage, women, old people, children were squashed together, some sitting, others lying, some in a daze, some sleeping, a few eating, many famished. There were Parisians and people from the suburbs, who'd been camping in the station for days; people from the north of France, from Belgium, from the Meuse department in northeastern France, and from Luxembourg, who had stopped in Paris believing that their exodus was over. They were there watching out anxiously for the arrival of a train, but when one did arrive they found they no longer had the strength to fight their way on to it."[69]

Latvian journalist Arved Arenstam had a similar experience on June 10 at the Gare d'Austerlitz railway station. "The train leaves in four hours' time," he noted in his diary. "About 20,000 people are massed in front of the station, most of them seated on their belongings. It is impossible to move and the heat is unbearable. . . . I have now been standing wedged in this seething mass for over three hours. . . . A woman standing near us has fainted. Two *agents* [policemen] force their way through, and carry her off over the heads of the crowd. Children are crying all round, and the many babes in arms look like being crushed to death."[70]

Such was the size of the crowds at the Paris stations that the station-masters soon had to close access to the platforms, fearing that people would be pushed onto the track in the inevitable surge forward as a train approached. On June 10 about 120,000 Parisians managed to leave the capital by train; the following day trains were fewer, and, on June 12, the mainline stations were closed.[71] This decision provoked a mad stampede to Charenton, near the Bois de Vincennes, when a rumour spread that some trains would be leaving from there.

Those who managed to board a train found the experience worse than on the stations. Nicole Ollier describes the trains going west as "a closed, Kafkaesque hellish world [where] you cannot wash or eat, but nor can you leave."[72] Passengers were forbidden to get off the train before it reached its final destination, although they ignored this rule whenever possible. However, armed guards at the stations frequently took up positions outside the train doors, which were often locked from the outside. Underfed, with no chance of attending to personal hygiene, the refugees felt they were becoming "pariahs treated like criminals."[73]

Berty (Berthe) Albrecht, a feminist anti-Nazi and future member of the Resistance, together with her daughter Mireille, managed to catch one of the last trains out of Paris, which was bound for Nevers, about 150 miles south of the capital. The heat in their packed compartments and corridors was so intense that several female passengers stripped down to their underwear. It was impossible to use the lavatory, since several passengers were perched on the toilet, using it as a seat. The first time the train stopped, the men in the compartment helped the female passengers out through the windows. Since the train could start off again at any moment, the women crouched down in a single line alongside the train and urinated right next to the railway track.[74]

So much for those who chose to leave Paris: for others the choice was made for them. On June 10 detainees from the Cherche-Midi prison, like those in other prisons in Paris, were taken from their cells and out of the city. Some of the Cherche-Midi inmates were put on buses and driven to the prison in Orléans, which refused to take them. The members of this curiously eclectic convoy, consisting of militants of the Far Right, anarchists, dealers in contraband, spies, and thieves, were then marched in handcuffs to a camp in Grues in the Vendée region. The convoy also included half a dozen Communists, four of whom were only eighteen years of age; they had been sentenced to death for committing acts of industrial sabotage and were executed ten days later. On the forced march to Grues, Thierry de Ludre, a leading contributor to the Far Right newspaper *Je suis partout* and who suffered from asthma, was struggling to keep up; he was shot dead by the guards.[75]

And then there were those who could not leave. A decision was taken to evacuate the Orsay Hospital in the southwestern suburbs of Paris, whose patients included eighty or so who were very sick and elderly, as well as civilian and military victims of the war brought there by the Red Cross. About half a dozen patients were deemed too ill to be moved and nurses were instructed to kill them with massive doses of morphine and strychnine; this they duly did, before heading off to join the exodus. Two years later the nurses were tried and received suspended sentences of between one and five years, because of the "extenuating circumstances" of the killings.[76]

Meanwhile, the tardy and inadequate defence of Paris was further undermined by arguments, which had been going on since early June, as to whether the city should be defended at all. On June 4, according to Roger Langeron, General Héring, the military governor of Paris, told General Weygand, the new chief of staff of national defence, "I have decided on an all-out defence of the capital."[77] On June 9 Héring broadcast a radio appeal to the unemployed to defend Paris, leading Parisians to believe, according to Langeron, that Paris would be defended "street by street, house by house."[78] However, on June 10—just hours before the government abandoned Paris and while Reynaud was apparently telling President Franklin D. Roosevelt that "he would fight in front of Paris, in Paris and behind Paris"[79]—Weygand wrote to Reynaud explaining that Paris would not, after all, be defended; rather, it would be declared an open city. In other words, Paris would offer no resistance to the German army, which, in turn, undertook not to launch an attack on the city and its inhabitants.

On June 11 Léon Blum, a Socialist statesman and former head of the 1936 Popular Front government, was back in Paris, where he sought out Héring. "So, is Paris to be abandoned?" asked Blum. According to Blum, Héring replied, "What can I say? We don't know anything. We have no instructions. We have no orders."[80] That same day Héring made a radio broadcast ordering all workers who had been given exemption from the general call-up to join the armed forces immediately; the following day a notice appeared across Paris in his name countermanding his own orders.[81] Even before this latest confusion, Langeron had been complaining that "unofficial government statements [had] announced successively that the capital would not be defended, then that it would be, then that it would not."[82]

This obvious state of confusion heightened the apprehensions of the million or so Parisians who were still in the capital and its suburbs. Nobody would tell them what was happening; nobody could tell them what they should be doing. The government ministers, senior (and less senior) civil servants and almost every elected parliamentary and most council representatives had fled. No wonder most of the citizens who remained behind felt frightened, angry, and betrayed.

True, Achille Villey, the prefect of the Seine department, and Roger Langeron, who as prefect of police was responsible for the Paris police force, had remained at their posts. So, too, had seven elected representatives,[83] who opted to stay and form a "permanent commission," working closely with Villey and Langeron to represent the people of Paris. But the government was divided even on the issue of what these seven men should do. On June 10 Georges Mandel, the minister of the interior, strongly suggested they should leave; the following day they received a handwritten note from Reynaud congratulating them on their decision to stay.[84]

Finally, on June 12 came the definitive ruling: Weygand announced that the capital would *not* be defended. General Dentz was appointed military governor of Paris, while Héring was packed off south of the city to take charge of a section of what remained of the French army. Dentz confirmed the decision not to defend Paris to William C. Bullitt Jr., the American ambassador.

It was also on June 12 that the last edition of a Paris newspaper went on sale before the Germans arrived. And what a pathetic publication it was. Calling itself the *Édition parisienne de guerre* (Paris War Edition), it consisted of a one-page, recto-verso sheet produced in the name of three Paris papers, *Le Matin*, *Le Journal*, and *Le Petit Journal* with a slogan on the masthead calling on its readers to "Hold Fast . . . Even Though. . . ." Its two pages carried precious little news: a fanciful piece, still spreading misinformation, reported that "Our divisions are mounting a relentless counterattack and inflicting serious losses on the enemy." A declaration to the British House of Commons by Churchill's deputy Clement Attlee was printed as well as an appeal from Héring for all able-bodied men over seventeen to leave the Paris region and proceed to the southern gates of Paris (Porte d'Italie, Porte d'Orléans, and Porte de Châtillon), where they would receive further instructions, presumably on how and where to join the French army. Colonel de La Rocque, the leader of a prewar political grouping on the Far Right, contributed an article complaining that Parisians were still being kept in the dark. Well-known journalist Géo London had phoned in a piece from Limoges about Italy's entry into the war, while a journalist in Paris wrote about how the city had awakened under an "apocalyptic sky . . . thick smoke that blocked out the sun";[85] he was describing smoke rising from local oil refineries, which had been set alight to stop the Germans from appropriating the fuel.

While confusion reigned and the French government and military top brass dithered, the German army advanced ever closer to the city. On June 13 a letter from Dentz, signed under his newly acquired title of military governor of Paris, appeared as a poster instructing Parisians to hand in any weapons they had at their local police station; that same day another poster, this time in Dentz's own name, informed Parisians that "Since Paris has been declared an 'open city,' the military governor calls on the population of Paris to abstain from any hostile act and relies on them to maintain their sang-froid and dignity which the present circumstances demand."[86] With very few exceptions, the announcement that Paris had been declared an "open city" was greeted with relief by civilians as well as any officials left in the city, who saw it as an indication that they would be spared the horrors of war. To their relief, Paris would not become another Warsaw.

One incident, however, occurred that threatened to bring the whole might of the German army down on the city. By June 13 German units had reached the eastern Paris suburbs of Pantin, Aubervilliers, and Bondy. At 5:10 P.M. a radio message from the Germans was received at the Paris police headquarters on the Île de la Cité, calling for somebody authorised to represent Paris to go to a specified street in the northern suburb of Moisselles[87] at six o'clock.

Left in charge of an open city by an absent government, Dentz saw it as his responsibility simply to maintain order until the enemy arrived. It was not his job to start negotiations with the enemy; he decided to ignore the message. At 11:25 P.M. a second message came from the German team of negotiators. They said they had come under fire and claimed (incorrectly, as it turned out) that one of their members had been killed.[88] They now informed Dentz that if by 5 A.M. no response was made to the call for a representative from Paris to meet them, German forces would launch an all-out artillery and air attack on the city. Dentz quickly agreed to send an officer and an interpreter to meet the German delegation.

The Germans escorted the Paris delegation to a house in the village of Ecouen, twelve miles north of Paris, which they were using as a temporary headquarters. Here the German military commanders agreed not to attack Paris on four conditions: (1) there was to be no resistance; (2) order was to be guaranteed both in the city and in the surrounding areas; (3) there was to be no destruction of bridges, public utilities, especially water and electricity, or of the broadcasting facilities; (4) Parisians should stay indoors for forty-eight hours after the Germans entered the city.

If any resistance was offered, the Germans said, it would be crushed by "the most rigorous means both on land and in the air." The Paris police should remain on duty and take responsibility for protecting property and preventing sabotage and looting.[89]

So it was that at dawn on June 14 German troops entered Paris unopposed. In April Goebbels had boasted in a Swiss newspaper that Paris would be under German occupation by June 15. His prediction had come true, with a day to spare.

3

Parisians and Germans, Germans and Parisians

$\mathcal{I}$N THE EARLY HOURS of Friday June 14 Pierre Guillemor, a retired railway worker, watched as a column of smartly turned-out German troops made its way through the northern, working-class Paris suburb of Argenteuil, where he lived. They exuded youth, efficiency, and discipline, and Guillemor paused to admire their "magnificent military equipment." He was relieved to see that the Germans showed no signs of hostility towards the French.[1]

In the city itself, Roger Langeron, the prefect of the Paris police, was aghast: "The thing we were dreading has happened. The German troops are in Paris."[2] At 8 A.M. he received news that what seemed like interminable phalanxes of motorised troops were pouring into the city from Saint-Denis and other northern suburbs. He noted: "First motorcyclists in their leather coats with their side cars, then an eruption of weaponry and tanks."[3]

On the day before the Germans arrived, the guardian of the flame at the Tomb of the Unknown Soldier, beneath the Arc de Triomphe, had likened Paris to a desert.[4] The Germans agreed; they felt as if they were entering a ghost town. As his unit made its way through Paris, German author and poet Wilhelm Ehmer observed that the streets and houses were dead and most of the shops were boarded up; an "eerie silence"[5] surrounded him and his fellow soldiers as they headed south through the city. Ehmer's unit came down the boulevard de Sébastopol and across the place du Châtelet, before halting briefly on the pont Saint-Michel to admire, to the left, the magnificence of Notre-Dame Cathedral on the Île de la Cité. They continued up the boulevard Saint-Michel and on to the Porte d'Orléans, one of the gateways to the south. There, General Erich Marcks, their commanding officer, stood up in his car and, like a human signpost, pointed in the direction of the River Loire. He watched as his men surged southwards.

As Marcks's men pressed on, farther to the west a second column of Germans entered the city. It passed through the place de la Concorde and over the River Seine before it, too, headed south towards the River Loire. A third column came in even farther to the west and assembled at the Arc de Triomphe, at the top of the Champs-Élysées. It was met by General Georg von Küchler, commander of the 18th Army and General Fedor von Bock, his superior. Both men were now joined by General Marcks, who had sped over by car from the Porte d'Orléans. A German military band struck up, and the first of many interminable German army parades began. By 9:45 A.M. a swastika flag was fluttering on the Arc de Triomphe[6] above the Tomb of the Unknown Soldier, a memorial to those Frenchmen who had fallen in the last war against Germany only a quarter of a century earlier.

Some Parisians defied the German army's order to remain indoors and cautiously ventured out to see what was happening. One German soldier described Parisians staring at him and his fellow soldiers "with a mixture of panic and curiosity." Some brave souls stood on the edge of the pavement; others swiftly withdrew under the entrance porches of their apartment blocks; mothers dragged their children inside and doors and windows were snapped closed. "But nothing happened," the soldier reported. "Nobody opened fire on us. The column rumbled slowly and calmly on its way."[7] Apart from somebody taking a potshot at the German negotiating team in the northern suburbs before the army entered the city, the German invaders encountered no resistance.[8] However, a local head of police from the 14th arrondissement met a French colonel and two or three soldiers with a machine gun near the Porte d'Orléans; they had no idea Paris had been declared an open city and they intended to attack the Germans. The police chief managed to convince them that this was against orders and they abandoned their plan.[9]

General Bogislav von Studnitz was the temporary military governor of the city and his 7th Infantry Division had overall responsibility for the occupation of Paris. Tanks were dispatched to encircle the city's administrative centre in the Hôtel de Ville, a late nineteenth-century, neo-Renaissance building on the north bank of the Seine across from Notre-Dame Cathedral. Inside the Hôtel de Ville the battalion commander was received by Achille Villey, the prefect who was responsible for the civil administration of the Seine department, including Paris. Villey had dressed up for the occasion and was wearing his ceremonial uniform complete with a bold red sash across his chest. The commander "invited" Villey, along with police chief Langeron, to meet General von Studnitz at 11 A.M. at the Hôtel Crillon, which the general had requisitioned as his headquarters. While this exchange was taking place, German soldiers removed the French national flag from the roof of the Hôtel de Ville and replaced it with one bearing a swastika.

By midday the German army had taken control of the centre of the city and the tank commander set off to watch the 9th Infantry Division march across the place de la Concorde with General von Külcher and General Stumme, head of the 7th Panzer Division, taking the salute, before the division goose-stepped up the Champs-Élysées to take part in yet another parade around the Arc de Triomphe. The Parisians were to be left in no doubt that the Germans had arrived and were now in charge. The German invaders even considered a gigantic triumphal procession through Paris, attended by Hitler himself, but, fearing an attack by the British Royal Air Force (RAF), they reluctantly abandoned the idea.

Achille Villey and Roger Langeron, the two representatives of the French state who had remained in Paris, arrived together and on time at the Hôtel Crillon for their meeting with Studnitz. Although Paris had been declared an open city, Studnitz remained worried about possible anti-German disturbances, and his main priority was to ensure that the city remained peaceful and free of incidents. The German general, who, with his monocle and little moustache looked like a caricature of a Prussian army officer, asked Langeron if the head of the Paris police could guarantee order. "I guarantee it if I'm allowed to get on with my job in peace," replied Langeron. Studnitz considered this for a moment. "If order is maintained and if I can count on my troops being safe," he said, "you won't hear anything from me."[10] He realised by now that resistance was unlikely and rescinded the order that

Parisians remain indoors, which was already being ignored anyway. Studnitz probably realised as well that if everyone stayed at home it would be impossible for the city to function properly, as the Germans wanted it to.

The two most senior French army officers in the city, General Dentz and Colonel Groussard, his deputy, were nervous that meeting the German top brass might be interpreted as colluding with the enemy. So, for their encounter with Studnitz, Dentz and Groussard were smuggled into the Hôtel Crillon under cover of darkness. The French government (which had left Cangé near Tours for Bordeaux on the day the Germans entered Paris) had instructed Dentz to maintain order and to ensure food supplies in the city and its suburbs. Now that the German army had arrived, Dentz believed he had no further obligations. Studnitz did not dispute this. However, he held the French army responsible for setting fire to the oil depots on the outskirts of the city shortly before the Germans arrived. He informed Dentz and Groussard that their fate would be decided by the German High Command.[11]

France's military collapse had been so swift and so comprehensive that Parisians in the city remained stunned; despite what they could see around them, they found it difficult to grasp that Paris was now under German control. Many of the German soldiers stationed in the city, too, found it hard to believe that they had seized the capital of France. "We are the victors," wrote one of them, a Lieutenant von Wedel. "My mind can understand that all right. But our hearts are not yet able to take in the importance of these events, the full significance of our victory. We talk about it among ourselves, we try to find ways to make sense of it, but we're not able to do so."[12]

Wedel was ordered to take up position at the top of the steps of the Madeleine Church,[13] which offered him the opportunity to place the German victory in historical context: "Napoleon built this impressive edifice as a temple to his Great Army. From here the view stretches out towards the rue Royale, which at the moment is full of German soldiers waiting to march past their officers, across the vast expanse of the place de la Concorde and as far as the golden cupola of Les Invalides.[14] I can't describe what it feels like to be here, as a member of the victorious German army, and find myself face to face with the silent witnesses of the greatest glory of the French army."[15]

Those German units detailed to remain in the city were soon requisitioning buildings, including any private properties that appeared to have been abandoned. On the day the Germans arrived the writer Paul Léautaud was visiting a friend in the rue Saint-André-des-Arts, near the place Saint-Michel. His friend looked out of the window and, spotting a German soldier opening up a house with a bunch of keys, told Léautaud that the Germans were doing this whenever nobody answered the door. Léautaud immediately thought of his own empty, locked house in the southern suburbs and headed straight for the Métro.[16]

When Simone de Beauvoir returned to Paris at the end of the month, she saw houses in the northern suburbs that had home-made signs on their front doors written in French, or more often in German, indicating that the houses were still occupied.[17]

Peter de Polnay, who lived in Montmartre, was out and about early on that historic Friday morning when the Germans entered the city. He walked to the nearby boulevard de Clichy, where a crowd watched as the impressively armed and disciplined Germans marched past in "a grey stream; and the first day of occupation it was an endless stream."[18] Another Parisian watching the advancing soldiers took them to be British troops and burst into tears when a French policeman told him they were Germans.[19]

Others were more relaxed. As Paul Léautaud crossed the boulevard Saint-Michel near the Luxembourg Gardens he noticed a French policeman showing a German soldier how to use a telephone. "It didn't bother me in the slightest," he wrote in his diary. "I didn't even stop to look at him."[20] When Ferdinand Dupuy returned to the *commissariat* (police station) in the 6th arrondissement where he worked, he was told that the Germans were on all the main streets, but that they were showing absolutely no signs of aggression towards the city's inhabitants. Based on what he had seen and heard, he described the general reaction of his fellow Parisians to the German presence as "consternation mixed with a sort of fearful curiosity."[21]

These smart, well-disciplined, healthy—and mostly young—Germans were the very antithesis of the images of starving, demoralised soldiers or raping, pillaging hordes that the French government propaganda had been drip-feeding Parisians for months. They were also quite unlike the dirty, bedraggled remnants of the French army the Parisians had seen wandering about in the city shortly before the Germans arrived. Many Parisians were astounded to discover how courteous, friendly, and helpful the young German invaders were: virtually all the Parisians that de Polnay met on that first day of the Occupation referred to the Germans' correct behaviour. "Correct was a word I was to hear *ad nauseam*," he wrote.[22] A couple of days into the Occupation, Ferdinand Dupuy contrasted the German presence with what many had expected. He noted: "Let's be honest about it. The Germans have demonstrated correct and polite behaviour that was, to say the least, unexpected from soldiers from across the Rhine."[23]

Some of the Parisians that de Polnay met even said they were relieved to see German troops in the city since they believed it meant that Paris would not be bombed or gassed. Others seemed to welcome the invader. Colonel Groussard, Dentz's deputy, was appalled to see Parisians of all social classes laughing with German soldiers and offering to help them.[24] De Polnay saw several members of a crowd watching the Germans march past rush forward to help a German officer when he was thrown from his horse.[25] Some in the crowds on the Left Bank (probably pro-Mussolini Italians), even cheered and applauded as the Germans made their way along the boulevard Saint-Germain.[26]

But for some a Paris occupied by German soldiers proved too much. Sixteen suicides were recorded that day, a record number. They included Thierry de Martel, an eminent brain surgeon and son of the Countess de Martel de Janville, a celebrated, anti-Semitic novelist who wrote under the pseudonym "Gyp," and Maurice Maile, the deputy mayor of Clichy, who had resigned from the French Communist Party in December 1939.[27]

Since there was no fighting as the Germans entered the city, they did not have to deal with any material damage or civilian casualties. Gas, water, and electricity supplies continued uninterrupted and the Métro still ran—after a fashion. It carried only 300,000 passengers a day; by the end of the year, the figure would be almost three million.

The German authorities imposed a 9 P.M. curfew, although this was extended to 11 P.M. in July and in November to midnight, "as a reward for the peaceful and understanding attitude adopted by the Parisian population."[28] Before the war, France and Germany were in different time zones, but German insistence that clocks in Paris be moved forward one hour to correspond to German time meant that, during much of the year, many adults and children would start their day in darkness. With the Germans also insisting on maintaining the blackout, signs outside cinemas and cabarets remained unilluminated. At night the only lights visible were the ghostly blue street lamps and the torches carried by some lucky pedestrians.

Langeron ordered special units of ex-civil defence personnel to open locked shops, requisition any food they found, and take it to local town halls to be sold at affordable prices. Cafés on the Champs-Élysées started to fill up again as uniformed German soldiers sat in the sun on the terraces alongside Parisian women in their summer finery. The Pigalle cinema reopened, and Parisians could feel that some life was returning to the city even if, according to Langeron, people were on the whole subdued, speaking little and quietly, as a result of the trauma they had just experienced.[29]

Two days later more shops were opening—notably those of bakers, grocers, and butchers—and also shoe stores and shops selling household goods; others announced they would be reopening soon. Owners of food shops purchased their supplies from the fruit and vegetable market in Les Halles[30] and from stocks held in Paris mainline railway stations, but Parisians found shortages in some parts of the city, notably of coffee, milk, wine, some tinned goods, and pasta; however, according to Langeron, fruit, green vegetables, and dairy products could be easily found.[31]

On June 17 two newspapers, *Le Matin* and *La Victoire*, went on sale. The latter was published for only three days before the Germans closed it down.[32] *Le Matin*, which had last appeared on June 11, came out as a two-page edition. That it was available at all was thanks to the efforts of its owner, the octogenarian megalomaniac Maurice Bunau-Varilla. So keen was he to restart production that he and his son operated the presses themselves. But even an anticommunist, anti-democrat, and anti-Semite like Bunau-Varilla was quickly cautioned by the Germans as to what he could print. Lieutenant Weber, the prewar head of the German News Bureau,[33] now attached to the German press service in Paris, told Bunau-Varilla that he expected *Le Matin* to present news objectively—in other words, as the Germans saw it.[34]

From the start of the Occupation the German military made it clear that it preferred editors, publishers, and journalists to exercise self-censorship rather than having to undertake the censoring themselves.

Newspaper editors toed the line, knowing that failure to do so could result in their paper allocation being reduced or in their newspaper being closed down altogether. *Le Matin* was the newspaper with the biggest circulation (more than half a million at the beginning of July), although it would soon be overtaken by *Paris-Soir*. Whether Bunau-Varilla needed Weber's nudge or not, when Georges Benoît-Guyod, a recently retired officer in the French Republican Guard, bought a copy of *Le Matin* the first day it appeared he thought it "looked just like a German newspaper."[35] After her return to Paris, de Beauvoir referred to it as "the German *Le Matin*."[36]

In mid-June Paris stood as an occupied city that had been spared any fighting and was trying to get back to some kind of normality. But France was still at war with Germany, and beyond Paris French military units were still engaged in combat with the invading army. In Bordeaux, Reynaud favoured honouring France's alliance with Britain and carrying on the fight against Germany, possibly from North Africa. However, Pétain and General Weygand wanted to put an end to the fighting as soon as possible. On June 16 a beleaguered and demoralised Reynaud resigned and Marshal Philippe Pétain, the hero of the First World War, took his place as head of the government.[37] The following day in Paris a poster from General von Bock, the commander-in-chief of the Group of Armies, appeared on the walls of the city, setting out his instructions to its inhabitants:

PEOPLE OF PARIS

The German troops have occupied Paris.

The City is placed under military Government.

The Military Governor of the Paris Region will take the necessary measures to ensure the security of the troops and the maintenance of order.

The orders from the Military Authorities must be obeyed unconditionally.

Avoid any hasty actions.

Any act of sabotage, be it active or passive, will incur severe punishment.

The City of Paris's ability to take advantage of being an Open City depends on the prudence and sensible behaviour of its Population.

The German Soldiers have received orders to respect the Population of Paris and their property, on condition that the Population remains calm.

Everyone should remain in their home or workplace and resume their activities.

This is the best way for each person to serve the City of Paris, its inhabitants and themselves.

—The Commander in Chief of the Group of Armies[38]

That same day (June 17) Pétain made the first of his many national radio broadcasts. He announced "with a heavy heart" that it was "time to stop fighting."[39] This tragically ambiguous phrase, combined with Pétain's admission that he was already seeking an honourable solution to the conflict, was taken by many French soldiers to mean that they should stop fighting immediately; consequently, nearly one million French soldiers were captured between his radio broadcast and the armistice agreement that was signed five days later.

Langeron and his police colleagues were flabbergasted when they heard what Pétain appeared to be proposing;[40] the news was also relayed to Parisians by German loudspeaker vans stationed in squares across the city. William Shirer, an American journalist, found himself in the heart of the city when the news broke: "The Parisians, already dazed by all that has happened, can scarcely believe it. Nor can the rest of us . . . I stood in a throng of French men and women on the place de la Concorde when the news first came. They were almost struck dead. . . . They stared at the ground, then at each other. They said 'Pétain surrendering! What does it mean? *Comment? Pourquoi?*' And no one appeared to have the heart for an answer."[41]

Meanwhile, Charles de Gaulle, an almost unknown French army officer who had been a junior minister in Reynaud's government, had made it to London. The day after Pétain's radio broadcast de Gaulle sent out his own message over the airwaves to the French people via the British Broadcasting Corporation (BBC). Unlike Pétain, who was seeking to strike a deal with the enemy, de Gaulle passionately urged French men and women to join him and his nascent Free French movement in London, concluding his broadcast with the words, "Whatever happens, the flame of French resistance must not and shall not be extinguished." He would make further broadcasts in the same vein.

Whereas millions of Frenchmen and women listened to Pétain, almost nobody heard de Gaulle. One of the very few Parisians who did

hear him was the banker and economist Charles Rist, who noted in his
diary: "Last evening on the radio heard the courageous and moving
appeal by General de Gaulle, which gives us hope and confidence."[42]
BBC broadcasts by the Free French who had rallied to de Gaulle would
become an invaluable source of information as well as a vital morale
booster for those in France opposed to the Occupation.

Another Parisian who heard de Gaulle was a forty-four-year-old left-
wing divorcée named Agnès Humbert. Before leaving Paris in the
exodus, she had worked at the National Museum of Popular Arts and
Traditions in the Palais de Chaillot, across the Seine from the Eiffel
Tower. She was in a cousin's house in a village near Limoges, fiddling
with the knob on the wireless set, when she suddenly stumbled upon
an appeal by a French general whose name she did not catch, but who
was urging all Frenchmen to rally round him to carry on the struggle.
It made her feel that all was not lost. "I feel alive again. A feeling I
thought had died forever is born again within me—hope. There is one
man after all—just one perhaps—who understands what my heart keeps
telling me. It's not all over."[43] But when she rushed to tell a veteran
French army captain in the village about the broadcast, he dismissed
de Gaulle as "a crackpot."[44]

On the day of de Gaulle's first broadcast, Langeron reported that the
Germans in Paris were still busy requisitioning buildings for their own
use, including ministries, large and small hotels, industrial and commercial buildings, and hospitals.[45] Journalist and author Pierre Audiat
commented on the speed with which they were doing so. The most important requisitioned buildings were immediately guarded by armed
sentries. Swastika flags flew from their roofs, while in front of many of
their facades, enormous blood-red, black, and white Nazi banners
flapped in the wind. As Audiat commented: "The Chamber of Deputies, the Senate, the Ministry of War and the Ministry of the Navy, the
biggest hotels on the Champs-Élysées, on the rue de Rivoli and in the
area around the Opéra, were immediately marked by the sinister flag,
where, on a red background, in a white circle, lay the swastika, looking
for all the world like a black hooked-leg spider."[46] Another constant
reminder for Parisians that their city was under German control were
the white signposts with black German Gothic lettering that appeared
on all the main boulevards to guide the occupying forces around the
city or to places farther afield.

Unless Parisians had a special pass, they were banned from German-controlled buildings; indeed, whole areas of the city were out of bounds to them. Some public parks, including the Bois de Boulogne, stayed closed for several weeks. By the time the Luxembourg Gardens re-opened, Hermann Göring had requisitioned the sumptuous Luxembourg Palace, which had previously housed the Senate, the upper chamber of the French parliament. German guards and high railings now kept Parisians well away from the palace and from the whole of the northern part of the gardens.[47] A week after the arrival of the Germans, Langeron visited a bourgeois quarter of the city near the Parc Monceau only to discover that the Germans were entirely in charge. He noted: "All my officers had been moved out of the area."[48]

As Parisians waited anxiously for news of the German response to Pétain's overtures, they were subjected to incessant propaganda: loud-speaker vans on the streets and broadcasts in French on Radio Stuttgart insisted that Pétain spoke for the vast majority of the French people, who saw no reason to sacrifice any more soldiers and just wanted an end to hostilities and to any more pointless sacrifices.[49]

On June 19 the German government agreed to discuss a possible armistice. Two days later, a loudspeaker van parked outside the Hôtel de Ville in Paris informed a small crowd that the purpose of German conditions was to prevent hostilities breaking out again and to give Germany the security it needed to continue the war against Britain.[50] On the same day, those schools in the city with enough teachers and pupils reopened and the *baccalauréat* examination[51] was rescheduled for the end of July. Langeron was informed that the health services in the city were working more or less as they should, although doctors and surgeons, who were among the few Parisians now allowed to drive in the city, were having difficulty obtaining enough petrol for their cars.[52]

On June 22, representatives of the French and German governments met and signed an armistice agreement. Hitler attended the ceremony, which he insisted take place at the exact spot, indeed in the very same railway carriage, as the one in which French marshal Ferdinand Foch had imposed his country's terms on a defeated Germany in November 1918.[53]

The armistice agreement set out the terms for a cease-fire, but it was not a full peace treaty, which would have settled, for example, the issue of what was to be done with the nearly two million French prisoners of war (POWs), almost half of whom had been captured in the five days between Pétain's June 17 broadcast and the signing of the armistice agreement. The terms of the agreement did not, as is sometimes thought, simply divide France into two zones; rather it dismembered it.

The largest zone was the Occupied Zone, which covered some three-fifths of the country. Its function was "to protect the interests of the Reich," and Paris, which became in effect the German capital of France, lay at its heart. The Occupation was to be a military one and the German army, the Wehrmacht, swiftly established its main administrative head-quarters for the whole of France—the Militärbefehlshaber in Frank-reich (MBF)—in the Hôtel Majestic on the avenue Kléber. (The Mil-itärbefehlshaber in Frankreich was also the title that designated the general at the head of the MBF.) The Occupied Zone was separated from the Unoccupied Zone by an arbitrarily drawn demarcation line. This was not just some German administrative convenience: it ran for more than 1,000 kilometres, snaking its way across the country, split-ting a dozen departments, cutting through towns and villages, and in some cases individual farms, separating friends and families, and de-stroying the fabric of the social life of the country.

In addition, the two northern departments of the Nord and the Pas-de-Calais were attached to, and governed by, the German military com-mand in Belgium. A Forbidden Zone, sometimes called the Reserved Zone, was set up in the east, to which refugees were banned from re-turning. This, and an adjacent Prohibited Zone (shown on some maps as a single zone), were earmarked by the invaders for German coloni-sation.[54] A small Italian Zone, occupied by the Italian army, was es-tablished close to the Franco-Italian frontier. A de facto annexation of parts of Alsace and Lorraine took place in the summer of 1940 when two departments in Alsace and one in Lorraine were placed under two German *Gauleiters*, the name given to political chiefs of regions under Nazi control. The three departments were Germanised: French civil servants were expelled, the inhabitants were obliged to speak German—they faced heavy fines if they spoke French—while towns and villages assumed German names and public services were placed under German control. This annexation was not part of the armistice agreement. In addition, in 1941, a Coastal Zone was established. Be-tween 10 and 20 kilometres wide in size, it ran from the border with Belgium along the English Channel down the Atlantic coast to Hen-

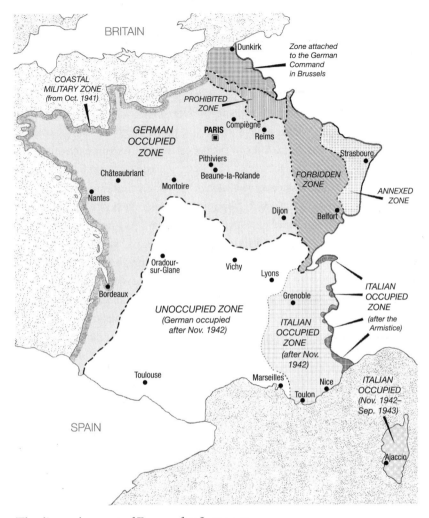

The dismemberment of France after June 1940

daye, near the Spanish frontier putting Germany in charge of France's northern and western coastline. It was out of bounds to all except current residents; those without permits, and "undesirables," notably Jews, were expelled from the area.

In an arrangement unique among Nazi occupation schemes, France would continue to have its own national government. According to the armistice agreement, it could retain a small "armistice army" and choose whether to establish itself in the Occupied or the Unoccupied Zone. In theory the government had sovereignty in both zones, although the

armistice agreement also stated that, in the Occupied Zone, the
German Reich would exercise "all the rights of an occupying power."
Nonetheless, this meant that Parisians, like other inhabitants of the
Occupied Zone, would now be subject to laws passed by the French
government as well as directives issued by the Germans. Under the
terms of the agreement, the French government agreed to hand over
to the German authorities all German nationals who had sought asylum
in France after the Nazi takeover in Germany, many of whom were
living in Paris.

Crucially, the armistice agreement determined that employees of the
French state in the Occupied Zone would work with the German authorities, help them enforce German directives and maintain law and
order. This provision was vital for the Germans, since they simply
lacked the manpower to police the Occupied Zone and were dependent
on the cooperation of the French police. The fine details of the armistice agreement would be decided at meetings of a Franco-German
Armistice Commission held at Wiesbaden, in southwestern Germany,
once the armistice was signed.

The recent turbulent weeks had thrown the lives of all Parisians into
chaos, whether they had fled the city or they had stayed behind. Many
had family members among the 90,000 French soldiers killed in action,
and Parisians accounted for about a quarter of the nearly two million
French POWs. The armistice held out hope for an end to the trauma of
a people whose country had collapsed in defeat in a mere six weeks. It
meant an end to the fighting, the killing, the turmoil, and the uncertainty. It also held out the hope that a full peace treaty and a speedy
return of the POWs would follow.

Besides wanting an end to the fighting in France, many Parisians
were resigned to seeing the whole of Europe under the Nazi jackboot;
in addition, a pro-Nazi minority actively sought this goal. But a comprehensive peace treaty was an unlikely prospect as long as Britain remained undefeated. Hitler was planning an imminent air assault on
Britain, followed by a sea invasion. Considering the speed with which
German forces had crushed not only France, but also Poland, Denmark,
Norway, Belgium, the Netherlands, and Luxembourg and since the
United States remained neutral and the Nazi-Soviet pact still held,
it was hard for Parisians to believe that Britain would be able to resist
Nazi domination for long.

Most Parisians, like the rest of their countrymen and women, were so relieved at what the armistice appeared to offer that they were prepared to pay the price—any price—for peace, stability, and an opportunity to start putting their lives back together again.

For other Parisians shame—rather than relief—was the dominant emotion. Teacher and essayist Jean Guéhenno, whose school had been evacuated to the Auvergne, admitted that the ringing of the Clermont-Ferrand church bells to signify the official end of the fighting filled him "with pain, anger and shame."[55] Flora Groult, still in Brittany, had been overwhelmed with shame—and despair—when she heard Pétain's speech; she and her sister Benoîte broke into floods of tears when they heard that the armistice had been signed.[56]

On Sunday, June 23, the day after the armistice was signed, a letter from Cardinal Suhard, who in April had replaced Cardinal Verdier as Catholic archbishop of Paris, was read out at churches across the city. The letter called on the faithful to remain calm, go about their work, and pray.[57] But not all the clergy supported this appeal to piety and passivity. Monseigneur Chevrot was a priest at the Saint-François-Xavier church near Les Invalides, where Bernard Pierquin, a medical student and active member of a Catholic student organisation,[58] was a regular worshipper. According to Pierquin, Chevrot was scandalised by the signing of the armistice agreement, which he saw as a betrayal, and he was vehemently opposed to a passive acceptance of the new status quo; the priest believed that Pétain had set France on a road of shame.[59]

On the other hand, Cardinal Baudrillart, the ultraconservative head of the Catholic Institute in Paris, positively welcomed the armistice. "At the present time," he said, "we need the Germans here to reestablish some order."[60] Another conservative, Paul Claudel, the Catholic right-wing diplomat, dramatist, author, and poet, also supported the armistice, believing it would lead to the demise of the Third Republic, which he described as "that obnoxious parliamentary regime which has been devouring France like a cancer for years and years."[61]

In London, de Gaulle, of course, rejected the armistice. In another radio broadcast he once again urged the French to fight on. This did not go down well with the troops, as Paris conscript Georges Sadoul, now in a village in southwestern France, observed. Around him soldiers were shouting, "*You* go and fight, then, you bastard! You've got your backside stuck in an armchair and you want other people to carry on getting killed. You'll be lucky!" Sadoul noted: "It was the soldiers who spoke, but the locals and the refugees agreed. The soldiers and the civilians had all had enough. They wanted peace at any price."[62]

June 28, 1940, marked the twenty-first anniversary of the Treaty of Versailles, the peace treaty that formally ended the First World War. It was also the day Adolf Hitler chose to pay a surprise visit to Paris.[63] "Paris has always fascinated me," he told the sculptor Arno Breker. "For years I've been desperately keen to go there. . . . Now the gates of the city are open to me."[64] Hitler's small entourage, including Breker and the Führer's favourite architect Albert Speer, flew to Le Bourget and arrived in Paris at the crack of dawn. They then set off in a five-car motorcade—led by the Führer's convertible Mercedes—on a whistle-stop tour calling at most of the iconic spots in the city—the Opéra, the Madeleine Church, the place de la Concorde, the Arc de Triomphe, the Trocadéro, the Eiffel Tower, Les Invalides, the Luxembourg Palace, Notre-Dame Cathedral, and the Tuileries Gardens. The visit was filmed and shown in cinemas across Germany portraying Hitler as conqueror, a man of action speeding masterfully and effortlessly through a Paris that had fallen to his army.

According to Breker, very few Parisians caught sight of Hitler and his party; just a couple of newspaper sellers, a policeman, and some women near the market of Les Halles. Speer's account includes a few early morning worshippers around the Sacré-Coeur basilica; the actor-playwright Sacha Guitry mentions an angler near the Trocadéro, who, he claims, saw Hitler but ignored him. The closest encounter with a Parisian took place when Hitler's party visited the Opéra, where they were met by the janitor, known as "Glouglou" because of his resemblance to a character in a well-known advertisement for Nicholas wine merchants. "Glouglou" switched on the lights for Hitler and his party, who were struck by the dignity with which he refused a tip. Serge Lifar, the Paris-based Ukrainian ballet dancer, later wrote that "Glouglou" failed to recognise Hitler, taking him to be a singer or an actor. Lifar claimed, somewhat implausibly, that when the identity of his early morning visitor was later revealed to him, "Glouglou" promptly fainted and had to be revived by having a bucket of water poured over his head.[65]

By the end of June life in Paris was slowly returning to something resembling its prewar existence: filmgoers had a growing number of cinemas to choose from and by the end of the month the banks were once again open for business; trains were again running into and out of the Paris railway stations, more Métro stations were operating, and the Germans had ordered the opening of the city's public museums, including the Palais de la Découverte, a science museum near the Champs-Élysées.[66] Meanwhile, on July 1, the French government took up residence, for what it assumed would be a temporary stay, in the sleepy spa town of Vichy, which lay in the Unoccupied Zone just south of the Demarcation Line.

Three days later in Paris, Langeron reported that the German military supported any measures to assist in making Paris look like a city operating normally and had already sanctioned the removal of sandbags from around public monuments. "The face of the city is being transformed once again," Langeron wrote in his diary.[67] With plans to invade Britain at an advanced stage, Germany needed France—and Paris in particular—as a stable and secure continental base. The German authorities hoped that if there were plenty of distractions on offer, Parisians would be convinced that the city was rediscovering its old self and this would reduce the chances of any public discontent or resistance. This is why the Germans sanctioned the reopening of as many theatres and cinemas as possible, although what was on offer did not meet with universal approval.

One of the first theatres to open its doors was Les Ambassadeurs, showing a farce, *Nous ne sommes pas mariés* (We're Not Married), about a man undecided as to whether he should ditch his mistress. The posters for the play guaranteed "three hours of uproarious laughter,"[68] but an article in *La Gerbe*, a literary weekly recently founded by the Catholic author and future arch-collaborator Alphonse de Châteaubriant,[69] claimed that a play about a man who could not decide whether or not to be faithful to his mistress was a poor reflection on French theatre and could only confirm the Germans' view that the French were not to be taken seriously.[70] That such material did not bother the German authorities is unsurprising. After all, when Albert Speer had asked Hitler, "Does the spiritual health of the French people matter to you?" the Führer had replied, "Let's let them degenerate. All the better for us."[71] More light comedies followed, offering relatively cheap entertainment since theatre tickets had been frozen at September 1939 prices.[72]

The German authorities also took to the airwaves to encourage the idea that in Paris very little had really changed. In June they closed

down all the existing radio stations and replaced them in July with a
single station, Radio-Paris, run under the auspices of the Propaganda
Bureau of the German military command in France (MBF). The choice
of Radio-Paris, the name of one of four publicly owned, prewar radio
stations in Paris was another bid to emphasise continuity, as was the
decision to locate it on the Champs-Élysées in what had been the premises of one of Paris's two private radio stations before the war.[73] Radio-
Paris's broadcasting range extended far beyond Paris itself and the station hoped that if the radio repeated often enough the message that life
in Paris had not really changed, people in the city would come to believe it and those who had fled Paris would return. In late summer
1940, for example, a broadcaster informed his audience: "Throughout
the afternoon we were out and about all over Paris and we observed that
life is almost back to normal. The cinemas are open, the café terraces
are full of people, the theatres—or rather the cabarets—have already
reopened. And you feel that nothing has fundamentally changed, except that in the street you see the uniforms of the German soldiers mingling with the dresses of pretty women."[74]

As part of this "return to normality" strategy the Germans encouraged entertainment associated with France before the Occupation to
help Parisians forget their current problems. Radio-Paris broadcast
plays starring celebrated prewar actors, such as Charles Dullin and Jean-
Louis Barrault, as well as variety shows with singing stars that included
Maurice Chevalier and Tino Rossi. During the summer and early autumn, Radio-Paris broadcast mostly light entertainment; in October,
for example, Benoîte Groult listened to Belgian accordionist Gus
Viseur playing *Porto japonais* and other swing numbers all through
the night.[75] As autumn progressed, Radio-Paris became more "political"
and it began to broadcast more "news" programmes, prepared and presented by French journalists who were recruited mainly from the ranks
of the Far Right.

The Germans could count on newspapers to encourage Parisians
to see continuity between life in their city before and after June 14.
Paris-Soir—Paris's best-selling evening paper before the invasion and
which had reappeared on June 23—was a good example.[76] The newspaper used the same typeface as before the invasion and was printed on
the same presses. The July 2 issue highlighted the similarity between
the old and the new versions, insisting that, "the Paris paper would be

identical to the one we love."[77] *Paris-Soir* denied that it was a German newspaper. It touted that it was thoroughly French and that Paris itself was still fundamentally French. "Policing in Paris is done by Frenchmen. . . . Life in the theatre and cabarets has returned, thanks to French people . . . *Paris-Soir* is a French newspaper produced by French people . . . Paris is still Paris."[78]

In 1939 Parisians could choose from more than 200 daily newspapers and periodicals.[79] In July 1940 they had four,[80] all produced under the watchful eye of the German army's propaganda bureau. However, Parisians were sceptical about what they read in the press and heard on Radio-Paris. On July 1 a journalist for *La France au travail*, one of the four Paris dailies, reported seeing some people in Montparnasse gathered around a car, listening to the radio. One of them commented, "They can say whatever they like. It's all propaganda." The following day the same journalist heard a passer-by who had just bought a paper also muttering that it was just propaganda. He concluded, "The Parisians used to be too open, today they are suspicious. . . . They think we are just trying to deceive and bamboozle them."[81]

The German army was making a sustained effort to persuade Parisians to accept the German soldier as a trusty friend. In the early days of July a poster appeared on the walls of the city. It depicted a handsome, young German soldier who had removed his helmet, gazing at a smiling boy whom he is holding in his arms and who is eating a slice of bread. Two girls are standing below: one looks up admiringly at the soldier and the little boy; the other seems less sure. The slogan reads: "Abandoned people! Put your trust in the German soldier."[82] The poster also appeared on the front page of *Le Matin* under the heading "The Truth" with the caption, "Here is proof that German soldiers are coming to help those who have been abandoned."[83]

This idea of "abandonment" was a recurring theme of German propaganda in the Paris press as well as on posters and on the radio in the early weeks of the Occupation. The Germans hoped to exploit the bitterness felt by Parisians who had not joined the exodus, many of whom believed they had been betrayed by their government and their civil servants who had fled Paris after promising to stay. The Germans wanted to reassure Parisians that Germany would not let them down and that it was in their own interest to align themselves with Germany.

The Germans offered Parisians a taste of German culture, too. They staged concerts by German army or air force orchestras in bandstands, parks, squares, and other open spaces across the city.[84] Advertised in the press as showcases of German music, these concerts were free unless you chose to pay two francs to sit on a folding metal chair. They were the only "spontaneous" outdoor gatherings permitted by the authorities and took place weekly (weather permitting), usually during the weekend in the late afternoon, and they were attended by thousands of Parisians.[85] Ferdinand Dupuy, an administrator with the Paris police, went to one such concert in the centre of Paris on July 3, describing it as "An hour of beautiful music that it was impossible not to have enjoyed." However, after the concert, as he wandered home, humming the refrain from a sleepy Viennese waltz, the strangeness of it all struck him like a bad dream. "Just think of it: German music on the place de l'Opéra!"[86]

In their attempt to woo Parisians, the German authorities made strenuous efforts to dissuade them from considering the British as their friends or saviours. They played on a longstanding view in France of Britain as "Perfidious Albion." Britain had revealed its true duplicitous nature at Dunkirk, they said, abandoning the French army and ordering its own troops to scramble back home. The Germans insisted that the current difficulties faced by the Parisians were all the fault of Britain, the Jews, the Freemasons, and the corrupt politicians of the Third Republic, who had all pushed France into war against Germany. French perceptions of Britain were not helped when, on July 3 more than 1,200 French sailors died as British planes sank part of the French fleet in the Algerian port of Mers-el-Kebir, near Oran. The British felt they had to take action to prevent the ships from being used by the enemy, but in Paris the Germans immediately seized on this incident. A poster appeared all over Paris showing a wounded French sailor in the sea and carrying the slogan "Don't Forget Oran."

Although the French state was represented in Paris by the prefect of the Seine and the prefect of Police, the French government did not initially have its own representative in the city. This changed on July 9 when Léon Noël arrived in Paris with a brief to liaise with the German military on behalf of the French government in Vichy.[87] Noël, a tall, distinguished former diplomat, had been present at the signing of the armistice. He believed that by standing firm and acting with dignity, he could ensure that Franco-German cooperation would be confined strictly to the terms of the armistice agreement. He thought such an approach would benefit France and naively believed it would be possible "to slow down, to attenuate certain [German] demands and lead the enemy to abandon others."[88]

By the time Noël arrived in Paris, most of the legislators sitting in the Chamber of Deputies in 1939 had managed to reach Vichy. On July 10 they voted 569 votes to 80 to give Pétain a free hand to revise the constitution. Pétain promptly abolished the Third Republic and created a new regime, *L'État français* (the French State), underpinned by traditional conservative values that would inform its social and economic policies. The Third Republic was dead; seventy years of parliamentary democracy were at an end. The republican slogan of "Liberty, Fraternity, Equality" was replaced by that of "Work, Family, Fatherland." Pétain promised a "National Revolution" that would sweep away the "decadence" of the Third Republic, the parliamentary regime deemed to have corrupted and weakened France and that had led the country to the crushing defeat of June 1940.

Pétain proclaimed himself head of state and appointed as prime minister *(vice-président du Conseil)* Pierre Laval, a scheming politician who had played a vital role in helping Pétain secure power. Laval was also officially named as Pétain's successor should the head of state die or be unable to carry out his duties. Under the rules of the new authoritarian constitution Pétain had full powers to appoint and dismiss ministers and to pass laws through his personally appointed Council of Ministers. However, despite Parisians being subject to French government legislation as well as German directives, Vichy seemed a long way away and they showed little interest in what was happening there. "The transfer of presidential power to Pétain is rarely a subject of conversation,"[89] observed Langeron. Parisians were more concerned about the German military presence in their city.

Out of a total of about two and a quarter million people living in the city in 1936, only between 700,000 and a million were still there when the Germans arrived on June 14, 1940.[90] But even before the armistice was signed, sad, defiant, anxious, or hostile refugees began drifting back to Paris. As the weeks passed, this trickle turned into a steady flow that lasted into the autumn. Some people made their own way; others travelled on special trains departing daily from the Unoccupied Zone;

others went by car, sometimes with the help of German soldiers. In January 1941, the population of Paris was two and a half million; that of the suburbs was just under two million.

Simone de Beauvoir had left La Pouëze, near Angers, for Paris at the end of June with some people who had a car—although not enough petrol for the whole journey. She ditched her companions on the second day and came back to Paris, first in a German truck and then in a Red Cross car.[91] Another woman returning to Paris was helped by the occupying forces: "They gave us petrol which allowed us to continue on our way and they wouldn't take any money. What a contrast with our fellow countrymen, several of whom demanded 50 francs for a little bit of petrol."[92]

German troops helped the refugees as part of the army's campaign to boost its popularity, and because it was not in Germany's interest to have hordes of people wandering about the country. German propaganda emphasised German magnanimity, while still foisting responsibility for the refugees' return onto the French government. A statement from the German authorities published in the French press at the end of July referred to newspapers devoting more and more space to the refugee problem, suggesting that it was a matter for the German occupying forces alone. The German statement could not resist a dig at France's treatment of German citizens after the First World War: "We Germans know all about the misery and distress of refugees and we know about the terrible consequences of that condition. But because we, as a cultured society, have done everything we could to lessen this misery and distress, this should not mean that the French can hold Germany responsible for the terrible difficulties affecting the refugees."[93] The statement went on to say that every French person was responsible for what had happened: it was their elected government that had been mad enough to declare war on Germany, and it was "the French people who had allowed the Freemasons, the Jews and the friends of Britain to run France." In other words, blame your government for the plight of the refugees, blame yourselves for voting for them and for letting the enemies of France take over, but don't blame us.

Soon the Paris railway stations were packed once again, with thousands of passengers arriving daily.[94] These refugees were returning to a city under German control, but Paris was nevertheless "home," offering the possibility of work, the support of family and friends, and the hope of some sort of a stable existence. Most Parisians believed it was a better option than the uncertainty, fear, and deprivations of a life on the road, and they found it preferable to trying to start afresh in the Unoccupied Zone, where, even if it was free of Germans, they might not know anyone.

Langeron reported that returning refugees were astonished to find Paris intact with no sign of unrest and pillaging.[95] Retired schoolmistress Berthe Auroy, for example, was deeply relieved to find that nothing had been stolen from or damaged in her home in the rue Lepic in Montmartre. "It feel as if I have awoken from a horrible nightmare," she wrote.[96] But the returning refugees still had to come to terms with a city which told you at every turn that it was under German control. Micheline Bood described the Champs-Élysées as "full of Boches" and recorded how the sight of "a Boche sentry" outside the old Ministry of the Interior building made her feel sick.[97] Flora Groult was appalled by all the evidence of German occupation, but the shock soon wore off. "It's a disgrace to get used to seeing the swastika flying over the Chamber of Deputies. But you do get used to it. The nightmare becomes completely normal."[98]

When Simone de Beauvoir reached Paris she did not know what had happened to Jean-Paul Sartre. She heard rumours that French POWs in camps in the Paris suburbs of Garches and Antony were being fed dead dogs and, according to her parents, the prisoners would be held there until the end of the war.[99] Nevertheless, it was a relief to find that Montparnasse, one of her old stamping grounds, had rediscovered its old individuality and was once again a place to which she could retreat.[100] Writer Maurice Sachs,[101] a self-confessed bisexual crook, arrived back in Paris on the same day as de Beauvoir. He decided to go for a quick tour of the capital, which he described as "a dead city, quite a fine sight actually—like a civilisation that has been destroyed."[102] He saw a few people in the Latin Quarter, a handful of girls sitting with German officers at tables at the Capoulade Café on the boulevard Saint-Michel, and one or two pedestrians on the boulevard Saint-Germain. On the rue de Rivoli and the place de la Concorde there was no one except the odd German, but, like many, Sachs was taken aback to see the huge red banners decorated with swastikas waving in the wind.

Metalworker Georges Adrey arrived back in Paris at the Gare d'Austerlitz railway station half an hour after the curfew, and so he had to spend the night in the train. Despite the hustle and bustle around the station early the next morning, he, too, found Paris sad and deserted. "It looked as if the city had felt obliged to dress in mourning to welcome us home."[103] Berthe Auroy described Paris as "still deserted and so sad," and so quiet that you could hear your own footfall on the pavement.[104]

Benoîte Groult was nervous about returning to Paris, likening it to meeting again someone she had once loved and whom she hadn't seen for years. However, she found the streets less empty than she had expected. She noticed the large number of bicycles, big German cars on the road, and, especially, the German planes flying low over the city as if they were keeping an eye on its inhabitants.[105] On her return to Paris, schoolgirl Micheline Bood wrote in her diary that not a single car was to be seen, let alone a taxi, and she had to take the Métro home.[106] When Madeleine Gex le Verrier came back to the city she saw only one "taxi"—a sort of sedan chair pulled by two men on a tandem. Few vehicles were on the roads because buses and trucks had been requisitioned by the French army before June 14 or by the Germans afterwards. The Germans had reduced the number of French cars by restricting driving permits (*Ausweis*) to those Parisians who needed a car for work. Madeleine Gex le Verrier was met at the train station by an old friend and a man she did not know. "You're really lucky," the friend said. "I ran across my doctor on my way to meet you. As he has a permit allowing him to drive in Paris, he has offered to drive us home and take your luggage."[107]

The scarcity of cars meant more Parisians walked or took the Métro. Or they cycled—provided they could find a bicycle. In July Benoîte and Flora Groult's father was repairing his bicycle, believing he would soon need it to go out in search of food. On August 5 Benoîte wrote: "You can no longer find a single bicycle in Paris. I treasure my old wreck as I would a Rolls Royce."[108] The Groults' fine Vivasport car was requisitioned by the Germans, but it was returned because of its high petrol consumption. It ended up "on blocks in the courtyard, like a great useless cow."[109] Many of the small number of cars that began to be seen on the streets were converted to run on *gazogène;* a cylinder or tank was attached to the roof or back of a car, truck, or one of the few remaining buses and it was used to generate a gas that could be used instead of gasoline to power the vehicle. A small number of electric cars also appeared.

Horse-drawn vehicles started replacing taxis and buses, a development applauded in an article headed "Resurrection 1900" in the weekly *L'Illustration*, which warned of the potential health hazard of animal droppings. When the Groult family met a friend at a railway station in August, they took her home in a horse-drawn cab.[110] *Le Matin* revived a nineteenth-century horse-drawn omnibus service between the Madeleine and Bastille, which was free for passengers with a copy of that day's newspaper. There was another reason why Parisians saw more horses on the streets: as there were very few trucks to take animals to abattoirs, they had to make their final journey on their own four legs.[111] Motorised taxis were also soon replaced by *vélo-taxis*, or bicycle taxis: of varying quality and levels of comfort they consisted of a small trailer for the passenger or passengers that was attached behind a bicycle or tandem.[112]

Although getting around Paris had become increasingly difficult, good train services made travelling within the Occupied Zone relatively easy. Berthe Auroy left Paris in August for a summer break. On her return, like many of her fellow Parisians, she took day trips into the countryside around the city to buy food directly from farmers. However, crossing into the Unoccupied Zone was another matter altogether. To do so legally meant obtaining a travel permit from the German offices in the rue du Colisée, which was almost impossible. To cross the Demarcation Line illegally meant finding a *passeur*, or guide, to smuggle you across, which was as expensive as it was perilous.

To make matters worse, from July all written communication between the Occupied and Unoccupied Zone was outlawed; anyone caught trying to make contact across the Demarcation Line risked serious punishment, even the death penalty in serious cases, such as suspected espionage. "Sending letters between the Occupied and Unoccupied Zones is still banned," Benoîte Groult wrote in August. "What are the Germans afraid of?"[113] About the same time, Berthe Auroy was distressed that she had received no more news from her friend Loïs, who had written to her from the Unoccupied Zone a month or so earlier. "Everyone is coming back to Paris, everybody. . . . But Loïs! Loïs! I haven't heard a thing since her little card written from Luchon at the beginning of July. This silence is just awful. I curse that demarcation line between the two zones which stops letters getting through. It's like the Great Wall of China."[114] Edmond Dubois, a Swiss journalist who had left Paris in the exodus, was in Béziers in the south of France when he heard news of the ban on postal traffic between the two zones: "We are on the other side, cut off from Paris, isolated from a circle of friends who opened the door to fifteen years of Paris life, as well as being isolated from what was our place of work."[115]

Increasing numbers of Parisians made their way back to the city over the summer. They had been reassured by what they had heard about the city and German propaganda insisting that life there had already returned to what much of it was like before the war. At any rate, many wanted to return before the deadline expired: the German authorities had given those Parisians who had fled in the May–June exodus until the end of September to come home.

Relations were often tense between Parisians who had left and were now returning and those who had stayed behind. Many of those who had stayed not only felt abandoned but also viewed those who had left as cowards; the handful of officials who had stayed in Paris were later praised by Pétain for their devotion to duty. A class dimension reinforced these suspicions. In general, it was the most affluent who had left, since they had somewhere to go and the means to get there, while those who stayed in Paris were often from more modest backgrounds, who lacked the money needed to leave and the funds to support them when they reached their destination.

Those who stayed behind were sometimes accused by those who fled of being Nazi sympathisers or perhaps members of the "fifth column" so often mentioned in German propaganda broadcasts before the Occupation. According to one official report from the suburb of Versailles, it was not until September that tensions between those who had left and those who had stayed died down.[116]

Many had stayed in Paris because they had no other option. "I'm staying," Paul Léautaud wrote on June 11. "I decided that I always was going to stay. I am even more determined than ever to do so. I don't want to give up my pets. I would not know where to go."[117] Others, like one café owner and his wife, stayed for financial reasons and because of their age: "To have left would have meant financial ruin, so we stayed. And also, my wife and I were sixty-five years old."[118] Others were too ill to leave. Some 200 patients in a hospital in Argenteuil in the northwestern suburbs were abandoned to the care of a single nurse. So many had died that the hospital had run out of coffins and bodies were buried in old flour sacks.[119]

On a visit to the northern suburbs of Paris, de Beauvoir met many people who had fled, but who told her that if they had known the outcome they would never have left.[120] A man from the northern suburb of Saint-Leu-la-Forêt, who gave her a lift, certainly regretted leaving: a 450-mile trip on a motorbike back from Montauban, in the south of France near Toulouse, had left his wife with a twisted spine and him "suffering from a terrible pain in his private parts."[121]

On Bastille Day (July 14) 1940 Léon Noël, Vichy's man in Paris, joined a tiny delegation to lay a wreath at the Tomb of the Unknown Soldier. There were no fanfares, no processions, no crowds. Who among those cheering crowds on July 14, 1939, watching French and British troops march past, seeing the tanks rumbling along as the RAF aircraft flew overhead, could have predicted that one year later Parisians would be living under German occupation? No one knew how long the present state of affairs would last. No one knew if or when the French POWs would come home. No one knew what would happen next.

4

Paris, German Capital of France

$\mathcal{H}$ITLER HAD assured the German High Command that the army would have sole responsibility for managing the occupation of France. Several senior army officers wanted a guarantee from him that Heinrich Himmler's armed secret police units[1] would not be unleashed on murderous rampages, as had happened in Poland, and which had tarnished the reputation of the German army in the eyes of the world.[2]

At first, responsibility for running the Occupied Zone fell to the commander-in-chief of the German army, the phlegmatic General Walther von Brauchitsch. Until October he also doubled as the Militärbefehlshaber in Frankreich (MBF), the military commander for France. Brauchitsch was answerable to Hitler, the supreme commander of all German combat forces,[3] but it was the Führer's chief adjutant, Field Marshall Wilhelm Keitel in Berlin, who dealt directly with the military in Paris.

Somewhat confusingly, the MBF refers both to the general in charge of German forces in France and the organisation for which he was ultimately responsible. The MBF took as its headquarters the luxurious Hôtel Majestic on the avenue Kléber in the 16th arrondissement, where the British delegation to the Paris Peace Conference in 1919 was based. Although Brauchitsch formally remained MBF until the appointment of General Otto von Stülpnagel in October, he spent most of his time either at the château of Fontainebleau, forty-five miles southeast of Paris, or in Berlin. The MBF was marked by a cumbersome, complex, and unstable command structure. A plethora of units and subunits with overlapping responsibilities meant that from the very start the organisation was plagued by interdepartmental and interpersonal rivalries, seething tensions between Nazi and non-Nazi members of the army, and constant conflicts between the army and other nonmilitary German agencies.[4] This arrangement conformed to Hitler's preference for dysfunctional organisational models, which allowed him control through divide and rule.

The MBF's chaotic structure reflected, in part, the German army's lack of preparation and planning. The unexpectedly rapid fall of France gave the top brass little time to think through the administrative structure it needed for Paris and Occupied France, or which individuals it wanted to place in which posts. Much of the early chaos, then, resulted from hasty improvisation. To make matters worse, the generals had no clear idea about Hitler's long-term plans for France. In the short term, of course, the country would provide a vital launch pad for the invasion of Britain, which was scheduled to take place after the Luftwaffe had knocked out the RAF.

Brauchitsch needed somebody in Paris to take responsibility for the day-to-day running of the nest of intrigue that was the MBF. At the end of June, after two stop-gap appointments,[5] Alfred von Streccius, a sixty-five-year-old general, was brought out of retirement to be put in charge. The bearded Austrian had been a military adviser in China, where his fascination with the writings of the philosopher Lao Tzu had led him to prefer inaction to action whenever possible.

The army may have been officially in charge of the Occupation, but from the start it had to defend this claim against several members of the Nazi elite in Berlin, who schemed to undermine the MBF to their advantage. As a result, power struggles, quarrels, and clashes within the Nazi hierarchy in Berlin were played out in Paris challenging the power and authority of the military.

The two MBF propaganda organisations[6] were formally answerable to the military: in practice they were in competition with each other and both were briefed by Josef Goebbels, Hitler's propaganda chief, when he was in Paris in July, and they continued following his secret instructions after his return to Berlin. The Abwehr, or German military intelligence, with its headquarters in the Hôtel Lutetia on the boulevard Raspail was responsible for information-gathering, sabotage, and counterespionage. As the intelligence branch of the military it was officially answerable to the MBF. However, its Paris head, Lieutenant-Colonel Friedrich Rudolph, actually took orders from Admiral Wilhelm Canaris, the head of the Abwehr, who, like Goebbels, had visited Paris and was now back in Berlin. Joachim von Ribbentrop, the German minister of foreign affairs, had his man in Paris. Otto Abetz, Ribbentrop's "adviser to the MBF" arrived in Paris the day after the German army. Along with a hand-picked team of German cronies, most of whom he had known since the mid-1930s, Abetz established his headquarters in the former German embassy on the rue de Lille in the 7th arrondissement.[7]

In September 1939 Heinrich Himmler, the much-feared head of security in the Third Reich, brought the different paramilitary, police, and security units together under a single umbrella organisation, the RSHA, and put his right-hand man, Reinhard Heydrich, in charge.[8] Despite Hitler's ban on nonmilitary police or security units accompanying the army into the capital, Himmler arranged to have some twenty members of the RSHA smuggled into the city in June, wearing uniforms of the GFP, the German military secret police;[9] they soon established their base in the Hôtel du Louvre, on a square just behind the museum.[10] This Sonderkommando (independent commando) was led by an SS major, Helmut Knochen, a slim, thirty-year-old who had forsaken a career in journalism to devote himself to the Nazi cause.

The men in Knochen's unit were drawn from different sections of the RSHA, namely, the SS, the elite Nazi paramilitary force; the Sipo-SD, which brought together the Nazi Party's own intelligence and investigation agencies and those of the Reich. The State Secret Police, the Gestapo,[11] now a department within the RSHA, had one representative, Karl Boemelburg, who was initially in the city in a consultative role. Knochen's group was in Paris (according to Reinhard Heydrich) to identify, keep an eye on, and fight the Reich's "ideological enemies," especially Jews, Communists, anti-Nazi Germans, and Freemasons. Parisians made no distinctions between these various competing groups and tended to refer to all the German security units as "the Gestapo."

Determined to maintain its own tight control over policing and security, the MBF kept a close watch on Knochen's shadowy group and insisted that its activities be strictly limited to information-gathering and that the fruits of any investigations be handed over to the MBF. Himmler's men grudgingly accepted this—for the time-being—and were soon busy pursuing suspected anti-Nazis, seizing records, and dutifully calling in the German military police to carry out arrests or house searches. But they were biding their time, positioning themselves and waiting for an opportunity to move in and snatch responsibility for security matters away from the army. Knochen was soon supported by a second unit, and in August a third contingent arrived. It was based in the Hôtel Boccador with offices in the French Sûreté building, 11, rue des Saussaies, where Boemelburg was now based, representing two branches of the secret security forces (the Gestapo and the Sipo-SD).

Meanwhile, the German military continued urging its troops to behave courteously towards the Parisian population, many of whom continued to testify to the politeness—even the kindness—of German soldiers, who gave up their seats for old ladies on the Métro and offered children chocolate bars and sweets. But of course, there was a much darker side to the German occupation of Paris.

On June 15, the day after the Germans arrived in the city, Roger Langeron was visited by a member of Knochen's unit. This man, described by Langeron as a member of the Gestapo, wanted to know if, as prefect of police, Langeron was still under the orders of "the Jew Mandel,"[12] a reference to Georges Mandel, who served briefly as minister of the interior in Paul Reynaud's government. The German wanted to know where the police files were being held. Langeron feigned ignorance and the man stormed out, threatening to return.[13] Two days later, Langeron learned that four of his police superintendents (*commissaires de police*) had been taken away for questioning "by the Gestapo" and had not been seen again.[14] Five days later three more were arrested and all seven were taken to Germany. Langeron himself was removed from office and put under surveillance. However, he soon resumed his duties and remained in post in Paris until February 1941, when, under pressure from the Germans, the Vichy government dismissed him. All seven police superintendents were released in mid-July after the intervention of Léon Noël, the French government's representative.

A unit of the Einsatzstab Reichsleiter Rosenberg (ERR)—a rival outfit to that of Knochen—established itself in Paris at the very start of the Occupation. Founded by Alfred Rosenberg, the chief Nazi ideologue, the ERR was in the city with Hitler's blessing to amass Jewish and Masonic books, artefacts, and treasures for a proposed postwar Nazi university in Germany. In practice, it was nothing but a looting agency, committed to pillaging works of art and books belonging to "enemies of the Reich," namely, Jews, Freemasons, and members of "degenerate races" from central and eastern Europe who had settled in Paris. The ERR raided the headquarters of the two largest Masonic orders in the country, the Grand Orient de France and the Grand Loge de France,[15] and by the end of June Rosenberg was gloating that, thanks to the alacrity of his men, a significant hoard of Masonic treasures had been seized in Paris[16] as well as artefacts that Germany claimed had been stolen by France or which were of particular historical importance to the Reich.[17]

A month later German pillaging and requisitioning of premises owned by Jews, Freemasons, and other "undesirables" was still continuing. On July 15, for example, the ERR raided the famous Lipschütz bookshop on the place de l'Odéon; the owner had fled and the ERR removed the 65,000 books he had left behind.[18] Author Paul Léautaud visited the now empty shop; he knew Lipschütz personally and considered him to be extremely charming, courteous, helpful, and fair, and he damned the Germans' action as "pure theft."[19]

While the ERR and Knochen's unit did their dirty work, the German army did not simply restrict itself to cosy public relations exercises. The MBF, too, was quite prepared to intervene if it found something offensive. At the end of June German troops demolished and then blew to pieces a statue of General Mangin, a French hero of the First World War, that stood on the place Denys-Cochin (7th arrondissement).[20] On July 5, two days after the British scuttled the French fleet at Mers-el-Kebir, the MBF ordered the demolition of a bas-relief in the wall of the Jeu de Paume Museum in the Tuileries Gardens; the sculpture honoured Edith Cavell,[21] the British nurse in occupied Belgium executed for "treason" by the Germans for saving the lives of soldiers from both sides during the First World War; on July 26 German soldiers blew up a First World War memorial in Vincennes because they deemed the inscription to be "insulting."[22]

Of all the Germans working to undermine the military in Paris, the most effective and therefore the most dangerous was Otto Abetz,

Ribbentrop's representative in the city. Abetz, a thirty-seven-year-old former art teacher and self-proclaimed Francophile whose wife was French, joined the Nazi party in 1937.[23] Before the war he had been an indefatigable promoter of Franco-German understanding, trying to persuade influential Parisians that a rapprochement between France and Germany was in the interest of both countries. A frequent visitor to Paris until June 1939, when he was expelled from the country for political meddling, Abetz could be suave, sophisticated, and charming, but he also had a fiery temper. General Benoît-Léon Fornel de la Laurencie, who would replace Léon Noël as the Vichy government's representative in Paris, described Abetz as "a Nazi, but a second-rate one both in terms of character and physique, a sort of brute bursting with arrogance. . . . When you meet him you are struck by the crudeness of his way of thinking, his ideas and his manners."[24] The military, anxious to protect its own authority, watched uneasily as Abetz set about building his own power base in the city, reestablishing links with his old French contacts and Nazi sympathisers, catching up on the gossip, and helping acquaintances obtain driving permits, passes to the Unoccupied Zone, much sought-after petrol coupons, or the release of friends and relatives from POW camps.[25] He was also scheming to subvert the still-banned French Communist Party by backing its bid for to publish its newspaper *L'Humanité* legally rather than clandestinely.

The French Communist Party—banned by the French government in September 1939 and hounded by the French police since then— hoped that things would change now that the Germans had arrived. Assuming it could count on the protection of the Nazi-Soviet Pact, the clandestine PCF, headed by Jacques Duclos, had called on its members and supporters to come out of hiding to lobby Léon Noël, Vichy's representative in Paris. They sought the reestablishment of the municipal councils that had been dissolved, plus the reinstatement of all the Communist councillors who had been sacked. This directive by the PCF leadership (who remained in hiding) resulted in thousands of Communists coming out into the open, who were then promptly arrested by the French police and interned in French concentration camps.

The Communist Party was reeling: many members had resigned in disgust after the signing of the pact; thousands more had been killed in action, were behind barbed wire in POW camps, or had been arrested and interned by the French police. Now even more party members were being rounded up. The PCF leadership desperately wanted *L'Humanité* to publish legally again to help it reconnect with what was left of its rank and file.

Two members of the PCF Central Committee, Jean Catelas and Maurice Tréand—nicknamed "Fatman" *(le Gros)*—delegated a young female militant, Denise Ginollin, to sound out the German authorities.[26] She contacted Lieutenant Weber, a member of the Press Unit within the main MBF propaganda bureau.[27] Weber told her he had no objection in principle to the paper going on sale legally. However, Langeron, now back in office, and the Paris police had other ideas and stepped in and arrested Tréand, Ginollin, and another female militant.[28]

Abetz was enraged and had the Communists released immediately. As a true Nazi he loathed communism, but he wanted to use an authorised *L'Humanité* for his own ends: not only to counter the power of the MBF propaganda organisations, but also to reach out to French workers, hoping to persuade them to drop Marxism in favour of Nazism, thereby undermining the PCF's influence.

In a meeting with Abetz at the former German embassy on June 26, Tréand and Catelas emphasised how the PCF had opposed the war and had been persecuted for its pains. They stressed that the newspaper would promote the economic reconstruction of France, denounce British imperialism, and campaign for a lasting peace. But the plan fell through; Berlin did not back Abetz's plan, and Duclos and the PCF leadership (who later denied any knowledge of these discussions) had second thoughts. The plan was, in any case, vetoed by the Comintern.

After the collapse of these negotiations,[29] Abetz funded a new Paris-based paper, *La France au travail*, which, apart from its strident anti-Semitism, bore a striking resemblance to *L'Humanité*.[30] He hoped that this faux Communist newspaper would woo French workers away from the PCF, and to an extent he was successful: *La France au travail*'s attacks on the bosses, those who took France to war, and on incompetent state functionaries, coupled with its support for the unemployed and women struggling on their own—widows or those with husbands in POW camps—were so similar to articles in the clandestine *L'Humanité* that the latter had to assure its readers there was no PCF involvement whatsoever in *La France au travail*.

Abetz had other concerns beyond subverting the French Communist Party. On June 23, the day after the signing of the armistice agreement, he proposed confiscating private property owned by Jews and by those French politicians deemed to be "responsible for the war."[31] A week later, Ribbentrop informed Abetz of Hitler's decree that works of art and historical documents belonging to private individuals, especially Jews, should be taken and "put into safe-keeping." Abetz reacted by immediately telling the German military in Paris that it was he who had been charged by the Führer with the auditing and seizure of Jewish-owned works of art in Paris and the Occupied Zone.[32]

Thanks to his prewar visits to Paris and his training as an art teacher, Abetz not only knew something about art, but knew where the most interesting Jewish art galleries in the city were to be found. He enlisted the help of some members of the secret military police (GFP), gave them the addresses of some fifteen Jewish-owned galleries, and instructed them to confiscate their contents and transfer them to the embassy.[33] After two days of raids the building began to resemble an Aladdin's cave, stacked high with paintings, jewels, tapestries, sculptures, and antique furniture. Abetz then told the military that a special commando unit under Baron von Künsberg, who had already seized archives in Lille, Boulogne, and Calais, would soon be coming to Paris to help him appropriate even more of the works of art in the city.

At the Hôtel Majestic, Count Franz Wolff-Metternich, the head of the Art Treasures Protection Unit of the MBF, was appalled. Abetz and Künsberg considered art to be war booty and were keen to get their hands on as much of it as they could; Wolff-Metternich, a descendent of the celebrated statesman, was a specialist on mediaeval architecture and a professor of art at Bonn University. He had been seconded to the military and saw his role as a protector of works of art, insisting that the Paris occupation should be conducted in strict accordance with the 1907 Hague Convention. This stipulated, among other things, that any seizure of works of art was strictly forbidden under threat of punishment. By taking artworks Abetz had provided the first serious challenge to the MBF's authority in the city.

Even if the Germans were engaged in turf wars among themselves, nobody could deny they were in charge. As well as flags and banners on all the main buildings, the city seemed to be full of Germans soldiers: walking along the pavements, sitting in cafés, attending the theatre, or coming in and out of shops or the Métro, on which they travelled first class. Large groups of them could always be found near the Eiffel Tower, Sacré-Coeur, Notre-Dame, and the Arc de Triomphe, having their photographs taken to be sent back home to their proud families. Germans rarely ventured into the more dangerous working-class areas in Paris itself or the northern and eastern suburbs unless they were billeted there.

The soldiers were quick to discover the famous Pigalle nightspots, such as the Moulin Rouge with its topless beauties, as well as other less reputable venues where women wearing a lot less offered a lot more. The troops frequented the cabarets of Montmartre up the hill close to Sacré-Coeur. Retired schoolmistress Berthe Auroy, who lived nearby, wrote of large numbers of trucks, full of soldiers, parked in front of the Moulin de la Galette, the Montmartre cabaret immortalised by Van Gogh, Toulouse-Lautrec, Renoir, and other artists.

Soldiers had venues for their exclusive use or tailored to their needs: cinemas, such as Le Rex on the boulevard Poissonnière, and theatres, such as Le Théâtre de l'Empire on the avenue de Wagram, were requisitioned, reclassified, and open only to German soldiers or to a few Parisians with special passes.[34] To encourage healthy pursuits, German soldiers were strongly urged to spend their free time in *Soldatenheime*, "soldier homes," where they could relax, have a bite to eat, read newspapers, and play parlour games. When horse racing resumed, Auteuil and Longchamp proved to be very popular with the German soldiers, who had their own reserved enclosures. Some restaurants, including the exclusive Tour d'Argent near Notre-Dame, started producing menus in German for wealthy officers who could afford to eat there; they did a roaring trade—as did cafés, bistros, and other restaurants that swapped their "English Spoken Here" signs for "Man Spricht Deutsch" (German Spoken).

All German personnel in Paris were given 50 Reichsmarks spending money *(Reichskasswenscheine)*, which, at the new more favourable exchange rate of 20 francs to the mark, allowed them to spend liberally.[35] They spent money on food, drink, clothes, and entertainment, but also on luxury and household goods, which they sent to family and friends in Germany, where such items had long since disappeared from the shops. Journalist and author Pierre Audiat described soldiers weighed down with parcels of fabrics, silk stockings by the dozen, perfume by the litre, and whole lines of women's shoes,[36] and Berthe Auroy saw Germans "coming out of the shops, their arms full of packages."[37] A joke went around Paris concerning two British spies disguised as German soldiers who were immediately identified by the Gestapo as British agents. When asked how the Gestapo knew they weren't German soldiers, the reply came, "Because you're not carrying any packages."[38]

The Parisians had various terms for the ubiquitous Germans. In their diaries, Micheline Bood and Charles Braibant both refer to Germans as *les Boches*, but this pejorative term, common during the First World War, was rarely used in public.[39] The Germans found it offensive; Pierre Audiat referred to women being arrested for using it and having to spend a whole day in custody polishing soldiers' boots as punishment.[40] A more common term was *les Fritz*, which the Germans tolerated, and *les Fridolins*, with which they were quite happy; they were also referred to, ironically, as *ces messieurs* ("these gentlemen"). Later, when food became scarce, they were sometimes called *les Mange-Tout* (a type of pea which translates literally as "the Eat-Everythings"), and blaming them for the absence of potatoes, *les Doryphores* (Colorado Beetles).

Male soldiers were not the only Germans on the streets: there was a female "army" of military support staff,[41] comprising typists, secretaries, and telephonists who were nicknamed "the mice" *(les souris)* on account of their grey uniforms. They were housed in requisitioned hotels across the city, with a large concentration of them in the international halls of residence on the Cité Universitaire student campus, opposite the Parc Montsouris, near the Porte de Gentilly. There were nurses staffing hospitals requisitioned by the Germans who were nicknamed *boniches* (maids) because of the large white bonnets they wore. They were generally older than "the mice" and, according to Audiat, "lacked both charm and beauty, making the hypothesis of any flirting between an invalid and his guardian angel most unlikely."[42]

Germans in Paris had their own fortnightly magazine to guide them around the city.[43] The first issue, which appeared in July 1940, had two prefaces, one in German and the other in French. The German preface claimed it was the exemplary behaviour of the German soldiers that had hastened the reopening of restaurants, clubs, theatres, and museums; the French preface asserted that a German guide book aimed at helping soldiers with shopping and excursions would hasten the return of prosperity and help give "our old adversaries" an enhanced appreciation of the city. The guide gave a list of recommended tourist sites.[44] The second issue highlighted the opening of the Folies Bergère, reinforced the message that Paris was starting to live again, and carried advertisements for racetracks, fashion boutiques, theatres, restaurants, and nightclubs.[45]

The German military authorities remained fixated on the behaviour of their soldiers. They insisted they behave correctly in public at all times. Uniformed personnel were forbidden to smoke in the street or even to loosen their ties; they were not to swim in the Seine, dance in public, sing in the streets, or buy pornography or drugs. The authorities tried, but with very limited success, to keep German soldiers isolated from the Parisians—especially Parisian women. In theory, an absolute ban was in place on any contact at all with black or Jewish women, and one early instruction (largely ignored) forbade German soldiers from even walking arm in arm in the street with a French woman. Despite these strictures, Paris police reports were full of the sorts of incidents one might expect to find whenever large groups of male soldiers have lots of money to spend in a city far from home: rowdy behaviour, drunkenness, fighting, and sometimes worse.

The top brass considered that fraternisation between French women and German soldiers (which began as soon as troops arrived in the city) reflected badly on the army and on the Reich and that it threatened to undermine discipline. It was also considered to be unpatriotic. France and Germany may have signed an armistice agreement, but without a full peace treaty both countries were technically still at war. Fraternising with the French was fraternising with the enemy, an enemy that had (in German eyes) forced a war on the German people.

To regulate and monitor sexual activity the military authorities requisitioned some forty Paris brothels to be patronised exclusively by German soldiers. Clearly displayed rules set out how the customers were expected to behave: no alcohol, no civilians, condoms to be used. Every soldier had to note the reference number of the woman with whom he had sex: the charge was 1 Reichsmark 50, or 30 francs.[46] Paul Léautaud discovered one of these brothels while out for a stroll with a friend near the boulevard Saint-Germain: "Walking down the rue Grégoire-de-Tours we saw on the door of a brothel a notice printed in German, which we couldn't understand. Underneath was another sign, this time in French: NO ENTRY FOR CIVILIANS OR FOREIGNERS."[47]

A German army report in July revealed what the authorities were up against in trying to control the behaviour of troops. The report complained about the behaviour of German soldiers in Paris and specifically referred to "the most disgusting dance halls with the worst sort of French tarts in Montmartre and elsewhere" that were "packed full of German soldiers whose behaviour is as bad as the company they keep." It added that such places were also frequented by officers, who did not appear to be shocked by the conduct of the troops.[48] An Austrian lieutenant visited one of these Montmartre dives with his company commander. He noted: "Two ravishing young women—one dark-haired, the other a blonde—named Cécile and Yvonne. The commander is a discreet fellow and soon left. I took a room for Cécile and myself and spent a delicious night there with her. She surpassed my expectations. Her father was a Parisian, her mother Tunisian. A very good mix."[49]

Many of the German soldiers in Paris were young men from rural parts of Germany who had rarely, if ever, left the family farm; they were overwhelmed by the sights of a city whose name they knew but which they had never thought they would see for themselves. It was not just the country lads who were impressed. An infantryman from the 30th Division wrote: "I am a native of Hamburg and so not a country bumpkin, but I have never seen such a beautiful city." He was impressed by the city's cultural heritage and the efficiency of the Métro.[50] Like many of his comrades, he climbed the Eiffel Tower, where he scratched the name of his wife on one of the supports. He also visited a cabaret, where "they showed us things on the stage that we only imagined in our wildest fantasies." He rounded off the day with a visit to a brothel. "Ah, soldiers," he wrote, "they always find a whorehouse more easily than they do a church."[51] However, the German military disciplined its soldiers swiftly and severely if they stepped too far out of line: on July 15 a German sergeant was executed by firing squad for the attempted rape of a fifty-seven-year-old concierge in the rue d'Alésia.[52]

However hard the military authorities tried to regulate and control the sexual behaviour of the German troops they were doomed to fail. One of the main reasons was the sheer number of "freelance" and part-time prostitutes working in Paris and the Seine department; they did not work in official brothels and, according to German estimates, numbered between 80,000 and 100,000.[53] Some of them worked the streets, from exclusive areas, such as the avenue Wagram, to poor areas, such as those around the Porte Saint-Denis and Les Halles. Others sought out customers in cafés on the Champs-Élysées and in Montmartre and

Montparnasse, which were subject to frequent raids by the French police.[54] Many of these part-time prostitutes were the wives of French prisoners of war who could not survive on the meagre allowance they received from the French government. Wives of French private soldiers held in POW camps received about half what a male factory worker could expect to earn, plus a small amount for each child—out of which they were expected to pay rent and buy food, clothes, and day-to-day products like razors, which they dispatched regularly to their husbands in parcels. At the end of 1940 a woman in Paris with one child received 28.50 francs a day, when meat cost 22 francs a pound and a bunch of carrots cost 4.50 francs.[55] The Vichy government's financial support for POW wives was in essence an extension of the rights of mobilised men enacted by the Third Republic after the declaration of war in September 1939; it was posited on the assumption that "the POW question" would soon be resolved in a formal peace treaty resulting in the prisoners being sent home very soon. By 1941, it was clear that Hitler had no intention of freeing these men who could serve as a source of labour and, if necessary, as a bargaining counter. In July 1941, Jacques Chevalier, the Vichy family and health secretary, wrote that "the nation has a debt to prisoners' families and this debt has not been paid."[56] This triggered a battle within the Vichy government with Chevalier asserting that widespread deprivation among the wives of POWs was resulting in the "considerable development of prostitution of women and minors" and the large number of actual or expected births of children with German fathers.[57] At the end of 1941 and the beginning of 1942, ministers campaigning within the Vichy government for an increase in allocations for the wives of POWs claimed variously that 60 or even 75 percent of prostitutes working in Paris were wives of POWs; most of whom, they claimed, had been driven into prostitution by hunger. Although these claims were certainly exaggerated in pursuit of higher allocations for POWs' wives, it has been estimated that the wives of POWs numbered at least 3,000, namely, 10 percent of the clandestine prostitutes working in the Seine department.[58] Eventually in July 1942, the daily allowance for a POW wife living in Paris or the Seine department was raised from 16 to 20 francs a day, but in a context of raging price inflation this was still wholly inadequate.

When rationing was introduced in September 1940, the wives of POWs received no extra rations for the monthly packages they were allowed to send to their husbands, whose contents could cost as much as 250 francs.[59] Some POW wives like Odette P., a twenty-one-year-old factory worker, worked as a prostitute in the Ternes area near the Arc de Triomphe whenever she needed extra money to cover the cost of items in a parcel for her husband.[60]

Shortage of money and the resulting deprivation were not the only problems the wives of POWs had to face. Initially weeks and sometimes months of emotional agony were endured before the prisoner's wife received confirmation that her husband was alive. On July 1 Simone de Beauvoir wrote of a prostitute at the Dôme in tears because she had no news of a lover, being comforted: "He hasn't written, but nobody's writing. Don't worry." "It's the same old story everywhere," added de Beauvoir, "women in the Métro, on the doorstep. 'Have you heard anything?' 'No, he must be a prisoner.' 'When will the lists come out?'" De Beauvoir was pessimistic about the POWs being released. "I am once again convinced that they won't release a single one before there's peace."[61]

Most wives had to wait until August before being notified that their husbands were held prisoner; for some the news did not come until the autumn of 1940 while others did not hear until the end of January 1941.[62]

Many wives thought that since the armistice was signed the war was over, and, encouraged by Vichy propaganda, they believed they and their husbands would soon be reunited. As time passed and nearly all the POWs remained in captivity, POW wives became increasingly anxious about how long this separation would last. Even Marie-Hélène Corbel, a Communist Party sympathiser from Paris, who understood better than most that her husband's fate depended out the outcome of the war, was wracked with anxiety: "When would the war ever end, when? And how, and in what way"? A friend of another POW wife turned to tarot cards to try to determine the date when her husband would return.[63]

POWs were allowed to write two letters and two postcards home a month, which could take up to a month to arrive. This delay was another cause of acute anxiety. Josette Lorin, the wife of a POW who lived in the suburb of Nanterre, recalled, "Scarcely had we read and reread them [the letters], than we asked ourselves, 'Is he still alive?'"[64]

Along with concern for the welfare of their husbands, the wives of POWs had to make an often massive adjustment to being on their own and, along with it, the solitude that came from being so. Simone, who married in 1930, lived in Paris, where she worked restoring tapestries for antique dealers. She found herself alone with her son, who was only two and a half, when her husband was taken prisoner. She felt she was unable to care for him and sent him off to a family in the countryside near Belfort, and later in Switzerland, who had agreed to look after him. "What loneliness for me. During the day I had my work but in the evening, news about my husband and son did not make up for their absence. The housing block I lived in was empty—all my neighbours who were self-employed artisans had left for the provinces. I used to get so frightened at night! You can never overestimate how precious it is to hear a reassuring voice. You have to be alone to know just how much that is worth."[65] Even women such as Martine Lombardi, who lived surrounded by her family—mother, grandparents, and children—and who worked full time in an office, felt "alone to face all the difficulties, no one to give me moral support. On the contrary I had to help my family to bear their sorrow and, moreover, I had to hide in my letters to my husband how bad I felt about his absence and my loneliness."[66]

Estelle Sergent, another Parisian married to a POW, recalled that part of the reason she had fewer problems than many other such women was because "my parents provided me with a great deal of support." For others, like Madeleine Capot, parental support came at a price—the loss of autonomy. She came from a very conservative Parisian family, and she and her husband, who married in March 1940, lived with Madeleine's mother. Madeleine continued living with her mother after her husband's capture, "My mother would not have liked me to live alone. I was young and had to be protected to remain worthy and faithful." The parents of Yvette Giraud, a Parisian who was engaged to a POW, maintained total control over her social life until she was twenty-seven.[67] It was not just parents, but also parents-in-law who could apply pressure: the in-laws of Gisèle Desbois, who lived in the countryside, refused to send her food in Paris as a way of pressuring her to move to live with them.[68]

Wives of POWs in Paris whose children stayed with them also reported difficulties: they regretted the absence of a man in the house as detrimental to the welfare of their sons and they themselves wanted an authority figure to maintain discipline. Estelle Sergent's daughter called her grandfather "daddy" while young children whose only image of their father was a man in uniform saw any soldier as a potential father.

Anne Devron's son, for example, saw a German soldier in the street in Paris and, to Anne's great embarrassment, asked his mother if the soldier was his daddy.[69]

☞ COOPERATION BETWEEN THE German military police and the Paris police as set out in the armistice agreement was positively encouraged and initially relations were generally good. The Germans relied on the Paris police to help keep order on the streets, to conduct house searches, and to direct what little road traffic there was. Some Paris policemen enthusiastically saluted the German officers,[70] but German military chiefs often complained that too few did so or that their salutes were lackadaisical and slovenly.[71]

Although some Parisians threw in their lot with the occupying forces, Parisians as a whole were not keen to ingratiate themselves with the occupiers. They settled for coexistence with the occupiers while waiting to see what happened next. From the very start of the Occupation some Parisians engaged in acts of passive resistance. In July an anonymous, illegally produced four-page pamphlet entitled *Conseils à l'occupé* (Advice to Those Living under Occupation) was circulated in the city. Written by Jean Texcier, a fifty-one-year-old left-wing trade unionist employed at the Ministry of Trade, the pamphlet constituted a mini-manifesto of passive resistance setting out in thirty-three short paragraphs how Parisians should behave towards the occupying forces. If a German addressed them in German, he suggested, they should pretend they did not know the language; if a German asked them a question in French, they did not have to give a truthful answer. The final paragraph called on the reader to make copies of the text and pass them on.[72] Texcier's ironic, low-key text also advised Parisians to keep contact with Germans to an absolute minimum. "Outwardly show indifference, but inside, hang on to your anger. It might well come in handy."[73] To Texcier's delight, a copy of the text found its way to London, and in October it was featured in one of the Free French BBC broadcasts to France.[74]

A common tactic of passive resistance was to deliberately avoid eye contact with Germans and to behave as if they were not there. This behaviour started within days of the Germans arriving and became increasingly common throughout the summer. As early as June 16 Langeron wrote that the Parisians "look straight ahead as if the green uniforms were invisible and transparent."[75] In July, young Benoîte

Groult wrote, "We're practising never to catch their [the Germans']
eye. We have to give ourselves the illusion that we're resisting."[76] In August medical student Bernard Pierquin observed, "One thing that is
striking: the Parisians are in close contact with Germans without
looking at them,"[77] and a month later, teacher Jean Guéhenno noted
with satisfaction: "I am pleased with the Parisians. They walk past the
Germans as they would past a dog or a cat. It looks as if they neither
see nor hear them."[78] According to Pierre Audiat, the Germans were
very quickly only too aware that the Parisians were blanking them and
called Paris *Die Stadt ohne Blick* (the city that refuses to look at you).[79]

Women on the Métro turned down offers of seats made by German
soldiers; Parisians deliberately let doors in the Métro corridors swing
back into the Germans' faces; and people on the street deliberately mis-
directed them.[80] The German-controlled Radio-Paris complained
over the airwaves that French people had forgotten how to smile; they
had forgotten the most basic notions of politeness, it said, and it accused
them of "taking advantage of the magnanimity of the victor."[81] Other
Parisians went further, ensuring that Germans were never served first
in shops. At the end of July a German soldier who tried to push to the
front of a long queue in a dairy was told by the owner to get in line like
everybody else. "The soldier joined the queue without causing any fuss
and resignedly waited his turn."[82]

A tiny handful of Parisians were determined to do more than engage
in passive resistance. Poet and novelist Claude Aveline later recalled
how, on a beautiful evening in July in a flat on the boulevard Montparnasse, "three friends discovered their mutual disgust at Pétainist cowardice and decided they had to prepare the fight-back."[83] The trio of
Aveline and his writer friends Jean Cassou and Marcel Abraham was
soon joined by Agnès Humbert, described by Cassou as "an outgoing,
impetuous and courageous woman."[84]

Humbert had returned to Paris from a village near Limoges. Inspired
by de Gaulle's broadcast, she had been so shaken by the sight of the occupied city and the complacent passivity of her colleagues at work
that she wondered if there was something wrong with her. She decided
they were the abnormal ones and that the best way to maintain her
sanity was to join others who wanted to oppose the Occupation. She
wrote in her diary: "The only remedy is for us to act together, to form
a group of ten or so like-minded comrades, no more. To meet up on

pre-agreed days to swap news, to write and distribute leaflets, and to share summaries of French radio broadcasts from London. I don't have many illusions about the practical effects of our actions, but if we manage simply to stay sane, that will be a success of sorts."[85]

The earliest opponents of the Occupation were all too aware of their isolation. Their sense of alienation from the rest of the population meant that they kept their heads down, engaged in low-level resistance, and hoped for the best. It is easy to understand Humbert's delight in coming across a copy of Texcier's pamphlet: "Will the writers of *33 Conseils à l'occupé* [*sic*] (Advice to Those Living under Occupation) ever know what they have done for us and doubtless for thousands of others? A spark in the darkness. . . . Now we know for sure that we are not alone. There are other people who think as we do, who are suffering and organising the struggle."[86] The seeds of active resistance were being sown.

During the early weeks of the Occupation, Paris posed no serious threat to the Germans. Official German reports described the Parisians as "quiet and correct" or "reserved and cautious." Nonetheless, some isolated acts of sabotage—the cutting of telephone wires, for example— were carried out mostly outside Paris and often by dissident Communists. Still, it was enough to make the German military authorities in Paris jumpy about anything that might possibly be a case of anti-German activity, and, whenever there was such an incident, they unfailingly assumed the worst.

A few days into the Occupation, the body of an NCO from the Adolf Hitler Regiment billeted in the southern suburb of Montrouge was found near a railway track not far from the Porte d'Orléans in the south of the city. The German authorities immediately assumed he had been murdered and threatened reprisals. They eventually established that the soldier had been hit by a train while returning drunk from a visit to a brothel. The German authorities overreacted again when another German soldier's body was discovered in Versailles.[87] They were also alarmed in mid-August when someone opened fire on a German army post in the Bois de Boulogne. Although Langeron suspected it had something to do with the longstanding rivalry between the German army and navy, the response of the German authorities was to ban Parisians from the area.[88] In Sarcelles, a few miles north of the city, ten days or so after the Bois de Boulogne incident, three soldiers were killed and others were seriously wounded in an explosion when a German truck accidentally ran into a pile of mines stacked by the roadside. The Germans were adamant that the troops had been targeted and told the local police chief that thirty local inhabitants would be taken as hostages and shot if the perpetrators of "this criminal act" were not found. Eventually, and reluctantly, the Germans accepted it was an accident rather than an act of armed resistance and exacted no reprisals.[89]

As the summer progressed, German reports noted the mood of Paris changing as the initial shock of occupation wore off. There were no signs of any peace treaty, which meant no prospect of POWs returning home; it was becoming increasingly difficult for Parisians to find what they needed in the shops; it was all but impossible to visit, write, or telephone anyone in the Unoccupied Zone—all of which fuelled resentment against the invaders. At the end of August, Helmut Knochen, the head of the secret police in Paris, reported "a growing anti-German tendency," and Streccius's staff at the MBF were also warning that an anti-German attitude was beginning to gain ground. A few weeks later, Otto Abetz agreed, adding that relations with French citizens had "considerably soured" since June and that one could indeed speak of "passive resistance." Professor Grimm, one of Abetz's German sidekicks, concurred, adding that if an initial stupor or depression could be detected after the Germans had arrived, it had long disappeared and been replaced by a sense of bitter recrimination. Genuine reconciliation with France was, he concluded, not possible.[90] In early August Hitler formally appointed Otto Abetz as Germany's official ambassador to Paris, although Abetz, in a typical display of arrogance, had been describing himself as German ambassador since his arrival in the city in June. He had happily been signing letters to this effect as he worked to undermine the MBF and turn Paris into the hub of Franco-German collaboration with himself at the centre.

German relations with the French government were supposed to be conducted via Léon Noël, Vichy's representative in Paris, who had been having a hard time of it since arriving in the city at the beginning of July. He found himself marginalised by the German military, shunned by Abetz, and undermined by General Charles Huntziger, France's representative at the Franco-German Armistice Commission in Wiesbaden. Noël correctly believed that Huntziger was conceding too much, too easily. Concluding he could not do the job to which he had been appointed, Noël resigned on July 19.[91]

On that same day Abetz held his first meeting with Pierre Laval, Pétain's prime minister and official successor and the first Vichy minister to arrive in the city. Laval was a passionate believer in close Franco-German collaboration, posited on his conviction that Germany would soon be victorious across Europe and that it was in France's national interest to ally itself with the Third Reich. The two men hit it off immediately and Abetz oiled the wheels of cooperation by giving the portly, chain-smoking political wheeler-dealer a travel pass *(Ausweis)*. This allowed him to move freely between Paris and Vichy, which he did several times over the summer, much to the fury of other ministers to whom this privilege was not extended.

Laval and Abetz were indeed well suited. Each man sought to use the other to strengthen his own position and bring about a Franco-German collaboration in line with his own desires. Both were from modest backgrounds, both had been teachers, and both had flirted with socialism before shifting to the Right. Both had spoken publicly in favour of Franco-German collaboration and both disliked war as an instrument of policy. They were great talkers, too, with hugely inflated notions of their own importance and their ability to engineer the political solutions they wanted; both could be bullies.[92] Furthermore, both were mavericks who liked to plot and scheme while paying scant attention to organisational or bureaucratic protocol.

The members of the German High Command in Paris were infuriated that Abetz had a direct personal link with Pétain's second-in-command—who was a civilian to boot. At the same time, Laval's freelancing diplomacy ruffled a lot of ministerial feathers in Vichy, not least those of Paul Baudouin, the French government's foreign minister, who felt, rightly, that Laval was trespassing on his domain.

While Abetz and Laval were scheming in Paris, life began to take a turn for the worse for ordinary Parisians. During the first few weeks after the Germans arrived, it had not been too difficult for residents to find the food they wanted in the shops. On July 11 de Beauvoir wrote to Jean-Paul Sartre, who had been taken prisoner in June and was in a German POW camp: "Paris is still itself. Food supplies are as they should be—to tell the truth, I don't even notice any restrictions."[93] Benoîte Groult felt the same, writing on July 19, just after her return to Paris, that the shops were full of fruit, vegetables, and chocolate, enough for everyone, the victors and the vanquished. But she wondered how much longer this would last.[94] At the same time, Berthe Auroy was already having trouble trying to replace bed linen and some essential clothing she had lost in the exodus. "It's not easy. The shelves are already almost all completely empty. The Germans, the refugees, not forgetting those people who are careful and sensible, had made a beeline for the goods. To find a pair of shoes I had to go to six, seven, eight shops. Maybe more."[95] Supplies were becoming unreliable and availability varied from one part of the city to another. Jacques Biélinky was a Jewish-Russian émigré who arrived in France in 1909. He was granted political refugee status on arrival and then French nationality in 1927, and worked in Paris as an art critic and journalist.[96] On July 26 he wrote in his diary that butter was easy to find, but eggs and cheese had completely disappeared. Milk was still available but was limited to half a litre per person. Three days later he was unable to find any coffee anywhere.[97] Meanwhile, Micheline Bood, who lived a few miles away in the west of the city, wrote that obtaining food was fairly easy, except for butter and milk. But, she added, "everything is very expensive."[98]

On July 31, in a desperate attempt to reduce consumption, the French government decreed that bread could go on sale only twenty-four hours after it had been baked, when it was already starting to go stale. Very soon, with shelves in the shops ever more depleted and queues outside increasingly common and growing longer by the day, the government started introducing further restrictions. On August 1 the sale of croissants and pastries was banned in both zones, and an attempt was made to lay down strict rules for the serving of meals (excluding wine) in restaurants: a starter—raw vegetables or soup—and a main course—an egg- or fish-based dish with vegetables or pasta or meat and vegetables, cheese or fruit (cooked or raw). No butter or crème fraîche were to be served separately. Shop prices were in theory fixed for basic goods, but, as different prices were set for each administrative department, some people travelled to nearby departments in search of cheaper items.

On August 13 Pétain delivered a speech in which he acknowledged that the government was struggling to resolve the problem of food distribution and that of other essentials. However, he insisted that the government's top priority was "to ensure that everyone, rich and poor alike, had their fair share of the nation's resources."[99] A Paris police report a week later confirmed that the situation in the city was deteriorating, but, unlike Pétain, it concluded that the Germans were the main cause of shortages. The report noted, for example, that only limited quantities of butter were on sale, "above all because large amounts had been requisitioned by the German authorities." In addition, egg deliveries were few and far between, milk could be delivered only in the afternoon and had usually turned before it could be consumed, and cheese, except for Gruyère, was in very short supply while the same went for fresh and dried pasta.

The report further noted that while supplies of tomatoes and fruit—especially grapes and peaches—were "abundant," only a small quantity of wine had arrived because of the difficulty in getting enough petrol for the wine-tankers on which delivery depended. Supplies of fresh meat were just about sufficient, "despite the [German] requisitioning." Large and small grocery wholesalers and retailers were unable to meet the demand of their customers. Many shopkeepers had no tinned meat or tinned fish, rice, coffee, chocolate, or tea. Salt and tea were in great demand, although deliveries were "expected," and many smaller food shops opened for only a few hours a day because of reduced stocks. The report insisted the German army was to blame for the shortages: "The purchases by German military units have affected all categories of goods."[100] A month later another Paris police report referred to Germans buying up everyday items, such as sheets, napkins, tablecloths, wool, shoes, cotton goods, socks, and stockings.[101] A bank manager in the northwestern suburb of Pontoise reported: "All the shops selling food, clothes, and shoes have been cleaned out by German civilians and military personnel."[102] The volume of goods bought in Paris to be sent to Germany was so great that a designated postal service was created; parcels were stamped and wrapped in special paper to ensure a smooth passage through customs.

By early August Benoîte Groult was having to wash her hair with a tar-based concoction;[103] later that month, there was no butter for breakfast and while out shopping she bought the last bar of soap, the last but one bar of chocolate, and just one kilo of noodles—the shopkeeper would not let her have anymore. "The future looks grim," she wrote.[104] At home in Fontenay, Paul Léautaud, who had been stockpiling tobacco since June, was down to just one egg.[105]

☞ IN THE SECOND HALF OF JULY, with many Parisians seriously beginning to feel the pinch, the Vichy government began to flex its legislative muscles. Vichy may have been a hotbed of personal rivalries and competing policies,[106] but a consensus existed that Jews, foreigners, Communists, and Freemasons were to blame for subverting and weakening France. They had to be rooted out and dealt with. The prewar Daladier government had already started hunting down Communists and interning foreigners. Now it was Vichy's turn to deal with "the traitors" and "the enemies within."

On July 18 the Vichy government ruled that any citizens who had left the country between May 10 and June 30 would be stripped of their French nationality. This included numerous wealthy Parisian Jews, who, unlike the poorer Jews in the city, had fled abroad with many crossing the Pyrenees into Spain. This piece of legislation made Abetz's pillaging of Jewish-owned art treasures even easier because he could now claim that their former owners were stateless. Charles de Gaulle, in Vichy's eyes the most infamous and dangerous traitor of all, would be sentenced to death in absentia on August 2, 1940.

On July 17 the Vichy government passed a xenophobic law, applicable in both zones, banning all individuals without a French father from being employed by the state. Five days later it announced a review in both zones of all naturalisations since 1927. A commission headed by Justice Minister Raphaël Alibert, a royalist and failed businessman, began the daunting task of examining thousands of dossiers of refugees and their dependents who had been granted French nationality in the last thirteen years. Although Jews were not specifically cited in the legislation, the law disproportionately affected foreign Jews who had settled in France and acquired French nationality; they made up about a quarter of the 200,000 Jews living in Paris—itself the city where the biggest concentration of Jews in all of France lived. The first step in the "purification" of the French state had been taken.[107] On July 28, in another move against "outsiders," the French government instructed the Paris police to order all foreigners of both sexes aged over fifteen living in the Seine department to register with the authorities. All completed registration forms had to be handed in to the foreigners' landlords or concierges by August 6.

Meanwhile, Abetz was consolidating his position both in Paris and in Berlin. He tried to impress Hitler and so secure the Führer's backing for his challenges to the military in Paris by sending Hitler approximately fifteen of the biggest, most beautiful carpets from the embassy;

they left for Berlin in a convoy of trucks on August 1 under Künsberg's supervision.[108] While this was happening Abetz met Hitler in his "Eagle's Nest" near Berchtesgaden, where the two men discussed the future of France.[109] It was during these meetings that Hitler formally confirmed Abetz as German ambassador to Paris. Shortly before the two men met, Abetz had sent a memorandum to Ribbentrop, his boss, setting out what he thought should happen to France: "Germany's interests demand, on the one hand, that France be maintained in a state of internal weakness and, on the other, that France be kept at a distance from foreign powers hostile to the Reich. *Everything must be done on the German side to bring about the internal disunity and weakening of France.*"[110] Hitler, who had still not publicly clarified exactly how he envisaged France's future, warmed to this approach and decreed that in the future Abetz, rather than the German military, would be responsible in Paris for all political matters, including those relating to the press, publications, radio, film, and theatre. He added, according to Abetz, that "the censors from the army high command should restrict themselves to ensuring that nothing in the newspapers, books, films or on the radio will get the French politically worked up or threaten the security of the occupying army."[111] When Major Heinz Schmidtke, head of the MBF's main propaganda bureau, heard the news he rushed to Berlin in a failed bid to have this ruling reversed. On Abetz's return to Paris, the ambassador informed General Streccius that the MBF's propaganda offices would be allowed to deal only with censorship: henceforth, all other cultural matters were his responsibility.

Abetz strengthened his position by creating two new bodies based in Paris: the Deutsches Institut (German Institute) and the Informations-Abteilung (News Department). The institute, headed by Karl Epting, another of Abetz's associates from the 1930s, was located in the sumptuous Hôtel de Sagan on the rue Talleyrand, which, until recently, had been the Polish embassy. Its role was to promote German language and culture and to bring together German and French intellectuals from the arts, sciences, and literature. The News Department, headed until May 1941 by the Francophile Rudolf Rahn, would concentrate on mass propaganda and, in particular, ensure that the press and publishing output conformed to German wishes.

Abetz rightly believed that Goebbels's men in the MBF propaganda offices knew little and cared even less about French culture: their aim was simply to crush France's cultural supremacy. Abetz, on the other hand, feared that such a full-frontal attack on French culture ran the risk of provoking revolt and resistance. Instead, he favoured a softly-softly policy of "collaboration by seduction" to win over Parisians to a German worldview. He viewed this approach as a complement to his discussions in Paris with Laval and as contributing to his strategy to weaken and divide France, which he had set out in his July memorandum to Ribbentrop.

Abetz and his wife hosted lunches and extravagant soirées at the embassy on the rue de Lille and in a beautiful eighteenth-century house at Chantilly, placed at the ambassador's disposal by the Vichy government. These social occasions brought together people Abetz had known in Paris before the war as well as singers, actors, dancers, artists, and literary figures, including Abel Bonnard (poet, novelist, and later education minister in the Vichy government) and authors Robert Brasillach, Céline, Alphonse de Châteaubriant, Henri de Montherlant, Alfred Fabre-Luce, Sacha Guitry, and Paul Morand; sculptors Paul Belmondo and Charles Despiau; actresses Arletty, Edwige Feuillère, and Yvonne Printemps; and dancer and director of the Paris Opera ballet Serge Lifar.

As Abetz mingled with *le tout Paris* he presented himself as the good, civilised German, the friend of France, committed to striking at the Jews and Freemasons, the common enemies of Germany and France. With a gracious smile, he would gently point out to his French guests that France had declared war on Germany, not the other way around. But he was always quick to add that Hitler sought a peaceful settlement with France; adding persuasively, if mendaciously, that Hitler wanted France and Germany to become equal partners in the "new Europe" that the Nazis were building. Abetz believed that if large numbers of French people could be persuaded that Germany wanted a partnership with France, they would be more likely to be passive and malleable, more willing to collaborate and accept German diktats as being in their own long-term interest. Behind all the soft soap, Germany wanted a trouble-free France from which to launch the next planned military offensive against Britain. Even though these invasion plans were postponed and finally abandoned, France still offered Germany a rich resource to support its war effort.

As well as wooing Laval and overseeing his propaganda offensive Abetz kept his eye on art booty. Once again he clashed with Wolff-

Metternich as he turned his attention to French national treasures evacuated from the city in 1939 and now sitting in thousands of crates in various châteaux to the south of Paris. Shortly after Abetz had returned from his meeting with Hitler, the military got wind of a plan cooked up by the ambassador and Künsberg to send to Germany some 1,500 artefacts previously housed in French state museums that included the table on which the Treaty of Versailles had been signed. General Brauchitsch, head of the German army in France, immediately ordered that Ribbentrop's "representatives" (i.e., Abetz, Künsberg, and their minions) should stick simply to compiling inventories of any works of art that had been evacuated from French state museums for safekeeping, and that the seizure of any works of art would not be tolerated.

Abetz tried to circumvent Brauchitsch's directive by having Wolff-Metternich's team transferred to work under Künsberg, but the MBF would not hear of it. Abetz, dependent on the army for transport to move the treasures, was stymied. Undaunted, he organised raids on the private homes of wealthy Jews in Paris and again used the embassy to store stolen treasures, often without sufficient care or record of their provenance.[112] Wolff-Metternich carried on challenging and opposing Abetz,[113] and he may have been behind Künsberg's recall to Berlin at the end of the month.

In mid-September the two-month wrangle between Abetz and Wolff-Metternich over who was responsible for the artworks of Paris was resolved when Hitler ruled that the Einsatzstab Reichsleiter Rosenberg (ERR) would transport valuable artefacts to Germany and keep them safe. Hitler would decide what happened to them after that.[114] The ERR, which had already been at the forefront of the pillaging of libraries and Masonic temples in the city at the start of the Occupation, had established its Paris base in the former library of the Universal Israelite Alliance in Pigalle. The Paris ERR unit was headed by the absurdly vain Baron Kurt von Behr, who, in an attempt to impress, liked to strut around in an ostentatious uniform of what was actually the German Red Cross.

As soon as the Führer gave the ERR the green light, Behr ordered French removal firms in the city to transport seized works of art to the Department of Eastern Antiquities in the Louvre Museum; in October they were taken instead to the nearby Jeu de Paume Museum overlooking the place de la Concorde. Behr had realised the advantages of the Jeu de Paume for hoarding stolen art treasures. Not only was it located in the centre of Paris, securely situated behind the railings of the Tuileries Gardens, but it needed fewer security guards than the Louvre. It offered an easier locale from which to exclude Abetz or any of his associates and to enforce Behr's edict that it was off-limits to all French officials, even Jacques Jaujard, the French director of national museums. The only exception Behr allowed was Rose Valland, a meek-looking, bespectacled forty-two-year-old who had worked at the Jeu de Paume since 1932, a woman whom Behr considered no threat at all. But appearances can be deceptive.

As well as seizing art treasures from galleries and private houses, Behr also set his sights on the works of art that Abetz had stashed away in the embassy; although the ambassador did manage to hold on to more than one hundred artefacts, claiming that they were the property of the Reich, were reserved for decorating the embassy, or were "Jewish-owned works of degenerate art" that could be traded for artistically valuable works.[115]

⮞ THE VICHY GOVERNMENT had begun its legal assault on the "enemies within" by discriminating against foreigners and those who had become naturalised French citizens relatively recently; now it was the turn of Freemasons. Although not explicitly named, they were the principal target of a law of August 13 applicable in both zones outlawing "secret societies." The Freemasons were historically associated with republicanism, secularism, and anticlericalism; their opponents accused them of using secret rituals as a cover for all sorts of depraved and lurid activities. In 1940 these opponents, which included traditional conservatives, large sections of the Catholic hierarchy, and many supporters of Pétain's National Revolution project, railed against the alleged Freemason influence in the hated 1936 left-wing Popular Front government. These groups attacked the Freemasons for allegedly contributing to France's prewar decadence, to the country's lack of military preparedness in 1939, and thus to its military defeat in June 1940. Pétain's antipathy towards Freemasons was well known. As one of Pétain's ministers, Adrien Marquet, observed, "For the Marshal, a Freemason is the classic bête noire. A Jew, he says, is never responsible for his origins; a Freemason is always responsible for his choice."[116] Pétain's views were reinforced by the virulent anti-Masonic opinions of his wife as well as his personal doctor and confidant Bernard Ménétrel. The Vichy government's offensive against the Freemasons presumably came as something of a blow to the majority of Freemason parliamentarians from different political parties who had voted to give Pétain full powers only a month or so earlier.[117]

The August 13 law also stipulated that all employees of the French state in both zones were required to swear in writing that they were not—or were no longer—members of the Masonic Brotherhood; a false declaration could result in a prison sentence of between six months and two years and a fine of up to 6,000 francs. On September 19 Jean Guéhenno wrote in his diary: "Today I had to sign a piece of paper declaring 'solemnly and on my honour' that I had never been a Freemason and that I had never been a member of a secret society. Ah! What stupidity."[118]

The collaborationist press in Paris viewed Freemasonry as a dangerous and unpatriotic force and applauded Vichy's offensive against the Brotherhood. "The dissolution of Freemasonry has not been an act of partisan revenge, but a necessary public-cleansing measure taken against the most pernicious penetration of our national life by outsiders."[119] In November, *Au Pilori*, a Paris-based anti-Semitic weekly rag launched on July 12, started publishing the names of Freemasons preceded by an editorial, which concluded, "People of France! Here are the murderers of France and their names! The list begins today. It will be a long one. Keep it. We're going to need it."[120]

The crackdown on Freemasons in Paris also involved seizing more Masonic archives and artefacts; they were stored in the national library, the Bibliothèque nationale in the rue de Richelieu, pending their transfer to a proposed Museum of Secret Societies. Overall responsibility for this operation was handed to Bernard Faÿ, the new head of the library; he had recently replaced Julien Cain, who was sacked because he was Jewish. Faÿ, officially known as the "Delegate of the French Government for the Liquidation of Masonic Lodges," was an ideal candidate for the post. He believed the French Revolution was an abomination and he was as fervent a supporter of Pétain as he was of General Franco in Spain. In other words, he was a dyed-in-the wool reactionary and a monarchist to boot.[121]

While Laval and Abetz were meeting in Paris, as naturalisations were being reviewed and Freemasons and Communists were being pursued and harassed, German officials at the Franco-German Armistice Committee in Wiesbaden dropped a bombshell. Article 18 of the Armistice Agreement stipulated that France would meet the cost of maintaining German troops in the country. The head of the German delegation at Wiesbaden informed the French that Hitler had set the figure at an eye-watering 20 million Reichsmarks (400 million francs) a day. The money was to be paid in ten-day instalments into a special "Occupation Costs" account in the Banque de France in Paris to which the MBF would have unrestricted access.

General Huntziger, the head of the French delegation, protested that this was an exorbitant sum that made no distinction between German occupying forces and those stationed in France, poised for an invasion of Britain. His objection was dismissed out of hand. While Huntziger was spluttering about French sovereignty and denouncing the German demand as a "diktat," the head of the German delegation simply informed him that if the French government did not *that very day* provide the 220 million Reichsmarks (RM) for the period 21–31 August, plus the 1,140 million RM it owed for the period from 25 June, it would face "the most serious consequences." Huntziger, afraid that Germany would invoke Article 24 giving it the right to annul the whole armistice agreement if France failed to meet its treaty obligations, meekly agreed that the French government would pay up.

As if that wasn't bad enough, the French delegation was horrified to discover that these exorbitant payments did not even include the costs of accommodation and furnishings. The French government was soon receiving invoices for the refurbishment of requisitioned buildings in Paris, including the purchase of luxury rugs and carpets, paintings, mirrors, armchairs, radios, and refrigerators. The Germans embarked on an extravagant spending spree with money provided by the French government, but in truth they had more money than they could spend. At the end of 1940 the occupying forces had "only" spent just over 620 billion RM (31 billion francs) of the 1,600 billion RM (80 billion francs) that the French government had handed over; by June 1941, the German bank account at the Banque de France stood at 1,200 billion RM (60 billion francs).[122]

This episode revealed that the much vaunted "sovereignty" of the Vichy government really was nothing more than a fig leaf. The requirement to find such a colossal sum, day after day, for an indefinite period

would bleed the French economy dry. It deprived the Vichy government of much needed funds, which in turn had a devastating effect on
men, women, and children in Paris as it did in the rest of the country.

On August 27 the Vichy government abrogated a law, known as the
Marchandeau Law,[123] which had made it illegal to incite hatred against
any group of people based on their racial or religious origins. This
opened the floodgates for anti-Semitism, allowing the press to indulge
in vicious attacks on Jews without fear of prosecution. It was not just
the written word: anti-Semitism now was on open display on the streets
of Paris as well. The city's anti-Semites connected with a powerful current of anti-Jewish sentiment within French culture as a whole. It had
never completely disappeared since the Dreyfus affair, which convulsed
France, and particularly Paris, between 1894 and 1906; indeed, an up-
turn in anti-Semitic activity had occurred in the 1930s.[124]

Anti-Semitism had raised its ugly head even before the abrogation
of the Marchandeau Law. On July 29 Langeron wrote of anti-Jewish
stickers appearing on walls.[125] Further anti-Semitic incidents were reported on the boulevard de Ménilmontant; in the flea market at Saint-
Ouen; outside Jewish-owned shops, such as the Lévitan furniture store
in the 10th arrondissement; and in cafés on the place de la République.[126]
Over two days in late August militants from Jeune Front, Robert
Hersant's small gang of anti-Semites, systematically smashed the windows of Jewish-owned businesses on the Champs-Elysées.

Jacques Biélinky's diary recorded a rash of anti-Semitic incidents over
the summer months, many involving people selling *Au Pilori* who came
into Jewish areas to provoke trouble. In August, for example, Biélinky
noted the following: a fight between Jewish war veterans and vendors
of *Au Pilori* in the passage du Carreau du Temple;[127] half a dozen youngsters arriving in the Jewish quarter of the 4th arrondissement, shouting
"Read *Au Pilori*, the anti-Semitic newspaper, against the Jews!";[128] and
a clash in the rue des Rosiers, another street where many Jews lived,
again involving *Au Pilori* supporters and a Jewish woman whose three
sons had been conscripted and were now prisoners of war.[129]

But Biélinky recorded instances when French (and even German)
police officers stepped in to arrest anti-Semitic thugs or support Jews
who were being insulted or threatened or to arrest anti-Semitic troublemakers. When a war veteran was attacked after he challenged some *Au
Pilori* vendors in the market at Fontenay-sous-Bois where he worked,

the German police arrived and arrested the aggressors.[130] A French café owner in the rue de Châteaudun put up a notice banning Jews from his establishment; a young Jew entered, ordered a beer, and told the owner he was Jewish. The owner insulted him and told him to get out. The German police were called; they asked the owner if he had permission from the German authorities to throw Jews out of his premises. The owner did not and the young man left the café peacefully in his own time.[131] Biélinky noted that groups of French police were starting to patrol the streets in the 4th arrondissement with high concentrations of Jewish inhabitants, including the rue des Rosiers and the rue Ferdinand-Duval, to prevent attacks on Jews living there. This action, he said, impressed the locals.[132] In July and August Langeron himself reported Paris police officers intervening to arrest anti-Semites who were blocking the entrance to a Jewish shop[133] and others who had ransacked or smashed the windows of Jewish-owned shops.[134] He also ordered his officers to investigate those who were behind the anti-Semitic posters and leaflets that continued to appear.[135]

Instances even occurred of German soldiers fraternising with Jews: Biélinky knew a fancy restaurant by a lake in what was then the spa town of Enghien-les-Bains, about eight miles north of central Paris, which advertised the fact that it sold Kosher food.[136] A few German officers regularly ate there and when the owner pointed to the Kosher sign and asked them if they knew where they were, they replied, "Of course we do, but we come all the same because we really like your food."[137] In the summer Robert Birenbaum was helping his Yiddish-speaking parents in the family grocery shop in the north of Paris. German soldiers, stationed in a requisitioned school in the nearby rue de Tanger, liked to drop in and chat in German with his parents; the soldiers were scrupulous about always paying for their purchases. In the evening Robert and his friends met up near the rue d'Aubervilliers, in front of the Stalingrad Métro station, and talked with young Germans. He recalled, "The atmosphere was pretty friendly."[138] And so it appeared, for the time being at any rate.

∾ 5

Unemployment, Rationing, Vichy against Jews, Montoire

*O*N SEPTEMBER 1 Roger Langeron, the Paris prefect of police, summed up how life in the city had changed since June and identified a clear shift in the outlook of most Parisians. Anxiety had been followed by relief when the feared German violence did not occur. A formal cease-fire between France and Germany appeared to be imminent and people thought the Occupation would not last long. But, Langeron added, it continued.

At first life was not too hard, but it became harder and harder, especially economically. There was much requisitioning of buildings and merchandise, while unemployment rose and the supply of food and household goods became increasingly problematic. More Parisians began to return to the city and a pro-British feeling started to grow. "Hostility towards the occupying forces is very clear," Langeron wrote. "Paris has not got used to—and will not get used to—the heavy beat of German jackboots on its streets." As Langeron observed, this hostility towards the Germans had not led to a surge of support for the French government in Vichy, although Pétain was still held in high esteem by many. However, Langeron conceded that "some people say that if the government came to Paris it would make it easier to deal with the German authorities, tackle unemployment and food shortages, and improve the position of the prisoners of war."[1]

Lack of work was a key problem. At the end of July more than 150,000 Parisians were receiving unemployment benefit and, in August, figures showed that the number of people employed in the Seine department was less than half the monthly average for the first six months of 1939.[2] The German authorities tried to take advantage of this and appealed to French workers to go and work in Germany, but few Parisians took up the offer.

From mid-July the German military had taken direct control of a number of important factories in Paris and the suburbs to support its war effort: these included the Citroën, Renault, and Simca car plants; Gnome and Rhône (aeroplane engines); Hispano-Suiza (vehicles and weapons); Farman (aeroplanes); the cartridge factory at Vincennes; and the arsenal at Puteaux. However, taking control did not mean that production had greatly increased.

The war had had a devastating impact on the number of workers in the factories in and around Paris. In August, the workforces at Renault and Citroën, for example, were only 10 percent those of prewar levels;[3] half a million or so Parisians were still held in POW camps in Germany;[4] hundreds of thousands more were still stranded in the Unoccupied Zone or had been killed in the battle for France in June. However, the unemployed could not just step in and fill the vacancies. Even if they had the right skills, the factories were unable to take on more workers and were putting those they had on short-time contracts. Factories were short of managers and supervisors, and stocks were low or nonexistent, often as a result of pillaging by the occupying forces or by locals. Contacting suppliers was extremely difficult, especially if they were in the Unoccupied Zone or overseas, and, when contact was made, the factory often lacked the funds to pay for supplies while even those with the necessary money still had to find ways of transporting the merchandise to Paris.[5]

At the Unic car works in the western Paris suburb of Puteaux all 800 employees (out of a prewar workforce of 2,200) were paid at the rate of a manual worker and given menial tasks to do such as sweeping and clearing up. As workers gradually returned, many found themselves on short-time contracts as at Renault, where they were employed every other day, or at Citroën, where they worked a twenty-four hour week. Some factories were closed down by the occupying authorities and their plant and stock taken to Germany. This happened, for example, at the

Masson factory in the northern suburb of Gennevilliers; at another factory in the suburb of Argenteuil, 300 machines were removed and, at a
stroke, hundreds of workers were made redundant.[6]

Department stores also found it difficult to replace stock. When they
did, German customers snapped up items that had disappeared from
the shops in the Reich and sent them home. Many Parisians employed
in the big stores, like those in the factories, faced a cut in hours; employees at La Samaritaine had to take ten days off a month without pay,
while those at the Bazar de l'Hôtel de Ville (BHV) worked only three
weeks out of four; at Galeries Lafayette and Au Bon Marché a third of
the staff were laid off completely.[7]

Many of the shops selling luxury goods around the place Vendôme
or on the rue du Faubourg Saint-Honoré went bankrupt. Few of their
wealthy customers had returned from the exodus, either fleeing abroad
or staying in the Unoccupied Zone; and their goods were priced beyond the wallet of the ordinary German soldier, even with the advantageous exchange rate. The shortage of raw materials combined with
the German requisitions drove many small businesses into insolvency:
people selling bed linen were hit by a slump in the textile industry; sta-
tioners could not find any paper; French shoe factories were suffering
not only from a shortage of leather, but also because they were con-
tracted to supply Germany with a huge volume of footwear.[8] In addition, the near impossibility of foreigners holidaying in Paris led to the
closure of travel agencies, while the British blockade proved ruinous for
any company importing from the French colonies in North Africa and
the Far East.

Workers were laid off as the Germans closed down prewar, state-
funded building projects, which had employed some 13,000 workers in
Paris in 1939; bus and taxi drivers found themselves out of work as there
was almost no public motor transport; truck drivers, too, were out of
work since most civilian trucks had either been requisitioned by the
French army before June or by the Germans thereafter. Maids and other
live-in domestic staff were laid off as employers could no longer afford
to pay them or feed them.

The Occupation did bring more job security for some workers: the
staff in luxury hotels were now employed all year round by the Germans, and so they no longer risked being laid off out of season. An
absence of foreign tourists meant many smaller hotels were forced to

close, although some survived, particularly near railway stations, offering accommodation to travellers arriving in Paris after curfew. Cobblers prospered as Parisians discovered that new shoes were difficult to find and so they needed to have existing pairs repaired; the boom in bicycle ownership meant that those running bicycle repair shops and selling spare parts like inner tubes and tyres, were very busy, while stocks lasted.[9]

The "return to normal" that the German authorities had been encouraging since June continued apace, helped by the authorities' decision to put the start of the curfew back to 11 P.M. On September 7, Paris's world-famous theatre the Comédie-Française held a reopening ceremony, addressed by Abel Bonnard, a minor poet and one-time rabble-rouser for Jacques Doriot's Far Right, collaborationist Parti populaire français (PPF), and Jacques Copeau, the theatre's administrator. Both stressed the continuity between the present and a Vichyist vision of the past. Bonnard emphasised the themes of work, family, and the land, while Copeau waxed lyrical about the deeply embedded power of the homeland, the soul of the French race, and the survival of the national spirit. A fortnight later the Comédie-Française reaffirmed its own continuity with the past by promoting a repertoire of works by Corneille, Racine, and other classical French playwrights on which its reputation had been built.

Later in the month Langeron listed more theatres that had opened,[10] and many of the productions offered a link with the past while providing a distraction from current problems. These displays were not restricted to theatres. In September, for example, the newspaper *Aujourd'hui* described L'Aiglon, a cabaret that had recently reopened on the Champs-Élysées, as a place "where you can forget the tough difficulties of the present time, unless you want to go there to rediscover your memories and friendships from before the war."[11] Cinemas, too, continued to attract customers, although from September 9 the choice of films was limited, as British films and those featuring Jewish actors were banned.

Parisians were also limited in what they could read. Paris was historically the undisputed centre of French publishing. It was here, and mostly in the 5th and 6th arrondissements, where all the great French publishing houses were based, many of them family firms such as Gallimard, Hachette, Armand Colin, Bernard Grasset, Arthème Fayard, and Robert Denoël. This literary concentration together with the nearby long-established seats of learning, notably the Sorbonne University, the Collège de France, the Institut de France, and the École normale supérieure, formed the intellectual and cultural hub of the nation.

Publishers had been under French government surveillance since mid-September 1939, when they needed official approval to publish any new book or republish one that was out of print.[12] Now, all publishers were subject to German control and the Nazis had made a virtue in Germany of not only censoring books, but also publicly burning them. Almost all the big publishing houses were soon falling over themselves to comply with the constraints laid down by the occupiers.

At the end of September René Philippon, the head of the guild of French publishers, came to an agreement with the German military authorities whereby publishers would be allowed to continue with their work as long as they agreed not to produce anything that could be construed as damaging to German prestige or interests or to publish the works of any author whose books were banned in Germany. As with the press, self-censorship was the German authorities' preferred option, but if any publisher wanted any clarification he could always refer to the propaganda bureau.

The occupying authorities were also determined to ban any "unsuitable" books already on sale. In September Philippon helped expand a list of some 140 books already banned by the Germans[13] into the more extensive "Otto List"—possibly named after German ambassador to Paris Otto Abetz—of more than 1,000 works deemed to be either offensive to German sensibilities or likely to poison the minds of French readers. In an attempt to win over these readers a preface to the Otto List explained that it was drawn up to create "a healthier atmosphere" and establish "a more objective appreciation of European problems." It added, "The German authorities have noted with satisfaction this initiative taken by French publishers."[14]

The two thousand or so Paris bookshops, newsstands, libraries, and *bouquinistes* (sellers of second-hand books that can be found in those dark green boxes along the banks of the Seine in the centre of Paris) received copies of the Otto List as part of 40,000 that were distributed throughout the Occupied Zone. The banned works listed included those by "unacceptable" German writers such as Thomas Mann and

Heinrich Mann, Stefan Zweig, and Erich-Maria Remarque (the author of *All Quiet on the Western Front* [1929]). French writers on the list included Charles de Gaulle, Louis Aragon, Georges Duhamel, and André Malraux. Books by foreign Jewish authors, including Sigmund Freud and Franz Kafka, were banned.[15] So, too, were works by French Jews, including Max Jacob, André Maurois, and Marcel Proust.[16] Jewish writers and political refugees stood accused by the Germans of having "betrayed the hospitality offered by France" and "of having unscrupulously agitated for a war which they calculated would benefit their own selfish interests."[17] English authors on the list included William Shakespeare, Virginia Woolf, and G. K. Chesterton. In the spirit of the Nazi-Soviet Pact, works by anti-Stalinists such as Leon Trotsky and Boris Souvarine were also forbidden. The Otto List was enforced by French police officers, who inspected booksellers' premises across the city, seizing and impounding nearly three quarter of a million books and closing down eleven of the seventy or so publishing houses they raided.[18] Other Otto Lists followed, and at the Liberation a French government commission estimated that in the course of the Occupation over two and a quarter thousand tons of books had been seized.[19]

Meanwhile, public discontent grew over food shortages, and the French and German authorities decided something had to be done to avoid civil disorder. In mid-September the Jewish-Russian émigré Jacques Biélinky wrote of Parisians descending en masse on food shops as soon as word spread that food rationing was about to be introduced. One shop selling sixty quarter-pound portions of butter attracted a queue of 350 people.[20] On September 17 the Vichy government officially introduced an extraordinarily complicated system of rationing. It was hopelessly inadequate as a solution to the problem of shortages.

Everyone had a right to a four-page ration book, distributed by the town halls *(mairies)* in each arrondissement, but a shortage of personnel meant a long wait before receiving it. Schoolteacher and essayist Jean Guéhenno queued for five hours at his local *mairie* before collecting his family's cards.[21] Once you had a card you had to return to the town hall on dates announced in the press to claim coloured ration tickets with which to buy various foodstuffs. "I had to queue and even queue several times in succession in order to receive a bundle of multicoloured sheets that we will cut out throughout the month so we don't starve to death," Georges Benoît-Guyod wrote. "The daily allowance of rations is totally inadequate. How was it fixed? A total mystery."[22]

Here are the individual adult rations: 350g bread a day (today's equivalent of about a baguette and half), 250g pasta a month, 50g cheese a week, 200g *matières grasses* (cheese with more than 25 percent fat) a month, 200g margarine a month, 300g meat on the bone a week, 500g sugar a month, and 50g rice a month. This represented around 1,300 calories a day, compared with an average consumption of some 3,000 calories before the war.[23] Some foodstuffs escaped rationing, the most famous of which was swede (rutabaga). Previously used only for feeding cattle, it was as bland as it was ubiquitous. It was universally disliked and became a symbol of food deprivation throughout the Occupation.

Like their compatriots in both zones, Parisians had to learn how to make their ration tickets last until another batch was issued. This cumbersome system was a failure: shortages persisted and long queues soon became a semi-permanent feature outside most food shops—especially bakers, butchers' shops, and dairies. It was difficult finding some vegetables—even potatoes, which could be bought without ration tickets. Within days of the introduction of rationing, Jacques Biélinky queued for an hour and a half outside a shop in the rue Mouffetard near where he lived just to buy three pounds of potatoes.[24] These queues all over the city reminded medical student Bernard Pierquin of engravings he had seen in his history textbooks of the 1870 siege of Paris.[25] Jean-Louis Besson later recalled what it was like for a child: "You spent ages queuing outside the shops, especially those which sold products that did not need tickets like leeks or potatoes. Often you had to wait for a *very* long time and Maman would ask us to go and stand in for her. A folding stool became indispensable."[26]

Despite high levels of male unemployment, queuing was mainly a female activity. Women bore the brunt of the exhausting search for food and other necessities. They queued for hours, often in vain if the meagre stocks ran out before they could be served. Queuing was fast becoming something of a social institution with its own etiquette and conventions; women would use the time to share their experiences or pass on rumours, cooking tips, and local gossip. According to Roger Langeron, queues were also "centres of good [i.e., anti-German] propaganda, but also centres of intrigues, provocation and denunciations."[27]

Polish immigrant Andrzej Bobkowski, drawing on his experience waiting in a queue of women, took a more jaundiced view: "Each of them tries to outdo the others over the number of queues she's been in already that day and how long she's had to wait. . . . Suddenly there's a fight. Someone's trying to push to the front of the queue." He goes on to describe much shouting and many insults, accompanied by grumbling from the rest of the shoppers. "It's all clear now. The woman who tried to get to the front without queuing is pregnant. She sticks her belly out and shouts back at the gossips."[28] In October pregnant women were issued with special priority ration cards. Before then, according to Bobkowski, some women pretended to be pregnant by stuffing a cushion under their dress or coat and heading for the front of the line.

One area of the city known to be a likely place to find food was the concentration of small shops around the Carrefour de Buci, in the 6th arrondissement.[29] "At this time when it is difficult to obtain food," Georges Benoît-Guyod wrote, "when so many Parisians are queuing on the pavement, the area is invaded from daybreak by crowds of people, men and women of all ages and all social backgrounds, looking for food to buy."[30]

Everybody sought someone else to blame for the food shortages. Shopkeepers accused the farmers and the wholesalers of hoarding and of price manipulation; shoppers accused the shopkeepers of profiteering; the collaborationist press blamed the Jews, while the French government and the German authorities blamed the British maritime blockade. However, this last ploy, amplified by the pro-German Paris press, to fuel Anglophobia failed to convince, not least because Parisians were only too aware that French-made produce, like wine, was also proving more difficult to find. In Paris it was commonly believed that the shortages arose from Germany's determination to exploit France for all it was worth, a view summed up in the oft-heard refrain "Ils nous prennent tout" ("They're taking everything we've got"). This perception was confirmed by a Paris police report in September: "Vegetables have become rare: leeks, carrots, turnips and cabbages in particular are in short supply. . . . There is an almost total lack of potatoes, all this *above all because of the requisitioning by the army of occupation either where the food is grown, while the goods are in transit, or in Les Halles market.*"[31]

The food shortages in the shops were made worse because some 450,000 farmers and farm workers were still being held in POW camps[32] and Vichy still had to meet exorbitant "Occupation" costs. In addition there was the impact of the German so-called purchasing offices (*bureaux d'achats*), which were springing up all over Paris. Eventually numbering more than two hundred, they were run as lucrative rackets by various branches of the German civil and military authorities. They accessed the money that the Vichy government paid into the German account at the Banque de France every week to cover "Occupation costs," then spent it on almost anything they could lay their hands on. The goods they bought were then sold at a huge profit to the military or exported to Germany, again at a huge profit. Thus the Vichy government ended up handing over millions of francs in cash, which the purchasing offices used to buy goods at bargain basement prices. The Vichy government was stung again when the different branches of the military presented it with bills for everything it had bought from the purchasing offices. As most Parisians struggled to find enough to eat, those running the purchasing offices were making themselves a small fortune.

The most infamous purchasing office of all was run by an Abwehr officer named Hermann Brandl and known as "Otto." His office acted as a cover for the Abwehr's spying activities and as a source of extra secret funding for the Abwehr that was not subject to any external scrutiny. People with goods to sell would queue outside Brandl's offices in the square du Bois de Boulogne, near the exclusive avenue Foch, between 2 P.M. and 5 P.M. every day, waiting to show samples of their wares. Many of these would-be sellers had hidden their stocks of merchandise when the Germans arrived; now they wanted to sell the goods before they were discovered and confiscated. Brandl and his staff bought anything and everything, provided it was in large quantities. Leather and leather goods were especially popular, but they also bought metal, tools, vehicles, machine tools, textiles, office equipment, household goods, domestic equipment, soft furnishings, medicines, perfume, foodstuffs, and even toys and sweets. Brandl did not care where the goods came from or whether the seller had the right to sell them—all of which helped keep the paperwork to an absolute minimum.[33]

☞ FROM SEPTEMBER 26 a postal service of sorts was established so that friends and family could communicate across the demarcation line. Correspondents could use only official cards, obtainable from the post office for 90 centimes, to send minimal information to relatives in the other zone. The pro-forma card, similar to cards used by soldiers and POWs, allowed the sender to give only very limited news about the

person named on the card: in good health/tired/slightly ill/seriously ill/
slightly wounded/seriously wounded/dead. Other spaces allowed
senders to specify material needs (including money), to say where they
were working, or, in the case of children, which school they were attending. Senders were also allowed to mention any cards they had received. There was just room for a couple of lines of news, followed by
a choice of two valedictions and just enough space for a signature.[34] All
cards carried a warning that if the sender misused the card, it would be
destroyed. In November, Jean Guéhenno learned that his grandfather,
who lived in the Unoccupied Zone, was ill. His grandfather decided to
send a card to Paris every Monday: no card would mean he had died.
Speaking to his grandfather was out of the question since telephoning
was virtually impossible for civilians and sending telegrams between
zones was banned until December 1940. "I could only send him one of
those printed official cards issued by the Germans. It will arrive in a
week," wrote Guéhenno. "If he dies, I won't even be able to go to the
funeral. Living like this in a prison is grinding me down."[35]

It was thanks to one of these cards that Berthe Auroy got in touch
with her dear friend Loïs, who was in the Unoccupied Zone. "I finally
managed to contact her in Marseilles with one of those 'inter-zone
cards,' which are such a pain to complete. When you haven't got an ill-
ness, or someone who's been killed or who's died to write about, you
just get two lines, whereas you need pages and pages. . . . In a telegraphic
style you fill these two lines saying nothing of what you would like to
say. And they call them 'family cards.'" In October she received a reply
from Loïs, who informed her in a couple of lines that she and her children were leaving France for America.[36]

☞ The Nazis' murderous, anti-Semitic policies in Germany and
Poland meant that Jews in Paris rightly felt they had more to fear than
most from the Occupation. In September 1939 approximately 300,000
Jews lived in France, two-thirds of whom lived in Paris. About half the
Paris Jews were foreign, Yiddish-speaking Ashkenazi Jews from Russia
and eastern and central Europe. Many had recently arrived from Poland, having fled the Nazis. They lived mainly in the poorer areas in
the east and north of the city.[37] About a quarter of the Jews in Paris
were French-born Sephardi who came originally from the Iberian
Peninsula; most had been in France for generations and were well in-

tegrated. Many of the wealthy Sephardic Jews lived in the bourgeois arrondissements in the west of the city as well as the well-heeled suburbs of Neuilly and Boulogne.[38] The other quarter of the Jewish population in Paris comprised foreign-born Jews who had acquired French nationality.[39]

Paris did not, therefore, have a single Jewish community; rather, several different Jewish communities existed. Even if they knew about it, the mostly poor Jewish refugees living in the north and east of the city were not affected by the Germans seizing the possessions of wealthy Jews. These refugees, especially those who were Communists, inhabited a different world from that of many Sephardi, whom they viewed as wealthy bourgeois who happened to be Jewish.

After the armistice, tens of thousands of Jews who had fled south made their way back to the Occupied Zone, most of them returning to Paris. The chief rabbi came back in August, although other rabbis stayed in the south or chose to return later. Given the centrality of anti-Semitism to Nazism, it may seem odd that so many Jews opted to return to the Occupied Zone, which was administered by the Germans, rather than staying in the Unoccupied Zone. They included Russian Jews who thought the Nazi-Soviet Pact would protect them; Jews such as Marcel Abraham, a university education inspector, who came back "simply to do what he considered to be his duty, namely to return to work."[40] Others lacked the means to stay on in the Unoccupied Zone or they felt isolated or uncomfortable in an alien and sometimes downright hostile region of France.

Armand Kohn, a banker who had left Paris with his family when war was declared, was typical of those well-established, wealthy Jews who were driven to return by a sense of patriotism. He had never denied he was Jewish, but he considered himself first and foremost to be French. He was proud of his service in the 1914–1918 war, for which he had been decorated. He remained cautiously optimistic about the future: "As long as we stay together, nothing can possibly happen to us. I'm a wounded war veteran. I have fought for my country. We have nothing to fear. As long as we do what is asked of us, no harm can come."[41]

Other Jews refused to be intimidated. Why should they stay away? Paris was their home. Robert Debré, a professor of medicine, defiantly made his way back from Bordeaux despite having been tipped off by a former Paris prefect of police that the Germans were about to turn on the Jews. "I took my decision at once," he recalled. "I would return and would not leave my city."[42] In contrast to this bravery, France harbored those who viewed the Jews as duplicitous, mendacious schemers who had been responsible for the nation's decline. The Nazis, of course, conceived of the Jews as subhuman, a people utterly incapable of patriotism.

Paris Jews were greatly relieved that, thus far, neither the Vichy government nor the German authorities had introduced any explicitly anti-Semitic measures; many drew the conclusion that if one looked beyond the German soldiers and flags, banners and signs, nothing had fundamentally altered in Paris. "Life has started again." "Life carries on." "Nothing in daily life has really changed, at least it doesn't seem to have," such were the refrains that were commonly heard.[43] Any difficulties Jews faced, it seemed, were the same as those confronted by most Parisians. Gentile or Jew, almost everyone was hungry, could not find what they needed in the shops, and had to queue.

However, this sense of nearly everybody being in the same boat was vocally and sometimes violently contested. In Paris in the autumn of 1940 there were plenty of people who felt they had little, if anything, in common with Jews, especially foreign Jews; moreover, the newspapers constantly blamed the Jews for France's present plight.

Speaking out against the "Jewish threat" to France was not new, nor was it the preserve of extremists of the Far Right. In 1939, shortly before he took over as head of the CI, the French state news and information service, Jean Giraudoux wrote: "Hundreds of thousands of Ashkenazi Jews who have escaped from the ghettos of Poland and Romania have arrived here." He went on to accuse "these hordes" of undercutting the wages of French workers, of not integrating, of being involved in illegal and corrupt dealings and, because of their poor health, of filling up the hospitals.[44] This widespread perception that France had been "invaded" by poor, desperate, Yiddish-speaking immigrants who would "swamp French culture" says more about the power of the media to play on people's fears than it does about the reality. It has been estimated that between 1933 and 1939 only about 55,000 Jews of *all* nationalities arrived in France; many of them did not settle but emigrated farther afield, notably to the United States and Palestine.[45] But at the same time anti-Semitism would have had little or no purchase if it had not been a cultural current entrenched in French society, one that had remained widespread throughout the life of the Third Republic.

On August 17 Otto Abetz, in his capacity as adviser to the MBF, pressed Werner Best, a committed Nazi and head of the MBF's Administrative Section, to ban any more Jews entering the Occupied Zone from the Unoccupied Zone, to secure the removal of any Jews already in the Occupied Zone, and to consider measures to expropriate their businesses and property.[46] Three days later, Abetz was urging Berlin to introduce enforced identification for Jews and Jewish shops.[47]

The MBF was keen to introduce anti-Semitic measures in the Occupied Zone, but it also wanted to be seen to be doing things by the book. Possibly too it was wary of alienating French citizens who were not anti-Semitic since this could threaten the peace in the city that they were so determined to maintain. The military's prime objective remained to win over the people of Paris and to encourage Franco-German collaboration. In addition, the MBF still felt the need to distance itself from the murderous rampages of the Polish invasion and to give every impression that it was running the Occupation in accordance with international law. So it appointed a multitude of jurists who spent hours poring over war treaties and other documents hunting for legal and international precedents that might be used to justify anti-Semitic policies.[48] The solution that emerged was to classify all Jews as "a security threat," which meant that under Article 46 of the Hague Convention they could be legitimately targeted.[49]

Armed with this legal justification, the German military authorities were ready to strike. On September 27 the MBF published a legal definition of a Jew[50] and banned any Jews who had left the Occupied Zone from returning. Less than a week later, on the eve of Rosh ha-shana, the Jewish New Year, announcements in the press and leaflets distributed near synagogues informed Jews that they had to register at their local police station by October 30. The same directive ruled that Jewish owners of businesses and shops had until the end of October to display in the window of their premises a yellow poster with a text in French and German indicating that the business was owned by Jews.[51]

Despite the unease this announcement generated within the Jewish communities of Paris, about 90 percent of Jews registered, each one giving the French police their name, address, nationality, and profession.[52] Their identity papers were stamped with the word *Juif* (for men) or *Juive* (for women) in bold red letters: now any French or German official who asked to see their papers could not fail to know that they were Jewish.

It is easy to understand why almost every Jew in Paris chose to register. First, people have a tendency to conform, to obey official directives and orders. Also, no Jewish leader had spoken out against registering; thus, it seemed quite acceptable, especially since under the Third Republic foreign Jews were used to reporting to police stations to renew their residence and work permits. And, after all, it was quite clear that the Jews were registering with the French police and not with the German authorities. Added to this, many foreign Jews would have had difficulty passing themselves off as non-Jewish Parisians. As David Lemberger, a Communist refugee recently arrived from Poland, put it: "How could you not declare yourself to be Jewish, when you've been born in Poland, you speak hardly any French and you're a trouser-maker from the rue des Immeubles-Industriels?"[53]

Parisian Jews sometimes registered out of a sense of pride in their Jewish identity. The eminent and elderly French philosopher Henri Bergson was among a small minority of Jews not required to register; nevertheless, he insisted on shuffling down to report to his local police station in his dressing gown and slippers. Others wanted to show they were proud to be both Jewish and French: Colonel Pierre Brisac registered wearing his French military uniform. Armand Kohn registered, still believing that if he behaved like a law-abiding citizen all would be well. Vidal Nahoum registered because he was afraid of what would happen if he did not. His son, the future sociologist Edgar Morin, recalled his father insisting. "We must do as they say because just imagine if we were stopped in the street and we hadn't obeyed the law and hadn't got our papers stamped!"[54] This fear of disobeying the law was reinforced by articles in the anti-Semitic press threatening dire consequences for any Jew who failed to register.

Some Jews did not register before the deadline expired, but they were counted all the same. Rabbi Apeloig arrived in Paris clandestinely in June 1941, eight months after the registration deadline had passed. Although his papers showed he was a rabbi, the vital *Juif* stamp was missing. He enlisted the help of friends, relatives, and even the chief rabbi in his vain efforts to rectify this omission. In despair he went to his local police station, where he eventually persuaded the police to record his name and to stamp his papers. He even made the duty officer promise that he would inform the German authorities.[55]

A tiny minority stayed away, like the father of nine-year-old Roger Herman: "I remember the stamp on our identity cards. Only my father obstinately refused to register, despite the advice of people around him. He thought, and rightly so, that if he had the word JEW on his papers he would have problems finding work."[56] Sometimes sympathetic French policemen discreetly discouraged Jews from registering if their names were not "typically Jewish"; although impossible to quantify, it would seem that, overall, the number of Jews who chose not to register as a result of this was very small.[57] Little did they dream what use the German authorities, aided by the French police, would soon be making of the data that had been amassed.

Just as most Jews complied with the order to register, so a majority of Jewish shopkeepers displayed a yellow sign, in French and German, indicating that their business was Jewish-owned. These signs were much more numerous in the poorer parts of Paris and the vast majority of them had links to the rag trade; for example, out of a total of 740 shops displaying a yellow poster in the 3rd arrondissement, 622 dealt in clothing and a further 31 sold shoes.[58]

On October 4 Jacques Biélinky was near the synagogue in the rue Notre-Dame-de-Nazareth when he met a French café owner whom he described as "100% Catholic." The man was loudly denouncing the persecution of the Jews and declaring that the locals, who were "truly French and truly Parisian," were not bothered about what happened to the wealthy Jews like the Rothschilds but openly supported Jews from modest backgrounds.[59]

The collaborationist press and radio bombarded Parisians with propaganda: the Jews were parasitic aliens, incapable of being integrated, and thus of being patriotic, and who worked only in the pursuit of self-interest to the detriment of France. On October 5, when Jacques Biélinky went out to see the reactions of those shopkeepers who now had to advertise that their shops were Jewish-owned, he discovered many of them using it as an opportunity to counter anti-Jewish propaganda by asserting their patriotism.

One wounded 1914–1918 veteran had posted details of his war decorations alongside the yellow poster, and other Jewish war veterans did the same.[60] Rabbis also talked up the patriotism of France's Jews: on October 12, the chief rabbi of the synagogue in the rue de la Victoire in the 9th arrondissement reminded his audience of 6,000 (including Biélinky) of the Jewish contribution to France's scientific, artistic, and literary heritage, not to mention the thousands of Jews who had died for France in the Great War and in the recent battle for France.

As the end of October deadline drew closer, Biélinky noticed more and more yellow posters appearing—along with ever more declarations of patriotism. A poster at a baker's shop in the 4th arrondissement read: "Three sons called-up"; another in a hat shop near the place de la République proclaimed: "Business founded in 1909 by Maurice Lévy, died for France at Douaumont in 1916. Company taken over by his son, veteran 1939–1940, awarded military medal with commendations"; another in a clothes shop in the Carreau du Temple[61] said: "Boss volunteered to fight in 1914–1918 war; his two employees war veterans 1939–1940."[62]

Many of the Jewish-owned small shops had a reputation for selling goods that were difficult to find elsewhere, and few customers were put off by the yellow posters. According to Biélinky, Jewish shopkeepers in the Carreau du Temple were saying, "Everybody knows we are Jewish and the Christians will always come flocking here to get a bargain in clothes, bed-linen and so on. The posters don't tell our regular customers anything new."[63] "I've had the poster up for three days," one owner of a clothes shop confided to Biélinky, "and I can tell you that my sales, far from dropping, have gone up a lot. I've never done such good business as I have these past few days, and none of my customers has been Jewish."[64]

But things were about to get worse as the next measure aimed at removing Jews from the economic life of Paris and the rest of the Occupied Zone was announced. In a directive dated October 20 the German military authorities announced that by December 26 all Jewish-owned businesses opening onto the street would have to be sold or placed in the hands of non-Jewish commissioner-administrators. Once this had been done, a red poster would replace the yellow one.

By February 1941, red posters were commonplace in shops previously owned by Jews.[65] The German directive applied to commercial enterprises big and small. Galeries Lafayette, Paris's third biggest department store after La Samaritaine and Printemps, displayed a red poster, and it passed into the hands of a succession of commissioner-administrators.[66] Berthe Auroy's Jewish friend Hélène Isserlis, who owned a small bookshop, had to work under the supervision of an administrator, who took charge of everything. She was ordered to dispose of her shop as soon as possible and there were people, Berthe observed, "who are hoping to take advantage of the situation and get it for a song."[67] She added: "Even my little shoemaker in the rue Tholozé, who can only just about afford his own last hammer, nails, and glue has a commissioner-administrator. What in God's name is there to administer?"[68]

The Vichy government was busy passing anti-Semitic legislation of its own. Its repeal of the Marchandeau Law, followed by its decision to review all post-1927 naturalisations, may not have targeted Jews explicitly but of those who lost French citizenship almost half were Jews. Jews were also disproportionately affected by laws restricting entry into various jobs and professions to those with a French father— French public service (July 1940), the medical profession (August 1940), and law (September 1940). These measures paved the way for Vichy's first Jewish statute (Statut des Juifs) applicable in both zones, passed on October 3, 1940, *without any prompting from the Germans.*[69] In a clear rejection of republican values and practice, it singled out one section of the population and passed a law defining a Jew, using racial criteria.[70] Henceforth, all Jews, foreign and French alike in both zones, were banned from working as senior state officials at departmental or national levels or as officers in the armed forces. Jews teaching in schools and universities had until the end of the calendar year to resign their posts. Jews were also banned from working in the press and radio. More than a hundred Jewish painters were barred from exhibiting in Paris, and the statute promised a limit on the number of Jews allowed to practice law and medicine—these quotas were introduced between June and December 1941. French prefects were also given the power to intern Jews in special camps or place them under house arrest.

The Parisian collaborationist press in Paris greeted the news of Vichy's anti-Semitic legislation with glee. The front page of *Le Cri du Peuple*, the newly founded paper of Jacques Doriot's PPF, triumphantly proclaimed: "The Jews have finally been driven out of public service!" *Le Matin* applauded the spirit of dignity and serenity shown by the government as it put an end to "the pervasive and ultimately poisonous influence" of Jews in French society.[71]

There was virtually no public reaction to these new laws from non-Jewish Parisians. Many were still putting their lives back together after the traumas of May and June. They were struggling with shortages, still worrying about family and friends in the Unoccupied Zone, grieving for their loved ones killed in battle, or concerned about those hundreds of thousands still held as POWs. For its part, the Catholic Church, with the exception of a tiny minority of priests, either openly applauded the anti-Semitic laws or remained silent.

Although the bulk of the population seemed to be indifferent, in private some people expressed other emotions. "The victors are infecting us with their illnesses," Jean Guéhenno wrote in his diary. "The Vichy government has this morning published its statute for Jews in France. There we are, anti-Semites and racists. . . . I feel full of shame."[72] After a friend of the economist Charles Rist was sacked from the École des Mines because he was Jewish, Rist described the Vichy laws as "ignominious." "It's clear that the government is getting itself entangled in a policy it believes will please the Germans," he said, "and which, moreover, will gain support from the most extreme elements of the French people."[73]

The Groult sisters seemed more concerned about Vichy's discriminatory policies against married women—who were banned from working in a range of professions if their husbands were employed—than about what was happening to the Jews. But they still drew a parallel between this discrimination and the anti-Semitic laws. "It's now illegal to employ married women in the state sector," Benoîte Groult wrote. "No entry for women and dogs. We are the Jews of the sexes."[74]

Discriminatory measures against the Jews did not mean the Freemasons had been forgotten. Shortly after Bernard Faÿ became head of the Bibliothèque Nationale he was approached to help in the preparation of a Paris exhibition exposing Freemasonry. Abetz believed too many Parisians were unaware of the "evils of Freemasonry" and hoped that this exhibition would rectify this. It also contributed to Abetz's strategy of divide and rule in French society.

The free exhibition billed as "Freemasonry Laid Bare" ("La Francmaçonnerie dévoilée") opened at the Petit Palais on October 13.[75] Huge boards at the entrance informed visitors that for 150 years Freemasonry had conspired not only to cover up what was really happening in France, but also to drag France into war. The exhibition was intended to cast a light on what Freemasons had been up to and expose the "grotesque, lying, dishonest, pseudo-democratic jiggery-pokery used to deceive, rob and ruin a nation."[76] The propaganda message was clear: France's only hope for salvation was to crush the Freemasons and their co-conspirators the Jews, thus preventing them from doing any further damage.

One visitor observed that among the exhibits were "the interiors of Freemason temples, initiation rites, triangles, skulls, ceremonial ornaments and clothing, various accessories . . . a board denouncing the Freemasons through history . . . and a little directory of Freemasons costing 40 centimes in which everyone hoped to find the name of a colleague or a pal."[77] An illustrated catalogue by one of Bernard Faÿ's associates was on sale for 50 centimes, as were books written by Faÿ and copies of *Au Pilori*. Early in October *Au Pilori* had called for the names and addresses of all Freemasons to be displayed in their local *mairie* and the names of the Freemasons to be publicised for a month on their front door and at their place of work.[78]

Parisians unable to visit the exhibition could read lurid accounts of alleged Masonic activities, rituals, and ceremonies in *Au Pilori* or in *L'Illustration*, which offered its own extensive coverage of the exhibition complete with photographs. When the exhibition closed at the end of November the organisers claimed it had attracted some 900,000 visitors, almost certainly a vastly inflated figure. In any case, by the time the exhibition closed the cold weather and a shortage of fuel had driven Parisians out of their freezing homes and into warm places such as cinemas, libraries, and exhibitions. It is fair to assume that for at least some of those who spent time in the Petit Palais it was merely a way of escaping the cold.

Meanwhile Faÿ continued to receive and catalogue documents and artefacts stolen from Freemasons. In November, the German authorities offered him use of the building on the rue Cadet formerly occupied by the Grand Orient de France, the biggest Masonic organisation in the land, for his work. The German authorities would retain the right to "visit the building at any time and to be kept informed on a permanent basis of the work being carried out there."[79] It is unclear whether the Germans knew that Vichy was secretly funding Faÿ's activities; it is clear that they were happy to let Faÿ and his staff do all the donkey work while they retained overall control.

By October it was clear that rationing had failed to make much difference to food shortages. On the day the Freemasonry exhibition opened, Paul Léautaud wrote in his diary, "It is getting harder and harder to obtain food. Quite a few days ago I used up the last of my ration tickets for butter, cheese, and most of those for bread and meat. . . . Sometimes my lunch is just a couple of cooked apples and some bread. . . . It's even worse for my pets."[80] Liliane Jameson, a young Parisian woman with an American father and a French mother, was finding it almost impossible to track down coffee, soap, potatoes, or rice.[81] Berthe Auroy told a similar tale: "No more potatoes, dried vegetables, butter, eggs, cheese, meat, fish. A total absence of coffee, cooking oil and soap."[82] There were occasional pleasant surprises; Gilbert Badia recalled happening upon some dried bananas in a shop on the boulevard de Sébastopol, and his recollection of his surprise and excitement at this find confirms just how drab and difficult life had become.[83] Many people had to make material sacrifices to survive; for example, Gilbert Badia's wife sold the piano given to her by her parents and in its place several kilos of potatoes were spread out on the floor.[84]

In an attempt to direct scarce resources to those most in need, the rationing system was modified on October 20. Parisians were separated into different categories according to age, plus subcategories for pregnant women and those with particularly demanding jobs.[85] The system may have been tweaked a little, but the allocations remained as inadequate as ever, and finding any food in the shops was becoming ever more of a challenge. More and more, Parisians were relying on trips to the country to find food or on friends and relatives in rural areas who could send it to them.

Berthe Auroy, for example, travelled to Épernon, about sixteen miles from Chartres, where she had spent the summer. She discovered that although produce was not always easy to come by, it was at least easier than in Paris; there was always something she could buy in Épernon. There was usually an element of barter in these transactions: Auroy brought knitting wool from Paris and small presents for the children of those with whom she did business. She returned to Paris laden with tins, pasta, honey (very expensive), potatoes, rice, beans, and cheeses. When, after a considerable struggle, she finally made it back to her home in Montmartre, she took great pleasure in writing the name of the contents on her boxes and tins. "It represented a bit of security for the difficult days ahead."[86]

Micheline Bood's family were lucky to know someone who lived in Brittany. "We have received 50 kilos of potatoes from Nounou [Nanny] who is Breton and lives in Brest," Micheline wrote in October. "At the moment in Paris you can't even find a single potato, so they're really valuable. We wonder how on earth they made it to here. We've also received butter and eggs: we haven't set eyes on any of these since we came back to Paris on July 30. God has been good to us. When I think of all those people who have nothing to eat and who have lost everything."[87]

Sending food through the post did have its problems. Gilbert Badia's father-in-law, who lived in the country, would occasionally catch a wild boar and send some of the meat to the Badias in Paris. "But the post was slow . . . my father-in-law wasn't always careful, so when the pieces of boar arrived they were alive with maggots. There was no question of throwing the meat away . . . we cleaned it with vinegar and ate it without a moment's hesitation."[88]

☞ MEANWHILE THE POWER PLAY in Paris continued. Otto Abetz and Pierre Laval had marginalised General de la Laurencie, Vichy's representative in Paris; they had also largely side-lined the work of the Armistice Commission at Wiesbaden; and they had realised Abetz's dream of turning Paris into the centre of Franco-German collaboration with him and Laval in charge. On October 22 Hitler met Laval at a railway station in the unassuming little town of Montoire about thirty miles from Tours; two days later Hitler met Pétain in the same town. These meetings, especially the one between the two heads of state, put the notion of Franco-German collaboration on the map and all over the front pages of French newspapers in both zones.

The encounter between the Führer and Pétain at Montoire was highly symbolic, but almost totally devoid of content: it was not until October 27 that the Paris press published a very bland press communiqué stating that Hitler and Pétain had agreed in principle on a policy of intergovernmental Franco-German collaboration (*collaboration d'état*) and that details would follow. The absence of any concrete measures did not stop the collaborationist press from hailing the meeting as a turning point. *Paris-Soir* told its readers that the future of France would be largely shaped by this meeting,[89] while Jacque Doriot's *Le Cri du Peuple* anticipated that the Hitler-Pétain conversations could well mark "the end of France's historic decline and the start of its recovery."[90]

The Paris press was full of homages to Pétain's wisdom and courage, painting him, yet again, as the saviour of France. A front-page article in *Le Petit Parisien* declared that no Frenchman or woman would ever forget the debt they owed to Pétain, described as "the incarnation of the soul of France. . . . It is to him, to this pure and great man, to the respect that his name and his life inspire, that France owes her survival at a time when all seemed lost."[91]

However, according to both de la Laurencie and Langeron, many in Paris and in the rest of the Occupied Zone were decidedly uneasy about Montoire. "The events of these past days have troubled hearts and minds in the Occupied Zone," de la Laurencie wrote in a letter to Pétain, adding that Hitler's meeting with Laval, who was already widely distrusted and disliked, had produced "an extremely violent psychological shock." While de la Laurencie conceded that the Hitler-Pétain meeting had initially produced a slight feeling of relief, it was very short-lived and he regretted to report that the meeting was the first blow to the marshal's prestige.[92] For his part, Langeron wrote on October 29 that the vast majority of Parisians "were indignant about the meeting at Montoire and the damaging effects it could have on the country."[93]

Jean Guéhenno wrote in his diary on October 26 that based on what he heard in the streets of Paris and in the Métro, "people are outraged at what is being done in their name."[94] That same day the economist Charles Rist expressed a fear of "another humiliation" and "sliding further into the abyss."[95] Georges Benoît-Guyod wrote that according to what he heard in the queues, approval of Montoire was far from unanimous, with many Parisians either opposed to Pétain's meeting with Hitler or sceptical about it. Benoît-Guyod also believed that the timing of the meeting, which coincided with an announcement of a derisory coal allowance and the Third Reich's arbitrary annexation of three French departments made a mockery of the German assertions that Franco-German collaboration was between equals.[96] Young Benoîte Groult made no mention of Montoire in her diary. Her strategy for coping with the difficulties of life in Paris in the autumn of 1940—the continued presence of the Germans, the food shortages, the measures taken against women and Jews, the detention of French soldiers in German POW camps, and the uncertainty about what would happen next—was to retreat into her own teenage world: "I never get bored with my own company; I've got an electric record player and lots of records, loads of books. . . . Does all of this make up for all of the other stuff? A dreadful admission. Yes, it does. That's youth for you."[97]

Pétain was clearly bothered that his meeting with Hitler had prompted apprehension and even hostility in some quarters. On October 30 he explained in a radio broadcast that he had willingly chosen to meet Hitler and embarked on a policy of collaboration with the Reich. He insisted that the policy of collaboration was his and his alone and that he was pursuing it to maintain the unity of France and to make a positive contribution to the building of the new European order. He conceded that there were "those whose noble scruples distance them from our way of thinking," but he insisted that "the first duty of every Frenchman and woman is to have trust."[98]

Montoire certainly marked an important turning point. The word "collaboration" had already appeared in the armistice agreement (where it was used to describe administrative and material cooperation between the German and French authorities) but at Montoire French collaboration with Germany was elevated to a political principle. It became a sort of moral and political commitment.[99] It was posited on the belief that Britain would soon be defeated and that France would have a seat at the high table of Nazi Europe. In the meantime, collaboration was nurtured by the illusion that it would be a two-way process, one reciprocated by the Germans.

In his October 30 broadcast Pétain thus raised hopes, albeit tentatively, that Franco-German collaboration would bring improvements to the lives of his listeners: "In the near future, the burden of the country's suffering could be lightened, the lot of our prisoners improved and the cost of the Occupation reduced. Furthermore, the crossing of the demarcation line could be made easier as could the running of the country and the distribution of food within it."[100]

In Paris, Pétain's broadcast to the nation was followed by more glowing praise of Pétain in the city's press. In *Aujourd'hui*, Paul Derval, the *directeur* of the Folies-Bergère cabaret, gushed that everybody had a duty to put their trust in Pétain and follow him. André Brunot, of the Comédie-Française, referring to Pétain as "a great Frenchman at the head of our country," added that he bowed before him and followed him "in total confidence and even love."[101]

Not everyone believed that Pétain was doing his best to protect France from the worst excesses of the German occupation. Roger Langeron wrote that the emotional impact of Pétain's broadcast was to make many Parisians variously more indignant, disappointed, and discouraged.[102] The Germans also noticed this change of mood. A report in October compiled for General Streccius, the MBF commandant, talked about a slump in morale among Parisians. Over the next few months these feelings deepened as citizens failed to see any benefits from the Montoire meeting or the French government's policy of collaboration. Meanwhile Free French radio broadcasts from London calling for resistance, and the failure of Hitler's plan to invade Britain, brought glimmers of hope that perhaps all was not lost. On November 11, less than three weeks after the Montoire meeting and Pétain's speech promoting collaboration, the Germans in Paris were confronted by a massive demonstration of students and school children gathering by the Arc de Triomphe at the top of the Champs-Élysées. Less than six months after the start of the Occupation, thousands of Parisians had dared to take to the streets and defy the German occupiers.

September 1939: As France prepared to go to war, boards like this one on the place de l'Opéra appeared all over Paris indicating routes out of the city to be taken by those leaving by road. Credit: Mary Evans Picture Library.

Parisians were legally obliged to carry their gas masks at all times but this stricture was soon ignored when the much-feared German gas raids from the air failed to materialise. Credit: Mary Evans Picture Library.

CINÉMA SAINT-CHARLES
72, RUE ST-CHARLES   TÉL. : VAUGIRARD 72-50

En cas d'ALERTE, les spectateurs sont invités à gagner les **ABRIS** suivants :

16   14   12   10   8   6   4

RUE BEAUGRENELLE

15   13   11   9   7   5   3

CINÉMA

ST-CHARLES

AVIS
Nous prions notre aimable clientèle de conserver ce billet avec lesquelles elle aura droit à assister à la fin du même spectacle, sauf les Samedis soir Dimanches et Fêtes.

Imprim. M. HALLOUIN, 35. av. Aristide-Briand, Arcueil. (Alésia 20-42)

A leaflet distributed in a Paris cinema showing the whereabouts of local cellars serving as shelters to be used in the event of an air raid. If the film was interrupted by a raid, customers could present the leaflet at a future date (except Saturday evenings, Sundays, and public holidays) and watch the rest of the film. Credit: Jean-Baptiste Ordas, www.occupation-de-paris.com. All rights reserved.

Mass exodus from Paris June 1940. Credit: Anthony Potter Collection, Hulton Archive, Getty Images.

June 28, 1940. Parisians flock to consult lists of the names of soldiers taken prisoner during the recent fighting. Credit: Mary Evans Picture Library.

June 28, 1940. Hitler visited Paris with a small entourage that included Albert Speer and the sculptor Arno Breker. Very surprisingly, there is no agreement about the exact date of this visit. Credit: The Art Archive.

Three German officers in front of the Opéra. Credit: Jean-Baptiste Ordas, www
.occupation-de-paris.com.

As part of their campaign
to win hearts and minds of
Parisians, the occupying
forces issued this poster.
It aimed to exploit the
feeling of abandonment felt
by many Parisians who had
remained in the city and
called on them to trust the
German troops. Credit: Mary
Evans Picture Library.

August 1940: German military band in concert in the Tuileries Gardens.
Credit: Mary Evans Picture Library.

With petrol in short supply and permits to drive in Paris difficult to obtain,
horse-drawn and cycle-driven vehicles became ever more common. Credit: Mary
Evans Picture Library.

Entrance to the anti-Masonic exhibition "La Franc-maçonnerie dévoilée" ("Freemasonry laid bare") held in the Petit Palais. It opened in October 1940 and closed at the end of November.
Credit: The Art Archive/Kharbine-Tapabour/Collection IM.

July 1941. The occupying forces attempted to subvert the "V" campaign launched from London by de Gaulle by initiating their own campaign. Parisians awoke on July 21 to find the Eiffel Tower (like the Chamber of Deputies) adorned with a giant "V" and the slogan (in German) "Germany is winning on all Fronts."
Credit: Mary Evans Picture Library.

The anti-Semitic exhibition "The Jew and France" opened at the Palais Berlitz on September 5, 1941, two weeks after the second roundup (*rafle*) of Jews in the city. The exhibition closed in January 1942. Credit: Mary Evans Picture Library.

The cover of the official programme for the exhibition "Le Bolchevisme contre l'Europe" ("Bolshevism against Europe"), which was staged at the Salle Wagram from March to June 1942. Credit: Jean-Baptiste Ordas, www.occupation-de-paris.com.

A queue outside a baker's shop on the corner of the rue Lepic and the rue Tholozé in the 18th arrondissement, not far from where Berthe Auroy lived. Credit: Collection Musée de la Résistance nationale, Champigny-sur-Marne.

Family food parcels being pushed along inside a Paris railway station under the watchful eye of a German soldier. As food became increasingly difficult to find, Parisians had to rely more and more on these so-called family food parcels sent from friends and relatives living in the countryside. In October 1941, the French government legalised this practice laying down conditions (frequently ignored) limiting what the parcels could contain. Credit: Mary Evans Picture Library.

A Zazou. Credit:
Roger-Viollet Collection, Getty
Images.

Agnès Humbert in 1938.
Agnès was an art historian
and a member of the Musée
de l'Homme Resistance
group, one of the earliest
Resistance groups in Paris.
Some twenty members of
the group, including Agnès,
were betrayed and went on
trial in February 1942.
Agnès was sentenced to five
years' imprisonment in
Germany but was deported
into slave labour, where she
was forced into dreadfully
dangerous factory work
until her release in 1945.
Credit: Photo published here by
kind permission of her grandson
Antoine Sabbagh.

Boris Vildé, a Russian ethnographer and linguist, as he appeared on a student card issued by the University of Helsinki, Finland, on January 15, 1939. Vildé was the driving force behind the Musée de l'Homme group and the initiator of its newssheet *Résistance*. He was executed by firing squad along with six other members of the group on February 23, 1942. Credit: Collection Musée de la Résistance nationale, Champigny-sur-Marne.

BEKANNTMACHUNG | AVIS

1. Der Jude SZMUL TYSZELMAN aus Paris
2. Der HENRY GAUTHEROT aus Paris

sind wegen Begünstigung des Feindes, begangen durch Teilnahme an einer gegen die deutschen Besatzungstruppen gerichteten kommunistischen Kundgebung, zum Tode verurteilt und erschossen worden.

Paris, den 19. August 1941.

Der Militärbefehlshaber in Frankreich.

1. Le Juif SZMUL TYSZELMAN de Paris
2. Le nommé HENRY GAUTHEROT de Paris

ont été condamnés à mort pour aide à l'ennemi, ayant pris part à une manifestation communiste dirigée contre les troupes d'occupation allemandes. Ils ont été fusillés aujourd'hui.

Paris, le 19 Août 1941.

Der Militärbefehlshaber in Frankreich.

Poster in German and French, dated August 19, 1941, announcing the execution of Samuel Tyszelman and Henri Gautherot, two young Communists who were arrested after taking part in a street demonstration against the occupying forces. The poster emphasises that Samuel Tyszelman was Jewish. Credit: Collection Musée de la Résistance nationale, Champigny-sur-Marne.

The Gaullist symbol—the Cross of Lorraine—and a "V" (for victory) carved into a tree next to a poster advertising the exhibition "Bolshevism against Europe," held in the Salle Wagram from March to June 1942. Credit: Collection Musée de la Résistance nationale, Champigny-sur-Marne.

Reconstruction (by the GFP?) of the assassination by a member of the Resistance of Corporal Rohland in the rue Erlanger (16th arrondissement) on April 20, 1942. © Préfecture de Police. Tous droits résérvés/All Rights Reserved.

6

From Mass Street Protest to the "Führer's Generous Gesture"

*T*HE MEETING at Montoire had failed to produce any tangible concessions and life in Paris was just more of the same. One thing Montoire had provoked, however, was an upsurge in anti-German feeling. In his letter to Pétain shortly after the Montoire meeting, General de la Laurencie, Vichy's official representative in Paris, observed that support for de Gaulle in the Occupied Zone was increasing.[1] Nowhere in Paris was this more evident than in the student area of the Latin Quarter.

As the new academic year began, some students dared to stage anti-German protests. Just over a week before Montoire, a small group of them demonstrated against the Occupation by trying to force their way into two German-only brothels on the rue Grégoire-de-Tours. Having failed to get in, they tore down posters announcing that the buildings had been requisitioned by the Germans and shouted insults at the Germans inside. On October 25 students attending a class at the Sorbonne walked out, protesting at the presence of three German officers in the lecture hall. When two female French students were later seen talking with the officers, they were booed and insulted by fellow students; the following day the women asked the dean for protection.[2]

By the autumn, de Gaulle, the leader of the Free French based in London, was emerging as a powerful symbol of resistance. As a man he remained an enigma: Gaul is the old Roman name for France and

143

many Parisians hearing his name in the broadcasts from London wondered if de Gaulle was a *nom de guerre* or if indeed there was any such person at all. The Free French broadcasts from London, which the Germans never managed to jam completely, lambasted the defeatist worldview of the Vichy government and the crowing triumphalism of the pro-Nazi collaborationist Paris press. Broadcasts offered a glimmer of hope to those longing to be free from German domination. Support for the British and for de Gaulle grew when Parisians realised that Hitler had failed to invade and conquer Britain: the Free French were still broadcasting from London and the newspapers carried no news of a German landing across the Channel. Yet despite de Gaulle's increased popularity and the absence of any improvements in the life of most Parisians after Montoire, plenty of people in both zones still believed Pétain was a hero, doing his best to protect them from the worst of German excesses. Indeed, the Free French in London received letters from listeners in France complaining that the broadcasts were too critical of Pétain. Some people mistakenly believed that de Gaulle and Pétain were secretly colluding to outwit the Germans.[3]

Towards the end of October Roger Langeron also noted an upsurge in Gaullist propaganda since Montoire in the Latin Quarter. He wrote of a proliferation of pro-de Gaulle stickers and of pro-de Gaulle leaflets left around buildings, placed in textbooks in the student libraries, or posted on walls alongside Gaullist slogans and symbols scrawled in chalk; a few young people were seen wearing de Gaulle's insignia: the two-barred Cross of Lorraine.[4]

But anti-German feeling was not restricted to the Latin Quarter. More and more Parisians were finding little ways to contest the Occupation and annoy the Germans. From October, according to the Paris police, cinema audiences began to show their disapproval during the propagandist newsreels by laughing, succumbing to "coughing fits," blowing their noses loudly, or "sneezing." Cinema owners appealed to patrons to desist, warning them that any disruption could mean the closure of the cinema and the punishment of those the authorities deemed responsible—starting with the cinema's owner. In a vain attempt to prevent the protests, cinemas took to leaving the house lights on when newsreels were being shown.

In February 1941 a number of Paris cinemas showed footage of Gontier de Vassé, a French pilot claiming to have been imprisoned in

England and mocking those who continued to believe that Britain was a friend of France. "It was almost impossible to hear what he was saying," a policeman at one cinema reported. "As soon as he appeared on the screen, 80 percent of the audience started systematically sneezing, noisily blowing their noses and snorting. The usherettes tried 'shushing' the audience to calm things down, but this only added to the noise that drowned out what Gontier de Vassé was saying."[5]

Some Parisians went further. One man was arrested for imitating a sheep during a filmed extract of a speech by the arch-collaborator Alphonse de Châteaubriant.[6] Another was arrested for whistling and for barking like a dog. At one cinema a pigeon was released into the auditorium, a French tricolour flag attached to its leg.[7] The authorities became absurdly sensitive about the behaviour of cinema audiences and often overreacted. Liliane Jameson and her mother went to the cinema together and when her mother powdered her nose during the German newsreel she was promptly arrested as was a man who slid down in his seat and pulled his hat over his eyes. Liliane's mother, along with Liliane, were taken to a nearby police station, but they were released without charge after two hours.[8] From June 1940 the German authorities had closed cinemas where anti-German protests had been reported, usually for a week; by early November 1940, twenty-six cinemas had been affected. However, from February 1941 there appears to be no record of cinema closures.[9]

Passive resistance was not just restricted to cinemas. The writer and critic André Thérive was in a crowded café when he claimed to see a German in uniform offer a cigarette to a man sitting next to him. "No thanks. I don't smoke," replied his neighbour, blowing clouds of smoke into the soldier's face.[10] Another time Thérive relates that he was outside the Abwehr headquarters in the Hôtel Lutetia when a German car drew up: the German officers alighted with much clicking of heels, unaware that someone had spelled out *Vive de Gaulle* in the dust on the back of the vehicle.[11] On another occasion, Thérive saw customers at a café table on a crowded pavement take great delight in stretching out their legs, forcing uniformed Germans to step out in the road.[12]

Signs were also clearly evident that the Germans were less "correct" towards Parisians than they had been immediately after they arrived. By late autumn, many complaints were being made about German soldiers in the Métro occupying seats designated for the elderly, pregnant women, or the infirm, including war veterans. In November Ernst Schaumburg, the German commandant in Paris with responsibility for day-to-day issues in the city, clarified the situation: he told the head of the Métro that all German military personnel, who already travelled first class for free, took priority over the French.[13]

Tensions were running high as Armistice Day approached. November 11 had been a public holiday in France commemorating the day in 1918 when France and Germany signed an armistice agreement marking the end of the First World War.[14] Every year since then, France had officially remembered the 1.7 million French people, including 300,000 civilians, who had lost their lives in the carnage as well as the 3.5 million soldiers who had been wounded, a third of whom had lost a limb.

In 1940 Armistice Day was an even more highly charged date than usual. It was a time for Parisians to remember France's dead and wounded, but it was also an uncomfortable reminder for the Germans of their defeat and humiliation just over twenty years earlier. Little wonder that the German authorities declared that November 11 would not be a public holiday and that no demonstrations would be tolerated. However, university students and especially secondary school pupils at the *lycées* had other ideas.

Early in November a group of university students distributed handwritten leaflets calling on fellow students to gather at the Tomb of the Unknown Soldier, under the Arc de Triomphe on the place de l'Étoile at 5 P.M. on November 11.[15] This politically disparate group included dissident Communists, who disapproved of their leadership's passivity; nationalists and royalists from Charles Maurras's Action Française, who deeply resented the German presence on French soil; and a new grouping of "Gaullists," inspired by de Gaulle's determination to fight on.

Many of those who responded to the call and headed for the Arc de Triomphe were politically motivated, but some had more personal reasons for going. Jacques Fragnier and his mother, who lived in the rue de Rome, were still awaiting news of Jacques's father, a war veteran stranded somewhere in the Unoccupied Zone. Jacques and his father had always attended the Armistice Day ceremonies together. "It had always been a moment when we felt intensely close," Jacques recalled. "At the thought of my absent father, a mysterious force was driving me to go to the Étoile on that 11 November, as I had done on all those other 11 Novembers with him. It took only a vague rumour going round my class for me to make up my mind to go."[16]

News of the gathering at the Arc de Triomphe reached the *lycées*, where boys and girls, who were educated in separate schools, were planning to play truant and join in. On November 6 schoolgirl Micheline Bood wrote excitedly in her diary: "A bit of paper's doing the rounds at school: 'People of France, the Bochs [*sic*] don't respect November 11. *Rendez-vous* at the Arc de Triomphe at 5 P.M.' . . . We're nearly all going to the Arc de Triomphe. It'll be fun. If anything happens we'll all be thrown in prison. No more homework, no more teachers and no more school punishments. That would be great."[17]

On the same day that Micheline was writing this, fighting broke out between students and German soldiers inside the Café d'Harcourt at the corner of the boulevard Saint-Michel and the place de la Sorbonne in the Latin Quarter. The German authorities responded by promptly closing all the cafés in the area. On November 7, *La France au travail* reported that for the past few weeks a handful of troublemakers had been involved in what the paper called "Gaullist activity," namely, disrupting lectures that were delivered in "the spirit of European collaboration" to which the "agitators" objected.[18]

At 4 P.M. on November 8 a small group of mostly Communist students gathered in the cold and dark outside the Collège de France, next to the Sorbonne. They were protesting against the arbitrary arrest of Paul Langevin, an internationally renowned professor of physics, who, had he not been locked up in the Santé prison, would have been giving a lecture at that time.[19] French police officers and German soldiers stood around and kept a careful eye on this small gathering, but they did not intervene and no one was arrested.[20]

From 8:30 A.M. on Armistice Day Parisians of all ages defied the German ban on public demonstrations and turned out to pay their respects to the dead and wounded of the 1914–1918 war. At the bottom end of the Champs-Élysées, they laid flowers at the statue of Georges Clemenceau, the French prime minister in 1918, and at the top of the avenue on the Tomb of the Unknown Soldier. The morning was fairly quiet, although the police broke up a group of about twenty students at around half-past ten and another 100 or so truanting school students, who arrived shortly before midday. René Beaudoin,[21] a thirty-two-year-old science teacher from their *lycée*, was stopped by the French police as he made his way down the Champs-Élysées. He had a blue, white, and red rosette pinned to his raincoat.

"What are you doing here?" the police asked him.

"I'm coming down the Champs-Élysées, having left my flowers. I bumped into my students by chance."

"So you consider it normal to incite your pupils to commit an offence?"

"I've just told them not to gather as a group under the Arc de Triomphe, to behave with dignity and not to provoke trouble. I don't think I've overstepped the mark as far as my duties as a teacher are concerned."

"And why did you go and leave flowers?"

"I wanted to pay my respects to those who died in 1914–1918."

"What are you doing wearing that emblem on your raincoat?"

"I'm paying homage to the colours of France."

"As a teacher, don't you think you should rather be setting a good example to your pupils?"

"My role is to teach them to be good French citizens and fulfil their patriotic duty."

"It is officially forbidden to demonstrate, as you well know!"

"Well, if just walking down the Champs-Élysées constitutes demonstrating, then so be it. Anyway, that's what I came here to do."

Beaudoin was subsequently tried, found guilty, and sentenced to eight months in prison.[22]

The French police had heard rumours that students from the universities and secondary schools were planning to gather at the Arc de Triomphe, but they were uncertain how best to respond. Seventeen-year-old Igor de Schotten, who had witnessed Stukas bombing the Renault and Citroën factories in June, attended the Lycée Janson-de-Sailly, within walking distance of the place de l'Étoile. According to de Schotten, at about 3 P.M. he skipped classes and popped into the florist's near his school to collect a wreath he had ordered a few days earlier. To his astonishment, the florist, Monsieur Landrat, produced an enormous blue Cross of Lorraine, which stood about two metres high. Landrat, who had guessed what Igor was up to, refused any payment: "It's not for you, *mon vieux*. It's for de Gaulle. It's for France."

Igor met his classmates: he and a pal named Dubost carried the cross along the avenue Victor Hugo, leading to the place de l'Étoile. They were followed by a group of fellow pupils. As they advanced, shopkeepers on both sides of the avenue lowered the metal shutters over their shop windows and most of Igor's classmates slowly melted away. A hundred metres from their goal they were stopped by the French police. Now there was just Igor, Dubost, and one enormous blue Cross of Lorraine. Again, according to de Schotten, the police accompanied the duo to the Tomb of the Unknown Soldier, where they left their cross. The two boys then headed off down the Champs-Élysées, where they were once again stopped by French police—in plainclothes this time. Dubost was arrested for wearing a small Cross of Lorraine badge and spent a month in the Santé prison. De Schotten continued unimpeded down the Champs-Élysées, which by now, as darkness fell, was rapidly filling up with more people, most of them school children. De Schotten was later arrested as well but is reported to have escaped from the police station where he was being held.[23]

Around 5 P.M. there were clashes on the Champs-Élysées at the Brasserie Tyrol, a meeting place for members of Far Right groups. Students responding to the call to meet at the Arc de Triomphe confronted 150 or so French pro-Nazi elements, including supporters of the group Jeune Front, whose members had smashed the windows of Jewish shops back in August. On this dark, drizzly evening, the two sides traded insults and hurled missiles at each other. A quarter of an hour later there were more clashes between students and Jeune Front members at the corner of the Champs-Élysées and the rue Balzac, followed by more confrontations at the Brasserie Tyrol.

By 6 P.M. the place de l'Étoile around the Arc de Triomphe was packed with thousands of people, mainly school students, while others were still making their way there. A resounding rendering of the Marseillaise filled the air, as did cries of "Vive la France!" and "Vive de Gaulle!" People were waving blue, white, and red flags; others threw paper crosses of Lorraine and bouquets of flowers towards the Tomb of the Unknown Soldier. The French police had lost any semblance of control. Suddenly, armed German soldiers, who had been waiting in covered trucks parked all around the place de l'Étoile, jumped out of their vehicles and stormed into the crowd. Jean Guéhenno, who earlier had watched French police removing flowers from the foot of Clemenceau's statue, was now near the Arc de Triomphe: "I witnessed the German soldiers with fixed bayonets charging at the school children on the pavements of the Champs-Élysées and saw officers hurling them to the ground."[24] Shots rang out as the soldiers waded in, beating demonstrators with rifle butts, often full in the face. Three demonstrators were shot, none fatally, although one remained in hospital until the end of January. But the students bravely fought back. Micheline Bood wrote in her diary of Germans injured in the fighting and of ambulances being called to take them away. "The French were elated and the Boches were miserable." She then bumped into a group of students who had surrounded a German and were treating him like a punchbag. He was almost in tears. Micheline and her sister were jubilant: "Tough on him, but he's a Boche," she wrote.[25]

About 125 student demonstrators—of whom about 100 were schoolchildren—were dragged away by the Germans. They were taken to the Cherche-Midi and Santé prisons where they were left standing in the dark, the rain, and the cold, before being kicked and beaten by German soldiers desperate to find out who had organised the demonstration. At the Cherche-Midi prison, five of those arrested were picked out at random and faced a mock execution.[26] Most of them were then released. Those arrested by the French police generally fared better than those rounded up by the Germans. The estimated number of demonstrators ranges from around three thousand to nearly six thousand; over a thousand were questioned at police stations, but most were released the same night.[27] However, about thirty were handed over to the Germans and most of them ended up spending up to five weeks in prison. An unknown number of demonstrators had been picked up by the Paris police, shoved into vans, driven away from the area, and released. When it was all over, Micheline Bood, who had not been arrested, wrote: "We are going to have to pay for this. But I can say 'I WAS THERE.'"[28]

In response to this demonstration, the German authorities ordered the closure of all Paris universities. All students who were Paris residents had to report daily to their local police stations, while all students whose main residence was in the provinces were ordered to return home.

Micheline Bood lived near the Champs-Élysées and faced further restrictions: she wrote in her diary that it was now forbidden to walk on the Champs-Élysées, around the Latin Quarter, and on the *grands boulevards*. Those who lived in these areas had to obtain special cards. "That's all because of the demonstrations," she wrote. "The Boches can be a real pain in the arse."[29]

The arrests continued after November 11. One student, Edwige de Saint-Wexel, was found to have lied when she claimed she had not been at the demonstration. A search of her apartment revealed leaflets and a diary full of anti-German sentiments. Two men from the German secret police beat her, stubbed out cigarettes on her chest and forehead, scarring her for life, and threw her in a cell, where she remained until February 1941. "I lived like an animal," she wrote, "unwashed, famished, lapping up my own soup, no one to talk to, no idea what was happening, nor orientation beyond my cell. It was like living in a cold, black hell. I was less than human."[30]

The Paris media was subject to a total news blackout on the November 11 demonstration, but news spread by word of mouth and through radio broadcasts from London, which claimed, incorrectly, that there had been ten fatalities. When Léautaud announced that he thought the demonstration had been "pointless" and "harmful," a colleague replied, "I don't agree. We don't want them [the Germans] here. People show them that. I think that's a very good thing. It's good that they see that not everybody is resigned to accepting the situation."[31]

Others who were not prepared to accept the situation included the tiny Resistance group founded in the summer by Claude Aveline, Jean Cassou, and Marcel Abraham that Agnès Humbert joined. Over the past few months it had grown through chance encounters and with members recruiting trusted friends. Germaine Tillion, an anthropologist at the Musée de l'Homme, had joined; she, in turn, brought in the museum's librarian Yvonne Oddon and her partner, a Russian exile named Anatole Lewitsky. In September the group wrote its first leaflet, which it printed off on the museum's duplicator.[32] Shortly afterwards the group was joined by the tall, strikingly good-looking Boris Vildé. Born in St. Petersburg, Vildé had arrived in Paris from Estonia in 1932 aged twenty-four, worked as an ethnographer at the Musée de l'Homme, and had recently been enrolled as a student in Finland. It was Vildé who, through sheer force of personality and apparently unlimited determination, energy, vision, and intelligence—as well as sheer chutzpah—became the de facto leader of the group. In November Agnès Humbert described him as "A marvellous fellow—the man here that I admire the most—his warm-heartedness is matched by his intelligence and his energy. He's a great guy."[33]

The group's modest expansion was largely thanks to Vildé's contacts in Paris and in the provinces, who fed him information about German plans and troop movements.[34] Vildé also claimed (almost certainly correctly) to have links with British Intelligence. Vildé linked up with an escape line in the Occupied Zone to the north of Paris, helping British soldiers and airmen to get home. He also recruited René Sénéchal, a young trainee accountant, nicknamed *le Gosse* (the Kid) and Albert Gaveau, an unemployed flight instructor, both of whom would play significant roles within the organisation.

Vildé insisted that the group needed its own newspaper and on December 15 he oversaw the production of the first issue of the four-page *Résistance*, which described itself as the *Bulletin officiel du comité national de salut public* (Official Bulletin of the National Committee of Public Safety). This grandiose title—complete with its nod towards the committee that was the de facto executive of revolutionary France between 1793 and 1794—was quite deliberate. Vildé believed that if the group gave the impression it was a large organisation, then current members would be more likely to stay and other people would be more likely to join. In late December, Sénéchal worked tirelessly firming up contacts in cities in the Unoccupied Zone, while Gaveau joined André Weil-Curiel, a Gaullist Free French agent, in a bid to escape to London by boat from Brittany. The attempt failed when the fisherman they had enlisted was arrested, although Gaveau and Weil-Curiel avoided capture.

Meanwhile, Otto Abetz was energetically promoting Franco-German intergovernmental collaboration through his meetings with Pierre Laval. Above all, Abetz wanted to use Pétain when it suited him while, at the same time, driving a wedge between Parisians and the Vichy government. Hitler's decision to give Abetz overall responsibility for the Paris press explains the anti-Vichy tone of most of the newspapers, which attacked Vichy's collaboration for being far too timid and half-hearted. Abetz understood that Pétain was too conservative and traditionalist to embrace the sort of far-reaching collaboration he believed was possible with Laval. For this reason he was keen to build up an alternative French power base in Paris, which could be used to threaten or put pressure on Pétain.

Abetz knew the editors and leading journalists on most of the Paris newspapers and having different newspapers target different sections of the population served his strategy of encouraging division and fragmentation. While press censorship was mostly self-censorship carried out by editors and journalists who knew what was expected of them, Abetz still reserved the right to intervene whenever he wanted them to give the news a particular spin. On the first anniversary of France going to war against Germany, for example, he had instructed editors to emphasise that France was as guilty as Britain in waging war on Germany; that the French and their prewar political leaders, whom they had elected, were equally responsible for France's aggressive policy towards Germany; so if the French were badly off, they only had themselves to blame.[35]

Abetz had especially close links with the newspaper *La France au travail*, which he had financed from July. He and the embassy were also providing almost half the funding for *Les Nouveaux Temps*, an evening newspaper edited by Jean Luchaire, an old pal from the prewar days and the former boss of Abetz's French wife Suzanne. The weekly literary review, *La Gerbe*, thought by many Parisians to be the personal property of the celebrated novelist and collaborationist Alphonse de Châteaubriant, actually originated from the German embassy. Rudolph Rahn, one of Abetz's close associates, later admitted that it was "the only creation of the Embassy's in the early days."[36] It received an allocation of paper that was disproportionate, in terms of circulation, to that granted to other collaborationist publications.[37]

Abetz's greatest coup in the world of Parisian intellectual publications was to seize on Jean Paulhan's resignation as editor of the *La Nouvelle Revue française* (NRF), France's top prewar literary publication, and replace Paulhan with the pro-Nazi novelist Pierre Drieu La Rochelle. Before the war the NRF had been a showcase of French literary excellence, so control of the review satisfied both Abetz's intellectual snobbery and his political ambition to use the paper as a vehicle to promote Franco-German intellectual and literary collaboration. The first issue of the "new" NRF was published in December, but it was soon clear that Abetz had established the continuity of the paper in name only. It was a pale imitation of the original and was swiftly boycotted by most of the established figures in the world of letters as well as by the rising stars.[38]

Meanwhile, the Propaganda Units of the MBF promoted cultural collaboration in the field of music. In addition to the free outdoor concerts, German musical ensembles soon arrived in Paris. Within weeks of the start of the Occupation the Berlin Philharmonic Orchestra had given two concerts in Paris and a third in Versailles; by November other German orchestras could be heard in concert at the Palais de Chaillot and the Théâtre des Champs-Élysées. In March 1941 when the Mannheim National Theatre performed Wagner's *Die Walküre* at the Opéra, huge swastika banners were hung above the main staircase; two months later the German Institute sponsored a visit to the Opéra by the Staatsoper Berlin, which performed works by Mozart and Wagner.[39] Abetz was not going to be left out of organising classical concerts and, in December, the German Institute hijacked the sponsorship of a Bach concert conducted by Herbert von Karajan at the Palais de Chaillot at which Abetz delivered the welcoming speech. Karl Epting, director of the German Institute, hailed this event as "a rousing success of cultural prowess and effective propaganda."[40]

The German Institute was also busy promoting German-language classes. Signs or menus in German were in bars, cafés, restaurants, shops, and hotels across the city. The Occupation had thrown Parisians and Germans together at shopping, food, drink, and entertainment venues and Parisian staff found it advantageous to know at least a few words of German. There was a sharp rise in the number of students taking German in schools and universities—a working knowledge of the language increased their chances of finding employment—while private German-language classes also flourished. In addition, more than 5,000 students enrolled for free classes run by the German Institute at the Sorbonne, which even offered cheap public transport for those travelling to and from courses.[41]

Before the war, fewer than a fifth of schoolgirls studied German; by 1941, the figure had risen to about a half. It has been suggested that this upsurge reflected their parents' hope that their job prospects would improve and their chances of marrying a German would increase.[42] It was not just students. In December Andrzej Bobkowski discovered that several of the female employees in the factory in the Paris suburbs where he worked as a social worker had signed up to learn German.[43] Middle-class men, too, were enrolling to learn the language. "The French bourgeois may rail against collaboration," Alfred Fabre-Luce noted, "but he's learning German: that means he thinks it [the Occupation] is going to last."[44]

Parisians had too many things to worry about in the present for them to think much about the future. Rationing had failed to solve the shortage of food and other necessities. By the end of November Micheline Bood had lost a lot of weight, "probably because of the restrictions," she wrote in her diary, although she was pleased because it gave her a good figure;[45] by January she found that over the past three months she had lost 2.5 kilos.[46] Food shortages led to an increase in *le troc*, or barter. Teacher Gilbert Badia, for example, gave Latin lessons to the daughter of the woman who ran a dairy in exchange for milk and butter. Badia recalled: "A quarter of a litre of milk a day without having to give her a ration ticket."[47] Some Parisians were soon using some items, especially tobacco, as an alternative currency.[48]

Alongside the growth in barter came an increase in black-market transactions. The collaborationist Paris press had started referring to the "black market" in September;[49] by October one newspaper was calling it "the number one problem of the moment."[50] "Black market" was a fairly elastic term. It included, for example, freelancing individuals—often employees of the state railway company, the SNCF, who had the right to free travel, which gave them easy access to the countryside. There they bought small, easily concealed amounts of produce from local farmers, which they brought home and sold to friends and family without having to bother about ration tickets.

Some operations were more structured, such as the one run by a certain Michel from Villejuif in the southern suburbs. He used a small truck to bring various produce from the countryside into Paris; he stored the food in a small lockup before selling it in a local café where customers also placed their orders.

Larger-scale operations, almost industrial in size, were scarcely distinguishable from organised crime. A police report at the end of January recorded seven men and one woman who had run a clandestine company selling rationed goods at inflated prices. When they were caught with a haul that included 6,500 tins of pâté and 2,250 kilos of salt, the police reckoned they had already netted several million francs.

The same report revealed that on January 22, 1941, Paris police arrested nine men and two women, two of whom had (illegally) founded a company in the rue Réaumur purportedly dealing in textiles. The police discovered the shop was being used as a cover to sell what their report described imprecisely as "all sorts of goods" and that two million francs worth of articles had been seized.[51]

The expansion of the black market saw the emergence of "fake policemen" (les faux policiers). A police report of January 20, 1941, recorded one of many similar cases: a man who persuaded people to buy black-market produce from him; then, falsely claiming to be a police officer, he kept the money, took back the goods, and threatened to arrest them if they objected.[52]

For the sellers, the black market was a quick, if risky, way to make money. Reactions of the Parisians to these illegal transactions depended, in part at least, on how much money they had. For the better off with no scruples, it was a way of ensuring they could continue buying whatever they wanted; others saw it as a regrettable necessity that saved them from going cold and hungry. Then there were those who saw it as an absolute final resort (if you could afford it), while yet others considered it an abomination and refused to have anything to do with it. Overall, with the exception of those who profited from it, the black market had very few friends. A survey of intercepted letters during the second half of January and early February 1941 concluded that "The black market, which enables a few well-off people and a few sharks to get rich, is particularly loathed by most of the population."[53] However, the longer the Occupation dragged on and the scarcer food became, more and more Parisians felt forced to use it in order to stave off malnutrition.

Many Parisians misunderstood the relationship between the black market and food and fuel shortages: they blamed the black market for the shortages, whereas it was largely a consequence of them. The combination of unofficial and official expropriations of French raw materials, goods, and cash by the occupying forces generated chronic shortages, which, in turn, had created the conditions for the rapid development of the black market. By constantly accusing black-market profiteers of sabotaging food supplies, the French government perpetuated the myth that the black market was responsible for the difficulties in people's daily lives. This accusation also served to deflect criticism from the government's own failings to distribute food equitably and to conceal the fact that the root cause of the problem lay with the economic consequences of the 1940 defeat, the ruthless requisitioning by the Germans, and especially the Vichy government's crippling weekly payments to the Germans, which were officially made to cover the cost of the Occupation.[54]

Meanwhile, making money out of food shortages and rationing became more and more widespread. One common illegal scheme was for shopkeepers to sell goods above the official price. In January, for example, a M. Boden admitted selling 100 kilos of rabbit and 200 kilos of chicken up to two or three times the official price.[55] Besides illegal buying and selling—and overcharging—a thriving trade was also carried on in forged ration tickets. In November the French minister for supplies reported an extensive network around Les Halles market trading in forged and stolen ration tickets for meat.[56] Two months later police arrested four people for dealing in forged ration tickets, which they had been producing at the printing works where they were employed; the work was done on Sundays, when they could be sure the boss would not put in an appearance. By the time of their arrest they had produced some 12,500 tickets, which made possible the purchase of 75,000 kilos of meat.[57]

Restaurants provided an ideal environment for the black market. In theory all were subject to restrictions: customers had to use ration tickets to pay for their meal; some foodstuffs like meat were not available on certain days; menus had to be displayed and adhered to by the establishment. In addition, restaurants were placed in one of five categories, each of which had an official ceiling on the amount that could be charged for a meal; these ranged from those in the cheapest category (D: maximum price 18 francs) to the most expensive (E: "Exceptional" at 75 francs). However, restaurants were soon subverting these rulings by charging more than the official menu price, providing extra dishes, serving meat on days when it was forbidden—sometimes hiding it under fried eggs—and accepting cash payments without tickets.[58]

Some restaurants like the Madeleine, a few hundred metres from the exclusive La Tour d'Argent and Le Catalan, an eatery frequented by Pablo Picasso in the rue des Grands-Augustins, were among "the high spots of clandestine gastronomy."[59] Many restaurants that flouted the regulations about sourcing its food and what could be served and when were frequented by members of the German military elite, which usually meant they were safe from investigation by the Paris police. One establishment that was illegally resourced was the infamous brothel with the English name One Two Two at 122, rue de Provence in the 8th arrondissement. Located in the former home of Joachim Murat, Napoleon Bonaparte's brother-in-law, with its twenty-two rooms and sixty "girls," One Two Two received about 300 customers a day. It also boasted its own fine restaurant, the Boeuf à la Ficelle, where food and drink were supplied courtesy of the black market. When the brothel's manager "Fabienne" (a former prostitute named Georgette Pélagie) and owner Marcel Jamet married they held their wedding reception there during which their guests downed 176 bottles and 34 magnums of champagne; the party ended with people slumped all over the floor.[60]

Vichy tried to win popular support by urging the French police to clamp down on the black market, but the Jamets viewed such efforts with irritation and pseudo-patriotic outrage. "There was a special section [of the police] devoted to cracking down on the black market," Fabienne Jamet complained. "Helped by the gendarmerie and the regular police, it carried out checks on all the roads, at the exits to every railway station and on every road into Paris. Confiscating goods, fines, closing down businesses, those were the weapons they used . . . Incredible! To think that there were French people trying to stop other French people from eating."[61] One Two Two had an official allocation of "only" 100 bottles of champagne a month, but their customers sometimes got through 150 a night. Regular German clients at the brothel— among them Wilhelm Radecke, head of the Abwehr in Paris—were only too happy to help One Two Two obtain more. They secured an *Ausweis* for Marcel Jamet, who, having bought as much petrol as he needed on the black market, would drive off to a wine-producer contact near Rheims and bring back some of the thousand bottles his supplier had set aside for his brothel.

☞ IN THE AUTUMN PARISIANS had to face a new peril: winter was looming. "In Paris the situation is incredibly difficult," Berthe Auroy wrote. "The market in the rue Lepic, which used to have so much, now has so very little. . . . Despite the food shortages everybody is still hoping to get in some provisions for the terrible winter which has been officially forecast."[62] Winter arrived early. "Here comes winter," Jean

Guéhenno wrote on October 16. "We are slipping gently into the grey and the cold."[63] On October 25 it was so cold that Berthe Auroy and a friend had to cover their freezing legs in an eiderdown as they sat indoors.

Collecting dead wood was strictly forbidden, so scavenging for firewood was a risky business. On November 4 *Le Petit Parisien* reported that a couple had been stopped with two bags of firewood; they had been treated leniently in court only because the man had been awarded the Légion d'honneur.[64] Berthe Auroy realised that her miserly monthly gas allowance was woefully inadequate: "How are you supposed to heat yourself *and* take a bath?" she asked herself.[65] She finally managed to track down a 1,000-watt electric radiator, and a month later she found an electrician willing to install it—for an exorbitant fee.

She had accumulated some coal earlier in the year, but when coal was rationed at 50 kilos a month she realised she would not have enough to see her through the winter. Luckily, a neighbour managed to obtain some huge lumps of coal for all the tenants in the house. This meant Berthe would be less reliant on the radiator and gave her hope she might stay warm enough until spring arrived. With great difficulty she broke the coal into manageable pieces, covering her kitchen in black shards and dust. For the first time in more than twenty years she lit the stove in her kitchen, where she pretty much lived all winter. "Dressing, undressing, washing, eating, socialising, writing letters, etc.—everything happens in the kitchen."[66]

In November Liliane Jameson loved the coal fire burning in her grate. She was less thrilled when she realised she did not have enough ration tickets to keep it burning throughout the winter. The other tickets had been allocated to her landlord, but there were only enough to keep the coal-fired radiators in the building working for two months.[67] Under the Occupation, coal had become a valuable commodity. The author Georges Duhamel observed a pedestrian spot a tiny piece of coal on the pavement, pick it up, study it carefully, pop it in an envelope, and put in his pocket.[68] The German occupiers had plenty of coal, so for some people stealing from them was almost a duty. When he was a boy René Omnès, the son of a gendarme and himself a future captain in the gendarmerie, was sent by his mother to a friend of hers who worked as a butler for the German navy.[69] René came home with two shopping bags full of coal, which the butler friend had stolen from his

German employers. When René's father learned what had happened, he forbade his son to return for more.[70]

⌇ Since Montoire, Pierre Laval, Pétain's prime minister and, since October 28, foreign minister, had met regularly with Abetz. Laval hoped that Hitler would soon announce measures to ease the problems faced by the French. This, he believed, would soften French opinion towards Germany and lay the foundations for a solid partnership between the two nations. But Hitler had other ideas.

In November the Führer revealed to his military commanders how France figured in his plans. "The aim of my policy towards France is to cooperate with this country in the way that will most effectively support the future conduct of the war against Britain."[71] There was no question of France becoming Germany's partner as the collaborationists and Laval hoped. Hitler considered Montoire to be a purely symbolic gesture of Franco-German friendship aimed at boosting pro-German feelings in France. He hoped to keep the French docile with a steady flow of anti-British, anti-Gaullist propaganda, combined with vague allusions to improving their lot if they backed Germany and did not cause trouble. In this vein, it was deemed time for a symbolic gesture on the Führer's part.

On December 10 Laval told General de la Laurencie that Hitler had graciously offered to transfer to Paris the ashes of Napoleon Bonaparte's son, Napoleon II, the duke of Reichstadt, nicknamed *l'Aiglon* (the Eaglet). His ashes were currently in Vienna, but the plan was that they would be placed in Les Invalides on the night of December 14–15, a hundred years to the day after his father's ashes had been interred there.

The Germans were counting on Pétain's presence at the ceremony and rumours began to circulate that the French government was preparing to leave Vichy. Medical student Bernard Pierquin noted in his diary that at the beginning of December "everyone had been talking about Pétain coming to the Occupied Zone, and possibly basing himself in Versailles."[72]

However, on December 13, the day before the transfer of the ashes was due to take place, there was high drama in Vichy: Pétain sacked Laval and had him placed under house arrest.[73] Pétain had been growing increasingly suspicious of—and irritated by—Laval, who was becoming ever more unpopular with the French in both zones. In Pétain's eyes

Laval had failed to secure any post-Montoire concessions from the Germans that Pétain could sell to the French as the fruits of collaboration; furthermore, Laval increasingly behaved as if he were a law unto himself, with his frequent trips to Paris and private meetings with Abetz. Pétain also thought that Laval had failed to use his influence with Abetz to stop anti-Vichy stories appearing in the collaborationist press, especially in Marcel Déat's *L'Œuvre*.

Déat believed that France should collaborate as closely as possible with Germany and rebuild itself broadly on the Nazi model. After Pétain rejected his proposal in the summer of 1940 to found a new French fascist party, Déat returned to Paris and took over the editorship of *L'Œuvre*, which became one of the most violently anti-Vichy papers in the city. Abetz wanted a divided France, subordinated to Germany, but he played along with Déat's vision of a new, Nazi-style France taking its place as Germany's closest ally in a new European order. Déat was reluctant to attack Pétain personally, mainly because of his First World War record, but he used his newspaper to mock those he saw as the fuddy-duddy politicians of the Vichy government and the conservative administrators of the defunct Third Republic with which it had surrounded itself. According to Déat, Vichy was riddled with inertia and indecision inherited from the Third Republic that needed to be radically purged at all levels. As Déat wrote in his diary in November, "It would be crazy to imagine a foreign policy of collaboration with Germany and integration with [Nazi-dominated] Europe with the same bunch of people, with the very same civil servants, with the same stereotypical attitudes running from the top to the bottom of the state hierarchy. The useless leftovers of the old regime must be eliminated."[74]

By December, Pétain had had enough of Déat and decided to retaliate. De la Laurencie, Vichy's representative in Paris, was told to expect a coded message by telephone from Vichy, which would be his cue to instruct the Paris police to arrest Déat. The message duly arrived—"The Marshal's wife crossed the demarcation line at 5 P.M."—but de la Laurencie forgot about his instructions and took it literally. He promptly started ringing the German authorities to protest at this treatment of Pétain's wife and to seek an apology. Luckily for him, before he had gone too far, he realised his mistake. He contacted Langeron, instructing him to arrest the editor of *L'Œuvre*. Langeron agreed to have

Déat arrested at dawn the following day, although he was concerned about how the Germans would react. Pétain had already moved against Laval, and Déat's arrest would take place on the day when Napoleon II's ashes were to be returned.

Despite these reservations, Déat was arrested at dawn on December 14. De la Laurencie visited Abetz to remind the German ambassador that he (de la Laurencie) was Vichy's sole representative in Paris. Abetz was furious and de la Laurencie found himself "in the presence of a man foaming with rage . . . a raving brute," who threatened to take him hostage if Déat was not released immediately.[75] Abetz's friend Jean Luchaire also recalled Abetz beside himself with rage as he railed against the French government and threatened to have de la Laurencie and other leading Vichy personalities arrested and shot.[76] Abetz was just as angry about Laval's sacking and tried to prevent Parisians learning of it by imposing a news blackout on the Paris press, insisting that he expected to see Pétain at Les Invalides for the return of Napoleon II's ashes. Within hours, General Otto von Stülpnagel, the new head of the military in Paris, countermanded the French police warrant for Déat's arrest and he was released. So much for the Vichy government's sovereignty in the Occupied Zone.

Around 9:30 P.M. on December 14, Pétain made a radio broadcast and Jean Guéhenno heard enough of it to realise that "for domestic political reasons" Laval was no longer either a member of Pétain's government or indeed any longer Pétain's designated successor, and that he had been replaced by Pierre-Étienne Flandin.[77] Charles Rist complained that no reason was given for this change at the very heart of the Vichy government. Flandin was even more pro-German than Laval, but Rist was glad, nevertheless, to see the back of Laval, whom he described as "that bastard son of a gypsy and a butcher-woman from the Auvergne . . . that agglomeration of personal, parliamentary, journalistic and financial corruption."[78]

Despite all this high drama behind the scenes, the torch-lit ceremony at Les Invalides went ahead on the night of December 14–15, albeit without Pétain, who declined the invitation to attend. The French government was represented by de la Laurencie, Admiral Darlan, and General Émile Laure. Laure described the scene: "At 1 A.M. the funeral procession of the ashes of the duke of Reichstadt arrived. The heavy coffin was presented to the occupying authorities outside the courtyard

where General von Stülpnagel and Abetz stood in the front row. . . .
Twelve Republican Guards took the precious cargo and passing between
two rows of torches that were crackling and spitting as the snow fell,
carried it up towards the chapel."[79] Abetz gave a speech praising Laval
as the man "who created the atmosphere of collaboration and who is,
for us, its sole guarantor."[80] Everything probably passed off as smoothly
as it could, given the circumstances, although the prevailing atmosphere
was as cold and frosty as the weather.

The next day any Parisians who had heard rumours of political tensions between Vichy and the Germans and who hoped to learn in the
press more about what was going were disappointed; Abetz had got
the news blackout he wanted. "They [the newspapers] arrived a good
two hours late," Jean Guéhenno observed. "Not a word about Laval;
no trace of Pétain's message."[81] Soon, however, more rumours spread. The
medical student Bernard Pierquin heard that Laval had put together a
daring plan to lure Pétain to Paris and then "to hold him in Versailles,
force him to sign a peace treaty with the Krauts, which would have
thrown France into the enemy camp."[82]

Early on Sunday morning, a few hours after the ceremony had ended,
Pierquin emerged from the Saint-Francois-Xavier church where he
had been attending Mass into the half-darkness, the freezing fog, and
the melting snow. Behind the railings of Les Invalides he saw, in the
distance and ghostly in the fog, Republican Guards in full uniform
with their swords drawn. He went into a nearby café, where he found a
newspaper referring to the transfer of the ashes under the headline "A
GESTURE BY THE FÜHRER." Around him people were saying they couldn't
care less.[83]

Langeron confirms this reaction: "The population of Paris attaches
absolutely no importance—and I mean absolutely none!—to this 'magnificent' gesture by the Führer."[84] As Jean Galtier-Boissière ironically
noted, "Great brouhaha about the return of Napoleon II's ashes. . . . But
the cheeky Parisians say they would rather have coal than ashes."[85]
Commenting on the event, the author Alfred Fabre-Luce wrote: "The
significance of the ceremony seemed to have changed. It no longer
looked as if it was to celebrate a gesture of rapprochement but rather to
bury the politics of Montoire."[86]

Once the ceremony was over, Abetz acted to secure Laval's reinstatement. He had been wooing Laval since July and their partnership had

established Abetz's reputation as the German in Paris with the best contacts at Vichy. This helped preserve Abetz's high standing in Berlin, as well as that of Ribbentrop, his boss. It also helped him to maintain an edge over his German rivals in Paris, especially the military propaganda units. He was outraged when Pétain sacked Laval and masterminded what Bernard Pierquin described as "an extremely violent anti-Vichy press campaign over the days that followed. Our Nazified newspapers accused Pétain's new government of being pro-British and pro-Jewish."[87]

On December 16 Abetz, along with a dozen SS men, sped off to Vichy to confront Pétain; Pétain refused to reinstate Laval but, as a concession, agreed to Abetz's demand to replace de la Laurencie with Fernand de Brinon,[88] the man Laval had chosen to act as his representative in Paris whenever he was in Vichy. Pétain also agreed that Laval could leave Vichy and go to Paris. Abetz still wanted to punish Pétain for ordering Déat's arrest, for refusing to attend the ceremony, and for sacking Laval. So he secured German backing from the MBF in Paris to ban any member of the Vichy government from crossing the demarcation line into the Occupied Zone. This move demonstrated once again how it was Germany that held the whip-hand: in theory, the Vichy government had sovereignty in both zones, but its ministers were now confined to the Unoccupied Zone.

☞ DECEMBER 1940 MARKED TWO IMPORTANT deadlines for Jews in Paris. If they worked in the state sector, they had until the end of the month to resign their posts. Jewish shopkeepers had until December 26 to place their businesses in the hands of non-Jewish administrators. A red poster on the premises would indicate this transfer had taken place. Parisians registered no public outcry at the dismissal of Jewish teachers: any reaction was restricted to schools and universities. The experience of Jewish teachers varied. Étienne Weill Raynal, who taught history at the Lycée Voltaire, was insulted and humiliated before he resigned; other teachers were given farewell gifts by their students: books, money, cigarettes, and fountain pens. Marguerite Glotz, a history teacher at the Lycée Molière, used her last class to pay a patriotic homage to France. As one of her pupils later recalled, "It was a paean to our country, to its history, to its values which she concluded with a vibrant 'Vive la France!' that I shall never forget. We never saw her again."[89] At the Lycée Henri-IV, near the Sorbonne, in a rare example of a collective protest, sixty-seven colleagues and almost all of the final-year pupils of Michel Alexandre, the head of philosophy, wrote to Jérôme Carcopino, rector of the Académie de Paris,[90] calling for Alexandre and two other Jewish teachers to remain in their posts. A second petition followed a fortnight later, signed by the head teacher and more students. It was sadly all to no avail. Alexandre and his two colleagues had to go. His one consolation was a gift from his students of a favourite book by the poet Paul Valéry, signed by the author.[91] It seems only one member of staff in all of Paris resigned in protest at the expulsion of Jewish teachers: Gustave Monod, a university inspector. On the other hand, several teachers denounced colleagues who had "forgotten" to declare they were Jewish, and plenty of teachers and school and university staff cold-shouldered their Jewish colleagues before they left.

This forced resignation of Jewish teachers and other public servants coincided with an escalation of anti-Semitic propaganda, which was even more sinister and virulent than before. On December 20 *Au Pilori* ran an end-of-year competition, aimed particularly at women, offering three pairs of silk stockings as the first prize. Entrants had to come up with the best proposal for what should be done with the Jews. Mademoiselle Gisèle X suggested dumping them in the jungle without food and dressed only in loincloths, leaving them exposed to wild animals and leprosy; another entrant thought that the crematorium would be a good destination, "and for all of them, from the oldest to the newborn." *Au Pilori* thought this was a good idea as well but wondered about the smell this would create in the neighbourhood. Yet another entrant thought the Jews could be used for leather goods. "I can see myself wearing shoes and a matching handbag made from the skin of a Lévy."[92] It is unclear whether these were genuine submissions or products of the warped minds of the *Au Pilori* staff. These repulsive ideas were expressed five months before any Jews in France had been rounded up, and a full eighteen months before plans for the "Final Solution of the Jewish Problem" in Europe were agreed at the conference at Wansee in the outskirts of Berlin. However, they served to legitimise the anti-Semitic laws that had been passed and helped to create a receptive climate for further measures. If genuine, they also revealed the deep-rooted anti-Semitism that pervaded some sections of Parisian and French society.

On December 24 small posters in French and German appeared on walls and fences across the city, announcing an execution: "Engineer Jacques Bonsergent of Paris has been condemned to death by a German military tribunal for an act of violence against a member of the German army. He was shot this morning." It was dated December 23 and signed by the MBF, the head of the German Army in France. Few of those reading the posters knew the story behind the announcement.

On Sunday, November 10 Bonsergent had been one of seven people in their twenties returning to Paris from a wedding just outside the city.[93] They were in high spirits as they left the Gare Saint-Lazare railway station and made their way home. It was after curfew and in the blackout it was difficult to see where they were going. The exact details of what happened next are unclear,[94] but it involved a brief scuffle with three German soldiers they had bumped into. Jacques Bonsergent was seized by the soldiers and frogmarched into a nearby café requisitioned by the Germans.[95] He was then taken to the Cherche-Midi prison and locked up.

Bonsergent appeared before the German military tribunal on December 5, but it was not he who had jostled one of the German soldiers; during a prison visit from his aunt, Bonsergent told her it was another member of the group who was wearing a hat and coat similar to his, who had clashed with the German. Bonsergent had refused to blame this friend and was sentenced to death.

Bonsergent had been arrested the day before the November 11 protest at the Arc de Triomphe, but his trial took place a little over three weeks after the event when the Germans were still seething about the demonstration. During the first few months of the Occupation the MBF had been willing to commute the relatively few death sentences that had been passed in the Occupied Zone, mostly for acts of sabotage. But the November 11 demonstration had changed all that. As a result, Bonsergent's appeal for clemency was rejected and he, an innocent man, was executed. It was almost certainly a warning from the Germans to all Parisians of what might happen if something like the November 11 protest reoccurred. It was possibly also another reminder to the Vichy government that the Germans were in charge and were quite willing to demonstrate this publicly by executing French civilians for the most minor of incidents and on the flimsiest of evidence if they chose to do so.

Christmas and the New Year are usually times for celebration, but not in Paris in 1940: the shortages of fuel and food put paid to any festive notions. On December 21 Liliane Jameson noticed that the trees on the avenue Niel were being trimmed and people were scrabbling for the smallest piece of bark, the tiniest twig to burn and keep themselves warm.[96] Jean Guéhenno wrote on that freezing December 25: "It's Christmas. We're being stifled."[97] Jacques Biélinky noted on the same day: "It's the saddest Christmas I have experienced in Paris since I arrived in 1909."[98] On Boxing Day he wrote of an acquaintance, a father of three, who had no coal and had already "broken up his chairs to make firewood . . . today he demolished an old chair: the old wood was very dry and burned well."[99] On December 31 Liliane Jameson described her New Year's Eve meal, "Soup, cabbage and sausages . . . a bit of foie gras (Oh! Happy days are here again!), and some cakes—but it's best not to ask how they were made."[100] Micheline Bood noted in her diary in the way that only a self-obsessed teenager can: "How awful 1940 has been. For everyone, for France, and for me."[101]

7

Protests, Pillaging, "V" for Victory, the First Roundup of Jews

GENERAL DE GAULLE and his followers in London had been stunned by the success of the November 11 demonstration, which they had supported but had neither planned nor organised. Now they had an idea for another mass protest against the German occupation.

In the dying days of December 1940, Free French broadcasts from London had repeatedly called for people in both zones to stay indoors for an hour between 3 P.M. and 4 P.M. on January 1, 1941. The hope was that the Germans in the Occupied Zone, having the empty streets to themselves, would realise just what isolated pariahs they were.

In the run-up to New Year's Day a young female teacher was arrested on the pont Saint-Michel in Paris as she put up stickers calling on Parisians to stay indoors. On the day itself an inhabitant of the 16th arrondissement, who leaned out of his window and shouted at passersby to go home, was taken into custody.[1] It is hard to say whether this protest could also be described as a success. Few people were out of doors between 3 and 4 on that freezing cold day, but the Paris police attributed this to the weather, a view endorsed by the pro-German Cardinal Baudrillart: "Wouldn't the snow have been enough to keep people indoors?" he asked.[2] It is impossible to say how many Parisians stayed away in protest but some certainly did. Berthe Auroy and her sister, for example, battled through the snow to see a play in Montparnasse on the other side of the city, determined to arrive at the theatre "before

3 P.M., when the English radio had asked us to demonstrate against the Germans by being off the streets."[3] Micheline Bood took great pleasure in writing "Vive de Gaulle" in the snow, while walking her dog earlier in the day; later, she remained indoors with her family between 3 P.M. and 4 P.M., as London requested.[4]

The severe weather conditions continued, making it even harder to find food. "Almost 40 centimetres of snow in Fontenay," wrote Paul Léautaud on January 2. "Nothing to eat. Not even bread. . . . All day long and into this evening the wind howled, getting everywhere in the house; spent my time shivering with cold despite my clothes, and my hands frozen despite keeping on the move."[5] The following day Jean Guéhenno wrote, "Life in Paris is getting very difficult. We have the tickets, but you can't get anything with them anymore. The shops are empty. At home for the last fortnight we've been living entirely off what friends and our cousins in Brittany have sent us."[6]

On January 5 the snow was deep enough to hold a skiing competition on the edge of the city at the Porte de Saint-Cloud. Benoîte Groult and a friend went skiing in the woods near Chaville in the southwestern suburbs, which felt almost like a mountain village.[7] But such fun moments were rare. Paul Léautaud was by now holed up in his bedroom with numerous pets: his monkey was on the radiator; one dog was on her couch with two or three cats sprawled on top of her; another dog was at the foot of his master's bed. Three or four cats were in the bed with Léautaud, not to mention another dog in his workroom next door.[8]

On more than sixty nights during the winter of 1940–1941, the temperature in Paris dropped below freezing, sometimes reaching temperatures of minus 17°C. The cold made people feel hungrier than ever, as they burned up energy trying to keep warm. Pupils at one *lycée* were given biscuits fortified with vitamins by uniformed employees from the city council, but this did not stop some of them fainting from hunger and cold; the boarders were so cold that they slept on the bed-base under their mattresses.[9] At the beginning of January at the Sorbonne all heating in the classrooms was cut off, although, much to the annoyance of the students, not in the administrative offices. In the freezing cold classrooms, lecturers could keep warm by walking up and down as they talked, unlike the students who had to stay in their places, freezing cold despite being wrapped up in hat and coats.[10]

Despite receiving a parcel of food from the Auvergne just before Christmas, Berthe Auroy still needed to go shopping. At the beginning of January, she observed, no new deliveries had been made to replenish the stocks in the shops. The lines of people queuing in the snow outside the shops looked even more pitiful. Parisians, many of them suffering with chilblains, queued for hours in temperatures of minus 10°C "to obtain . . . well! Not much and sometimes nothing at all if the stocks had run out."[11]

The arctic-like weather conditions affected how people dressed. Over time, Berthe Auroy had perfected her queuing outfit: "Two or three layers of woollen garments, a small scarf pointing out from under my cape. My head wrapped up in a woollen hood. Thick knitted stockings, so thick in fact that they stay up on their own and look like a pair of boots that someone working in the sewers would wear. Fancy fur-lined shoes that I call 'Mademoiselle Thérèse's bootees,' after a character painted on an old plate we used to have. Best of all is my big grey shawl with pink stripes that I wrap around myself, but which still lets me stuff my hands into a threadbare old muff."[12] Micheline Bood, writing during a week when meat was impossible to find, noted in her diary that she liked to wear her father's military-style hobnailed boots when she went out, even though they were "as heavy as her rollerskates." In fact, they were both practical and, she claimed, fashionable: "All the women in Paris are wearing shoes like these. . . . They keep you really warm."[13] The Parisians needed to keep themselves warm for longer that year than most years. February 1941 began with what Berthe Auroy called "a new cold offensive" complete with thick snow and ice. "The misery has started all over again."[14] Potatoes were "a rare luxury," and she reported apartments being used to house rabbits and poultry. "One day I was giving a lesson in a smart apartment on the rue Blanche when suddenly a resounding "cock-a-doodle-do" sounded from the room next door. A cockerel and a hen had been caged under the sink for over a month and the poor old hen was still able to lay an egg in this apology for a hen house. Lots of top-floor maids' rooms were home to rabbits and poultry, which were killed on the days when it was impossible to find any meat to buy."[15]

On January 10 Liliane Jameson noted that everything was in short supply; it was almost impossible to find butter, cheese, meat, and not even worth looking for fish or any fruit and vegetables other than apples, lemons, and swede. "A kilo of potatoes can only be found extremely rarely, with luck and if you have tickets. . . . Every week there's a new restriction. A fortnight ago we were saying 'We really can't live on less than this.' We're saying the same thing again now."[16]

Food was so scarce that people started queuing outside shops as early as they could; some concierges rented out their cellars to people who wanted to be outside the shops the moment the curfew ended at 5 A.M.[17] Unsurprisingly, tempers flared and there were often accusations of queue-jumping, especially when there were several queues for different items. "'Excuse me, *Madame*, is this the queue for potatoes?' 'No, *Madame*, can't you see this is the queue for fish? And here, next to it, is the queue for onions.'" Berthe Auroy was mistaken for a queue-jumper and at once became the object of howls of protest from those around her. "'Hey! You there! The little woman in the grey coat. No pushing in. Get to the back!'"[18] Some people, mainly women, charged for queuing for others with their children often providing a home-delivery service. Anyone suspected of shopping for someone else frequently incurred the wrath of fellow shoppers, as Léautaud discovered when he was wrongly accused of doing this.[19]

Not all Parisians were struggling to find food and keep warm. While the many shivered and went hungry, a few lived as well as ever. When Galtier-Boissière was invited to a fashionable restaurant he found the "nouveaux riches" enjoying themselves. "The finest of wines are flowing. The rich are triumphant in the New Order. With money, lots of money, you can always eat until you're fit to burst, while housewives queue for hours in the snow to get a slice of swede."[20] The collaborationist newspaper *La Gerbe* wrote of customers in the fashionable bistro Le Nid tucking into oysters in tomato and garlic sauce with brown bread and salted butter, and of sumptuous evenings at the Lido cabaret with diners "finishing up their third evening meal and their tenth bottle of champagne."[21]

Access to food gave people power, as Benoîte Groult discovered. When a rather ugly fellow student at the Sorbonne gave her some roast veal (his father worked in the Les Halles market) she felt obliged to accept his invitation to the cinema. "He has rough, hard hands and he didn't even wait until the film credits were over before he was clamping one of them on my knee. I was asking myself how far he thought he had the right to go for a piece of roast veal. I didn't know what the going rate was." She managed to keep him at bay and he stormed off, furious.[22]

In early 1941 hunger and cold were major preoccupations for Parisians, but there were other difficulties too. In January the Vichy government passed a law allowing individuals to obtain one pair of shoes using special coupons *(bons d'achat)*, which were allocated to suitable applicants by the local *mairie*. Liliane Jameson wrote of having to wait for ages to discover if she qualified for a pair of what were called "national shoes."[23] Benoîte Groult was asked to give a reason for wanting a new pair of shoes: "As if walking wasn't reason enough."[24] Like others, she turned to the black market: "Made to measure on the rue Orfila by a shoemaker who, like a man of the world, meets all the Paris big shots in his premises above the shop. You have to give the password before you go in, as you do when you go to some low dive."[25] In December the sale of leather-soled shoes was banned and shoes with wooden soles, sometimes referred to as "armistice shoes," started to take their place. "Every woman will start growing taller as she puts on her wooden-soled shoes—the only ones you can buy without tickets—since the treads are 2 to 3 centimetres thick," trilled the women's magazine *Marie-Claire* in March 1941.[26] The shoes, which the manufacturers tried hard to make as stylish as possible, were soon to be seen everywhere, and the following year Maurice Chevalier recorded a hit song called "The Symphony of the Wooden Soles." These hard-wearing shoes were also heavy and cumbersome, as Micheline Bood later realised when, in possession of a forged German travel pass, she was stopped by the German police: "I would have run away but with my wooden-soled shoes it wouldn't have been easy and they would have quickly caught up with me."[27]

Meanwhile, business in the unofficial "purchasing offices" was booming. Between January and March 1941 Hermann "Otto" Brandl's Bureau was spending 15 million francs a day on goods and materials that were sold at a hefty profit; by the autumn the bureau was spending 50 million francs a day.[28] Brandl's operation became so successful that by the spring of 1941 "Otto" had taken over several acres of property in the northern suburb of Saint-Ouen. Soon the area was crammed with shops buying and selling goods, as well as warehouses and quaysides piled high with merchandise, plus a sprawling packing and dispatching department with exclusive use of rail and canal links. Some 400 packers, dockers, drivers, and gangers were working for Brandl's organisation. Finding a job in this shady enterprise was easy since there were few formalities, making it very difficult for French or German officials to find out who was working there and what exactly they were doing. Employees did not even have to provide proof of identity; they were expected to do what they were told, work hard, put in long hours, and ask no questions, but they were well paid—between 5,000 and 12,000 francs a month, compared with a factory worker's salary of around 1,500 francs.

Brandl did not just wait for potential sellers to approach him: he had his own local "intermediaries" or buyers, one of the most celebrated of whom was Joseph Joinovici, known as "Monsieur Joseph." Joinovici had left his native Bessarabia and arrived in Paris in June 1925. Illiterate and penniless, he had set up as a rag and bone man and, after fifteen years of astute trading, was a self-made millionaire. Like other prewar dealers, he always had his ear to the ground; he had a good idea of who had what goods stashed away and who could be "persuaded" to sell. It was thanks to shadowy figures like Joinovici that Brandl and the heads of other German "purchasing offices" could run their operations on a gigantic scale.[29]

Another important trader in this murky world was the Russian Michel Szkolnikoff. Before the war he sold textiles to some top Paris stores, including Galeries Lafayette and Au Bon Marché. Now he was doing a roaring trade selling goods to the purchasing offices, especially the one run by the German navy, the first *bureau d'achat* to be established. In January 1941 it paid Szkolnikoff 10 million francs, followed by 20 million in February and another 60 million in March.[30] In the spring of 1941, 800,000 metres of material, of which no trace appeared in Szkolnikoff's books, were found on his premises. During the Occupation he was reckoned to be the biggest black-market dealer in textiles, owning more than fifty buildings in the select area around the Champs-Élysées, as well as having shares in the up-market Hôtel Regina.[31] The Germans' willingness to do business with Joinovici and Szkolnikoff, both of whom were Jewish, shows that, for some members of the occupying forces, greed and pragmatism outweighed any ideological considerations.

During May–June 1940 many traders and industrialists had hidden their goods to prevent them falling into the hands of the invaders. In the autumn of 1940 others followed suit, this time in response to the French government's attempt to halt price inflation: all privately held merchandise had to be declared. Hanging on to stock was now a risky option: if goods were discovered the owner could end up in prison and have everything confiscated. Many were glad to accept an offer for their merchandise, and it helped that some of Brandl's intermediaries were French, or at least not German, since this eased the conscience of the more patriotic seller. After the French government's introduction of the new statute pertaining to Jews in October, Brandl's intermediaries turned their attention specifically to Jews they suspected of holding stock. It was in their best interest to sell, Brandl's men said, since even a low price for their goods was better than seizure without compensation, especially if this was accompanied by a prison sentence.

Brandl had acquired his own mob of vicious ex-convicts. They appropriated suitable buildings in Paris and the suburbs for him, and they also provided "security men" to protect both these premises and the vast sums of money that Brandl was moving around the city. After the war a police superintendent would qualify the activities of the "purchasing offices" as "the most extensive network of corruption, trafficking, treason, blackmail, and denunciation that our country has ever known."[32]

☞ THE GERMAN SCRAMBLE to seize France's art treasures continued apace and in early 1941 moved into a new phase following the intervention of Hitler's deputy Hermann Göring. In September Abetz had grudgingly accepted Hitler's ruling that the Einsatzstab Reichsleiter Rosenberg (ERR), headed in Paris by Kurt von Behr, would be responsible for seizing art, but at least Abetz was able to keep some of his booty. On November 1, in the Jeu de Paume Museum, white-coated art experts, members of the ERR and the Luftwaffe, emptied hundreds of wooden crates stuffed with art treasures, putting the contents on display, ready for inspection. Three days later Reichsmarschall Göring arrived at the museum with members of his senior staff. He strode around the museum, a cigar in one hand and a glass of champagne in the other, scarcely able to believe his eyes as he examined the priceless treasures laid out before him. Göring offered his personal support to the ERR, on condition that he had first pick from the treasure trove—after the Führer, of course. Under a directive dated November 5, Göring specified that the art treasures "saved" by the ERR, as well as those under army protection, should be distributed as follows: Hitler had first pick, then Göring, then the ERR, then German museums; the remainder, he said, would be sold at auction open to German and French art dealers and French museums.[33]

In February Göring was back in the Jeu de Paume to inspect a new haul of art treasures. Wolff-Metternich, the MBF's representative, who was still trying to keep works of art out of the clutches of the ERR and away from Hitler, talked to Göring about protecting the works of art. Göring, he recalled, told him "to get lost in terms that were far from polite and then sent me on my way."[34] Shortly afterwards, Göring ordered that a consignment of art treasures stolen by the ERR be sent to Hitler; it was made up of more than thirty paintings from the Rothschild collections, including Vermeer's *The Astronomer*, portraits by Hals and Rembrandt, and Boucher's famous *Madame de Pompadour*.[35]

The German military—keen as always to be seen as behaving honourably, but also covering its back—produced documents stating that the army would not be held responsible for Göring's actions. In their view, the behaviour of this morphine-addicted kleptomaniac ran counter to Hitler's September directive authorising art works of value to be transported to Germany and held there in safekeeping. Nor would the military be held responsible for the actions of the ERR. It made clear it considered itself exempt from any responsibility for contraventions of the Hague Convention by Göring or the ERR.[36]

The army's desire to absolve itself of any responsibility played to Göring's advantage. With the risk of interference from the military removed, he ordered art raids all over the country. So many truckloads of Jewish-owned art treasures arrived at the Jeu de Paume that the whole of the ground floor was full to overflowing. "So frenzied was this scavenging that several non-Jewish collections belonging to people with suspicious names had to be returned with sheepish letters of apology."[37] In all, Göring made more than twenty visits to the Jeu de Paume and managed to get his hands on almost as many works of art as Hitler.[38]

The ERR, now with Göring's support, seized, stored, and dispatched thousands of works of art. Meanwhile Rose Valland, who was still working in the Jeu de Paume museum, described 1941 as "a year of crucial importance for the Einsatzstab Rosenberg marking the peak of its activity and power."[39] Thanks to Göring's protection, the ERR in Paris was free from "interference" by the German military; nothing during this second year of Occupation, it seemed, could interrupt or even slow down its activities. More and more trucks continued to arrive at the Jeu de Paume, which was scarcely big enough to hold all the paintings, pieces of furniture, sculptures, clocks, and ornaments taken from apartments and furniture warehouses. Initially the Rothschild family was targeted, yielding over 5,000 artefacts. Whatever the Nazis' objection to "degenerate" modern art, they knew only too well the high sums of money people would pay for these works, leading them to seize collections by impressionists such as Monet and Sisley as well as more than 200 modern paintings from the Paul Rosenberg Gallery. But there were times when ideology trumped private gain as in July 1943 when between 500 and 600 works by painters who were classified as dangerous, including Pablo Picasso, Max Ernst, Fernand Léger, and Paul Klee, were burned in the garden of the Jeu de Paume.[40]

Most members of the ERR at the Jeu de Paume ignored Rose Valland or dismissed her as a foolish woman, although legitimate German art experts were more cordial. But nobody realised that she was secretly recording the destinations of the artworks that were being dispatched from the museum. To do so was extremely dangerous in itself but Rose had no doubt about what the Germans had planned for her once all the works of art had been disposed of—even if they had not discovered what she was up to. "Increasingly, they considered me to be an awkward witness," she wrote later. "Von Behr had decided to do away with me before the war ended. I was to be taken off to Germany and killed once we were over the border."[41] In the meantime she fought hard to remain in her post. No other French citizen was allowed into the Jeu de Paume, which was guarded by armed sentries. Little did the Germans realise that there was already a spy in the Nazi camp.

Beginning in the autumn 1940 more and more Parisians were tuning into the BBC. The German authorities in Paris were divided about how to respond: the MBF banned listening to foreign broadcasts—unless they came from Germany or other occupied countries—and threatened dire punishment for anyone caught listening to broadcasts from London. Abetz cautioned against a severe crackdown, arguing it would be counterproductive and that in any case a ban was unenforceable. The Vichy government legislated against listening to the BBC or to any radio station broadcasting "anti-national propaganda" in public places; anyone caught could spend up to six months in jail and ran the risk of having their radio impounded.[42] But these attempts to stop people listening to the BBC were in vain. Although the Germans did manage a partial jamming of the Free French broadcasts from London, towards the end of 1940, the MBF had to admit that "after 6:30 P.M. English radio rules the airwaves."[43] In January 1941, having more or less given up trying to stop Parisians listening to the BBC, the German authorities tried to neutralise the impact of the broadcasts by making it illegal to pass on information gleaned from any radio station not subject to German control. Notices posted across the city by the French police on behalf of the occupiers read: "Beware of tall stories. Surveillance carried out in public places over the past few days has led to the arrest of individuals spreading information which is completely false and likely to generate public anxiety. The prefect of police warns the public that anybody indulging in such behaviour will be taken to court and severely punished."[44] About two weeks later, Paul Léautaud was having coffee near the Odéon Métro station with a friend, who was loudly voicing his anti-German views. "A young man who was sitting near us came over and whispered that we should be careful, adding that he had just spent 24 days in the Santé prison for speaking too freely in a place just like the one they were in."[45] Expressing anti-German opinions in queues could be dangerous as well. Louise L., a cleaning lady, was arrested in a queue in January for complaining that the Germans took 65 percent of everything and were pushing the Parisians into starvation, while the French government did nothing.[46]

☞ THROUGH THE WINTER, the Musée de l'Homme Resistance group had been expanding as Boris Vildé and his fellow resisters made contact with other individuals and nascent networks; but in January things started to go wrong. A police raid in Paris early in the new year yielded the names of the distributors of the group's newspaper *Résistance*. Léon-Maurice Nordmann, a thirty-two-year-old socialist lawyer, was on the list; he was arrested several weeks later on a train half an hour out of Paris as Albert Gaveau, another Musée de l'Homme member, was trying to help him reach Britanny and cross the English Channel by boat to Britain.[47] On February 5 Agnès Humbert wrote: "It looks as if we are going to have to be extremely careful: it seems that specialist police have arrived from Berlin. Pass it on!"[48] Her fears were soon confirmed as other arrests followed. Yvonne Oddon and Anatole Lewitsky convinced

Vildé that it was too dangerous for him to stay in Paris: he left for the Unoccupied Zone. Two weeks after his departure, Oddon and Lewitsky were arrested.

In March, Humbert was in her flat typing out the forthcoming issue of *Résistance* when the doorbell rang. She opened the door and was astonished to see Vildé standing there. It was bad news: René Sénéchal (the Kid) had failed to turn up at a rendezvous in the Unoccupied Zone and Vildé assumed he had been arrested.[49] Albert Gaveau had urged Vildé to come back to Paris and take stock of the situation. On March 26, shortly after his return, Vildé had lunch with Gaveau and Pierre Walter, another member of the network. He then left them for a meeting at a café on the place Pigalle with yet another member of the group who was charged with obtaining some false papers for him. He never made it: he was picked up by plainclothes German security police. Vildé was interrogated and taken to the Santé prison before being transferred to Fresnes jail.

Three weeks later Agnès Humbert was visiting her mother in hospital[50] when she was accosted by two German policemen. They insisted that she take them to her flat. There they discovered a part-written front page of *Résistance* with the exhortation: "Copy this and pass it on." A quarter of an hour later she was in custody. Shortly afterwards, Pierre Walter and his girlfriend Jacqueline Bordelet were arrested. The network had effectively been dismantled, with many of its members now behind bars awaiting trial.

Albert Gaveau was not arrested. Back in October 1940 he had been recruited as a double agent by the German secret police (Sipo-SD) and had been steadily passing on information ever since. He did it for the money rather than out of any ideological zeal. His German paymasters were so pleased with his "performance" that Gaveau's monthly pay (excluding expenses) rose rapidly from 2,500 francs to 10,000 francs— over six times what a Paris manual worker might expect to earn.[51]

By the time Gaveau's betrayals had effectively destroyed the Musée de l'Homme group, other Resistance groups based in Paris had begun to appear or were about to do so. The early Resistance groupings in Paris were very small and, like the Musée de l'Homme group, claimed publicly to be larger to encourage members to stay, attract new recruits, and impress the enemy. They were mainly concerned with producing anti-Nazi, pro-Resistance news sheets and, in some cases, collecting information that would be useful to the Allies.

In September 1940, Raymond Burgard, a French teacher at the Lycée Buffon, had linked up with four members of Jeune République, a progressive Christian organisation of which he was an active member. They started putting anti-German stickers in the Métro and on walls and public benches. Their slogan was "Just one enemy: the invader." In January 1941, they began producing a newspaper called *Valmy*, named after a battle in September 1792 when the French army thwarted a Prussian attempt to march on Paris; Valmy was also the name of their group.[52] In April 1942, Burgard was arrested (see Chapter 10). The group did not survive his arrest but its members joined other Resistance organisations.

In October 1940, Raymond Deiss, a patriotic music publisher, produced the first issue of his "information sheet," entitled *Pantagruel*, in his bookshop in the rue Rouget-de-Lisle, just off the rue de Rivoli. The news-sheet declared its opposition to the armistice and highlighted the 400 million francs a day Vichy was paying for "Occupation costs." It warned its readers not to forget Germany's war aims, however friendly German soldiers in the city might appear, denounced anti-Semitism, and asserted that France's best hope lay with a British victory. Sixteen issues of *Pantagruel* would appear before Deiss was arrested a year later and deported to Germany; he was decapitated in Cologne in August 1943.[53]

In December 1940 seven typed copies of the first issue of *Libération* were produced at Christian Pineau's flat in the rue de Verneuil. Pineau had been an active trade unionist before the war, and the members of the small Libération-Nord Resistance group that was created around the newspaper were mostly Pineau's trade union contacts. They included Jean Texcier, author of *Conseils à l'Occupant*. One copy of the first issue of *Libération* was hidden in Pineau's cellar: the other six were sent anonymously to friends, who were asked to produce multiple copies and pass them on. Showing great courage, commitment, and energy, the group succeeded in producing a copy of the newspaper every week until the end of the Occupation. The newspaper helped the movement to grow in size and significance, and, by the end of 1941, Pineau had established contacts with other Resistance groups on both sides of the demarcation line. In March 1942 he flew to London for a series of meetings with de Gaulle.

In March 1941 Jean-Paul Sartre made his way back to Paris after his release from a POW camp in Germany. Before the war he had been a political observer but not a participant, so his close associates, including de Beauvoir, were astounded to hear him say on his return that he was determined to found a Resistance group. Sartre and his close friends joined forces with the philosopher Maurice Merleau-Ponty and some of his students, who had founded a tiny Resistance grouping called Sous la Botte (Under the Jackboot), to form a Resistance group called Socialisme et Liberté (Socialism and Freedom). Socialism and Freedom's members were almost all students and intellectuals. They included a mix of socialists, anarchists, orthodox Marxists, and anti-Stalinists. This inexperienced group counted some fifty members in Paris and another twenty in Grenoble, organised in cells of five members each.[54] The group prepared and distributed leaflets, some of which were written in German by Dominique Desanti, one of the group's members. The German leaflets, specifically aimed at members of the occupying forces, were usually left in first-class Métro carriages in which German soldiers could travel free of charge. The leaflets were framed in humanistic terms and stressed that the resisters were not their enemies. The group also devoted considerable time to envisaging what a post-liberation France would look like with Sartre drawing up a constitution for the future French state. In the summer of 1941 Sartre and de Beauvoir travelled into the Unoccupied Zone hoping, in vain as it turned out, to secure support for their group from novelists André Malraux and André Gide, and from Daniel Mayer, who had replaced Léon Blum as leader of the French Socialist Party. According to de Beauvoir, Socialism and Freedom was disbanded in the autumn, soon after Sartre and de Beauvoir returned to Paris. They had concluded that the group was ineffectual and were also shaken by the deportation of one of its members.[55] After the war Dominique Desanti insisted the group continued as late as the autumn of 1942.[56]

Another early Paris Resistance group that had its roots in the student and intellectual milieu was Défense de la France (In Defence of France), of which Philippe Viannay, a Sorbonne student, was the prime mover. Thanks to funding provided by an industrialist friend of Viannay's, the group was able to produce its own newspaper, which first appeared in August 1941. A printer, Jacques Grou-Radenez, whom Viannay met through a friend agreed to teach typesetting skills to two members of the group. Thanks to another of Viannay's contacts who provided ink and other material, *Défense de la France* became one of the most widely read and professionally produced clandestine Resistance newspapers in the Occupied Zone. In 1942 General de Gaulle's niece joined the group, although it was not until January 1, 1943, in the twenty-fifth issue of the paper, that the general's name first appeared.[57] The group was infiltrated and, in raids during July 1943, most of its members were arrested and deported (see Chapter 12).

☞ AFTER HIS DASH TO VICHY in December when he failed to persuade Pétain to reinstate Laval, Otto Abetz returned to Paris, pleased to have secured the sacking of de la Laurencie, whom he personally loathed, and the appointment of Fernand de Brinon, Laval's right-hand man, in his place. Holding Pétain and his government in even greater contempt than before, Abetz was running a new anti-Vichy campaign through the collaborationist Paris press on the theme "Vichy is betraying France's national interests."[58] He also tried to destabilise Laval's replacement Pierre-Étienne Flandin, who had formed a governing triumvirate with Admiral Darlan and General Huntziger. Abetz had only contempt for Flandin;[59] instead, he supported Darlan, whom he considered the only military man at Vichy with enough political breadth and sufficient leadership qualities to be a possible replacement for Laval.[60] Thanks to Abetz, it was Darlan, not Flandin, who met Hitler near Beauvais on Christmas Day when the Führer visited the troops.

On February 4, 1941, Laval turned down Pétain's offer of a minor post in government. Abetz was keen to keep Laval in Paris and use him to threaten Pétain by proffering him as the possible head of an alternative French government if it became necessary to force Pétain's hand. On February 9 Abetz's anti-Flandin campaign finally paid off. Flandin, who had been systematically shunned by the MBF, Abetz, and de Brinon since his appointment, resigned and was replaced by Darlan, who now became prime minister (*vice-président du Conseil*), as well as foreign minister, minister of the navy, minister of war, and minister of the interior; he was also appointed Pétain's successor.

Marcel Déat's newspaper *L'Œuvre* had been at the forefront of the Paris collaborationists' anti-Vichy offensive; now Abetz planned to enlist the support of its editor himself. Déat was still seething with rage at Pétain because he had refused to let Déat build a Nazi-style party to energise Pétain's National Revolution, and especially for ordering his arrest in Paris in December. In February Abetz gave his full backing to the Rassemblement national populaire (RNP), a new, Paris-based collaborationist party that Déat founded at the beginning of the month.[61] Abetz's ability to ignore the army's ban on political organisations in the Occupied Zone showed that he retained his power and influence, despite the debacle over the transfer of Napoleon II's ashes and the sacking of Laval.

The creation of the RNP in Paris on February 1 was announced to a fanfare of publicity on Radio-Paris, in Déat's newspaper *L'Œuvre*, and on posters that showed what the RNP thought of the Vichy government: "Vichy wants to reinstate some outdated past and make us look ridiculous with its parody of a revolution. Vichy is plotting with Jews and Freemasons."[62] Déat hoped the RNP would help him to further his ambition to found a Nazi-style regime in France by championing Laval against Pétain. Georges Albertini (writing as Claude Varennes), one of Déat's close associates, explicitly linked the creation of the RNP to the sacking of Laval on December 13: "13 December 1940 marked the starting point of the RNP. . . . The aim was to launch a movement to promote the politics of Montoire and Pierre Laval's return to power."[63] Abetz was perfectly happy to use Déat and the RNP to secure the return of Laval, but he had no intention of allowing Déat to build an ersatz Nazi regime.

The RNP was based at 128, rue du Faubourg Saint-Honoré, and its membership was drawn from the ranks of First World War veterans, syndicalists, and former Left deputies; it also included members of the thuggish Mouvement social révolutionnaire (MSR), led by Eugène Deloncle, who had founded the prewar right-wing terrorist group La Cagoule. The presence of Deloncle and his men prompted the early departure of other RNP members and generated ongoing tensions between the intellectual Déat and the bruiser Deloncle. As the British historian Julian Jackson puts it, "While Déat aspired to build a mass party, Deloncle was more interested in an elite force of shock troops; Déat's supporters wore suits, Deloncle's uniforms."[64]

While the Paris pro-Nazi collaborationists were plotting and squabbling, the Free French in London launched another initiative against the German occupying forces. On March 22 the "V" (for Victory) campaign called on people in occupied France to make Vs wherever and however they could. Very soon the letter started appearing all over Paris in what Berthe Auroy called "an orgy of Vs."[65] Sometimes Vs were chalked or painted on walls and pavements or the letter V in a German poster would be circled in ink, chalk, or paint; since the German for "forbidden" is *Verboten*, posters featuring the word were in abundance. Vs were scratched into the paintwork of German vehicles and cut out of paper and left scattered around while the BBC was soon opening its broadcasts to France with the first four notes of Beethoven's Fifth Symphony, which spelled out V in Morse code.

A young Parisian woman got word to the BBC that she had seen a V on a vehicle belonging to the German press service and another painted on the wall of the Hôtel Lutetia, home of the Abwehr and German military police.[66] Jean Guéhenno wrote on March 24 that a child had scrawled an enormous V on the door of his house,[67] and in the Métro Liliane Jameson spotted tickets on the ground which had been torn into "wonderful little 'home-made' Vs."[68]

Micheline Bood's history teacher drew a huge V on the blackboard and talked to the class about George I, describing him as "a perfect German—stupid and a boozer." Returning from school, Micheline and her friend Yvette drew Vs all the way home. "In the rue d'Astorg I was making a V on a German car. I heard the sound of boots behind me and made off in a hurry, as Yvette put it. The Boch [*sic*] drew nearer, saw the V on the car, then, turning to Yvette, gave her a broad smile. My God! We had made hundreds and hundreds of Vs. I would have never thought it was so easy in broad daylight."[69]

The German authorities were nowhere near as relaxed about the Vs as the soldier who smiled at Yvette. On April 1, in an attempt to stamp them out, the Paris press announced a measure to reduce the number of slogans and stickers in Paris, which were deemed to be an eyesore and a threat to public order. Henceforth, the owners or concierges of buildings on which they appeared would be responsible for removing them; failure to do so would result in prosecution. Four days later, Parisians were informed that 6,200 people—property owners, concierges, and shopkeepers for the most part—had been fined for not removing slogans.[70] Most but by no means all of those drawing Vs were youngsters like Micheline Bood. Berthe Auroy wrote that for several days her concierge Mme R. stood guard outside the building where Berthe lived when the children came out of school.[71]

It was clear that the mood in Paris was changing. The collaborationists like Déat and Deloncle were consolidating their forces in the city;

but at the same time, de Gaulle's Free French could inspire a successful campaign on the theme of "victory," and anti-German protests were becoming more common and more daring. The French government's inability to tackle the problem of shortages or to secure the return of French POWS dented its credibility. However, the public almost always continued to blame Vichy government ministers rather than Pétain himself. Despite all the difficulties faced by Parisians, Pétain remained popular and not just with "old generals and bigots," as Bernard Pierquin put it. He wrote in his diary that many Parisians, excluding collaborationists and Communists, thought Pétain was doing his best to protect them against the Germans and keep the Nazi influence at bay as he tried to revive France's fortunes. Because many still thought that behind his façade of hostility to the Free French, Pétain was secretly colluding with de Gaulle, whose role was to keep France in the fight and defend its honour, Pierquin believed he and his friends could be "in a way, both Gaullists and Pétainists."[72] The quite mistaken belief that de Gaulle and Pétain were working together against the Germans appeared to Pierquin and his friends to be confirmed by "the daily attacks in the Nazified Paris press on Vichy's Anglophile and Gaullist manoeuvring."[73] However, Pierquin freely admitted in his diary that a good number of Parisians "only listen to the English radio and think that 'Monsieur Pétain' is nothing but a marshal who has sold us down the river."[74]

☞ WHILE PIERQUIN AND HIS FRIENDS tried to work out what they thought about de Gaulle and Pétain, Micheline Bood's personal attitude towards individual Germans in the city was being put to the test. In February Micheline and her friend Yvette visited the Neptuna swimming pool and were shocked at the sight of young French women cavorting in the water with German soldiers. Later that day, Micheline's father taught her some useful German phrases (of varying degrees of politeness) should a German try to chat her up. But on a subsequent visit to the pool in April, Micheline struck up a conversation in English with a young German soldier. His name was Walter and he insisted on leaving the pool with her and catching the same Métro. They met again a few days later on her fifteenth birthday. Walter asked her to go out with him. Micheline explained it was not possible, because French people would not approve and also because her brother was in England in the Royal Air Force.[75]

Meeting Walter had painful repercussions for Micheline. While she kept him at a distance, her friends Monique and Yvette, her sister (Nicole), and her mother all accused her of being in love with him. She regretted having spoken to them about Walter; her mother said it was a pity Micheline had spoken to Walter in the first place. Micheline found it hard to reconcile the polite young man with the cruel and treacherous barbarians she had been told about for so long. She had been taught to detest Germans and she loved stories from the 1914–1918 war in which Germans died in their thousands. "I hated Germans without even knowing who they were, because of their crimes."[76] Micheline tried talking to a priest about her mixed-up feelings for Walter, but the priest, perhaps assuming more had gone on than was the case, discussed the matter in such frank terms that she blushed with shame.

By early June Micheline had found some clarity: "I have always hated 'the Boch' [*sic*] . . . but can you hate somebody you do not know? Or that you only know through stories which date back to so many years ago?" She added: "I hate and will always hate 'the Boch,' who has been our enemy for centuries, but there is a huge difference between a mass of people and an individual who is part of the mass. The Germans, taken individually, are generally well behaved and correct."[77]

However, Micheline's continued support for Britain also created problems: Monique and another friend were adamant that the British were terrible and wanted to kill more French people.[78] This idea was apparently prompted by their parents who had their own reasons, unspecified by Micheline, for wanting the war to end and the British to be defeated.

Although no new overtly anti-Semitic measures were introduced during the winter, the German authorities had not been idle. Theodor Dannecker, a protégé of Adolf Eichmann, had been in Paris since September. As head of the Department of Jewish Affairs he was charged with implementing his master's anti-Semitic policies in France. Dannecker was nominally answerable to SS Captain Helmut Knochen, the head of the cluster of Himmler's secret police agents operating in Paris, but Dannecker actually received his orders directly from Eichmann himself. Dannecker, described by a French anti-Semite as "a fanatical Nazi who went into a trance every time the word 'Jew' was mentioned,"[79] had largely been held in check by the military. However, early in 1941 he started to flex his muscles and began plotting to establish a French organisation to coordinate the French government's anti-Semitic measures in both zones. He was also working to establish an anti-Semitic propaganda unit in Paris. Eichmann's man was ensuring that anti-Semitism was pushed up the agenda.

Along with Otto Abetz and Carlo Zeitschel, Abetz's representative for Jewish affairs, Dannecker began applying pressure on Vichy to create its own Central Jewish Organisation. This German initiative strengthened the links in Paris between the embassy, the secret police, and Vichy, while marginalising the military. In March Abetz persuaded Darlan, who had been appointed Pétain's prime minister a month earlier, to back the proposed organisation. At the end of March the Vichy government duly announced the creation of its Commissariat général aux questions juives [CGQJ] (Commissariat-General for Jewish Affairs). The CGQJ would coordinate the French government's policies concerning Jews in both zones[80] and would, Dannecker envisaged, play a leading role in the "final solution," which at this time was taken to mean ridding Europe of all Jews through a carefully established colonisation plan in a territory yet to be determined.[81] The French government hoped that its involvement meant that it, rather than the Germans, would receive any assets seized from expropriated Jewish property and businesses.

Dannecker had successfully persuaded Vichy to form a French organisation to centralise and coordinate anti-Semitic activity on both sides of the demarcation line, but he had doubts about Xavier Vallat, the man appointed by Vichy on March 29, 1941, to serve as its head. Vallat, who had not been on Abetz's list of favoured candidates, was Pétain's choice. He was a militant Catholic and a wounded First World War veteran. Although Vallat was a committed anti-Semite, his antipathy towards the Jews was inspired by his interpretation of Christian texts and papal bulls rather than Nazi ideology. He viewed Jews essentially as foreigners who could not be assimilated and therefore posed a threat to French national interests.

Dannecker also provided funds for the establishment in Paris of the violently anti-Semitic Institut d'étude des questions juives, or IEQJ (Institute for the Study of Jewish Questions), located at 21, rue la Boétie, a requisitioned building that formerly housed the art gallery of Paul Rosenberg, one of the leading prewar art collectors in the city. The IEQJ served as a centre for the city's anti-Semites, who remained, at best, sceptical about and, at worst, contemptuous of Vichy's CGQJ. Paul

Sézille, a leading Paris-based Jew-hater, a violent former captain in the colonial infantry and founder of the anti-Semitic Communauté française (French Community) group, was placed in charge of the IEQJ.[82] The IEQJ devoted itself to spreading anti-Semitic propaganda and publicly denouncing Jews or people they believed to be Jews; IEQJ members also joined von Behr's ERR squads, helping to search houses owned by Jews and confiscating their property.

The inaugural meeting of the IEQJ on May 11 attended by Paris's leading anti-Semites, including the novelist Louis-Ferdinand Céline and the journalist Lucien Rebatet, was marked by Sézille physically attacking one of the guests, whom he alleged was a Jewish spy; on another occasion he accused Laval of being a Jew. Sézille's erratic behaviour led to the disappearance of the IEQJ in 1942. It was replaced by an institute for the study of Jewish and ethnoracial issues, headed by another notorious anti-Semite, George Montandon.[83]

In May 1941 several thousand Jewish men, mostly Poles, received a green card from the French police summoning them to report to their local police station at 7 A.M. on May 14, bringing proof of identity. The card warned of serious consequences if they failed to attend. Most of these men assumed it was just another identity check. However, when they arrived at their neighbourhood police station, French policemen immediately arrested them, bundled them into green Parisian buses, and drove them off to the Gare d'Austerlitz railway station. At the station, just over 3,700 Jewish men were packed onto trains and taken to French internment camps in Pithiviers and Beaune-la-Rolande, some 60 miles south of Paris. The camps had been built by the Daladier government before the fall of France to hold "undesirables"—mainly French Communists and Republican refugees from Spain.[84] The roundup of Paris's Jews had begun.

An anonymous "group of Jewish women and children" circulated a leaflet: "Appeal to the French" that recalled France's glorious past as a defender of human rights and called on Parisians to protest at the arbitrary arrest and internment of the group's husbands and fathers. It marked a desperate attempt to counter the lies of the collaborationist press, which made out that those who were arrested were black-market dealers; on the contrary, far from being speculators, they were mostly self-employed artisans and traders—tailors, carpenters, dealers in furs—the majority of whom had been volunteers in the French army, the leaflet said.[85] It is not known how many people saw this "Appeal to the French," but it certainly went unheeded: nobody in Paris seemed to care. However one (non-Jewish) Parisian in the 17th arrondissement felt angry enough to write to Xavier Vallat personally at the CGQJ in May about the effect of the mass arrests on him. He wrote that he could not care less if thousands of Jews had been locked up; however, he cared very much that he had taken two pairs of shoes belonging to him and his wife himself to a local shoe-mender and when he went to collect them he discovered that the shop was closed and the cobbler was being held in a camp. He bemoaned the fact that it would be almost impossible to find other pairs of shoes and said that his wife and he could not be expected to go outdoors in their slippers. He explained that he had gone to the local police station but they were unable to help and told him it could take months for the matter to be resolved.[86] Relatives of those arrested travelled to the camps to try to contact their loved ones. One of these was fourteen-year-old Jacques Adler, who recalled seeing his father standing behind barbed wire. They spotted each other and tried to speak over the voices of hundreds of others all around, while French gendarmes lashed out, driving everyone back from the perimeter fence. Adler never saw his father again.[87]

On May 14, most of the Jewish men who had received a green card had obediently reported to the police, but a tiny minority had not. One of these was Joseph Minc, a thirty-three-year-old Polish Communist dentist. He had arrived in France in 1931, reaching Paris in 1937. He fought against the Germans in 1940, was captured, but managed to return to Paris in September.

Minc overslept on May 14 and when he learned from his wife that all those who reported were being detained he decided to lie low; Minc and his family left where they were living and moved into an apartment lent by friends for several weeks. Another friend, Lieber Rymland, was not so lucky. He had reported to the police and was held at Pithiviers. Like Minc, he was a member of the Communist Party, which instructed its members in the camps to "stay with the masses" and not to try to escape. Minc later wrote that this "incomprehensible" directive had "disastrous results." He was absolutely right. After the war it was revealed that almost all of those who were rounded up on May 14, 1941, and interned were deported and exterminated. At the end of the war, Minc's friend was freed from the camp where he had been held and, by chance, was reunited with his wife, who had also been deported. It was, however, a tragically brief reunion. On his way back to France, Lieber Rymland died of exhaustion.[88]

☞ WHILE THE GERMANS WERE confident they could remove the city's Jews with barely a whisper of opposition from non-Jews, they were clearly rattled by Parisian support for the Free French in London. De Gaulle had called for another day of action on May 11, the day on which France traditionally remembers Joan of Arc. The heroine of the Hundred Years' War was now being promoted by both London and Vichy as a symbol of French national unity. "On May 11, Joan of Arc Day, all French people will come together with but a single thought: the freedom of their homeland," de Gaulle explained in a broadcast from London. "On that day, between 3 P.M. and 4 P.M., they will go out onto the public thoroughfares of our towns and villages. They will walk around on their own, in family groups or with friends. They will not form a procession and there shall be absolute silence. But making eye contact with others doing the same thing will be enough to express their shared aspirations and fraternal hopes."[89]

The Germans banned all marches, meetings, banners, and flags in honour of Joan of Arc and, in an attempt to undermine any protest, *Paris-Soir* reminded its readers that Joan of Arc had kicked the English out of France.[90] The Paris police were out in force on May 11, especially around probable rallying points such as the place des Pyramides near the Louvre with its statue of Joan of Arc astride a horse, and the Arc de Triomphe, where they stood several ranks deep around the Tomb of the Unknown Soldier. Meanwhile, trucks packed with German soldiers made a great show of driving noisily through the city, presumably in an attempt to intimidate potential marchers.

None of this prevented Parisians turning out in great numbers, strolling around in silence, alone, or in small groups. Those who tried to reach the place des Pyramides en masse were channelled away by police barriers into the nearby Tuileries Gardens. Some witnesses reported that de Gaulle's call for absolute silence was respected; others recall shouts of "Long Live de Gaulle!" and "Up with England!" and people singing the Marseillaise.[91] According to the police, forty-two people were arrested. At 6:15 P.M. everything was back to normal after another mass demonstration of patriotism.

In May when the first roundup of the Jews took place it looked as if the Germans in Paris were having it all their own way. Aided by the French government in Vichy, they moved against the Jews with impunity and nobody outside the Jewish communities seemed to care. Resentment certainly simmered across the city at the German presence, but opposition had so far been largely passive and symbolic. All that was about to change because of events thousands of miles away to the east.

8

Resistance and Repression

SINCE AUGUST 1939 Nazi Germany and the Soviet Union had been bound by a non-aggression pact, honoured by each side. In June 1941 that agreement was blown apart by the most dramatic development of the war since the fall of France a year earlier.

On June 21 a Communist worker from Berlin, Alfred Liskov, one of millions of German soldiers stationed along the Russian border, deserted and swam across the River Prut. On the other side he informed the Russians that his unit had been told to prepare to invade their country. When this news was relayed to Stalin he ordered that Liskov be shot for spreading misinformation.[1]

A few hours later, after months of planning, the German army began a massive shelling offensive along a front stretching more than a thousand miles along the Russian border from the Baltic to the Black Sea. Over three million German troops, along with some forty divisions of Finnish, Italian, Romanian, Hungarian, and Slovakian soldiers, stormed into Russia. They were supported by more than 3,500 tanks, 600,000 motor vehicles, 700,000 field guns and other artillery, and more than half the entire German air force. Operation Barbarossa[2] was the largest invading force ever seen. After Poland, Denmark, Norway, the Netherlands, Belgium, and France it was now Russia's turn to experience blitzkrieg.

The Red Army was wholly unprepared as German land forces, backed by dive-bombers, smashed their way through the Russian defences. The sheer size of the advancing army was as exhilarating and exhausting for the Germans as it was terrifying for the Russian soldiers, who surrendered in the hundreds of thousands.[3] As the tanks forged across the baked-dry ground in the blistering summer heat they threw up thick clouds of yellow-brown dust visible for miles. The tanks advanced so fast that the German infantry had to cover 25 to 30 miles a day on foot to keep up. As one German general wrote, the invasion "for us means running, running, until our tongues hang out, always running, running, running."[4] Most of the petrified Russian civilians who found themselves in the path of the invasion had nowhere to run: in accordance with German invasion guidelines they were killed and their villages set ablaze.[5] Any Russians who did manage to escape were nearly always caught and finished off by members of the Einsatzgruppen, Himmler's SS special security units, who behaved even more barbarically in Russia than they had in Poland.

Hitler had been toying with the idea of invading Russia as early as July 1940.[6] Russia's defeat, he calculated, would prompt Britain to sue for peace; in addition, it would secure Germany's eastern borders and rule out any future possibility of Britain and America (not yet in the war) building an anti-Nazi front in Russia. The invasion would be a "crusade," a war of annihilation that would destroy Bolshevism, which, Hitler was convinced, was in league with Jews and hell-bent on world domination. The invasion was also the latest instalment of Germany's *Drang nach Osten* (March to the East) to secure more land for German settlement *(Lebensraum)*, seize mineral deposits, and gain access to agricultural produce.[7]

The invasion may have been months in the planning, but Stalin had refused to believe his own intelligence reports about the impending offensive. When he finally realised what had happened, members of his immediate circle described him variously as "subdued," "depressed and nervy," and "pale and bewildered."[8]

It was not just Stalin who was taken by surprise. Back in France, Vichy immediately broke off diplomatic relations with Moscow and hoped that since Germany was now at war with Britain and the Soviet Union, this would take pressure off France. From London, de Gaulle sent a telegram of support to Stalin and hoped to establish permanent contacts between the Free French and the latest country to fall victim to Nazi aggression.[9] In a radio broadcast, Churchill declared that Britain and her empire were totally aligned with the enemies of Germany, and thus with the Soviet Union, prompting Paris-based economist Charles Rist to comment wryly that this news would have Vichy accusing Churchill of being a Bolshevik.[10]

Most Parisians, including the prefect of police, were astounded.[11] They were generally overjoyed by the news, but for many different reasons. The invasion released the French Communist Party (PCF) from the straightjacket of the 1939 Non-Aggression Pact; with the "socialist motherland" under attack, out went references to an "inter-imperialist war" and in came the notion of an "anti-fascist war" and a war of national liberation. After Stalin's call on July 3 for the peoples of all countries occupied by Germany to join Russia in the fight against the invader, PCF propaganda was soon explicitly linking Russia's armed struggle with the liberation of France. "Long live the Red Army, which by valiantly defending the land of the Soviets is fighting to rid France of its fascist invaders and rid Europe of Nazism!"; "French people, the Red Army is fighting to break your chains!"; "The Russian soldiers are dying for our freedom!"[12] Very soon, this support for the Red Army would not be limited to words alone.

Many Parisians joined with the Communists in hoping that the Wehrmacht would be crushed by the Red Army; a Russian victory would put paid to Hitler's plans for European domination and the liberation of France would surely follow. Berthe Auroy wrote that people of different political opinions were rejoicing now that Russia was in the war.[13] Micheline Bood described the news as "marvellous," adding that "hope is born again."[14] Liliane Jameson's neighbour greeted her on the morning of June 22 with the triumphant shout: "Have you heard the good news? Chancellor Hitler has declared war on Russia!"[15] Awaiting trial in her cell in the Cherche-Midi prison, Agnès Humbert, a member of the Musée de l'Homme Resistance group, was "delirious with joy" when she heard the news. "I can't sit still: I walk up and down, I jump about, I sing."[16] Her main concern was to get the news to her imprisoned comrades as quickly as possible as well as to a young German prisoner, a veteran of the Spanish Civil War, who was due to be executed shortly.

Maurice Goudeket, who had married the novelist Colette in 1935, was also overjoyed: "The war is over! It might still last three or four years more, but for me, secure in the absolute, Hitler has already disappeared and the German soldiers you see passing by are nothing but phantoms." Colette told him he was crazy.[17] Others, like Benoîte Groult, while hopeful, also realised what it would mean if Hitler's gamble paid off. "If Russia is defeated, it is slavery for us for decades to come."[18] Communist sympathiser Edith Thomas conceded that pro-Pétain bourgeois Parisians backed the invasion and this meant that "Bolshevism was once again 'the enemy of humankind,' the plague from which the Nazis would save the world."[19] However, generally speaking, resentment towards the occupier easily outweighed any fears raised by Bolshevism.[20]

The invasion meant some Parisians now felt less isolated; inspired by the adage "my enemy's enemy is my friend," Jean Guéhenno wrote in his diary: "We now have 180 million more friends than before." However, he feared that a defeat of Hitler would make Europe vulnerable to a Communist takeover.[21] Although Charles Rist observed that everybody was happy about Germany's declaration of war on Russia, he was concerned that people could be overestimating Russia's ability to withstand the German onslaught.[22] Medical student Bernard Pierquin thought that ultimately Germany would probably defeat the Soviet Union, but he hoped that Britain might benefit in the process as the two great enemies—Pan-Slavism and Pan-Germanism—fought each other to a standstill. However, he did add a prophetic rider: "Napoleon should not be forgotten,"[23] a reference to Napoleon Bonaparte's disastrous invasion of Russia in 1812.

The news of the invasion turned Parisians with no military knowledge or experience into self-proclaimed experts. For example, the woman who owned the hotel where Andrzej Bobkowski had been living since January told him that she thought the Germans were going to get a good hiding, before going on to discuss with him the Soviet Union's military potential.[24]

Understandably unenthusiastic about the news were those German soldiers stationed in Paris who were now likely to be sent from summer in the City of Light to fight on the bleak Eastern Front. Author César Fauxbras noted that large numbers of German soldiers were leaving, and he recorded that a German soldier who had been living with the wife of a Parisian POW for seven months had been sent off to fight in Russia.[25] A friend of Paul Léautaud's was employed by a *mairie* in the southern suburbs of Paris to liaise with the Germans: when he asked two German officers if they were being sent to Russia they burst into tears.[26]

In contrast, news of the German offensive triggered an explosion of joy among the city's collaborationists.[27] Lucien Rebatet, the pro-Nazi journalist and cinema critic, wrote that the German attack against Russia changed everything for him, driving him wild with enthusiasm.[28] Like Hitler, the collaborationists believed that the invasion marked the beginning of the end for Bolshevism and some even started planning to give the German army a helping hand.

With Abetz's support, the main collaborationist leaders in Paris came together to promote the Légion des volontaires français contre le bolchevisme (LVF), a legion of French anti-Bolsheviks who volunteered to fight against the Red Army on the Eastern Front alongside their German "comrades."[29] Pierre Costantini, one of the more eccentric of the Paris collaborators (he had personally declared war on Britain after the sinking of the French fleet at Mers-el-Kebir in July 1940), saluted LVF members as "the crusaders of a new order against Anglo-Jewish-Bolshevik disorder."[30]

Hitler was initially unenthusiastic about the prospect of a French anti-Bolshevik force joining his troops in battle as he had no intention of sharing the glory of a Russian defeat with Vichy or of letting Vichy use the LVF's participation as a future bargaining counter. In the end, prompted by Abetz, Hitler agreed. However, he insisted that the fighting force be initiated by the Paris-based collaborationist parties and not by Vichy; that it remain limited to 15,000 men; and that the French government would not seek any concessions in return.[31] The Vichy government said it had no objection to the creation of the LVF but the German military in Paris were totally opposed to the whole idea. Once again Abetz brushed aside the spluttering objections of Otto von Stülpnagel, the MBF, by asserting he was acting on personal instructions from Hitler.

On July 8 the announcement of the creation of the LVF, which claimed to have the backing of both Pétain and Hitler, was greeted rapturously in the Paris collaborationist press.[32] It was followed by an intense, embassy-funded publicity campaign and recruitment drive using posters, newspaper articles, cinema newsreels, and radio broadcasts, in which LVF recruits were once again referred to as "The New Crusaders." One LVF propaganda poster actually showed a crusader in shining armour, standing proudly against the backdrop of blazing Russian buildings, a sword in one hand and a shield bearing the letters LVF in blue, white, and red in the other. Immediately behind him was the silhouette of a German soldier.[33] Abetz handed over offices previously occupied by Intourist, the official Russian Tourist Organisation, to the Legion to use as its headquarters.[34] The LVF also took over some eighty empty shops, most of them formerly owned by Jews, to use as recruitment stations.

The collaborationist press gave euphoric coverage of an LVF rally held on July 18 in the Vélodrome d'Hiver (the Vél'd'Hiv'). In front of a massive tricolour flag hung the huge letters LVF; the rest of the stadium was festooned with giant banners proclaiming "Down with Bolshevism, France Arise!" and "Bolshevism Defeated Means a United Europe!" According to the collaborationist press, 15,000 people listened enraptured, when they weren't cheering, applauding, stamping their feet, or chanting the names of their leaders, who took turns to denounce Bolshevism and call for its obliteration.[35] If France was to take its rightful place in the new Bolshevik-free Europe of the future, the speakers insisted, France had to be part of the anti-Communist crusade in Russia *now*. The police report of the event was less ecstatic, recording that only about 9,000 people were there, specifying that a quarter of them were women.[36]

Of all the Paris collaborationist leaders who spoke at the Vél'd'Hiv' meeting, the burly bruiser and former Communist Jacques Doriot was most closely associated with the LVF; and, indeed, he enlisted and went off to the Eastern Front in September.[37] His personal commitment contrasted with that of Marcel Déat, his arch-rival among the collaborationist leaders, who wrote in his diary, "No question of my going."[38] Although Déat had acquitted himself well in the First World War he preferred to stay and pursue his political ambitions in Paris rather than fight on the cold distant Eastern Front with the LVF, which, apart from anything else, was too closely associated with Doriot.

Doriot, the son of a blacksmith and a seamstress, had been a former rising star in the French Communist Party, but he was expelled in 1934 for building alliances with other left-wing groups and parties in his fief in the northern suburb of Saint-Denis. This was at a time when the PCF, following the Comintern policy, was vehemently opposed to such a strategy. Not surprisingly, in June 1936 Doriot was disgusted by the cynical hypocrisy of the PCF when it changed its political line and itself began to advocate building leftist alliances. Seething with resentment at how the party had treated him and desperately needing an outlet for his political passions and ambitions, Doriot founded the Parti populaire français (PPF), the French People's Party, which evolved from an anticommunist organisation into a pro-Nazi one.

Doriot's strategy after the armistice and Montoire was to publicly back Pétain while simultaneously planning to rid Pétain's entourage of the conservatives, reactionaries, and dead wood he believed were blocking the founding of a dynamic, authoritarian Nazi-style regime. In the Occupied Zone the PPF had its own paper, *Le Cri du Peuple*, and its headquarters were at 10, rue des Pyramides in the 1st arrondissement, although the German authorities did not officially sanction the PPF's existence until December 1941. At the beginning of 1941, according to the police, the PPF had 10,000 members, of whom just over a quarter were from Paris; although it attracted members from all walks of life, about half the delegates who attended the May 1941 congress were workers and about a third of them were former Communists and socialists.

Doriot had a number of points in common with his rival Marcel Déat: they were of the same generation (Doriot was four years younger than Déat); both had fought with honour in the First World War; both came from the Left (Doriot from the PCF, Déat from the Socialist Party, the SFIO); both had been highly regarded, before being expelled from their respective parties; and both had marched from the Left of the political spectrum to the Right, where each had founded a political organisation and each nursed the ambition to be the leader of the single neo-Nazi party in the new France.

There the similarities ended: Doriot, nicknamed Big Jacques, was a self-educated, brawny womaniser from a working-class background, who loved both being in crowds and addressing them and was always on the look-out for a fight. Déat was short and tubby, a brilliant but shy intellectual who had attended the prestigious École normale supérieure; he was a solitary man who neither drank nor smoked and was ill at ease with crowds of people. While Doriot was a star orator who could talk for hours—and often did—Déat was most at home with his faithful old typewriter, bashing out one of the 1,200 articles he wrote during the Occupation. Not surprisingly, perhaps, they loathed one another.

Of the leading Paris collaborationists, only Doriot went off to fight alongside the Germans, but this did not stop the others from using the LVF recruitment drive to publicise their own organisations. Even before the LVF rally at the Vél'd'Hiv', Déat claimed that 10,000 RNP members had volunteered and he promised 20,000 more. Eugène Deloncle, leader of the Mouvement social révolutionnaire (MSR), committed 10,000 from his organisation. Not to be outdone, Doriot promised that the Parti populaire français would provide more volunteers than all of the other groups put together. This was pure fantasy and completely academic, since Hitler had imposed a ceiling of 15,000.[39]

The LVF was open to healthy, non-Jewish French males aged between eighteen and thirty (extended to forty for officers), but by the end of July barely a thousand men had volunteered, according to a report by Admiral Bard, the new prefect of police for Paris.[40] In January 1941 Roger Langeron, who had held the post since the Germans arrived, had been arrested by the German authorities. He had long been suspected of harbouring Gaullist sympathies and his ordering of Déat's arrest in December 1940 had been the final straw. After a short spell in the Cherche-Midi prison Langeron was compelled to retire.[41]

Some of the LVF recruits were driven by fanaticism and bloodlust, like the unnamed LVF lieutenant, a member of Doriot's PPF and a practising Catholic, who would later write home from the Eastern Front: "Our leader, Chancellor Hitler, can give whatever orders he likes. We will carry them out with our eyes closed, since we have confidence in him." He also hoped that once Russia was defeated a campaign of mass blood-letting would turn Britain and France into Nazi states.[42]

Another volunteer, Christian de la Mazière, attributed his joining up to his traditional, conservative upbringing, imbued with anti-Bolshevism; he had grown up surrounded by newspaper portrayals of Communists as murderous, anti-Christian monsters.[43] He also admitted to being thirsty for adventure as a young man tired of just sitting around in Paris and talking politics with friends. In an interview in 2001 he declared, "We all believed in a German victory and in our view Bolshevism represented a real threat to freedom in Europe. You just had to go. There was no choice."[44] Some anti-Semites who volunteered shared Hitler's belief in a worldwide Jewish-Bolshevik conspiracy; they believed that by fighting communism they were simultaneously waging war against world Jewry.

As one LVF recruitment slogan put it: "For a Frenchman, fighting in the LVF is a duty, but it is also in his own interest." These included economic interests and it was economics, rather than ideology or politics, that prompted many recruits to enlist: a German report in the autumn estimated that only about a third of recruits were "idealists" (i.e., believing in the cause); the rest were either looking for adventure or were drawn from the ranks of the unemployed.[45]

Some recruits signed up out of curiosity: one such LVF recruit, who had been unemployed for months, expected to be surrounded by fanatics and staunch Doriot supporters. He was surprised to discover how many other similarly apolitical recruits there were. He reckoned that for every one who was genuinely committed, there were a hundred who were like him.[46] All successful recruits received the same rate of pay as their German fellow soldiers,[47] getting the first tranche when they signed up. A number enlisted, took the money, and promptly disappeared; some even returned a couple of months later to sign up again under another name.[48]

Hitler's invasion of Russia appeared to be going to plan, and on July 8 the Führer told his propaganda chief Josef Goebbels that the war in the east was in the main already won.[49] News of Germany's triumphs in the east reverberated throughout Paris, thanks to Radio-Paris and the collaborationist press. Parisians hoping for a German victory were beside themselves with joy; those rooting for Russia and a German defeat consoled themselves by dismissing these reports as Nazi lies. Sadly, they were not. Things were going so well for Hitler that the LVF organisers feared the recruits would arrive too late and Stalin would surrender before they reached the Eastern Front.[50]

Meanwhile, the German authorities in Paris, in a burst of public self-confidence, co-opted de Gaulle's V campaign. The Free French had encouraged Parisians to make letter Vs everywhere in anticipation of an Allied victory. At the end of July, the Germans launched a "V" campaign of their own. As Edith Thomas observed on July 23, "Goebbels, no doubt fearing this show of hostility, had Vs—this time symbols of a *German* victory and the relief of Europe *by the Nazis*—plastered over German offices, the front pages of the newspapers, and even the Eiffel Tower and the Chamber of Deputies."[51]

Besides a gigantic V on each of these two iconic buildings there hung a huge banner with the slogan DEUTSCHLAND SIEGT AUF ALLEN FRONTEN

("Germany Is Winning on All Fronts") in bold capital letters. The economist Charles Rist found the German V campaign puerile (as did Berthe Auroy),[52] but he added that at least it showed that the London-inspired V campaign had had an impact on the Germans.[53] Jean Guéhenno referred to "a veritable battle of the Vs" and described the Germans trying to appropriate the V by insisting, rather unconvincingly, that it stood for an old German word, "Victoria."[54] All the while, as Guéhenno observed, Parisians continued to cut Vs, Hs (for "Honour"), and the Cross of Lorraine out of their Métro tickets—the pavements were covered with them.[55] It was also becoming increasingly common to see the Gaullist Cross of Lorraine chalked on walls inside a V.[56]

Communist Party members and supporters in Paris refused to be demoralised by news of Germany's early military successes or by the Nazi propaganda offensive. Following Stalin's call for the inhabitants of Nazi-occupied countries to oppose the invader, the PCF decided to throw itself wholeheartedly into overt, anti-Nazi direct action. Or, to be more precise, it decided to throw members of its youth organisation, Les Bataillons de la jeunesse (Youth Battalions) into the front line. Thus it was that in the summer of 1941 a handful of Parisian youngsters, for the most part from poor, working-class backgrounds, briefly became the vanguard of the struggle in Paris against the occupying forces.[57]

While the Nazi-Soviet Pact held, Communist political action usually meant scrawling slogans on walls and distributing leaflets denouncing Vichy and the "inter-imperialist war," while also attacking de Gaulle as a lackey of British capitalism.[58] These were risky activities since any militant who was caught was likely to end up in prison or in a French internment camp, as happened to Guy Môquet, a sixteen-year-old arrested giving out leaflets near the Gare de l'Est railway station in October 1940.[59] Following the German anti-Russia offensive, the Communist militants' actions became more daring in form and overtly anti-Nazi in content: they began organising surprise demonstrations when they symbolically seized public space and occupied it for as long as they felt they could. As one of the participants, twenty-three-year-old Liliane Lévy-Osbert, recalled, "We were moving to a higher level. We were demonstrating in the street in broad daylight."[60]

The first of these events was set for July 13, but the sudden appearance of the French police meant the action had to be abandoned almost as soon as it started. As the fifteen or so demonstrators made themselves scarce, a few were arrested, but they were quickly released by the police, who did not take them or their protest very seriously.[61] The Germans had banned all demonstrations on the following day, Bastille Day, but this did not stop a group of youngsters, mostly from the 11th arrondissement, many wearing blue, white, and red clothing, from converging on the place de la République and running westwards; they shouted slogans and threw leaflets around as they ran before they were blocked by French police pouring out of the police station at the back of the *mairie* of the 9th arrondissement, just around the corner from the Richelieu-Drouot Métro station. Four demonstrators were arrested, but they were released after serving four-month sentences.[62]

On July 15 a poster appeared across Paris signed by Otto von Stülpnagel, the MBF, that carried a chilling message: "Since the Communist Party has been banned, all Communist political activity in France is forbidden. . . . Anyone found guilty should expect to be sentenced to death by a German military court."[63] On July 24 André Masseron, who had been arrested at the Bastille Day demonstration for whistling the Marseillaise, was executed;[64] less than a week later, posters in French and German appeared announcing the execution of José Roig, accused of being a Gaullist recruiting agent.[65]

☞ IN JULY THE JEWS who had been rounded up in May were still held in internment camps at Pithiviers and Beaune-la-Rolande. Their wives demonstrated outside police stations and town halls in Paris and in the suburbs demanding the release of their husbands. They were told to take their grievances to the offices of a Jewish Co-ordinating Committee for Greater Paris.[66] There were violent demonstrations outside the committee's offices in the rue de la Bienfaisance and many Jews viewed the committee with deep hostility, correctly regarding it as a puppet organisation under German control. When Leo Israelowicz, one of the two Jewish stooges appointed by Dannecker to head the committee, spoke to the demonstrators on July 24 he made no criticism of the German and French authorities. Instead, he implied that somehow the arrests were the fault of the Jewish community and claimed that the men who had been arrested and thrown into camps were "martyrs who are atoning for others," and that "without their sacrifice there would have been pogroms."[67]

The demonstrations continued over the next few days, sometimes with as many as 500 women taking part, all now blaming the committee for the arrests of their husbands. The protesters managed to get inside the building, where they went on a rampage, smashing up chairs, equipment, windows, and mirrors and trying to break down doors. On one occasion Israelowicz had to barricade himself in his office; he telephoned Dannecker, who told him to call the French police. Instead, two of Israelowicz's colleagues joined some of the women in a delegation to the Prefecture of Police, where they were told that the arrests of their husbands had been ordered by Dannecker himself and the matter was out of their hands.

During another protest, demonstrators hurled anything they could get their hands on at Israelowicz and set upon one of his colleagues. Again Israelowicz called the police, who cleared the demonstrators out of the building and drove them out of the street. Later in the day a hundred or so women, many of them pregnant or with small children, returned and stood outside the building chanting, "We want our husbands back!" "We can't survive like this!" "We're starving to death!" Two women were arrested for refusing to move on when ordered to do so by the police and another for resisting arrest.[68]

According to the German-run Radio-Paris, the wives of internees were demonstrating "to protest at the amount of money they have been allocated."[69] That was nonsense, of course; it was an attempt to play on the stereotype of the grasping, ungrateful Jew. Jacques Biélinky got it right when he wrote in his diary, "The wives of the internees who went to the rue de la Bienfaisance did so to protest against the internment of their husbands, not to ask for help."[70] In November 1941, the Co-ordinating Committee along with all other Jewish organisations was subsumed into the Union générale des israélites de France (UGIF), an organisation created by Vichy under pressure from the Germans. It operated in both the Occupied Zone and the Unoccupied Zone and in the latter was under tight German control. All Jews had to belong to the UGIF, whose role was ostensibly to represent Jews to the public authorities. UGIF leaders hoped the organisation would help to protect Jews but in practice, especially in Paris, it served as an instrument of control and repression cynically manipulated by the Germans in pursuit of their vicious anti-Semitic policies.

Meanwhile the young Communists refused to be intimidated and planned another demonstration for August 13. On the day protesters were given conflicting instructions as to where the demonstration would start—possibly a deliberate ploy to confuse the Paris police. Following a tip-off, however, the police placed the area around the Havre-Caumartin Métro station under surveillance, and around 6:30 P.M. they moved in and arrested seventeen young Communist militants. At about the same time, another group of protesters gathered around the Saint-Lazare railway station.

Other militants, including Liliane Lévy-Osbert, were grouping at the Strasbourg-Saint-Denis Métro station.[71] "Suddenly we set off along the boulevard Saint-Denis, just like that," she later wrote, "in the middle of the traffic, among the cars. The same tactic as before. Those in the front charged forward, the rest followed. The body of the demonstration took shape. We'd scarcely covered a few hundred metres when a convoy of German cars overtook us.[72] Bad luck—and that was the end of the demo. They turned round and drove straight at us. The French police were there as well. This changed the balance of forces completely. Shots rang out. The Germans were firing at us. I remember the panic in our ranks. Some people ran onto the right-hand pavement and disappeared into the little streets leading off the boulevard; others ran onto the pavement on the left and took refuge in the doorways. They were the ones who were caught. I was so taken aback that I was glued to the spot. In front of me everything was so confused. It all happened so quickly."[73]

The Paris police report on this demonstration records a hundred or so young people, three of whom were carrying French national flags, trying to march towards the place de la République. "Soldiers from the occupying army intervened and fighting took place, during which shots were fired. Two demonstrators were wounded and taken to l'Hôtel-Dieu.[74] A German officer and a French policeman were also injured. . . . Six individuals were arrested; four were taken into custody; two others placed under guard in the hospital."[75] The German military had finally had enough of street protests. The crackdown the Communists were expecting and fearing had arrived. But worse was yet to come.

The following day Pétain announced the creation of special tribunals, empowered to issue death sentences, that would try Communists and other Resisters. But still the protests continued. The lightning demonstrations that had started in July continued in street markets, mostly in the working-class areas in the north and east of the city. But there were protests elsewhere as well. On August 15 about fifty people demonstrated outside a sports arena in the southern suburb of Antony with banners and leaflets proclaiming: "Kick Out the Invader!" "The Victory of the Red Army Means Independence for France!" "Out with the Army of Occupation!" Two days later a dozen youngsters brandishing two tricolour flags and singing the Marseillaise appeared in the rue Daguerre in the south of Paris; they threw leaflets to the ground before fleeing. On the same day in the north of the city some fifty young men and women marched down the boulevard Barbès singing the Marseillaise and shouting slogans until the police appeared and they ran for it. There were no arrests.[76]

Some actions were more radical and daring. An arson attack on August 12 damaged the cabs of trucks requisitioned by the Germans and parked near the Porte de Choisy in the south of the city. Two days later material used in submarines and aeroplanes was destroyed at a factory in Vitry-sur-Seine. As twenty-five-year-old Jacques d'Andurain, one of the three perpetrators,[77] fled from the scene, he shot one of the workers who had given chase, using a 6.35mm lady's revolver belonging to his mother, a marchioness and society hostess.[78] The man was not seriously hurt and d'Andurain managed to get away. He later recalled that his heart was pounding so fast that he was shaking for the rest of the day.[79]

A police report of August 18 noted this escalation of Communist activity. It observed that actions during the previous week by Communists included attempted sabotage, demonstrations on public highways, and increased distribution of leaflets, stickers, and posters.[80] Andrzej Bobkowski, a Polish refugee writing in his diary on the same day, noted, "Stickers with the hammer and sickle have appeared on German posters. The Communists have declared war on the Germans in occupied French territory."[81]

The members of the Bataillons de la jeunesse remained at the forefront of this new offensive against the Germans. They were nearly all in their late teens and early twenties, idealistic, and, like many young people through the ages, believed they were invulnerable. They were not poker-faced, sanctimonious militants, but youngsters who enjoyed socialising, going camping together, swimming, messing about on the river, and flirting. Over the summer, despite their inexperience and strong reservations, they started wondering if they should go further than street demonstrations and sabotage. Should they try and turn Paris from a city where the Germans could relax into one where they always had to be on their guard? Should they, in other words, start executing German soldiers in the street?

One of the most passionate advocates of this type of direct action was a twenty-two-year-old Parisian named Pierre Georges. Georges, later known as Colonel Fabien, was already a veteran of the Spanish Civil War with a well-deserved reputation for being a hard man. He had recently been appointed head of the military wing of the Bataillons de la jeunesse. Gilbert Brustlein, a leading militant in the 11th arrondissement, recalled Georges's argument as he tried to convince Brustlein's fellow militants that they should start killing German soldiers in cold blood.

The Nazis were using the same tactic of organised terror in France as they used in Germany, and they had already started killing Parisians: one only had to think of the posters announcing the executions of Jacques Bonsergent, José Roig, and André Masseron. Terror had to be met with terror, argued Georges. If we Communists do not hit back in kind, the Germans will be able to create a climate of fear and use their grotesque anticommunist propaganda to isolate us. However, if we manage to kill some Nazi officers, it is the Germans who will be frightened.[82]

Brustlein later described the heated discussion that followed among his comrades. Christian Rizo, a nineteen-year-old student who had participated in the Armistice Day street protest in November, argued that the young Communists were not killers and that Communists, unlike anarchists, were against provocation and individual acts of violence.[83] His reasoning strongly echoed that of Lenin, who had said that violence is only truly revolutionary if it is an integral part of a mass political movement, and it is counterrevolutionary if carried out by a tiny minority cut off from the population.

Asher Semahya, a twenty-seven-year-old mechanic of Greek-Jewish extraction, the leader of the Communist youth organisation in the rue de la Roquette area, near la Bastille, was also in Brustlein's group. He protested that many German soldiers were workers in uniform and that they might inadvertently kill a German Communist; Brustlein pointed out that very few German officers would be Communists. Brustlein also insisted that armed attacks would undermine German morale and strikingly expose the myth of the invincible Nazi army.[84]

There were powerful arguments in favour of taking up the gun. Communists and Nazis were at war, and while the Red Army killed German soldiers on the Eastern Front, it was surely perfectly legitimate for French Communists to do likewise in Paris. But what finally clinched the matter was a dramatic move by the German military authorities.

On August 19 blood-red posters with black lettering appeared across Paris in French and German announcing that Henri Gautherot and Samuel Tyszelman,[85] two of the youngsters who had been arrested after the August 13 demonstration, "had been condemned to death for aiding the enemy by taking part in a Communist demonstration against the German military forces of occupation" and had been shot that day. Henri was only twenty-one years old and Samuel (known as "Titi") was just twenty. In an attempt to link "terrorist" and "Jew" in the minds of Parisians the posters pointedly stated that Tyszelman was Jewish. If some of the street protests had been a bit of a lark, the "game" was now deadly serious; the rules had radically changed. That two of the young Paris Communists had been executed by firing squad had a devastating impact on their comrades, many of whom knew the two young men personally. "We were traumatised, sad, demoralised, distressed," Liliane Lévy-Osbert remembered. But after a period of reflection, the resolve of these young people to carry on the fight against the Germans was greater than ever.[86]

The occupying authorities had not finished yet. On August 20, the day after Gautherot and Tyszelman were executed, Otto von Stülpnagel, without bothering to consult Vichy, ordered the Paris police to carry out a massive roundup of Jews in the 11th arrondissement as a further punishment for the August 13 demonstration.[87] The area was chosen because of its high concentration of Jews, mainly from eastern and central Europe, and its deserved reputation as a hotbed of Communist activity.[88] No attempt was made to link the arrests in the 11th arrondissement with any particular crime or offence; being Jewish was reason enough to be arrested. The Germans believed that a mass roundup in the area of Paris with the greatest concentration of so-called Judeo-Bolshevik criminals would allow them to strike with a single blow at their two main enemies in Paris at the same time that the Wehrmacht and Himmler's SS units were massacring the same "foes" thousands of miles away.

The orders went out. The German army would oversee the roundup, but the arrests would be made by nearly 2,500 members of the Paris police force. From 5 A.M. all roads in and out of the 11th arrondissement were sealed off and all the local Métro stations were closed.[89] Using lists based on information gleaned from the mass registration in October 1940, the French police set off to the homes of all French and foreign male Jews aged between eighteen and fifty living in the area,[90] but they were also under orders to arrest any male Jews they stopped in the street as well. If the police could not find a Jew who was on their list, a male relative could be taken instead. This happened in the rue des Immeubles-Industriels, a street with a high concentration of Polish Jews, when the police failed to find David Lemberger. They arrested his son Jean instead, even though he was only seventeen.

By the end of the day almost 3,000 men had been detained, but this was scarcely half the original target of 5,784. The roundup was therefore extended for another five days and broadened to include male Jews aged between fourteen and seventy-two from the whole of Paris, including the affluent western suburbs.[91] One Jewish man who was arrested in the Saint-Paul area asked the police to wait: he reappeared wearing his French army uniform, complete with medals, including two *croix de guerre*, but he was taken away nonetheless. In the end 4,230 men were arrested. Unlike the earlier "green card" roundup, this one included a thousand Jews who were French, of whom about forty were well-known lawyers. The Vichy government had been quite relaxed about the Germans arresting and interning foreign Jews; indeed, it had passed its own laws allowing foreign Jews to be interned. Although the French government had passed its own laws excluding French Jews from various professions and was planning to impose quotas on others, it was opposed to French Jews being arbitrarily arrested and detained. But the German authorities simply brushed aside Vichy's objections.

All those arrested were bundled into green buses requisitioned from the STCRP,[92] the public transport company for the Paris region; they were driven to Drancy, a small town to the northeast of the city. In Drancy the buses made their way to what looked like an abandoned building site—which is exactly what it was. In the mid-1930s work had started there on an ultra-modern social housing project in the form of a horseshoe-shaped block, complemented by five fourteen-storey towers. The war had interrupted the building work, and the half-completed estate was first used by the French government to intern Communists. In June 1940 the Germans used it as a transit camp for British and French prisoners of war. In 1941 Theodor Dannecker, Eichmann's man in Paris, commandeered the camp, but until 1943 it was run entirely by the French. Admiral François Bard, the prefect of the Paris police, was ultimately responsible for its day-to-day running; the head of the camp was a French police superintendent; the gendarmerie, France's national military force charged with police duties among the civilian population, provided the camp guards, who answered to Admiral Bard. The provision of food and bedding and the general maintenance of the camp were the responsibility of the prefect of the Seine Department, Charles Magny, whose pleas to Pierre Pucheu, the French minister of the interior, for extra funds to cover this expenditure fell on deaf ears.[93] Pucheu, appointed in August, was determined to take the toughest possible line against those, like Jews and Communists, whom he considered to be France's enemies.

More than 4,000 Jewish men now found themselves prisoners in this desolate abandoned building site with its unfinished housing blocks, cut off from their families, not knowing why they were there or what was going to happen to them. They were distressed, fearful, and disorientated. Jean Lemberger recalled waiting apprehensively in the courtyard as those around him expressed their anxieties: "This is unfinished public housing, nobody's ever lived here ... I hope we shall soon get something to eat. . . . How can we contact our families? . . . My wife will be worried sick."[94]

Some of those arrested at home had been able to pack a bag; those detained in the street had nothing but the clothes they were wearing. For two weeks no one had blankets, sheets, or soap. The men's ration cards were confiscated and they were packed, about forty at a time, into cold, draughty barrack rooms; the spaces between the wall and window were wide enough to pass your hand through, and the walls were bare except for rusty iron rods protruding from concrete pillars. There was nothing to sit on and for most of the prisoners nothing to sleep in, just the bare, cold concrete floor with all its bumps and cracks; some were fortunate enough to have one of the bunk beds provided by the Prefecture of the Seine Department.[95] Some of the men arrested feared they would be sent to work in Germany, others asserted confidently that Pétain had already intervened to have them released; others claimed they were going to be exchanged for French POWs.[96] In truth nobody knew. No one told them why they had been seized, how long they would be staying, or what was going to happen next.

The prisoners spent the whole day cooped up indoors, except for one hour's exercise and the camp roll calls, and they were strictly forbidden to look out of the windows whenever Dannecker visited the camp. All personal visits were forbidden; prisoners were allowed to write to their families once a fortnight, but it had to be in French; playing cards and reading were banned, although some reading matter did circulate secretly.

The French gendarmes had licence to slap, beat, kick, whip, or insult any prisoner who broke the camp rules,[97] but since these rules were never published it meant they could ill-treat whomever they wanted whenever they chose—and, with one or two honourable exceptions, this is just what they did. In 1942, when there were female and male prisoners in the camp, the French commandant of the camp, Marcelin Vieux, was seen whipping a woman for being too slow to move away from the middle of the yard.[98] Another inmate remembered Vieux punching inmates and beating them with his truncheon. He also vividly recalled his two violently anti-Semitic French subordinates, who never went on patrol without their truncheons at the ready.[99] Dr. Falkenstein, another prisoner, saw one of these men hit a four-year-old girl so hard that he knocked her unconscious.[100]

A special punishment cell was known as Le Gnouf (the nick). It measured 3 metres by 4 metres into which up to thirty inmates at a time could be crammed: no room to lie down or even sit down unless the prisoners took it in turns and only a single bucket as a lavatory. A gendarme could have a prisoner sent to the Gnouf for any "offence": stealing a vegetable when on vegetable peeling duty meant two days in the Gnouf; anyone caught smoking in a dormitory room risked one or two weeks; dealing in tobacco meant a month's incarceration,[101] as did waving or making other gestures to somebody outside the camp.[102] Some of the Drancy inmates who had been held in Dachau said that conditions in Drancy were even worse.[103]

Roll calls were also used as a punishment. Ostensibly held to make sure nobody had escaped, the roll calls meant prisoners were forced to stand outside in all weathers for up to three hours while the name of every single prisoner, however sick or infirm, was called. Sometimes the guards miscounted and the whole procedure started again; sometimes the sick were forced to attend, even if this meant carrying them out on stretchers.[104] But, as one prisoner put it, all the other deprivations in the camp would have been bearable if it wasn't for the hunger they had to endure. "People were so desperately hungry that they would throw themselves on any crumb of bread that fell on the ground. Our stomachs were so empty that we did not have the strength to think about anything but food."[105]

In the early months, prisoners were expected to survive on a daily ration of just two bowls of clear soup, 150–200g of bread, and 200g of unpeeled vegetables. Twenty-year-old Gabriel (Gaby) Ramet used an official card to write to his mother and sister on September 1 telling them that both he and his father, who had also been arrested, were in good health and in good spirits, although they were having to share a bed; it was forbidden for relatives to send in any food or tobacco, but he asked them to send a blanket, as it was already starting to get cold.[106] Unless things changed, the prisoners faced the risk of a long, lingering death from starvation, aggravated by the cold weather.[107]

☞ AT EIGHT O'CLOCK in the morning on August 21—the day after the start of the 11th arrondissement roundup—two young Communists, Pierre Georges and Gilbert Brustlein, were waiting on the Line 4 platform of Barbès-Rochechouart Métro station in the north of Paris. Both enjoyed a reputation for courage and had a taste for action; they were now about to strike a blow in the heart of Paris against the German occupying forces.

Pierre Georges insisted that the action had to take place in rush hour, in public, in a working-class area. At 5 past 8, a Métro train rattled into the station and a group of German sailors prepared to climb aboard: one of them, Alfons Moser, a quartermaster, wearing a splendid blue uniform, looked very important to Georges and Brustlein. As he stepped into the first-class carriage, Georges drew his gun and shot him twice in the back. As Moser collapsed forward into the carriage, Georges and Brustlein made their getaway. When they finally stopped to catch their breath in the square Willette, below the Sacré-Coeur basilica, Georges turned to Brustlein and said, referring to their pal Samuel "Titi" Tyszelman, "Titi has been avenged."[108] The first fatal shots in the Communists' armed struggle in Paris had been fired. Armed resistance had begun.[109]

The Germans authorities were swift to react and responded with bullets of their own. Otto von Stülpnagel, the MBF, was absent from Paris on a short term of leave, but his deputy Ernst Schaumburg issued a terrifying warning. From now on anyone held in prison for whatever reason would be treated as a hostage. If there were any similar attacks on Germans in the future, an unspecified number of hostages would be taken out and executed.[110]

Pierre Pucheu, Vichy's new minister of the interior, a member of Doriot's PPF before the war and a fanatical anticommunist, proposed that the Vichy government create new "special tribunals." These would make it possible for prisoners who had already been tried and sentenced to be "retried" and retrospectively sentenced to death for their original offence. Thus on August 28, in response to Moser's killing, three prisoners were hauled before one of Vichy's "special tribunals."[111] Two had been sentenced to fifteen months and two years, respectively, for spreading propaganda; a third, a Jew, had been sentenced for possession of forged identity papers. They were now tried again in front of French judges for the same offences, found guilty, sentenced to death, and guillotined the next day. The Germans rejected Vichy's gruesome and repulsive proposal that the trio should be decapitated in a public square in Paris.[112] The day after the trio went to the guillotine, the German authorities announced that three Gaullists found guilty of spying and five Communists found guilty of participating in demonstrations against the German army had been executed on August 24.[113]

☞ ON AUGUST 27, a small crowd of people gathered outside the Borgnis-Desbordes barracks in the Paris suburb of Versailles. They were there to watch the passing-out parade of the first contingent of LVF volunteers about to leave for their training camp in Poland before travelling on to fight against the Red Army on the Eastern Front. Jacques Doriot, head of the Parti populaire français (PPF) and the Parisian collaborationist most associated with the LVF, was in Brittany, but two of his lieutenants were present in their black uniforms, as was a large number of the PPF rank and file. Marcel Déat, leader of the other big collaborationist party the Rassemblement national populaire, was also there, even though he still had no intention of enlisting. Also in attendance was Fernand de Brinon, Vichy's man in Paris, General Otto von Stülpnagel, and a representative of Otto Abetz. Pierre Laval, the former French prime minister, was also present, later claiming that he had been viewing property in Versailles and decided to drop in on the ceremony.[114]

As people in the crowd raised their arms in a Hitler salute and sang the Marseillaise,[115] the French tricolour flag was slowly raised for the first time in the Occupied Zone since the defeat of May–June 1940 and the LVF flag was ceremoniously handed over to its soldiers.[116] Those attending the ceremony found no contradiction in giving a Nazi salute while singing the French national anthem. They firmly believed that France's national interests lay in supporting—and indeed fighting for—a Nazi-dominated Europe. They believed in an authoritarian, nationalistic France, a France, which, having crushed its enemies the Freemasons, the Jews, and the Communists, and having ridden itself of all vestiges of corrupt parliamentary democracy, would take its rightful place alongside its natural ally the Third Reich.

After a brief visit inside the barracks, the dignitaries were making their way through the crowd outside when five shots rang out. In what was almost certainly a copycat action of the Communist armed attack at Barbès-Rochechouart, a loner named Paul Collette, who had prewar connections with the Far Right, had shot and wounded both Laval and Déat: Laval was hit in the arm and chest, Déat in the stomach. Two other men were slightly wounded, one of whom was nineteen-year-old Serge Basset, the youngest LVF recruit in the barracks.[117]

Laval and Déat both needed to be hospitalised, but they survived. "Providence did not want me to die, as I have to save France," Laval is supposed to have declared.[118] In an interview he said he was targeted because he advocated collaboration, whose highest aspiration was, he believed, reconciliation between the people of Germany and France. "This is the only goal that counts for me," he said.[119] In private, Laval believed the attack was an assassination attempt masterminded by Eugène Deloncle, leader of the MSR, but this was never proven.

In a vain (in both senses of the word) attempt to boost his image in the eyes of the Germans, Vichy's representative in Paris, de Brinon, claimed that it was he who was the target. He unsuccessfully tried to persuade Collette, who had been arrested just after the shots were fired, to support this interpretation. Déat, like Laval, strongly suspected Collette was working for Deloncle, but the would-be assassin insisted that he acted alone. Laval was his target and he claimed he had been motivated by patriotism.

Teacher Jean Guéhenno wrote in his diary that when Parisians learned that Laval had been shot they "had great difficulty concealing their joy."[120] Naturally, the Paris collaborationist press made political capital out of the attack. On August 28, *Le Petit Parisien* said the attack had "the hallmark of an Anglo-Judeo-Soviet crime." Two days later the same paper expressed the hope that the attack might "finally make the maniacs on Gaullist radio think again," describing the Free French as "the valets of Judeo-British capitalism," who, "no longer content with sowing discord and hatred through inflammatory broadcasts several times a day, were now encouraging assassinations."[121]

On September 3 Gilbert Brustlein and two associates, Ascher Sema-hiya and Fernand Zalkinov, unsuccessfully attempted to assassinate a German officer outside a hotel in the 10th arrondissement;[122] two days later, as a reprisal, the Germans executed thirteen hostages at Mont-Valérien on the capital's northwestern extremity. On September 6 someone opened fire on a German officer in the 16th arrondissement; four days later a naval officer was shot and wounded at the Porte Dauphine Métro, and another attack occurred the following day.

Since Schaumburg's declaration in August after the first German soldier was shot, anyone found guilty and imprisoned even for a trivial offence automatically became a hostage and was at risk of being executed by a German army firing squad. In mid-September, General Keitel transmitted Hitler's instructions to the Wehrmacht in Paris that for every "terrorist" attack, between fifty and one hundred Communists should be executed.[123] Stülpnagel and the military authorities in Paris, were now in a quandary. The MBF had no objection in principle to executing civilians as it had already shown, starting with Jacques Bonsergent in December 1940. However, he feared that executions carried out on the scale that Hitler demanded would simply fan the flames of anti-German resentment and fuel the Resistance. Paris would thus become even less safe for Germans. This in turn would undermine the policy of collaboration to which the army was committed, support for which was already fragile because it had yielded no significant benefits for Parisians or the French. Even a die-hard Nazi like Werner Best, the head of the Administrative Section of the MBF, had his doubts: a memo from his office written after the September 3 assassination attempt in the 10th arrondissement noted that it would be unjust and regrettable if the Paris population as a whole were blamed or if innocent lives were destroyed as the result of deeds almost certainly committed by Communists.[124]

As the attacks on Germans continued, Stülpnagel responded by executing hostages as a reprisal even if they were not on the scale that

Hitler was demanding. On September 17 the newspapers informed their readers that ten hostages had been executed in reprisal for attacks on German soldiers on September 6, 10, and 11;[125] five of the hostages were Jewish. That day Benoîte Groult commented on this outrage in her diary, naming seven of those who had been executed and giving their dates of birth as printed in the official declaration. "Most of these twelve [*sic*] guys whose lives have just ended and whose names are made public as if they were criminals, are the same age as I am. I want to remember you Libermann, David, born on 1 January 1920,[126] and you Joly, René, and you, old Lucien Blum, shot aged 62 for something you didn't do."[127]

More posters in French and German signed by Stülpnagel followed. They appeared all over the city bearing the names of executed hostages. In the course of a week, starting on September 22, César Fauxbras kept a note of them: "Yesterday, a new poster: 12 people executed."[128] "Twenty Communists shot in reprisal for attacks against trains."[129] "Now we are getting public announcements almost every day about people being shot [by the Germans]."[130] In all, more than fifty French hostages were executed between late June and the end of September.[131]

Paris had become very dangerous for everyone. After the shooting of Déat and Laval the collaborationists were jittery; the attacks against the Wehrmacht personnel made the German soldiers jumpy. Parisians were increasingly nervous as the risk of being arrested increased as the number of police raids and stop-and-search operations rose. At the end of September, Edith Thomas wrote of French and German police stopping people in the Métro and searching them, looking for weapons and leaflets. In some parts of the city, she noted, whole housing blocks were surrounded by police and the inhabitants held while the buildings were searched from top to bottom.[132] An official report for September referred to 76,567 people being stopped, resulting in nearly a thousand detentions.[133]

In October, the Communist Party tried to divert German attention away from Paris by attacking German soldiers in the provinces. The most spectacular of these actions occurred in Nantes on October 20 when Gilbert Brustlein shot and killed a German officer who turned out to be Karl Hotz, the local regional commander and one of the most senior members of the German military outside Paris. When news reached Hitler, he demanded that at least fifty hostages be shot, followed by a further fifty if the perpetrators were not caught within forty-eight hours. That same evening (October 21) came news that a German military adviser had been assassinated in Bordeaux.

Brustlein made it back to Paris, where the special brigades of the French police were working hand-in-hand with the German military secret police (GFP), frantically arresting anybody they thought was a member of, or was linked to, the Bataillons de la jeunesse.[134] By the following Easter, some thirty young militants had been executed. Brustlein, like Pierre Georges, managed to avoid capture. Brustlein eventually made it to England via Gibraltar while Georges remained in France and continued to be active in the armed resistance.

On October 22 and 23 the Germans shot ninety-eight hostages in retaliation for the shootings in Nantes and Bordeaux. Twenty-seven of these individuals were chosen from the prisoners held in a camp at Choisel, near Châteaubriant, where more than 500 political prisoners were being held. The group included Parisian Guy Môquet, now seventeen years old, who had been arrested distributing leaflets when he was just sixteen.[135] All twenty-seven were taken to a quarry just outside Châteaubriant and shot in three groups of nine. All the prisoners refused to be blindfolded. Bernard le Cornu, Vichy's subprefect (*sous-préfet*) based in Châteaubriant, claimed that Vichy minister of the interior Pierre Pucheu was fully implicated in the selection of those to be executed. Pucheu persuaded the Germans to reduce the number of Châteaubriant hostages originally singled out for execution; in exchange, he gave the Germans the names of those he thought were the most dangerous Communists in the camp. The Germans then included them among the twenty-seven prisoners chosen to be shot.[136] Sixteen hostages were executed in Nantes: one of these, André Le Moal, who had been arrested for shouting "Vive de Gaulle," was, like Guy Môquet, only seventeen years old.[137] Five other hostages, originally from Nantes, were shot at Fort Romainville in the eastern Parisian suburb of Les Lilas where they were being held in prison. The remaining fifty hostages were executed in Bordeaux in reprisal for the assassination there of the military adviser. The names of those who were shot were published in newspapers and on posters. The execution of so many innocent people, and especially that of Môquet, shocked the young Parisian Communists profoundly. Yet most of them remained convinced that to stop assassinating German soldiers now would be a betrayal of those who had been executed. They were aware, however, that their armed attacks made them unpopular with the wider Paris population.

The response of Micheline Bood to these attacks was typical: "There have been more murders of Germans lately. I think it's truly disgusting to do that, because there are terrible reprisals and lots of hostages are shot."[138] After the war Liliane Lévy-Osbert, one of the members of the Bataillons de la jeunesse, acknowledged this public disapproval. She wrote of her friends being isolated from their fellow citizens, most of whom disapproved of their anti-German actions. Parisians, she said, categorically rejected any act of rebellion. A fear of reprisals terrorised the population, which turned into anger and was then directed at these "adventurers" who were seen as putting the lives of decent folk in danger. As she noted, "This was just what the Germans wanted."[139]

Another militant, Maroussia Naïtchenko, was employed in a small factory and, in a memoir published in 2003, she recalled the reaction at work on the day that the list of forty-eight executed hostages was published. Most people in her workshop expressed their horror at the attacks, which they had learned about, as had Maroussia and her political comrades, through the press. "But most of them condemned 'the terrorist attack which had provoked the reprisals,' taking up the same terms as used by the collaborationist press. For some people it was not the occupying forces who were responsible for their killing of the hostages, but the members of the Resistance themselves."[140]

The Communist Party's own cynicism added to the isolation experienced by the Bataillons de la jeunesse. The PCF leadership sanctioned the assassinations of Germans and privately thanked Brustlein on his return to Paris from Nantes.[141] However, the level of disapproval among the population was so high that while PCF propaganda exploited to the full the Germans' execution of Communist hostages, it refused to take public responsibility for the attacks it had initiated and even claimed that they were provocations carried out by the Nazis themselves.[142] After the war, Brustlein alleged that the PCF leadership came to consider him such an embarrassment that they tried to dispose of him permanently by sending him on a suicide mission. It was shortly after this that he fled to London.[143]

Although most Parisians opposed the assassination of German soldiers, Jean Guéhenno respected the actions and sense of solidarity of those responsible, whom he imagined to be a group of determined, disciplined, and experienced militants: "The assassin could be in the place of the hostage; the hostage could be in the place of the assassin. It's a matter of chance."[144] Little did he suspect that these "Communist terrorists," as the authorities referred to them, were young, brave but inexperienced idealists driven by a passionate desire to "do something" to help the Soviet Union and to drive the invader out of France.

A tiny minority of Parisians looked favourably upon the Communists' armed actions. Gilbert Badia, a teacher who joined the PCF in 1935, was not impressed by the argument that an anti-Nazi German soldier might get shot, or by those who said the attacks were not worth it because the retaliatory measures of the Germans were decimating the armed Resistance. "It was war," he wrote later. "I admired the bravery of those who carried out the attacks; I knew that I would be incapable of doing so myself."[145]

Pétain, of course, was vehemently opposed to any resistance and especially armed resistance. On August 23 he sent a telegram to Hitler deploring the shooting of Moser. A month later, following other anti-German attacks in Paris and elsewhere in the Occupied Zone, he broadcast a radio message to the Occupied Zone warning that these "criminal attacks" would lead to disunity and disorder. He called on his listeners to do everything in their power to help the government find the perpetrators, who could only be, he asserted, "foreign agents."[146] As Guéhenno noted, "Doesn't utter a word about the thirty hostages shot last week."[147] In another broadcast, just after the attacks in Nantes and Bordeaux, Pétain once again blamed these "crimes" on "foreigners" who cared nothing for French widows, orphans, and prisoners, and he again called upon his listeners to denounce those responsible.[148]

De Gaulle, in stark contrast, had no moral objection to German soldiers being gunned down in France. In a radio broadcast from London on October 23 he told his listeners it was absolutely normal and justifiable for French people to kill Germans. In his view, if Germans did not want to be killed by French people, they should have stayed in Germany and not waged war on France. But at the same time, he tried to discourage further bloodshed. It was too easy, he said, for the occupying forces to take reprisals against innocent French men and women. He therefore advocated "patience, preparation, and resolution," and assured his listeners they would receive their orders when the time came for a coordinated attack from outside and inside France.[149] De Gaulle was uncomfortable with armed attacks being organised in France by Communists, over whom he had no influence or control. He admired their courage, but he did not trust them. When he considered the right time had come, he wanted the country's internal resistance to be mobilised as part of a coordinated effort under his leadership as the head of the Free French forces.

In late summer and early autumn, as German repression increased and the armed resistance continued, Parisians grew ever more fearful. A word out of place, an anti-German comment overheard, to be caught with a Communist (or Gaullist) leaflet, or to be the victim of a misplaced or malicious denunciation could mean prison and with that the possibility of being executed in reprisal for an armed attack you knew nothing about.

Although Parisians may not have approved of the Communists' attacks, neither were they inclined to help the Germans catch those who carried them out. As a way of punishing Parisians for refusing to cooperate in the fight against terrorism, the German authorities frequently extended the curfew. "As from tomorrow evening until September 23, everybody has to be indoors by 9 P.M.," wrote Micheline Bood in her diary on September 19, "and anyone caught on the street after that time will be considered a hostage."[150] As Pierre Audiat noted in his account of Paris during the Occupation, it was frighteningly easy to be caught out after curfew. "A moment of absent-mindedness, an accident, being unavoidably delayed, bad luck, or getting caught up in a demonstration or a fight could turn the most peaceful of Parisians into a hostage and end up with them being executed."[151]

These bullying tactics by the Germans were largely ineffective: Parisians, on the whole, refused to give the Germans information about the attacks. On September 20 Jean Guéhenno wrote: "We're being punished as if we were children—'for our own good' declares General von Stülpnagel. We are guilty of not denouncing the perpetrators of the attacks against German soldiers. 'The occupying authorities' haven't managed to capture a single one of them.'"[152]

For some Parisians it didn't matter whether they supported the Communists or not: the authorities bore down on them simply because of who they were. In June 1941 Vichy published a second Jewish statute, adding a religious dimension to the racial one contained in the October 3, 1940, statute; and over the next three months, Vichy introduced quotas for Jewish students, lawyers, and doctors. On August 13 all Jews in the Occupied Zone were further marginalised when the Germans gave them until the end of the month to hand in their radio sets at their local police station. The victimisation of the Jews made them ever more fearful and vulnerable: Jacques Biélinky wrote in his diary of men posing as police officers turning up at Jewish homes and searching them for valuables and money.[153] As before, this discrimination against the Jews went hand in hand with intensive anti-Semitic propaganda aimed at softening up public opinion for the introduction of further discriminatory measures.

A poster campaign ran throughout the summer. In one poster an image was used which Berthe Auroy described as "perhaps the most vile and disgusting ever to have disgraced the walls of Paris."[154] It showed a Jew with greedy, cruel eyes, dressed in trailing robes, his long dirty hair in ringlets, biting into a symbolic representation of France, the blood running down his chin. Another depicted a prostrate woman lying on the French flag; a giant vulture, its wings spread, is perched on her, about to attack her chest: the bird's head is a caricature Jew, the Star of David on a chain round its neck.[155] "People of France! Help!" read the slogan. In the Métro, Berthe Auroy watched to see how other Parisians responded to these revolting displays: she did not hear the slightest reaction; nothing but impassive and impenetrable faces. "The Occupation has turned us into wooden automata," she concluded. She remained convinced, however, that most Parisians resented and saw through this grotesque propaganda. "As a result," she wrote, "even those who in the past showed little sympathy for the Jewish cause now feel inclined to support it."[156] Sadly, she offered no evidence for this optimistic view.

The Germans' new poster campaign was reinforced by a nauseating exhibition. "Le Juif et la France" ("The Jew and France") was organised by the IEQJ, the German-funded, Paris-based organisation specialising in anti-Semitic propaganda, with extra financial support from the German secret police. The exhibition opened on September 5, 1941, in the Palais Berlitz, in the 2nd arrondissement.[157] A giant poster depicting a caricature of a grasping Jew hung above the entrance. Inside, over two floors, statues, texts, cartoons, photographs, and dubious "statistics" supported the Nazis' central theme of why and how Europe should rid itself of the Jews.[158] Rooms were devoted to anti-Semitic interpretations of the history of the Jews, focusing on their alleged atrocities. There was a graphic denunciation of the "Jewish domination" of French cinema and exposés of the alleged links between Jews and Bolsheviks and Jews and internationalism, plus a section showing how different states in Europe had started to address the "Jewish Problem."

The cover of the exhibition catalogue featured a caricature of a grubby Jew in a prayer shawl holding the world in his grasp. The whole exhibition was designed to spread the poisonous lie that the Jews were a race apart, scheming with the Communists and the Freemasons in pursuit of world domination. In so doing, according to the vile anti-Semitic fantasists, Jews corrupted and debased everything they touched and Parisians needed to look no further for the root cause of France's and, indeed, the whole world's problems.

The newspapers, the radio, leaflets, and even a loudspeaker outside the Palais Berlitz urged Parisians to visit the exhibition. According to the IEQJ, this publicity campaign was wholly successful: it claimed that more than a million visitors viewed the exhibition by the time it closed on January 15, 1942, although the German Institute put the figure at 250,000.[159]

☞ ON OCTOBER 3, the German High Command in Berlin received a telegram from Stülpnagel in Paris: "NIGHT OF 2–3 OCTOBER. EXPLO-SIVES USED IN ATTACKS ON SEVEN JEWISH SYNAGOGUES. APPARENTLY ANTI-SEMITIC GROUPS. PERPETRATORS NOT YET APPREHENDED."[160] In a letter dated October 6, Stülpnagel gave more details confirming that seven synagogues had indeed been targeted,[161] with explosives placed adjacent to external walls. One device had failed to explode,[162] but the others had caused extensive damage not only to the synagogues themselves, but also to nearby buildings. Several French people had been injured in the explosions, as well as two German soldiers.

A few days later Jacques Biélinky went to the synagogue in the rue des Tournelles, near the place des Vosges in the Marais district. Looking through holes in the external doors he could see that the bomb had destroyed the interior of the building, and shattered the glass in all the windows. Across the way, he noticed a small café; its doors and windows had been blown away and were replaced by material stretched over the openings; nearby were several other buildings with broken windows.[163] It must have been quite an explosion.

Stülpnagel set up an inquiry. He discovered to his fury that not only had the attacks been carried out by some of Deloncle's MSR thugs, but that the explosives used had been specially ordered by SS First Lieutenant *(Obersturmführer)* Sommer, Himmler's representative in Belgium and France, and sent from Berlin to Paris specifically for bombing the synagogues.

Stülpnagel also learned that Helmut Knochen, the head of Himmler's secret police in Paris, had been involved. Stülpnagel, was beside himself with rage that Himmler's men had dared to carry out bomb attacks without telling him. He wrote in his report that it was intolerable that German units, in an occupied country, were going behind his back to plan actions that were at odds with his own intentions and which, moreover, were likely to sabotage initiatives for which he was responsible.[164] He managed to have Sommer recalled to Berlin, but he failed to have Knochen removed. Knochen was a protegé of Reinhard Heydrich, Himmler's right-hand man, and this connection carried more weight than Stülpnagel's protestations. Knochen remained in Paris.

Relations in Paris between the army and Himmler's men had been strained ever since 1940, when Himmler's men had been smuggled into the city wearing army uniforms. They were now close to breaking point. The army in Paris rightly saw the secret police's bombing of the synagogues as confirmation that Himmler's men were determined to make inroads into issues of "security," which the army continued to insist was its prerogative. Himmler's men would surely try again.

ᴇ9

Resistance, Punishment, Allied Bombs, and Deportation

*A*s autumn 1941 approached, most Parisians were still struggling to find enough to eat. A police report in mid-August noted that people were already apprehensive about how they were going to manage when winter came, and were blaming the French authorities as well as the occupying forces for the food shortages.[1] Another report a week later was even gloomier and referred to "the ever increasing scarcity of basic foodstuffs." Mothers, worried that insufficient food left their children weak, were especially anxious with another winter on the way. In addition, the ongoing problems with footwear and clothing meant concern was widespread that many children would have no shoes or warm clothes and so would be unable to go to school.

The shortages had political consequences. As the report noted, most people's purchasing power had fallen as a result of the rise in the cost of living; they were now spending the last of their savings. The report suggested that if things continued in this way more Parisians might start looking to Britain and de Gaulle for a solution to their problems.[2]

By the autumn food supplies had still not improved. However, for those lucky enough to have family in the country, life became a little easier on October 13 when the Vichy government finally authorised the posting of "family parcels." Country residents had been unofficially sending food parcels to family members in Paris since the early days of the Occupation. Now they could do so officially, provided their parcels weighed less than 50 kilos and contained only limited amounts of certain permitted products.[3] In practice, parcels were rarely checked and Parisians did not even have to prove the parcels came from relatives. Although food parcels meant Parisians could get up to 300 extra calories a day,[4] wealthier Parisians were twice as likely to receive them than those living in poorer areas.[5] Some people did well out of delivering food parcels; the Swiss journalist Edmond Dubois, now back in Paris, wrote of postmen in the 16th arrondissement receiving small tips for trudging up several flights of stairs with deliveries of vegetables or dead rabbits. But the tips soon added up to a handsome sum. "They were receiving 20,000 francs a day in the Passy district where 10,000 parcels arrived every day."[6]

One unfortunate consequence of making family parcels legal was that it dramatically reduced the volume of food on sale on the open market and, as a result, prices in the Paris shops went even higher. Family parcels also took up space in trains that would otherwise have carried food destined for the open market. In one instance, three out of five trains intended to take artichokes to Paris from a station in Brittany were full of family parcels.[7] Furthermore, as people did not have to prove that family food parcels were for relatives, many were diverted, their contents were sold on the black market in Paris and often turned up on restaurant menus in expensive dishes.

Parisians still had to go to the *mairie* every month to queue for ration cards. Berthe Auroy queued for almost three hours to get a card for milk; she observed her fellow Parisians "weary, exhausted, demoralised, waiting in gloomy silence." She felt frustrated that they had become too patient: most people, she said, had suffered so much they ended up looking like cattle, meekly waiting in line.[8]

Shortages also affected the lives of street traders: the chestnut-seller at the corner of Berthe's street was a familiar fixture every autumn. This year, however, he had not even bothered to light his brazier. "So where are our chestnuts, our apples, our nuts?" she asked in her diary. "And where are our onions?" The rumour mill had a bizarre answer: "People say the Germans are extracting the alcohol from them to make explosives."[9]

But it was not just finding food that was a problem. As autumn took hold there was also the cold to deal with once again. When Berthe returned to Paris towards the end of October after a short stay in the country she wrote that winter had suddenly arrived: icy winds, the first fall of snow on October 24, and the temperature dropping to zero. All she had for heating, she wrote, was the electric radiator she had bought the previous year; it struggled to raise the temperature to between 7° and 10°C in her "kitchen-cell," where she was condemned to spend the whole winter. "Not surprisingly, my feet are already puffed up with chilblains."[10]

Other measures were soon announced which would make life even more difficult. In mid-November Liliane Jameson wrote that further reductions in the supply of gas and electricity had been introduced;[11] according to Jean Galtier-Boissière this was because British bombing raids over the German Ruhr region had resulted in French electricity being diverted to Germany.[12] Liliane Jameson also wrote of Métro stations being closed, lifts no longer working, factory output falling, and a ban on the installation of any new domestic electrical appliances. There had even been talk of cutting off the gas altogether.[13] The height of luxury, wrote César Fauxbras, was to be invited to somebody's home where there was a fire burning to listen to the BBC.[14]

In 1941 the Germans were doing all they could to ensure that Armistice Day on November 11 passed off without incident. Formal orders banned any public gathering or displays and it was strictly forbidden to lay flowers at the Arc de Triomphe.[15] The Germans were not taking any chances. But nor, apparently, were the Parisians. "We haven't yet heard of any incidents,"[16] Liliane Jameson wrote the following day. However, Micheline Bood recorded in her diary that somebody had carved "Avenge Us!" into a statue of Joan of Arc on the place Saint-Augustin, in the 18th arrondissement, and that a dozen policemen kept people away from the statue while a group of workers struggled to erase the slogan.[17]

By December getting around Paris had become much more difficult. The number of carriages on Métro trains was cut from five to four, sometimes three; the number of trains had also been drastically reduced; half the light bulbs in the trains and the station were missing; lifts and escalators were still not working. "Between 6 and 7 in the evening the Métro is hell," wrote Andrzej Bobkowski. He described a trip from the Porte d'Orléans: "Even by the time we reached Denfert-Rochereau [three stations away] the train was jam-packed. It was hard to breathe. At each station one group of people were propelled out of the door like a cork from a champagne bottle while another group tried to push its way on board. . . . Everyone was sweating. The carriage was stinking."[18] Travelling in these conditions frayed the passengers' nerves. When Bobkowski changed lines at Strasbourg-Saint-Denis station he found the corridors packed with people shouting and complaining. A woman with a child in her arms wanted to use the exit tunnel to reach the platform and thus avoid a long queue, but a Métro worker was having none of it. The people in the queue started shouting at him to let the woman through. "The crowd was ready to tear the Métro employee limb from limb. In the end a few men grabbed him and some women shouted 'Throw him onto the track!' The woman eventually went through, the crowd expressed its satisfaction, the Métro official was showered with insults."[19]

Travelling by bicycle was still the quickest, cheapest, and easiest way of getting around, but demand was so high that owners constantly worried their bikes would be stolen. At the end of December Bobkowski was pleased to see that specially designed bicycle shelters had sprung up in front of all the main administrative buildings and the big cafés. "A little old man gives you a ticket and you go on your way without worrying."[20] However, a couple of weeks later the tyres on Bobkowski's bicycle had completely worn through: there was almost no chance of finding any replacements, so he was forced to walk or go back to enduring the bad-tempered atmosphere in the Métro or in the bus, where he noted that everybody shouted at the ticket-collector.[21]

The face of the city had changed since the German authorities removed some eighty statues from across the city, which they allegedly melted down for the metal.[22] Jean Guéhenno saw a statue of the philosopher Jean-Jacques Rousseau being removed from the place du Panthéon;[23] Berthe Auroy mourned the loss of the composer Hector Berlioz from the square Vintimille and the disappearance of the early socialist Charles Fourier from the boulevard de Clichy;[24] Jacques Biélinky noted that a bronze statue of Théophraste Renaudot, the founder of *La Gazette de France*, the first Paris newspaper, no longer stood in front of the Palais de Justice opposite the Prefecture of Police building.[25]

A short spell of milder weather set in at the start of December, but then it turned bitterly cold again. Just before Christmas Jacques Biélinky wrote that his small supply of coal would run out in a few days and there was no point hoping for any more.[26] Berthe Auroy had to abandon her electric radiator as there was scarcely enough electricity in her building even to make the lights work. Over at her friend Hélène's, the central heating boiler, which had blown up the year before, had still not been repaired. Hélène's family was reduced to a single wood fire on the ground floor and for the first time in her life Hélène's hands were covered with chilblains.[27] Towards the end of January Micheline Bood was also complaining about the cold. It had dropped to minus 10°C but she willingly admitted that this was nothing compared to the Russian front, where she had been told it was minus 35°C.[28]

But however bad things were in Paris, they were as nothing compared to life for the 4,000 Jews packed into the camp at Drancy. For the first two months many of them had no change of clothing. They scraped any food they were given out of old tin cans left behind by former detainees. On October 1, when members of the Red Cross were finally granted access to the camp, they were met by prisoners demonstrating and demanding more food; the ringleaders were locked up in the cell block. Meanwhile readers of *Paris-Soir* and *Le Petit Parisien* were told that Drancy's Jewish prisoners lived in luxury, eating to their heart's content, while most Parisians struggled to survive, often with their loved ones held in German POW camps.[29]

In truth, some prisoners in the Drancy camp had lost more than 30 kilos since they had arrived. There had been a flu epidemic in October and there were already teenage prisoners who were pretubercular; there were more than 300 cases of men with TB and no effort was made to isolate them from their fellow prisoners.[30] Drancy itself was becoming life-threatening. Prisoners were starting to die of starvation and serious illnesses, some forty deaths recorded over ten days at the end of October and beginning of November.[31] It was virtually impossible to maintain any degree of personal hygiene. Noël Calef was held with about fifty other men in a dirty, noisy, smelly room, where arguments were always breaking out. He was tortured by hunger pangs, but the mere sight of the soup made him want to vomit.[32] The showers did not work and it was so cold it was impossible to wash all over; a third of the internees had succumbed to a diarrhoea epidemic.

At the beginning of November a doctor from the Prefecture of the Seine and two German army medical officers visited the camp, where they found hundreds of emaciated inmates so weak from starvation they could barely stand. Dannecker, the man ultimately responsible for the camp, was in Berlin getting married; taking advantage of his absence, the German military decided to release 1,500 internees, prioritised by Jewish detainees who were doctors. Nearly 400 inmates left Drancy on November 4 and another 550 the following day. However, on his return on November 12, Dannecker immediately "suspended" this release programme. On the day of Dannecker's return, Jacques Biélinky met some of those "skeletal beings" who had been freed who were almost too weak to stand.[33]

Two days later he wrote that seven people freed from Drancy had come to the Jewish hostel in the rue Lamarck, but they were all sick and were taken to hospital. Biélinky heard that conditions in the camp had improved slightly in that all prisoners had been given mattresses; the prisoners were now also allowed to receive food from outside. "So, they are no longer condemned to die of hunger."[34] After another devastating outbreak of diarrhoea a few more inmates were released on health grounds.

☞ Brustlein's assassination of a German officer in Nantes was supposed to take the pressure off Paris, where the French police were closing in on members of the Bataillons de la jeunesse. Ironically, it had the opposite effect: the French anti-terrorist units, the Brigades spéciales (Special Brigades), assumed, correctly, that those involved in the Nantes attack had gone to ground in Paris, and so this was where they continued to concentrate their anti-terrorist offensive. Those who carried out attacks on the Germans continued to feel socially and politically isolated. There was always the danger that those who were interrogated and tortured by members of the Special Brigades might give up the names and addresses of comrades still at large; this meant that anyone suspected of being associated with an armed attack ran the risk of being picked up by the French police at any moment.

The youngsters' situation was made even more precarious because the PCF had neither trained them in basic security measures before they started targeting German personnel and property nor offered them any protection afterwards.[35] At the same time, the Special Brigades of the Paris police were getting more proficient at tailing and then arresting suspects. By the end of November about half of the members of the Bataillons de la jeunesse were in custody, which largely explains the fall in the number of anti-German actions carried out in the Paris area between September 1941 and the end of November 1941.[36]

The assassination strategy of the Communists remained unpopular, even though most Parisians opposed the Occupation. Brustlein's mother later told the police that she was unaware of her son's part in the Nantes attack when he returned to Paris and told him that whoever had done it should have given himself up.[37] Even sabotage was frowned upon because of Germans reprisals against innocent hostages.

The young Communists might have been down, but they were not out. Those still at liberty were more determined than ever to show the Germans they could still mount a guerrilla offensive, hoping their actions would fool the Germans into thinking they had more members than was the case. The numbers involved in armed attacks had always been small, but now they were tiny. On average an armed Communist resister lasted just over seven months on "active service" before being arrested, and if the leaders were excluded, it fell to about five months.[38]

On November 21 seven militants attacked the Rive Gauche bookshop on the corner of the place de la Sorbonne and the boulevard Saint-Michel.[39] The building had previously housed the Café d'Harcourt, a favourite meeting place for students until the German authorities closed it down, shortly before the big demonstration of November 11, 1940. The bookshop was a favourite meeting place for collaborationist writers and journalists, such as Robert Brasillach, whose brother-in-law Maurice Bardèche was the shop's manager. The bookshop was nominally protected by the French police, but this did not stop Pierre Georges, who had assassinated Moser at Barbès, running towards it and throwing a bomb through its window. As the policeman on duty gave chase, Louis Coquillet, another Communist militant who had been waiting opposite the shop, raced across the boulevard Saint-Michel and threw a second bomb before being chased down the rue Racine. There was a brief exchange of fire but nobody was hit: the bomb did some damage to the bookshop, but not enough to keep it closed for long. After the attack the German military authorities decided to punish the Parisian population as a whole rather than execute selected hostages. The city was fined one million francs and the curfew was imposed an hour earlier. In early December Jean Galtier-Boissière, who ran his own bookshop close by, wrote that the Rive Gauche owners had told their staff that the bookshop received letters every day threatening to blow it up and any employees who wished to stop working were free to do so.[40]

On 28 November, a week to the day after the Rive Gauche bookshop attack, Communists threw two bombs into the Hôtel du Midi, a brothel in the rue Championnet in the 18th arrondissement. Three German soldiers and a French prostitute were killed; five soldiers and three women were injured.[41] This time the authorities decided to punish the local population.

All inhabitants in Montmartre (the 18th arrondissement) were or- dered to be off the streets from 6 P.M. and told to keep their doors and windows closed. One of them was Berthe Auroy, who learned of the directive by chance when talking to a neighbour. She returned home about 5:30 but was concerned for her sister, who had set off that after- noon to visit a friend on the other side of the city near the Buttes- Chaumont. As the 6 P.M. deadline approached there was still no sign of her. Berthe checked with her concierge and rang her sister's doorbell. No reply. She started to panic. It was nearly six o'clock and all the shops were already closed. Loudspeaker vans drove through the streets, telling people to go home and close their windows. Berthe had no choice but to return to her apartment. However, defying orders, she stayed at the window, hoping to spot her sister returning. "The last latecomers are running breathlessly down the street," she wrote. "The bell in the Sacré-Coeur basilica is sounding six o'clock. The street is totally de- serted. At 6:15 the great silence is broken by the sound of the heavy boots of our masters as they leave the Moulin de la Galette cabaret. But where is my sister?"[42]

Berthe later discovered that her sister, knowing nothing of the curfew, had emerged from the Métro station on the place Blanche at about 6:45 to find herself in a crowd of terrified people hemmed in by the police. She wanted to cross rue Lepic but was turned back like everybody else. Women in tears were pleading to be allowed to go and fetch their chil- dren, who were at home alone. A heavily pregnant woman told a French policeman she was about to give birth: the officer hesitated before let- ting her through, only to be given a severe telling-off by a German policeman for doing so. Berthe's sister decided to book into one of the nearby hotels, but they already had long queues outside them, so in the end she went back to her friend's home and spent the night there.[43] Berthe wrote of scuffles and arguments between the police and people who were prevented from returning home, of children having to depend on the kindness of neighbours, and of a woman near the place Blanche who had taken in fourteen women and children whom she had never seen before. From December 3 things returned to normal, but rumours circulated that some people had been shot for being out after the new curfew.

In early December, despite the arrests of Communist militants, anti-German activity continued. On December 2 a German captain was shot and wounded in the street in the 10th arrondissement.[44] In the 13th arrondissement a centre where staff sought to recruit volunteers to the LVF to fight on the Eastern Front was bombed.[45] The same sanctions were applied in these two arrondissements as in Montmartre and posters appeared warning that very severe measures would be taken against Parisians if the bombers were not found. Rumours promptly spread that the German authorities were planning to ban the sale of bread, cut off all electricity supplies, or place the city under a state of siege. In the event none of this happened.

On December 5, the day that a major in the Luftwaffe was shot,[46] Admiral François Bard, who had become prefect of the Paris police in May, broadcast on Radio-Paris asking the whole population of Paris to help "stop those following the orders of a foreign power being able to cause any harm."[47] His request was ignored. The following day, another German officer was shot and seriously wounded in the 17th arrondissement.[48] On December 7 a dynamite attack was launched at lunchtime on a junior officers' canteen.[49] In response, Otto von Stülpnagel decided it was time to punish the whole city.

The MBF decreed that from December 8 until further notice, all restaurants, cinemas, theatres, and other places of entertainment would close at 5 p.m.; all inhabitants of the Seine department were to stay indoors with their windows closed from 6 p.m. to 5 a.m. Anyone found breaking these rules would be severely punished and Germans soldiers would use their weapons if necessary.[50]

"It is now 6:30," wrote Jean Guéhenno on December 8, 1941. "I am watching the end of the day. Not a sound, not a whisper. This is Paris!"[51] On December 9 Jacques Biélinky observed that around 4 p.m. the Métro trains and stations were packed with people rushing to get home in time; by 5 p.m. most bakers had not a crumb of bread left and the shops and restaurants had abruptly closed; after 5 p.m. he saw police patrols on bicycles, guns on their backs, and the last stragglers leaving the Métro. At 6 p.m. the city was "plunged into a macabre silence"[52] or, as Berthe Auroy put it, "reduced to an enormous black and silent hole."[53]

However, not everybody objected to the new curfew: Micheline Bood and her schoolmates were thrilled to bits: "Until further notice, we have two hours fewer lessons. We leave school at a quarter-past four instead of quarter-past six."[54]

The Germans were determined to stamp out the attacks, which undermined their authority in the capital. Not only was it a matter of pride, but also battle-weary troops were sent on leave to Paris for rest and recuperation. It had to be safe. On December 8 Radio-Paris broadcast a chilling announcement. Since not a single perpetrator of the latest anti-German attacks had been arrested, Stülpnagel, the MBF, had personally ordered that one hundred Communist, Jewish, and anarchist hostages were to be taken out and shot. Furthermore, a fine of one billion francs was to be imposed on the Jews of Paris and a thousand Jews from the city would be deported.[55] Four days later, shortly before one hundred hostages were executed, a thousand Jews were rounded up.

This time the German military police and the secret police took the lead, helped by the Parisian police.[56] French and German police worked in pairs or in threes, arresting 743 men in their homes: nearly all of them were French Jews, mainly members of the social and political elite of the city. Those arrested were held at the École Militaire before being taken (along with 300 Jews who had been in Drancy since August) to a camp at Compiègne-Royallieu. This camp (sometimes referred to simply as Royallieu) lay just to the north of Paris near the forest of Compiègne where the 1918 and 1940 armistice agreements had been signed. The camp had been opened at the end of June for the internment of "active enemies of the Reich"[57] and its prisoners included Russians who had been resident in France, "communist agitators," trade unionists, and socialists. Unlike Drancy, which was managed by the French, the camp at Compiègne-Royallieu was managed directly by Germans and the guards were soldiers from the German army.

One of those arrested was the playwright Jean-Jacques Bernard. He watched as fellow prisoners who had been brutally taken from their homes gathered in twos and threes and calmly tried to work out why they had been arrested. "I have never seen so many Jews together," he wrote. "But with one or two exceptions, you could not discern a typical Jewish type."[58] The Germans wanted to start deporting Jews immediately, but this plan had to be postponed because of a shortage of trains.

It was not until March 27, 1942, that the first Jews were deported from France.[59] More details are given further on in this chapter.

On December 14, 1941, a German army detachment arrived at Drancy with a list of fifty inmates who were to be taken away and shot. They could find only forty-four of them: the others had either died or been released. The unfortunate forty-four were transferred to the Santé prison. They were given a last meal of sauerkraut before being taken to Mont-Valérien the following day and shot along with fifty-one others.[60] Unsurprisingly, executing hostages had the full support of the collaborationist newspapers: those who were shot were Jews, Communists, or anarchists, they wrote, so they were "not really French" anyway.[61]

Even before the latest mass execution of hostages, signs were growing that Parisians were becoming less hostile towards those involved in armed resistance. On December 8, for instance, Andrzej Bobkowski observed a degree of solidarity between the population and the perpetrators; people were even pleased about the repeated anti-German attacks.[62] A police report at the end of the month confirmed that the German tactics had backfired. It stated that the Communists were hoping to exploit to the full the Parisians' growing indignation at the executions and persuade them to identify with the armed actions and "avenge the innocent victims of German repression." The report concluded that Communist propaganda was likely to strike a chord among the population and, "given the disapproval and hostility that the repressive methods used by the German authorities is provoking, we should expect an upsurge in acts of terrorism."[63]

Responding to this shift in public opinion, in late December the PCF abandoned its policy of denying any involvement in the armed attacks against the Germans and finally acknowledged responsibility for actions against German property, equipment, and personnel. Through its clandestine newspaper *L'Humanité* the PCF now argued that it was the Germans who were the terrorists and the German tactic of executing innocent hostages legitimised anti-German attacks. After all, the occupying army had started executing innocent Parisians before the Communists had killed any Germans.

On New Year's Day 1942 Parisians listened to Pétain's New Year broadcast in which he complained that despite "this partial exile which has been forced upon me" and "the half-freedom which I have been allowed," he was continuing to do his duty.[64] He recognised the high levels of bitterness and apathy across the country, where people were living a wretched existence in their second winter since the armistice. He castigated the anti-Vichy collaborationists in Paris and the Gaullists in London, both of whom he described as "deserters," for using the press and the radio to undermine national unity. He also attacked the minority of black-market dealers and others who had made a fortune out of the suffering of the French population as a whole. Not only did Pétain's broadcast spare Germany any responsibility for France's plight, but Pétain also reiterated the view that France's salvation lay in ever closer rapprochement between the peoples and governments of the two nations.[65]

Jean Guéhenno described the speech as "a strange admission of powerlessness and a half-desperate plea to the French"; the Paris collaborationist "deserters," he wrote, were seething.[66] It was probably because of Pétain's attack on his Paris collaborationist opponents that not a word of the speech appeared in the city's press.

Parisians had more than enough preoccupations of their own without worrying about Pétain's troubles. The teenager Micheline Bood vowed that she would never allow a German boy to kiss her;[67] Paul Léautaud was desperately trying to lay his hands on some coal. Berthe Auroy turned her back bedroom into an allotment, where she grew carrots and parsnips in a strip of damp sand; she had potatoes germinating behind a big armchair and under a wardrobe near a bed of onions; she also had leeks "spread out in front of the fire-place like a present for Father Christmas."[68] Jacques Biélinky noted that there were no more queues outside the shops because the shops were all empty;[69] the Groult sisters were having family lunches in their mother's bedroom—the only room with a fire—wearing gloves converted into mittens, and balaclavas—and they were still so cold they were unable to think straight.[70] Jean Guéhenno wrote how hard it was to live without having at least one certainty on which he might pin his hopes; he found it intensely difficult to function in a sort of mental cloud of vague rumours, lies, misinformation, and foolish dreams.[71]

And yet, despite all this, there was a hint of optimism in the air among the opponents of the Occupation. "Will we see the end of the war this year?" wondered Andrzej Bobkowski on New Year's Day.[72] "The coming year is bound to be better than the old one," Jean Guéhenno wrote, "we are nearer the end."[73] Three weeks later, he was daring to write that the defeat of Germany was now a certainty.[74]

There were at least two reasons for this cautious optimism. First, Hitler's armies in Russia had failed to reach (let alone take) Moscow, and now they were having to confront not only the Red Army, but also, like Napoleon nearly a century and a half earlier, the terrible Russian winter. Second, it was no longer just Britain, the Soviet Union, and the Russian winter with which Hitler had to contend; after the Japanese attack on Pearl Harbor on December 7, the United States had officially entered the war.

The conflict had now gone truly global. For Americans living in Paris it had serious implications. Liliane Jameson's mother had married a U.S. citizen[75] and had to report to the German authorities. She and Liliane joined a motley crew of people—"Americans by accident" Liliane called them—who spoke perfect French with a true Parisian accent. There were also "proper Americans." She found them to be "pretty pathetic on the whole, very strong accent, big shoes, lipstick, wearing baggy check raincoats and munching peanuts to replace their beloved 'candies.'"[76] Liliane's mother was ordered not to leave the Seine department without permission and to report to the police every week.

But Benoîte Groult had little faith in an imminent American victory: "America will win," she wrote in her diary on Christmas Day, "but only when hens have teeth and when I don't have any left." On New Year's Eve she was unable to decide which year was the bleakest: the one just ended or the one ahead. "Never have we wished people a happy new year with less conviction," wrote Benoîte.[77]

Those with little reason to be optimistic about their own fates were Boris Vildé, Agnès Humbert, and the other members of the Musée de l'Homme group of resisters. They had been arrested almost a year earlier and their trial was scheduled to begin on January 8, 1942. While they had been in prison, armed resistance had begun, followed by mass executions: the whole atmosphere in which they were to be tried was very different from the relatively peaceful one that had prevailed when they were arrested. Their crimes were related to the distribution of leaflets and a newspaper, plus obtaining information about German troop movements and military installations.[78] Their actions may have been less flamboyant than the anti-German attacks that followed, but this courageous group still acted knowing they risked being shot as spies if they were caught.

Nineteen alleged members of the Musée de l'Homme group were assembled at Fresnes prison in the Val-de-Marne, just south of Paris.[79]
As they stood in front of their cells in a dimly lit corridor, Agnès Humbert was surprised to see how many of them there were, many of whom
she did not know at all. They were marched off by armed German soldiers to a purpose-built courtroom, complete with swastika flags, but
with, Agnès noticed with surprise, no portrait of Hitler.[80]

Four Germans were officiating: Captain Ernst Roskothen, the presiding judge, was "a tall, slim, young man who had an intelligent and
distinguished air about him;"[81] Captain Gottlob, the prosecutor, a Nazi
hack who became apoplectic with rage at the defendants' refusal to be
intimidated; and "two assessors, both of them old, fat and flabby, with
shaven heads and faces like pigs."[82] The defendants were all charged
with working for the enemy as part of a Gaullist conspiracy: they stood
accused of spying, spreading enemy propaganda, aiding escaped prisoners, and other miscellaneous illegalities.[83] They all faced the death
penalty. Roskothen attempted to run the trial by the book, consistently
treating the defendants and their lawyers with courtesy and civility.
Gottlob, on the other hand, ranted and sneered at them, insulting them
at every opportunity.

The trial effectively ended on February 14, when the defendants
heard Gottlob's summing-up: with typical theatricality he pulled his
dress sword out of its scabbard and slammed it down on the table to
emphasise a point. This performance was followed by the defence lawyers' pleas for clemency. Roskothen told the prisoners he would deliver
his verdicts in a few days. On February 17 a pale Roskothen appeared
in the courtroom. He had a difficult duty to carry out, he said, especially since he admired the prisoners he was about to condemn. Five
of the accused were acquitted; four received prison sentences: Agnès
Humbert was sentenced to serve five years in Germany. Ten others
were sentenced to death, including three women, Boris Vildé, Anatole
Lewitsky, René Sénéchal (the Kid), and Léon-Maurice Nordmann and
Pierre Walter.

After the sentences were announced, Vildé made a powerful but
unsuccessful plea for clemency for the Kid. Next he asked to shake the
presiding judge's hand, thanking him for his courtesy and consideration.
Roskothen then allowed the defendants some time alone together to say
their farewells. Roskothen was so affected by the trial that he headed
straight to the lavatory, where he vomited.[84]

The death sentences of the three women, of whom Yvonne Oddon was one, were commuted to deportation, but on Monday, February 23, 1942, the seven men who had been sentenced to death were driven along icy roads to Mont-Valérien, where they were executed by firing squad. Their bodies were then removed and buried in the cemetery at Ivry, in the southeastern suburbs of Paris. The following evening Jean Paulhan, the former editor of the *Nouvelle Revue française*, telephoned Jean Guéhenno: "It's all over, for our friends. It's all over. Since yesterday afternoon."[85]

By the time Vildé and his comrades were shot, Otto von Stülpnagel had resigned as the MBF and had been replaced by his cousin Carl-Heinrich von Stülpnagel. The "hostage policy" had caused serious tensions between the MBF and Berlin, with Berlin accusing Paris of being too "soft." While it is true that Stülpnagel protested at the high numbers of executions that Berlin was calling for, it should not be forgotten that he and he alone was responsible for the executions of ninety-five hostages on December 15, shot in reprisal for attacks carried out in Paris between November 28 and December 7.[86]

Any doubts Otto von Stülpnagel harboured about the mass executions were based on pragmatism rather than morality: he feared they would be counterproductive and might drive the French into the arms of Germany's enemies, thus wrecking the spirit of Franco-German collaboration he tried so hard to foster. However, he also claimed, shortly before his resignation—thus very late in the day—that he opposed the mass executions on moral grounds. Such protestations have to be nuanced by his advocacy in December 1941 of a policy of mass deportation. In February 1942 he wrote: "I believed it was possible to use other means to punish, as it was absolutely necessary to do, attacks on members of the Wehrmacht, namely by fewer executions but above all by mass deportations of Jews and Communists."[87]

Otto von Stülpnagel was wont to challenge Berlin directly over the policy of mass executions (when it suited him), but his cousin was less confrontational. Carl-Heinrich tended to agree with the number of hostage executions demanded by Berlin, although he usually failed to proceed with the second wave of executions supposed to take place if the perpetrators had not been caught. Official posters signed "von Stülpnagel" continued to appear all over Paris and few Parisians were aware that one MBF had been replaced by another with the same name. On

March 3, 1942, the moon was shining brightly over Paris as Captain Ernst Jünger of the Wehrmacht dined with a friend at Le Ramponneau, a chic restaurant on the avenue Marceau in the 16th arrondissement.[88] "After the meal," he wrote in his diary, "there was a dull sound outside which made me think of an explosion." It was followed by more rumbles. He concluded it was one of those springtime storms quite common in Paris. When Jünger's companion asked the waiter if it was already raining, the man replied with a discreet smile, "These gentlemen take that to be a storm; I'd say it's more likely to be bombs."[89] He was right: the Royal Air Force had just carried out its first bombing raid on Paris.

Roger Vabre lived on the first floor of a building opposite Workshop 26 of the Renault factory in the southwestern suburb of Boulogne-Billancourt. He and his wife were in the middle of their evening meal when they heard their concierge shout "This time it's our turn!" They quickly left their apartment, hoping to make it to the shelter on the other side of the road, but when they reached the ground floor, they realised it was impossible to leave the building. "Outside it was as bright as day and the sound of aircraft was getting louder and louder. By now everybody was piling into the cellar and the couple was swept along in the crowd."[90]

Two days after the armistice, the Renault car factory at Boulogne-Billancourt had been taken over by the Germans and placed under military guard. It became the responsibility of a German commissioner and his deputy, drafted in from the Mercedes offices in Paris.[91] By February 1941 around 16,000 workers were employed there and, as its contribution to the German war effort, Renault was planning to deliver some 13,000 trucks to the German army by the end of the year.

In June 1941 the British war cabinet had approved daytime bombing raids on factories in German-occupied countries in Europe, but raids on Paris were initially ruled out because of fears about civilian casualties. Since November 1941 the Air Ministry had been pressing to carry out nighttime raids and in February 1942 permission was finally granted. The first target selected was the Renault factory at Boulogne-Billancourt. The purpose of the raid was not just to strike a blow at the German war effort by disrupting vehicle production at the plant, but also to gauge the French reaction to Allied bombing raids on their country.[92]

On March 3, 235 bombers left Britain in three waves, the first of which reached the Renault works shortly after 9 P.M. The bombers combined the Gee technique—a new method of radio navigation—with the use of flares in an attempt to make bombing from medium altitudes more accurate.[93] The planes dropped more than 400 tons of bombs from between 2,000 and 4,000 feet. The British hailed the raid as a huge success and the technique was subsequently rolled out in raids over Germany. Almost all the planes claimed to have hit the factory buildings and only one plane, a Wellington flying in the third wave, was reported missing.

The RAF raid was heard or seen all over Paris. On the Left Bank in the 5th arrondissement the sound of the bombing was so loud it made Jacques Biélinky's windows rattle;[94] Andrzej Bobkowski, at home in the southern suburb of Montrouge—and much closer to the Renault works—went up to the top floor to watch what was happening. The whole of the west of Paris was lit up and he watched as the flares dropped from the planes burst into life; they looked like stars as they hung in the sky for a long time.[95] In Montmartre, in the north of the city, Berthe Auroy, like Jünger, had at first taken the rumbling noise to be thunder, but when she looked out of her window she could see, in the beautiful moonlight, "fireballs miraculously suspended in the air."[96] It gradually dawned on her that, despite no alert having been sounded, it was indeed an Allied bombing raid. Soon people were at their windows or out in the street, while others, including Berthe, went up to the Sacré-Coeur basilica, just as they used to do before the war to watch firework displays.

As Jünger and his companion left their restaurant they heard some anti-aircraft fire; as did Jean Galtier-Boissière, who was leaving another restaurant near the Opéra at about the same time. When Galtier-Boissière reached the pont Neuf, it was full of people who were watching the bombing over in the west. He, like Berthe, was reminded of crowds watching firework displays, specifically those held on Bastille Day before the war.[97]

On the night of the raid the Germans had failed to sound any air-raid alert and many of the inhabitants of Boulogne-Billancourt and the surrounding areas were literally caught napping. The Allied bomber crews had been ordered to keep their bombs on board rather than release them over residential areas and, according to one Canadian pilot, it was so bright you were unlikely to make a mistake.[98] This breezy complacent confidence was at odds with an official British evaluation of the risks, which concluded that civilian casualties were inevitable. Bombing was notoriously inaccurate and in September 1941 a report on British bombing raids over Germany (admittedly from higher altitudes than during the Renault raid and with pilots contending with anti-aircraft fire) found that *only 15 percent* of aircraft were bombing within *five miles* of their targets.[99] In the Renault raid, bombs rained down not just on their target, but also on workers' houses nearby. Nearly 400 civilians were killed and nearly 600 were seriously injured. In all, more than 200 homes were destroyed; these included some buildings near the factory, which, although they did not take a direct hit, were blown away in the bomb blasts. The casualties were twice as high as those inflicted thus far in the war on any one night of bombing over Germany.[100]

The morning after the raid Admiral François Darlan, the French prime minister, paid a brief visit to Boulogne-Billancourt. He then sped back to Vichy, where a government statement in Pétain's name was issued denouncing "these cowardly killings," which, it said, would provoke "general outrage." The Paris authorities and the collaborationist press made every effort to wring as much propaganda advantage from the raid as they could. There followed a violent anti-British campaign, which focused exclusively on the civilian deaths and the destruction of people's homes but failed to mention any damage to the Renault factories. A communiqué from the Prefecture of Police in Paris published in the newspapers on March 4 referred to "cowardly aggression by the RAF." Having failed to hit German ships in Brest and in the Channel, it said, the RAF had decided to target civilian districts of Paris instead.[101] The following day the raid was front-page news in the collaborationist press under lurid headlines: "British planes massacre civilians in Paris suburbs" *(L'Œuvre);* "Churchill organises bombing of Paris" *(Paris-Soir);* "Odious British aggression: more than 1,700 French victims" *(Le Cri du Peuple);* "I saw British massacre Parisians" *(Paris-Midi).*[102] *Le Petit Parisien* called the raid "Another of Churchill's crimes" and gave it front-page coverage over five days. In the evening Vichy's representative in Paris, Fernand de Brinon, took to the airwaves on Radio-Paris to offer his own idiosyncratic analysis of the attack. Describing the British government led by Churchill as "Communistic" *(bolchevisant),* he accused it of resorting to "weapons of despair" and of responding to Stalin's call to arms by striking at random. "It was those French families referred to in Communist propaganda as 'proletarian families' who were the main victims."[103] German-produced posters proclaiming ASSASSINS in huge letters appeared across the city, and wounded survivors of the raid were featured on Radio-Paris but, according to Berthe Auroy, the interviewers were not able to get much out of them to help the German campaign.[104]

The press outrage continued over the next few days. One newspaper article resurrected an old stand-by of anti-British propaganda: because Britain had experienced stunning failures in all theatres of war, it said, "the City of London coldly organised the large-scale massacre of peaceful French people."[105] France was not at war with Britain, but this did not stop some papers calling for retaliation through a counterattack. The newspaper *Les Nouveaux Temps* trumpeted that "France attacked by Britain must defend herself against Britain and take her revenge against Britain."[106] Marcel Déat's newspaper *L'Œuvre* suggested rounding up all the British spies who were allegedly at large in the Unoccupied Zone.[107]

Pétain and his entourage tried to use the bombing to boost Pétain's prestige by stressing Pétain's denunciation of Britain and his solidarity with the victims. On Saturday, March 7, in the areas where the bombs landed, Joseph Barthélemy, the French minister of justice, and Jérôme Carcopino, the minister of education, each read out a message from Pétain. It referred in passing to an act of "criminal aggression by a former ally," but dwelled mainly on a graphic and probably accurate description of the human and material devastation: "Streets blown apart, areas flattened, families decimated, babies thrown from their cradles into their tombs, pathetic human remains pulled from the ruins in suffocating smoke."[108]

Vichy designated Sunday, March 8 as a day of national mourning, but Paris saw two competing events to commemorate the victims: Vichy and the Germans each wanted to promote their own response to the raid. The main Vichy-sponsored memorial was a Mass for the victims in Notre-Dame Cathedral, after which Cardinal Suhard, the archbishop of Paris, gave a brief address saluting "the sacrifices of our dead."[109] Meanwhile, further down the Seine on the place de la Concorde, the German propaganda organisations, with the active involvement of Goebbels, were organising their own ceremony. The Germans constructed a huge temporary cenotaph draped in black on the square, scornfully described by Bobkowski as "a joke in bad taste."[110] Pétain tried to veto the German-sponsored event, but as was usual in his dealings with the Germans, he came out second best.

According to the organisers of the German event, tens of thousands of Parisians responded to the call to file past the cenotaph and pay their respects to the people killed in the raid. Among those attending were the leaders and members of the main Paris collaborationist organisations, who turned out in force to march past, notably the PPF (without Jacques Doriot, who was on the Eastern Front), Deloncle's MSR, and Déat's RNP.

Following the raid, Allied planes dropped thousands of leaflets over Paris and the suburbs where the bombs had landed. One leaflet saluted the efforts of French workers to undermine the German war effort and presented the bombing raids as vital to that struggle. Another leaflet was headed: "The Renault factories are working for the Germans. The Renault factories have been hit"; it reproduced aerial photographs of the damage and underscored the importance of Renault's truck production for the German army. The text also asserted that only victory over Nazi Germany would bring "a measure of consolation" to the French families and workers who had died.[111]

The Germans retaliated by distributing their own propaganda leaflets, mimicking those dropped by the RAF but highlighting the civilian deaths and injuries and the devastation of residential areas to denounce the British action.[112] A number of leading pro-Nazi Parisian intellectuals published an open letter protesting that the bombing flew in the face of the claim that Britain could and would come to France's aid;[113] for his part, the fascist Lucien Rebatet accused the RAF of cynically "killing Parisians in cold blood."[114] Jacques Doriot's PPF produced a leaflet that said "ENOUGH! . . . Assassins! The British are being beaten in Europe, Asia, Africa, America, Australia, everywhere, but are victorious in the Paris region." The PPF ensured it played a leading role setting up and running a Workers' Committee for Immediate Assistance (COSI), created immediately after the raid, which it used to maintain Doriot's and the PPF's high profile among collaborationists in the city. Fernand de Brinon, Vichy's representative in Paris, was made honorary president of COSI. Carl von Stülpnagel, the new MBF, who had been asked to keep a low profile, authorized the allocation of one hundred million francs to those whose homes had been damaged or destroyed during. The press carried a photo of de Brinon accepting a cheque for this sum: the money came from the billion-franc fine that had been earlier imposed on the Jews of Paris.[115]

Despite the casualties, the damage to homes, the blood-curdling media coverage, and the anti-British propaganda, Parisians appear to have largely supported the raid. Medical student Bernard Pierquin, who visited Boulogne-Billancourt in the aftermath of the bombing, described being very pleased at the sight of dozens of burnt-out tanks all along the avenue de Sèvres and of Germans rummaging about in the debris.[116] He also discovered that the locals were not fooled by German and collaborationist propaganda; the anger of those living nearby was directed not at the British, who they thought did their best to hit only the Renault factories, but at the Germans, who they believed deliberately chose not to activate the air-raid sirens, thus leaving the population open to being killed in large numbers.[117]

Liliane Jameson, a supporter of de Gaulle, referred to an impressive press onslaught with articles, photos, and posters all aimed at castigating the raid as a British crime. She wrote that, according to the newspapers, the one and only reason the British had come to Paris was to bomb the civilian population, the wives and children of their former ally. "And to cap it all ... no newspaper mentioned a single military target that was hit."[118] But she made the point that the coverage by the collaborationist press was so crude and Parisians were so aware of the RAF's actual target, the anti-British propaganda failed to have its intended results. "'It's war, what do you expect.' Such was the sensible conclusion most French people came to," Liliane wrote.[119] This view was echoed by Bobkowski writing the day after the raid, when the death toll was feared to be higher than it later proved to be: "Generally speaking, people are satisfied, and even if people are talking about 2,000 dead, they approve of this action."[120] Berthe Auroy concurred and wrote that the raid had done nothing to change the opinion of the Parisians. Most people seemed resigned about the casualties and few blamed the British. However, she noticed that terrified inhabitants of the working-class suburbs, fearing more air raids, were starting to leave and that the schools were emptying.[121] Galtier-Boissière commented on the hypocrisy of the press outcry about Anglo-Saxon barbarism. "As if the Germans had never bombed civilians. What about the 30,000 killed in Rotterdam and the columns of civilians who came under [German] machine gun fire during the exodus [of 1940]?"[122]

☞ ON MARCH 1, 1942, a German sentry was shot dead outside a Wehrmacht billet.[123] Three days later, which was the day after the Renault bombing raid, General Schaumburg, the German commandant of Greater Paris, announced that twenty Jews and Communists would be executed and a further twenty shot if those who killed the soldier were not found by March 16. In addition, all theatres, cinemas, and other places of entertainment would be closed on March 4, the day of the sentry's funeral. March 4 was also the day when the Palais Bourbon, former home of the Chamber of Deputies, the lower house of the French parliament, was turned into a courthouse.[124] On July 19, 1940, it had served as an auditorium, when German dignitaries in Paris gathered to hear the transmission of a speech by Hitler. Now, to coincide with a giant anticommunist exhibition that opened three days earlier in the Salle Wagram, the Chamber of Deputies was set to be the stage for a three-day trial of seven youngsters from the Bataillons de la jeunesse. The defendants had been arrested in Paris by French police officers, who, in accordance with a German ruling, had handed them over to the German military authorities.[125] The defendants were accused of having carried out seventeen attacks on German soldiers and military equipment between August and October 1941. Only one of the seven was aged over twenty and all but one lived in the 11th arrondissement. The defendants included Christian Rizo, who had been in Nantes with Brustlein when Hotz was assassinated, and Tony Bloncourt, who had taken part in a number of actions, including the attack on the Rive Gauche bookshop.[126]

The trial of the Musée de l'Homme group in January had been given little press coverage. This time, however, the German military authorities wanted as much publicity as possible. They paraded some of these Communist "terrorists" in front of the press, using every opportunity to highlight that two of them were Jewish.[127] The first day of the trial was taken up with personal details of the accused, none of whom had a criminal record, and a description of the methods, weapons, and materials they had used in the actions. The second day was given over to the attacks themselves. The confessions of the accused were then read out: none denied the charges. The verdict was a forgone conclusion: all were found guilty and sentenced to be executed by firing squad at Mont-Valérien. Each defendant was allowed to write a letter to loved ones. They expressed their pride in dying as men of France for their country, their only regret being the pain and distress they knew their death would cause their nearest and dearest. They were shot on March 9. Only five execution posts were available to which the prisoners could be tied; thus, two of them, Roger Hanlet and Robert Peltier, had to watch their comrades being shot before meeting the same fate.[128]

Death by firing squad was not the only punishment meted out to enemies of the Reich. On March 27, 1942, buses requisitioned by the French police brought a group of 565 male Jewish internees, their heads recently shaved, from the camp at Drancy to the nearby railway station of Le Bourget-Drancy, where they were bundled into a waiting train. Each man was allowed to take a small suitcase or knapsack, a blanket, a tin dish, a spoon, and a set of clothes. Their first stop was Compiègne, where another group of Jews from the nearby camp of Royallieu, including French Jews arrested in the roundup in December 1941, was forced onto the train, along with thirty-four Yugoslav Jews. Dannecker accompanied them to their destination. This, the first convoy of Jews deported from France totalled 1,112 men: they were of-ficially being deported as a reprisal for Communist attacks on German property and personnel.[129] The prisoners knew neither their destina-tion nor what awaited them on arrival; they were sent to a camp in a small Polish town near Cracow named Oświęcim or, as the Germans called it, Auschwitz. Only twenty-three deportees survived to return to France.

While the deportees were making their fateful journey eastwards, cinema audiences in Paris were watching newsreel footage of a small group of celebrities who had left Paris on March 18 on a very different sort of train journey. Four of France's favourite female screen stars posed, pouted, and fluttered their eyelashes at the cameras before they set off with actor Albert Préjean on a goodwill visit to Austria and Germany.[130]

☞ CONTINUING FOOD SHORTAGES left more and more people with no option but to trade illegally. By the summer of 1941 Parisians were making a clear distinction between the black market—a large-scale, profit-driven professional operation—and what was being called "the grey market" *(le marché gris):* the huge number of small-scale transactions often carried out between people who knew each other. The grey market was widely accepted as a necessary part of life. However, even if Parisians made a distinction between the two, the law did not.

"From mid-1941," in the words of the Dominican priest Raymond Bruckberger, a future member of the Resistance and close friend of Albert Camus, "a whole nation stepped outside the law."[131] Whereas previously a relatively small number of Parisians had gone to the countryside in search of food, now hordes of them left the city to buy produce directly from farmers without using their ration tickets. Very few of these small-scale operators had a car, petrol, or a driving permit, so most of them travelled by train. The most popular routes were Paris-Orléans, Paris-Chartres, and Paris-Rouen; some trains were nicknamed after the produce most likely to be brought back to Paris, so there was the Bean Train and the Spud Train. According to the author Alfred Fabre-Luce, it was better to pay a lot and buy direct from a farmer rather than pay a crazy price to a middleman. He envisaged a more egalitarian black market: "Our aim is not so much to do away with the black market as to make it more democratic."[132]

Parisians returning from their sprees in the country risked being searched and having their haul confiscated: the total weight of the produce seized from searches of a single train could run into hundreds of kilos. However, these checks did not deter Parisians from taking food trips; they calculated there was a fairly good chance of not being stopped and searched because the police simply did not have the manpower (or, hopefully, the motivation) to search every carriage and every passenger. Even if one were stopped, there was always a possibility the policeman would be sympathetic and would take no further action when he saw how little food one was carrying; or he might be open to a bribe (money or food) to turn a blind eye. To minimise the risk of getting stopped at a mainline station, Parisians often alighted from the train at small suburban stations and made their way home by foot or on bicycle, often under cover of darkness, even though this might mean being out after curfew.

However, enough people were still being caught by the police to generate a wave of resentment among the population. Why should people buying and selling on the "grey market" be prosecuted and punished? they asked. Especially now that family food parcels were legal. Shortly before Christmas in 1941, Cardinal Suhard, the archbishop of Paris, pleaded with the authorities to ignore small illegal transactions on the grey market because of their relative unimportance to the overall economy and because people relied on them to obtain the basic necessities of life.[133]

To many angry Parisians it looked as if only "the little people" were being targeted. A January 1942 police report noted many complaints that inspectors were picking on the small fry while letting the real black-market racketeers operate with impunity.[134] In an attempt to win readers and as a stick with which to beat Vichy, the collaborationist press stressed how important the grey market was for ordinary Parisians struggling to get by. At the end of January, *Paris-Midi* claimed that searching parcels brought back from the country often took the form of bullying and suggested that inspectors would be better employed trying to catch the big operators.[135] In February, an article in *Le Temps* argued that the small-scale illegal transactions of the grey market were completely different from the big black-market operations: "Leave the poor city dwellers—who all too often cannot find enough of what they want on the open market—free to buy what they can, as best they can, in their own way."[136]

The French government in Vichy eventually decided it needed to do something and perhaps win back some of the popularity it had lost over time, largely through its failure to secure adequate food stocks or establish an equitable system of distribution. On March 15 it finally succumbed to public pressure and passed a law differentiating between three types of black-market dealing: large-scale black-market dealing driven by profit, fraudulent activities carried out by producers and traders, and "unlawful acts committed to meet personal or family needs." Even so, unless things improved on the Eastern Front, Berlin would almost certainly soon be making even more demands on French resources. This meant things could only get worse for the people of Paris.

10

SS Seizure of Security, the Yellow Star, the Vél'd'Hiv' Roundup, La Relève

$\mathcal{B}$RITISH PLANES have flown over Paris almost every night for the past fortnight, wrote Jean Guéhenno in his diary on April 9, 1942.[1] The bombers had been targeting factories in the north and eastern suburbs, including the Matford and Ford truck plants at Poissy,[2] but casualties were nowhere near as high as during the raid on Renault.[3] The RAF made two unsuccessful attempts at bombing the Gnome and Rhône aircraft engine factories at Gennevilliers, during which the nearby suburb of Colombes was hit. Civilian casualties were incurred and homes were destroyed but, again, not on the scale of the Renault raid.[4] A schoolmate of Micheline Bood's, whose friend had seen the wreckage of a bomber that had been shot down, insisted on passing on a gruesome description of the body of one of the four Wellington crew-members who had perished.[5]

Micheline Bood was due to take a physical education test[6] in Colombes the day after the raid when the suburb was hit. When she arrived in Colombes, she heard that the test had been cancelled because bombs had hit the stadium where it was to take place. Keen to see the damage, Micheline ran to the stadium and found two enormous craters, fires still ablaze and smoke everywhere. There were also apparently twelve unexploded bombs. Wandering around the town before catching her train home, she felt indifferent about what she saw, and experienced no real sense of connection with the locals. What most upset her was that two British planes had been brought down.[7]

Despite the casualties of the latest bombing raids, many Parisians—especially those living away from where the bombs fell—felt the attacks were somewhat unreal. They even regarded them as free entertainment. According to Jean Guéhenno, people no longer scurried for the shelters when they heard the air-raid sirens. Instead, they opened the curtains and watched the fireworks display from their beds. "Unfortunately," he added ruefully, "our house is too low down and I can see only the reflection in the sky of the exploding bombs."[8]

Berthe Auroy, who lived closer to the bombers' targets, seemed more bothered by the noise and the lack of sleep it produced than anything else. She was prepared for an emergency, staying in bed with a bag containing all her precious things, plus a fur coat she could slip on quickly, kept at the ready in case a fire broke out or the house was in danger of collapsing. But, she added, "They've set up an anti-aircraft battery on the hill which makes a real racket whenever a plane drones overhead. God! What an infernal din there is then. Windows and doors shake. I just bury myself further under my bedclothes. . . . My neighbours upstairs sometimes hear pieces of metal falling on the roof. But in the end you get used to anything. I try and grab a nap between two waves of planes going over and sometimes I manage it."[9]

☞ ON APRIL 7, 1942, in a blaze of publicity, a second trial opened of more Communist resisters, this time at the Maison de la Chimie, established in 1934 to promote research in chemistry.[10] Of the twenty-seven Parisians in the dock, who were charged with attacks against German personnel and property, over half were under the age of twenty-five.[11] One was a twenty-three-year-old fine-leather craftsman named Georges Tondelier. He had been a Communist activist since the age of fourteen and had taken part in more than a dozen actions, including the bomb attack on the Rive Gauche bookshop in November. After his arrest he betrayed his comrades, hoping his life would be spared. At the end of the trial, four of the accused, including the youngest, fifteen-year-old André Kirschen, were deported to Germany;[12] the rest, including Tondelier, were sentenced to death. On April 17 all of them—except Tondelier—were taken to Mont-Valérien to face a firing squad. Franz Stock, the German chaplain at the Santé prison, was present and he later testified that the Communists, about to die, raised their clenched fists and, before the shots rang out, filled the air with cries of "Long live freedom!" "Long live the USSR!" "Long live a strong and free France!"[13] As at the earlier Bataillons de la jeunesse trial, the condemned were allowed to write farewell letters to their loved ones. Twenty-one-year-old Louis Coquillet, a French railway worker and volunteer fireman, whose many armed anti-German actions also included the attack on the Rive Gauche bookshop, wrote to his girlfriend, telling her he had no regrets.

> Don't let despair take over, my dear one, but be strong and proud of me. I played, I lost, I'm paying the price. . . . I will nonetheless have the consolation before dying of knowing that I didn't give my life for nothing and that I worked for the happiness of all those dear to me. . . . I want you to use all your willpower to drive me out of your mind so that my death becomes a normal death, a memory that fades over time. You have your whole life in front of you, a life full of promise and happiness, as long as it's not spoiled by you always thinking about me. I think you know what I mean. My greatest happiness before dying would be to know for certain that you will meet a man with whom you will rebuild your life and who will be as faithful to you and as keen to make you happy as I was.[14]

The traitor Tondelier remained in the Santé prison, ostracised by his fellow inmates because of his treachery. But he did not have to contemplate his betrayal of his comrades for long; despite having assisted the Germans so diligently, a couple of months later, on June 11, the Germans shot him too.

The trial of what the newspaper *Au Pilori* called "a miserable herd of delinquents, degenerates, monsters . . . soldiers of Communism in the pay of the Jews," was supposed to act as a deterrent. But just after it ended another anti-German demonstration took place, this time at the Lycée Buffon, a boys' secondary school in the 15th arrondissement.[15] On April 16, their first day back at school after the Easter holidays, a small group of pupils protested at the arrest of one of their teachers, Raymond Burgard, the founder of Valmy, one of the earliest underground Resistance networks and newspapers (see Chapter 7).[16] Five of his pupils were so outraged when the police stormed into the school to quell the protest that they decided to go underground and commit themselves to the armed struggle against the German occupying forces.[17] During the next few weeks, until they were captured, they participated in attacks against German-occupied buildings and German soldiers; they also acted as a protection squad at a Communist-led demonstration in the rue de Buci.[18]

For months the Communists had staged meetings in street markets, hammering home the message that the shortages were caused by the occupying forces requisitioning vast quantities of food, clothing, and fuel. The Communists knew that demonstrating, haranguing crowds, or distributing leaflets in broad daylight was riskier than ever, and that anyone caught doing this would almost certainly be shot. However, they refused to cede public space to the occupiers and their French accomplices; instead, they planned a spectacular outdoor gathering to boost the morale of PCF members and supporters and to show that the Communists would not be cowed. So as to ensure a good crowd would be on hand to hear what they had to say, they decided to stage their demonstration outside the Eco foodshop in the rue de Buci on May 31, just when a consignment of tinned sardines was due to go on sale there. Fish was by now so rare it was a luxury and the Communists knew that news of the sale would attract a large crowd of shoppers.[19]

Madeleine Marzin, a seasoned thirty-three-year-old Communist militant from the 15th arrondissement was given the task of organising the demonstration and addressing the crowd. Because this was so dangerous, she would be covered by two armed protection groups, one of which included four of the pupils from the Lycée Buffon.[20] Communist militants mingled with the crowds inside and outside the shop. At about 10:15 A.M., Madeleine and another comrade, Marguerite Bonner, grabbed handfuls of tins and tossed them into the crowd of waiting shoppers. Other militants began shouting anti-German and anti-Vichy slogans and throwing around leaflets. All hell broke loose. Eco employees tried to detain Madeleine and Marguerite, while the first protection group rushed forward to free them. Someone in the shop alerted the nearby police station and soon the *flics* arrived. The lads from the Lycée Buffon were briefly overpowered, but they managed to escape. Members of the second protection group opened fire, trying to stop any additional arrests, shooting dead two French policemen and injuring another.

This second protection group was then also overpowered and its members arrested. Marguerite lost her bag in the melee, providing the police with an easy trace and thus leading to her arrest the following day. In all, nineteen militants, including Madeleine, were taken into custody. Because of the deaths of the French policemen, the demonstration was classified "a terrorist attack" and Madeleine and three militants from her protection group were sentenced to death. Following Pétain's intervention, Madeleine's sentence was reduced to life imprisonment. Her companion (and later husband) was given twenty years' hard labour; other women who had been arrested received a sentence of five years each.[21]

A few days later the five Lycée Buffon students were denounced to the police and four were arrested. The youngest, seventeen-year-old Pierre Benoît, managed to remain on the run until August 28 when he was picked up by the police and sent to join his comrades in prison.[22] In October all five were hauled before a special Luftwaffe tribunal, which condemned them to death and ordered their transfer to the Santé prison. On February 8, 1943, they were all executed by firing squad on a rifle range in the south of the city and were buried in the cemetery at Ivry.

☞ FOR MONTHS, OTTO ABETZ, the German ambassador in Paris, had been manoeuvring to bring Pierre Laval back to power. By the spring, Admiral Darlan, the French prime minister, had lost the confidence of the Germans, and so, on April 18, 1942, under German pressure, Pétain sacked Darlan and brought back Pierre Laval. The darling of the Germans was back, now formally nominated by Pétain as head of the government *(le chef du gouvernement)* with responsibility for domestic and foreign policies.[23] However, the public's attitude towards Laval had not changed: he was still generally loathed and despised. BBC broadcasts from London greeted his return with the ditty "Laval, Laval, Laval who just loves the Boche, Laval, Laval, Laval who just loves the dosh."[24] Berthe Auroy spoke for many when she described him as "the most loathed and detested man in the whole of France, who's been imposed on us by the Germans."[25] The mere sight of his photo in a newspaper made her feel like vomiting.

As well as the changes at the top of the French government, important developments were underway in Paris concerning the German security services, although the details were not known by most Parisians.

Ever since June 1940 when Heinrich Himmler, the head of the SS, had used Helmut Knochen to establish a bridgehead in Paris, the various agencies of the German secret police that included the Gestapo, had been looking for ways to undermine the army's power and assume responsibility for all matters relating to security. When Himmler learned of Otto von Stülpnagel's resignation as MBF in February, he requested a meeting with Hitler and persuaded the Führer to transfer responsibility for security-related matters in France from the army to the SS by appointing an individual as supreme SS and head of police (HSSuPF) for occupied France.[26]

The HSSuPF would be based in Paris and would report directly to Himmler. This dramatic development meant that the Nazi Party (NSDAP), through its own security service, namely, the SS, was now responsible for all issues related to policing, security, and "racial preservation" in occupied France.

Himmler's head of police and security arrived in Paris in May. He was forty-five-year-old Carl Oberg, a chubby former fruit importer. Oberg wore Himmleresque wire-rimmed spectacles and was a long-standing admirer of Hitler. He had joined the Nazi Party in 1931; the following year he joined the SS, the party's paramilitary organisation whose members swore a personal oath of loyalty to Hitler. Oberg had then shot up through its ranks after the Nazis' accession to power in 1933. He had a justified reputation for savage brutality from his posting as an SS chief in Poland, where he oversaw programmes of extermination of Jews and the forced conscription of Polish workers in the part of the country under his control. His lack of French, and especially a lack of local knowledge, meant that he was dependent on the man who had headed the secret police since June 1940 and who now became his deputy, Helmut Knochen.

Oberg set up his own headquarters on the boulevard Lannes, a broad avenue running along the eastern edge of the Bois de Boulogne, and even before June 1, when his appointment officially took effect, he began dismantling the directorate of the army's secret police force (GFP). He placed himself firmly at the head of the German secret security forces in Paris, which had grown both in size and in importance since the start of the Occupation. He further marginalised the army by ensuring it was he—and not the MBF—who reported to Berlin on developments in France. This allowed him to put a positive spin on what his men were doing and to minimise the army's contribution.

In case the German army in Paris failed to get the message about who was now in charge of security matters, Reinhard Heydrich, Himmler's right-hand man and one of Hitler's most loyal henchmen, endorsed Oberg's appointment on a visit to Paris in early May. A fortnight later Heydrich was targeted in Prague by two members of the Czechoslovakian Resistance and died of wounds sustained in the attack.[27]

In 1941 the Vichy government passed a law creating a centralized police force but the Paris police was exempted and continued to enjoy a certain autonomy and close cooperation with the German security forces in the capital.[28] From the autumn of 1941 there were regular meetings between the German police, the prefect of police, and the head of the Renseignements géneraux; a German police officer was based permanently in the Prefecture of police and senior members of the RG met with the heads of the German secret police (Sipo-SD) every Wednesday at the German police headquarters in the rue de Saussaies.[29]

Heydrich and Oberg both wanted to strengthen French and German cooperation on security matters, especially concerning the resolution of the "Jewish problem." On May 5 they held a meeting at the Ritz Hotel in Paris with René Bousquet, whom Laval had recently appointed to head the police force created by Vichy a year earlier and through whom Laval intended to tighten his grip on the French forces of repression. The trio were joined at this meeting by Fernand de Brinon, Laval's old confidant and Vichy's official representative in Paris, and Louis Darquier. Darquier—or Louis Darquier de Pellepoix, as he pompously liked to call himself—was a notorious anti-Semite who had just replaced Xavier Vallat as head of the Commissariat général aux questions juives (CGQJ), the German-backed but French-run organisation for coordinating Jewish policy in the two zones. Darquier's savage hatred of all Jews was much more to the taste of Dannecker, Abetz, and Oberg, the key players in Paris dealing with the "Jewish problem," than Xavier Vallat's anti-Semitism, which was inspired by Christianity, one that differentiated between French and foreign Jews.[30] Hard-liners, of course, thought this attitude was far too wishy-washy.

Heydrich had not visited Paris just to show his support for Oberg: he also gave him feedback from an ultrasecret meeting he had called in the Berlin suburb of Wannsee in January.[31] At this meeting, targets had been set for the number of Jews to be rounded up and deported from all the Nazi-occupied countries of Europe, as well as other countries

as yet unconquered by Germany. After the Wannsee meeting, Heydrich
had instructed Adolf Eichmann to "clean up the record" and the word
"extermination" does not appear in the formal minutes; instead phrases
such as "deportation to the east," "expulsion," and "resettlement" are
used. However, those who attended were left in no doubt whatsoever
that the plan called for the mass extermination of Europe's Jews. At his
trial in Israel in 1962, Eichmann admitted that at the end of the meeting,
as tongues were loosened by cognac, the participants had spoken openly
of "killing," "liquidation," and "extermination," and at about the same
time as this meeting, Hitler had publicly demanded that the Jews be
"annihilated."[32]

Addressing the "Jewish problem" in France lay at the heart of Oberg's
responsibilities, and the shortage of German police available meant he
needed French cooperation. Cooperation between the French police
and the German authorities had formed part of the June 1940 armistice agreement. Now Oberg was particularly keen to strike a deal with
Bousquet since formally securing cooperation of the French would
implicate them in events. At the meeting at the Ritz, according to de
Brinon, Heydrich was glad to see how committed Bousquet was to close
collaboration with the German security forces. He agreed to Bousquet's
request that while the French police should work closely with the
German authorities they should continue to appear to be independent.
The German authorities had been pleased with the measures the French
government had already taken, unprompted by the Germans, against
the Jews in Paris and the rest of the Occupied Zone. However, Vichy's
tackling of the "Jewish problem" was too haphazard and amateurish for
the likes of Abetz, Oberg, Knochen, Darquier, Dannecker, and their
minions. The Wannsee conference had given them targets for the
number of Jews to be deported. Now they had to meet them.

In Paris, as in the rest of the Occupied Zone, Jews had already been
economically isolated: their businesses had been taken away from them;
they had been driven out of state employment. Quotas had been introduced to limit the number of Jews allowed to enrol in the liberal professions or as university students, and some had already been rounded
up and deported. Now, with Himmler's SS in charge of Jewish policy
in Paris, the time had come to marginalise all the Jews socially, to identify them as the pariahs the Nazis believed them to be. The plan was
to convince non-Jewish Parisians that the city's Jews were not a part

of Paris, but were to be kept apart *from* it. Once the Jews had been socially and economically marginalised, they would be removed altogether.

The initiative was driven by Dannecker, Oberg, and Abetz, but it was the MBF that obediently announced the momentous news that would apply to the whole of the Occupied Zone. As from Sunday, June 7, 1942, all Jews aged over six years would be obliged to wear a six-pointed yellow star, the Star of David, whenever they went out of doors. The star was stamped with the word *Juif* (Jew) in mock Hebrew lettering and was to be worn on the left-hand side at chest level.[33] All Jews would collect their stars from local police stations but the cost of manufacturing them—300,000 francs—would be borne by the Union générale des israélites de France (UGIF), the German-inspired Jewish organisation. On the same day the German authorities instructed the prefect of the Seine to ensure that Jews would be allowed to travel only in the last (second-class) carriage in the Métro.[34]

About 80 percent of the Jews in the Occupied Zone, nearly all of whom lived in Paris and its suburbs, complied with the directive, just as they had registered at police stations in October 1940,[35] and for broadly the same reasons: a belief it was right to obey the law; a fear of what would happen if they did not; and a fear of being seen as cowards if they refused to show they were Jews. This time, unlike in October 1940, the UGIF, a nominally Jewish organisation, was in place to urge Jews to comply with the German directive and to wear their stars with pride.

Most Jews seem to have done so. A member of the German secret police was shocked to report the "unacceptable spectacle of Jews sitting in cafés and restaurants near German soldiers and officers. The Jews say that they are proudly wearing the Jewish star, which is the symbol of Nazi oppression."[36] Another member of the secret police reported women in the working-class areas of La Goutte d'Or, Barbès, and La Chapelle in the north of the city who were "talking loudly so that people could hear that they were proud to wear the insignia of their race (*l'insigne de leur race*)."[37]

A survey conducted long after the event by Léon Poliakov among Jews who had worn the yellow star confirms this widespread pride in wearing the star,[38] as does Jacques Biélinky's observation in his diary at the time: "No one was going to opt out, since they felt no shame in being Jewish. Those people who said they would not collect their star or would not wear it if they did—these were very rare exceptions—were accused of being cowards."[39]

The thought of being considered a coward certainly troubled Hélène Berr. A twenty-one-year-old Jewish student from a wealthy family in the 16th arrondissement, she was studying English at the Sorbonne[40] and could not decide what to do. Her first reaction was to refuse to wear the star. After all, the German directive was outrageous and to wear it, she reasoned, would be a sign of submission to the occupier. On the other hand, it seemed to her cowardly not to wear it when so many others did. In the end courage won out. "If I wear it," she wrote, "I always want to be very elegant and dignified, so people can see what it is. I want to do what is most courageous. This evening, I think that means wearing it." She was, however, still very apprehensive: "The only thing is, where might all this be taking us?"[41]

Jews were banned from wearing war medals alongside the star, but some of them bravely insisted on doing so. They wanted to show they were both Jewish and French patriots. The penalties for this could be severe. René Bloch, a surgeon at the Necker hospital in the 15th arrondissement, was caught wearing both his star and his First World War decorations, including the *Légion d'honneur*. He was sent to Drancy and deported shortly afterwards.[42]

A minority of Jews did not wear a star, either out of defiance or because there were none left when they went to their local police station to collect them. Many of those who refused made it to the Unoccupied Zone (where they did not have to wear a star) or moved from the area where they were known and lived a semi-clandestine existence in another part of the city, away from family and friends. Jews caught not wearing a star ran a terrible risk. A French police report dated June 12 noted that the Paris police had arrested sixty-six Jews for not wearing a star. They handed over every one of them to the German secret military police.[43] Seventeen-year-old schoolgirl Louise Jacobson was arrested by French police near her home in the rue des Boulets in the 11th arrondissement for not wearing a yellow star; after spending time in prison at Fresnes and the camps at Drancy and Beaune-la-Rolande, she was finally deported to Auschwitz, where she was murdered on arrival.[44] Tamara Isserlis, the twenty-five-year-old niece of Berthe Auroy's Jewish friend Hélène, wanted to go to a concert on July 8.

Unfortunately for her this meant being out after 8 P.M. when all Jews had to be indoors. She left her papers bearing the stamp "Jew" at home but was stopped by a German officer as she was about to climb into the first-class compartment on the Métro. She was also wearing a blue, white, and red ribbon. She was arrested and held in prison at Les Tourelles, near the Porte des Lilas. She was then taken to Drancy. On June 22 she was deported to Auschwitz, from which she never returned.[45]

This new legal requirement for Jews served as a wakeup call for many non-Jewish Parisians, who were shocked to see fellow citizens—men, women, and especially children—wearing a yellow star. One Paris informant working for the German secret police reported to their masters that the yellow stars had provoked "outspoken and unanimous indignation. Even the anti-Semites are against this measure, above all because children have to wear the star."[46] Another Paris informant concurred, noting that the general feeling in Paris was one of "sentimental pity for the Jews," adding that people tried not to stare at them although the star was very obvious.[47]

This came as a relief to Jews in Paris, who had "feared they would be treated like wild animals, stared at by thousands of eyes, wherever they went, wherever they were—even if this was accompanied by sympathetic looks and a compassionate smile."[48] Henri Szwarc, a Jewish worker at the Renault factory in Boulogne-Billancourt, decided to be brazen about it when he first went out wearing his yellow star near his home in the 15th arrondissement. He stared down passersby and if they continued to look he shouted at them: "What do you think I am? Some sort of a freak?"[49] Hélène Berr, having decided to wear the star, found doing so much harder than she had imagined and was on the verge of tears when she ventured outdoors. However, most people did not stare at her as she walked through the streets, proudly holding her head high, and some fellow pedestrians even gave her a friendly smile. A minority did stare and she just stared back; a few even pointed at her. She suffered the humiliation of being ordered into the last carriage by a ticket collector in the Métro. On June 9, surrounded by fellow students in the sun-lit courtyard of the Sorbonne, she realised just how much the experience of wearing the star had affected her: "It suddenly felt as if I was no longer myself, that everything had changed and I was in the middle of a nightmare. I saw familiar figures all around me but I was conscious of the sadness and astonishment they all felt. It was as if I had been branded on my forehead."[50]

Yellow stars appeared all over Paris at a time when many Parisians were losing patience with Pétain's policy of collaboration, which had still failed to provide them with any tangible benefits. The argument that it was in France's best interest to align itself with the future masters of Europe had begun to ring hollow. Parisians listened to the broadcasts from London and read between the lines of the collaborationist press: it seemed obvious things were unravelling for Germany on the Eastern Front. Perhaps Germany was not so invincible after all. Perhaps Germany would not win the war. Many Parisians still had reservations about armed resistance on the streets but, just as Abetz and Stülpnagel had feared, the ferocity of the German reprisals had destroyed for good any campaign to win their hearts and minds. It reminded Parisians of the old archetype of the Germans as barbarians.

The German plan to isolate the Jews of Paris and show them as a race apart backfired. Non-Jewish Parisians could see for themselves that the Jews on the streets with their yellow stars were a far cry from the grotesque caricatures that had been on show at the "The Jew and France" exhibition or were painted in the collaborationist press. Biélinky wrote in his diary that an objective observer visiting the Jewish quarters of Paris would soon see through the Germans' lies. Were it not for the star, he said, nobody would know these young men and women were Jews.[51]

For Parisians committed to democracy, the yellow star directive was reactionary, offensive, and the very antithesis of the republican values of liberty, fraternity, and equality. A Communist youth newspaper called on young Parisians to take every opportunity to show solidarity with the Jews. "The yellow star: badge of the persecuted," it said. "The swastika: a target for bullets from patriots' guns!"[52] Others were equally scathing about the yellow star. "Right back to the Middle Ages," wrote Galtier-Boissière.[53] Andrzej Bobkowski compared it to the medieval treatment of lepers.[54] Flora Groult described it as an act of "infamy"[55] while Berthe Auroy, thinking about Jewish children being forced to wear the yellow star, wrote that she was ashamed that humankind had stooped so low.[56] On the day after the star became obligatory even Ernst Jünger, a German army officer and well-known writer, claimed he felt embarrassed to be in a Wehrmacht uniform when he passed Jews in the street wearing a yellow star.[57]

Non-Jews showed solidarity in deeds as well as words. The daughter of a Jewish friend of Jacques Biélinky was worried that her Catholic friends would shun her; instead, they all came to her house and wanted to show their solidarity by accompanying her whenever she went out wearing the star. Henri Szwarc was very apprehensive about how his workmates at Renault would react. He was relieved to discover "they behaved like real pals and friends: I didn't sense any change at all in their behaviour towards me." After a medical checkup at work, a doctor whom Szwarc did not know gave him his card and told him to come and see him if ever he needed help.[58] Jacques Biélinky, queuing for milk wearing his star, found that fellow shoppers greeted and chatted to him as usual. In one shop, however, a man told him to his face that Jews should not be allowed to queue, but another shopper told the man to shut up, and the shopkeeper served Jacques as usual.

It may have been partly wishful thinking on Jacques's part when he wrote on June 8 that most non-Jewish Parisians sympathised with the Jews, but it is clear genuine and widespread compassion was exhibited for them.[59] At the Jewish centre in the rue Lamarck, where everybody wore a yellow star, Jacques heard similar stories: "Different accounts showed that the treatment of those wearing their 'decoration' has—with a few rare exceptions—been friendly."[60]

A small number of Parisians dared to go further in showing their solidarity with the Jews of the city. Their actions mark a clear break with the silence and indifference that had greeted earlier anti-Semitic measures. Indeed, the yellow star directive provoked the first open opposition by non-Jews to the persecution of the Jews of Paris.

On June 7, the very first day on which Jews were ordered to wear the star, Henri Moratet, a thirty-nine year old architect living in the north of Paris, went out into the streets wearing a yellow star bearing the word "Auvergnat" (meaning, born in the Auvergne—a region of central France). A passerby insisted he remove it. He refused. A fight broke out and Henri was arrested and taken into custody.[61] The police arrested other non-Jews wearing plain yellow stars or stars marked "Buddhist," "Zulu," "Goy" (a Jewish word for a non-Jew), and "Swing." Students were in the forefront of the protesters wearing mock yellow stars: one, for example, wore a yellow star and a belt with eight stars, each inscribed "Victory."[62] There were also reports of other students wearing stars with the inscription "*Juif*," purporting to stand for Jeunesse universitaire intellectuelle française (French University Intellectual Youth).[63]

On June 7 Flora Groult reported that a classmate wore a red star with "PHILO" on it, because he was a philosophy student. "We all decided to make stars for the following morning," she wrote. Two days later she noted: "People say that students have been arrested in the Latin Quarter for wearing made-up stars and Papa has forbidden me to wear the one I had made for myself."[64] Berthe Auroy wrote that she thought about wearing a fake yellow star and hoped that this practice would spread. However, she makes no further mention of this so presumably she decided against the idea.[65] Micheline Bood wrote that girls in her secondary school were going to wear home-made stars but that she was not, finding such behaviour "excessive and pointless."[66]

The Germans were very jumpy about non-Jews wearing the star. Théo Tobiasse, a Jewish teenager from a Lithuanian background, had blue eyes and blonde hair. On his way home from school he and a Jewish classmate were stopped by a German military policeman. Théo—but not his friend—was asked for his papers. "He suspected I wasn't Jewish," Théo wrote, "and thought I was wearing the yellow star to be provocative or out of solidarity."[67]

Nineteen-year-old Françoise Siefridt, a Catholic student, was arrested by a French policeman in June for wearing a fake yellow star with the word "Papou" ("Papuan") on it. She thought she would probably receive a reprimand and be released. Instead, she was taken from the local police station to the Tourelles military camp, one of several assembly points during the roundup of Jews in May 1941. Here Françoise was held with other "Jews," as the Paris police called those who had been arrested for wearing home-made stars. Her fellow-detainees included Henri Moratet, the man from the Auvergne; a respectable, middle-class lady in her late fifties, who had worn a yellow star with a crucifix on it; a post-office employee engaged to a Jew; a couple of office workers; a secretary; and a female newspaper-seller, who had tied a yellow star to her dog's tail. Françoise and other "Jews" were then transferred to the camp at Drancy, where they were held until August.[68]

Opposing this new current of sympathy for the Parisian Jews, the collaborationist press in Paris worked hard to fan the flames of a deep-seated fear or loathing of Jews that prevailed in some sections of Parisian society. Appeals in the collaborationist press for the German and French authorities to remove all Jews from France or even to kill them grew shriller still. Everyone in Paris sensed that more anti-Semitic measures were on the way. They were about to be proved right.

On July 3 uniformed and plainclothes French police surrounded the Jewish Rothschild hospital in the 12th arrondissement.[69] The building had been requisitioned by the Prefecture of the Seine to treat sick Drancy inmates whose illnesses risked triggering an epidemic in the camp. The hospital's director was Armand Kohn. Despite losing his job as a banker because he was Jewish, Kohn, now a leading member of the UGIF, persisted in believing that an accommodation with the Germans was possible. The French police ordered Kohn to hand over the Drancy patients, all of whom were seriously ill. The police then beat the patients, bundled them into police vans, and drove them back to Drancy: one patient died en route, others died in the camp shortly after arrival. The remainder were among members of a convoy of deportees that left Drancy on July 19 for Auschwitz, where it arrived two days later.[70]

On July 8 the German military authorities signed a new directive: Jews were banned from all public places: restaurants, cafés, tea rooms, and bars; they were forbidden from entering theatres, cinemas, music halls and all other places of entertainment as well as museums, swimming pools, libraries, public exhibitions, châteaux and other historic sites, sporting events (either as spectators or participants), race courses, campsites, or parks.[71] Their home telephones had already been confiscated: now they were banned from using public telephones as well. Furthermore, they could go shopping only between 3 P.M. and 4 P.M., when, as the Germans well knew, almost everything would be sold out.

In early July 1942 members of the Resistance in Paris heard (possibly from sympathisers in the Paris police) that a massive roundup of Jews was being prepared for the night of July 16–17. They distributed leaflets in Jewish areas, warning the local inhabitants of a forthcoming raid. The resisters believed that—as with previous mass arrests—only men would be targeted, so they also went door-to-door, urging male Jews not to sleep at home that night.

In the short term, it might be possible to hide in another apartment or to stay with a non-Jewish friend for one night, but leaving an area permanently was fraught with danger and difficulty. Since February it was illegal for Jews to change their address; if they were caught so doing they risked being sent to Drancy. Even those prepared to break the law still needed somewhere to go and somebody to support them when they got there. This was also true if they could reach the Unoccupied Zone, but to do this they needed to find the money to pay a *passeur*, or guide, to take them across the demarcation line. Jacques Biélinky was lucky enough to have a Protestant friend who was willing to shelter him and, on July 12, he moved in to stay with her in the suburbs. Three days later, he wrote in his diary that some people were saying women as well as men were about to be arrested and sent off to Germany as forced labour.[72]

At 4 A.M. on July 16, while Paris slept behind closed shutters and locked doors, the familiar green buses of Paris and the blue police vans left their garages and depots. With their blue-tinted headlights, they made their way across the city and took up position in parts of the city with a high concentration of Jewish immigrants. Detachments of French police armed with rifles sealed off whole areas, setting up barricades and closing Métro stations. Once everything was in place, some 900 two- or three-men arrest teams of French policemen got to work; they were often accompanied by thugs from Jacques Doriot's Parti populaire français. The police officers were under orders to arrest everyone on lists compiled using the data collated during the mass registration of October 1940. They were under strict instructions to work as quickly as possible and not to waste any time discussing what was happening with the people they were to take away.[73] A couple of weeks earlier, René Bousquet, head of the national police, had readily agreed that the French police would provide the manpower for the *rafle* after Oberg gave him an assurance that no French Jews would be taken. What has gone down in history as *la Rafle du Vél'd'Hiv'*—the Vél'd'Hiv' roundup—sometimes referred to as Opération vent printanier (Operation Spring Wind) had begun.

The Reiman family lived in the rue du Temple in the 3rd arrondissement. Abraham Reiman had worked making fur coats until the "economic Aryanisation" directives made this impossible. In May 1941 he was one of those who had received a green card summoning him to his local police station, where he was arrested; he was now interned in the camp at Pithiviers. In the early hours of July 16 Malka, his wife, and her two young daughters, Madeleine and Arlette, were awakened by a loud knocking on the door: two French police officers were looking for Abraham Reiman. When they learned he had been sent to Pithiviers, they ordered Malka and her daughters to come with them, giving them five minutes to get ready. Malka started screaming at the policemen and throwing things at them. The police restrained her, saying they were following orders. Malka and her two daughters were then marched out into the courtyard, where other local Jews had been marshalled, before they were all herded into a waiting bus.[74]

Elsewhere the police were even more ruthless. In the suburb of Montreuil, for example, Cyrla Zylberberg watched from a hiding place inside her apartment as French police broke down her door with an axe. In Vincennes the police smashed their way into Henri Leder's apartment.[75] Annette Muller was just nine years old at the time; she recalled a thunderous knocking on the door of her flat and two men in tan raincoats bursting into the room. "Get a move on, get dressed we're taking you in," they said. "My mother threw herself to the floor and wrapped her arms around the legs of one of the men, sobbing, 'Take me, but please, I beg you, not my children!' They pushed her away with their feet. I looked at my mother. I felt ashamed."[76]

Sometimes the police were so keen to meet the targets they had been given that they arrested people who were not even on their lists. A policeman appeared at Sarah Lichtsztein's apartment to take away her mother; spotting Sarah, he asked who she was. Sarah had never registered, so she was not on the policeman's list. He simply added her name and marched her off as well.[77] In the buses, armed police had instructions to open fire if anyone tried to flee. "If there was the slightest attempt to escape," one of them recalled, "we were to fire into the crowd. That's what the submachine guns were for."[78]

This latest raid, during which around 13,000 Jewish men, women, and children were rounded up, came after months of fear, anxiety, persecution, and deprivation. For some Jews it was simply too much to bear: an estimated 100 Jews killed themselves rather than be taken. There were several cases of people committing suicide by throwing themselves out of the windows of their homes; a woman in the 14th arrondissement killed herself and her children in this way. In Montreuil, a Jewish doctor injected his family and then himself with poison;[79] a Russian Jewish doctor injected herself with a massive dose of chloroform.[80]

On April 9, 1942, in response to the attacks on German personnel in France, Hitler had ordered that deportations of Communists, Jews, and "anti-social elements" should be added to the execution of hostages in the arsenal of repression.[81] Preparations for mass deportation started in earnest at the end of April 1942 and Oberg even temporarily suspended executing hostages between May 30 and August 11.[82]

Single men and childless couples who were seized in the *rafle* in July were bussed directly to Drancy, which now became a holding camp for prisoners prior to deportation. The first train of deportees packed into cattle-trucks after the July 16–17 roundup left on July 19 with 879 men and 121 women on board, including the patients who had been brought to Drancy from the Rothschild hospital.[83] When it reached Auschwitz two days later, 375 members of the convoy were gassed on arrival.[84] Between July 19 and November 11, 1942, a total of 29,878 Jews were deported from Drancy in thirty-one convoys.[85] Most deportees were murdered on arrival or shortly afterwards.

Those with children were driven at gunpoint in buses straight to the huge indoor Vélodrome d'Hiver, commonly referred to as the Vél'd'Hiv', in the 15th arrondissement; over the past two years the cycle stadium had been a favourite venue for collaborationist meetings, such as the one to launch the LVF in July 1941. The seated areas were soon packed with Jews, mainly women and children, who would be held there, in inhumane conditions, before being taken to an unknown destination; it could be in France or one of those "resettlement areas in the east" that people spoke of. Nobody knew. By the end of the day on July 17, about 7,000 people were packed into the stadium: soon more than 8,000 Jews—including some 4,000 children—would be held there. At first sight it appeared that absolutely every seat was taken, but closer examination revealed that some of the "people" in the seats were actually bundles of clothes, small bags, or suitcases—the few possessions some of the detainees had been allowed to bring; others had only the clothes they were wearing.

The conditions were appalling: the people held in the Vél'd'Hiv' had only a dozen lavatories, and these soon became blocked and nobody came to mend them. The stench in the sweltering heat of the airless stadium was overwhelming: whole areas were awash with urine and excrement as people had no choice but to relieve themselves against the walls. There was nowhere for people to wash and nothing for them to wash with. Madame Matthey-Jonais, who had been a volunteer nurse in the First World War, was one of the handful of French Red Cross workers allowed inside the stadium. She described what she saw. "No washbasins or toilets; the water had been cut off and we had to go and fetch water in jugs to assuage people's thirst. . . . No food except soup sent in by the Red Cross, but nowhere near enough for everyone. A stifling, foul-smelling atmosphere; people having hysterics, people screaming, children crying, and even adults as well, whose physical or psychological resources were simply exhausted. Several crazy people were spreading panic. Everybody was crammed together, unable to stretch out; no mattresses, just piled up together."[86] She was working nonstop, but without medicine or medical equipment.

Rosette Shalit, one of those who had been arrested, was puzzled to see bundles of clothes occasionally fall from the seats higher up in the stadium. She later learned it was women trying to commit suicide by jumping from the upper sections, often with their children in their arms.[87] Most of the thirty or so suicide attempts inside the stadium followed this pattern; ten were successful. As the people landed with a dull thud on the ground below, the crowd would back away, screaming. The desperate and unfortunate people were then picked up, wounded, gasping, dying, or dead.[88]

"I shall never forget that crowd, those cries, that crying," wrote Hélène Zytnicki, who was one of the children held in the stadium. "I will never forget either the stink, the heat, . . . It was madness everywhere. No preparations for us to sleep or to go the lavatory or do anything at all actually. . . . Add to that the thirst, the hunger, the shouting, the impossibility of moving or sleeping and you have a picture of the situation we found ourselves in."[89]

Those in the Vél'd'Hiv' were held prisoner, although some did manage to escape.[90] Twenty-year-old Anna Traube, arrested at home in the 10th arrondissement, made two unsuccessful attempts to get away before being bundled into a bus and taken to the Vél'd'Hiv'.[91] According to her testimony, when she was in the stadium she managed to wangle a pass, complete the details with a false name, and persuade one of the few Red Cross staff in the stadium to stamp it. Another French official helped her to clean and tidy herself up. She now had to get through three police checks inside the stadium. At the second one she was stopped by a policeman who knew her. He looked at her. He looked at her papers with the false name. A pause. Then he whispered, "Bravo, how did you manage that?" and waved her through. She made it to a local café that the French official had described and her mother and sister came to collect her there the following day.[92]

The thousands of Jews imprisoned in the Vél'd'Hiv' were stuck there, terrified, for five long days. They were forbidden to receive any news, food, or clothing from the outside or to contact friends or family. They were hungry as never before, their throats parched from the dust and lack of water. Babies were born in the Vél'd'Hiv'. Women had miscarriages. People died, others went insane. And still nobody knew what their fate would be. But when the chief adviser to Darquier, the head of the French Commissariat général aux questions juives (CGQJ), visited the stadium he declared that everything was fine and that the two overworked doctors present were all that was needed.

One of the handful of firemen on duty at the Vél'd'Hiv' to carry out safety checks was Fernand Baudvin. He and his colleagues had no idea who all these people were or why they were there, but almost immediately the firemen found themselves besieged by individuals pleading to get them out of that hell-hole. This was clearly impossible, but soon Fernand and his colleagues were smuggling messages to friends and family on the outside. They began discreetly, accepting letters along with a few centimes—if people had them—to pay for a stamp, and, between them, they had soon collected about 500 letters. Their captain gave them the next day off and a free Métro pass, advising them, strictly unofficially, to post the letters in as many different post boxes as possible and to steer clear of the chic areas. This they duly did.[93]

The Jews of Paris had been forced to wear a yellow star; now came this latest offensive against them. As news of the roundup spread, many non-Jewish Parisians were outraged. Berthe Auroy wrote in her diary about the police operation, the anguish of mothers and children, the suicides, and she asked, "Is it possible that we have plumbed the depths of such barbarism?"[94] Charles Rist was similarly appalled: "Everyone is reeling from the terror and horror generated by these measures."[95] Like Berthe Auroy, Andrzej Bobkowski referred to a new "Saint Bartholemew's Day massacre," which should really be called Saint Adolf's Night.[96] The July roundup was shocking enough to rouse some leading figures of the Catholic Church to protest—albeit in private. Laval was in Paris during the operation, but he appears not to have taken much interest in what was happening. Nonetheless, it was to Laval, as French head of government, that Cardinal Suhard wrote, saying that he was "deeply affected by the family dramas that the deportations were creating."[97] A week later, at a meeting in Paris, cardinals from the Occupied Zone drew up a declaration, which they asked Cardinal Suhard to send to Pétain. This declaration referred to the mass arrests of Jews and the harsh treatment to which they had been subjected, in particular in the Vélodrome d'Hiver. It continued, "In the name of humanity and Christian principles that we raise our voices to defend the inviolable rights of every member of the human race."[98] Each bishop was charged with drawing the contents of the declaration to the attention of the clergy for whom he was responsible; the declaration was not, however, published. It is not clear whether the cardinals knew about the French government's collusion in the roundup of the Jews or about Drancy, but no reference was made to either in the letter. The feeble response from the Catholic hierarchy to what was happening to the Jews in Paris reflected its deep-rooted anti-Semitism and its support for the Vichy regime, whose commitment to traditional conservative values it shared.

It was the first roundup of Jews since Oberg took over as head of the German secret police with responsibility for issues of security and "racial preservation." Of the 13,000 Jews arrested during the roundup, nearly two-thirds of them were women and children, but this total fell far short of the 28,000 the Germans had hoped for from Paris, a figure they derived from the data amassed in the 1940 registration.[99] Some Jews had been tipped off by policemen they knew and made sure they were not at home when the raids took place.[100] Others had been alerted by members of the Resistance or the staff of the UGIF, some of whom had been told about the roundup by the Germans. Almost nobody had anticipated that women and children would be taken, so it was mostly men who had gone into hiding before the raids began. Once the roundup began, more Jews found refuges away from home, leading to a shortfall of nearly 70 percent of anticipated arrests on the second day.

Between July 19 and July 22, the 8,160 parents and children who had been held in the Vél'd'Hiv' were sent by train to internment camps at Pithiviers and Beaune-la-Rolande in the Occupied Zone south of Paris. On July 22, an anonymous functionary from the Prefecture of Police wrote a laconic note informing his superiors that the Vél'd'Hiv' "had been emptied." The note added that there were just fifty sick Jews and some lost property left behind: the Jews and the lost property were sent straight to Drancy.[101]

On July 6 Theodor Dannecker, the German head of the Department of Jewish Affairs (Judenreferat) in Paris, had sent a telegram to Adolf

Eichmann, telling his boss that Pierre Laval had proposed that Jewish children, as well as their parents, should be deported. Even Dannecker and Darquier, the head of Vichy's CGQJ, baulked at sending children under the age of twelve to Drancy, let alone directly to Auschwitz, without approval from Berlin. Thus when the adults at Pithiviers and Beaune-la-Rolande were about to be deported, their children remained behind. It fell to the French gendarmes who ran the camps to forcibly separate young children from their parents. The air was full of shouting and wailing; French gendarmes beat hysterical mothers (some of whom were still lactating) to the ground with their rifle butts in order to wrench them from their screaming children and toddlers. At the end of July and the beginning of August, five rail convoys of adult deportees and youngsters over twelve years of age left Pithiviers and Beaune-la Rolande and went directly to Auschwitz.[102] The little ones remained behind. However, towards the end of July, Eichmann instructed Dannecker to begin the deportation of the little children from Pithiviers and Beaune-la-Rolande.[103] A fortnight or so later some 4,000 grimy, traumatised skeletal little children aged between two and twelve began arriving by train at the Gare d'Austerlitz in Paris, where they were put on buses and taken straight to Drancy.

Georges Wellers was a Russian-born Jew who arrived in France in 1929. He was granted French nationality in 1938 and worked as a senior researcher at the National Centre for Scientific Research (CNRS). He was arrested in Paris in December 1941 and interned at the Royallieu-Compiègne camp before being transferred to Drancy. As head of the totally inadequate "Hygiene Service" in the camp, he was one of the very few adults allowed into the children's sleeping quarters after 9 P.M. He later described how those bewildered, distressed, and utterly disoriented children, forcibly separated from their parents, were packed a hundred and twenty at a time into rooms, each child with nothing but a filthy mattress to sleep on. Buckets were placed in the corridor since the toilets were too far away for the little ones. The children were given cabbage soup, which provoked attacks of diarrhoea that soiled their clothing and bedding. "There was no soap, so you had to rinse out their clothes in cold water, while the child, almost naked, waited for them to dry."[104]

Wellers was a witness at the 1962 trial of Adolf Eichmann in Tel Aviv where he described how at night many of the children "cried, they became agitated, they called for their mothers. It happened a number of times that a whole roomful of 120 children woke up in the middle of the night; they completely lost control of themselves, they screamed and woke the other rooms. It was frightful." There was nobody to care for the children, although three teams of female inmates volunteered to do what they could; when they were deported, others replaced them.[105] Members of the French Red Cross who had been allowed into the camp also tried to help. One of them posted a letter from a seven-year-old girl to her concierge in Paris: "Madame la concierge—I am writing to you because I have nobody else. Last week Papa was deported. Mama has been deported. I have lost my purse. I have nothing left."[106] At Drancy, to try to reassure the children, adults told them they were off to PitchiPoi,[107] a magical land of Yiddish folklore. The children did not stay long at Drancy. Two or three days after they arrived, half of them were deported, mixed in with 500 foreign Jews; two days later it was the turn of the other half.[108] Not one of them returned. Anti-Nazi activist Edith Thomas described in her diary how she felt when she happened to see one of the deportation trains rattling past her. "I saw a goods train. In the cattle trucks there were some children. Their hands were poking through the barred windows. For the first time in my life I felt a cold shiver of horror run down my spine."[109]

☞ THE NAZIS WERE FORCIBLY DEPORTING Jews from France for ideological reasons; now for economic reasons they were desperate to recruit Frenchmen to work in Germany. Ever since the Occupation began, France had provided Germany with workers, but on a small scale and on a "voluntary basis" (although in practice many workers were coerced into leaving).[110] Most French citizens were uneasy about, or hostile to, the idea of French people working in Germany. In the early months of the Occupation most of those who left for Germany were foreigners, picked up as the Germans trawled the internment camps in search of volunteers.[111] As the Occupation dragged on, some Frenchmen, especially among the unemployed—who numbered about a million in the Seine department—were seduced by German promises of high salaries and good working conditions. However, numbers were still insufficent to meet the needs of the German war economy, even when added to workers brought into Germany from other occupied countries, such as the Netherlands, Belgium, and Denmark.[112]

By early 1942 the labour shortage in German factories was becoming desperate in the extreme. Things were going so badly for Germany in Russia that Hitler was forced to accept that what was planned as a lightning war was going to be a protracted one. Furthermore, furtive and treasonable mutterings in Berlin dared to suggest that Germany might not actually win. Germany badly needed more workers to take the place of those who had been sucked away from its factories to the Eastern Front to replace the 1.3 million German soldiers who had been killed in the so-called "anti-Jewish-Bolshevik crusade."

In March 1942 Hitler made forty-seven-year-old Fritz Sauckel, a former governor of the German province of Thuringia and long-serving member of the Nazi Party, responsible for recruiting and employing labour; this meant bringing suitably qualified foreigners from German-occupied countries to the armament factories in the Reich. Pierre Laval, as ever anxious to ingratiate himself with the Germans, was keen to help. On May 12 he wrote to Ribbentrop, the German foreign minister, saying he wanted France to contribute to what he called Germany's giant struggle against Bolshevism. To this end he wanted as many French people as possible to take the place of those in German factories who had been moved from the production line at home to the front line in the East.[113]

On June 16 Laval met Sauckel and accepted his proposition, underwritten by Hitler, that 50,000 Frenchmen currently held in POW camps would be released in the autumn in exchange for 150,000 skilled French workers, who should be sent to Germany at once. Laval dubbed this programme—whereby one POW would be exchanged for every three workers—La Relève (the Relief). On June 22, two years to the day after the armistice in what *Le Matin* called an emotional appeal, Laval made a radio broadcast urging workers from both zones to sign up to the scheme. It would liberate French POWs, he said, and help to build the Germany of the future. In a phrase that would return to haunt him, Laval insisted, "I want Germany to win because tomorrow, without that victory, Bolshevism will establish itself everywhere."[114]

Paris, like the rest of France, was soon covered in posters promoting La Relève. Berthe Auroy spotted one: it depicted a German worker extending a hand to his French counterpart. On the right, the sun shone brightly on Germany, but on the left, France was cast in darkness; in the background was a young woman, smiling and holding a beautiful baby. "When you see such tempting possibilities, you're surprised there's a single worker left in France,"[115] Auroy noted ironically.

Another poster showing the faces of three women of different ages called on French mothers, wives, and fiancées to encourage their menfolk to enquire about the Relève scheme. Yet another poster had religious undertones and a subtext suggesting that good actions resulted in deliverance. It showed a hand holding up a key towards a source of bright light, above which ran the slogan: "You Hold the Key to the Camps!" Below it said: "French workers, you are setting the prisoners free by going to work in Germany!"[116]

In the first week of July, some thirty recruitment offices for La Relève opened in the Seine department. Retraining centres were also established, like the one at Courbevoie, to the west of Paris, offering a course that would, it claimed, turn successful applicants into metal workers in just six weeks.[117] However, despite all the publicity, the campaign yielded meagre results. Between April and July only 31,300 Frenchmen volunteered: far short of the 250,000 Sauckel was demanding.[118] A Paris police report in mid-July dryly observed that Laval's appeal to French workers and a much-publicised open letter to factory bosses promoting La Relève, which appeared in the press, "do not, so far, appear to have been greeted with enthusiasm."[119] Clearly, if propaganda had failed to recruit enough workers, another approach would be needed.

☞ In July the German security forces gave another turn of the screw showing the influence of their new SS commander Oberg. A poster in French and German and issued by Oberg's office on July 10 informed Parisians that henceforth the relatives of anyone believed to be involved in anti-German activities would be severely punished. The move was based on the premise that it was usually close relatives of the perpetrators of armed attacks or acts of sabotage who helped them before or after the event. The text read: "1. All close male relations aged 18, be they younger or older [than the presumed perpetrators], including brothers-in-law and cousins will be shot. 2. All corresponding female relatives will be sentenced to forced labour. 3. All children (up to the age of 17) of the men and women affected by these measures will be sent to a state institution for young offenders."[120]

This intimidation appears to have had very little effect: the attacks continued—but so did the executions. On August 11 Oberg announced that he had ordered the execution of ninety-three "terrorists" convicted of having committed acts of terrorism or of being associated with these actions. He also threatened Parisians that if he did not receive more help in tracking down "terrorists," he would be obliged to adopt measures that would bring pain and suffering to the whole population.[121]

After the virtual decimation of the Communist youth organisation, the Bataillons de la jeunesse, the PCF had reorganised its armed resistance groups in the city. The Bataillons de la jeunesse had operated with a high degree of autonomy under the auspices of the PCF's Organisation spéciale. With the Bataillons de la jeunesse smashed beyond repair, another PCF group stepped into the breach, this time a shadowy group known as the Détachement Valmy (the Valmy Detachment), which had nothing in common—except the reference to the Battle of Valmy in 1792—with the small Resistance group founded at the Lycée Buffon by Raymond Burgard.

The Valmy Detachment had come into being a year earlier and, carrying out orders issued by the clandestine PCF leadership, had executed those whom the PCF leadership considered to be traitors. The Valmy Detachment was responsible, for example, for the assassination in September 1941 of Marcel Gitton, who had been number three in the party's hierarchy before the war. After the defeat of June 1940, Gitton became an outspoken critic of the PCF, the Soviet Union, and the Comintern. Although not officially a member of Doriot's Parti populaire français, he published a letter in its newspaper *Le Cri du Peuple* in August 1941 calling on Communist workers to join the PPF. The following month he was gunned down by a two-man unit[122] from the Valmy Detachment in the street near his home in Les Lilas, an eastern suburb of Paris. Over the next ten months members of the Valmy Detachment carried out another eight assassinations or attempted assassinations on designated "traitors."[123]

From the summer of 1942, the Valmy Detachment, working along with the newly formed Francs-tireurs et partisans français (French Sharpshooters and Partisans), commonly known simply as the FTP, carried out attacks on German soldiers and property. On August 5 the FTP threw grenades at members of the Luftwaffe who were training in a stadium in the 16th arrondissement, killing eight of them. It was the highest number of fatalities in a single action in Paris during the Occupation. Between the end of July and the end of September, the

Valmy Detachment carried out at least fifteen anti-German actions in the Paris area. On September 8 they exploded a bomb in the cinema Garenne-Palace, killing a German soldier and wounding four others; two days later a grenade was thrown at a detachment of the Wehrmacht in the rue d'Hautpoul in the 19th arrondissement, injuring nine soldiers; and on September 16 a bomb exploded in the huge Rex Cinema in the centre of the city, injuring five soldiers.[124] Overall, fatalities were rarely incurred, relatively few soldiers injured—and then only slightly—and usually little damage inflicted. This did not prevent Oberg from responding by ordering the execution of 116 "Communist terrorists."[125]

Many of the attacks may have been less dramatic than the militants had hoped, but they were enough to rattle the occupying forces. "Valmy" raised its head in a different context when Oberg's security agents intercepted Communist leaflets calling for demonstrations in Paris and the suburbs on September 20: the anniversary of the Battle of Valmy in 1792 when revolutionary French forces defeated the Prussians. The Germans were nervous enough about what might happen to impose draconian restrictions on all Parisians. The authorities again ordered the closure of all theatres, cinemas, cabarets, and other places of leisure used by residents between 3 P.M. and midnight on September 19 in the Seine, Seine-et-Oise, and Seine-et-Marne departments; they also imposed a ban on all public meetings, including sports events. The following day, in the same three departments, French civilians who were not on official business were forbidden to be on the street between 3 P.M. and midnight.[126]

The Germans were hell-bent on pursuing the "enemies of the Reich." The Jews of Paris were in more danger than ever before, while the Communists, in the forefront of the armed resistance, were relentlessly pursued and innocent hostages risked being executed at any moment. The Vichy pipe dream of trouble-free collaboration was in tatters and the German authorities were about to embark on a policy that would alienate the people of Paris—and indeed the rest of France—more than anything they had done so far.

☞ *11*

Denunciations, Distractions, Deprivations

*T*HE VÉL'D'HIV' ROUNDUP and the deportations that followed terrorised the Jews of Paris. Worse was to follow: between July 19 and July 29, five convoys carried 5,000 inmates from Drancy to Auschwitz, although none of the Jews in the convoys knew what their destination was or what awaited them when they arrived.[1] Until the Vél' d'Hiv' *rafle* it was mostly French Jews who had fled Paris for the Unoccupied Zone and then, in many cases, further afield; now all Jews, and especially immigrant and stateless Jews, wanted to leave. However, fleeing south was not an option for all: travel was expensive and a *passeur* had to be found to get one across the demarcation line. As Jacques Adler, whose father had been rounded up in 1941, has put it: "Survival through escape was the privilege of those who could afford it."[2] Some Jews who had enough money to leave decided nevertheless to stay put: Sorbonne student Hélène Berr, who worked as a volunteer at the offices of the Union générale des israélites de France (UGIF) helping fellow Jews in Paris, stayed in the city out of a sense of responsibility. She felt that to leave would be an act of cowardice: she was not willing to take advantage of her relatively privileged social position and abandon those who were held in detention or were too poor to leave.[3] She had also become increasingly attached to Jean Morawiecki, a young Catholic student, and that may have also influenced her decision. Others stayed because they had responsibilities to elderly or sick relatives: the father of Denise Lefschetz, also a volunteer at the UGIF, was convinced that as a war veteran he had nothing to fear, but he also refused to abandon his eighty-two-year-old mother, who was in no state to travel; François Lyon-Caen had to abandon his plans to cross into the Unoccupied Zone when his wife was diagnosed with cancer.[4]

Even those who could afford to engage a *passeur* had no guarantee they would reach their destination. Bianca Bienenfeld's father, who had given Simone de Beauvoir a lift out of Paris during the exodus, was now in the Unoccupied Zone with Bianca's mother. Bianca raised a tidy sum of money and paid a *passeur* to guide her into the Unoccupied Zone. The *passeur* put Bianca up in a hotel in Moulins, just to the north of the demarcation line, promising to come back, but she never saw him or her money again. It seems this sort of deception was commonplace.[5] However, Bianca did manage to reach the Unoccupied Zone later, making her way to Aix-en-Provence, where friends helped her obtain false papers.

For the Jews still in Paris, life was extremely dangerous, but more so for some than for others. In spite of all the constraints imposed by Vichy and the German authorities, many French Jews remained hopeful that they would be left alone; after all, almost all the Jews who had been rounded up thus far were either foreigners or stateless. Both French and foreign Jewish staff working for the UGIF as well as their families were exempt from arrest, as were Jews working for German-run factories in the city. Certain Jewish foreign nationals living in Paris were also "protected," but the Germans were steadily reducing the number of nationalities on the protected list, and each reduction was marked by a new roundup.[6]

The options for those who stayed in Paris and were not "protected" were to go underground, to go into hiding, which usually meant being supported and hidden by non-Jews, to acquire false papers, or to join the Resistance. One of the Jews who chose to go into hiding was Albert Grunberg, a Jewish Romanian hairdresser who lived and worked near the Sorbonne. In September 1942 two French policemen came to arrest him at his home at 14, rue des Écoles; Grunberg gave them the slip and took refuge in his shop a few doors down the same street. With the help of his concierge, a few trusty neighbours, and his (non-Jewish) wife, who kept the hairdressing business going, he remained in hiding in a sixth-floor room above the shop at No. 8 until the arrival of the

Allies in August 1944.[7] All Jews who went into hiding or who carried false papers were constantly haunted by the nightmare of what would happen if they were denounced or discovered. Grunberg kept a diary providing a fascinating account of his two years in hiding. It reveals that he was terrified of being denounced by a fascist couple living on the floor below in the same building, whom he correctly believed to be paid informers.[8]

Jews had been vulnerable to denunciation ever since the introduction of the first anti-Semitic measures in the autumn of 1940. Each new anti-Semitic directive or law meant there were more things Jews had to do or were forbidden to do, which meant a greater risk of noncompliance—either deliberate or by oversight—and a greater chance of being reported to the authorities. There were various motivations for denunciations of Jews: it could be naked anti-Semitic hatred as with an anonymous letter sent to the Commissariat général aux questions juives (CGQJ) in October 1943 that began, "Dear Sir, I hate the Jews who have done us so much damage, and this is why it gives me great pleasure to unmask one of them for cheating by dodging the laws which are there to stop them harming us."[9] Another letter written to the CGQJ in the same month began: "Dear Sir, As someone who loathes Jews," before naming a foreign Jew who, he alleged, had not registered and went out without wearing a yellow star.[10] Others sought to damage a commercial competitor, like the stamp dealer who, in August 1941, wrote to *Le Matin* newspaper denouncing a rival who, he alleged, had a Jewish business partner.[11]

A denunciation could be motivated by a combination of anti-Semitism and resentment, as with a letter sent in October 1941 to the then head of the CGQJ Xavier Vallat. The writer, a Parisian woman, described herself as "a true Frenchwoman who is sick and tired of seeing our poor country being eaten away by Jews." She was writing to denounce one particular Jewish tailor whose address in the 20th arrondissement she gave and who, she claimed, was still working, even though his shop displayed a red notice indicating it was under "Aryan" management. She complained that this man could find fabrics to work with while it was impossible and forbidden for others to do so. She concluded by calling on the police to raid his premises and carry out an identity check.[12]

A denunciation could have a strictly personal motivation. Jean Kanapa, a Jewish author and future leading member of the PCF, had a non-Jewish fiancée. His putative father-in-law was so enraged at the thought of his daughter marrying a Jew that he threatened to denounce Kanapa to the Gestapo; the couple wisely fled to the Unoccupied Zone.[13] Whatever their actual motivation, those who denounced others could rationalise their actions by claiming that by bringing breaches of the law to the attention of the authorities they were merely doing their duty as good citizens.

A particularly tragic case was that of Annette Zelman.[14] Simone de Beauvoir knew Annette slightly and she was, like Sartre and de Beauvoir, an habitué of the Café de Flore on the boulevard Saint-Germain. Sartre and de Beauvoir had first met Annette and her boyfriend Jean Jausion at the demarcation line when Sartre and de Beauvoir were crossing back into the Occupied Zone after their abortive attempt to drum up support for their little Resistance group Socialism and Freedom (see Chapter 7). Twenty-year-old Annette and Jean, the only son of an eminent doctor, Hubert Jausion, who was in charge of the research laboratories at the Franco-Muslim hospital in the Paris suburb of Bobigny, planned to marry. Annette's parents were not overjoyed at the prospect of their daughter "marrying out," but this was nothing compared to the reaction of Jean's father. Hubert had contacts among the German High Command and called for Annette to be arrested. The arrest was carried out on May 22, 1942, on the orders of Theodor Dannecker, head of the Jewish bureau of the Gestapo in Paris. She was initially held in the sordid cell block of the French police headquarters[15] before being moved to the camp at Tourelles in the east of the city. There she joined other Jewish women, as well as other detainees, including the Catholic student Françoise Siefridt, who had been arrested for wearing parodies of the yellow star.

On June 18, eighty or so Jewish women, including Annette, were isolated from the other detainees and put under guard in a single dormitory. Françoise Siefridt wrote in her diary of terrible rumours circulating that the group of women who had been singled out were going to be shot;[16] a few days later they were transferred to Drancy. Meanwhile, at the Café de Flore, Annette's fiancé and her friends knew only that Annette and Bella Lempert, another young Jewish habituée of the café, had disappeared. "Jausion and his friends still come to the Flore and sit in the same seats," wrote de Beauvoir, "They speak amongst themselves in a state of slightly dazed agitation."[17] What they did not know was that on June 22 Annette was one of sixty-six women among nearly 1,000 Jews at Drancy who were forced onto the train that made up Convoy Number 3 to Auschwitz. This was the same convoy that included Tamara Isserlis, the niece of Berthe Auroy's Jewish friend Hélène, who had been caught out after curfew and without her star (see Chapter 10). Like Tamara, Annette never returned.

Bella Lempert was due to be deported in the same convoy as Annette, but at the last minute her name was removed from the list. She was later deported to Auschwitz and murdered shortly after she arrived. Annette's fiancé, Jean Jausion, depressed and suicidal, wrote a novel that was published after the war. He participated in the Liberation of Paris in August 1944, but he was caught in a German ambush in Lorraine a few weeks later. He was almost certainly shot by the Germans, dying soon afterwards from his wounds. His body was never found.[18]

It is impossible to be sure how many anti-Semitic denunciations were made during the war.[19] Laurent Joly believes that estimates of three to five million (for France as a whole) for denunciations of Jews, Communists, Gaullists, members of the Resistance, that have been claimed are much too high; he suggests that hundreds of thousands would probably be nearer the mark.[20] He also argues that denunciation happened across the social spectrum and was not, as is often claimed, a predominantly female act.[21]

The French and German authorities devoted plenty of manpower and time to hunting down Jews in Paris,[22] but they had by no means forgotten their other principal target—the Communists. Here, too, denunciation played an important role; indeed, according to Joly, most denunciations were not of Jews but of alleged Communists or people believed to have committed "economic offences," that is, black-market activities.[23] In May 1941, for example, Jean Catelas, who was responsible for the clandestine organisation of the PCF in the Paris region, was arrested following a tip-off by two women in the suburb of Asnières, who gave the local anti-Communist unit of the Paris police the address where Catelas was hiding.[24] It was another tip-off from a member of the public that put the police on the trail of the three members of the Bataillons de la jeunesse. In October 1941, the female owner of a café-bar called La Boîte à Sardines that was frequented by members of the group contacted the police. She gave them the names of the three militants who had gone to Nantes when Brustlein killed the local regional commander in exchange for the release of her son-in-law from a German POW camp.[25]

Communist activists belonged to clandestine networks so the police tended to wait patiently and observe rather than pounce immediately. The police were smart enough to realise that playing the long game and tailing suspects would lead to more arrests. The police drew up complex diagrams showing the network of links between militants, and this helped them to prepare mass arrests. For instance, putting Jean Catelas under surveillance rather than arresting him immediately led to the arrest of twenty or so other activists, including Gabriel Péri, another leading member of the PCF.[26] Interrogation and torture of arrested militants could yield yet more names and information, which, in turn, resulted in another wave of arrests. In contrast, most of the Jews who had gone underground—except for those who joined the Resistance—broke off all contact with family and friends and moved to another part of the city. The police soon learned that if they put such Jews under surveillance, it rarely led them to any others; once the police had spotted a Jewish "target," they therefore tended to move in and arrest the person straightaway.

☞ IT MAY SEEM UNLIKELY but by the summer of 1942 Paris was the focus for an unprecedented youth craze in Paris based on fashion and music. Flamboyant young Parisians calling themselves "Zazous" were making their presence felt in the city, especially around certain cafés on the Champs-Élysées and in the Latin Quarter where they would congregate and listen to their favourite music: swing.[27] The word "Zazou" derived from the swing number *Zah Zuh Zah*, recorded in New York by Cab Calloway, a black American band leader and scat singer, shortly before his band played in Paris in 1934.

Swing and jazz were banned in Germany because the Nazis considered them to be degenerate. Were they not tunes written by Jews and performed by "Negroes"? To make matters worse, the man who was about to become one of the European stars of swing was yet another degenerate—a gypsy—from Belgium named Django Reinhardt. Swing originated in the United States, so after America's entry into the war in 1941, swing also became "enemy music." But the knowledge that swing had been proscribed in Nazi Germany, together with its association with the anti-conformist Zazou youth meant that, for many, swing music was associated with rebellion. Unsurprisingly perhaps, the words *Swing* and *Zazou* each appeared on yellow stars worn by non-Jewish Parisians in July 1942 expressing solidarity with the Jews.[28]

Hitler's head of propaganda Josef Goebbels tried to subvert swing music by promoting a band performing under the name of Charlie and his Orchestra. The band, whose name derived from its singer Karl "Charlie" Schwedler, performed swing classics but with anti-American, anti-British, and anti-Jewish lyrics (in English), which were broadcast on short-wave radio targeting the United States and especially Britain.[29]

Although jazz and swing were banned in Germany, no such prohibition was enforced by the German authorities in France, who were also far more relaxed about the Zazous than were the French authorities and the collaborationists. Indeed, swing in particular enjoyed something of a golden age during the Occupation. As early as December 1940 a "Festival of French Jazz" was held at the Salle Gaveau in the rue La Boétie, in the 8th arrondissement. The Salle Gaveau could seat over 1,200 spectators and the event was so popular it sold out in twenty-four hours and a second concert had to be scheduled for two days later.[30] The German military took the pragmatic view that jazz was useful: it promoted the notion that Paris had returned to normality and this outweighed any ideological objections. Jazz musicians took advantage of this tolerance and soon jazz was to be heard in venues small and large across the city. Jazz flourished in Paris because it was also popular among the German occupying forces (and much later, among the American liberating forces).

After the entry of the United States into the war at the end of 1941, French bands continued to play American jazz and swing tunes, although their titles were often "Frenchified." It is unlikely the Germans were fooled: it was a charade in which everyone colluded for form's sake.[31] When war broke out, Django Reinhardt was touring in Britain with the Quintette du Hot Club de France (Quintet of the Hot Club of France). The violinist Stephane Grappelli stayed in England, but Django, who spoke almost no English, returned to France. After Pearl Harbor, Django reduced the number of American tunes in his repertoire and included more of his own compositions, including one haunting melody "Nuages," which enjoyed three encores at the Festival of French Jazz, became his signature tune and helped propel him to stardom.

All the jazz orchestras and groups included swing numbers in their repertoire, but it was a young French singer named Johnny Hess who spread the appeal of swing far beyond the ranks of jazz aficionados (much to the chagrin of jazz purists) and coined the word "Zazou" in his 1938 hit "Je suis swing" ("I Am Swing"). In January 1942, the weekly magazine *Vedettes* reported that ever since the success of "Je suis swing" young people had made Hess their idol. They tore photographs of him out of magazines and fought to get his autograph, and the same magazine reported that "the rallying cry of all those under twenty is the famous *Zazou! Zazou!* as shouted out by Johnny in his popular song."[32]

Hess's success peaked in 1942 when he appeared at four concert halls in Paris[33] and recorded yet another hit "Ils sont zazous" ("They Are Zazous"). Hess's former partner, the energetic and exuberant singer Charles Trenet, also climbed on the Zazou bandwagon by recording "La Poule zazoue" ("The Zazou Hen") with Django Reinhardt and by declaring himself to be an honorary Zazou.[34]

Along with a devotion to swing came the distinctive Zazou way of dressing. Male Zazous, usually in their late teens and early twenties, grew their hair long at the back and with a quiff in the front; they wore tight-fitting trousers that stopped just above the ankle, thick-soled shoes, shirts with high collars, a tie with a small knot, and a three-quarter length drape Zoot suit-style jacket with broad sloping shoulders; they frequently wore sunglasses and carried a furled umbrella.[35] Female Zazous wore short, pleated skirts, a bag slung over the shoulder, high-heeled wooden shoes—if possible—and plenty of makeup.[36] Their clothes were either handmade or bought on the black market and re-fashioned accordingly. The young men spoke with high-pitched voices; the women affected a deep sort of growl. This was the very antithesis of the traditional, conservative style and behaviour associated with discipline and clean living, promoted both by the Vichy government and by Nazi ideology and iconography.

The Paris Zazous were asserting their own youthful sense of identity in strained circumstances; they wanted to distance themselves from the conservatism of the older generation, the puritanism of the Vichy government, and the oppressiveness of Nazism. Unsurprisingly the Vichy government portrayed the frivolous dandyism of the Zazous as an affront to a population suffering from the effects of the world war. Other conservatives saw them as a challenge to traditional gender differences, which troubled them no end. For some it seemed that male Zazous with their long hair, tight trousers, and squeaky voices were not just being effeminate but were openly homosexual.

Collaborationists were quick to contrast these "decadent" Zazous with the virile models of manhood found in the German army. The leader of one of the collaborationist movements pontificated: "Have you not compared our Zazous with the twenty-year old Hitlerians who have returned from fighting in the frozen mud of Russia? When you see the former trotting along the boulevards wiggling their backsides and twirling their umbrellas and the others, with their cut-away shirt collars, their boots proudly pounding the ground, looking impassively ahead, do you not have to admit that, between that heroic and conquering race and our vacuous and pretentious one, lies the difference between life and degeneration."[37]

For conservatives and members of the Far Right, the Zazous were shameful, decadent, and narcissistic nihilists with no respect for anything, not even the plight of the *patrie*. However, not everyone disapproved. Simone de Beauvoir felt that in their outlandish way the Zazous were expressing their disgust with the Pétainist National Revolution and all staunch defenders of the deeply conservative "new morality." Watching the Zazous around the Café de Flore, she wrote that despite their affected airs, she and Sartre rather liked them.[38]

By the spring of 1942, the Zazou phenomenon with its Dadaist-sounding call for "a 'swing' France in a Zazou Europe" had become widespread enough for some collaborationists to decide it was time to teach these degenerate wastrels a lesson. On May 25, 1942, fights broke out on the boulevard Saint-Michel between Zazous and the police, who were joined by some 300 or 400 members of the Jeunesses populaires françaises (JPF), the youth wing of Doriot's Parti populaire français, which had just held its inaugural meeting in the nearby Mutualité hall.[39] Roger Vauquelin, the leader of the JPF, described the Zazous as the triumph of democratic mindlessness and Jewish decadence; they were living proof of the physical and moral degradation of a section of the nation's youth. He issued orders for anti-Zazou punishment squads to be sent out to Neuilly, the Champs-Élysées, and the Latin Quarter. A few days later a group of JPF thugs set about some Zazous near one of their favourite meeting places, the Pam-Pam café on the Champs-

Élysées. This was followed by police raids on the Pam-Pam and another Zazou haunt, the Colisée on the boulevard Saint-Michel, when about a hundred Zazous were taken into custody by French police before being released. The pro-Vichy newspaper *Gringoire* congratulated the police for putting an end to the eccentricities of these "depraved kids" and "idle little girls" who hung out in the cafés of the Champs-Élysées and the Latin Quarter.[40]

On July 5, *Jeunesse*, a JPF publication, carried a report of JPF members physically attacking male Zazous in the Latin Quarter and on the Champs-Élysées and forcibly shaving their heads. The report concluded, "Decadence must be halted and the decadent must be punished."[41] Shortly afterwards, the PPF's own newspaper, *Le Cri du Peuple*, started a regular column headed "JPF in Action," carrying reports of attacks on Zazous in Paris and the suburbs. Readers who wished to "join the band of hairdressers" were encouraged to report to the JPF headquarters in the rue Cimarosa in the 16th arrondissement.[42]

The Zazous were rebels, not resisters, and clearly the anti-Zazou attacks were qualitatively different from the roundups of Jews and the anti-Resistance repression: Zazous were not sent to Drancy, tortured, deported, or executed by firing squad. However, arrests of Zazous and attacks on them by pro-Nazi thugs contributed to an atmosphere of foreboding among some of the youth in Paris: it was clear that public displays of individuality and deviance from conservative norms could mean trouble.

While some of the Zazous continued to meet in their usual hangouts, fear of police harassment and attacks by JPF gangs drove others away. Many now retreated to clandestine dance halls that had sprung up all over the city. A ban on dancing in public had been introduced by Georges Mandel, the minister of the interior in Paul Reynaud's government back in May 1940 when the Germans invaded France. Vichy had no intention of rescinding the ban, believing that to do so would be an insult to the French soldiers who had been killed or who were still held in POW camps. Furthermore, the French government considered that dance halls represented a moral danger for the wives of POWs since it risked promoting fraternisation or worse between French women and German soldiers—not at all the sort of collaboration Pétain wished to encourage. Above all, in the eyes of the Vichy government, dancing and its association with pleasure and laxity recalled the hated, self-indulgent, dissolute, and decadent Third Republic. It threatened to undermine Pétain's deeply conservative National Revolution project.

Whatever Vichy might have felt, reality was somewhat different. No sooner had France surrendered than German soldiers were blatantly ignoring orders from their superiors banning them from dancing with Parisians in the city's clubs and bars. By April 1941 the German military authorities had given up trying to stop them and rescinded its own ban: trying to enforce it was simply more trouble than it was worth. At the same time the German military authorities also adopted a fairly relaxed attitude towards French people dancing in public. "If [they], in spite of the disgraceful defeat of their country, wish to dance, it is in the German interest not to prevent them from doing so," reported the Schools and Culture Department within the MBF.[43] As far as the Germans were concerned, as long as Parisians were dancing indoors they were not causing trouble outside.

The Vichy ban on dancing did not mean it was forbidden to *learn* to dance. As early as October 1940, premises offering "dancing classes" started opening across Paris. Soon hundreds of places offered Parisians the chance to "learn to dance," out of sight and reach of the Paris police.[44] The following year, the police were so concerned about the proliferation of these "dancing classes," many of which were simply clandestine dance venues, that they introduced a raft of regulations to try to ensure that only genuine classes could operate. For example, all classes had to be registered with the police; the number of couples attending each class was limited to fifteen; students had to enrol in advance for at least five lessons and have a valid membership card; there were to be no live bands—the only music allowed was to be provided by a pianist or by a gramophone.[45]

These regulations made little difference. For example, a young musician turned businessman Édouard Ruault, calling himself Eddie Barclay,[46] under which name he would play a key role in postwar popular culture, offered "dancing lessons" at 37, rue Boissière in the 16th arrondissement. Barclay ignored the ban on live music, so his establishment provided plenty of work for musicians, including Emmanuel Soudieux, a double-bass player with Django Reinhardt.[47] Barclay did not bother to register the venue with the police and soon he was publicising dance *sessions* (rather than *classes*). Barclay's club attracted young, well-heeled Parisians and for the local Zazous it was a place of refuge. "We preferred to meet up amongst ourselves so as not to get beaten up," said Jean-Louis Bory, a former Zazou.[48]

The collaborationist press was outraged by the large number of clandestine, unregistered "dancing classes." On June 11 *La Gerbe* published an investigative article entitled "The Great Scandal of the Dancing Classes." It painted a picture of grubby, seedy dives charging membership fees of 100 francs, plus a 10 franc entrance fee per visit. *Au Pilori* went further, publishing the addresses of places that were offering "dancing classes" and reporting how young Zazous danced the night away while French prisoners languished in the German *stalags* (POW camps).[49]

The ban on public dances led to a boom in private dancing parties in Paris and the suburbs. The poet, song-writer, novelist, and trumpet player Boris Vian and his wife Michèle hosted weekend parties in Ville-d'Avray, a short train ride from the Gare Saint-Lazare. Some of the Zazous from the Champs-Élysées Pam-Pam café came to these parties, although Vian assailed their knowledge of jazz, or rather their lack of it.[50] Along with such semi-bohemian private parties that spread across the city and the suburbs, suave and sophisticated musical gatherings were held for *le tout Paris*. They included those such as the ones hosted by Porfirio Rubirosa, a diplomat from the Dominican Republic who later married the actress Danielle Darrieux,[51] where guests could dance the night away to tunes played by well-known musicians, including Django Reinhardt.[52]

☞ ALTHOUGH SOME PARISIANS were able to grab a few hours of fun and dancing, a police report of August 10, 1942, painted a sober picture of life in the city. The "terrorist attacks" were continuing, and the report mentioned specifically another gunfight between police and an armed PCF group: this time as speakers were addressing an impromptu street meeting outside a big grocery store in the rue Daguerre in the south of the city.

The report added that Parisians who saw German military vehicles pouring across the city on July 29 wondered if this meant a second front would soon be opening up. If so, they asked themselves where would it be and how might it affect them. Few Parisians had signed up to work in Germany, so many now wondered if compulsory recruitment was on the way. "In general," the report stated, "the population is expecting difficult times ahead, and is anxious and on edge." Food as always remained the Parisians' main concern.[53]

The report stressed that "the problem of supplies is still at the top of the list of the Parisians' preoccupations." It asserted that the people of Paris were far from convinced that the government was doing enough to crack down on fraud and the black market, and they believed that the huge number of counterfeit bread tickets in circulation had distorted the rationing system. Parisian housewives complained that fruit was too expensive and fresh vegetables hard to come by and that it was difficult to find fish or cooked meats. They blamed these shortages on the Germans, who, they said, were busy stockpiling everything.

But it was not just food. The report noted that a serious lack of clothing and footwear was having a catastrophic impact, especially on lower-income households; in addition, the constant rise in the cost of living while salaries remained low had generated an attitude "susceptible to extremist [i.e., Communist] propaganda." Both Abetz and the military had always been aware of this danger if life was made too difficult for the French. However, such arguments cut no ice with the Nazi elite in Berlin, who planned to appropriate even more French food, raw materials, and manpower to compensate for shortages of supplies and workers in Germany.

La Relève—the voluntary system of exchanging French workers for French POWs—had not been the success for which Laval and Sauckel had hoped. Numbers had fallen far short of German expectations; nonetheless, Laval persevered in promoting the scheme. In August he was at Compiègne railway station, along with other Vichy and German dignitaries, keenly awaiting the arrival of the first train bringing French POWs home. Their return was planned to coincide with the departure of a trainload of volunteers, choreographed to give the impression that La Relève involved an equal exchange between departing workers and returning POWs, although, in reality, it was one POW for every three French workers.

The media were out in force ready to capture this historic moment. "Joy is written on everyone's face, and hearts are gripped by emotion," reported *L'Illustration* from the crowded platform.[54] It was probably more than joy that was written on the faces of some of the returners. There were 600 or so POWs on the train, but 1,000 rations of red wine had been laid on for them. Many of the men drank several rations each and, accustomed only to weak German beer, they arrived in Compiègne completely drunk.[55] Jean Guéhenno was disgusted by the labour exchange programme, observing that the phrase "Bringing Back the Prisoners" ("La Relève des prisonniers") was a cover for the vilest sort of blackmail, which only someone like Laval could have come up with.[56]

But Germany wanted more than just workers. In the summer the MBF told Gabriel Le Roy Ladurie, since April Vichy's minister of agriculture, that Germany needed more meat from France. However, this was nothing compared to what Hermann Göring, the head of the Reich's Four-Year Plan, had in mind. In a speech in Berlin to military commanders and senior Nazi administrators in early August he made clear his attitude towards France and the French. The French were, he claimed, "stuffing themselves with food," and yet France was a conquered country. "In the past you just pillaged," he said, "if you conquered a country you got all its wealth. These days, things are done more humanely. As far as I'm concerned I plan to pillage—and to do so with a vengeance." Complaining that "Monsieur Abetz" acted as if he held a monopoly on the definition of collaboration, Göring then summarised his own view: "When the French hand over everything they've got until they have nothing more to give, and if they do that voluntarily, then I'll say I'm collaborating."[57]

A week or so later Göring met Stülpnagel in Paris and told the MBF that he had a fortnight to let Berlin know how he was going to meet the demands of the Nazi leadership. Göring wanted the French to hand over more than two million tons of grain, 350,000 tons of meat, 300,000 tons of potatoes, 150,000 tons of vegetables, 300,000 tons of fruit and 600 million litres of wine—all for German consumption.[58] Stülpnagel was appalled. The increases were not only unrealistic, but also they posed potentially an extremely dangerous threat to law and order. It would mean further cuts in rations, in addition to the 12 percent reduction that had already been announced. This would increase the risk of social unrest and drive more French people into the arms of the Resistance. Göring brushed aside Stülpnagel's objections. But German plundering of France was not limited to foodstuffs: in late September it was estimated that 55 percent of France's aluminium production, 80 percent of its magnesium, all locomotives, and countless machines would be requisitioned by Germany. Seventy percent of French woollens would be sent to Germany, as would 84 percent of the country's cotton goods and 87 percent of its linen goods. Food requisitions would total more than five million tons.[59] Even before these new demands were taken into account, the MBF calculated that, leaving aside the black market, the cost of living in Paris had already risen by more than 65 percent between August 1939 and July 1942—a jump of nearly 50 percent in the inflation rate since the start of the Occupation.[60] Most Parisians were slowly but steadily being driven towards destitution.

While Göring demanded more French produce, Fritz Sauckel wanted more French workers for German factories. By August the number of workers participating in the Relève "voluntary" POW exchange scheme had only reached about 10 percent of German expectations and Sauckel threatened to make the system compulsory.[61]

Realising this could trigger labour unrest, strikes, and sabotage, Laval objected, and Abetz supported him. Nevertheless, on September 4 Laval signed a new labour law, applicable in both zones, giving the French government powers to specify the deployment ("in the national interest") of men and women workers, including the option of sending workers to Germany. All men aged between eighteen and fifty who were not in regular employment for at least thirty hours a week were required to register at their local *mairie*.

Laval and the collaborationist press continued to pretend that La Relève was voluntary and warned about what would happen if it failed to meet its targets. In a radio broadcast in October Laval warned his listeners, "Either La Relève will be voluntary with all the material advantages that brings to the workers, or people will be forced to leave with all the humiliation that that will mean for the worker who will be the victim."[62] Notwithstanding Laval's claims for La Relève, the September 4 labour law had brought a systematic and compulsory deployment of workers to Germany one step closer. Indeed, less than three weeks after it was passed, a Paris police report described the law as "instituting a national and obligatory labour service," adding that the new law had become the main talking point of the moment among Parisians. Although opposition to working in Germany was generally high, the report noted some people supported the law, arguing either that it meant that everyone, including "slackers" and "parasites," would have to join in the national effort or that it increased the French government's power at the expense of the cartels.

Opponents of the law, the report stated, saw it as yet another infringement of personal freedom and, according to the report, the numbers of workers visiting the German recruitment offices was as low as before. Not only were the overall numbers of workers well below what Germany expected, but so too were the number of skilled workers: in October Jean Bichelonne, the French minister of industrial production, admitted that only 17,000 skilled workers had volunteered—133,000 short of the number Germany was expecting.[63] This was despite the German tactic of closing down factories in France in the hope that those made redundant would volunteer for work in Germany. The police report recorded that the vast majority of workers viewed the new law, above all, as an act of weakness on the part of Vichy, or rather an act of obedience to German wishes, and they were fearful that La Relève was the prelude to workers being sent off en masse to Germany, where they would contribute to the Reich's industrial war machine.[64]

At the beginning of October, according to another police report, the new labour law had increased the level of disquiet and unease among the workers. To make matters worse, under another provision of the law factories were given a quota of workers they were expected to send to Germany, sparing if possible married men and those with large families. "Everywhere workers showed their hostility to groups of workers being identified to go and work in Germany; in some factories they did this by working slower than usual or even breaking off from working entirely."[65] However, with one or two notable exceptions, such as Michelin and Peugeot, lists of those selected to go were drawn up and posted by the factory management. The same police report noted that La Relève was still very unpopular with workers, who remained sceptical that French POWs would be sent back to France.

Should any workers identified by factory managers for work in Germany refuse to go, the Germans were always on hand to help out. In November the German military police arrived at the Citroën car factory in Paris and took away a group of workers who refused to leave to work in Germany. Forty-eight hours later their families were told that the men had been sent to a car factory in Saxony. Some workers from Paris factories, fearing they would be forcibly conscripted, took refuge in the countryside, finding jobs as agricultural workers.[66] Escape was not always possible. One Citroën worker who fled to his mother's native village in the provinces found it impossible to stay there and a fortnight later returned to work at Citroën. He was packed off to Germany in the next convoy of workers from the factory.[67]

Meanwhile the Vichy government and the Paris media did everything they could to persuade workers to leave for Germany. Cinema newsreels hailed the benefits of La Relève; the collaborationist press published articles urging workers to leave—like the one on the front page of *Le Matin* headed: "Why people have to go and work in Germany."[68] In an open letter to the press purportedly from French POWs, the prisoners wrote that they were worried that not all French people had understood what it was like to be in a camp and that every day that passed made the prisoners a little more bitter.[69] In an article published alongside the letter, two Vichy ministers promised that the French government would take responsibility for the well-being of the families of skilled workers who went to work in Germany.[70]

Between October and December 1942 some 180,000 French workers did leave Paris to work in Germany. However, their doing so did not constitute an unqualified boost to the German war effort. These departures resulted in a fall in output at factories in France, which were working for Germany, especially in the armament and aeronautical sectors.[71]

Alongside the fears Parisians harboured concerning the introduction of a comprehensive compulsory labour scheme, anger and resentment remained ongoing about shortages, especially as the third winter of the Occupation approached. Anger was directed at the Vichy government, the German occupiers, and the continued black-market profiteers, especially when Parisians discovered that goods they could not find in the shops were still available illegally at prices that were beyond their reach.

Shortages once again brought to the surface underlying tensions between Paris and the provinces, the city and the countryside. According to a police report in October 1942, strong feelings of animosity were widespread towards the farmers. In the autumn that year, dairy produce and meat were still in very short supply, but Parisians taking a summer break in the countryside had seen for themselves no shortage of meat, milk, or cheese existed there. Paris retailers were also unpopular with their customers, who accused the shop owners of swapping produce among themselves, which, shoppers believed, meant that customers were being denied access to large quantities of goods.[72] Shopping was as exhausting and frustrating as ever. Here is one Parisian woman's account of her time shopping in October:

> 7:30 Go to the baker's. Buy some bread. They will have some *biscottes*[73] at 11 o'clock.
>
> 9:00 Today is a day you can buy meat. The butcher tells us that it will not be delivered until Saturday.
>
> 9:30 At the cheese seller's. The cheese will not be here until 5 o'clock.
>
> 10:00 At the tripe shop. My ticket is Number 32. I won't be served until 4 o'clock.
>
> 10:30 At the greengrocer's. There will be vegetables at 5 o'clock.
>
> 11:00 Back to the baker's. No *biscottes* left.[74]

Her morning consisted, in total, of six trips, three and a half hours of waiting, and almost nothing to show for it; she had another "shopping trip" planned for the afternoon. And the next day it would start all over again, without any guarantee she would be able to buy anything. On an almost daily basis female heads of the household had to deal with a thousand and one problems, which were worse for those who were short of money.[75]

The shortage of food took its toll on the most vulnerable. A police report in September noted the concern expressed by medical specialists about the rise in the number of cases of TB in Paris since the end of 1940. "The victims are mostly young people who have not been fed well enough during their growth spurts," it said, "and wounded veterans from the First World War."[76]

☞ PARIS POLICE REPORTS in the autumn recorded how interested Parisians were in the war on the Eastern Front and how surprised they were that the Russians' apparent success in defending Stalingrad, which has led them to wonder what the outcome of the battle would be.[77] The tenacity of the Russians was encouraging to those who wanted the Germans to lose and gave the collaborationists pause for thought. But it was events closer to home, in French territories on the southern shore of the Mediterranean, that gave the biggest boost to the hopes of those Parisians longing to see the end of the German occupation.

Between 2 A.M. and 4 A.M. on the night of November 7–8, Operation Torch began: a total of 270 boats landed more than 60,000 soldiers, mostly Americans, on the north coast of Africa. They landed in the French protectorate of Morocco and in Algeria, which was constitutionally part of France. Both Morocco and Algeria had remained loyal to the Vichy government but in Algiers, on November 7, some 500 anti-Vichy locals seized important buildings in the city and held pro-Vichy military and civil leaders prisoner. This action helped the Allies to seize the city the following day, despite Pétain's ordering the 120,000-strong French army in North Africa to resist the Allied invasion. The Allies sustained 1,500 casualties in the early armed clashes and hit back hard. For once Pétain stood firm and resisted German pressure for France formally to declare war on the Allies; both he and Laval realised by the end of 1942 that a German military victory was becoming increasingly unlikely and that they needed to keep all their options open, including being prepared to cut a deal with the Allies. However, they did allow the German air force to land in Tunisia.

Parisians reacted with joy on hearing of the Allied landings. "Those who heard the news on the radio were unable to keep it to themselves and telephoned their friends," wrote the schoolteacher Jean Guéhenno. The landings were of enormous importance, he said, and could change the speed at which the war would now be pursued. On the streets of Paris the good news could be read on people's faces and by the way people moved—"their eyes were shining and they had a spring in their step," wrote Alfred Fabre-Luce. He noted how joy trumped everything: "Joy at seeing, at last, some light at the end of the tunnel of war."[78]

Perhaps it was the beginning of the end, said Benoîte Groult. "We certainly have the impression that Germany is going to get its comeuppance. The Valkyries will go back into their hole and die like something out of one of Wagner's operas."[79] Hélène Berr's parents were "very excited": she knew she should be as well, but could not adjust to the news, even though it suggested "perhaps the beginning of the end."[80] In a speech at the Mansion House in London on November 10, 1942, Winston Churchill also expressed the hope that the war was moving into a new phase: "Now this is not the end. It is not even the beginning of the end. But it is, perhaps, the end of the beginning," he said.

Other Parisians were frightened by the actions of the Allies. One of Galtier-Boissière's friends was scared that the French government would declare war on the United States and that within forty-eight hours the British would bomb Paris.[81] Georges Benoît-Guyod was concerned for the safety of his brother Jean, last heard of in Algiers commanding a regiment of Algerian colonial infantrymen loyal to Vichy. Georges dreaded the idea that Jean might have to fight his own nephew, who had joined the Free French.[82]

Micheline Bood was "really excited" about the landings and wrote in her diary that people were "glued to radio broadcasts from Britain," despite German attempts to jam them. The collaborationist newspapers were claiming that "the American aggression" meant "we will have no more wheat, coffee, chocolate, wine, etc." But this was strange, thought Micheline, as most Parisians had not seen chocolate since the early months of the Occupation.[83] If they wanted coffee they had to make do with ersatz "National Coffee." Micheline said that the Parisians' main topics of conversation were "grub, heating and clothing." It was virtually impossible to find shoes any more or even tokens for shoes from the *mairies*; leather-soled shoes had all but completely disappeared. Daily food rations for young people like herself had fallen to 350g of bread and a quarter of a litre of milk. Adults received even less—275g of bread and no milk at all.[84]

A FEW DAYS AFTER the start of Operation Torch came the German response. Following Laval and Pétain's refusal to sign a military alliance with Germany, Hitler decided to invade the whole of the country. At 7 A.M. on November 11 (Armistice Day) German troops swept across the demarcation line into the Unoccupied Zone. Hitler claimed it was not an occupation: German troops were merely stationed there to defend France against a possible Allied invasion from the south. In a letter to Pétain, Hitler insisted that his decision should not be taken as anti-French, and that he wanted the French government and administration to remain in place. However, he told the German High Command that French sovereignty would be recognised only if it served Germany's interests. "It will be abolished as soon as it is no longer compatible with the needs of the military."[85] For its part, Germany's Axis partner Italy invaded the French island of Corsica as well as parts of France near its borders and Italian troops were dispatched to Tunisia to confront the Allied armies.

Pétain gave instructions that the French armistice army, which Vichy had been allowed to retain, should not engage with the German troops as they moved southwards; only General de Lattre de Tassigny, a divisional commander in Montpelier, disobeyed, and he was promptly arrested. Two weeks later Hitler ordered the armistice army to be disbanded. On November 26, Admiral Laborde, not wanting what was left of the French fleet to fall into the hands of the Germans or the Allies, scuttled most of it in Toulon.[86] By the end of the month, Vichy's reputation was in tatters. Its fig leaf of sovereignty had been ripped off. "So, no more army, no more fleet," wrote Georges Benoît-Guyod, "not a square inch of free land in mainland France. North Africa in the hands of the British and the Americans; Savoy, Nice, Corsica, and Tunisia handed over to the [Italian] fascist buffoons. Such is the dreadful balance-sheet of the month of November."[87] The German occupation of the whole of France meant that although Germany still relied on the French government for administrative support and especially policing, there was little need now to discuss anything with the Vichy government; in future, Pétain's government would be simply informed of German decisions.

Benoîte Groult optimistically hoped that Pétain would decamp to North Africa, since he might possibly decide to rally the country from there.[88] Jean Guéhenno had no such illusions, noting that recent events proved that the 1940 armistice was an act of stupidity as well as a betrayal. "All we gained from it was shame." He concluded that, ever since 1940, Pétain had thought only about himself and never, in Guéhenno's view, had a head of state been so ignorant about his people.[89]

The Germans knew that the Allied landings in North Africa had provoked a marked rise in anti-German feeling. Members of Himmler's secret security forces reported to him that Operation Torch had unleashed "a hitherto unknown Germanophobia in France," with as many as 95 percent of the population now expecting an Allied victory. The military in Paris were equally downbeat: "Today Germany no longer has very many friends," complained one German officer based in the Paris suburbs. German optimism was rapidly dissipating, and the swagger was gone.[90] This pessimistic outlook was reinforced by the ongoing problems on the Eastern Front and the growing intensity of Allied bombing raids on Germany. From 1942 these raids were less restrictive: they no longer targeted only military installations, they included factories and, subsequently, civilian areas.

The Paris collaborationists had to consider how Operation Torch affected their plans and ambitions. Marcel Déat continued to support Laval, even though the prime minister was loathed by many Parisians—not just Gaullists and Communists—and deeply mistrusted and detested by members of Pétain's entourage at Vichy. Déat persisted in thinking that an alliance with Laval, and possibly other collaborationist parties, could still bring about the totalitarian state of his dreams. His hopes were raised further when, on November 18, Pétain signed a decree stating that future laws required only Laval's signature to be valid.

Jacques Doriot, the leader of the PPF and Déat's great rival, on the other hand, was plotting to step into Laval's shoes. He wanted to beef up Vichy's policy of collaboration, which he considered too mild and vague, and transform France into a Nazi-style state. Doriot had the backing of some sections of the German secret security forces in Paris, which fuelled his mistaken belief that he was Berlin's man in France. He emphatically ruled out an alliance with Déat or any other collaborationist leader and hoped that, with the backing of his Nazi allies in Paris, he would become the French Führer at the head of a single party controlling an utterly ruthless and ideologically committed security apparatus.

While Déat stuck with Laval, Doriot and the PPF had been staging meetings across France since the end of the summer that Doriot hoped would pave the way to ousting him.[91] On November 4 more than 7,000 PPF delegates converged on the Gaumont-Palace cinema in Paris for the start of a five-day "Congress for Power." Doriot delivered an eight-hour [!] speech in which he developed his ideas for a totalitarian France of the future. However, his plans for a triumphant climax to the congress were thwarted when Laval banned the final day's proceedings, giving as his reason the Allied landings in North Africa, which had just taken place. Doriot and his supporters responded by taking to the streets. They marched down the Champs-Élysées, shouting "Laval out! Laval Traitor! Put Doriot in Charge!" After Operation Torch, Doriot publicly demanded that Laval immediately declare war on Britain and the United States and that France seize North Africa back from *les Anglo-Saxons.*

If Doriot hoped the Allied landings and the German occupation of all France would lead the Germans to dump Laval and support him instead, he was sorely mistaken. Otto Abetz wanted to see a united front of collaborationist organisations in Paris, which also had representatives in the French government in Vichy. Hitler, like Abetz, wanted to keep France compliant and divided; he feared that backing Doriot might result in the creation of a rival Nazi-style state in France, which could ultimately challenge the Third Reich. Berlin considered banning the PPF altogether, but in the end settled for reducing its German funding.[92]

Ironically, the main German casualty of Operation Torch in Paris was Otto Abetz. His relations with Ribbentrop had been strained for several months. The German foreign minister had become ever more exasperated by Abetz's growing tendency to act as a law unto himself and by his ardent support for Laval. The North Africa landings had dramatically altered the political landscape: the rationale for Abetz's "softly-softly" approach to collaboration had evaporated. Those among the Berlin elite, like Goebbels and Göring, who had always distrusted Abetz, were quick to claim that if Berlin had not listened to Ribbentrop's man in Paris and had dealt with France more firmly, things would be a lot easier now: for example, they would not have had to tolerate a Vichy government that refused to declare war on the Allies.

"Indeed we can well and truly say that every aspect of Abetz's policy is in ruins," Goebbels noted. "He was too committed to Laval and his groups of collaborationist friends."[93] Göring, who openly mocked Abetz's interpretation of collaboration, and Fritz Sauckel, still smarting from France's failure to come up with enough workers, were both delighted to see Abetz humiliated. Ribbentrop gave Abetz his marching orders and recalled him to Berlin.

Three elements of the German forces in Paris were also glad to see Abetz sent packing: firstly, the German secret police, because Abetz consistently blocked Jacques Doriot, whom they wanted to see at the head of a National Socialist France; secondly, members of the MBF's propaganda units with whom Abetz had been in conflict ever since the start of the Occupation; and thirdly, General Friedrich-Carl Hanesse, Göring's man in Paris and the Luftwaffe's chief of staff, who had set himself up in Baron Rothschild's mansion on the avenue de Marigny. "All the hateful campaigns directed at me emanated from these three services," Abetz later claimed. He also alleged, with some justification, that these three services plotted with two of his enemies, Josef Bürckel, Gauleiter in Lorraine, and Fritz Sauckel, Hitler's foreign labour recruiter, to have him summoned back to Berlin.[94] However much Abetz wanted to blame others for his return to Berlin in disgrace, few could disagree that his policy of collaboration had failed: it had not delivered the peaceful and stable, if fragmented, France that his masters in Berlin wanted nor had it generated much French enthusiasm for a close association or alignment with the Third Reich. Most Parisians, like many of their countrymen, resented Abetz's close association with Laval and deplored the utter failure of both men to bring about any improvement in their lives. Indeed, for most people the Abetz-Laval inspired "collaboration" had meant ever-increasing misery.

Since the German invasion of Russia, life in Paris had undergone a number of major changes. The self-confidence of the German occupiers had been severely dented by a combination of defeats on the Eastern Front, the Allied landings in North Africa, and the growing intensity of Allied bombing of Germany. It remained to be seen how the Germans in Paris would react. It seemed probable that they would respond to the setbacks in the only way they knew how: with increased brutality and repression. The collaborationists in Paris also had to decide whether the game was up. Had they backed the wrong horse all along? And what would happen to them if the Allies were victorious? Any Parisian opposed to the Occupation was greatly cheered by developments on the international front. In the past one could be dismissed as a foolish idealist for even suggesting that Nazi Germany might be defeated or that the Germans might withdraw from Paris. Now it had become a real possibility. And yet, if Parisian spirits were raised, their living standards remained rudimentary: the majority of Parisians still struggled to find enough to eat; they still lacked clothes to wear and enough fuel to keep them warm; they were still waiting for loved ones to return from German POW camps; and for able-bodied men the horror of being forced to work in Germany remained a distinct possibility. Against this backdrop of hope and hardship, the Resistance improved its organisational and financial prowess (thanks to money from London).[95] However, French and German police forces were still busy tracking down, arresting, imprisoning, deporting, and executing "undesirables" and "terrorists." In 1942 thousands of Jews continued to be deported to eastern destinations from Drancy, although events in North Africa forced the Germans to suspend deportations from November 1942 until February 1943 as they were compelled to turn their attention southwards.

The month of November 1942 was perceived at the time to be a significant moment. "What will happen now?" wondered the retired schoolmistress Berthe Auroy. "We are having to learn more and more to expect the unexpected and it is with trembling fingers that I turn the knobs on the wireless set each morning. The prognoses about how long the war will last have taken off again with a vengeance. Generally speaking, most people agree that the end will come during the summer of 1943. But you ought to see the pessimists shaking their heads and sighing, 'We've got years more of this yet.' . . . In the meantime, this sad life of ours carries on."[96]

Two young Jewish women walking on the street wearing the yellow star. From June 7, 1942, all Jews over the age of six were required to wear a yellow star when they went out of doors. Many Jews reported that they were not stared at in the street but, as this photo shows, this was not always the case. Credit: Mary Evans Picture Library.

Two mock yellow stars worn by non-Jews in Paris in protest at the discriminatory edict forcing Jews to wear yellow stars and to show solidarity with the Jews. These stars are on display at the Museum of the Prefecture of Police, 4, rue de la Montagne-Sainte-Geneviève, 75005 Paris. Tous droits de reproduction réservés à la Préfecture de Police de Paris / These images may not be reproduced without permission from the Paris Prefecture of Police.

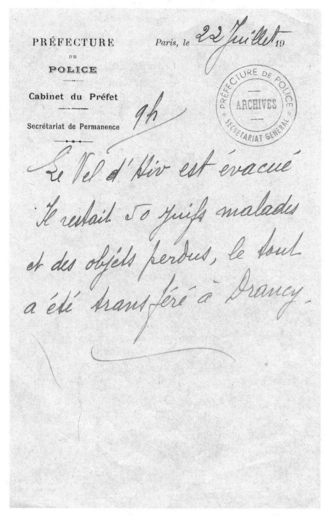

A note dated July 22, 1942, written by a French policeman informing his superiors that the Vél'd'Hiv' cycle stadium was now empty except for "50 sick Jews and some lost property. They have all been transferred to Drancy." During the night of July 16–17, 1942, the biggest round up of Jews *(la Rafle du Vél'd'Hiv')* in Paris was carried out by the Paris police. Some 8,000 Jews were held in dreadful conditions in the Vél'd'Hiv' before being sent to internment camps in France and then deported.

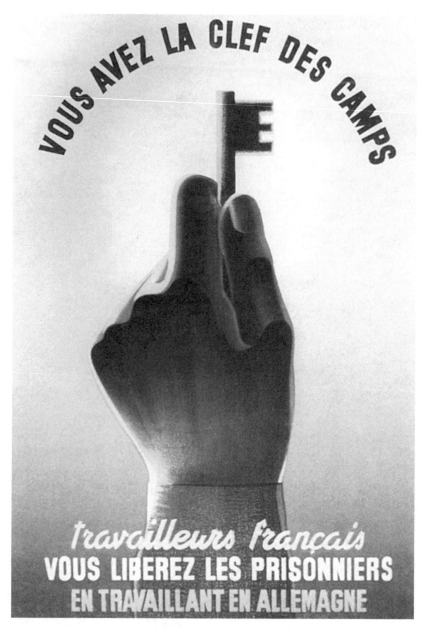

"You hold the key to the camps. French workers, by working in Germany you will be setting the prisoners free." This poster encouraged French workers to sign up for *La Relève* (The Relief), a labour programme proposed by Pierre Laval whereby one French prisoner-of-war would be released for every three French workers volunteering to work in Germany. Credit: Mary Evans Picture Library.

Frenchmen recruited to the Service du travail obligatoire (STO), on the
platform at the Gare de l'Est. The STO, a system of labour conscription forcing
French workers to go and work in Germany, was introduced by Pierre Laval in
February 1943 after *La Relève* failed to attract enough volunteers.
Credit: Roger-Viollet.

This red poster (*l'affiche rouge*) appeared on the walls of Paris in the spring of 1944 aimed at discrediting a Resistance group led by an Armenian named Missak Manouchian. The poster was reproduced as a leaflet which claimed that the group's members were unemployed or professional criminals who were inspired by Jews.
Credit: Mary Evans Picture Library.

In 1956, a street in the 20th arrondissement was named after the Manouchian group. To mark the occasion Aragon wrote a poem loosely based on Manouchian's last letter to his wife. The poem was put to music and recorded by Léo Ferré with the title "L'Affiche rouge" (The Red Poster).

The domes of Sacré-Coeur rise above a heap of rubble, the result of an Allied bombing raid. The most devastating Allied bombing raid on Paris during the war was the one on April 20–21, 1944, targeting the railway yards at La Chapelle in the north of the city. Bombs also rained down on Montmartre and on the suburb of Saint-Ouen, killing 670 Parisians. This was enough to bring Pétain to Paris—his only visit to the city during the Occupation. Credit: The Art Archive/ Mondadori Portfolio.

Two children standing among the wreckage of their home after an Allied bombing raid. Credit: Mary Evans Picture Library.

Building barricades which sprang up across the city, mainly in poor and working-class areas, provided Parisians of all ages with a way of opposing the occupying forces during the Liberation of Paris. Credit: Mary Evans Picture Library.

A barricade on the rue Saint-Jacques. "The defenders have stuck big portraits of Hitler, Goering and Mussolini on the barricade Saint-Jacques so that the Boches will riddle their heroes with bullets." Jean Galtier-Boissière, *Mon Journal sous l'Occupation* (1944). Diary entry 24 August 1944. Credit: Mary Evans Picture Library.

A plaque in memory of Victor Rastello, one of over 2,800 Parisians killed in August. Victor, a local concierge, was standing between the rue des Quatre-Vents and the rue Saint-Sulpice, just off the Carrefour de l'Odéon, on August 24 when he was shot dead by an enemy sniper.

August 25, 1944: French troops in front of Notre-Dame Cathedral. Credit: Mary Evans Picture Library.

August 25, 1944. German soldiers and civilians being taken prisoner near the Opéra. Credit: Musée de général Leclerc de Hauteclocque et de la Libération de Paris—Musée Jean Moulin, Paris-Musées. Collection Gandner.

August 26, 1944. Gun battle on the rue de Rivoli. Two police officers crouch behind a car requisitioned by the Paris Liberation Committee (Comité parisien de la Libération, or CPL), while a civilian uses the roof of the vehicle to steady his automatic weapon. Credit: Musée de général Leclerc de Hauteclocque et de la Libération de Paris—Musée Jean Moulin, Paris-Musées. Collection Gandner.

August 26, 1944. Parisians in the place de la Concorde seeking shelter from German sniper fire. Credit: The Art Archive/National Archives Washington DC.

August 26: Crowds waiting on the Champs-Élysées to cheer de Gaulle.
Credit: Mary Evans Picture Library.

August 26, 1944. Crowds massing in the centre of Paris to celebrate the liberation of the city. Credit: AFP Collection, Getty Images.

⌢ 12

Labour Conscription, Resistance, the French Gestapo

$\mathcal{T}$HE ALLIED landings in North Africa had switched the focus of the war from the Eastern Front back towards Europe. They marked an important shift in the balance of power against Germany and had triggered a German occupation of the whole of France. The course of events carried dramatic implications for the German war machine, the Vichy government, the Resistance movements, and the collaborationists as well as for "ordinary" men and women in Paris and beyond.

The need for the MBF to stretch its administrative structure to cover what had been the Unoccupied Zone led to novel and awkward interactions between the German military and secret police, on the one hand, and local French officials in the "Southern Zone," notably mayors and prefects, on the other. It also raised political, practical, and moral issues for the inhabitants of the Southern Zone, who now had to resolve how to behave towards the Germans.

The issue of who was to meet the cost of the German expansion was settled on December 19. The Germans simply informed the Vichy government that the cost of the Occupation, for which it remained liable, would rise from 300 million francs a day to 500 million. This diktat confirmed yet again Vichy's vassal-like status; it also meant the French government would have even less money available to try to meet the needs of the French people.[1]

Most Parisians opposed to the Occupation took some cheer from Hitler's decision to occupy all of the country since it showed how seriously he took the threat of an Allied landing on France's Mediterranean coast. They were overjoyed at the Allied landings in Algeria and Morocco but, as few new Allied advances followed, their attention shifted once again back to the Eastern Front. Here it was increasingly clear the German army was still in deep trouble. On January 1, 1943, for example, one broadcast from London informed listeners that in the past six weeks 175,000 German soldiers had been killed in the battle for Stalingrad. Even if this was an exaggeration, Hitler's New Year's Day proclamation to the German people—carried on January 2 by the French collaborationist newspapers in Paris—showed much less of his usual bravura and triumphalism: Under the headline "Victory!," Hitler was reported as saying, "After the winter we shall be on the march again, concentrating all our efforts on serving freedom, in other words the life and freedom of our people. The day will come when one side will be crushed. We know that will not be Germany."[2]

At the turn of the year both Jean Guéhenno and Andrzej Bobkowski noticed a change in the articles that Goebbels wrote for a German publication *Das Reich*. Guéhenno noted the Nazi propaganda minister's increasing pessimism with each passing week, while Bobkowski concluded that Goebbels did not know what to write anymore;[3] in mid-January Jean Guéhenno told his diary that he believed Nazi Germany was doomed.[4] The banker and economist Charles Rist now took the view that the war might not last as long as people feared. At a meeting at the Banque de Paris the economist noted that those he referred to as "collaborators" had long faces; some were already preparing to change sides and had started speaking of the Russians with respect.[5]

Interest in events in the Soviet Union had turned into an obsession. On January 14 Andrzej Bobkowski wrote in his diary that it was impossible to find maps of the Soviet Union anywhere in Paris and that everyone who had one was consulting it as they listened to the radio.[6] Indeed, the very next day he called on his landlords and found them stretched over a map of Russia listening to the BBC as it announced the names of towns and villages that had been retaken from the Germans. "The Russians are advancing everywhere," he wrote.[7]

Predictably the collaborationist newspapers devoted much less space to events in Russia than they had during the early weeks of the German invasion. Then, the German authorities had insisted that French news-papers publish six columns of news a day about the Eastern Front, but from January 24 they imposed a strict limit of two columns. In an abor-tive attempt to stop Parisians tracking the successes of the Red Army, German communiqués stopped mentioning place-names.[8]

At Stalingrad the Wehrmacht found itself encircled by the Red Army. The prospects for Germany could scarcely have been worse, as even Hitler was now forced to concede. On January 30, 1943, on the tenth anniversary of his appointment as Reich chancellor, the Führer pro-moted General Friedrich Paulus, his most senior officer at Stalingrad, to the rank of field marshal. This was intended as an invitation to Paulus to commit suicide "with honour." The following day Paulus decided this was an offer he could refuse and chose instead to surrender, which he did on February 2. Some sections of the German army followed Hitler's orders to fight on, but Soviet forces mercilessly bombarded them into submission. More than 200,000 German soldiers died in the abortive attempt to secure Stalingrad; another 235,000—in rags, filthy, unshaven, starving, demoralised, and ridden with lice—were taken prisoner; fewer than 6,000 of them would eventually make it home to Germany. Although the Russian campaign would grind on for months to come, the great Wehrmacht had been humbled at enormous human and material cost. Charles Rist hailed what he called "the end of the tragedy of Stalingrad," adding that this was the first time German generals had surrendered to the Russians since the Seven Years' War of 1756–1763.[9]

The Wehrmacht may have been beaten at Stalingrad, but the Nazi elite in Berlin refused to contemplate defeat at the hands of the Bolshe-viks. They resolved to throw even more men and machines against the Red Army. Desperate for military success, Berlin planned to put tens of thousands more German workers into uniform and send them off to the Eastern Front. Since many had been employed making weapons and equipment, which were also needed at the front, this in itself was scarcely a solution. Replacement workers had to be found elsewhere.

Despite all the suspicion and resentment in France surrounding La Relève, Pierre Laval's "voluntary" exchange programme, between June 1, 1942, and December 31, 1942, nearly 240,000 French workers, including almost 85,000 from the Greater Paris area, left France to work in

Germany.[10] However, Laval realised that a scheme relying on volunteers and hand-picked workers from certain factories would not be
enough to satisfy Sauckel's demand for another 250,000 workers between January 1943 and the end of March. On February 16, two weeks
after the German army's capitulation at Stalingrad, Laval took the step
that many had been dreading: he introduced, a nationwide, *compulsory*
labour conscription programme called the Service du travail obligatoire
(STO) that ran in tandem with La Relève. Under the STO, young men
(initially those born between January 1, 1920, and December 31, 1922)
would be sent to work in Germany for two years. Failure to comply
could mean imprisonment for between three months and five years and
a fine of between 200 and 100,000 francs. Some occupations and social
groups were initially exempted—farmers, miners, police officers, students, and railway workers—but, as German demands for French labour increased, many of these exemptions were modified or abolished
altogether.[11]

Towards the end of February Jean Guéhenno reported that the
system for deporting STO conscripts was working ever more efficiently.
He wrote of sullen young men lining up like convicts outside the *mairies*
in Paris, waiting to register for the STO. He longed for a spirit of resistance: if only French police would refuse to help, the Germans would
need a whole army of policemen to round up the conscripts.[12] The
banned Communist daily *L'Humanité* went further. It claimed that the
dreadful sight of dozens of young men being marched along by four or
five gendarmes would become a thing of the past if the crowd, rather
than remaining passive, "gunned down the cops or gave them a good
hiding."[13] In May a friend of Charles Braibant saw a truckload of workers
in the Latin Quarter about to be sent to Germany. They were chanting
the slogan "Laval to the shithouse!" at the top of their voices. "All the
shopkeepers standing on their doorsteps were clapping. The police
could not join in, but you could tell they would have liked to."[14]

The introduction of the STO caused widespread anger and dismay.
Jean Guéhenno wondered how he and his fellow citizens would ever
recover from the shame of it.[15] From April 1, all French workers aged
between eighteen and fifty had to carry a workplace certificate detailing
their place of employment and job title. Some Parisians continued to
respect Pétain, or view him with affection, but Pétain's meek acceptance
of Germany's occupation of the whole of France and his silence when

Laval launched the STO seriously damaged his reputation in the eyes of many who had previously looked up to him: he was increasingly seen as a puppet of Laval or a tool of the Germans. As one Parisian listener to the BBC wrote in April, "Marshal Pétain is, in the opinion of his most faithful followers, nothing but a pathetic old man, who, when not being accused of being unable to understand anything at all anymore, is charged with being in love with Germany."[16] For student Bernard Pierquin, the introduction of the STO destroyed Vichy's credibility completely. "The answer to the question, 'What would we have become without Pétain?' is very simple. 'Exactly what we are now—slaves.'"[17] Yet some Parisians still insisted that Pétain was doing his best for France. The greatest threat to France and Europe was not Nazism, they said, but Bolshevism, which had to be crushed whatever the cost. If part of that cost was Frenchmen going to work in the Reich to support the German war effort, so be it.

Between January 1 and the end of March 1943, 250,000 more French workers were packed off to Germany, including about 70,000 from the Greater Paris area. Still Sauckel was not satisfied. He demanded another 220,000 workers by the end of June. Laval was by now only too aware how much the STO was stirring up anti-German feeling and he warned Sauckel that he was unwittingly becoming de Gaulle's accomplice. Nevertheless, after much huffing and puffing, Laval caved in: he agreed to try to meet Sauckel's demands. However, between May and the end of 1943, only around 170,000 workers left for Germany, of whom fewer than 30,000 came from Paris. Paris workers made up a third of STO recruits between June and December 1942, a quarter between January and March 1943, and only a fifth between March and December 1943.[18]

Dr. Hermes, the MBF head of censorship in Paris, confidently predicted that the STO "would, by itself disorganise the army of the Resistance" by sending would-be and active resisters to Germany, and some members of the Resistance also feared this would happen.[19] But they were both wrong. While many young men dutifully, if resentfully, responded to the call-up, thousands of others refused. In both zones of France the STO became a focus for anti-Vichy and anti-German activity and propaganda. Refusal to join the STO offered a chance to resist that went beyond passive resistance or publishing a newspaper but did not necessarily mean taking up arms. In the Southern Zone, the

unfamiliar presence of the German occupiers further helped to gal-
vanise the Resistance.

Those who did not want to go to Germany under the STO had several options. Some refused to register. Others registered but did their
best to be turned down at the medical examination: the lucky ones were
examined by sympathetic French doctors who, keen to subvert the
system, accepted tales of exaggerated or invented symptoms and certi-
fied them unfit for work. The less fortunate were examined by pro-Nazi
French doctors, who deemed them fit for work whatever their condition. One such was Louis-Ferdinand Destouches, better known as the
novelist Céline, who conducted STO medicals at Bezons, a town about
six miles to the northwest of Paris. However, even conscripts who
passed the medical still had a chance to "disappear": they could simply
fail to report when it was time to leave.

Some young Parisians were officially excused. Bernard Pierquin,
like other medical students attached to hospitals in Paris, obtained an
exemption certificate from his local *mairie*.[20] Others tried to sidestep
the recruitment procedure by taking a job in one of the factories under
German control or even a German organisation like the Nazi Party's
military transport division (NSKK),[21] which meant they were unlikely
to be sent to Germany. Some Parisians dodged the STO by signing up
with Doriot's PPF, where they were not only safe from conscription, but
were fed and paid as well. From September 1943 students were no longer
exempt from the STO.[22] Jean Guéhenno wrote of Paris students escaping the clutches of the STO by taking jobs in mines or factories
offered by anti-Nazi French bosses. To Guéhenno's great regret, he
was aware of at least one case where the experience of being a manual
worker reinforced a student's feelings of superiority towards his fellow
workers, for whom he felt contempt rather than a bond of solidarity.[23]
It is not clear how common this reaction was. A friend of Bernard Pierquin was taken on in the mines at Monceau-les-Mines. Others obtained
certificates excusing them from the STO or went into hiding.[24]

Some Parisians left the city altogether, either for the Southern Zone
or farther afield. The son of Berthe Auroy's neighbours somehow managed to make it to Africa, where he joined one of the anti-Vichy French
army units fighting alongside the Allies.[25] Others decided to stay put
but to go underground. This was not easy since anyone seeking a new
ration card had to produce a work certificate clarifying their status or
an official letter exempting them from the STO. Going underground

in Paris usually meant finding a refuge and relying on someone willing to offer protection and share their meagre food allowance. The Paris police responded to the large number of Parisians dodging the STO call-up by increasing the number of spot checks on young men, especially in and around the Métro stations and cinemas. Any man unable to produce his employment documentation was promptly arrested. Even the Germans admitted that the STO was so unpopular among Parisians that a conscript on the run almost always found support among the local population, especially in working-class areas. One planned STO holding centre was scrapped because it was surrounded by workers' houses, making it too easy for a conscript to escape into an area that was particularly hostile to the STO.[26]

In March 1943 a twenty-two-year-old acquaintance of Jean Guéhenno told the schoolteacher that he was being sent to Germany. Soon afterwards Jean received a letter: the young man was working in an explosives factory in the outskirts of Berlin. He worked with three Ukrainian girls aged between twelve and fifteen filling and pushing trucks. They all knew that if there was the slightest suspicion of sabotage they would be immediately handed over to the Gestapo. In the autumn the young man was back in Paris: the work on the nightshift in the factory had been so demanding he had developed serious heart problems and had been sent home.

Broadcasts from London and Resistance propaganda exploited the widespread anger felt about the STO. When Charles Braibant went to the Sorbonne a few days after the STO was launched he found the university in uproar and its walls covered in stickers reading "Resist! Don't Go!" (even though students at this time were exempted).[27] In the summer, *L'Avant-Garde*, the clandestine newspaper of the Federation of the Young Communists of France, reported on protests against the STO in three Paris cinemas under the headline: "BRAVO, YOUNG PEOPLE OF PARIS!"[28] The Free French in London were already in good spirits after the Allied successes in North Africa and Germany's defeat at Stalingrad. They now used their broadcasts to urge young Frenchmen not to go to Germany and called on their families to encourage them to stay: in 1943 the phrase "Ne va pas en Allemagne" ("Don't go to Germany") was used almost 1,500 times in broadcasts.[29] The BBC broadcasts also emphasised Vichy's loss of legitimacy: after all, it had stood by and let the Nazis occupy all of France and it was behind the hated STO. The broadcasts exhorted French civil servants to commit acts of "administrative sabotage" by, for example, slowing down the process of STO registration and call-up, and not asking for proof of STO registration when issuing ration tickets.

The STO provided plenty of opportunities for members of the Noyautage des administrations publiques (NAP), a clandestine organisation of French officials devoted to subverting the work of the French administrative machine from within that was created in September 1942. One of its members in Paris who did most to undermine STO recruitment in Paris was Jean Isméolari. He worked, as he had before the war, as a government inspector specialising in work-related issues. With amazing guile and chutzpah, he succeeded in creating two new organisations within the Ministry of Labour.[30] The aim of the first was to cause as much confusion as possible in the STO recruitment process so as to generate the maximum number of appeals; the second unit oversaw the appeal panels: packed with anti-STO sympathisers, it issued official letters of exemption to as many people as possible.[31] One historian has calculated that Isméolari was personally responsible for saving nearly 14,000 young men born in 1920, 1921, and 1922 from being sent to Germany, and the total number of STO exemptions resulting from "administrative resistance" has been estimated at around 100,000.[32]

When the student exemption was removed in September 1943, help was at hand for those who wanted to dodge the STO call-up. Law students at the Sorbonne, for example, were helped by Georges Ripert, the dean of the faculty. Ripert was Vichy minister of education between September and December 1940 when Jews were being driven out of the teaching profession; but in 1943 the same Ripert was, according to French historian Robert Aron, willing to back-date university registration forms and allow students to enrol under false names. He also let them cut classes if they needed to "disappear" for a while and authorized them to sit exams even if their identity papers lacked the official stamp proving they had registered in the STO census.[33]

Far from decimating the ranks of opponents of the Occupation, as many Germans hoped and some Resistance leaders feared, the STO proved, on the contrary, to be a fillip for the burgeoning Resistance movements. By the spring of 1943, the Resistance was less fragmented and in both zones it was becoming possible to join the Resistance rather than simply come together with a few friends to form a small group, as had happened in the early days. Now, especially in the Southern Zone, many young men on the run from STO conscription took refuge in the countryside. Here some made contact with nascent rural Resistance groups known as the *maquis*, a term unknown in January 1943 but common currency six months later.[34] It is doubtful the *maquis* would have grown as fast as they did without the STO, but the STO's significance has sometimes been overstated; one study suggests that only about 10 percent of those who refused to submit to the STO joined the *maquis*.[35]

In Paris, Sauckel's obsessive recruitment drives were ruffling feathers in the senior ranks of the German military. General Stülpnagel was angered by Sauckel's presumption that he had unrestricted authority over the French economy. He was further outraged when Sauckel, explicitly ignored his wishes and appointed Julius Ritter to be his personal representative in Paris. Once in post, Ritter held private meetings with Laval, leaving Stülpnagel vainly protesting that the MBF was the only representative of the Occupation authorised to negotiate with the French government.[36]

Sauckel's manic recruitment of French workers ultimately foundered. He was determined to send as many French workers to Germany as possible, but in reality the Germans also needed French workers to be employed in French factories, working for Germany or on German projects like the Atlantic coastal defence wall being built by the (German) Todt Organisation. Hitler seemed to believe that half a million French workers could be transferred to Germany while at the same time French factories could increase arms production. It was pure fantasy.[37] In September 1943 Sauckel was side-lined when Albert Speer, the recently appointed German armaments minister, and Jean Bichelonne, Vichy's secretary of state for industrial production, agreed to exempt 600,000 French workers from transfer to Germany and to redeploy them in France in sectors where at least 75 percent of the output was produced for the Reich; by January 1944, more than one million French workers were employed in these sectors.[38] Although some labour transfers to Germany continued, the signing of this agreement explains why the number of workers who were subsequently involved was relatively small.

☞ BEFORE NOVEMBER 1942 the absence of Germans in the Unoccupied Zone and the French authorities' obsession with catching Communists had allowed non-Communist resistance groups to operate relatively openly. When Christian Pineau, founder of the Resistance group Libération-Nord in the Occupied Zone, visited Lyons, he was shocked to discover leaders of the Resistance walking around unhindered and openly meeting one another in cafés or restaurants. "It was almost as though they had visiting cards printed with their underground title."[39] When the Germans occupied the whole of France, however, tighter security was required and closer cooperation developed between the different Resistance movements. This is what Jean Moulin, de Gaulle's personal envoy and former provincial prefect, had been tirelessly working for since his return to France from London early in 1942.

In January 1943 the three largest Resistance networks in the south—Libération, Combat, and Franc-Tireur—came together in an umbrella organisation called the Mouvements unis de la Résistance (United Movements of the Resistance, or MUR). The now formally coordinated Resistance in the Southern Zone was better equipped to campaign against the STO. It supported conscripts from both zones who refused to be sent to Germany by forging identity papers, work certificates, and ration books, as well as feeding, housing, and arming those who opted to become active resisters.

In the spring of 1943, just over six months after German troops occupied the Southern Zone, cooperation between the different movements moved to a higher level. After months of stormy negotiations riven by interorganisational suspicions, political differences, disagreements over strategy, and disputes about structures and procedures, as well as personal rivalries and clashes of egos, Jean Moulin finally succeeded in convening a historic meeting in a small street in the Saint-Germain area of Paris.

In a first-floor flat at 48, rue du Four in the 6th arrondissement on May 27, 1943, eight representatives from the main Resistance organisations, six others from the banned political parties, and two from the trade unions (also banned) came together. The Communist Party was represented twice: once in its own right and once through le Front national (the National Front), a broad-based Resistance movement that it initiated in 1941 using republican rhetoric and calling for the unity of all "patriots." Moulin convinced the representatives that the Resistance would be more effective with a single coordinating body rather than each group going it alone. Those present voted unanimously to found the Conseil national de la Résistance (CNR), the National Resistance Council. They also voted unanimously to recognise de Gaulle as the leader of the French Resistance.[40]

Moulin stressed that de Gaulle, despite his difficulties with Churchill and especially with Roosevelt, was recognised nationally and internationally as a symbol of the anti-Nazi Resistance in France. Moulin also emphasised how every Resistance group within the CNR would benefit from financial, military, and air support from Britain if they recognised de Gaulle as its head. Furthermore, de Gaulle had access to the BBC, whose broadcasts could reach the whole of France and could serve to inspire and coordinate actions across the country. The broadcasts would also continue to give credibility to the Resistance by publicising anti-German letters from "ordinary" men and women throughout the country; since the autumn of 1941 broadcasts had been used to send coded messages to Gaullist supporters in France and this could be extended to all Resistance groups within the CNR.

From de Gaulle's perspective the CNR would provide the foundations for a broad-based post-Liberation French government. It would boost his own credibility and authority in the eyes of the British and maybe, eventually, the Americans. The Resistance movements' recognition of de Gaulle as their leader gave him a trump card to play against his rival General Henri Giraud. Giraud, a fellow French army officer, who had escaped from prison in Germany. Just after the Allied landings Giraud reached North Africa, where he had tried to secure American backing to replace de Gaulle as the Allies' main interlocutor. In the event, de Gaulle completely outmanoeuvred him. Even before the creation of the CNR, the Resistance movements were becoming better organised and attracting more members and supporters—although only a tiny percentage of Parisians or the French population as a whole could ever be described as "active resisters."

The early Resistance groups had been small, often short-lived organisations that were essentially devoted to spreading propaganda against the occupying power and collecting information potentially useful to the Allies. By 1943, especially after the German defeat at Stalingrad, the tide of war seemed to be turning in the Allies' favour. Resistance attacks on German personnel and property continued as did sabotage actions but now Resistance groups were receiving funding and arms from London. In Paris, the cultural hub of the nation, the intellectual

Resistance had also opened up its own offensive, first with *La Pensée libre* and then with *Les Lettres françaises*.

La Pensée libre was a Paris-based clandestine literary journal sponsored by the PCF and spearheaded by three of the party's intellectuals. The first, Jacques Decourdemanche (known as Jacques Decour), was a novelist, the editor of the prewar literary review *Commune*, and a teacher of German at the Lycée Rollin. The second was a Marxist philosopher named Georges Politzer and the third was Jacques Solomon, a researcher in quantum physics. The first issue of *la Pensée libre*, running to ninety-six pages, appeared in February 1941, but despite claims to be open to non-Communists, it had all the appearances of a party publication. Pressures from within the party for a more literary and less rigidly orthodox publication resulted in Pierre de Lescure taking charge of the production of the second issue. De Lescure had moved in literary circles in Paris before the war and had been published with the famous publishing house of Gallimard; however, more importantly, he had good contacts with the party. From October 1940 de Lescure was engaged in intelligence gathering; he worked closely with British Intelligence and also had dealings with the Musée de l'Homme Resistance group.[41] De Lescure teamed up with Jean Bruller, a journalist and illustrator before the war who worked as a carpenter during the Occupation. When all the material for the second issue of *La Pensée libre* was destroyed during a German raid on the premises where the journal was printed, Lescure and Bruller resolved to find another outlet for literary resistance. *La Pensée libre* did not reappear.

Meanwhile, Jacques Decour had fully embraced the idea of bringing together anti-Nazi writers from across the political spectrum; later in 1941 he, Jean Paulhan, former editor of the *Nouvelle Revue française* and novelist François Mauriac, cofounded the Comité national des écrivains, or CNE, which would have its own newspaper: *Les Lettres françaises*. This new clandestine literary publication would offer a platform for writers to denounce the occupying forces, their supporters in France, and the ideas that underpinned Nazism.

Decour had assembled the texts for the first issue of *Les Lettres françaises* (including a book review by Pierre Lescure), but was arrested in February 1942 before he could produce it; he was shot by the Germans three months later, a week after the executions of Politzer and Solomon, his colleagues on *La Pensée libre*. Responsibility for producing *Les Lettres françaises* passed to Claude Morgan and it was not until September 1942 that the first issue finally appeared; all six pages were written almost entirely by Morgan, but the editorial Decour had prepared for the first issue was given pride of place on the front page. *Les Lettres françaises* was typed and duplicated monthly using stencils until October 1943 when it started appearing in a professionally printed form. Besides Morgan, its contributors included Jean-Paul Sartre, Albert Camus, Jean Guéhenno, Raymond Queneau, Paul Éluard, Aragon, Elsa Triolet, and Jean Paulhan. Edith Thomas was also involved in the project: besides contributing to the publication, it was at her home in the 5th arrondissement that the meetings of the CNE were held.[42] It was the CNE that gave Sartre the green light to stage his play *Les Mouches* (The Flies). A favourable review of Sartre's play by surrealist writer and ethnographer Michel Leiris appeared on the front page of *Les Lettres françaises* in December 1943.[43]

After the loss of all the material for the second issue of *La Pensée libre*, Bruller and Lescure co-founded an independent clandestine publishing house, which they called Les Éditions de Minuit (Midnight Editions). Its aim was to allow authors to publish short works of literature without risking contamination of their literary output or reputation through contact with German censorship; it would also challenge Vichy's claim to represent France and show that democratic and republican values had not been crushed. The most famous book Les Éditions de Minuit produced was its first, published in September 1942, written by Bruller under the pseudonym Vercors and entitled *Le Silence de la mer* (The Silence of the Sea). The story is told in the first person by a man who lives with his niece in a house in the provinces where a cultured, Francophile German officer has been billeted. The officer talks about French and European culture and tries to engage his hosts but his words are met with a wall of silence. After a trip to Paris, the officer tells his hosts that he was so disgusted by what other Germans were saying about Paris and France that he had asked for a transfer to the Eastern Front. He says that he will be leaving the following morning. He bids his hosts good night as he has done very night but adds "Adieu." Then, after a poignant pause, the young woman breaks her silence for the first and last time and whispers "Adieu" in return. A review in *Les Lettres françaises* early in 1943 described it as "the most moving, the most deeply human book that we have had read since the start of the German

Occupation."[44] Les Éditions de Minuit clandestinely published some twenty books and it, like *Les Lettres françaises*, survived to continue after the Liberation.

⊱ THE GERMAN INVADERS were increasingly on edge. They were rattled by continuing setbacks on the Eastern Front and viewed the Allied presence in North Africa with foreboding. The German forces, now spread across the whole of France, were more exposed and vulnerable to attack from the Resistance, which was growing ever stronger and more confident. In December 1942 Hitler told Laval that he wanted him to create a new French paramilitary force to work alongside the occupying forces in the fight against anti-German "terrorism." Otherwise, Hitler warned Laval, he might have to treat France like Poland and send in the SS. According to Marcel Déat, the leader of the RNP, Laval had been already planning just such a force for at least a month. Laval knew it would give him dominance over his opponents and protection from his enemies. "He is still at the planning stage of his project," wrote Déat in his diary on November 23, 1942, "but he is envisaging a French Militia that would operate in both zones."[45]

Laval was starting to feel ever more threatened by the Paris-based collaborationists; he believed a French national militia under his control would protect him should the collaborationists decide, as he feared, to form a French pro-Nazi front. Laval worried, in particular, that Marcel Déat's RNP and Jacques Doriot's PPF might link up with the Service d'ordre légionnaire (SOL), a paramilitary grouping in the south led by Joseph Darnand. The SOL had initially supported Pétain's National Revolution, but Darnand, already impressed by what he saw on a visit to Germany in the summer of 1942, deplored Vichy's refusal to back SOL members fighting the Allies in North Africa a few months later. He wrote to Laval complaining of the government's "inertia" at a time when firm action was required. Darnand believed that an Allied victory would mean a return to the bad old days of corrupt democracy. It was time to stand firm alongside Germany. Pétain was tainted in the eyes of the collaborationists by what they saw as Vichy's feeble response to the Allied landings, its general lack of resolve, and its refusal to proclaim unconditional support for Germany.

Laval believed that a national militia built around the SOL with Darnand at its head would enable him to uncouple Darnand (based in the south) from the Déat's RNP and Doriot's PPF, each with their own militias, in Paris. In December 1942, PPF members again demonstrated, demanding Laval's resignation as head of government and even calling for him to be shot as a traitor. Darnand also threatened to join Doriot in a march on Vichy.

Laval exploited the Germans' obsession with their troops' security, claiming that a national militia proved his practical commitment to the fight against Germany's enemies within France. Pétain had lost his "Unoccupied Zone," his fleet, and his armistice army, and he looked on helplessly as France's colonies were occupied by the Allies or went "Gaullist." He welcomed the creation of the militia, hoping it might prop up the crumbling edifice of his National Revolution. He also thought it might be used as a bargaining counter with Hitler at some point in the future.

Early in 1943 Laval's dream was realised. On January 5, 1943, Pétain, announced the creation of La Milice française, a national militia, directly answerable to Laval and headed by Darnand. Its official brief was to "contribute to France's recovery" (as defined by Vichy), using propaganda, surveillance, and political mobilisation, as well as combatting communism and "the Jewish plague." The Milice counted about 15,000 members by the end of the year, about 10 percent of them women. They included Catholic fundamentalists, monarchists, pro-Nazis, and other right-wing extremists. Some still believed in Pétain's National Revolution; others, like Darnand, were more explicitly pro-German. All were committed to hunting down France's "enemies within," notably resisters, Jews, Communists, and STO-refusers.

When Darnand addressed the founding meeting of the Milice in Vichy on January 30 he told his audience that by working closely with the French government they would bring order, clarity, and coherence to their currently divided and disorganised country. Darnand said his ultimate aim was to "establish in France an authoritarian, national-socialist regime, enabling France to be an integral part of the Europe of the future."[46] Members of the Milice passed on information about Resistance activities to the German secret police and the Abwehr, and they were directly responsible for killing resisters in Lyons, Grenoble, and Marseilles. On April 29 came the first reprisal from the Resistance: the deputy leader of the Milice in the Bouches-du-Rhône department in the Southern Zone was gunned down. Pétain's predictable response

was to publicly back the Milice, describing it as "the crucial weapon in
the fight against all dark forces."[47] In June the Milice's own uniformed
fighting force, La Franc-Garde, was founded. Laval mistakenly thought
that by putting Darnand at the head of the Milice he would restrain a
man whom he saw as a threat and neither liked nor respected. However, Laval's sentiments about the Milice were those that Dr. Franken-
stein harboured about his "monster": he realised his creation was taking
on a life of its own.

⯈ ALLIED ADVANCES AND SUCCESSES in Russia, North Africa, and Italy
had hardened the resolve of the collaborationists, encouraged the resisters to become more daring, and given extra hope to all those who
opposed the Occupation. Growing numbers of Parisians, hitherto
attentistes—those who had adopted a wait-and-see-stance—and those
who, without being out and out collaborationists, had made an accommodation with the Occupation, were reexamining their position. The
Paris police were no exception: as 1943 progressed, signs of tension and
dissension in their ranks were growing. In August Helmut Knochen,
the deputy head of the German secret police, wrote a report deploring
passive resistance and a lack of commitment among the French police.
He floated the idea of the Gestapo sacking unreliable policemen and
deporting them to Germany, although this did not happen. In a second
memorandum in the same month, Knochen warned that if (or when)
the Allies invaded, the French police would probably stab German soldiers in the back. He also noted a shift in the popular mood away from
the Communists and towards the more moderate de Gaulle. It seemed
to Knochen beyond doubt that even in the upper echelons of the police sympathy could be found for the Gaullists. The staff at the Paris
Prefecture of Police, he firmly believed, had become "predominantly
anti-German."[48]

But as sections of the Paris police became more anti-German, the
Brigades spéciales (BS), the police anti-Resistance squads, aligned themselves even closer to the occupying forces and were ever more energetically tracking down "the enemies within" and becoming increasingly
brutal in their interrogation methods. The German secret police, too,
became even more vicious often recruiting French criminal gangs only
too willing to help them carry out their dirty work. The most noto-

rious of these, known as "the French Gestapo from the rue Lauriston," was headed by Henri Chamberlin, now known as Henri Lafont.

As the Germans advanced on Paris in June 1940 Chamberlin, then a thirty-eight-year-old small-time French crook, was one of a cohort of prisoners evacuated from the Cherche-Midi prison in Paris to a camp at Cepoy in the Loiret. In the subsequent chaos that swept through France that summer, Lafont made his way back to Paris with a couple of fellow prisoners, who had been imprisoned for spying for Germany. When they arrived in Paris, one of them introduced Lafont to "Otto" Brandl, the spy's superior within German military intelligence (Abwehr). Brandl was already making a fortune buying and selling goods through his "purchasing office" and Lafont became a member of his heavy mob, dealing with anyone who owed money to Brandl or tried to sell him short.

Lafont also drew on his knowledge of the Paris underworld to provide Brandl's "purchasing office" with the names of shady dealers, what they dealt in, and where they stored their goods. In August 1940, Lafont presented himself at Fresnes prison claiming to be a member of the German police, and he managed to secure the release of some thirty criminals. At a stroke Lafont acquired a band of ruthless crooks who owed him their freedom as well as simultaneously gaining a reputation as someone who was well regarded by the Germans. This made him both powerful and dangerous. A few days after the Fresnes coup, thanks to a recommendation from Brandl, Lafont enlisted in the German police force. In 1941 Lafont took German nationality, was appointed captain in the Wehrmacht, and later became an officer in the SS.

Lafont established his gang headquarters at 93, rue Lauriston, an early twentieth-century townhouse in the 16th arrondissement and, even before the summer of 1942 when Knochen's secret police finally wrested responsibility for security and policing away from the military, Lafont had sensed which way the wind was blowing. He had started moving away from the Abwehr and began cultivating leading members of the secret police, especially the Gestapo, headed by Karl Boemelburg, which was based in the rue des Saussaies and the avenue Foch.

It was about this time, in April 1942, that Lafont was joined by a man with whom his name would become inextricably linked: Pierre Bonny. Bonny, once described by a government minister as France's top policeman, made his name in the 1930s during a sensational case involving the suspicious dealings and mysterious death of a swindler, Alexandre Stavisky. However, Bonny's reputation was shattered shortly afterwards when he was drummed out of the police force for embezzlement and bribery, before being found guilty in court of misappropriating public funds.

Superficially, the two men could not have been more different: Lafont, the abandoned child who became a street hoodlum, a chancer, a fixer, and a manipulator, who lived by his wits; and Bonny, the outwardly respectable, obedient, and zealous bureaucrat, albeit a corrupt and greedy one, a man who was most at home at his desk with his files and reports. Bonny introduced systems procedures and protocols, bringing a sense of order to the gang's activities, while Lafont provided the cruel and ruthless flair. "Monsieur Henri," as Lafont liked to be called, was the undisputed boss, feared and admired by Bonny in equal measure; however, together they formed a redoubtable duo.

Lafont fêted and flattered the head of the Paris Gestapo, catering to Boemelburg's every desire, even allegedly finding him male prostitutes. Lafont showered him with gifts, many of them stolen, like the beautiful pieces of silver lifted from a collection worth millions of francs once belonging to the American ambassador to Poland.[49] Boemelburg was in Lafont's debt and under his spell, but he also understood how useful Lafont's gang could be to him and to the Gestapo. Thanks to Bonny's organisational skills the gang had become a ruthlessly efficient and effective organisation. It was feared and respected in gangland Paris, where it had extensive contacts and influence, as it did within the many branches of the occupying forces.

Once the Bonny and Lafont gang aligned itself with the Gestapo, its leading members were officially allowed to carry weapons. They were issued with German police identity cards and travel passes giving them unrestricted travel within and beyond the city. Their official German papers and the support of the German secret police meant the gang could operate with impunity, putting it beyond the reach of the French police and giving it an edge over rival gangs.

It was illegal for Parisians to deal in foreign currency (or gold) in occupied France and one of the gang's early lucrative activities was tracking down Parisians who had gold they wanted to sell. Gang members posed as discreet buyers wanting to offload some cash, but when the seller showed them the gold, they produced their police cards, confiscated the gold, and took the seller back to the gang's headquarters on the rue Lauriston. Any Jews were handed over to the Gestapo; others who had been duped were released but were too frightened to complain, believing they had been caught trading illegally by the official German police. The gold was duly delivered to the German foreign currency office in the 9th arrondissement and Lafont received up to 30 percent of its value as a reward.[50]

Lafont's men used the same tactic to confiscate goods from big-time black-market dealers. They took the seized goods either to one of Brandl's "purchasing offices" or to Lafont's other Abwehr contacts at the Hôtel Lutetia. Lafont also worked closely with General Behr in pillaging raids on Jewish homes. He provided Behr with security guards for his new headquarters on the avenue d'Iéna and Lafont's men either took part in raids on Jewish homes themselves or passed on the addresses to Behr.[51]

Lafont's gang also tracked down members of the Resistance. One of Lafont's earliest assignments for the Abwehr was the capture in Toulouse of Otto Lambrecht, a key member of the Belgian resistance. Lafont handed him over to the German authorities in Bordeaux, who went on to arrest more than 600 members of Lambrecht's network. One of the gang's greatest coups was the infiltration of the Paris-based Resistance group Défense de la France (In Defence of France), which produced a newspaper of the same name. (See Chapter 7).[52] Émile Marongin, a student working for Lafont, penetrated deep into the organisation and filed reports to Bonny listing the personal details of members and sympathisers, addresses of letter drops, safe houses, and storage points for the group's newspapers prior to distribution. In July 1943, after three months gathering information, Lafont launched a raid that focused on a bookshop in the rue Bonaparte in the 6th arrondissement, which the Défense de la France militants used as one of their main letter drops. Some fifty members of the network, including General de Gaulle's niece, Geneviève de Gaulle, were rounded up. Lafont took them to one of his gang's premises on the place des États-Unis, where they were beaten up and then handed over to the Germans before being deported.[53] Geneviève de Gaulle was sent to Ravensbrück. She survived the war, but a dozen of her comrades did not. Marongin was paid 80,000 francs for his work. The German authorities later concluded (wrongly) that he was a double agent and deported him to Buchenwald. He was freed by the Americans, returned to France to stand trial, was condemned to death, and executed on December 26, 1946.

The headquarters of the Bonny-Lafont gang was in Paris but it also operated in the provinces. It was involved in at least fifteen actions with the German secret police when—allegedly abetted by a pro-Nazi British army officer and a renegade Gaullist resister—it helped to round up British agents and seized weapons that had been parachuted into France. The Allied agents often carried important military documents and sometimes huge sums of money, like the captured army colonel who was dropped into France with four million francs; another intercepted parachute drop about seventy miles south of Paris in June 1943 yielded more than four tons of weapons.[54]

Lafont had his own contacts in the provinces who kept him informed about what was happening, but any of his men found cutting a private deal with the local German secret police ran the risk of being killed. When Lafont discovered that Jean Leroy, one of his contacts in Limoges, was working independently with the local Gestapo he sent a gang member from Paris to kill him. The assassin allegedly returned to Paris with Leroy's decapitated head as evidence that Lafont's orders had been carried out.[55]

Lafont may have worked for the Germans, but he made sure he always had the upper hand. Just as he "bought" Boemelburg by showering him with lavish gifts, so he gave Helmut Knochen, the deputy head of the secret police, a Bentley car valued at 500,000 francs as a wedding present. A suspicious Knochen assigned two officers to keep an eye on Lafont, but within days Lafont had so corrupted them that they ended up spying on Knochen for Lafont. Among the Abwehr officers and leading members of the German secret police, only Carl Oberg refused all contact with Lafont and never accepted his presents.

It was not just the Germans who were in Lafont's power and debt: other shadowy figures could also find themselves beholden to him for a service rendered. One of these was the illiterate, multimillionaire rag-and-bone man Joseph Joinovici, who had made a fortune selling vast quantities of metal to Brandl's "purchasing office." In the early days Brandl had enough influence to save Joinovici from being rounded up because he was a Jew and to protect his company from requisitioning under the laws related to the "economic Aryanisation of Jewish businesses." By the summer of 1943, however, when the purchasing offices were being wound down, Brandl could no longer act as Joinovici's protector; in September the Amt IV-J, the anti-Jewish bureau of the Gestapo, issued a warrant for Joinovici's arrest. Brandl appealed to Lafont for help. Lafont agreed to protect Joinovici at a price—five million francs. Joinovici paid up and was not arrested. Lafont's ability to protect Joinovici from the Gestapo when even the Abwehr was unable to do so speaks volumes about the power and influence of the head of the "French Gestapo" in Paris. Three months later the Amt IV-J ordered Joinovici to attend a medical examination to see if he was circumcised. This time, Karl Boemelburg, the head of the Gestapo, almost certainly acting on instructions from Lafont, intervened and ensured that the matter was dropped.[56]

Lafont had a string of affairs with glamorous aristocratic and high-society women, including Benito Mussolini's mistress Magda Fontanges and one of the mistresses of the Prince of Monaco.[57] Another of Lafont's mistresses, Tatiana Murutchev, oversaw the luxurious refurbishment of most of 93, rue Lauriston, creating a sumptuous setting for the extravagant dinners and wild parties for which Lafont became famous. He loved to be surrounded by the glamorous and powerful, and his banquets were attended by the Gestapo and other sections of the secret police, selected members of his gang, actresses, models, collaborationist journalists, staff from the Abwehr and the German embassy, including Abetz before his recall to Berlin. French stars from the world of sports, cinema, and the music halls also enjoyed his hospitality or came to him to ask a favour, such as freeing a prisoner from jail or securing the release of a POW. The entertainer Maurice Chevalier visited Lafont shortly before the invasion of the Unoccupied Zone to obtain a pass allowing him to cross the demarcation line and visit a property on the Côte d'Azur.[58]

While *le tout Paris* was wining and dining in style, and taking part in orgies on the upper floors of the mansion on the rue Lauriston, it was quite a different story in the basement. This was where Lafont and his associates interrogated and tortured many of those they had "arrested," before handing them over to Boemelburg's men. Two maids employed at the house later testified to seeing severely beaten detainees being removed from the room; Joseph Joinovici claimed he saw Bonny strike a detainee so hard that Bonny broke a ring he was wearing. The worst treatment was reserved for suspected resisters who refused to talk. Electrical leads were attached to their genitals or they were subjected to the terrifying ordeal of the *baignoire*—an early version of "waterboarding"—whereby the prisoner's hands and feet were bound and their head forcibly held under ice-cold water until they passed out. If they still refused to talk when they regained consciousness, the procedure was repeated. Another method of torture was to cover the soles of the prisoner's feet in petrol and set them alight.[59]

☞ WHILE LAFONT AND HIS HENCHMEN entrapped and tortured resistance fighters in the basement at 93, rue Lauriston, the Brigades spéciales (BS) of the Paris police were hunting down members of the PCF's own clandestine immigrant worker organisation, the Main d'œuvre immigrée (Immigrant Workforce, or MOI); the MOI was subdivided into contingents based on language or ethnicity and was vital to the party's work of political education, agitation, and propaganda. In May 1942, the BS arrested a group of Yugoslav Communist workers who published their own news-sheet; this was followed a month later by the arrest of more than a hundred members of what the police called "the clandestine group of Spanish Communists in France." Despite these setbacks, in the summer of 1942 each of the MOI's remaining sections seconded 10 percent of its members to form armed detachments, collectively known as the FTP-MOI.[60] The activities of these armed FTP-MOI groups overlapped with those of the Valmy Detachment, which was smashed by the police in the autumn of 1942; most of the Valmy group were deported in March 1943.

Between September 1942 and the end of the year the armed FTP-MOI detachments carried out almost sixty spectacular attacks on German and collaborationist targets in Paris and the surrounding area.[61] Some members of the FTP-MOI detachments were arrested; although horribly tortured, they bravely faced a firing squad, having told their interrogators nothing. A dearth of information about the structure and membership of both the MOI itself and its armed wing, the FTP-MOI, left the BS struggling to break up both networks.

In January 1943, however, thanks to a tip-off, the BS started tailing eighteen-year-old Henri Krasucki, a leading member of the MOI's Jewish youth organisation, who lived in the largely immigrant Jewish 20th arrondissement. This secret surveillance of Krasucki and his girlfriend Paulette Silwka led the BS to other militants; this in turn, yielded yet more names and addresses, so that in March 1943, when the BS arrested Krasucki and Silwka they were also able to seize another sixty or so militants. Krasucki had been betrayed by Lucienne Goldfarb, a young Jewish woman from the rue des Immeubles-Industriels in the 11th arrondissement. She later claimed she informed on Krasucki and other young Jewish Communists from the 11th and 20th arrondissements whom she knew in exchange for the release of her parents, who had been arrested.[62]

The young militants were taken to the BS headquarters inside the Prefecture of Police, where their French interrogators stripped them naked, beat them using whips with pieces of lead attached to the lashes, and, in Krasucki's case at least, tortured him in front of his mother, Léa. One militant exempted from the beatings was the heavily pregnant seventeen-year-old Anna Neustadt. In April she gave birth to a baby boy and named him Gaby. She managed to get the news to Gaby's seventeen-year-old father, a fellow Communist militant named Thomas Fogel, who, like most of the MOI youngsters, was by then in Drancy. A long letter written by Thomas on May 31 concluded, "Just one word, my dearest Anna, and my little Gaby, be brave and don't give up hope, just keep thinking of our young and powerful love which will bury all these bastards. Because, Anna darling, it is our love which will be the constant bond in our march towards victory."[63] Shortly afterwards, Fogel was deported to Auschwitz and was later transferred to a labour camp at Jaworzno in southern Poland, where he died without ever seeing his son; his parents, who never saw their grandson, were on the same convoy from Drancy to Auschwitz as their son Thomas and were gassed on arrival. Anna and seven-month-old Gaby made it to the Vendée in western France, where they and a handful of Jews were sheltered by Protestant families in the hamlet of Le Noirvault.[64]

In November 1942, deportations from Drancy were temporarily suspended as the trains were needed to move men and materiel across France after the landings in North Africa. In February 1943 they resumed and three convoys left the camp that month taking some 3,000 French and foreign Jewish men, women, and children to Auschwitz.[65] Many of the deportees were sick or elderly and two women died in the bus taking them from Drancy to the nearby railway station of Le Bourget-Drancy. A month later, on March 23, a total of 994 prisoners left Drancy in Convoy 52 for the Sobibor extermination camp in Poland. Among them was Jacques Biélinky, the Jewish art critic and journalist whose diary gives a sober insight into life in Paris during the early years of the Occupation. Biélinky was one of 1,600 elderly Jews rounded up in Paris during the night of February 10–11.[66] No one in the March 23 convoy returned.

After three weeks in the hands of the French police, the MOI militant Henri Krasucki was moved to the German section of Fresnes prison near Paris, reserved for those condemned to death. He was held for two and a half months with no one knowing what had happened to him. He was then transferred to Drancy and deported to Auschwitz in June 1943 in a convoy of more than 1,000 people, including most of his comrades and his mother. Henri was one of only six of the young Jewish MOI militants who survived.[67] His mother also returned and both are buried in Père Lachaise cemetery in Paris.

When an MOI militant was selected to join its armed wing, the FTP-MOI, his or her life changed radically; those seconded were paid around 2,000 francs a month for subsistence; they had to live alone, often cold and hungry, with no human contact, except with a very small number of other designated FTP-MOI militants. They lived knowing that at any moment they could be arrested, tortured, executed, or deported be it through betrayal or carelessness or simply bad luck. And the tasks they were set to do could also be extremely hazardous.

A former chemistry student, Samuel Weissberg was seconded to the FTP-MOI Jewish detachment and became its bombmaker. In early December 1942 he was assembling a bomb in his "laboratory"—a kitchen in his small apartment—when it exploded.[68] Weissberg was thrown across the room, his clothes and hair ablaze. The room filled with acrid smoke. Somehow he struggled out of the apartment and staggered down a quiet side street. Luckily, a shopkeeper hid him in the back of her shop; six hours later, under cover of darkness, he reached a safe house, where he collapsed. A doctor was called and arranged for him to be taken to a hospital by the only means available—a bicycle rickshaw.

After a few days, Samuel learned that the doctor had been denounced for "treating terrorists" and was being hunted by the police. Samuel was moved to another flat, where he was nursed by Hélène Kro, a young Jewish wife of a POW and mother of a four-year-old boy, who had joined the armed struggle after the Vél'd'Hiv' roundup. Hélène was later caught transporting dynamite and taken by the police to her fourth-floor apartment while they searched it. She realised the game was up and, afraid of betraying her comrades under torture, she waited until the police were distracted, rushed to the window, and threw herself to her death.[69]

In April 1943 a BS report referred to an increase in armed attacks carried out by Communists in the Paris region since the start of the year. The BS responded by preparing a crackdown against the adult Jewish section of the MOI. Its agents once again secretly followed known and suspected militants, and in June they started to arrest them. By the end of July 1943 almost all the leaders of the Jewish MOI section were in the hands of the police, along with some 150 militants. Fewer than 100 of about 550 militants active at the beginning of the year were still at liberty.[70] In the roundup the police netted forty militants suspected of belonging to the FTP-MOI. It was a devastating blow to the armed detachment. However, while the armed resistance in Paris may have been down it was by no means out. It was about to regroup and strike back with a vengeance.

～ 13

Anti-Bolshevism, Black Market, More Bombs, Drancy

$\mathcal{B}$Y THE SUMMER OF 1943, the police had decimated the MOI organisation. The PCF dissolved the weakened FTP-MOI groups and replaced them with just two groups: one, comprising mainly Spanish militants that specialised in train derailments, mostly outside Paris, and the other that launched armed attacks in and around Paris itself. This second group was led by Missak Manouchian, an Armenian who had emigrated to France in 1925, worked at the Citroën car plant in Paris, and joined the PCF in 1934. Manouchian, like many of his group's members, was Jewish; most of the other members had Hungarian or Polish backgrounds, the others were Spanish, Italian, or Romanian. Despite the loss of members from its ranks, the FTP-MOI's armed offensive escalated: between June and October 1943 it carried out some seventy attacks.[1]

On July 28, an FTP-MOI unit bombed what they thought was the car of General Schaumburg, German commander of Greater Paris. However, not only was Schaumburg not in the car, he was no longer in post; he had been replaced two months earlier by General Boineburg-Lengsfeld, who was not in the car either.[2] This attack, requiring tremendous courage and nerve, was ultimately therefore largely symbolic; it illustrates how difficult it was for the Resistance to obtain reliable and up-to-date information about the Germans.

Another FTP-MOI attack two months later was more successful. Over a period of weeks, Cristina Boïco, the Romanian head of the FTP-MOI's intelligence-gathering unit, tracked the movements of a big official Mercedes. It carried an important German passenger— sometimes in uniform, sometimes in civilian dress—between his home in the 16th arrondissement and his workplace in the requisitioned Maison de la Chimie.[3] On September 28 an FTP-MOI hit squad was in position outside the man's home at 18, rue Pétranque at 8:30 A.M. when he stepped into his car, as he did every day at that time. The first shots missed their target, but a second volley hit the man in the stomach as he tried to make a run for it. The target was still alive. One member of the squad tried to finish him off, but his gun jammed. He resorted to stabbing the man in the chest; the man's bodyguard and chauffeur were also killed. The following day the FTP-MOI militants learned through the press that they had killed Julius Ritter, the Paris representative of Fritz Sauckel, the architect of the STO, the compulsory labour scheme.

Ritter's killing was at the top of an impressive list of FTP-MOI attacks that month, which also included the derailment of four trains outside Paris, the assassinations of German soldiers and police officers, and a series of grenade attacks on two German trucks, on a café frequented by Germans, and on the offices of Doriot's Parti populaire français (PPF). But, unsurprisingly, the police were closing in.[4] The Brigades spéciales (BS) once again resorted to tailing known or suspected militants and, as was their practice, patiently establishing links between members of the network. In October they arrested Joseph Davidovitch, the political head of the FTP-MOI for the Paris region. He talked, gave the BS information, most of which confirmed what they already knew, and was then allowed to "escape" and rejoin his comrades. A policeman sympathetic to the Resistance leaked details of Davidovitch's treachery: Davidovitch was interrogated by members of the FTP-MOI, confessed to betraying them, and was summarily executed. However, this understandably harsh punishment did nothing to save the group. On November 13 the BS, using the data collated over months of surveillance, confirmed and in some cases complemented by what Davidovitch had told them, arrested more than one hundred suspected militants, classified, according to police terminology, as fifty-eight Jews of various nationalities, twenty-nine foreigners, and twenty-one French "Aryans."[5] The FTP-MOI was destroyed. Three days later Missak Manouchian was also captured; all those arrested were tortured by the BS before being turned over to the Germans. This was quite an extraordinary moment. As the French historian Denis Peschanski later wryly observed, "Here we have foreigners fighting for the liberation of France being identified, followed, and arrested by French police officers working for the German occupying forces."[6]

After the war the PCF was accused of abandoning Missak's group to their fate. According to Missak's wife, Mélinée, her husband realised members of the group were under surveillance and asked the clandestine PCF leaders to smuggle the activists out of Paris, but they refused.[7] Adam Rayski, the political head of the MOI Jewish section, also pleaded for the resisters to be evacuated out of the danger zone, but only Rayski and two other political (rather than military) leaders were spirited out of Paris and away to safety. Those who carried out the attacks remained behind.

For both national and international reasons, the PCF believed it was imperative to maintain its armed groups in Paris and not pull them out of the city—even if the militants on the ground were almost certain the police were closing in. The date and place of the opening of the Allied second front were as yet unknown, but the Resistance was already making preparations for the Liberation of France and this meant maintaining a strong and active Communist presence in the city. In August 1943 a Paris Liberation Committee was created to organise efforts to liberate the city, and half its members were members or sympathisers of the PCF. Stalin, desperately wanting the United States and Britain to open up a second front with a landing in northern France, adopted a conciliatory stance towards the two countries. In France, the PCF leadership ruled out making a revolutionary bid for power and, instead, expressed a willingness to work closely with de Gaulle and his French Committee of National Liberation (CFLN), thus positioning itself to play a key role in politics after the Liberation. The PCF needed to remain at the cutting edge of the armed struggle in Paris to protect its own Resistance credentials; it could not afford to pay the political price of withdrawing its militants.

The PCF also hoped its armed attacks against the Germans would undermine enemy morale, show that the Germans were not invincible, and rouse Parisians, especially Parisian workers, out of what the PCF considered to be their lethargy to align themselves with the Communists in the fight against the occupying forces. With the hardening of anti-German attitudes in the city, the initial widespread disapproval of armed anti-German actions had dissipated; the PCF feared that to abandon the armed struggle, especially when a German defeat appeared increasingly likely, would diminish its political credibility in the eyes of the population. It is likely that the party also wanted to show Stalin that the comrades in France were prepared to risk their lives, just as soldiers in the Red Army were risking theirs.

In the summer of 1941 the PCF leadership had failed to take into account the inexperience and naivety of its brave young militants in the Bataillons de la jeunesse, thus putting their lives at risk. In the autumn of 1943 it refused to take seriously the precarious position of the Jews and/or foreigners who made up the Manouchian group and refused to follow the basic tenets of guerrilla warfare to protect them. Admittedly waging a guerrilla war in an city is more difficult than in the countryside, but as Rayski later wrote, "By stubbornly pursuing guerrilla warfare in Paris and not respecting the basic rules of this sort of fighting—harassment, withdrawal, pausing between attacks, movement—the PCF leadership committed a serious political error and is without any doubt partly responsible for the arrests."[8]

There is a strong suggestion that Missak Manouchian shared this view. In a final letter to his wife hours before his execution he wrote, "I will shortly die, along with my twenty-three comrades, with the courage and serenity of a man who has a clear conscience . . . I forgive all those who did me harm or who wanted to do so, except the one who betrayed us [presumably a reference to Davidovitch] and *those who sold us out*."[9] It has also been suggested that the PCF leadership was prepared to sacrifice the FTP-MOI militants because it believed that a band of mostly foreign Jews did not fit the image of the "Party of the Resistance" that it intended to promote after the war.[10] Although the Manouchian group was initially largely airbrushed out of the orthodox Communist narrative of the war, it is most unlikely that this would have been a conscious decision taken in 1943.

At the time of the arrests of FTP-MOI members, the Germans were desperately exploiting fears among Parisians that German setbacks on the Eastern Front meant France was in danger of being overrun by

Bolsheviks. This propaganda offensive had begun even before the German defeat at Stalingrad in February 1943: a month earlier, Andrzej Bobkowski noted in his diary that the German authorities were painting a grim picture of what life in France would be like if the Russians won.[11] Not everyone was convinced. Micheline Bood, for example, believed there was nothing to be afraid of: even if the Russians were victorious, she wrote in her diary, they would have suffered too much to pose a threat to any other country.[12] In contrast, the student Bernard Pierquin was worried about a sudden German collapse, followed by a Russian invasion unchecked by the British or the Americans.[13] An acquaintance of the Bood family even lost weight worrying about the Bolshevik threat.[14]

German propaganda campaigns portraying Germany as the leader of the struggle to save Europe from Bolshevism became ever more strident, and this message was broadcast on the radio and publicised in the press as never before. Posters appeared all over Paris showing Red Army soldiers scaling walls, kicking in doors, burning barns, shooting men, and assaulting women.[15] One in particular depicted a caricature Red Army soldier superimposed on a photograph of Notre-Dame with what looked like a bottle of vodka in his pocket. In one hand he carried a whole bag of looted religious artefacts, in the other he brandished a stolen crucifix. Behind him other Russian soldiers entered the cathedral. Many of the anti-Soviet posters carried the slogan "À bas le bolchevisme!" ("Down with Bolshevism!"), but the message was subverted; Parisians blocked out some of the letters of "bolchevisme" so it read "À bas le bo che!" ("Down with the Boche!").

This anti-Soviet campaign was still raging on February 19, 1944, when twenty-four FTP-MOI members of the Manouchian Group went on trial in Paris before a German military tribunal. The German authorities gave the case maximum publicity, hoping to "prove" that the famed French Resistance was nothing but a ragbag of foreign Jewish Communist criminals—a theme dutifully echoed in the collaborationist mass media. In addition, the occupiers produced a now famous red poster (*l'affiche rouge*), which appeared on walls all over Paris. It consisted of photographs of ten members of the FTP-MOI group appearing as wild and dangerous as possible, and drawing attention to their Communist and/or Jewish and foreign backgrounds. The poster ridiculed the idea that such people could possibly be described as "liberators" and dubbed the group the "Army of Crime" (L'Armée du crime).[16] The militants were found guilty after the shortest of deliberations by the court and twenty-two of them, including Manouchian, were executed by firing squad at Mont-Valérien on February 21, 1944. At their trial those who were executed took full responsibility for their actions without voicing any regrets or pleading mitigating circumstances. Olga Bancic, the only woman on trial, was also found guilty, deported to Germany, and was decapitated in Stuttgart on May 10, 1944. Another of the accused, Migratrice, was ordered to appear before a French court.

⮑ VICHY REMAINED DESPERATELY keen to show the Germans just how committed it was to the struggle against Bolshevism, a message reinforced by Laval's recent founding of the Milice with its mission to pursue "the enemies within"—in the Southern Zone. Pétain had always distrusted the Légion des volontaires français contre le bolchevisme (LVF) with its members fighting alongside the Germans against the Red Army, because of the LVF's close links with the Paris collaborationists, in general, and with Jacques Doriot, in particular. However in February 1943, in a gesture of solidarity with the Nazi anti-Bolshevik crusade, Pétain granted the LVF legal recognition.[17] On the frozen Eastern Front LVF members in German uniforms with little tricolour badges mercilessly hunted down and killed anyone they thought might be an anti-German partisan. Thousands of miles away in Paris the LVF maintained a sprawling, bureaucratic organisation that was a hotbed of intrigue and rivalry, staffed by collaborationist placemen on bloated salaries living and working in luxurious accommodation. As the RNP leader Marcel Déat wrote, "Anti-Bolshevism in Paris keeps its people well fed."[18] The head offices of the LVF were located in sumptuous premises on the rue Saint-Georges and the place Malesherbes, where vast sums of money mysteriously disappeared or were siphoned off into the coffers of the collaborationist parties or the pockets of their leaders.[19] Donations of coffee, chocolate, tobacco, cigarettes, and other items from LVF sympathisers, which those on the Eastern Font should have received, ended up in the hands of the members of the Central Committee or were sold on the black market; in one instance, a whole railway truck of cigarettes and tobacco disappeared without trace. Not surprisingly, LVF volunteers fighting in Russia felt abandoned by the corrupt pen-pushers back in Paris. Volunteers back on leave from the Eastern

Front called at the LVF headquarters in Paris to tell staff what they thought of them, often using their fists to reinforce their views.[20]

On August 27, 1943, the second anniversary of the founding of the LVF was celebrated at a ceremony in the courtyard of Les Invalides attended by three government ministers. This was followed by a Mass and a parade by LVF members and supporters. After a meal and a show for 1,000 LVF members and their families in the Grand-Palais, a huge exhibition hall near the Champs-Élysées, the legionnaires marched up the avenue to the Tomb of the Unknown Soldier. Here Fernand de Brinon laid a wreath, alongside two other wreaths in Nazi colours, deposited by German representatives. The legionnaires then marched down the Champs-Élysées, this time accompanied by small bands of LVF recruits who had come over from their barracks in Versailles and who physically attacked any passersby they felt were not showing sufficient respect or enthusiasm.

Although the Paris police had done so much of the Germans' dirty work for them, the collaborationists believed many of the rank and file were at best unreliable and at worst harboured Resistance or pro-Allied sympathies. The LVF louts set about police officers on duty on the Champs-Elysées, kicking, punching, and beating them with sticks. One LVF member shouted at them, "Bastards! We should finish them off. If it was the Americans, they'd be greeting them with open arms!"[21] In their hunt for police officers, one LVF volunteer threatened to stab a policeman to death; another officer was beaten in the face and neck before being thrown to the ground and stamped on. More than seventy police officers were injured in the course of the evening.

Parisians were not slow in showing their contempt for the Légion, leading many of the volunteers to conceal their LVF membership. A doctor friend of Charles Braibant met a German patient who spoke very bad German. It transpired that he was a Frenchman, a member of the LVF who was so tired of being insulted that he had removed the tricolour badge from his German army uniform and was trying to pass himself off as a member of the Wehrmacht.[22]

In another move designed to commit France to the German-led fight against Bolshevism, Pierre Laval signed a decree in July 1943 allowing men "to fight against Bolshevism outside France by enlisting in units constituted by the German government"—in other words to join the Waffen-SS. The Waffen-SS began as the military wing of the SS and became an elite fighting force, unconditionally committed to Hitler, that went into combat alongside the Wehrmacht. Hitler subsequently allowed the creation of foreign Waffen-SS units, who also swore unconditional allegiance to him. The Waffen-SS was soon calling itself the European political army.[23] A Waffen-SS regiment of French volunteers was founded in the summer of 1943, and, a year later, on Himmler's initiative, it became a designated French SS assault brigade.[24] A Waffen-SS recruiting office opened on the avenue du Recteur-Poincaré in the 16th arrondissement, and *Paris-Soir* declared itself thrilled that French Waffen-SS soldiers would be able to distinguish themselves in the European victory over Bolshevism alongside their German brothers.[25]

As in the rest of France, Paris was subjected to an intensive German propaganda campaign asserting that the Waffen-SS was bringing together citizens from across Europe to save their countries from the Bolshevik menace. One poster showed a French soldier standing erect in the gun turret of a German tank above the slogan "If You Want France to Live, Fight in the Waffen-SS against Bolshevism!"[26] Another showed a close-up of rows of smart young men with chiselled features wearing army uniforms and helmets bearing the SS insignia. The slogan: "With Your European Comrades under the Sign of the SS You Will Be Victorious!"[27] Another poster showed an SS soldier in combat dress above the inscription "Shoulder to shoulder against the common enemy," while yet another proclaimed "You too! Your comrades are waiting for you in the French Waffen-SS Division."[28] In January 1944 a ten-day photographic exhibition was held in Paris honouring the French Waffen-SS with the German organisers claiming it drew more than 2,000 visitors a day and more during the weekend.[29] The Frenchmen in the Waffen-SS believed they were destined to "purify" France and usher in a brave new Nazified world. One French Waffen-SS volunteer, who scornfully rejected Pétain's so-called National Revolution, wrote, "If we win this war it is we, the SS, who will sweep away all this filthy muck and build a National-Socialist France that is clean and healthy."[30]

By the end of September some 800 Waffen-SS volunteers had reported to the main recruitment centre in German-controlled Alsace. In August Joseph Darnand, leader of the Milice, gave the regiment a boost when he swore an oath of loyalty to Hitler and joined the

Waffen-SS as a lieutenant: in recognition of this gesture, the Germans supplied the Milice with a handful of weapons—fifty submachine guns.

According to a German communiqué of December 1943, almost half the Waffen-SS French volunteers who signed up in October were students, farmers, and young men aged between eighteen and twenty and about a third of the volunteers hailed from Paris.[31] Ideological conviction was more common than among the early LVF recruits, but there were also some, as with those who joined the LVF, who sought adventure or a break with their past.[32] By January 1944, the total number of those enlisted was around 2,500.[33]

The anti-Bolshevik campaign in Paris was complemented by anti-British and anti-American propaganda, which aimed at mobilising Parisians and their fellow countrymen and women against an invasion by Allied forces. Even before the fall of Stalingrad in February 1943, Paris had seen an anti-British campaign with posters of iconic figures from French history and literature appearing alongside anti-British phrases they had written or were alleged to have uttered. "I would rather give my soul to God than to be in the hands of the English" (Joan of Arc); "The New Europe will be built, but Britain and Russia will be excluded from it. We will pursue Britain on the high seas and the Russian Tartars in the Steppes" (Victor Hugo). German propaganda also presented Britain and the United States as rivals, one poster showing Churchill and Roosevelt each clutching Africa and trying to wrest it away from the other.[34]

☞ ALTHOUGH THE 1942–1943 WINTER was milder than those of 1940–1941 and 1941–1942, Bernard Pierquin and his fellow students were still gathering together in the only heated room they had, sitting close to a stove they fed with crumpled paper. They worked in their bedrooms wrapped in blankets; Bernard was one of the lucky few not to have chilblains on his fingers, which allowed him to write without pain.[35] It was not just Bernard and his fellow students who were short of fuel. In April Micheline Bood visited a woman who had a magnificent leather-bound encyclopaedia in her personal library. It was missing half its pages: the woman had been forced to use them to light her fire. She even offered Micheline a couple of her books so she could do the same.[36]

In 1943 France had the lowest food rations in Europe: 275–350g of bread a day, depending on the age of the recipient, 50g of cheese a week, and 500g of sugar a month. The meat ration, which had been reduced again in January, was a mere 120g a month. However, Paris received only half the amount of meat it needed to provide its inhabitants with even these meagre rations; as a result many Parisians either received less than their allocation or often nothing at all. Milk ration tickets for young children were often worthless because it was impossible to find shops selling milk. By June 1943 the volume of vegetables reaching Paris was 50 percent lower than it had been a year earlier.[37] "We are getting hungrier and hungrier," Charles Braibant wrote in his diary in January. "Nothing left in the shops. We're only surviving thanks to the parcels from the countryside, and those are arriving more and more irregularly."[38]

One reason for the shortages was Berlin's decision, as part of its strategy, to integrate the French economy into the "European war economy," that is, to requisition more goods, including foodstuffs, directly from the Vichy government to make up a shortfall in Germany. Agricultural output in Germany had fallen dramatically since early 1942 as ever more farmworkers were conscripted to fight on the Eastern Front, where the continuing conflict meant that the anticipated arrival of agricultural produce from the Soviet Union failed to materialise.[39]

Trips from Paris to the countryside to secure food became more hazardous and less common. Fewer trains were running and the risk was now greater of getting caught not just by French police, but also by the German secret police, members of Doriot's PPF, or freelancers and criminal gangs posing as French or German officials. Even those who made it to the country discovered it was ever harder to find food, unless they had family contacts or good friends living there; many Parisians stopped bothering to even try. In April 1943 Charles Braibant was in Thénezay, west of Poitiers, where he had previously found plenty of food. "No more butter to be found," he wrote, "no more goats' cheese and it's the devil's own job to lay your hands on a kilo of beans."[40] Besides the huge increase in the volume of food requisitioned for German consumption at home, the patterns of behaviour of many suppliers had changed. More farmers now dealt directly with German soldiers on leave in the countryside, who were willing to pay hugely inflated prices for food. This pushed the cost of food on sale in the countryside up to as much as twice the going rate on the Paris black market and well out of the reach of most Parisians.[41] Other suppliers had linked up with one of the big black-market organisations that flourished as food and other goods became ever scarcer. These criminal gangs were able to pay suppliers in the countryside good prices and provide them with a steady cash flow.

While the kings of the black market in Paris made fabulous personal fortunes, the "little people" not only ran their errands, but also ran the greatest risk of getting caught. Many of them were arrested as they collected goods at one of the mainline stations or transported them illegally across the city, A report on the social backgrounds of Parisians charged with low-level black-market activities in Paris between 1943 and 1944 found that 25 percent were out of work, like the unemployed taxi-driver immortalised by Bourvil in the film *La Traversée de Paris*;[42] many were young men, often based in small groups—frequently found hanging around stations or in working-class areas—whom dealers used to sell or deliver illicit goods. About 20 percent of those charged had fairly menial jobs, often in the food or restaurant sectors. As butchers' boys or waiters in restaurants and cafés, they were close to produce they could sell and were in daily contact with many potential customers.

About 15 percent were factory workers who had seen a 30 percent drop in the purchasing power of their wages since the start of the Occupation; this had forced many to find other ways of making ends meet. Charles Braibant wrote in his diary that life had become so expensive and difficult that even the most honest worker was tempted to become a black-market trader to feed his family.[43] Braibant also noted the growing number of minors involved in black-market trade: according to the chief of police in Versailles, he was told, it was common to find children as young as twelve or thirteen with 10,000 or 15,000 francs in their pockets. "They buy up food and sell it on to the Germans at ridiculous prices."[44]

About 10 percent of small-scale black-market traders arrested in Paris between 1943 and 1944 were drivers or delivery or removal men—men with jobs that required them to move around the city, bringing them into frequent contact with possible customers. About 7 percent of those arrested were white-collar workers in town halls, the post office, and other administrative centres where there were opportunities for stealing goods, ration books, or tickets. Concierges (4 percent) and other (unspecified) professions (19 percent) made up the rest.[45]

The black market operated all over Paris, but some places were especially associated with it. As early as October 1940, according to one journalist, it was possible to find as much of almost any foodstuffs that you wanted in Les Halles, the main market in Paris, which sold fruit, vegetables, dairy produce, flowers, meat, and poultry.[46] The flea markets were also a hive of black-market activity: sellers of textiles thrived at the Porte de Clignancourt; at the nearby market at Saint-Ouen it was possible—if you could afford it—to buy a bicycle tyre for 1,000 francs or a pair of shoes for 2,500 francs. Particular restaurants, from the most luxurious to the most modest, had a reputation for serving up food bought on the black market. Then as now sellers traded illegally in the corridors of the Métro but there were so many of them that the police more or less gave up trying to move them on.[47]

Getting around in Paris became more difficult. In early 1943 Charles Braibant spotted a poster in the Métro announcing the closure of yet more stations.[48] A 40 percent tax was applied to the sale of bicycles—if you could find one to buy. Smokers had to pay 10 francs to renew their tobacco ration card and, in April, tobacco rations were cut by a third; from now on, smokers had to get by with just two packets of twenty cigarettes a month or one packet of tobacco.[49] It was forbidden to transport rabbits, poultry, fish, or even snails without a special permit; the coffee content in the concoction known as "national coffee" dropped to 10 percent.[50] Wine had been rationed to four litres a month since October. The famous aniseed-based aperitif *pastis* had been banned in August 1940 and the factories closed. It was still possible to find it, but it cost 70 francs a glass. Parisians were warned to steer clear of an illegal "alternative" *pastis*, nicknamed *L'Assommoir '43*, which sold at between 15 and 20 francs a glass.[51] It could be fatal, the authorities warned, or could cause deafness, blindness, or insanity.[52] The fashionable drink in the select cafés of the Champs-Élysées was port, brought straight from Perpignan in the south of the country; those who could not afford the real thing could resort to an ersatz version made in Paris using red wine, blackcurrants, and saccharine.

However, not everyone in Paris was struggling: as always the wealthy Parisians found ways to continue living in a style to which they were accustomed—usually thanks to the black market in luxury goods. Some Germans also had the time of their lives. Ursula Rüdt von Collenberg was the twenty-one-year-old niece of a Luftwaffe general who had a job in the Archive Commission. In April 1942 she moved from a villa in Neuilly, formerly inhabited by a wealthy Jewish woman, to the

requisitioned Hôtel d'Orsay. Over the next eighteen months she enjoyed a large well-appointed room with en-suite bathroom and a telephone. She breakfasted and dined at the hotel and lunched at the German
embassy; she went regularly to the theatre, the opera, and art exhibitions at the Orangerie and the Musée de l'Homme. She bought lovely
material, which a White Russian dressmaker turned into clothes. She
later recalled the fantastic deals that were being struck all around her
on the black market for wine, food, and shoes. "We could buy what
we wanted, much more than the French." Not surprisingly, perhaps,
she described her stay in Paris as "the most wonderful and unforgettable
time of my youth."[53]

Another problem that most Parisians had to face—but the occupying
forces on the whole did not—was an unreliable supply of electricity.
This had been an issue in Paris since early in the Occupation, partly
because coal was no longer being imported from Britain. By 1943, the
problem had been exacerbated by the intensification of Allied bombing
raids over Germany, which had resulted in vital French electricity supplies being diverted to the Reich. Already in 1942, the sale and rental
of electrical appliances became illegal, as did illuminating shop windows; restaurants and cafés had to reduce their lighting by 50 percent.
More radical restrictions were imposed in January 1943 when it became
illegal for Parisians to use electric heating appliances in their homes;
in May hairdryers and coffee-makers were added to an ever-growing
list of proscribed domestic electrical appliances. Any domestic con-
sumer who used more than their electricity allocation faced a heavy
fine, and a repeat offence could result in the supply being cut off completely.[54] The number of cases of fraudulent use of electricity rose
sharply from 1942 as Parisians, desperate to save money, tampered with
electricity meters, replaced fuses removed by the electricity company,
and illegally bypassed the meters and connected appliances directly to
the mains. The extent of the fraud was so widespread that the prefect
of the Seine department personally led a campaign to try to stamp it
out, although this proved to be largely ineffective.

Interruptions in the supply of electricity became so common that in
September 1943 a list was compiled of "special customers" who would
continue to be serviced whenever a major power cut occurred. These
included hospitals, telephone exchanges, fire stations and, of course, the
Hôtel Majestic, Hôtel Crillon, the Chamber of Deputies, the Senate,
and other buildings requisitioned by the Germans.[55]

As if shortages of food, fuel, clothing, and energy, plus rising taxes and falling incomes, were not enough, in 1943 Parisians also had to endure more Allied aerial bombing raids on the city. On Sunday April 4 Parisians were out and about, taking advantage of a wonderful warm spring day. At about two o'clock in the afternoon Andrzej Bobkowski was at home getting ready to go for a bicycle ride. Suddenly a terrifying racket broke out that sounded as if all the German anti-aircraft guns in Paris had opened fire; then came a heavy rumbling that lasted a minute or so, followed by the muffled humming of engines.[56] The 8th U.S. Bomber Command had just carried out its first bomb attack on Paris, targeting the Renault factories, as the RAF had done just over a year before. Some 500 bombs each weighing over 1,000 pounds were dropped and, despite an initial American report that they had more or less fallen within the target area, it later transpired that only about half had hit the Renault works: the rest had landed in the nearby suburbs, killing some 300 civilians and seriously wounding another 400.

The German army captain and writer Ernst Jünger described Parisians out for a Sunday stroll coming face to face with groups of injured people gasping for breath, their clothes in tatters, holding their arms or their heads, a mother clutching to her breast a baby covered in blood. He wrote also of a bridge over the Seine being hit and bodies being fished out of the river.[57] Micheline Bood's sister Nicole was lucky. She was on an outing with fellow Girl Scouts, but as they went down into the Métro her picnic basket had sprung open, spilling the contents all over the steps. By the time she and her friends had picked up everything, the train had left: just minutes later the same train was in the Pont-de-Sèvres Métro station where it was hit by an Allied bomb and eighty people were killed.[58]

Seven people were killed when a bomb landed on the Longchamp race course in the Bois de Boulogne. The bodies of the victims were laid out on the track for an hour and a half before being taken away, thus allowing the first race to start. Jean Guéhenno considered this a sign of just how far standards of decency had fallen. He wrote in his diary the following day that not even the deaths of others could stop people betting on the horses and when the newspapers printed the names of the victims, they also published the results of the races.[59] On a lighter note, Micheline Bood described how a family friend at Longchamp had been so frightened he had pulled down his top hat over his ears. After the raid he was struggling to get it off; his friends tried to help but, worried he would never be able to find another, he was desperate for them not to cut it.[60]

Engineer Fernand Picard visited the Renault factory on behalf of the owner and his boss Louis Renault: Fernand reported that the latest raid had caused more extensive damage than the one in March 1942. The collaborationist press tried again to exploit the raid and turn public opinion against the Allies. The following day *Le Matin* carried a front-page article under the headline "A NEW CRIME BY THE ANGLO-AMERICAN ASSASSINS."[61] As a sign of respect, all places of entertainment in the city were ordered to close on April 7, when the funerals for the victims took place.

While the German authorities and Vichy did their best to inflame anti-Allied feelings in the city, it is unclear how many Parisians blamed the Allies for the raid and how many blamed the Germans. Liliane Jameson described the bombing raid as "one more sad and regrettable result of the German presence in our midst."[62] Charles Braibant initially castigated the American pilot who had dropped the bomb on Longchamp as "an imbecilic criminal." He said that people blamed the Americans for prolonging the war, first by waiting so long before joining in and then for dragging things out in Tunisia. However, later in the same diary entry he referred to the "painful accident" at Longchamp, which he now blamed on the Germans for installing anti-aircraft guns so close to the racecourse.[63] One man whose son had been killed in the raid was in no doubt who to blame. He was so outraged by the pro-Gaullist comments of his next-door neighbour that a few days after the raid he seized his man's three-year-old-son and strangled him with his bare hands.[64]

The next bombing raid, this time in the autumn, was even more punishing than the one in April. Again, it was a daytime raid but, for the first time, Allied bombs landed in Paris itself rather than on and around factories in the industrial suburbs. It was followed by two more raids (on the suburbs) within a fortnight. On September 3, Andrzej Bobkowski was near the place Saint-Germain-des-Prés, on the Left Bank, when the air-raid sirens started wailing. Anti-aircraft guns opened fire. Two squadrons of planes flew overhead, their underbellies glinting in the sun. The sound of exploding shells filled the air and Bobkowski ran for cover in the gateway of a nearby building. Suddenly people were fleeing the area around the Gare Montparnasse railway station and the rue de

Rennes was swallowed up in a cloud of dust.[65] A friend of Jean Galtier-Boissière's was almost killed on the rue du Départ at the top of the rue de Rennes when a nearby building collapsed; a woman standing next to him was struck on the head by a piece of flying masonry.[66] After the attack was over, Bobkowski cycled into the area where the bombs had fallen. He saw that a six-storey building near the Gare Montparnasse had collapsed and that bombs had fallen in both the rue de Rennes and the rue du Cherche-Midi. He saw police and firemen and the air reverberated with the sound of ambulance sirens.[67] Other bombs fell in the 15th arrondissement near the Porte de Versailles, in the rue de la Croix-Nivert, and in the 16th arrondissement near the boulevard Murat, where Charles Braibant lived.[68]

The American planes had once again been targeting the Renault (and Citroën) factories, but few of their bombs landed on or even near their targets; indeed, bombs were scattered over an area of about 750 acres—more than seventy times the size of the target area where the factories were located.[69] Even though the casualty figures were relatively low, 86 killed and 190 seriously injured) Fernand Picard was deeply shocked. The bombing caused widespread distress, he said, because people did not understand why the bombs were scattered over such a large area, far away from any military target and had landed in the middle of built-up urban neighbourhoods. Picard concluded that given the civilian deaths and how little of the Renault factory was actually hit the raid was a mistake, both militarily and psychologically. "People do not understand why a raid like this was needed in order to make progress in the war."[70] Andrzej Bobkowski, surely conscious of the rape of his native Poland, was scathing about what he saw as the Parisians fussing about nothing. Referring to his place of work he wrote "The whole factory is in uproar. Everybody's trying to get on the phone. The whole of Paris is on the phone calling family, relations, and friends. They've bombed Paris. Oh! là! là! Three little bombs! What a carry-on!"[71]

Six days later a raid targeted the Hispano-Suiza factory in the northwestern suburb of Asnières, which produced vehicles and weapons for the Germans, but bombs rained down instead on the nearby suburbs, killing almost 100 civilians. On September 15 the bombers were back, under massive anti-aircraft fire from the ground, as they sought once again to bomb industrial targets, this time once again in the southwestern suburbs. A church near the Renault factory that had been hit during the September 3 raid was now reduced to rubble. This time the intensive bombing succeeded in inflicting more damage on the Renault works than earlier raids: 15 percent of the floor space in the factory was destroyed, the workshops had to be closed, and not a single machine tool was in working order. It did not all go the Allies' way, however. Eye-witnesses spoke of planes bursting into flames in seconds and plunging to the ground and of pilots' parachutes catching fire as the airmen tried to escape the flying infernos in what Fernand Picard described as "the most violent air attack ever launched on the Paris region."[72]

That evening, when Picard arrived home in the western suburb of Bécon-les-Bruyères, he saw, in the light of a blaze that engulfed two neighbouring houses, his wife and children sitting in front of their home. Five bombs had landed within a fifty-metre radius of the house and eleven had fallen within a radius of 100 metres. Madame Picard and the girls feared their house had become so unstable it would collapse on them if they went inside.[73]

At about 1:30 A.M. on the night of September 23–24 a Royal Air Force Lancaster bomber was hit by anti-aircraft fire over central Paris. It burst into flames and crashed into a large department store near the Louvre. The body of the pilot, who had bailed out, was recovered from the roof of the museum; the dead crew members were retrieved from the plane's wreckage, which was scattered in nearby streets. Some bits of the plane were later seen suspended from the railings around the museum.[74] Georges Benoît-Guyod was part of a crowd that gathered outside the Louvre the following day. He noticed there had been a fire in the upper part of the building and was told six airmen had perished. Pierre Audiat wrote of a wave of emotion that swept through the crowd when their charred bodies were recovered.[75]

☙ EVER SINCE DRANCY had been established as an internment camp for Jews in August 1941 it had been managed by French administrators with guards drawn from the ranks of the gendarmerie. But in July 1943 the Germans assumed direct responsibility for the camp. Adolf Eichmann, who had attended the Wannsee Conference where Reinhard Heydrich had secured the support of senior German officials and politicians for the extermination of Europe's Jews, appointed the man to be in charge of Drancy. He picked Alois Brunner, a sadistic Austrian SS captain who had acquired a sinister reputation for the speed and efficiency with which he oversaw the roundup and deportation of Jews in Vienna, Berlin, and Salonica in Greece.

With Brunner in charge, Drancy was run by handpicked thugs from the SS and the French gendarmes were reduced to patrolling the camp on the outer side of the perimeter fence. In the early weeks of the new regime the SS took delight in finding especially cruel ways of punishing selected prisoners in the central courtyard in full view of their fellow inmates as a way of making sure that nobody could be in any doubt as to what would happen if they stepped out of line. The SS also resorted to brutally setting prisoners against each other: two inmates accused of trying to smuggle letters out of the camp were forced to beat each other repeatedly with clubs in front of the other prisoners.[76] Out of sight but not out of earshot, Brunner's SS thugs systematically tortured inmates in a special underground chamber nicknamed "the Bunker." Here, throughout the period when Brunner was in charge of the camp, those deemed guilty of minor infractions were stripped naked, starved, beaten, and hosed down with freezing cold water.[77]

Brunner imported a method of control used in the camps in eastern Europe, notably Auschwitz and Buchenwald. He cynically and cruelly exploited the demoralisation, despair, and fear that permeated the camp by recruiting guards from among the prisoners and making them responsible for day-to-day discipline within the camp. These guards acted as intermediaries between the SS and the bulk of the inmates, which made it possible for Brunner to run the camp with just a handful of SS henchmen.

Brunner tried to ensnare more prisoners by adopting a callous policy of "family regroupings." Prisoners about to be deported were offered a fake option: the chance to be deported with their family and "resettled in the East." All they had to do was write to family members, asking them to come to the camp and join them. An ailing sixty-four-year-old, Bernard Ivenitzki, who had been transferred to Drancy from the Rothschild hospital, was forced to write a letter to his wife: "The German authorities are inviting you to bring all your luggage and join me so we can be deported together. If you don't arrive within a week I will be deported on my own."[78] There was no reply. On July 31 he was deported—without his wife.

The internment of Jews in Drancy gave the SS a chance to collate up-to-date personal data on the prisoners. All new arrivals had to write a letter to their families, which meant the SS were able to obtain their addresses; any internee who refused to divulge their family's details was given a severe public beating. Some internees, nicknamed "missionaries," were even sent out from Drancy into Paris and beyond with the names and addresses of Jews still at liberty to encourage them to join relatives in the camp. The families of these "missionaries" remained in the camp as hostages, threatened with immediate deportation if the "missionary" failed to return. According to Drancy inmate Georges Wellers, a naturalised French Jew who was born in Russia, the project was a flop: in August more than 550 home visits by twenty-two "missionaries" yielded fewer than eighty people.[79] The scheme was soon abandoned and Brunner shifted his attention to rounding up Jews in the Southern Zone.

Brunner's cynicism knew no limits. The UGIF, the German-inspired Jewish organisation, was instructed to supply Drancy with goods that were virtually impossible to find in the Paris shops on the pretext that those being deported would need them when they reached their destination. Thanks to the black market, the UGIF was able to supply truckloads of blankets, sheets, shoes, and clothes, which were delivered to Drancy and distributed to those about to be deported. The deportees were forced to hand over all their money but were given a receipt (in zlotys), which they were told they could redeem when they arrived in Poland. Of course, no such reimbursement occurred and as soon as they arrived in Auschwitz the bed linen and clothing the deportees took with them was confiscated, down to the very last handkerchief. Their belongings were then sorted and forwarded to the Reich. Brunner had found an easy, cost-free way of transferring much needed merchandise—like clothes, shoes, and bed linen—back to Germany.[80]

In September Brunner left the camp to oversee a roundup of Jews in the south of France as well as in the former Italian Zone, which was now under SS control.[81] Around the same time a group of Drancy prisoners came up with an audacious plan to dig a forty-metre escape tunnel. It would stretch from the cellars at the far end of Drancy's west block to an air-raid shelter near the avenue Jean-Jaurès, beyond the confines of the camp. Three teams of about twenty prisoners each took turns using short-handled pick axes to hack their way through the clay subsoil and build a tunnel that measured about 1 to 1.3 metres high and 60 to 80 centimetres wide.

Many of the diggers had responsibilities within the camp that gave them access to areas that other prisoners did not have. If they were challenged by a member of the SS when acting as a lookout, for example, they could always dream up a plausible reason for being where they were. This relative freedom of movement also made it easier for the tunnellers to take what they needed from the mass of tools and building materials delivered to the camp. They helped themselves to planks to shore up the tunnel and electric cables to provide the lighting. When lack of oxygen in the tunnel became a problem, Claude Aron, a chemist, stole some oxylith, a substance that turns into oxygen on contact with water, which the SS stored in the infirmary. The excess earth from the tunnel was distributed throughout a network of cellars that the Germans never visited.

By November 8, the diggers had obtained a key to the air-raid shelter and were only a few metres away from their goal when the SS stormed into the cellars and discovered the tunnel. Apparently they had been tipped off by a prisoner at Compiègne, who had heard about the tunnel from a prisoner recently transferred from Drancy. Henri Schwartz— an owner of a furniture shop near Bastille and one of the leaders of the escape bid—was identified by some work clothes, which he had left in the tunnel. He was tortured into giving up the names of the other diggers, who then had to fill in and seal up the tunnel. The tunnellers were deported in a convoy of 1,200 Drancy prisoners, which left Bobigny railway station on November 20.[82] During that night, seventeen prisoners, including twelve of the tunnellers, escaped from the train near Toul while it was still rumbling through France. One of these was the chemist Claude Aron. He made it to southern France and joined the *maquis*, but he was arrested in Lyons. He was brought back to Drancy with his mother and members of his family. He was tortured and again deported, as was his mother. Neither returned.[83]

When Brunner and the SS took over the running of Drancy, the status of the camp changed. It was no longer an internment camp. It became an "emigration camp" *(Abwanderungslager)*. Although the number and rate of deportations fell compared with the previous year, the Germans remained as keen as ever to deport as many Jews as possible.[84] In response to the Vichy government's unease about deporting French Jews, the Germans, so as to deport as many foreign Jews as possible, proposed that the legal definition of "French" be changed. In

March 1943, Heinrich Röthke, who four months earlier had replaced Dannecker as head of the Department of Jewish Affairs in Paris, returned to an idea floated by Abetz in April 1941: he proposed that all Jews who had been naturalised since 1927 should be stripped of their French nationality. At a stroke they would no longer be French and Vichy should have no objection to them being rounded up and deported.

In June 1943 Laval signed a draft law to this effect. The Germans anticipated having extra French and German police in Paris for a mass roundup of those who were about to lose their French nationality. However, Laval then changed his mind. Pétain, he said, needed to give his approval and had refused to do so. This was true, although not because Pétain had suddenly turned against anti-Semitic policies that permeated the Occupation. Rather, in his letter of refusal, Pétain stressed that he had been willing to work with the Germans on countless other occasions, but he expressed his "inability to understand the sending of Jews of French nationality while there were still so many other Jews in France."[85]

Despite his failing intellectual faculties, Pétain, like Laval, was aware of how much had changed since the big *rafles* of 1942. Then they had been quite happy to see thousands of foreign Jews transferred from French camps to Drancy from where they were deported; but now the tide of war was running in the Allies' favour. In May the Germans had capitulated in Tunisia and in June de Gaulle had established his French Committee of National Liberation in Algeria. July saw the Wehrmacht's loss of Kursk and Orel on the Eastern Front, the Allied landings in Sicily, and the fall of Mussolini. Pétain now fretted about his declining popularity, while Laval remained universally loathed by the French public—even more so since he had introduced the STO. Both men calculated that they could not risk alienating public opinion further by denaturalising 50,000 French Jews. Nor did either man want to alienate the Allies: Laval, who still hoped to see Bolshevism defeated, was also already repositioning himself in relation to the United States and Britain, so he could act as broker of a compromise peace between the Western Allies and Germany if the circumstances demanded it.

Heinrich Röthke knew that the cooperation of the French government was essential if another large-scale roundup of Jews was to be organised, since, without the French police, the Germans simply did not have enough manpower. The shortage of German personnel was confirmed when Helmut Knochen requested 250 extra men and was told by the RSHA central office that it could spare only four. While the Brigades spéciales of the Paris police were still energetically rounding up Communist "terrorists," Carl Oberg, the German SS officer in charge of security, believed they now lacked initiative in the "struggle against Judaism." There was widespread discontent and even anger within the ranks of the French police at having to track down STO deserters. More and more Paris policemen, too, were reassessing their relationship with the occupiers, as the chances of a German victory receded with every passing month.[86]

This projected mass *rafle* of Jews in Paris never took place. The large number of deportations in 1942 had left a depleted Jewish population in the Occupied Zone, and although Oberg blustered that a new wave of roundups could be accomplished by German police forces alone, his deputy Helmut Knochen was more realistic. Knochen told Eichmann that the recent French recalcitrance and the shortage of German personnel meant that the prospect of a total elimination of all Jewish influence *(Entjudung)* in France in the near future was quite unrealistic.[87] Instead of concentrating on rounding up Jews in Paris, Brunner turned his attention to the Southern Zone and the former Italian Zone. Here, he had to rely on local denouncers, members of the paramilitary Milice, fascist thugs from Doriot's PPF, and other anti-Semites to help him and his band of SS brutes round up Jews of all ages and nationalities, including French. Countless Jews fled the area or were hidden, protected, or spirited away by locals, so that in March 1944, after five months of frenzied activity, Brunner had managed to arrest only 2,000 people—a far cry from the tens of thousands he anticipated. That said, by August 1943, according to Röthke, 52,000 Jews had been deported from Drancy, leaving 70,000 in the Occupied Zone (of whom 60,000 lived in the Greater Paris area) and some 200,000 in the rest of France. The total number of Jews deported from France has been reliably put at 75,721, of whom only about 2,566 returned.[88] However grotesque this unspeakably inhumane treatment and, in most cases, murder of innocent men, women, and children remains, these numbers mean that about three-quarters of the Jews in France were not deported.

Furthermore, as Brunner had found in the south of France, Jews were being hidden and protected by non-Jews, some of whom would gain official Israeli and French recognition after the war as *Les Justes* (the Righteous Among the Nations).[89] This happened also in Paris, where whole families, single women, and, less commonly, single men were hidden, fed, and protected, although the total number of Jews who were saved from deportation in this way is impossible to quantify as is the number of those who protected and supported them.[90] In her diary entry for April 16, 1943, Micheline Bood casually mentioned a family who were sheltering a Jewish girl who was in her second year of secondary school.[91] Eva, a young Polish woman, was taken in by a French couple in Paris in the summer of 1942 and stayed with them until May 1945. She later wrote of their courage and of the unconditional warm hospitality they offered her. A tailor named Joseph Leibovici and his wife and daughter were helped by one of Joseph's employees, who, with her husband, found the Leibovici family three hiding places in Paris and helped them move between them. One of these was in a building where the Germans occupied all the apartments except the one used by the Leibovicis. Moving between different hiding places was quite common even if extremely dangerous. A thirty-one-year-old Moldavian Jew, Monsieur Loudmer, was protected by Madame Germaine and her daughter, Mireille, who often accompanied him when he moved between his two hiding places: "She offered me her arm and spoke loudly with a strong Parisian accent when we passed any French or German policemen. This meant we avoided identity checks, which we would never have got through."[92]

In 1943, two annexes of the Drancy camp opened within the walls of Paris itself and a third opened in March 1944. In these annexes Jewish prisoners were made to sort and pack goods pillaged from Jewish homes in the capital and beyond by Behr's men, ready to be sent to Germans whose homes had been bombed. The number of homeless Germans had increased dramatically since the Allies' intensive air assault on German cities, which started in May 1942 when more than 1,000 Allied bombers pounded Cologne.

One of these new annexes was a huge former furniture store owned by Wolff Lévitan, which stood on the rue du Faubourg-Saint-Martin in the 10th arrondissement, not far from the Gare de l'Est railway station.[93] The requisitioned Lévitan building was renamed Lager-Ost (East Camp) and specialised in sorting and packing everyday household goods. In July 1943 120 Jews were transferred from the main camp in Drancy to live and work there.

Four months later, a second Drancy annexe opened in the industrial complex in the 13th arrondissement spawned by the Gare d'Austerlitz, which, like the Gare de l'Est, had a direct rail link to Germany. Yvonne Klug, a former inmate who was later deported to Auschwitz, described it as "The biggest organisation dealing in theft, removal, and trade in stolen goods that you could ever imagine. All the possessions and furniture stolen from Jews arrived there to be sorted and sent to Germany."[94] In March 1944 a third, smaller camp opened in a former private residence on the rue de Bassano in the 16th arrondissement that had previously been the home of descendants of the Meyer-Cahens, one of France's richest banking families. Usually known simply as Bassano, this annexe specialised in clothing and luxury items.

Most of the prisoners sent from Drancy to the Paris annexes were Jews who had been classified (for the time being) as exempt from deportation; they included the Jewish wives of French POWs and Jews married to non-Jews and their children. Between July 1943 and August 1944 almost 800 former Drancy inmates passed through the annexes. They worked on the lower floors and slept in "dormitories" above. The first contingent to arrive at Lager-Ost found their "dormitory" consisted of one large room, shared by male and female prisoners and divided only by a curtain; there were no beds, no mattresses, and only two wash basins. However, conditions did subsequently improve.

A steady stream of trucks rumbled into Austerlitz and Lager-Ost, bringing not only household furniture such as beds, sideboards, cupboards, wardrobes, tables, chairs, and writing desks, but also pianos, stoves, cookers, safes, and gramophones, all stolen from Jewish homes. In addition, thousands of crates contained a jumble of bedding, clothing, crockery, cutlery, silverware, glassware, kitchen utensils, rubbish bins, wastepaper baskets, toys, books, lamps, carpets, clocks, watches, pictures, photographs, and personal papers. The Jewish homes from which these had been stolen had been stripped bare. One prisoner, who was first at Austerlitz and then at Lager-Ost, estimated that 2,400 crates arrived each working day from Paris and the provinces.[95] The working day itself was largely determined by the number and frequency of the trucks; the prisoners usually started at 8 A.M. and worked for at least ten hours, often longer, carrying, unloading, and repacking crates that, when full, weighed between 35 and 60kg each. Sometimes, as a punishment, the Germans would wake up the inmates in the middle of the night and make them do a twenty-four-hour shift.[96]

Once the crates were unloaded from the trucks they were taken to the floors above. At Lager-Ost this was usually done mechanically, but frequent power cuts meant the inmates themselves had to carry the crates upstairs. This was also the case at Austerlitz, where for a long time there was no lift. The furniture and contents of the crates then had to be carefully sorted and packed, ready for transportation to the Reich. On occasion, as one former inmate, Gilbert Jacob, later recalled, "Inmates would recognise in among these objects, things that belonged to them which they were forced to wrap up for these 'gentlemen.'" Another inmate, Robert Fabius, realised his wife's father had been arrested when he saw items that had been in his father-in-law's home, including framed pictures of Robert's own wife.[97]

Because everything sent to Germany had to be in good condition, skilled workers and artisans among the prisoners at the main camp at Drancy were transferred to the annexes, where they worked carrying out repairs to items that were damaged. Erna Herzberg, for example, who had worked for a big Paris couturier, was sent from Drancy to Lager-Ost because of her dress-making skills; she was later moved to Bassano.[98] Dressmakers and tailors made, repaired, or refashioned items of clothing; watch and clock repairers mended timepieces; furniture restorers worked on items damaged in transit; carpenters built the crates used to take the pillaged goods to Germany, as well as stands and display shelves for the annexes themselves. Thousands of crates left these Paris camps every week for Germany. Top German generals had luxury items sent to their homes across the Rhine. General Guderian, for example, who had played such an important role in the defeat of France, furnished a property given to him by Hitler with items from the Drancy annexes in Paris.[99] As one former detainee recalled, "Every day crates with labels bearing the names of the most well-known members of the [Nazi] regime were sent off to Germany."[100] Members of the German elite visiting Paris or based in the city made sure they got their hands on some of the booty as well.

It was Kurt von Behr who oversaw this systematic pillaging of Jewish homes—an operation known as Möbel-Aktion. He made frequent "inspections" of the annexes, bringing guests and inviting them to pick out any items that caught their eye. Two workshops were supposed to be making trousers and skirts for German boys and girls, but, in reality, vast quantities of material stolen from Jews were used to produce dresses and suits for the wives of German officers and officials, including Behr's vain and capricious Australian wife. "Baron von Behr ordered dozens of pairs of boots, while the tailors never stopped turning out uniforms for him," one Jewish prisoner later recalled. "His wife was just as bad: she was mad about shoes and handbags, which were made for her by skilled inmates."[101] The prisoners were also astounded by the sight of Behr's wife rummaging up to her armpits in crates before hauling out a crocodile-skin handbag or silk trappings, which had "to be put on one side for Madame the Baroness."[102]

⪼ IN THE AUTUMN OF 1943 the Germans in Berlin wanted to keep Pétain as a figurehead and still considered Laval their best ally in France. French collaborationists, who were becoming ever more explicitly pro-Nazi, were also becoming ever more hostile towards Laval. Doriot had long opposed Laval and planned to oust him, but now other collaborationists, such as Marcel Déat, Doriot's rival, were becoming disillusioned with the prime minister. They saw how unpopular he was with the public and they considered him an unreliable opportunist whose policies lacked any dynamism and vision and who was interested only in saving his own skin. In his political memoirs, Déat described Laval as adopting a wait-and-see attitude. He wrote that Laval "did not get involved in anything, let events take their course, let the Germans slide towards their fate while he tried to pull his own irons out of the fire."[103] Déat also detailed how, in his opinion, Laval's vision of collaboration ("a sort of daily trade-off in France's interests") differed from his own, which demanded a radical political, economic, and social restructuring of France and a Franco-German entente within the "New Europe."[104]

In short, the collaborationists regarded Laval as an obstacle to the creation of their hoped-for Nazi-style France. In September five of them, including Joseph Darnand; Marcel Déat, the head of the RNP; and Georges Guilbaud, the head of propaganda in Doriot's PPF—put their names to what they described as a programme for the revival of France. They sent it to Hitler and members of his inner circle in Berlin, including Himmler. In this communication they called for Laval to be removed as head of government and to be replaced by a team of almost all of the collaborationist leaders (except Doriot, who was still on the Eastern Front). They called for the purging of the state apparatus—especially the police—and the creation of a single party and a single national militia operating across the country. Such a regime, they asserted, would provide the basis for a Franco-German collaboration worthy of the name. Their advances were rebuffed. Little did they realise that Hitler remained resolutely opposed to having a rival Nazi regime on his doorstep. For the moment it suited the Germans to work with Laval as a head of government and to keep Pétain, reduced to even more of a figurehead than before, as head of the French state.

The compliant and increasingly befuddled Pétain may have had virtually no power or influence, but he was still useful to the Germans as a symbol of stability. However, despite his weak position, Pétain was scheming to outmanoeuvre Laval and once again remove him from office. Pétain, the avowed anti-democrat, cynically planned to outline a new republican regime—with a national assembly, a strong executive, and a supreme court—in which Laval would play no part. Pétain hoped this initiative would counter the winds of democracy blowing across the Mediterranean from de Gaulle's French Committee of National Liberation in Algiers. Pétain also hoped that his apparent shift towards democracy would win Roosevelt's approval and support and secure his future in a postwar France. Pétain made preparations to announce his constitutional plans on the radio on November 13, but the Germans were having none of it. They banned the broadcast and insisted that Laval remain at the head of the government. Pétain rather absurdly went on strike and refused to carry out his duties—although it is difficult to say quite what they were except to give his approval as usual to whatever the Germans wanted or to be ignored if he demurred.

Abetz, once more in favour in Berlin, was back in France as ambassador, and on December 4 he visited Vichy, bringing Pétain a letter dated November 29 from Ribbentrop. Pétain was told to stop his "strike" and fall into line. Ribbentrop reiterated Berlin would in no way allow Pétain to proceed with his proposed constitutional reform, adding, for good measure, that *any* changes in the law envisaged by Pétain had first to be scrutinised by Berlin. Ribbentrop also instructed Laval to organise a ministerial reshuffle to produce the sort of government of which Germany would approve.[105] Berlin wanted a French government with collaborationists in key positions endorsed for public consumption by Pétain and which it could control through Laval. Pétain protested but backed down as usual and did what he was told. In December out went René Bousquet, the head of police appointed by Laval. He had served the Germans well in the *rafles* of foreign Jews but his reluctance to round up French Jews had branded him unreliable in the eyes of Berlin. He was replaced by Joseph Darnand. Ominously, Darnand, a Frenchman who held the post of head of the Milice and who had sworn a personal oath of loyalty to Hitler when he joined the Waffen-SS in August, was now in charge of all French law-and-order forces, notably the French national police force and the gendarmerie, as well as holding responsibility for prisons.[106]

A second ministerial appointment was that of Philippe Henriot, nicknamed "the French Goebbels," who also a member of the Milice. A talented broadcaster, he used his skills to spew out poisonous anti-Semitic and anti-Communist propaganda two or three times a day, initially on Radio France (Radio Vichy) and, from 1942, on Radio-Paris. In January Henriot became French minister of information and propaganda. The French government now included Darnand, an SS officer, who was already the head of an armed militia committed to hunting down Jews and members of the Resistance, in charge of internal security and Henriot, a skilful and persuasive broadcaster who could be counted on to pump out Nazi propaganda. Hitler also wanted Marcel Déat as a government minister, but Pétain protested at the promotion of the man he had tried to have arrested in December 1940 and who had been constantly attacking Vichy through the columns of his newspaper *L'Œuvre*. Hitler simply bided his time: in February 1944, Pétain said that if he accepted Déat's appointment as a government minister he would be denying everything he stood for and bringing discredit upon himself. Within weeks Déat became minister of labour with Pétain futilely refusing to endorse the appointment. In a final snub to Pétain, Déat did not even bother to leave Paris to take up his post in Vichy; he considered most of his fellow ministers to be, at worst, obstacles to the sort of collaboration he wanted and, at best, simply irrelevant. Déat's plans to send half a million more workers to Germany by recruiting those born in 1923, 1924, and 1925 and abolishing some previously exempted categories failed to materialise. Déat's appointment, coming so soon after the installation of Darnand and Henriot, marked a clear victory for the pro-Nazi collaborationists. Hitler's rejection of the collaborationists' manifesto showed he was not prepared to give them a free hand, but he was, however, willing to play on their hopes of close Franco-German collaboration while using them to recruit workers and reinforce the repressive and propaganda machinery within the French government. Vichy's complete subservience to Germany's wishes was encapsulated when Cecil von Renthe-Fink, a fiercely anti-French German officer, was sent to Vichy to keep a close eye on the now politically impotent and mentally fragile Pétain to ensure that he did not step out of line.

Pétain had put France on the road to state collaboration at Montoire in October 1940. He had made Laval his prime minister; both men had publicly backed Germany and had done its bidding in the hope of securing a place for France at the top table in the New (Nazi) Europe. They later added another reason for their support: Nazi Germany was the only hope of those who sought to stop the spread of communism. Unprompted by the Germans, the Vichy government had introduced overtly discriminatory laws targeting Jews, foreigners, and Freemasons; it was deeply implicated in tracking down and punishing those opposed to the Occupation; it had provided the manpower for the arrest of Jews and endorsed their deportation from France; it had organised the forced recruitment of workers for Germany and, more recently, had created the Milice. But by the end of 1943 both Laval and Pétain had lost almost all of their influence. Committed pro-Nazi forces had moved into this power vacuum. Vichy was becoming "Nazified."

For those in Paris opposed to the Germans, 1943 was marked by hope and disappointment. Throughout the year they had asked themselves if the much anticipated Allied landing was about to happen. "Will this be the crucial year, with the Allies landing and the opening of a second front in Europe?" student Bernard Pierquin wrote in his diary on January 5, 1943.[107] Even a cynical pessimist like Andrzej Bobkowski admitted that the war might end that year.[108] But the high hopes that followed the Allied landings in North Africa in November 1942 turned rapidly to frustration and disappointment, and the delight with which most Parisians had greeted Operation Torch soon evaporated. At the end of January 1943, shortly after a meeting in Casablanca at which Churchill and Roosevelt agreed that the war would end only when Germany had surrendered unconditionally, Charles Braibant observed that Parisians tried to suppress their anger and impatience at the lack of Allied progress in North Africa; they were hungry and no longer asking where or how the Allied offensive would be launched. Only one word was on everyone's lips: when?[109] By February, according to

Braibant, many Parisians believed the Allies were using the campaign in Tunisia to give their troops some fighting experience; others thought the Allies were dragging out the campaign to draw German troops away from the Eastern Front and so take pressure off the Red Army.[110] That same month, shortly after the Red Army's success at Stalingrad, Bobkowski wrote that British propaganda was again referring to an Allied landing, which "the whole of Paris" was convinced would happen in March.[111] In March itself Liliane Jameson, too, wrote of Parisians complaining about the Allies deliberately taking their time in Tunisia, keeping the Axis troops there, inflicting losses on them, lowering enemy morale, while preparing for something on a bigger scale.[112] Charles Rist also sensed something was in the offing. He wrote, "We are living in a frenzied state of anticipation, waiting for 'something.'" This imminent Allied landing would be the definitive breakthrough. "The more the British and Americans appear confident about the future," wrote Rist, "the more impatient we are to see them strike a decisive blow."[113] Bernard Pierquin, writing in March, looked forward to a big Allied landing in "June or July" and "definitely in France, somewhere on the Channel coast."[114] By the end of the month he was less optimistic: "What is certain is that there will be a landing one day, but when?"[115] In a broadcast on July 1, Churchill had raised French hopes once more when he predicted Allied landings before the leaves fell from the trees. However, the British prime minister was probably thinking of the landings in Sicily later that month, which were already at an advanced stage of planning, or he was possibly trying to placate Stalin and others, who were demanding the opening of a second front without delay. In early September, Bernard Pierquin wrote that everyone expected an Allied landing in mainland Italy "within a few days."[116] According to him, the news that Italy had surrendered unconditionally and that the Allies had landed near Naples raised the spirits of the Parisians, but, after all the disappointments, few dared to hope that the massive Allied bombing of airfields signalled the immanent opening of a new front in France.[117]

Parisians counting on the return of POWs, those deported to camps, or those taken German factories were becoming more depressed than ever, according to Pierquin. The German occupiers capitalised on what they presented as a rash promise by Churchill, which he had been unable to keep. They distributed leaflets in the form of leaves from the famous Parisian plane trees, bearing the slogan: "I have fallen, Churchill. Where are you? Where are your soldiers?"[118] Another propaganda leaflet showed the British prime minister at the microphone, with the caption, "Churchill promised liberation before the leaves fell." Below was a picture of a Parisian street-sweeper brushing up leaves with his broom, and another slogan: "The leaves have fallen."[119] Those longing for the Germans to be driven out of Paris hoped desperately that 1944 would be the year of their deliverance.

⤳ *14*

A Serial Killer on the Run, Pétain in Paris, the Milice on the Rampage, the Allies on Their Way

*A*s Parisians waited for news of an Allied landing, the city was gripped by the macabre goings-on in a street in the 16th arrondissement not far from the Arc de Triomphe. On March 11, 1944, the police were called to investigate thick clouds of black, foul-smelling smoke pouring out of the chimney at 21, rue Le Sueur. When the police officers entered the cellar of the boarded-up house, they were shocked and disgusted at what they found: body parts were scattered across the floor and piled up on the stairs. The charred remains of a human hand poked out of the door of a roaring stove.

Subsequent investigations revealed five kilos of hair and more than ten complete scalps, as well as a sack containing a body that had been cleaved in half—minus the head, foot, and internal organs; in the backyard two pits full of an obnoxious mix of quicklime and more body parts were discovered. There were so many chopped-up limbs and bones that forensic experts failed to agree on how many people had been killed or their gender, let alone the time and cause of death. Items of women's clothing, make-up, and perfume indicated that many of the victims were female, but why or how they had been killed remained an enigma. To add to the mystery, the police discovered a small triangular room with metal rings set into the walls and a spy hole in the door. They wondered if this was to allow the killer to watch the faces of his bound victims as they writhed in agony.

355

The owner of the property was the apparently conventional and respectable Dr. Marcel Petiot, who lived with his wife in the rue de Caumartin in the 18th arrondissement. The couple apparently doted on their only son, Gérard, entertained at home, played bridge, and often went out to the cinema and the theatre. Georges-Victor Massu, the French police officer in charge of the case and on whom Georges Simenon partly based his fictional Inspector Maigret, received a telegram from his superiors: "Order from German authorities. Arrest Petiot. Dangerous Lunatic." Massu immediately issued a description of Dr. Petiot, as well as a warrant for his arrest and for that of his wife and his brother Maurice.

A media frenzy ensued in the newspapers as they squeezed every drop of sensationalism from the discovery of the human remains. Petiot was dubbed "the New Landru" (a reference to an infamous French serial killer, convicted and guillotined in 1922 for murdering eleven people), the Butcher of Paris, the Scalper of the Étoile, the Monster of the rue Le Sueur, the Demonic Ogre, and Doctor Satan. In cafés, restaurants, and workplaces across the city, Parisians speculated about why Petiot might have killed all these people and where he might be now. News of Petiot's alleged exploits dominated the headlines in Switzerland, Scandinavia, Belgium, and even the United States, where *Time* magazine noted that the story had "crowded war news from the headlines" (although the journalist who wrote the story was one of many who believed that Petiot was a fabrication concocted by the Nazis to distract Parisians from their daily problems). In actual fact, unknown to the police or the media, Petiot was hiding in a friend's apartment in the rue du Faubourg-Saint-Denis in the 10th arrondissement.[1]

On March 15 the German secret police handed Massu a file claiming to show that Petiot had created an "escape line" out of Paris for Jews, Allied pilots who had been shot down, deserters from the German army, and anyone else who wanted to leave the city. Such escape lines had been operating since the start of the Occupation; for instance, in 1940–1941 the Musée de l'Homme group tried to help people reach Britain and had links with an escape line in northern France. The Germans were convinced enough of the existence of Petiot's escape line to release a Jew, Yvan Dreyfus, from the Royallieu-Compiègne camp in return for a pledge to infiltrate Petiot's organisation. Dreyfus disappeared and was later presumed to have been murdered by Petiot.

Within days of starting his investigations, Massu suspected that Petiot had invented his "escape line" as a means to lure people who wanted to flee the city. He promised would-be escapers a safe passage out of Paris, and then proceeded to murder them and steal their money and possessions, after which he cut up their bodies and tried to dispose of the pieces. This hypothesis appeared to be confirmed on March 15, when a man came to see Massu wanting to know what had happened to Joachim Guschinow, his Jewish friend and business partner from whom he had bought a leather-and-fur shop under the "Aryanisation laws" of 1940. Guschinow, desperate to leave Paris after the roundups of Jews in May and August 1941, agreed to pay 25,000 francs to his doctor (Petiot), who promised to smuggle him out of France on a boat leaving Marseilles for Argentina. All documentation would be provided. Guschinow hid some precious stones and more than a million francs in cash in his clothing and suitcase; he also took along some fur coats, so he could open a shop when he reached Buenos Aires. Just before his scheduled departure Guschinow and his wife dined together near the Arc de Triomphe. Guschinow's wife never saw or heard from her husband again.

Another case that came to the attention of the police was that of Joseph Récocreux, known as Jo the Boxer, who also needed to leave Paris—and fast. But, unlike Guschinow, he was fleeing not the Germans but rather his boss, Henri Lafont, the head of the French Gestapo gang from the rue Lauriston. Lafont had discovered that Jo, dressed in a German uniform, had been freelancing, extorting money and valuables from Jewish householders and keeping the proceeds for himself. Jo met Petiot, who was calling himself "Dr. Eugène," and accepted the doctor's offer to spirit him out of the city. Petiot asked Jo to return to see him alone, but Jo arrived with another gangster called François Albertini (François the Corsican), who also wanted to leave Paris—as well as their two mistresses. The two gangsters swapped women, probably trying to safeguard themselves from any double-crossing by the other, and François and Jo's mistress, Claudia, left first. Some time in the autumn, Petiot (still posing as "Dr. Eugène") told Jo he had received a letter from Argentina saying that the couple had arrived safely. At the end of October, Jo, François's mistress Annette, and a second woman set off to follow François and Claudia, but, like the latter, they got no farther than 21, rue Le Sueur. They were carrying cash and jewellery, including 1.4 million francs sewn into Jo's suit, which they planned to use to start a brothel in South America. A few weeks later, Petiot was seen wearing Jo's ostentatious gold watch, which he claimed Jo had given him as a present.[2]

Another member of Lafont's French Gestapo gang who was keen to put himself beyond the boss's reach was Adrien Estébétéguy, known as Adrien the Basque. He was one of the original members of the gang freed by Lafont from Fresnes prison in August 1940 (see Chapter 12). One of Adrien the Basque's jobs was "persuading" people to part with their gold, but Lafont suspected him of reselling some of it and keeping the proceeds, and of doing the same with valuables seized during raids on private homes. Adrien disappeared in March 1943, and Adrien's brother Émile later claimed that Lafont had used Petiot and his "escape line" as a ruse to dispose of his brother.[3]

It was not until October 1944, two months after the Liberation of Paris, that Petiot was arrested—in disguise and posing as a Resistance fighter from the Forces françaises de l'intérieur (FFI).[4] At Petiot's trial in 1946 it was revealed that Petiot had previously been convicted of embezzlement and carrying out illegal abortions. One of his former mistresses was found murdered; another had mysteriously disappeared, as had a key witness in a trial in which Petiot was charged with drug dealing. Petiot's protestations that he was a patriotic member of the Resistance and involved in an escape network going by the absurd name of Fly-Tox (the name of a popular insecticide) were not believed. Nor was his extravagant claim that the bodies in the house on the rue Le Sueur were the grisly remains of sixty-three Germans, collaborators, and other enemies of France whom he was proud to have killed. Petiot was found guilty of murdering twenty-six individuals, although the actual number killed was almost certainly considerably higher. Dr. Albert Paul, Paris's chief medical examiner and expert witness at the trial, thought the victims might have numbered as many as 150. Petiot's appeal was rejected and he was guillotined on May 25, 1946, with many questions about the whole affair still unanswered.

☞ By the spring of 1944, Parisians had become accustomed—as far as this was possible—to Allied bombing. Since March 1942, raids had taken place on the Renault and Citroën factories in the southwest; others had occurred in the northern and northwestern suburbs around

Gennevilliers, Colombes, Poissy, and Argenteuil, together with the raid when bombs fell on Paris itself in the rue de Rennes and the city's southern outskirts.

From early April Allied bombers pounded targets throughout France. Their aim was to cripple the rail network and destroy rolling stock in preparation for the Allied landings. Parisians knew by now that most of the recurrent air raid alerts were for real and they would race to the nearest shelter as soon as the sirens sounded. On April 9 in a shelter in Vincennes, a young man named Raymond Ruffin met a woman with a baby in her arms whose story encapsulated just how murderous the war had become for civilians. Her husband, sent to Germany under the STO scheme, had been killed there in an Allied air raid and her parents had both died in an Allied bombing raid on Nantes on the Atlantic coast of France. French civilian casualties were mounting across France, especially in residential areas near docks, factories, and railway hubs. On April 9, for example, the main target of a raid by Allied bombers was Villeneuve-Saint-Georges, a rail hub in the south of Paris, during which more than 250 civilians were killed and nearly 170 others were injured.[5]

On April 18 Raymond Ruffin was taking cover in Vincennes again, this time in a cellar on the avenue de Paris. When a bomb landed nearby, the cellar was plunged into total darkness; more explosions followed; dust poured from the ceiling and "over the terrifying sound of more explosions came an indescribable cacophony of wailing, shouting and coughing."[6] Luckily nobody in that shelter was killed or injured; other bombs fell on Noisy-le-Sec, destroying marshalling yards, locomotive sheds, and workshops. From inside the camp at Drancy, young Francine Christophe saw a pilot parachuting from his plane who landed next to the camp. She watched as the buildings and warehouses in Noisy burned all through the night. For reasons that are unclear she said the sight of the buildings ablaze made her laugh, but she added, "the noise of the ack-ack guns made me shake with fear."[7] The raid on Noisy destroyed or damaged almost 3,000 houses, and more than 450 civilians were killed and 370 injured.[8]

The same night bombs were dropped on Juvisy, another rail hub in the outer suburbs to the south of Paris. Nineteen-year-old Marcelle Thiou had travelled to Juvisy from Troyes to see her two-week-old niece. Around midnight the household was awakened by flares. Marcelle rushed with her sister, her brother-in-law, and the baby to a makeshift shelter across the road. When a bomb landed nearby all four of them were buried under rubble and debris. The baby was killed in the blast and Marcelle's brother-in-law died soon afterwards. Marcelle was trapped for three long hours with her niece's tiny body pressed against hers. Eventually, she and her sister were dug out from their dust-filled hell-hole. Later Marcelle saw the bodies of her niece ("her mouth open and twisted and her eyes rolled upwards") and her brother-in-law among those laid out in a line on the pavement. Marcelle's niece and brother-in-law were two of the 125 people who died in that raid; another 475 were injured. Marcelle was covered in bruises, incurred by the impact of the spades used to free her from the debris.[9] On April 20 Charles Braibant wrote in his diary: "The heavy bombardment of the railway yards in Noisy-le-Sec, Villeneuve-Saint-Georges, and Rouen which took place at night between yesterday and the day before have caused quite a stir. It has to be admitted it was terrible. Several hundred people killed."[10] Pupils from the Lycée Saint-Louis who were called in to help with the rescue work had to be sent home because of deaths and injuries as a result of bombs exploding up to a week after they were dropped.

But it was the Allied bombing raid on the north of Paris on April 20 that proved the most traumatic. What turned out to be an all-out attack on the city itself rather than the suburbs, combined with the large number of fatalities, was enough to bring Pétain to Paris for the first time since the start of the Occupation almost four years earlier.

On April 20 Maurice Toesca, the principal private secretary of the prefect of Police, was at home in Neuilly after a trip to the theatre; just after midnight he heard some anti-aircraft fire and the wail of air-raid sirens. He ran to the window and, against the backdrop of a starry night, watched as flares in the sky dissolved into what looked like floating pools of liquid light.[11] It was a prelude to a massive air raid on the marshalling yards at La Chapelle in the 18th arrondissement; as with earlier raids the flares were there to guide the bombers to their target. The flares were immediately followed by showers of thin aluminium strips designed to interfere with German radar systems and misdirect anti-aircraft guns on the ground. Then, flying in from the south, came the first wave of bombers.

The bombs fell so quickly after the alert sounded that there was no time for teacher Jean Guéhenno, who lived in the northeastern part of the city, to run to the shelter. He stayed indoors with the windows open to watch the spectacle, which he described as "magnificent but pretty terrifying," while reflecting that humankind was both incredibly powerful and stupid.[12] More flares were dropped but, carried by a northwest wind, they inadvertently extended the target area into residential areas. Berthe Auroy had been quite sanguine at the start of the raid, but soon realised to her horror that bombs were now falling in the part of Montmartre where she lived. Another witness, the author Alfred Fabre-Luce, described "a giant red glow lighting up the whole of Sacré-Coeur," while all around houses were shaking.[13]

Berthe Auroy was in one of them. When she looked through her kitchen window the sky looked as if it was on fire. She returned to her bedroom, trembling with fear and cold; the noise was deafening; she felt paralysed, expecting the building to collapse at any moment. She was too frightened to seek refuge with her neighbours on the floor above, but soon they were knocking on her door seeking shelter with her. "We huddled together . . . we felt better facing the danger together." The electricity cut out, but the bombing remained as heavy as ever and continued for a full hour. "Have they decided to destroy the whole of Paris?" Berthe wondered.[14] Then it stopped.

Berthe and her neighbours rushed to the window and to the north saw huge flames leaping towards the sky, although nothing in the immediate surrounding area seemed to have taken a direct hit. They smiled at one another with tears in their eyes. Then the sense of relief evaporated as it all started again. This time they could hear the high-pitched whistle of the bombs as they fell and were shaken by the devastating explosions that followed. Eventually the all-clear sounded. The bombardment was over. However, two weeks later Berthe wrote that whenever she thought about the raid, she felt as if she had been thrown into hell. The British high command concluded that the raid had been a success, with "only a few clusters of bombs falling off target."[15] Whether it was wishful thinking or ignorance on the part of the British is not clear but that was not at all what it looked or felt like on the ground.

Some 670 people had been killed "off target," mostly in buildings and cellars in the 18th arrondissement and a few in the nearby suburb of Saint-Ouen. Hundreds more had been injured, but an astonishing 4,530 inhabitants of Montmartre had been pulled unharmed from the cellars in buildings that had collapsed.[16] More than 2,000 bombs had fallen on an area of about two and a half square miles. The La Chapelle area, which stretched as far as the Butte Montmartre—the hill on which Sacré-Coeur stood—now resembled a lunar landscape, scattered with twisted railway tracks and locomotives, one on top of another, "as if engaged in some ghastly act of copulation."[17] Six Lancaster bombers had been lost to enemy fire.

Berthe Auroy ventured out into her neighbourhood the day after the raid. She found that a dozen or so bombs had fallen around the nearby Sacré-Coeur basilica. Behind the basilica a whole block had been hit; a sign warned of unexploded bombs; one badly damaged street was sealed off and an anxious crowd watched from a distance as teams cleared the rubble to free those trapped beneath; a friend who lived near the town hall told Berthe that one factory in Saint-Ouen had been completely destroyed. On Monday, Berthe saw hearses bringing coffins to the Sacré-Coeur ready for the funeral service. "Some of them must just hold bits of bodies," she wrote.[18]

Parisians living in Montmartre had always assumed they would be spared any bombing raid, as neither factories nor military targets could be found in their arrondissement. They had forgotten about the railway yards at La Chapelle. Berthe noticed a change in attitude around her after the raid: people who had been quite nonchalant about air-raid warnings in the past now fled to the cellars at the first sound of the siren. Now too, as soon as night fell, the Métro stations were packed with frightened families, who commandeered the benches. Berthe went to stay with her sister, whose nearby apartment block at 90, rue Lepic had a cellar that served as an air-raid shelter. The air-raid alerts grew more and more frequent. Every night Berthe would get up in a hurry, dress herself, and join the crowd of other inhabitants from the block, shivering in the cellar, each one clutching their bags of valuables.[19] The increased intensity and frequency of the bombing raids was seen as another indication that the Allied landings were imminent: even if many drew encouragement from this belief it was little consolation to the 1,500 people killed in Allied bombing raids on Paris and the suburbs of Juvisy, Noisy-le-Sec, and Villeneuve-Saint-Georges between April 10 and 25.[20] Parisians thought it very likely that the city's mainline railway stations—all of them in densely populated residential areas—would be the next targets.[21]

Predictably, the collaborationist press again used the raids to condemn the Allies, but even Parisians opposed to the Occupation were unsettled by them, especially the one on La Chapelle. The author César Fauxbras wrote that feelings were running high about the bombings and their probable consequences: many Parisians feared that the disruption of the rail networks would mean even less food reaching Paris and so further reductions in rations and the end of food parcels from the countryside.[22] Banker and economist Charles Rist understood that the purpose of the raid was to disrupt German troop and transport movements, but, given the lack of any activity from the British side, he wondered when the Germans would want to use the rail network. De Gaulle talked about an imminent offensive, the radio talked about Russian troops regrouping and preparing to march on Berlin. And all the while, wrote Rist, in Paris people were dying, were being forced into hiding, or were being arrested.[23]

Talk of Pétain returning to Paris had been heard ever since the fiasco in December 1940 when the ashes of Napoleon Bonaparte's son were sent from Vienna to be placed in Les Invalides. But it had remained just talk. At the end of April, however, Pétain visited the Northern Zone for the first time since the signing of the armistice on a trip undertaken with the blessing of the Germans, who appreciated its potential as a vehicle for anti-Allied propaganda. As part of a tour of several cities that the Allies had bombed, the head of the French state came to Paris on April 26 to pay his respects to those who had died in the air raids. Between the raid on April 20 and his arrival in the city almost a week later, Pétain had celebrated his eighty-eighth birthday. He still looked physically fit, but his mind was going and his grasp of what was happening around him had become increasingly tenuous.

On the morning of April 26, Pétain attended a memorial service in Notre-Dame Cathedral for those who had perished in the bombing raids and was then driven to the Hôtel de Ville. At around 3 P.M., after lunch with various dignitaries, he appeared on a specially constructed platform and addressed a crowd of about 10,000 people. Many of those present were children from local schools, who had been mobilised for the event, and he certainly received a warm—some claimed ecstatic— welcome. Maurice Toesca had a more nuanced view. He wrote that, in general, those aged over forty were passive and just curious; those between twenty and forty were interested and many seemed quite moved;

children between ten and fifteen were wildly enthusiastic and in a state
of frenzy.[24] In his short address Pétain promised the crowd he would
return and, to the fury of his German minder Renthe-Fink, Pétain departed briefly from his prepared speech to say that next time it would
be without the need to inform his guards.[25] Pétain kept his word about
returning, but probably not as he intended: the next time he was in Paris
would be in July 1945 when de Gaulle's provisional government put him
on trial for treason. After his speech at the Hôtel de Ville, Pétain visited the Bichat hospital in the north of the city, where many of those
injured in the bombing raids were being treated. At about 6 p.m. he
left for other cities in northern France that had been hit by Allied
bombs. During that night, within hours of Pétain's departure, British
and Canadian aircraft were back. They bombed marshalling yards and
factories in the suburbs of Choisy-le-Roi, Nogent-sur-Marne, Maisons-
Alfort, Alfortville, and Créteil in the eastern and southeastern suburbs
of the city. The Gare du Nord had been closed after the raid on La
Chapelle; on April 27 Parisians awoke to find that the Gare de Lyon
railway station had been closed as well.

The Paris media still believed that Pétain had a role to play as a
counter rallying point to de Gaulle and the Allies, and they went into
raptures over Pétain's visit; writer and journalist André Brissaud even
went so far as to describe the crowd's reception of Pétain as "a plebi-
scite."[26] This was clearly nonsense. However, the cheers that greeted
him were real enough and for a moment, it would seem, even among
those Parisians who had lost confidence in him, Pétain became a symbol
of French patriotism. From the early days of the Occupation, Laval had
acted as a lightning conductor for most of the dissatisfaction and disil-
lusionment with Vichy and many of those present in the crowd were
not aware just how closely Pétain had been willingly collaborating with
the Germans. Those who were there on the day were cheering France;
it was the Pétain who had been constantly attacked by the pro-Nazi
Paris press who was standing in front of them, the First World War
hero addressing the crowd under a French flag—and not a German in
sight. Brissaud expressed this attitude well. "We were listening to the
Marshal, we were looking at the head of state, but our eyes were drawn
to the French national flag that had been raised on the Hôtel de Ville
for the first time since the armistice."[27] Claude Mauriac, the son of the
author François Mauriac, wrote of a friend being overwhelmed by the

sight of a mother in the crowd pointing out the tricolour to her young child who had never seen the French national flag before.[28] The very fact that thousands of people turned out to welcome Pétain generated its own positive and patriotic mood. This even touched Claude Mauriac, who had opposed collaboration from the start and who was now drawn to the Resistance—he would become de Gaulle's private secretary a month later. He waited for two hours in a crowd on the street and when Pétain was driven past he admitted being "overwhelmed, not enough to shout out, but full of feelings of gratitude and love."[29]

Pétain had a very different reception in the former Unoccupied Zone. In Paris, the population was overwhelmingly aware of the inescapable German presence and had a tendency to believe, wrongly, that all French government legislation was passed under German pressure. In the Unoccupied Zone before the end of 1942 there had been no official German presence for Pétain to hide behind and the people there were better informed about the policies and personalities of the Vichy government. It is true that Pétain had enjoyed great popularity—early on—but in the south much affection, respect, and trust had disappeared by spring 1944. For example, when Pétain appeared in public in Saint-Étienne a few weeks after his rapturous welcome in Paris he was booed by large sections of the crowd.[30]

Some ministers in Vichy hoped that the marshal's Paris visit, followed by his trips to Orléans and Nancy, could be used to show that support for Pétain was not dead. It might even be exploited to smooth the way to some sort of an accommodation with the Allies. However, a radio broadcast on April 28, the day after Pétain's return to Vichy, showed that while he might retain some residual appeal, however symbolic or nostalgic, he remained firmly in the pocket of the Germans. In his broadcast he raised the spectre of a civil war in France and told his listeners that "this so-called Liberation" was but a giant mirage. To be a true patriot meant remaining unswervingly loyal to his government. Although Pétain did not identify de Gaulle and his followers by name, he warned his listeners against following those who, far away from the risks they were asking their countrymen and women to take, sought to drag France into a new venture whose outcome was extremely risky. He accused those drawn to the Resistance of "compromising the future of the country," adding that it was in their best interest "to adopt a correct and loyal attitude towards the occupying forces." He continued,

"When the current tragedy is over and when, thanks to Germany's defence of the continent . . . our civilisation is definitively safe from the danger of Bolshevism, it will be time for France to rediscover and affirm her rightful place."[31]

⌒ IN ALGIERS ON JUNE 3 de Gaulle renamed his French Committee for National Liberation (CFLN) the Provisional Government of the French Republic (Gouvernement provisoire de la République française, or GPRF) and flew from Algiers to London at Churchill's invitation. Although de Gaulle did not know it, he was about to be briefed about the D-Day landings in France, which were scheduled to take place within the next few days.

On June 6 those Parisians who had been longing for an end to the Occupation heard the news for which they had been waiting. The Allies had landed in France. Operation Overlord—the code name for the D-Day landings on the French side of the English Channel—had begun. More than 150,000 Allied soldiers, supported by thousands of aircraft, landed on five Normandy beaches between Caen and Cherbourg or were parachuted into the nearby countryside. Wave upon wave of soldiers and weaponry followed, and by the end of July almost one million Allied soldiers were in France engaged in fierce fighting against German armies that were determined to drive them back into the sea.

President Roosevelt, who viewed de Gaulle as a potential dictator, was determined to keep him firmly on the sidelines, and he strove to ensure that the role played by de Gaulle's Free French forces in the liberation of France should be minimal. The American leader refused to recognise de Gaulle's provisional government and insisted that any liberated areas would be administered by the Allied Military Government of Occupied Territories (AMGOT).[32] On June 14 de Gaulle, together with a large retinue, was grudgingly allowed to leave Britain to pay a quick visit to Bayeux in Normandy. Ignoring Churchill's instructions not to hold any public meetings there, the leader of the Free French forces addressed an enthusiastic crowd from an improvised stage erected in the town. De Gaulle concluded his speech with the phrase, "The French government salutes Bayeux—the first town in France to be liberated." There was no hint that the government to which de Gaulle referred was a provisional one. Importantly, when de Gaulle departed, he left four of his representatives behind to form the kernel of a new administrative structure, and Bayeux briefly became the capital of liberated France. This was the first step in de Gaulle's ultimately successful bid to prevent the Allies' imposing their own administrative organisation on "his" country.

Rumours of an Allied landing (or "invasion," as the Germans and the collaborationists called it) had been circulating ever since Operation Torch in November 1942, but now it was actually happening. Parisians had been disappointed so often that some, like a concierge near Charles Braibant's home, were sceptical. Braibant described Parisians as hopeful but, he noted, wary of having their hopes dashed again, they were staying calm.[33] Bobkowski also described the atmosphere in the city as calm, and he noted how the Germans had rewarded this attitude by pushing back the curfew an hour so that Parisians could go to the cinema.[34]

However, some city residents were positively excited about the news. "It really is *the* landing," Benoîte Groult wrote. "People say there are already 180,000 men on the Continent. What an amazing achievement. . . . This time it's the real thing. Hope is no longer up in heaven, it's within our walls."[35] Liliane Jameson was almost in tears she was so happy. A voice in her head kept repeating "They've landed! They've landed! They're here on French soil and they're coming our way. That's it! It's really happened."[36] Berthe Auroy heard the announcement on Radio-Paris, which presented the news as of little importance. When Berthe heard it she felt the blood rush to her heart.

At the same time, amid the general feeling of joy, Parisians were worried about the city running out of food. They asked themselves: "How are we going to get food supplies if there's no transport? How are we going to manage if there's no water, no gas, no electricity?"[37] Two days after the landings Berthe saw Parisians besieging bakers' shops, which by the end of the morning of June 8 were already displaying signs "No More Bread."[38] Berthe assumed that as the fighting drew closer to Paris she, like the rest of the Parisians, would be spending days and nights on end in air-raid shelters. She had already prepared some provisions and suitable clothing.[39]

As the fighting raged in Normandy where the Allied advance faced fierce resistance, the Germans in Paris did their best to keep their spirits up, to maintain the city's cultural life, and to sustain the sense of normality that they had tried to induce since they first arrived four years earlier. The Propaganda Section of the MBF announced over ninety concerts in June; state theatres opened during the week, and smaller private theatres put on shows at the weekends. There were art auctions at the Hôtel Drouot, where paintings by Matisse and Bonnard sold for hundreds of thousands of francs, and crowds flocked to art exhibitions at the Palais de Tokyo; even as late as the last day in July a new show of watercolours opened at the Orangerie.[40]

This desperate attempt to retain some sense of normality had a dark side. The Normandy landings had not led to an anti-German uprising in the city—much to the disappointment of some resisters in Paris. Amid rumours of attacks and insurrection, the German secret police continued to round up suspected resisters, Allied sympathisers, and secret agents. The French police, on the other hand—with the exception of the Brigades spéciales, who remained zealous and brutal until the bitter end—were increasingly keen to distance themselves from their German occupiers. Between June 30 and July 14 almost 400 Resistance suspects in the Paris area were arrested by the German secret police compared with only forty-six arrested by French police.[41]

The fanatical and ideologically committed Germans in Paris were enraged by the Allied landings, and abuse meted out by the secret police became more common and even more extreme than before, as the torturers vented their frustration and anger on their unfortunate prisoners. As revealed in evidence presented in Paris in 1954 at the trial of Carl Oberg, the Paris head of the German secret police, already disgusting and brutal attempts to extract information from suspected resisters now gave way to acts of pure, sadistic terror: prisoners had their eyes gouged out, their fingers sawn off with knives, or their genitals hacked off.[42]

The Milice had been officially operating in the former Occupied Zone since January 1944, but even before then Darnand's men could be seen strutting around the city, especially near their headquarters in the place de Châteaudun. They took over several secondary schools to house their members, including the Lycée Saint-Louis on the boulevard Saint-Michel opposite the Rive Gauche bookshop. Although the German military remained uneasy about the Milice, Darnand's paramilitary organisation cooperated closely with the German secret police, and Helmut Knochen, Oberg's second-in-command, described the thuggish Darnand as "politically absolutely irreproachable."[43]

In the Southern Zone, Darnand had introduced special Milice courts that would have made the German secret police proud. Each court had three judges; nearly all were members of the Milice, rather than the judiciary, and all were chosen by Darnand or one of his close advisers. The accused had no lawyer and no right of appeal. Any suspect found guilty was executed immediately. In Lyons, Milice trials rarely lasted more than fifteen minutes and there was no reason to suppose it would be any different once they started to be held in Paris.[44]

In Paris the Milice soon followed the example of the German secret police and the French Brigades spéciales in systematically torturing its opponents—real and imagined—at its headquarters at 44, rue Le Peletier in the 9th arrondissement. There, working as a team, a one-time barman and a former pimp took perverted pleasure in forcing prisoners to lie on a rack while being subjected to powerful electric shocks or being compelled to drink twenty or thirty litres of water. The torturers also liked to place metal rings around the heads of their captives and then tighten them, as one would a vice. These terrifyingly brutal scenes often took place in front of suspected accomplices in the hope they would be terrorised into giving information.[45]

Outside Paris clashes between the Resistance and the forces of the Milice were escalating. As the Allies battled their way through Normandy, it looked as if the rest of France was on the brink of civil war. On June 7 Darnand mobilised the Milice "to save the country"; the following day he announced menacingly that the so-called Resistance was made up of enemies who must be fought with the utmost determination. The Milice had already shown its ruthless and merciless nature: a few months earlier in February and March a full-scale battle raged on the Glières plateau high above Annecy in southeastern France. Some 500 resisters from the *maquis* were eventually beaten by a combined force of 3,000 German soldiers and members of the Milice. Three hundred resisters managed to escape, but 149 were either killed in the fighting or in the terrible reprisals that followed. It had been a serious strategic mistake to group so many resisters in one place, but the heroism of the *maquis* turned Glières into a symbol of French determination to resist the German invader whatever the cost.[46]

By June the Resistance had the Milice member and arch-collaborationist broadcaster Philippe Henriot in its sights. Following his appointment by Laval as French minister of news and propaganda, Henriot had continued to broadcast two or sometimes three vitriolic "editorials" a day. In these salvoes, he played on the fear of civil war, attacked the Jews, denounced the Resistance as a rabble of terrorists and Communists, and castigated the Allies as "invaders" or "murderers in the sky." A champion of all-out collaboration, Henriot was a compelling orator. The Free French in London took him seriously enough to lambast him personally as well as countering his pro-Nazi venom. Meanwhile, in Paris, a sixteen-man Resistance commando unit planned to kidnap him and send him to Algiers. If he resisted, they had orders to kill him.

On June 28, shortly before 6 o'clock in the morning, there was a knock at Henriot's bedroom door at his ministry in the rue de Solférino where he had spent the night with his wife. The callers announced they were from the Milice and slipped their identity papers under the door. When Henriot opened it, he found himself facing three men, each holding a machine gun. He tried to disarm them—and almost succeeded—when the leader of the group gave the order to fire. Henriot collapsed. He was too seriously wounded to be taken prisoner and was shot dead where he lay.[47]

Laval announced the news of Henriot's assassination during the radio slot usually occupied by his minister of news and propaganda. He reminded his listeners of Henriot's eloquence and passion. "Unable to reply to Philippe Henriot they silenced him," he said, "unable to make him shut his mouth, they shut his eyes."[48] This theme was repeated on posters that soon appeared all over Paris showing a photograph of Henriot accompanied by the slogan "He Told the Truth . . . They Killed Him."[49] The day after his death, a huge catafalque was erected outside the ministerial offices where he worked, which was later moved and erected outside the Hôtel de Ville. On June 30 a funeral service was held for him in Notre-Dame Cathedral.

Henriot was an established figure of the Occupation and his murder left few indifferent. Even François Mauriac, the celebrated author who published with the clandestine Éditions de Minuit and contributed to the underground Resistance press, fell under Henriot's spell. His son Claude wrote that his father had changed from tuning in to the BBC to listening to Henriot: "He cannot, despite everything, stop himself listening . . . refuting the arguments as he goes along, as if he needed to persuade himself."[50] Reactions to Henriot's death among Parisians ranged from disgust and horror to relief and hearty approval. His fans viewed him as all that was best about France and many queued to file past his body and pay their respects. Henriot's corpse was laid out in an open coffin inside the ministry building, watched over by a guard of honour made up of members of the Milice.

Others admired Henriot's eloquence, but they realised just how dangerous this talent had made him. Charles Braibant took this view and concluded, "The patriots who killed him have done the country a great service. And what's more here's at least one man who got what he deserved."[51] A leaflet distributed by the Front national denounced Henriot as "the traitor who had sold out to Hitler; the French Goebbels. He has paid the price for his treason."[52] Jean Guéhenno wrote that Henriot had a better death than he deserved, adding somewhat curiously, "It would have been better to have condemned him to live in a cupboard strung up by the neck."[53] François Mauriac was a little more indulgent, referring to Henriot as a "martyr for a bad cause which was already lost when he fought for it."[54] Georges Benoît-Guyod fundamentally disapproved of the assassination itself, but at the same time he was glad to see the end of Henriot. Henriot was, he said, "a pitiful pedlar of false ideas, who, as a government minister, dedicated himself to spreading enemy propaganda on the pretext of promoting Franco-German reconciliation within a new Europe; for a long time I have thought of him as nothing more than an unpaid agent of the Third Reich."[55] For his part, Pétain refused to broadcast a tribute to Henriot. Pétain had been marginalised by the appointment of pro-Nazis within his government, namely, Henriot, Darnand, and Déat, and his feeble comment on Henriot's assassination was simply: "He was not my minister; I had not approved his nomination."[56]

Marcel Déat, who himself had survived an assassination attempt in March 1943, denounced the killing of Henriot as odious and cowardly, and he called for revenge. The Milice too, vowed revenge, which they exacted through murderous rampages in Toulouse, Clermont-Ferrand, Grenoble, and Mâcon. But they were after a more celebrated scalp. Georges Mandel, briefly the minister of the interior in Paul Reynaud's 1940 government, had opposed the armistice of June 1940. He was part of a parliamentary delegation that tried, but failed, to reach North Africa in the hope of continuing the anti-German struggle from there. He was arrested, sentenced to life imprisonment, and was, like Édouard Daladier, Paul Reynaud, Léon Blum, and General Maurice Gamelin, incarcerated in a prison at Portalet in the French Pyrenees. In November 1942, Mandel was seized by the Germans and sent to Germany. On July 6, 1944, he was brought back to the Santé prison in Paris, and the following day the German secret police handed him over to Max Knipping, Darnand's ministerial representative in the Occupied Zone. Knipping in turn delivered Mandel into the hands to a small gang of Milice members *(miliciens)*, who drove him away, ostensibly towards Vichy. After about thirty miles Mandel's captors stopped their car in the Forest of Fontainebleau and murdered him, later claiming that they had been attacked by the Resistance. Mandel was buried in a cemetery in Versailles on July 13; only eight people were allowed to attend the funeral.[57]

The murder of Mandel by the Milice was not an isolated incident; sections of the German army too were now resorting to barbarous terrorist tactics. On June 8, 1944, an SS Panzer division was on its way to engage the Allies in Normandy when it stormed into Tulle, southeast of Limoges. The town had been occupied the day before by the FFI, the armed wing of the Resistance. In reprisal, the following day SS soldiers hanged ninety-nine hostages from balconies, trees, and streetlamps; they selected another 149 for deportation, of whom less than a third returned after the war.

On June 10 soldiers from the same SS division carried out one of the most appalling massacres of the war in France. At Oradour-sur-Glane— where, incidentally, no Resistance activity had been recorded—the men from the village were taken into barns, gunned down, and their bodies burned. All the women and children were herded into the church, where soldiers mowed them down with machine guns, deliberately firing low to hit the children, as bullet holes in prams later proved. The church was then torched: those who were not already dead were burned alive or suffocated to death. After pillaging the village, the soldiers burned what was left of it to the ground and went on their way, except for a small group that returned to bury the bodies in trenches.[58] Six hundred and forty-two villagers were murdered; five men and one woman—who escaped through a church window—were the only survivors (and local witnesses) of the massacre.

Meanwhile in Paris, the National Resistance Council (CNR) and Paris Liberation Committee (CPL) called on residents to take to the streets on July 14—Bastille Day. Some more timorous members of the CNR feared that the call would either be ignored, leaving the Resistance looking weak and foolish, or it would be followed and would result in bloodshed and reprisals. In the event, the street demonstrations were a huge success. Tens of thousands of people packed the streets all over Paris and in the suburbs. They wore blue, white, and red as they

marched, sang, and chanted. With a few exceptions there was little reaction from the German or French police although some arrests were
made, including a number of railway workers; indeed, people even talked
of the French police in the place de la Contrescarpe, behind the Panthéon, singing the Marseillaise and of demonstrators in Belleville
shouting: "The police are on our side!"[59] This relaxed attitude towards
the demonstrators was completely at odds with how the majority of
French police had behaved over the last four years. But this shift in outlook and behaviour was not limited to the police. Christian Chag-
neau, a leading Communist militant, noted that for the first time in
ages Communists, with warm support from the Parisians, had demonstrated freely in the city. He remarked: "Something in the situation
had changed and changed in everybody's consciousness as well."[60]

Parisians were celebrating an imminent victory, but they also viewed
their immediate future with some foreboding. Allied bombing and
fierce fighting between the Allies and the German troops following the
Normandy landings had, as they feared it would, seriously disrupted
road and rail links between Paris and the rest of France; the waves of
economic and social dislocation the war was generating meant that food
in the city was scarcer than ever. "From today's perspective, the extremely difficult months we've lived through look like times of plenty,"
Berthe Auroy wrote in her diary. "Out of ten food shops, nine are closed
and the tenth is more or less empty. NOTHING FOR SALE! Except
here and there on a little cart you find a bunch of parsley or some
fresh mint."[61] After railing against the black market (too expensive for
people like her on measly state pensions), the frustration of fruitless
shopping expeditions and the problem of not having enough gas with
which to cook, she admitted it would get even worse. "We have been
told officially that Parisians have got days with no food ahead of them.
Without the railways, we cannot hope to receive the vegetables needed
to feed the capital for much longer."[62]

She wondered: Would Parisians have to rely on grass and rats for
food? And then she noted what she thought was perhaps the cruelest
shortage that could possibly be inflicted upon her fellow citizens: "Wine.
There's no more wine getting through!"[63]

Despite these difficulties and the problems that lay ahead, many still
registered plenty of laughter and joy, as the Bastille Day demonstrations
showed. For others, Bastille Day 1944 told a very different story. When
the Germans had been approaching Paris back in June 1940, prisoners

from the Santé, Cherche-Midi, and Fresnes prisons were evacuated. Now with the Allies seemingly on their way, "ordinary" or common-law prisoners (those not convicted of "political crimes") at the Santé jail planned to "evacuate themselves" in a mass breakout. Just after 10 P.M. on July 14, rioting prisoners broke down the doors of their cells. As the guards dived for cover, the inmates ran riot. An hour later it looked as if the prisoners might actually succeed in breaking out completely. The governor of the prison decided to call for German help. Within half an hour Kommandant Neifeind, accompanied by Knochen and a hundred or so his men, arrived at the prison, along with Amédée Bussière, the Paris prefect of police, and four top-ranking members of the Milice.

It was agreed that the Milice should take responsibility for reestablishing order, and Neifeind told Pierre Gallet, one of the Milice leaders and a close associate of Darnand, "I want to go into the cells and see them running red with blood."[64] Jean Bassompierre, the commander of the Milice in the Occupied Zone, brought in two Milice detachments from their quarters in the Lycée Saint-Louis. The men were instructed to block all exits to the prison and drive the prisoners back into their cells. Order was swiftly and brutally restored; six prisoners were shot dead and another ten injured.

Fifty common-law prisoners were singled out to appear before a Milice special court, presided over by Pierre Gallet; Gallet's two assistants were Max Knipping, who had handed Mandel over to his Milice assassins, and Georges Radici, another leading member of the Milice.

The court-marshal sat in the afternoon of July 15. If it had been dealing with "political prisoners" the hearings would almost certainly have been much shorter and most, if not all, of the defendants would have been found guilty of mutiny and shot. The panel acquitted twenty-two prisoners, but the remaining twenty-eight were found guilty and sentenced to death: one was eighteen years of age, eleven were aged nineteen, and six were aged twenty. The executions began shortly after the last hearing ended. Those condemned to die were shot in batches of seven. The six-man execution squads of French Gardes mobiles were so disgusted by what they were ordered to do that some took aim so as to deliberately miss their human targets. Sadly, this only meant that the condemned men were forced to face another volley of shots.[65]

With the Allies advancing in northern France and in Italy and with any prospect of a "final victory" for German forces on the Eastern Front having evaporated, it was becoming increasingly clear to more and more Germans that the game was up, although any German daring to say so openly risked being shot for treason. In Paris the German military began to contemplate the possibility of leaving the city: Stülpnagel had men scouring eastern France for possible refuges and identified Saint-Dié, a town southwest of Strasbourg, as a suitable retreat in the event of a *Sonderfall*, or "special case" (a euphemism for Paris falling to the Allies). Stülpnagel was in touch with disillusioned Wehrmacht officers in Germany, who were convinced that Hitler, through his reckless policies and dogmatic refusal to seek any negotiated settlement with the Allies, was driving Germany to defeat and devastation. When Hitler's megalomania slid into paranoid madness, this small group of high-ranking officers became more convinced than ever that, for Germany's sake, it was imperative to assassinate the Führer.

The recently appointed colonel Claus von Stauffenberg was chief-of-staff to Colonel-General Friedrich Frimm, commander-in-chief of the Reserve Army. Stauffenberg had served in Poland and France and then in North Africa, where he lost his left eye, his right hand, and two fingers of his left hand. In September 1943 he met a group of nationalist, conservative army officers determined to remove Hitler, and he began to plot with them.[66] A few months later Stauffenberg was presented with an ideal opportunity when he was ordered to attend a briefing session on July 20 in the Führer's field headquarters at Rastenburg in northeastern Poland. He arrived at the wooden barracks hut for the briefing carrying a briefcase containing two bombs. Slowed down by his physical impairment, he had time to prime only one of the devices before placing his briefcase next to a large wooden table over which Hitler was leaning examining a map. He then left, saying he had to make a phone call. From a short distance he watched as the bomb exploded, wrecking the hut and, Stauffenberg assumed, killing Hitler. He sped by car to a nearby airport and flew to Berlin, where he assured his co-conspirators that Hitler could not possibly have survived the blast and must be dead. The conspirators in turn informed their associates that the coup had been a success.

One of the people Stauffenberg telephoned was his cousin Caesar von Hofacker, who was serving in Paris as adjutant to the MBF. Stauffenberg told his cousin that Hitler was dead and asked him to inform Stülpnagel. On hearing the news, Stülpnagel, the most senior army officer in Paris who was party to the anti-Hitler conspiracy, swung into action and ordered the arrest of all the members of the secret police in the city. Under cover of darkness, shock troops led by General Boineburg-Lengsfeld, the military commander of the city and the suburbs, arrested some 15,000 members of the security police, including its head, SS General Carl Oberg.

Micheline Bood was at home that night and realised something strange was happening. From the window of her family's apartment overlooking the rue du Faubourg-Saint-Honoré she saw a long convoy of trucks, their headlights extinguished, making its way from the rue du Cirque towards the avenue Matignon. "Scores of Germans poured out of the back of the trucks, ensuring they made as little noise as possible." Micheline thought it was another roundup of Jews, but then the soldiers lined up in single file while their officers gave orders in hushed tones. Then they all set off towards the rue des Saussaies "with fixed bayonets and heads down, as if they were going into attack."[67] The following day the trucks had disappeared. In her account, Micheline did not mention that the rue des Saussaies housed the headquarters of the Gestapo and other units of the German secret police. Most of those arrested were taken either to Fresnes jail or to the Fort de l'Est in the northern suburb of Saint-Denis.

By the time Boineburg-Lengsfeld reached the Hôtel Raphaël to report that the arrests had been successfully made, news had reached the MBF that Hitler had survived the assassination attempt. Shaken by this totally unexpected piece of news, Stülpnagel feared he was a dead man and immediately ordered Oberg's release. Boineburg-Lengsfeld now had the unenviable job of going to the Hôtel Continental, where Oberg and senior members of his staff were being held, to set them free. In the event, the encounter passed off without incident and Oberg even agreed to come to the Hôtel Raphaël to join Stülpnagel for a glass of champagne. The following evening, Boineburg-Lengsfeld threw another reconciliation party for Oberg and his senior staff at the end of which Oberg gave his host a fine box of black-market cigars.[68]

In Berlin some of the plotters committed suicide and four, including Stauffenberg, were shot. Hitler made a brief radio broadcast to decry what he called a crime without parallel in German history. He also wanted his listeners to know that he was alive and well. Three times he referred to his survival in taking it as a sign from Providence that he should, and therefore would, continue his work.[69]

In Paris Stülpnagel was suspended and summoned back to Berlin to explain himself. He travelled by car and, on the way back near Vacherauville, just north of Verdun, he said he would take a short walk. His escorts heard a gunshot and ran to find the general floating in the Canal de l'Est. At first they thought he had been shot by the Resistance but he was taken to a hospital in Verdun, where doctors discovered he had blinded himself in a botched suicide attempt. Oberg travelled to Verdun to interview Stülpnagel, who tried to take all the blame for the involvement of other Paris army personnel in the attempted coup. In August Stülpnagel and three others from Paris (including Caesar von Hofacker, Stauffenberg's cousin) went on trial in Berlin; all four were found guilty and hanged. Field Marshal Rommel, "the Desert Fox," was also implicated in the coup and committed suicide in October.

☞ THE ALLIED LANDINGS did not deter the Germans from continuing their roundup of Jews in Paris. Because of a shortage of German manpower and French failure to cooperate, Brunner, the commandant of Drancy, believed that the most efficient method was to raid known concentrations of Jews in the city. He targeted children's hostels and orphanages, claiming that this would eliminate "future terrorists." An SS officer liaised with the German-funded Jewish UGIF and came away with a list of half a dozen orphanages for Jewish children in Paris and the suburbs as well as the number of children registered at each address. Two buses set out and over two nights 250 Jewish children and some thirty staff members were rounded up and taken to Drancy. A few of these children along with the wives and children of Jewish POWs were deported to Bergen-Belsen on July 23; most of the children were sent to Auschwitz in Convoy 77, one of the biggest convoys of the war. Once it had set off on July 31 with its 1,300 deportees, only 871 prisoners were left in Drancy.[70]

⤐ 15

The Liberation of Paris

O_N AUGUST 1, 1944, 15,000 men of the Free French Second Armoured Division (Deuxième Division blindée, or 2e DB) landed at Utah Beach on the Normandy coast. Their commanding officer was General Philippe de Hauteclocque, a French aristocrat who had adopted the name Leclerc to protect his family from possible German reprisals. His division included men of different political opinions with a shared determination to play their part in the Liberation of France. Some, like Leclerc, joined de Gaulle in London, others were in Britain when France surrendered; there were also anarchists and socialists who had fought in Spain against Franco and who were grouped in a unit known as La Nueve under the command of a Frenchman, Captain Raymond Dronne. For all its pride in being a French division, the 2e DB was armed, clothed, equipped, and trained by the U.S. Army and was almost immediately assigned to General George S. Patton's Third Army.

Ferocious battles raged in Normandy and it was not until two months after the June landings that the Allies made a significant breakthrough. Marc Boegner, the head of the Protestant Church in France was in Paris on August 6. "The week that has just finished has left us stunned," he wrote. "The Americans have advanced 300 km with their tanks and the Russians have taken the war onto German soil."[1] The Allies had liberated Le Mans, which lies about midway between the Normandy beaches and Paris, but the human cost on both sides was high, not least among French civilians living in the area. By mid-August 40,000 Allied soldiers had been killed and 170,000 injured; some 240,000 Germans soldiers had been killed or wounded, and another 200,000 had been taken prisoner. More than 50,000 French civilians had also died, and many towns, including Caen, Argentan, Lisieux, Falaises, Coutances, and Saint-Lô, were reduced to smoking ruins.[2]

By early August the wily Pierre Laval was back in Paris plotting his political survival. He wanted Paris to be an open city as it had been in June 1940, and he envisaged a special sitting of the National Assembly to coincide with the arrival of the Allies. It would be chaired by Édouard Herriot, who had been president of the Assembly in June 1940 and who was currently being held in a psychiatric hospital near Nancy. Laval planned to welcome the Allies in the name of the French government, and he hoped the parliamentary session would lend him democratic credibility. An arch manipulator and opportunist to the very end, Laval believed the Americans would back him, largely because it would keep de Gaulle out of the political picture.[3] He also calculated that recognition of him as the powerbroker of this initiative would be enough to save his skin. Laval secured Abetz's support for the plan and Herriot was brought to Paris and given rooms in the Hôtel de Ville.

On August 5 General Dietrich von Choltitz was in Normandy when he received an unexpected summons to join Hitler in Poland. Two days later the Führer informed the general that he was to assume responsibility for all the German troops and police forces in Paris, emphasising that Choltitz would be directly answerable to him. Choltitz was ordered to organise the immediate evacuation of all nonessential administrative German staff from the city; the remaining German personnel were to stay and defend Paris to the bitter end. On August 9, Choltitz arrived in Paris and set up his headquarters in the Hôtel Meurice where commanders of Greater Paris, responsible for the day-to-day running of the city, had been previously been based.

On August 10, workers at the Noisy-le-Sec railway depot in the eastern suburbs went on strike, demanding better pay and protesting against the continued detention of fellow workers who had been imprisoned after the July 14 street demonstrations. As the movement spread, the Germans arrested strikers across the region, holding them as hostages. The momentum of the strike was broken only when the

German authorities agreed to release men taken since the strike began and to review the cases of those arrested earlier. Despite German success in defusing the situation, the revolt had started. Bernard Pierquin, who was now working in a hospital and who had been a messenger for a Paris Resistance group since February 1944, saw the strike as a portent of the fight that lay ahead.[4]

The next anti-German initiative took many Parisians by surprise because of whom it involved: the police. By August 1944 three Resistance movements were operating within the ranks of the police: the pro-Communist Front national de la police, the Socialist-influenced Police et Patrie, and the Gaullist Honneur de la police. For some time, the Germans had suspected that the Paris police had become unreliable, and on August 13, in a dramatic move by the occupying forces, French policemen in the suburbs of Asnières, Courbevoie, and Saint-Denis were disarmed in their own police stations by members of the German secret police.

The leaders of the Front national de la police called for a general strike of the Paris police to begin on Tuesday, August 15. The Socialist and Gaullist groups had reservations about the timing of the strike and objected to the tone of the leaflets publicising it, especially the threat that any policeman who refused to take part would be shot. However, neither the Socialists nor the Gaullists wanted to cause a division in the police Resistance movement, nor did they want to risk being outmanoeuvred by the Communists. The language of the leaflets was toned down, all three police Resistance groups backed the strike call, and more moderate leaflets were distributed to police stations across Paris.

On August 15 the organisers reported that support for the strike was almost unanimous. "As one, they suddenly left their posts, threw off their uniforms and disappeared from the streets of the capital as if somebody had waved a magic wand,"[5] wrote Ferdinand Dupuy, a senior administrator at the police station in the 6th arrondissement. In the afternoon more than 1,500 civil servants demonstrated in Paris outside the Hôtel de Ville. All were doubtless encouraged by the news that the Allies (this time including a significant number of French troops) had landed that morning on France's Mediterranean coast.

At first Parisians were puzzled by the sudden absence of policemen. A retired French military officer living on the boulevard Saint-Michel observed that his local police station was closed and that throughout the day there wasn't a single policeman to be seen on the streets. "It wasn't until the following day that we learned the truth, which was that the Paris police were on strike."[6]

The French police might have disappeared from the streets, but the German military and secret police were still active. "Everything necessary will be done to maintain order and to pitilessly repress disorder,"[7] Choltitz threatened on the day the police strike began, and he made it clear that maintaining the supply of food depended on order being maintained. Meanwhile, the Germans continued ridding the city of "undesirables." Thousands of resisters held in prisons in or near Paris were taken to the railway station at Pantin in the eastern suburbs. There they were packed into waiting cattle trucks and sent to concentration camps in Germany, the men to Buchenwald and the women to Ravensbrück.

The German secret police pressed on trapping and now murdering members of the Resistance. In one operation some forty résistants were caught and killed by Germans posing as fellow resisters, offering to supply them with much-needed weaponry. On August 16 thirty-four of them were driven in trucks to Les Cascades (The Waterfalls), a well-known beauty spot in the Bois de Boulogne. As they climbed down from the vehicles they were mown down by machine-gun fire; their corpses were then blown to pieces by grenades. Most of those murdered were under twenty-five; the youngest was just seventeen. Seven other resisters, also believing they were about to be supplied with weapons to turn on the occupier, were ambushed by Germans and shot dead in the rue Leroux in the 16th arrondissement.[8]

On August 17 Pierre Laval's desperate plan to secure his own survival began to unravel. An outraged Marcel Déat, now a French government minister, told SS Carl Oberg about Laval's plans and demanded that Laval, along with Herriot, be removed from Paris at once. Déat, like many other Paris collaborationists, had decided to leave the capital for Belfort, near the German border, and Déat had no intention of letting Laval take advantage of their absence.[9] Prompted by Oberg, Himmler ordered Herriot's arrest: the former president of the National Assembly was taken under German escort to Potsdam, where he was held until April 1945, when he was handed over to the Russians. On the evening of August 17 Laval held his last ministerial meeting in Paris at his offices in the Hôtel Matignon, attended by just five members of the Vichy government. Power cuts forced the ministers to work by candlelight and the setting was as gloomy as the mood. At 11:30 P.M. Otto Abetz interrupted the proceedings to inform those in attendance that members of the French government in Paris had been "invited" to leave the city.

Laval protested that he wanted to stay to represent the French government when the Allies arrived, but he and his wife were bundled into a German car and driven away; other Vichy ministers in Paris were picked up and joined what was now a German convoy, which arrived in Belfort on August 19. Laval's usefulness to the Germans had run its course. His bid to make overtures to the Allies had been a piece of egotistical opportunism that the Nazi elite in Berlin was not prepared to tolerate. On August 20 in Vichy a protesting Pétain was taken prisoner by the Germans and also driven to Belfort.

WITH THE COLLABORATIONISTS IN FLIGHT and the remnants of the Vichy government under German guard in Belfort, the fate of Paris now lay in the hands of five major forces: the Parisians themselves, de Gaulle's Free French, the Communists and other Resistance organisations, the Allies, and the German forces under General Choltitz.

In June 1940 those Parisians who had not fled had waited anxiously as the German army advanced. Now, in early August 1944, they once again waited and wondered about what lay ahead as another army made its way towards the city, or so they believed. This time it was the Allies who were advancing, and the Germans still in Paris gave every appearance of preparing for a major battle as they took up positions in key buildings across the city. In June 1940 travelling around the city had not been too difficult; gas and electricity supplies were reliable and people could still find most of what they wanted in the shops—even though that would soon change. By the summer of 1944, however, after more than four long years of occupation, life for most of the people of Paris was immeasurably harder.

At the end of July only eight Métro lines were still in operation; on August 6 trains in the Métro ran only between 6 and 11 A.M. and 3 and 10 P.M. On August 12 at 1 P.M. the network stopped altogether: normal services were scheduled to resume on Wednesday August 16 at 8 P.M., but nothing happened. The workers were on strike. Bicycles were more in demand than ever, and there was a thriving market in stolen bicycles, which now changed hands at between 8,000 and 10,000 francs each—between four and six times what a factory worker would earn in a month. Some Germans, already desperate to flee the city by any means, were stopping Parisians and confiscating their bicycles. Joseph Pot, who used his son's bicycle to get to work since the Métro had stopped running, did his best to evade them. "When I go to work I make my way through the back streets, where there is no risk of running into any Krauts," he told his diary.[10]

Power supplies were virtually nonexistent. Officially, electricity was available between 10 P.M. and 5 A.M.—but this was just a rough guide since power cuts could not be ruled out. Soon anyone not on a priority supply circuit often had just twenty minutes a day of electric light—the same twenty minutes to cook their food and listen to the radio. As it was not the same twenty minutes everywhere, Parisians tried to piece together Allied radio news bulletins by phoning friends in different parts of the city.[11] Desperate not to miss the news or the use of some electric light, people often went to bed leaving their lights and radio "switched on," hoping the current might be reinstated, however briefly. Victoria Kent, a refugee from the Spanish Civil War, had done this and was awakened round 1 A.M., when her room suddenly lit up and she heard the sound of the radio coming from different floors of the apartment block where she lived.[12] Because of this partial and unpredictable supply of electricity Parisians burned candles, resin, paper, or charcoal to give their homes some light.[13] Small heaters burning paper as fuel went on sale, allowing new mothers to warm a baby's bottle in about a quarter of an hour. Artisan workshops and small retail outlets installed bicycles on blocks and paid teams of people to pedal furiously to generate a steady supply of electricity to drive the company's tools or machinery.[14]

Electricity shortages made taking X-rays and sterilising medical equipment in hospitals almost impossible. Supplies of gas were also severely restricted. Joseph Pot, who took evasive action to stop the Germans stealing his bicycle, wrote, "All we have now is a tiny bit of gas in the evening for half an hour."[15] Soon the gas was cut off completely, and hospitals and clinics were allocated the few available bottles of butane gas. Jean Galtier-Boissière returned home on August 15 to discover that no more gas would be supplied to his home. Every resident could register with a local restaurant to receive one hot meal a day.[16]

Flora Groult and her father went to their local *mairie* to collect the so-called distress card required to claim a daily meal; there they found a long line of faces familiar from four years of queuing.[17]

Although the reports reaching the Allies of four million starving Parisians were exaggerated, food supplies had fallen to dangerously low levels. On August 17 flour stocks were sufficient to keep Paris in bread only for a week. Bakers' shops were closing one after the other and huge queues formed outside those that remained open. In all, there was only enough meat for each inhabitant to receive three 90g portions. As a final resort, enough pasta was available for twelve meals per person, but only 350g of biscuits per inhabitant. The amount of milk available was woefully inadequate and the hot weather meant much of it curdled before being distributed, reducing viable stocks even further.

There was, as always, the black market, but the extreme shortages pushed everyday food items far beyond the reach of most people. Butter, for example, officially cost 60 francs a kilo, but on the black market it could cost ten times that amount—in other words just one kilo cost almost a third of the monthly 2,000 franc salary of an office worker. Bread had a similar markup: the official price was 3.75 francs a kilo, but on the black market it cost 35 francs. In the first two weeks of August, following inspections of some 2,250 commercial outlets, more than 650 people were charged with black-market dealing; 7 million francs worth of goods were seized, including flour, razor blades, fabrics, bottles of cognac, soap, and sides of beef.[18]

Along with concerns about gas and electricity supplies and acute food shortages came wildly conflicting rumours about where the Allies were and when they would arrive in the city. One thing was certain: as the month of August progressed some Germans were taking up defensive positions in the city at the same time as large numbers of them were starting to leave. Just as in June 1940 a trickle of Parisians abandoning the city had quickly become a flood, so it was now with the occupiers. On August 8 and 9 Charles Braibant noted in his diary that the Germans were moving out of Paris, but according to Jean Galtier-Boissière August 17 marked "the mass flight of the Krauts." The Germans fled from the Sorbonne, the Gare de l'Est, and the Gare du Nord and sped down the boulevard de Magenta and the rue La Fayette. "On all these roads were dozens, hundreds of trucks and coaches full to overflowing, guns being towed, ambulances packed with their wounded, going every which way—following, overtaking, and passing other vehicles coming in the opposite direction," he wrote.[19] As all the French police were on strike, German police were having to direct the traffic. At the same time, outside the top hotels near the Arc de Triomphe, Galtier-Boissière saw monocled generals accompanied by elegant blondes dressed as if for a fashionable beach holiday, while other Germans were sitting around at pavement cafés drinking beer.

Many Germans may have been moving out, but those who stayed behind made their presence felt by firing indiscriminately at buildings and people. After the last truck left the place de la Sorbonne, Galtier-Boissière saw SS sentries open fire: bullets whistled through the air as passersby in the street scattered in all directions. Galtier-Boissière swiftly left his balcony overlooking the square and moved back inside his flat.[20]

Venturing outside the following day, he found nearby windows riddled with bullet holes and saw that the Sorbonne chapel had been scarred by gunfire. "A passerby told me there had been five or six people killed on the boulevard Saint-Michel yesterday," he noted in his diary. "Near the rue Racine a concierge was throwing a bucket of water onto a pool of blood on the ground, which she then brushed furiously. 'A woman had been killed,' she explained, 'and another one was killed in front of the tobacconists.' "[21]

The Parisians were at the mercy of random German attacks. Meanwhile, few of them had any idea of exactly what the Resistance within the city planned to do or when they planned to do it. On August 14 de Gaulle appointed Alexandre Parodi to be his minister in territories not yet liberated. Parodi was a civil servant who had been in the city since 1940 working for de Gaulle's Free French, determining the structure of post-Liberation political and administrative bodies; he was empowered by de Gaulle to speak in the name of the French state. The problem was that events were about to move so fast and communications with de Gaulle remained so slow that Parodi would find himself forced to take decisions on his own initiative. Alongside Parodi, de Gaulle's nominated national military delegate, Jacques Chaban-Delmas, had returned to Paris on August 16 after a month in London, where he met General Pierre Koenig, the commander-in-chief of the Forces françaises de l'intérieur (FFI). The FFI was formed in June 1944 when fighters from different Resistance groups across the country, including

Paris, came together to form a single armed organisation. The regional
FFI commander for the Seine and three adjacent departments[22] was a
Communist and a veteran of the Spanish Civil War named Henri
Rol-Tanguy.

The Resistance in Paris was made up of a bewildering diversity of
groups and committees. The National Resistance Council (CNR),
founded in Paris on May 27, 1943 (see Chapter 12), had expanded as the
Resistance movements grew in size and number. Georges Bidault replaced Jean Moulin as head of the CNR after Moulin was arrested and
tortured to death in the summer of 1943.[23] The members of the CNR
were even more heterogeneous than before and now included conservatives, Catholics, centrists, and socialists, although the Communists
retained a strong influence. The CNR had a military wing, COMAC,[24]
which also had a strong Communist core. Paris had its own Liberation
Committee (Le Comité parisien de la Libération, CPL), founded in
August 1943, half of whose members were either Communist members
or sympathisers.

The main fault line in the anti-German forces in Paris lay between
Communists and Gaullists, although other Resistance groups and individuals were aligned to neither camp.[25] The Communists were pushing
hard for a popular uprising to rid the city of the German forces while
de Gaulle's representatives, Parodi and Chaban-Delmas, were far more
hesitant—especially Parodi—and were constantly urging caution.

De Gaulle had declared on April 18, 1942, that it was the duty of every
Frenchman and woman to fight using any means at their disposal against
the German enemy and its accomplices in Vichy. "National liberation,"
he insisted, "cannot be separated from a national insurrection."[26] But
in Paris no consensus existed on when the uprising should start, who
should lead it, and how long it should last (as much as such events can
be planned).

The cautious Gaullists favoured deferring any uprising. "We believed," de Gaulle's national military delegate Chaban-Delmas recalled, "that the insurrection should kick off as the Allies approached
the city."[27] When Chaban-Delmas returned to Paris from London he
brought strict instructions from General Koenig that an uprising should
not be launched "prematurely." The Gaullists also envisaged that the
any insurrection should be short, no longer than forty-eight hours if
possible, and that it should stop as soon as the first Allied soldiers arrived and the Gaullist administrators for the city were in post.[28]

Unfortunately, even on the assumption that the Gaullists could orchestrate a short uprising timed to coincide with the arrival of the Allies, their plan had one glaring flaw: the American-led Allied armies had no intention of heading for Paris. During his visit to London, Chaban-Delmas had pleaded for them to alter their plans, but all in vain. Paris had no military strategic importance for the Allies whatsoever: General Omar Bradley, commander of the U.S. 12th Army Group, dismissed the city as representing "nothing more than an inkspot on our maps, to be bypassed as we headed toward the Rhine."[29] The Anglo-American priority was to pursue and crush the German armies as they retreated eastwards. To stop and fight in Paris would mean losing valuable time and manpower. It would also divert the Americans from another goal: seizing a port (ideally Antwerp) where they could land their supplies rather than having to bring them 400 kilometres by road from Cherbourg. In addition, the Allies had no wish to take responsibility for feeding four million Parisians, whom they believed to be on the point of starvation.

While the Gaullists in Paris were urging caution, Rol-Tanguy and forces within the FFI were agitating for an uprising. They were encouraged by the bullish mood across the city driven by the belief among Parisians that the Allies were heading their way and by the sight of large numbers of Germans scrambling out of the city. The pressure was clearly growing for an uprising that would drive out the remaining invaders. Some members of the Paris Liberation Committee (CPL) the National Resistance Council (CNR) and its military leadership, the Comité d'action militaire (COMAC), could scarcely contain themselves. They saw the uprising as an organic phenomenon that had been gathering momentum ever since the July 14 demonstrations and as an expression of the pent-up will of the people of Paris who had suffered so much. Despite this change in mood, Parodi and Chaban-Delmas remained nervous and still continued to counsel extreme caution.

On August 18 the German secret police chiefs Oberg and Knochen drove out of Paris. The German embassy closed its doors and the Hôtel Majestic ceased to function as the MBF headquarters, although it remained a stronghold with some 400 German soldiers who, positioned inside, were ready to defend it. August 18 was also the day on which the two big French labour confederations, the left-leaning Confédération générale du travail (CGT) and the more right leaning Confédération française des travailleurs chrétiens (Confederation of Christian Workers,

CFTC), called for a general strike. More than a whiff of insurrection could now be definitely detected in the air.

The CNR and CPL met to discuss whether it was now time to call for an uprising; however, Rol-Tanguy decided to wait no longer. As regional commander of the FFI he devised a poster calling on Parisians to join an FFI unit in their workplace or where they lived. They were instructed to take up arms and specifically to seize German weapons and use them to attack the occupiers, their vehicles, and fuel depots; they were also directed to take over food stores and to protect water, gas, and electricity supplies against possible sabotage attempts by the enemy.[30]

Early on August 19, however, before Rol-Tanguy could distribute his posters around the city or the CPL and the CNR managed to issue a joint call for an insurrection, the Paris police once again took everyone by surprise. At daybreak hundreds of them occupied the police headquarters in the Prefecture of Police building opposite Notre-Dame Cathedral. As one representative on the CPL noted in his diary: "The insurrection did not wait for us."[31]

At 11 A.M. Charles Luizet, a former prefect of Corsica and de Gaulle's nominee for prefect of police, arrived at the police headquarters and met no dissent as he assumed command.[32] This meant that a representative of the Provisional Government of the French Republic (GPRF), headed by de Gaulle, was in charge of a crucial building as the insurrection began in earnest. Rol-Tanguy and Luizet then met de Gaulle's representative Parodi and drew up a proclamation. Under the heading "République française" it declared that all forces in the Paris region, including the police resisters, were integral components of the FFI and thenceforth under Rol-Tanguy's military command. It ordered the mobilisation of all men aged between eighteen and fifty capable of bearing arms and ended with the words "Long Live de Gaulle! Long Live the Republic! Long Live France!"[33]

After much deliberative hesitation, Parodi had decided to back the insurrection. He had hesitated because he feared that an insurrection in Paris before the arrival of the Allies would result in countless civilian deaths and that German tanks and artillery would destroy the city's historic buildings. However, he had been cycling to meetings in different parts of the city and was aware of growing popular defiance of the occupying forces.[34] He was also aware that Rol-Tanguy and other Communists were pressing for an uprising. If the Gaullists refused to support it, the Resistance would be divided, and so he gave it his support. "I thought that one of my responsibilities was to sustain the unity of the French Resistance until the very end, right until the arrival in Paris of General de Gaulle," he explained twenty years later. "Otherwise we ran the very great risk at that time of smashing the Resistance, if there had been a deep split on the question of the insurrection."[35] There was also another reason: the Gaullists feared being overtaken by events and marginalised.

Across Paris members of local Liberation Committees seized control of the *mairies* and other public buildings: the tricolour was run up the flag pole, frequently accompanied by a heartfelt if off-key rendition of the Marseillaise. In most cases these takeovers met with little or no serious opposition from the Germans. By the end of the morning of August 19 there was a French flag flying over all twenty of the *mairies* in the city, and early the following morning five tricolours would flutter on the Hôtel de Ville, the administrative centre for Paris and the Seine department. A Resistance group had seized the building and arrested René Bouffet, Vichy's prefect of the Seine department, who was replaced by Marcel Flouret, another member of the Free French nominated by de Gaulle.

In most of these official buildings the civil servants of the Vichy regime meekly submitted to the new administration; some even offered to help the Resistance, as happened in the 19th arrondissement. In the 17th arrondissement a group of young resisters broke into the *mairie* on the night of August 18–19 and held a wild, celebratory party while outside some others seized local women suspected of *collaboration horizontale*—sleeping with German soldiers—and publicly shaved their heads as a punishment.

This gruesome spectacle occurred throughout France as towns and cities were liberated; women believed to have consorted with Germans were also marched half-naked through the streets. Berthe Auroy was told about a woman whose head was shaved and who had a swastika painted on her forehead. Berthe wrote that she went to the rue Tholozé, just round the corner from her home in the rue Lepic, where the punitive shaving had taken place, and found tufts of hair on the street. She reported claims that "scalps" of horizontal collaborators were hanging on railings outside the *mairies* in Batignolles and Montmartre.[36]

Edmond Dubois, a Swiss journalist, reported that "scalps" were put on the railings outside the *mairie* in the 17th arrondissement as well.[37] In the 16th arrondissement the local Liberation Committee distributed a poster warning the locals not to take the law into their own hands: "It is formally forbidden to take arbitrary measures (cutting off people's hair, arresting people, stealing their property) against those suspected of committing an offence. Any such actions will be punished with the utmost severity."[38] Near the home of Andrzej Bobkowski alleged collaborators were also arrested as were local shopkeepers suspected of having profited from the black market.[39]

In the 1st arrondissement a handful of Germans briefly occupied the abandoned *mairie*, but they soon retreated after a skirmish with a group of FFI. In the 20th arrondissement, the Resistance was driven out of the *mairie*, and in the suburb of Neuilly only the intervention of the Vichy mayor prevented the resisters being executed by the Germans. In the suburbs of Joinville, Alfortville, Rosny, and Neuilly-sur-Marne it was the Communists and not the Gaullists who reached the *mairies* first, took them over, and assumed responsibility for administration of the locality. The occupations at the local level may have been chaotic and may not have followed any clear plan, but by the evening of August 19 a number of important ministries and other major public buildings were occupied by GPRF nominees; other buildings, factories, depots, and installations were in the hands of the Resistance. The offices and printing presses of the collaborationist press were also occupied and handed over to various clandestine Resistance newspapers.[40]

The takeovers did not always proceed smoothly or without problems. It was obvious the Germans would not stand idly by and watch the city fall under the control of the Resistance and the Free French. Despite the evacuation of many German troops, Choltitz still had 20,000 men under his command, as well as some eighty tanks and sixty pieces of artillery. Serious clashes between the Germans and Parisian resisters broke out on and around the place Saint-Michel, just across the bridge from the Prefecture of Police, and, from inside the police Prefecture itself policemen took pot shots at passing German vehicles. In the afternoon of August 19 a German Tiger tank appeared outside the building; it fired a couple of shells, but the Germans lacked the manpower—and probably the willpower—to mount any serious follow-up assault. Instead they launched a relatively ineffective mortar-and-grenade attack.

Throughout the day (August 19) came other reports of armed clashes between Germans and Resistance fighters in different parts of Paris. Berthe Auroy noted in her diary the sound of fighting in the north of the city, which people said was coming from near Barbès. "The machine guns rattled away without stopping and the sound of revolvers being fired alternated with that of heavy gunfire."[41] Shortly after midday the Protestant pastor Marc Boegner was in the Grand Palais when he heard the sound of machine-gun fire coming from the place de la Concorde just to the east where Germans and the Resistance were fighting it out. "Bullets were smashing into the walls of the Grand Palais. I came out to collect my bicycle. People coming from the place de la Concorde said the Resistance was attacking the Naval Ministry."[42]

As well as street battles with resisters, German troops launched many unprovoked and indiscriminate attacks on unarmed civilians. Early that morning, Simone de Beauvoir had looked out her window and seen a sight that had become all too familiar—the swastika flag still flying on the Senate building, housewives looking for food in shops in the rue de Seine, and a long queue outside the baker's. Just another day in the life of occupied Paris. Suddenly two cyclists sped past, shouting, "The Prefecture has been taken!" Next a detachment of German soldiers left the Senate building and made its way on foot towards the boulevard Saint-Germain. "Before they turned the corner of the street the soldiers unleashed a volley of machine-gun fire," wrote de Beauvoir. "Passersby scattered in all directions, taking cover as best they could in doorways. But all the doors were shut. One man crumpled and fell while he was hammering on a door; others collapsed in the middle of the pavement."[43]

Flora Groult was cycling home along the boulevard Raspail with some "distress" meal cards when she heard the rattle of machine-gun fire. All around her people threw themselves to the ground, but she remained rooted to the spot with her bike. Then she too dived for cover. "I waited a few moments and everything was quiet again," she wrote. "The Germans in a car who had been picking off people in the crowd had moved away to carry on their killing somewhere else."[44] Andrzej Bobkowski also recorded random gunfire in his diary: "This afternoon sounds of shooting in the street. German cars firing at random every now and again. Nobody dares go outside."[45]

The events of August 19 and the days that followed did not constitute a *mass* uprising. "Ordinary Paris" continued to exist alongside the random shootings by German soldiers, the seizure of the *mairies*, and pitched battles between resisters and Germans. Jean-Paul Sartre wandered around the city during the uprising and his impressions were published in the first seven issues of *Combat*, a Resistance newspaper started in December 1941, edited by Albert Camus and which could now be sold openly. "The insurrection is not visible everywhere," Sartre observed. "On the rue de la Gaîté a blind accordionist is sitting on a folding stool playing music from *La Traviata*. People are darting towards a bistro for a quick glass of wine. Along the banks of the Seine men and women are swimming or sunbathing in their bathing costumes. And yet the battle is present everywhere."[46] Sartre watched a photo of Pétain being torn down inside a police station and noted that one could read anxiety, expectation, and joy on the tense faces of the people: "Many of them felt deeply that this was a historic moment and had instinctively put on their very best clothes."[47]

In fact, the dominant mood among Parisians was joy: the thrill of seeing the French flag flying in the city where for the last four years and more they had seen nothing but swastikas. "It's all over," wrote Bobkowski. "The [French] flags are flying."[48] Flora Groult wrote excitedly in her diary: "I saw the French flag today! I even saw two—the first on the *mairie* in the 6th arrondissement, then one which had just been raised on the *mairie* in the 7th. People were standing up, fired with emotion, singing the Marseillaise. I give thanks that I have been allowed to see that."[49] Some Parisians, like Berthe Auroy were getting together with neighbours to make their own flags, ready to hang out of their windows when the Allies arrived.

Believing that their liberation was at hand, some Parisians were filled with a new self-confidence. Berthe Auroy wrote of a Jewish neighbour beaming with delight as he dared to walk around without his yellow star.[50] Berthe, too, was pleased to see him in a jacket "without that horrible yellow star that he's had to wear for the last two years."[51]

It was still almost impossible for Parisians to know what was happening in their own city. Micheline Bood heard pistol shots and machine-gun fire coming from the Champs-Élysées and the avenue de Marigny, while the reverberations of heavy artillery rattled the windows of her family's flat. "I don't know what's going on," she wrote, "as we obviously can't go outside."[52]

The old sources of information were no more. Radio-Paris had gone off the air on August 18, its final broadcast claiming that the Wehrmacht would win, thanks to its secret weapons. Seemingly unconvinced by their own rhetoric, the radio station's employees promptly fled to Germany in trucks. The collaborationist newspapers had disappeared and the open Resistance press was still in its infancy. As Georges Benoît-Guyod wrote on August 19: "Still no newspapers, no radio, no reliable news."[53]

All sorts of wild rumours swirled around to fill this news vacuum. Micheline Bood's imagination ran riot: she speculated that there had been thousands of deaths in Paris, more than during all the Allied bombing raids. She told her diary that 400 people had been killed on the place de la Concorde alone and that the rue Royale was "running red with blood."[54]

On August 19 the only point on which there was any consensus among Parisians was that their city would soon be liberated by the Allies—or "les Américains," as they tended to refer to them. Little did they know that on August 19 the Americans still had no intention of doing any such thing.

☞ LATE IN THE AFTERNOON of August 19 Raoul Nordling received a phone call from a Frenchman (whose identity remains a mystery to this day) urging him to broker a cease-fire in Paris between the Germans and the Resistance. Nordling was the Swedish consul in Paris, Sweden having remained neutral throughout the war. Two days earlier he had used his neutrality to intervene with the Germans and save some 3,200 French political prisoners from deportation or execution.[55] It has been definitively determined that he was approached by a Frenchman and that he did subsequently engage in conversations with Choltitz. What happened next is unclear, but although Rol-Tanguy had not been consulted and no formal documentation was produced, a cease-fire came into effect that evening. Nordling welcomed the news of the cease-fire as did the Free French. Rol-Tanguy wanted to fight on but other Resistance leaders sought to extend the cease-fire. The next twenty-four hours were full of confusion with accusations of betrayal and counter-accusations of slander and calumny, of orders issued by some and then swiftly countermanded by others.

Supporters of the cease-fire were found mainly among the Gaullists and politically neutral Resistance groups, who argued again that the armed insurrection was premature. The superiority of enemy forces in the city, plus a shortage of weapons and ammunition among resisters, meant that the uprising would be crushed with a huge loss of life. But other members of the Resistance, with the Communists most prominent among them, feared the cease-fire was but a prelude to efforts to strike a deal with the Germans. This outcome, they argued, would be a betrayal of everything they were fighting for—and of their many comrades who had died at the hands of the Germans since the Occupation began. The Communists, most especially, still believed that the insurrection could snowball into a fully blown popular uprising, so powerful and widespread that the Germans would be swept out of Paris.

Choltitz clearly saw the advantage of a cease-fire, even though much later he claimed he had never agreed to one.[56] Convinced by now that Germany was going to lose the war, he was primarily concerned with salvaging his reputation and securing his personal safety. He knew he would probably have to face awkward questions about his war record on the Eastern Front, the recent murder of the resisters in the Bois de Boulogne, and indiscriminate shootings by his troops on the streets of Paris.[57] Choltitz calculated it was in his best interest not to add to this long list of charges that he feared the Allies would bring against him after the war by ordering his soldiers to defend Paris to the end: he had no intention of being held responsible for the destruction of revered landmarks and the deaths of thousands of Parisians no matter what Hitler might order him to do.

On August 20 cars and vans traversed the city with loudspeakers, announcing a cease-fire. Marc Boegner saw two of them near the Champs-Élysées; Jean Galtier-Boissière saw a French police car and a green car with four Germans in it near the place de la Sorbonne.[58] A car with a loudspeaker in Montmartre provoked such a noisy reaction from the locals that Berthe Auroy thought the Allies had finally arrived.[59] Everywhere the message was the same: the German high command had agreed to preserve public buildings and treat prisoners according to the rules of war; resisters should not open fire on German troops until the evacuation of the city was complete.

While arguments raged in the Resistance, plenty of Parisians were thrilled at the news of a cease-fire, even if some had misunderstood what it meant. Jean Galtier-Boissière reported people on the street applauding and shouting: "Hitler has asked for an armistice! . . . The war is over!"[60] In Berthe Auroy's neighbourhood French flags flew at most of the windows and the surging crowds in the streets reminded her of the celebrations in the street when the 1918 armistice was signed.[61] Bobkowski again observed French flags flying on some houses.[62]

But no sooner had the cease-fire (or "truce" or "armistice," as some Parisians referred to it) been declared than it was broken. Flora Groult was told that German tanks were back in place in the Tuileries Gardens and near Les Invalides;[63] Benoît-Guyod got it right when he wrote: "A truce was indeed agreed, but it was just a flash in the pan . . . the street fighting carried on as before."[64] Benoît-Guyod wrote in his diary on August 20 that the FFI fighters were already doing the rounds telling Parisians to take down their French flags as the Germans were firing on any home that displayed them.[65] On August 21 the cease-fire was technically still in place but many resisters (especially among the Communist FTP and the FFI) ignored it; they remained steadfastly opposed to a truce and vowed to continue taking on and beating the Germans, thus making the cease-fire unworkable.[66]

After additional furious debate, the Resistance leaders who had supported the cease-fire were forced to recognise that fighters on the ground had, by fighting on, rendered it null and void, and they formally rescinded it. From August 22 the cease-fire was officially over. The Resistance was once again united and even more determined to end the German presence in the city. Rol-Tanguy subsequently remarked that during the so-called cease-fire 106 French people had been killed and 357 wounded, while five Germans had been killed and several wounded.[67]

It soon became abundantly clear that the fighting would continue and most Parisians bolted their shutters and stayed indoors for as long as possible. However, when their stocks of food ran out they were forced to dash outside to try to find something to eat. Others, despite the danger (or perhaps because of it) were fascinated by the dramatic events being played out in their streets and wanted to witness it firsthand. Photos, taken by amateur photographers, show groups of spectators gathering on street corners or watching the fighting from their windows. These civilian witnesses were a distinct feature of the uprising before, during, and after the cease-fire. Jean Galtier-Boissière saw some of them on the street in the Latin Quarter on Sunday, August 20, displaying what he called "a mixture of highly charged curiosity and incredible foolhardiness, interspersed with sudden bursts of fear. . . . The onlookers start out naively thinking that since they are spectators and not taking part in the fighting they are not in any danger. Then a bullet whistling by or a man falling to the ground brings home to them the risks they are taking. The group breaks up as its members rush for cover in doorways or disperse. In a flash the boulevard is empty. Five minutes later, driven by their irrepressible devilish curiosity, every onlooker is back, once more risking his life in the front row."[68]

Galtier-Boissière also noted how the degree of danger was affected by where one stood. During the fighting on the place Saint-Michel, for instance, the riskiest place was just behind the Resistance fighters themselves; other spectators watched from the boulevard Saint-Germain, while the more cautious ones observed what they could from the rue des Écoles, a hundred metres or so farther up the boulevard Saint-Michel. The most prudent Parisians followed the action as best they could from the place de la Sorbonne.[69]

On August 19 Micheline Bood watched from her flat as trucks full of Germans sped down the street, their rifles and machine guns pointing at anyone on the street. "This is all so exciting," she wrote, "I don't expect Maman will let me go to the dentist this afternoon."[70] Two days later she and her sister went out with a camera to photograph what was going on. They were frightened but also exhilarated. "It is extraordinary," wrote Micheline, "this engrossing game called war."[71] When the two girls reached the top of the rue de Rome, near the Gare Saint-Lazare, they were so excited it no longer occurred to them to be scared. But the streets were dangerous and death could strike randomly. One young man was shot dead on the steps of the church of Saint Thomas Aquinas just off the boulevard Saint-Germain when the Germans opened fire on worshippers who were leaving after attending Mass.[72] Flora Groult wrote of Philippe A., who was wearing a medical armband and on a bicycle near the Gare de Lyon when he was shot dead; a German woman in uniform who saw the shooting made off with his watch and his wallet.[73]

ON AUGUST 20 General de Gaulle flew into France for the second time since the Allied landings. His plane landed in Cherbourg and he headed straight to a meeting with General Dwight D. Eisenhower, the Allied commander-in-chief, at his headquarters near Le Mans. Eisenhower explained the Allied strategy, which de Gaulle felt was quite logical. However, as he later wrote, one point profoundly concerned him: nobody was planning to march on Paris.[74] He urged Eisenhower to send troops there, adding that the prime position should be accorded to the Free French Second Armoured Division (the 2e DB).

The following day (August 21) de Gaulle wrote to Eisenhower informing him that virtually no police force existed in Paris. This absence, he said, meant the risk of disorder was serious, a situation that could threaten future military operations. The Americans wanted to avoid a serious confrontation with German troops in Paris, so de Gaulle, still wanting to press Eisenhower to order the Allied troops to move on Paris, deliberately underplayed the strength of the German presence in the city. De Gaulle told Eisenhower that "the German forces had almost completely disappeared" and there was only a risk of "a few clashes and slight damage within the city."[75]

General Leclerc was also annoyed and frustrated with the Americans. He did not believe their assurances that French troops would be allowed to liberate Paris. American troops were moving eastwards, while Leclerc's tanks were still fighting Germans near Argentan, some 160 miles to the west of Paris. On the evening of August 21 Leclerc had had enough. Without telling his American superiors, he ordered a small detachment of French tanks to move towards Paris. Their mission was to evaluate the strength of the enemy's forces, to identify the best axes of attack, and, most importantly, to ensure that it was French troops who entered the capital first, should the Americans have a change of heart and decide to advance on Paris after all.

On August 22 Roger Cocteau (code-name "Gallois"), a special envoy sent by Rol-Tanguy, made it out of Paris through German lines and reached the headquarters of U.S. general Omar Bradley in Laval, a town about 190 miles southwest of Paris between Le Mans and Rennes. Cocteau briefed Bradley and some of his fellow generals on the situation in Paris: the German troops were demoralised and few of them remained in and around the city. He requested Allied support with the proviso that French troops be allowed to liberate the city. (Rol-Tanguy's decision to send messengers—the first one was killed—to contact the Allies and request their support rather undermines the view that the Communists in Paris were preparing an insurrection to seize power.)

Shortly after Bradley left for a meeting with Eisenhower, Leclerc arrived in Laval hoping to see Bradley and argue the case once again that
the whole of his Free French Second Armoured Division (the 2e DB)
should be given orders to head for Paris.

When Eisenhower and Bradley met, they decided that the Allies
would, after all, advance on Paris along with Leclerc's 2e DB, which
would enter the city ahead of the Allied troops. After the meeting,
Bradley flew back to Laval to find Leclerc waiting for him. Before the
French general could say a word, Bradley greeted him: "Ah, Leclerc!
Good to see you. I was just about to give you the order to head for Paris."[76]
Leclerc returned to Argentan and told his chief of operations what
the French soldiers had been waiting to hear: "We're heading straight
for Paris."

The relentless pressure from de Gaulle and Leclerc certainly contributed to this U-turn by the U.S. high command, as did Eisenhower's
promise to de Gaulle in December 1943 that the French army would
lead the Liberation of Paris. But it is unlikely that these points on their
own had changed the minds of the American commanders. Despite
incidents of barbaric cruelty and serious fighting by German soldiers in
the city, Choltitz's apparent willingness to sign a cease-fire strongly suggested that he would not defend Paris to the bitter end. It seemed clear
that it was highly unlikely Paris would be another Stalingrad, an urban
battleground that would entail protracted house-to-house fighting and
untold destruction and death.

The Allies were undoubtedly influenced by reports from de Gaulle
and Cocteau that only a small number of demoralised Germans remained in the city. It is also likely that de Gaulle's dark hints that Paris
could descend into chaos played a part, as did the realisation that although the armed insurrection was already underway, the Resistance
was low on ammunition and needed military support.

In Paris itself, about 160 miles away from Leclerc and the 2e DB, the
Resistance had its own ideas about boosting its supply of weaponry. On
August 22, the day the 2e DB finally got its marching orders, posters in
the name of the commander of the FFI for Greater Paris appeared all
over the city. Under the caption "Paris: The Fight Is On" *(Paris se bat)*
Parisians were again to join the FFI or form their own patriotic militia
unit. Under the slogan "Everybody Get a Kraut" *(Chacun son Boche)* Parisians were once more urged to attack Germans in the city and seize

their weapons.[77] On the same day a poster in Rol-Tanguy's name referred to the FFI and the city's people being engaged in "the battle for Paris." It called on Parisians to build barricades so as to isolate the Germans in a few pockets and thus ensure they would no longer be able to take reprisals. "EVERYONE TO THE BARRICADES" was the rallying cry.[78]

Men, women, and children responded by building barricades on boulevards, avenues, and even the smaller streets to stop or at least slow down any rapid deployment of German tanks or troops. Soon an estimated 600 barricades had sprouted up all over Paris. The geography of the barricade building corresponded to earlier uprisings and revolutions, and were built especially in the poor and working-class districts in the north and east, which had voted for the Popular Front in 1936; in contrast, relatively few barricades appeared in the fashionable 7th, 8th and 16th arrondissements.[79] The barricades were built out of anything that came to hand: cobbles torn up from the street, asphalt dug up with pickaxes, sandbags, old furniture, gratings, mattresses, car tyres, branches hacked or sawn from the city's trees. On August 21 Jean Galtier-Boissière took his dog for its early morning walk. "No question of there being a cease-fire," he concluded after seeing a massive barricade being built across the boulevard Saint-Michel near the junction with the boulevard Saint-Germain. "People were throwing on park benches, folding metal cots, potted trees taken from the front of cafés, metal fences used to protect trees. Anything and everything." Shortly afterwards on the nearby rue Saint-Jacques he saw another barricade made out of sandbags and cobblestones.[80] Three days later, he noticed that photos of Hitler, Göring, and Mussolini, which he presumed had been taken from a pro-Axis Italian bookshop on the boulevard Saint-Germain, had been stuck on the barricade so that if the Germans fired at it, they would end up making bullet holes in the pictures of their heroes.[81] On August 22, Bernard Pierquin, now a Resistance liaison agent, saw barricades going up as he cycled around the city carrying messages from one Resistance centre to another. Everybody was joining in: "It's one big party," he wrote in his diary.[82]

The barricades were intended to inhibit the movement of German troops but they were sometimes more symbolic than practical. They were a nod to Paris's revolutionary past—the French Revolution, the Revolutions of 1830 and 1848, and the 1871 Commune—but they also

allowed ordinary Parisians to become participants in their own liberation rather than merely remaining passive bystanders. At the same time,
barricades provided resisters with excellent cover when firing at Germans or attacking them with Molotov cocktails; they could also be used
to demarcate areas liberated by the Resistance or to block important
traffic routes—although few of these barricades would have been able
to withstand the tracks of a German tank.

Those manning the barricades wore a variety of armbands: some bore
the national blue, white, and red colours with the Gaullist symbol of
the cross of Lorraine, others the letters FFI. The fighters of the Communist FTP had been incorporated into the FFI, but some members
still preferred to wear their FTP insignia. These armbands were worn
only in safe areas and were removed when the resisters moved around
the city. Some men manning the barricades wore military-style khaki
uniforms and helmets; others looked as if they were going hunting;
many men resembled the revolutionaries of the Commune of 1871, a
scarf tied around their neck, a shirt open to the waist, and a tight belt.
August 1944 in Paris was exceptionally hot and many of the men and
women on the barricades wore light summer casual clothes; only a
helmet and boots revealed them to be fighters. People grabbed hold of
any weapon they could find, from old hunting rifles to an odd assortment
of pistols and revolvers, as well as a few machine guns and arms taken
from the Germans.[83]

The call to the barricades on Tuesday, August 22 was followed by
two more days of intense fighting. On Wednesday Parisians awakened
to the sound of explosions in the east: Micheline Bood's apartment
shook like jelly. People thought—incorrectly as it turned out—that the
German garrisons in the Senate building in the Luxembourg Gardens
had been blown up. Micheline's earlier somewhat ambivalent attitude
towards the Germans had now turned into pure loathing. "I hate them,"
she wrote. "I hate them. When I think that I used to believe those
people were men. We shall never forget. I hope we get our revenge."[84]

At around 9 A.M. on August 23 members of the FFI inside a police
station attached to the Grand Palais opened fire on some passing
German soldiers. The Germans promptly summoned reinforcements
from the nearby place de la Concorde, including two Tiger tanks and
two "Goliath" tanks—small, remote-controlled mobile mines, each
packing 75 kilos of explosives. According to a senior employee at the

Grand Palais, one of these Goliath tanks exploded against the outside wall of the building, setting the Grand Palais alight, releasing huge clouds of smoke into the Paris sky.[85] Firefighters arrived and came under attack from German soldiers. The inferno was brought under control only once the FFI fighters inside the blazing building had surrendered and the Germans had left with their prisoners. The interior of the Grand Palais, constructed for the Universal Exhibition of 1900, was completely gutted, but its famous glass roof and metal art deco framework survived.

One casualty of the incident was a horse, possibly a passing cart horse or one from the Houcke Circus, which had been performing in the Grand Palais: struck by a stray bullet, it collapsed on the nearby avenue Montaigne. Almost immediately, hungry Parisians descended on it and cut it up: all that remained, according to one eyewitness, was a pile of the animal's innards and the head, its milky eyes staring.[86]

As the fire in the Grand Palais was being brought under control, Berlin radioed a message to Choltitz ordering him to hold the city at all cost. Hitler and his entourage were apparently unaware of the insurrection that was well underway, and Choltitz was ordered to respond to any rebellion by blowing up city apartment blocks and publicly executing the ringleaders. Hitler ordered Choltitz to prepare the bridges over the Seine for demolition and insisted that he was not to let Paris fall into enemy hands, except as a heap of rubble.[87]

At lunchtime clouds of smoke billowed into the sky above the Grand Palais and Parisians wondered if this marked the start of efforts by the Germans to raze the city to the ground. However, when they tuned in to London radio they were flabbergasted to hear a newsreader announce that Paris had been liberated the previous day. The BBC had over-interpreted a communiqué prepared by a Free French agent, Georges Boris. In what was probably a bid to underline the part played in the Paris uprising by the FFI and ordinary Parisians, Boris deliberately implied that the city already had been liberated. "Yesterday, 22 August, after four days of fighting, the enemy was defeated everywhere. Patriots are in control of all the public buildings. Representatives of the Vichy government have either been arrested or are on the run. This is how the people of Paris have played a determining role in the liberation of the capital."[88] The news "PARIS IS FREE" flashed around the world and across France church bells rang out in celebration. Micheline Bood was "furious" with the BBC for saying that the bells were ringing in Paris;[89] Jean Galtier-Boissière wrote that London was a little ahead of Paris time, since in his district the fighting continued.[90] An outraged Jean Guéhenno insisted that these lies were not even good propaganda: "The truth is much, much better, namely that Paris has refused to be under German control any more, that the city has taken back its democratic institutions and that these gains alone are paid every minute with much bloodshed."[91] Berthe Auroy went to bed that night with no idea of what was happening. She knew that barricades had been erected across the city, she could hear heavy gunfire and small arms fire in the streets, and all the while the BBC claimed that Paris had been liberated and was playing the Marseillaise over the airwaves.[92] As Pierre Audiat recalled, "Torn between fear and hope, Parisians slept even less well during the night of 23–24 August than during the preceding nights."[93]

As if to mock the BBC's announcement, intense fighting persisted across the city, notably around the Luxembourg Palace, the place de la Concorde, and the Saint-Lazare railway station. Jean Galtier-Boissière heard bursts of gunfire throughout the day. Around 5 P.M. German tanks took up position on the boulevard Saint-Michel near the place de la Sorbonne and opened fire once again on a big barricade on this main route. "The noise of the first shell blew in all the windows of the German Rive Gauche bookshop," wrote Galtier-Boissière. "They had been a target for patriots on so many occasions, but it took a German gun to smash them all in one go."[94]

Near Micheline Bood's neighbourhood the fighting was so fierce that she could go outdoors only for a few minutes in the evening. "There was firing and fighting all day long in Paris," she wrote. "I wonder what is still left of the city. . . . Everybody is a bit gloomy. We are living too intensely in the present to think about the future and we cannot predict when all this will end—we wonder if they [the Allies] are ever going to get here."[95]

The fighting raged on the following day, Thursday, August 24. However, the Germans were being beaten back. After armed clashes around Le Parc des Buttes-Chaumont in the northeast, for example, the Resistance took 137 German prisoners. But the Resistance fighters still lacked the heavy weaponry they needed to dislodge enemy soldiers securely dug in at a number of redoubts; for example, more than a thousand German soldiers were lodged in their Prince-Eugene barracks near the place de la République. The Germans had barricaded off the square, which they defended with two tanks and artillery, including machine guns. They had largely been pushed onto the defensive, but they still occasionally mounted offensive actions, such as their attacks on the Resistance barricade on the rue du Faubourg-du-Temple and on the rue Voltaire in the 11th arrondissement.[96]

The Germans in Paris must have known that Leclerc and his tanks were moving ever closer, but in public Choltitz continued to bluff, bluster, and threaten. He had no intention of following Hitler's increasingly hysterical and, frankly, insane orders to reduce Paris to ruins. Even if he wished to do so, he had neither the manpower nor the materiel with which to do it. Neither the German army nor air force had enough men and machines to destroy the city, and the rumours that the Germans had mined bridges across the Seine and packed dynamite into buildings across the city were completely untrue. But at the same time Choltitz refused to call a halt to the fighting.

On August 24 a terrified friend telephoned Charles Braibant: he was stuck in an apartment on the boulevard Saint-Michel and "Nazi patrols" outside were laughing as they fired through windows and at passersby; he had just seen a body taken into the house across the street. That night Charles learned that German heavy weaponry was firing at Paris from the race course at Longchamp, and some shells had landed in the 15th arrondissement.[97] Out on the street it was still largely a matter of chance whether or not civilians were killed. On August 24 Jean Bedel, a member of the Free French in Paris (and later a well-known journalist and art historian), was standing on the place de l'Odéon next to Victor Rastello, his concierge and friend. Victor, a man in his mid-forties, had found an old rifle and was on the lookout for Germans. Suddenly he dropped to the ground, shot dead by a German sniper.[98]

Leclerc and most of the 2e DB approaching Paris from the south and southwest met with more resistance than they had expected; a third group in reserve headed for Versailles and the western side of Paris. As they advanced on the capital the Germans fled in an ever-more disorderly and undignified retreat. A small, three-tank detachment of Leclerc's forces led by Captain Raymond Dronne was ordered to go ahead and make for the Hôtel de Ville. As Dronne later explained, it was "the heart of the capital and the symbol of Parisian and national liberties."[99]

Dronne, his tanks and his men—mostly Spaniards from La Nueve unit—were at the Porte d'Italie on the southern edge of the city at 8:45 P.M. on August 24. Inside the city, the enemy troops seemed to have melted away and Dronne's tanks advanced through streets densely packed with people shouting, cheering, and throwing themselves onto the vehicles and their crews. The column made its way through the streets of the 13th arrondissement, over the pont d'Austerlitz and along the right bank of the Seine. At twenty-two minutes past nine the small multinational contingent of troops under French command was greeted in front of the Hôtel de Ville by Georges Bidault, the head of the National Resistance Council (CNR) and de Gaulle's two representatives Alexandre Parodi and Jacques Chaban-Delmas.

Rol-Tanguy was still in his vast underground bunker at Denfert-Rochereau, from where he had been directing Resistance military operations in the city.[100] In response to an appeal from the Resistance radio (which began broadcasting on August 21), the whole of Paris echoed to the sound of church bells, including the sonorous tolling of the huge bell of Notre-Dame. All over Paris people wept with joy, cheered, and embraced other family members, friends, or complete strangers. Some had even odder ways of celebrating. Monsieur Belleux, who lived in a narrow little street near La Madeleine, learned from the radio that Leclerc's division had arrived; he heard the bell of Notre-Dame tolling and then the sound of a rush of water in the street, followed by a man in the house opposite shouting to his wife, "I'm just so happy I'm pissing out of the window!"[101]

The first detachment had arrived. Then, on August 25, the remainder of Leclerc's tank division moved on Paris and at about 9:30 A.M. entered the southern part of Paris through the Porte d'Orléans and advanced towards the city's centre. Jean Galtier-Boissière and his wife raced from their flat on the place de la Sorbonne to the nearby rue Saint-Jacques. They witnessed "an unforgettable sight: a crowd pulsating with excitement, surrounding French tanks covered in French flags and bunches of flowers." Each tank, each armoured car with their khaki-clad soldiers, were being mobbed by groups of young girls, women, children, and people wearing FFI armbands. The crowds lining both sides of the street were clapping, blowing kisses, shaking hands, and shouting out to the victors their joy at being liberated.[102] Meanwhile, the U.S. Army's 4th Infantry Division led by Major General Raymond Barton was also making its way to and through the city. Barton's men kept to the east of the 2e DB's main thrust and swept through the southern suburbs and on into the eastern parts of Paris, taking the Bastille before moving on towards Nation and the German barracks at Vincennes. All along they found themselves in what U.S. war correspondent Ernie Pyle described as "a pandemonium of surely the greatest mass joy that has ever happened."[103] But despite all the cheering and celebrating, the battle for Paris was not yet over.

The Resistance continued to attack the Germans, but with the arrival of Leclerc and the Allies the nature of this conflict changed. Fewer Germans patrolled the streets as most remained barricaded inside the buildings they were committed to defending—and now they had French and American tanks with which to contend.

Not every German was holed up in a garrison. Jean Galtier-Boissière and his wife heard gunfire as they ran to see Leclerc's troops arriving: it was almost certainly German snipers, or possibly members of the Milice, on the tops of buildings firing into the street. Resisters were also out on the rooftops with their rifles hoping to pick off German snipers. Sadly, several civilians and other resisters were shot in the mistaken belief that they were the enemy. This almost happened to Bernard Pierquin, who described August 25 as the craziest and most extraordinary day of his life. When his concierge told him Nazi snipers were positioned on the roof he bravely picked up a revolver, put on his FFI medical armband, and, with his father, raced to the top floor of the building; here, with a leg-up from his father, Bernard managed to scramble up onto the roof. He could find nobody there, but almost immediately shots rang out all around him: he had been mistaken for an enemy sniper by some other FFIs down the street.[104]

Jean Galtier-Boissière's wife also had a narrow escape. She was sitting in their bedroom on the fifth floor when a dozen machine-gun bullets ripped through the window shutters and peppered the wall; had she been standing, she would have been killed. The shots had been fired by one of Leclerc's soldiers, aiming at snipers on the roof of their apartment building.[105]

The final anti-German offensive of August 25 began when the Resistance seized the telephone exchange in the rue des Archives to prevent the Germans from destroying it. More fierce battles raged around the two German strongholds in the south of the city: the Senate building in the Luxembourg Gardens and the École Militaire near Les Invalides. In the 16th arrondissement French troops and tanks led by Colonel Langlade took out three German tanks and other vehicles outside the MBF headquarters in the Hôtel Majestic, and the 350 Germans inside surrendered. Tanks and troops led by another of Leclerc's men, Colonel Pierre Billotte, closed in on Choltitz's headquarters in the Hôtel Meurice on the rue de Rivoli. Infantrymen from the 2e DB stormed into the ground floor firing machine guns and hurling smoke grenades.

Choltitz realised that his position was hopeless and, confronted by two of Leclerc's officers, he handed over his sword and pistol and agreed to tell his men to stop fighting. The German commander was then taken to the Prefecture of Police, where Leclerc and Chaban-Delmas were waiting. Rol-Tanguy and Maurice Kriegel (code name Valrimont), representing the FFI and COMAC, respectively, strongly protested when they were told to wait in another room. In the end they were allowed to witness Choltitz and Leclerc sign the document announcing the immediate capitulation of the Germans in Paris. This attempt by the Gaullists to exclude representatives of the FFI and COMAC was significant. It was the first indication of many to follow that, as hostilities ended, the Resistance, whose members had fought and died on the streets of Paris, would be systematically sidelined by de Gaulle and his followers.

Choltitz was taken to Leclerc's headquarters in the Montparnasse railway station. Here Rol-Tanguy managed to add his signature to the surrender document, thus allowing the radio and the Resistance press to announce that von Choltitz had surrendered not only to the head of the 2e DB, but to the leader of the Forces françaises de l'intérieur (FFI) as well. Choltitz then sent orders to any Germans still holding out in the Senate building, the Chamber of Deputies, and the Prince-Eugene barracks or elsewhere to surrender by the end of the day. Following some desperate and futile last-minute acts of resistance, all of the German strongholds in the city surrendered. Most of Choltitz's troops were taken prisoner, although a small number of diehards and SS fanatics were still on the loose.

De Gaulle arrived in the city at about 4 P.M. and briefly visited Leclerc's headquarters. Keen as ever to keep the Resistance in what he considered to be its place, de Gaulle was annoyed to discover that

Chaban-Delmas and Leclerc had allowed Rol-Tanguy to put his name to the surrender document and, what was worse, that his signature appeared above that of Leclerc's. However, significantly for de Gaulle's ambitions, both men had signed in the name of the Provisional French Government—not the Allies. In other words, the Germans had capitulated to the Free French and not to the "Anglo-Saxons." After stopping by at his old offices at the War Ministry and visiting the Prefecture of Police, de Gaulle arrived at the Hôtel de Ville around 7:15 P.M.

"Paris!" he proclaimed to representatives of the Resistance in a speech in the great hall. "Paris humiliated! Paris broken! Paris battered!—but now Paris liberated! Liberated by herself, liberated by her own people, with the help of the armies of France, with the support and backing of the whole of France, of fighting France, of the only France, of the true France, of eternal France."[106] Four days went by and it was only when de Gaulle made a radio broadcast paying tribute to all those who had helped to liberate Paris that he publicly recognised the part played by "the good and brave Allied armies and their leaders whose unstoppable advance made the Liberation of Paris possible and made the liberation of the whole country a certainty by joining us to crush the German forces."[107]

At the Hôtel de Ville, Georges Bidault, president of the CNR, urged de Gaulle on behalf of the Resistance to proclaim the Republic, but de Gaulle replied tartly that it had never ceased to exist. In his view, Vichy had always been illegitimate, and ever since the dark days of June 1940 he alone had represented republican France. Therefore, he did not see why, as the head of the government of the French Republic (albeit as yet still provisional), he needed to proclaim its existence.

De Gaulle then moved to the balcony of the Hôtel de Ville and raised his arms aloft to acknowledge the cheers of a rapturous crowd. Parisians could now put a face to the name and the voice that had for the last four years encouraged them to believe that all was not lost; the one man who had told them not to abandon hope and urged them to oppose the Occupation.

On Saturday, August 26 it seemed as if the whole of Paris had turned out to cheer de Gaulle, the national symbol of resistance, as he walked down the Champs-Élysées. De Gaulle, as always attuned to the importance of symbolism, understood how vital it was for his political future for him to be seen leading the parade, accompanied by Leclerc and members of the French army, and acclaimed by the people of Paris. Leclerc's 2e DB, still formally under Allied command, ignored American orders to go to the northern suburbs of Paris, where some Germans refused to surrender; instead, they followed de Gaulle's instructions to join the victory parade.[108] "It looked like the sea!" de Gaulle said later, recalling the moment when he stood at the top of the Champs-Elysées. "A packed crowd filled both sides of the road. Perhaps two million people. The roofs, too, were black with people. Groups of people, intermingled with flags, packed every window. Human clusters were clinging to ladders, flagpoles, and lamp posts. As far as my eyes could see, there was nothing but this swell of humanity in the sunshine, beneath the tricolour."[109] Huguette Robert, who lived in the rue de Varenne, was there: "It was boiling hot, sweltering. Standing, waiting for two hours. At last the procession arrived. The general is on foot in the centre. Shouts fill the air: 'Vive de Gaulle!' 'Vive Leclerc!' "[110]

De Gaulle embodied the reestablishment of French sovereignty, of national pride, and of the end of the Occupation. Hope had triumphed over despair; in place of despotism and servitude, democracy and freedom had found expression in the CNR Charter, a blueprint for post-Liberation political, economic, and social reconstruction. The Parisians cheering de Gaulle believed that at last they had a chance to build a future of their own rather than one in which they found themselves incorporated into the new Europe of the Nazis.

Micheline Bood sat in a parked truck at the corner of the avenue de Marigny and the Champs-Élysées to watch the parade. "General de Gaulle walked past. I'm still hoarse from shouting so much and my hands are sore with so much clapping." She described him looking both "unpretentious and magnificent" and "so immensely tall that he towered over everybody else."[111] Near the Tuileries Gardens de Gaulle climbed into an open car, ready to be driven past the Hôtel de Ville and on to Notre-Dame to attend a special Mass.

Not everything that day went according to plan. At the place de la Concorde members of the crowd scattered in terror as volleys of shots rang out and an unknown number of those celebrating the Liberation of the city fell to the ground dead or wounded; one woman was shot in the head very near where Micheline sat in the truck.[112] André Auvinet, who was also in the crowd, thought the shots came from the Naval Ministry building or the nearby Hôtel Crillon. Leclerc's tanks returned fire, blowing out windows in the Ministry building. André managed to leave the area unscathed, but he reported hearing more shots being fired from the Chamber of Deputies and nearby buildings on the other bank of the Seine.[113] It is most likely that the shots were fired by members of the SS, the Milice, or mavericks from the German army. It is also possible that some of the sound of gunfire came from weapons being fired into the air by celebrating members of the FFI. It is impossible to know exactly how many people were shot that day, although one historian claims as many as 300 were killed; she does not supply a source for this figure.[114]

De Gaulle reached Notre-Dame at around 4:15. Cardinal Suhard, the archbishop of Paris, was "advised" not to attend. He was too tainted by the Occupation, having welcomed Pétain to Paris and having conducted the funeral service for Philippe Henriot, the collaborationist broadcaster assassinated by the Resistance. As de Gaulle alighted from his car outside the cathedral more shots rang out. Members of the FFI and the 2e DB on the square in front of the building started firing wildly towards the cathedral's towers. Later more shots were fired inside the cathedral, with marksmen in the galleries joining in. Who started the shooting and why has never been satisfactorily explained. One theory is that the firing inside Notre-Dame began when nervous riflemen mistook the noise of pigeons flying high up inside the building for snipers moving around in the upper galleries. De Gaulle initially dismissed the incident, but he took the matter more seriously when he heard that firing had broken out in other parts of the city. He later wrote that he suspected the Communists of organising the shootings to show that the enemy was still active and that Resistance organisations like COMAC, the CNR, the Paris Liberation Committee, and local Resistance committees were still needed and should be responsible for policing, justice, and the purging of collaborators. De Gaulle gave no evidence for this view.

The day of celebration, August 26, ended on a sober and depressing note. Shortly before midnight German planes carried out a random punishment bombing raid on Paris. They killed 120 people in nine arrondissements, including some in the centre of the city, which had hitherto been spared. In the Seine department as a whole 190 people were killed, including staff, patients, and children at the Bichat hospital in the 18th arrondissement, which Pétain had visited in April.

The war against Germany lasted for another nine months. But the wild outpouring of joy with which Parisians greeted the Liberation of their city surpassed the celebrations that marked the official end of the war on May 8, 1945.[115] Some 3,200 Germans lost their lives during the Liberation of Paris and almost 15,000 were taken prisoner. The FFI were probably responsible for about a third of German casualties. Seventy-one men of the 2e DB were killed, 225 wounded, and twenty-one reported missing during its advance on Paris and the city's capture. Altogether 2,873 Parisians were killed during August 1944.[116]

De Gaulle moved swiftly to ensure that the Resistance could not disrupt his political ambitions. On August 28, 1944, he summoned the twenty or so most senior fighters of the Paris Resistance to congratulate them on their contribution to the Liberation of the city but also to tell them that their forces would now be absorbed into the regular French army. He then met the leaders of the National Resistance Council (CNR) to tell them their job was done. "I left them in no doubt as to my intentions towards them," he wrote later. "Once Paris was wrenched from the enemy, the CNR became part of the glorious history of the Liberation, but there was no reason why it should continue to exist as an instrument of action. The government would henceforth assume sole responsibility."[117]

France's new state administration would be one fashioned by de Gaulle. Paris was freed and once again became the capital of France. On August 31 de Gaulle moved his government from Algiers to the city. He swiftly appointed trusted personnel from Algiers to senior administrative positions. This meant ousting many of those drawn from the ranks of the Resistance (whom he neither knew nor trusted), many of whom had occupied government and state positions during and since the Liberation of the city. This was another sign that de Gaulle would brook no rivalry from the Resistance and would certainly not give the Communists any opportunity to stage the takeover he had always feared—especially since their role in the August 19 uprising.

He was mistaken about the threat of a Communist coup d'état. Certainly individual Communists hoped the national liberation struggle against Germany would turn into a full-blown revolution against the French ruling class, but this was not the intention of the PCF leadership in August–September 1944. The French Communist Party was, as always, loyal to the Soviet Union, and Moscow's priority was to maintain its alliance with Britain and the United States. In addition, any attempt to stage a national Communist uprising led by the working class against the French ruling class while France was still at war with Germany would almost certainly have meant conflict with de Gaulle and his supporters, and would, in all probability, have tipped France into a civil war. If this had happened it is inconceivable that the Allied troops in France would have stood idly by and a conflict between Communists and the Allies in France was absolutely not what Stalin wanted.

A postscript to the Liberation of Paris came almost eight months later. On April 2, 1945, de Gaulle, in his capacity as head of the Provisional Government of the French Republic, bestowed upon the city of Paris the prestigious Cross of Companion of the Liberation for the uprising of the summer of 1944 when ordinary citizens braved bullets to push back the invader.

Conclusion

ONCE LIBERATED, Paris again became the centre of French political power. Early in September de Gaulle announced the formation of the country's first provisional government in metropolitan France. De Gaulle had three main objectives: to restore order, to unite a geographically fragmented and politically divided country, and to reinstate France among the great nations of the world. After more than four years of deprivation under German occupation, the bulk of the Parisian population had less grandiose but more pressing concerns.

During the Occupation Parisians never stopped repeating that it was the Germans who were taking everything. Many therefore assumed that with the Germans gone shortages would disappear; some were so convinced that a new dawn had broken that they tore up their ration cards as Leclerc's tanks rolled into Paris.[1] However, bombed and sabotaged rail networks meant a greatly restricted movement of goods, food, and raw materials.[2] During the latter period of the Occupation, the Resistance encouraged farmers not to hand over produce as a way of countering German requisitioning. Now with the Germans leaving the countryside, farmers tended either to consume most of their produce themselves or to sell it for cash on the black market.[3] This further reduced supplies of food to the cities. Food production itself remained lower than prewar levels because of labour shortages (all those farmers who would stay in POW camps for another nine months or more) and shortages of animal power, especially horses, and fertilizer.

The euphoria at the Liberation of Paris soon evaporated, replaced by a generalised feeling of dejection. Parisians found themselves once again caught up in the depressing round of queuing for ration books, looking for food to buy and which they might (or might not) be able to find. On August 31 Berthe Auroy waited in line for six hours, including three hours outside a bakers' shop. The following day she had to queue again—for just six tomatoes and some pears; in the afternoon more queuing, this time for some cauliflowers.[4]

In October 1944, one Parisian, Fernand Picard, noted in his diary that bread rations increased from 300g to 350g a day and meat rations were set at 250g (about 8 oz.) a week "but there were still problems with butter, cooking oil and wine."[5] But in February 1945 he wrote that in Paris and other cities "most people were suffering more from hunger than ever before."[6] Rationing was no short-term measure: apart from a two-month break at the end of 1944 bread remained rationed until November 1, 1948, milk until April 15, 1949, and, the following month, coffee, cooking oil, rice, and sugar were still rationed. It was not until December 1949 that rationing finally ended: it lasted for five and a half years after the city had been liberated—longer than the Occupation itself.

The shortage of food was the main problem, but it was not the only difficulty Parisians had to face. In mid-September 1944, the theatres, cinemas, and music halls remained closed, and, although the Métro was running, it was offering only a restricted service. A limited postal service began operating in October, but electricity was still only available for forty-five minutes a day and gas for just half an hour at lunch times. The winter of 1944–1945 was grim. Janet Flanner, an American journalist, wrote in January 1945: "Parisians are colder than they have been any other winter of the war, they are hungrier than they have been any other winter of the war."[7] Although not a new phenomenon, housing conditions in the immediate post-Liberation period varied enormously from luxurious spacious apartments to cramped and squalid slums: about half the apartments in Paris had no WC or bathroom, and almost 100,000 furnished dwellings were deemed to be unfit for human habitation. This had obvious implications for health, especially with respect to medical conditions, such as tuberculosis, which are closely related to poor living conditions.

Rationing encouraged the growth of a market in forged ration books, which thrived as it had during the Occupation: in one infamous case, the police raided a hotel room where, over a two-year period, a single forger had produced over a million fake ration cards for bread.[8] The black market also returned: a report from the Prefecture of Police on September 4, 1944, noted that "the black market which seemed to be less in evidence at the Liberation is back in business: cigarettes, tinned food, meat . . . are starting to be sold again at exorbitant prices."[9] During the festive season at the end of the same year, restaurants offered meals costing as much as 7,000 francs, whose ingredients had been bought on the black market. Paul Ramadier, the unpopular minister of food (nicknamed "Ramadiet" or "Ramadan," after the Muslim fasting period), ordered police raids on a number of top Paris restaurants, and twenty or so were closed down. Family food parcels, another feature of the Occupation, were still being sent from the countryside to the cities. However, a Paris police report in August 1945 estimated that almost all the 540 tons of family food parcels sent to Paris were dispatched under false names and the produce ended up on the black market. As happened during the Occupation, some workers moved into selling on the black market because they either were unemployed or could only find part-time work. A police report dated April 9, 1945, noted:

> The factories in the Paris region are finding it extremely difficult to recruit workers. Among those workers made redundant because their factories had been destroyed [by Allied bombing] or because of the shortage of raw materials and who only receive 75 percent of their wages, there are quite a number who prefer to enjoy their freedom rather than go back to work. This freedom allows them to go to agricultural areas, bring back several kilos of foodstuffs which they sell across Paris at a profit and, which, when added to their unemployment benefit, gives them far more money than a regular job would do.[10]

Not all those who had made a fortune on the black market in Paris during the Occupation continued to do so afterwards. The mega-rich racketeer Michel Szkolnikoff, who fled to Spain, was assassinated in

Madrid in June 1945. Joseph Joinovici, the billionaire rag-and-bone man, who at the end of the Occupation sold weapons to the police and betrayed Bonny and Lafont, the heads of the French Gestapo, was nonetheless arrested in November 1947; two years later he was found guilty of economic collaboration, sentenced to five years imprisonment, and fined 600,000 francs; the court also ordered the seizure of his assets up to the value of 50 million francs. The trial of twelve members of the French Gestapo was held in December 1944; the leaders—Bonny and Lafont and seven others—were found guilty and were executed at Fort de Montrouge just after Christmas.[11]

The issue of dispensing "justice" after the Liberation proved to be a very complex and lengthy one, which ultimately satisfied almost no one. Before the legal system was once again functioning, members of the FFI arrested thousands of alleged collaborators, who were taken to the Vél'd'Hiv' stadium, where Jewish men, women, and children had been held in 1942. They were then driven to Drancy in the same buses used to take Jews to the camp during the Occupation. The prisoners were guarded by FFI resisters until September 20, when the FFIs were replaced by members of the prison service. Towards the end of October 1944 the camp held over 6,000 prisoners; four months later only 900 remained.[12] Some high-profile Vichyite collaborators were among the 4,500 prisoners held in Fresnes jail; others remained untroubled in their posts working as assiduously for the new government headed by de Gaulle as they had for the Vichy régime.

Paris did not escape the lawless purges (*l'épuration sauvage*) that swept through France in the wake of the Liberation. In Paris dubious and criminal elements attached themselves to the FFI and, claiming to be members of the Resistance, went on the rampage. The British writer Malcolm Muggeridge was invited to join one such group on their nightly purges. He wrote that, "considering their youth, they behaved with horrifying callousness, arrogance and brutality."[13] They boasted about their executions, and they stole cigarette cases, jewels, and money. Muggeridge later discovered that their leader, who was arrested, had been a collaborator during the Occupation.[14]

In the weeks following the Liberation of Paris, dozens of bodies were left around Paris with tags identifying them as Nazi collaborators; another twenty-eight, who had been shot through the head, were pulled out of the Seine. A rogue FFI unit was based in the Institut Dentaire

(the Dental Institute) in the 13th arrondissement, which was part of a
network of unofficial prisons in the Paris region where suspected collaborators were "interrogated," "tried," and then sentenced. In mid-
September the FFI leadership ordered the closure of the Institut Dentaire.[15] In early October, the government established three new courts
to deal with alleged crimes of collaboration.

A fundamental difference distinguished the approach taken by de
Gaulle and the Communists over the question of the purges. In his narrative of the dark years, de Gaulle insisted that with the exception of a
tiny number of collaborators, the French people had heroically resisted
the German occupier; hence, a radical purge was unnecessary. Whole-
sale purges would also damage his project of building national unity
and would run contrary to his belief that France needed "all her children" for the work of national reconstruction. The Communist Party,
on the other hand, having ruled out a revolutionary uprising, called for
a radical cleansing. This demand was made in the name of justice but
also to enable the PCF to place its members and sympathisers in key
positions in the world of culture,[16] the newly nationalised industries,
and the nascent political and administrative structures that were being
created.[17] This would complement its electoral strategy of presenting
itself as *the* party of the Resistance, which led to its emergence as the
biggest political party in the country after the parliamentary elections
of October 1945. The party was accorded four posts in de Gaulle's
government, but none of the key posts it hoped to secure.[18] In January
1946 de Gaulle, frustrated by what he saw as the selfish policy of all
political parties in putting self-interest before the national interest,
resigned. In October 1946 voters in a referendum approved a proposed
constitution for a Fourth Republic, and in January 1947 Vincent Auriol
became its first president.

The official purges were still taking place when Auriol was elected
and, indeed, they continued until the end of 1948. About 160,000 cases
across the country went to court, of which nearly half ended in acquittal;
a quarter of those accused were sentenced to deprivation of civic and
political rights (*dégradation nationale*) for varying lengths of time, 16 percent of those found guilty were imprisoned, 8 percent were sentenced
to forced labour, and 4 percent were sentenced to death, although more
than half of these 7,037 individuals were sentenced in absentia. The legal
purging process in France was much more moderate than in Belgium,

the Netherlands, Norway, or Denmark.[19] The war years were times that most people looked back on neither with pleasure nor pride, and sentiments were strong, and not just among those on the Far Right who hoped to escape punishment, to pay lip service to the Gaullist myth that the vast majority of the French had resisted *(la France résistante)* and look to the future rather than dwell on the past. Generally speaking, the later a trial took place, the more lenient the sentence was likely to be. This meant that individuals accused of economic collaboration tended to receive relatively lenient sentences or to have their cases dismissed altogether, because of the time it took to amass evidence from the company's order books, correspondence, and other documentation.

Amnesties began as early as 1947 for those who had lost their civic and political rights. By March 1954 all sentences passed in absentia were annulled; those who returned from abroad to stand trial faced sympathetic judges and were either acquitted or given suspended sentences. Prison sentences that had been passed were reduced on appeal and, by 1964, twenty years after the Liberation, not a single collaborator was still behind bars.[20]

Those who had publicly staked their reputations on collaboration or expressed pro-Nazi views in print were more likely to be tried earlier and to be sentenced to death. On October 23, 1944, Georges Suarez, editor of the collaborationist daily *Aujourd'hui*, became the first person to be condemned to death by a legally constituted court in metropolitan France.[21] He had advocated brutal reprisals against all opponents of the Occupation, had demanded that the relatives of Free French leaders be shot as hostages, and had poured lavish praise on Hitler.[22] Suarez was executed by firing squad on November 9, 1944. The journalist and author Robert Brasillach, who had spewed out anti-Semitic bile in the columns of *Je suis partout*, was also sentenced to death and executed on February 6, 1945, despite an appeal for clemency from fellow-writers, including Albert Camus and François Mauriac.

In April 1945, Philippe Pétain, who had just celebrated his eighty-ninth birthday, left Sigmaringen Castle in Germany and was taken under armed German escort to Switzerland, where he handed himself over to the French authorities. In August, after a three-week trial in the Palais de Justice in Paris, he was found guilty of treason and sentenced to death. De Gaulle commuted the sentence to life imprisonment, and Pétain died in jail six years later.

Pierre Laval was less fortunate. Thanks to a plane supplied by Ribbentrop he managed to fly from Sigmaringen to Spain, where he was arrested, then expelled, and flown to France via Austria. On October 9, 1945, Laval's trial began in Paris in the same courtroom where Pétain's case had been heard. If Pétain's trial had been thorough and dignified, Laval's was rushed and chaotic: in just five days Laval was found guilty and sentenced to death. The morning of his execution Laval tried to kill himself with cyanide; after the soles of his feet were slashed to increase circulation and his stomach was pumped out seventeen times, Laval was eventually revived and taken in a semi-conscious state to a small plot of land behind the prison, tied to a stake, and executed by a firing squad.

Jacques Doriot, the rising star within the PCF turned fanatical anti-Bolshevik and pro-Nazi, fled from Paris first to Neustadt (Germany) and then to an island on Lake Constance that straddles Austria, Germany, and Switzerland. It was here with Nazi support that in January 1945, he established the headquarters of his Committee for French Liberation, which had the crazy ambition of liberating France from de Gaulle and the Allies. In February 1945 he drove to a meeting with Darnand and Déat to discuss their participation in his new venture but he never reached his destination: on the way his car was strafed by two planes and he was killed outright.[23]

Joseph Darnand, the First World War hero who became head of the Milice, left Sigmaringen in April to fight alongside the Italian fascists against the partisans. Captured by British agents, he was handed over to the French. He was sentenced to death on October 3, 1945, and executed a week later.

Fernand de Brinon, Laval's right-hand man and Vichy's third and last representative in Paris, tried to flee to Switzerland. He surrendered to the American army in Bavaria and was sent to Paris, where he spent the next two years between his cell and a bed in the prison hospital. He went on trial in March 1947, was found guilty, and was executed on April 15. De Brinon's death sentence was the last one to be followed by an execution.

Marcel Déat, founder of the Rassemblement national populaire (RNP) and editor of *L'Œuvre*, also reached Italy, where he and his wife were helped by Catholic priests. The couple lived for two years in Genoa and then, from 1947, in Turin, where Déat died of natural causes in January 1955.

Louis Darquier (de Pellepoix), the rabid anti-Semite who replaced Xavier Vallat as general commissioner for Jewish affairs in 1942, fled to Franco's Spain. In 1947 he was tried in absentia, along with Vallat, who was sentenced to ten years' imprisonment but was released after two. Darquier was sentenced to death but all attempts to extradite him failed. He settled in Madrid, where he taught in a language school under an assumed name. He died peacefully in Spain in 1980 a couple of years after giving an unrepentant interview in the French magazine *L'Express* in which he denied the existence of the Holocaust and claimed that only fleas were gassed at Auschwitz.[24]

René Bousquet, Laval's appointment as chief of the French police, fled to Germany and was in Bavaria when the war ended. He was tried in France in 1949 and was given a sentence depriving him of his political and civic rights for five years; however, the sentence was never implemented since the court accepted his claim that he had actively helped the Resistance. Bousquet went on to build a successful postwar career as a banker and journalist. In 1991 he was indicted for crimes against humanity, but because of his long-standing close friendship with French president François Mitterrand the opening of the trial was repeatedly delayed. In June 1993, a few weeks before it was finally due to start, eighty-four-year-old Bousquet was shot dead in his apartment by a gunman who claimed to be avenging Bousquet's war crimes.

It is hard to argue that any of the key German personnel based in Paris during the Occupation were given the punishment they deserved. Otto von Stülpnagel, MBF, committed suicide in the Cherche-Midi prison in February 1948. Otto Abetz's trial opened before a military tribunal in Paris in July 1949. He was found guilty of involvement in the pillaging of Jewish property, the deportation of members of the Resistance, the deaths of hostages, and, in particular, the death of Georges Mandel. He was sentenced to twenty years hard labour and was banned from living in France for another twenty years. After vociferous campaigns in Germany and France, Abetz was released in April 1954; he and his wife died in a motorway crash in Germany in 1958. Foul play was suspected but never proven. Alois Brunner, who ran the camp at Drancy from June 1943 until just before the Liberation of Paris, was sentenced to death in absentia in 1954. By then he was in Egypt, where, on the CIA payroll he was also working as an illicit arms dealer.[25] He then moved to Damascus, where he instructed the security forces of Amin Havez, the then president of Syria, on torture techniques and was implicated in a plot to assassinate the head of the World Jewish Congress.[26] SS General Carl Oberg, head of the German secret security services in Paris, and his deputy Helmut Knochen were both sentenced to death by a French court in October 1954. In 1958 their sentences were commuted to twenty years hard labour (Oberg) and life imprisonment (Knochen). In 1962 both men were pardoned by de Gaulle, who had been elected president of the Fifth Republic in 1958, and released. Oberg died in 1965 and Knochen lived on until 2003.

While the new judicial machinery was straining to address the issue of justice, the new French state was trying to work out how to handle the thousands upon thousands of POWs, deportees, and STO conscripts who were arriving in Paris. The government's attitude towards these returnees reflected its commitment to building national unity: they were all people who had spent the war—or part of it—outside of France and they now needed to be reintegrated into postwar France.

The French government, aware that pro-Nazi elements were trying to sneak into France, set up processing and interviewing centres for POWs and STOs in the Vél'd'Hiv', the Gaumont-Palace Theatre, and the Rex Cinema. To accommodate the huge influx of returning "exiles," the government requisitioned over 770 hotels—almost half as many again as the Germans had taken over during the Occupation.[27]

Ideally, according to the government, social reintegration would take place through contact with family, friends, neighbours, and workmates. But this was difficult to achieve: prisoners, labour conscripts, and deportees had been cut off from their Paris worlds for years, with some, held in indescribably degrading and terrifyingly inhumane conditions, having had no contact with the outside world at all.

Those returning had not experienced Paris life during the Occupation and lacked the same reference points as those who had. Some of those who came back were surprised to discover that their joy at returning stood at odds with the gloom that had settled over Paris as people realised that everyday life was not about to improve.[28] Once familiar places now felt strange and alien. A student STO conscript returning to the Latin Quarter, which he had previously associated with studying, laughter, and being carefree, wrote, "What have I got in common with the young people on the Boul'Mich [the boulevard Saint-Michel] after two years . . . of STO? . . . Nothing—I don't belong here anymore."[29] Another returning STO worker wrote: "I'm returning from another world, a world where the values were different. I'm going to have to learn how to live life all over again."[30] Some returning STO workers were welcomed with open arms, but others found themselves suspected of being "unpatriotic" and were criticised for not staying in France and joining the Resistance. While some STO workers were able to return to their old jobs, others found themselves unemployed.

More than half the POWs, who had been held for up to five years, were married with children and all the members of their household had to adjust to their return. The young son of one POW's wife who had slept in his mother's bed since 1940 "was reluctant to yield his place to a prematurely aged man who had returned from his Stalag."[31] POWs (and to a lesser extent married STO workers, who had been absent for a shorter period) had to confront ways in which their roles as husband and father had changed. Men, who often felt shame or embarrassment at having been captured and having spent the war passively, found that their wives had been propelled into taking responsibility for the household and were now more active, more independent, and more used to taking decisions than before. The steep rise in divorce rates in the immediate postwar period stemmed, in part, from difficulties encountered by couples where the husband had been held in Germany.[32]

Whatever difficulties the STO workers and the POWs faced, they were as nothing compared to those deported for political reasons (affiliation with the PCF or being a member of the Resistance), or particularly the Jews. In the immediate post-Liberation period most attention was focused on workers who had volunteered or who had been coerced to work in Germany and on the POWs, who, taken together, massively outnumbered the number of "racial" and political deportees.[33] Whereas most of the 800,000 workers and the million or so soldiers still in camps at the end of the war came home, this was not true of the deportees, particularly the Jews. According to the most reliable figures about 140,000 individuals were deported from France; about 60 percent of the 65,000 of those deported for political activities came back but only about 3 percent (2,566) of the 75,721 deported Jews returned.[34]

The deportees from the camps arrived in Paris by train (usually at the Gare d'Orsay—today the Musée d'Orsay)—or they were bussed in from the airport at Le Bourget. They were then taken to the Hôtel Lutetia, which until recently had housed the headquarters of the Abwehr. From April to August 1945 the Lutetia operated as a reception centre for those returning from the concentration and extermination camps.[35] Here these refugees from hell, often with no identity papers, were further traumatised as they tried to convince their interrogators that they were not spies, SS members, or other Nazis trying to pass themselves off as returning deportees.

Many of the hotel's hundreds of spacious rooms had three or four beds installed, where returnees rested until reunited with their families; single rooms were for those without families whose stay was extended. Those in need of medical attention were taken to Bichat and Salpêtrière hospitals. The hotel was constantly besieged by crowds of people, many waving photographs of their loved ones and entreating the returnees to look at them and tell them if they recognised them and had any news of them.

While POW and STO returnees often found problems reintegrating into their families, in most cases they had families to whom they could turn. Many of the Jews who returned were the sole surviving members of their immediate family or even their extended family. Many Jews who returned to Paris also discovered that their apartments had been emptied and that somebody else was living there: the original owner usually succeeded in having the usurper evicted but this could be at the cost of a lengthy and expensive legal case.

Communists (and Jews who were Communists) had a "family" in the French Communist Party to whom they could turn but this was not always easy either. Pierre Daix, a Communist who had participated in the November 11, 1940, demonstration and later joined an armed Communist group, was imprisoned in France in 1942 before being deported to Mauthausen concentration camp in March 1944. Recalling his return, Daix wrote, "My life did not fit with the one I had left." He could not stop thinking about those who had died in the camp and he was unable to sleep in a bed (instead he slept on a rug on the floor). Deportees tended to seek out fellow deportees who had similar experiences and with whom they felt they could share their anxieties. They expressed such fears as "I don't know what to say to my wife," "I don't recognise my children anymore." A female deportee worried, "I wonder if it will work with my husband; he has become so much younger than I am."[36] In addition, hardened working-class militants steeped in the doctrines of Marx and Lenin could find themselves outnumbered in their local party branches by new recruits, drawn to the party because of its resistance to the Germans and who were often not only from a different class background, but also woefully ignorant about Communist history, culture, and theory.

The government's decision not to distinguish between POWs, STO workers, political deportees, and Jews made it difficult to highlight the experience of the minority of Jews who had survived the barbarous inhumanity of extermination camps like Auschwitz. They found it extremely difficult to talk about their experiences; they initially remained silent, in part, because they did not want to distress those who still hoped that members of their family would return and, in part, because their experiences were so unbelievably terrible that it was literally impossible for many to find words to describe them. Even if they could, nobody wanted to hear about them anyway. Simone Veil, a lawyer and politician who later became president of the European Parliament said in an interview in 1990, "If I take my case, I have always been ready to talk, to bear witness, but nobody wanted to listen to us."[37] Those tempted to speak out could even find themselves threatened and accused of special pleading. A leaflet addressed to "Jewish compatriots who have returned after four years" warned them against making too much of a fuss and asserted that *everyone* had suffered during the war. It threatened Jews that if they tried to present themselves as "privileged victims" they risked fuelling a wave of anti-Semitism which was perhaps already on the rise.[38] As far as schools were concerned, and to a large extent in the wider society as well, a veil was effectively drawn over the uniquely brutal treatment to which the Jews had been subjected and which remained in place for some thirty years after the liberation of the city. Jean-Marc Benammar, now a lecturer at Paris VIII University wrote, "When I was a kid (1968–1975) I was not taught anything about racial deportations. To boys of my age, Jews were deported for having fought the Germans. I learned what Auschwitz was by seeing the tattooed arm of the father of one of my friends."[39]

⌒ AND WHAT BECAME OF THOSE whose diaries provide such valuable insights into life in Paris between 1939 and 1944? Of those whom I have managed to track down, **Berthe Auroy** (1880–1968) continued living in Montmartre until her death. **Hélène Berr** (1921–1945) and her parents were arrested, taken to Drancy, and deported to Auschwitz on March 27, 1944, Hélène's twenty-third birthday. Hélène's parents were murdered in the camp and Hélène was transferred to Bergen-Belsen, where she died in April 1945, days before the camp was liberated. **Jacques Biélinky** (1881–1943) was deported from Drancy to Sobibor on March 23, 1943, and never returned. **Micheline Bood** (1926–1980) became a journalist and author. Polish refugee **Andrzej Bobkowski** (1914–1961), who found himself stuck in Paris on his way to South America when war broke out in 1939, left France in 1947 and settled in Guatemala. **Charles Braibant** (1889–1976) was appointed head of the French state archives (Archives de France) in 1948, where he remained until 1959. **César Fauxbras** (1899–1968), pseudonym of Gaston Sterckeman, had published widely before the war but found his works rejected after the Liberation for being too subversive. He returned to his job as an accountant and his diary was published posthumously. **Jean Galtier-Boissière** (1891–1966) published a continuation of his diary, which he had started before the war, covering the years up until 1960. After the success of *Journal à quatre mains*, **Benoîte Groult** (1920–) and **Flora Groult** (1924–2001) published two more co-written books marked by a commitment to feminism. Both worked as journalists and published other works written individually. Benoîte headed a commission for feminising the names of professions and job descriptions and was recently interviewed in a television programme *L'Occupation intime* (now available on DVD).[40] **Jean Guéhenno** (1890–1978) published accounts of his trips to North America, South America, Africa, and Japan, as well as a number of autobiographical works and essays. He was admitted to the Académie française in 1962. **Agnès Humbert** (1894–1963) was deported to Germany in 1942, where she spent three years working in dreadful conditions in a rayon factory. Back in Paris she refused to return to the National Museum of Popular Arts and Traditions and, despite severe health problems, published numerous books on art and sculpture. **Roger Langeron** (1882–1966) became a published historian specialising in the French Restauration period (1814–1830) and, in 1960, he was elected a member of the Académie des sciences morales et politiques. **Paul Léautaud** (1872–1956) remained a polemical and outspoken literary critic whose diaries were published in nineteen volumes between 1954 and 1966. **Georges Sadoul** (1904–1967) wrote numerous books on film, including a six-volume history of the cinema. **Edith Thomas** (1909–1970) was appointed head librarian at the state archives, where she worked until her death. After her resignation from the PCF in 1949, she remained a partisan of the Left, establishing a reputation as a fem-

inist author; in 1968, she was appointed one of the judges for the Prix
Femina, which is awarded each year for the best novel written by a
woman. In August 1944 **Rose Valland** (1898–1980) alerted the Resistance that a train full of art treasures was due to leave France, probably
for Mikulov, today in the Czech Republic. The Resistance blocked the
train at Aulnay-sous-Bois, where it and its contents were liberated by
the French army.[41] After the Liberation of Paris, Rose went to Germany
as a French army officer, where she played a crucial role in locating
stolen works of art. She was also a witness at the Nuremberg trials of
top Nazis. When she returned to France she was appointed head of a
department for the protection of art treasures. She retired in 1968. She
was awarded numerous French and foreign honours, including the *Légion d'honneur* (France), the Presidential Medal of Freedom (USA), and
the Order of Merit of the Federal Republic of Germany. **Alexander
Werth** (1901–1969) became Moscow correspondent of *The Guardian*
newspaper from 1946 to 1949 and published books on postwar France
and on Russian politics and society.

☞ IT IS NOW MORE THAN seventy years since the swastika flag flew
from the top of the Eiffel Tower and German soldiers of the Wehrmacht mingled with crowds on the Champs-Élysées. And yet the obser-
vant visitor to Paris will find plenty of reminders of the time that Paris
was at war.

Bullet and shell scars, still visible in the walls of the Prefecture of
Police, the Hôtel Dieu hospital, the Conciergerie on the Île de la Cité,
and the École des Mines on the boulevard Saint-Michel, bear witness
to the battle to liberate Paris. Métro stations are named after victims
and heroes of the war: Jacques Bonsergent, the first Parisian executed
by the Germans; Guy Môquet, the teenage hostage shot by a firing
squad in October 1941; Colonel Fabien, the nom de guerre of Pierre
Georges, who assassinated the first German in Paris in 1940 and who
was killed by a mine near Mulhouse in December 1944. HenriRol-
Tanguy's name appears under the Métro station name at Denfert-
Rochereau, which is near his underground headquarters, and General
Leclerc's name appears on signs at the Porte d'Orléans Métro stop at
the end of the avenue that now bears his name.

Dozens of streets across the city have also been named after heroes of
the Resistance: for example, the avenue Jean-Moulin in the 14th arrondissement is named after de Gaulle's representative who sealed the

unity of the different Resistance groups in a flat in the rue du Four in May 1943, and a street in the 20th arrondissement honours the "Manouchian group" of resisters. The five schoolboy resisters from the Lycée Buffon, executed by the Germans in February 1943 in a shooting range in the south of the city, have a square named in their memory in the 14th arrondissement.[42] Their remains were transferred from the cemetery at Ivry to the chapel at the Sorbonne and all five were each posthumously awarded the Légion d'Honneur, the Croix de Guerre, and the Médaille de la Résistance. There is also a plaque in their honour at the Lycée Buffon, and in 1959 they featured on a postage stamp in the series Heroes of the Resistance. In the Luxembourg Gardens stands a memorial to university and secondary school students in the Resistance who gave their lives for France. Walls all over the city have plaques with the names of those who were killed during the liberation of the city in August 1944 or earlier in the Occupation or who were deported. Flowers are placed at these sites on the day of their death and on public holidays.

Tucked away behind Notre-Dame Cathedral on the eastern tip of the Île de la Cité is a mostly underground memorial to all those deported by the Nazis, and 1994 saw the opening in Montparnasse of a museum honouring General Leclerc and Jean-Moulin endowed with a mouthful of a title (even for the French): Le Musée du Général Leclerc de Hauteclocque et de la Libération de Paris—Musée Jean Moulin.

For years, the role of the Vichy government in the deportation of the Jews and that played by foreign resisters in fighting the occupying forces were ignored, played down, or denied. In 1995, President Jacques Chirac delivered an historic speech on the anniversary of the Vél'd'Hiv' roundup of July 1942, making him the first French head of state to admit the culpability and complicity of Vichy in the deportation of thousands of Jews to Nazi death camps. "France, home of the Enlightenment and the Rights of Man, a country that welcomes others and offers them asylum, on that day committed the irreparable. It broke its word and handed those under its protection over to their executioners."[43] Plaques on schools and other institutions where Jews were seized and deported now make explicit the role of the French state in these operations.

As recently as June 2007, a decision taken by the newly elected right-wing French president Nicholas Sarkozy revealed just how sensitive a period the war and Occupation remain in France. Sarkozy declared that the inspirational letter written by seventeen-year-old Guy Môquet to his mother just before his execution in front of a German firing squad should be read out each year in every French secondary school on the anniversary of Môquet's death. This call unleashed a major outcry, with Sarkozy being accused of political opportunism and of trying to hijack the memory of the Resistance.

"What do all these reminders of the war years say about this troubled period in the history of Paris (and France)?" is a question that has provoked different responses over the years since the Liberation. For the first twenty-five years or so, one historical narrative held a virtual monopoly—the Gaullist myth, that Paris and France resisted and liberated themselves. When de Gaulle died in 1970, two years after his credibility had been dented by the student and worker revolt of May–June 1968, the story line changed. Marcel Ophuls's 1971 revisionist documentary *Le Chagrin et la pitié* (The Sorrow and the Pity), which was banned on French TV but eventually screened in cinemas, and Louis Malle's 1974 film *Lacombe Lucien* played a central role in opening up a new era during which the myth that "everyone resisted" was replaced by the fiction that "everyone collaborated." This book has tried to show that in Paris (as elsewhere) things were not that clear-cut: in Paris there were those (a tiny courageous minority) committed to resistance, many of whom paid the ultimate price; there were those (another tiny minority) who for ideological, opportunistic reasons, in pursuit of personal gain and/or enhanced status aligned themselves with the Nazis; there were also those who took advantages of wartime shortages to make money. But the energies of the majority of Parisians were focused on doing their best to survive increasing hardship and deprivation while making as few compromises as they could.

Notes

Introduction

1. Noth (n.d.), p. 43.
2. See Shirer (1970), p. 383.
3. See Crémieux-Brilhac (1990), p. 26.
4. France even specified that should Germany attack Poland, the French army would attack the Siegfried Line within thirteen days of mobilisation, while Britain promised to launch bombing raids against Germany.
5. Quoted in Weber (1995), p. 258.
6. In 1914, Déat, a small and tubby man from a modest provincial background, had gained a place at one of France's *grandes écoles*, the École normale supérieure in the rue d'Ulm. He served in the First World War which he began as a private and ended as a captain complete with the Légion d'honneur and five commendations. He then returned to his studies before embarking on a career as a philosophy teacher and making a name for himself as a political activist. Twice elected as a *député* for the French Socialist Party (SFIO) and tipped as a possible Socialist leader, he was expelled from the SFIO in 1933 after clashing with its leader Léon Blum over strategy and doctrine. He helped found a French "Neo-Socialist Party," and he was briefly a government minister. His pacifism was tinged increasingly with pro-German sentiments; he was violently opposed to France going to war with Germany over Poland, as his inflammatory article "Mourir pour Dantzig?" showed.
7. Déat (1939).
8. See Amouroux (1997), pp. 94–95.
9. Quoted in *Le Figaro*, 3 July 1939, p. 1.
10. When 14 July was introduced as a commemorative day in the 1880s it was to mark 14 July 1790—the date on which was held the *fête de la fédération*, a ceremony meant to promote national unity, and not 14 July 1789, the date on which

the Bastille fortress was stormed. However, although it remained a national holiday, 14 July became increasingly associated in the minds of most French people with the storming of the Bastille. Thanks to Simon Kitson for this clarification.

11. *Le Matin*, Saturday 15 July 1939, p. 4.

12. Named after André Maginot, the war minister who oversaw its construction until his death in 1932.

13. Stalin had been excluded from the negotiations at Munich and, fearing that France and Britain would do a deal with Hitler, he cynically struck first. From Hitler's perspective, the pact meant that he would not to have to worry about any interference, military or otherwise, from Moscow as he pursued his territorial ambitions.

14. See Charpentier (2008), p. 320.

15. Quoted in Duchatelet (2002), p. 348.

16. De Beauvoir (1960a), p. 428.

17. Amouroux (1997), p. 100.

18. In the nearby Seine-et-Oise department alone, the party had nine *députés*, twenty-nine municipalities that were either Communist-controlled or had a Communist mayor, and more than twenty local Communist publications, not counting those produced by local cells or factory committees. See Crémieux-Brilhac (1990), p. 175.

19. On 30 August 1939, the press reported that 90,000 Communist leaflets and 3,000 posters had been seized in Paris with an unspecified number of arrests in Versailles; the following day, 60,000 leaflets were seized in the southern Paris suburb of Montrouge, and on 1 September, a further 300,000 leaflets were seized in Paris at an address in the rue Haxo, in the working-class district of Belleville in the east of the city.

20. See Koestler (1941).

21. De Beauvoir (1960a), p. 431.

22. Braibant (1940), p. 21. Diary entry 28 August 1939.

23. "Une émouvante allocution du Cardinal Verdier au Sacré-Coeur de Montmartre," *Le Figaro*, 29 August 1939, p. 2.

24. "Une allocution du Grand Rabbin à un office solonnel," *Le Figaro*, 29 August 1939, p. 2.

25. Maurice Privat, *1940, une année de grandeur français* (Paris: Éditions Mondiales, 1939), quoted in Kupferman (1987), p. 207.

26. Amouroux (1997), p. 94.

27. *Le Matin*, 29 August 1939, p. 1.

28. Full name, Villey-Desmeserets.

29. See *Le Matin*, 31 August 1939, p. 1.

30. See *Le Matin*, 1 September 1939, p. 2. Initially it was thought 52,000 would be evacuated but by the time the evacuation plan was put into action on 30 August some 20,000 had already left. See *Le Matin*, 31 August 1939, p. 2.

31. By the middle of January 1940, more than 500,000 Parisian adult and child refugees were located in the twelve designated provincial departments. See Amouroux (1997), pp. 131–132.

32. See Alary (2010), p. 41.

33. Alary (2010), pp. 31–32.

34. Rayssac (2007), p. 96.

35. Rayssac (2007), pp. 98–99.

36. Anon., *Ce que le public doit savoir en matière de défense passive*, Préfecture de Police (Paris), 1938. Thanks to Emmanuelle Broux-Foucaud at the Service de la Mémoire et des Affaires Culturelles of the Paris Prefecture of Police for giving me access to this document.

37. *Le Matin*, 1 September 1939, p. 2.

38. De Beauvoir (1990a), p. 15. Diary entry 1 September 1939.

39. Anatole de Monzie, *Ci-devant*, p. 142, quoted in Crémieux-Brilhac (1990), p. 57.

40. *Akten*, vol. 7, no. 538, quoted in Crémieux-Brilhac (1990), p. 57.

41. Sartre was employed as a philosophy teacher and began to draw attention as a writer of existentialist fiction following the publication of *The Wall*, a collection of short stories, and especially with the appearance in 1938 of his novel *Nausea*.

42. Place Hébert in the 18th arrondissement.

43. De Beauvoir (1990a), p. 15. Diary entry 2 September 1939.

44. Twenty-nine "classes," namely, those who were twenty years old in 1909 to those who were twenty years old in 1939, were mobilised. See Buisson (2008), p. 10.

45. Alain Laubreaux, *Écrit pendant la guerre* (Paris: Éditions du Centre d'études de l'Agence Inter-France, 1944), p. 43, quoted in Richer (1990), pp. 32–33.

46. Letter to Armand Petitjean (6 September 1939), in Cornick (2010), p. 288.

47. Sartre (1976), p. 179.

48. Dubois (1946), p. 10.

49. See *Le Matin*, 2 September 1939, p. 2.

50. Alfred Fabre-Luce, quoted in Veillon (1995), p. 17.

51. Dubois (1946), p. 10.

52. Fabre-Luce (1947), p. 68.

53. Sadoul (1977), p. 15. Diary entry 2 September 1939.

54. De Beauvoir (1990a), p. 19. Diary entry 3 September 1939.

55. Léautaud, vol. 12 (1962), pp. 300–301. Diary entry 1 September 1939.

56. Dubois (1946), p. 11.

57. Georges Perec, *W, ou le souvenir d'enfance* (Paris: Gallimard, 1993), quoted in Ragache (1997), p. 8.

58. Its headquarters were in the rue Saint-Dominique in the 7th arrondissement.

59. Dupays (n.d.), p. 16.

60. Dupays (n.d.), pp. 7–8.

61. Braibant (1940), p. 28. Diary entry 3 September 1939.

1. The Phoney War

1. Paul Valéry, *Cahiers*, vol. 2 (Paris: Gallimard [Pléiade edition, 1974]), p. 1498, quoted in Charpentier (2008), p. 18. Emphasis in the original.

2. Quoted in Crémieux-Brilhac (1990), p. 55.

3. Quoted in Charpentier (2008), p. 18.

4. Léautaud, vol. 12 (1962), p. 302. Diary entry 5 September 1939.

5. Buisson (2008), p. 9, gives the figure of 8,000.

6. Amouroux (1997), p. 120.

7. De Beauvoir (1990a), p. 24. Diary entry 4 September 1939.

8. Stéphane (1946), p. 18.

9. Braibant (1940), p. 32. Diary entry 5 September 1939.

10. *Le Temps*, 6 September 1939, quoted in Richer (1990), p. 65.

11. Léautaud, vol. 12 (1962), p. 303. Diary entry 7 September 1939.

12. De Beauvoir (1990a), p. 27. Diary entry 5 September 1939.

13. Hastings (2011), p. 11.

14. De Beauvoir (1990a), p. 56. Diary entry 5 September 1939.

15. Quoted in Richer (1990), p. 66.

16. Quoted in Richer (1990), pp. 66–67.

17. *Les Veillées des chaumières*, October 1939, quoted in Veillon (1995), p. 19.

18. See Hastings (2011), pp. 16–17.

19. Braibant (1940), p. 45. Diary entry 14 September 1939.

20. Sartre (1983).

21. See Quintin Hoare's introduction in Sartre (1984), p. ix.

22. On 29 September the Communist deputies started calling themselves "the Worker and Peasant Group" *(le Groupe Ouvrier et Paysan)*.

23. Amouroux (1997), p. 101.

24. See Amouroux (1997), pp. 184–185.

25. De Beauvoir (1990a), p. 96. Diary entry 17 October 1939.

26. De Beauvoir (1990a), pp. 20–21. Diary entry 3 September 1939.

27. Braibant (1940), p. 88. Diary entry 10 October 1939.

28. Braibant (1940), p. 38. Diary entry 8 September 1939.

29. Léautaud, vol. 12 (1962), p. 319. Diary entry 29 October 1939.

30. Junot (1998), p. 23.

31. Missika (2001), p. 35.

32. De Beauvoir (1990a), pp. 111ff; Bair (1990), pp. 221–222.

33. It became *Le Bon Marché* in 1989.

34. An advertisement in *L'Illustration*, 23 December 1939, quoted in Veillon (1995), p. 25.

35. Veillon (1995), p. 24.

36. See Courtois (1980), esp. chapter 3, "À bas la guerre impérialiste," pp. 83–122.

37. Thorez made it to Moscow and was sentenced in absentia to six years imprisonment.

38. Sartre (1995), p. 205. Diary entry 20 November 1939.

39. Sadoul (1977), p. 89. Diary entry 12 December 1939.

40. Sartre (1995), p. 472. Diary entry 23 February 1940.

41. Mousset (1941), p. 95.

42. Sartre (1995), p. 430. Diary entry 17 February 1940.

43. Truffaut (1985), quoted in Ragache (1997), p. 11.

44. Quoted in Veillon (1990), p. 35.

45. Sadoul (1977), p. 106. Diary entry 16 December 1939.

46. Sadoul (1977), p. 109. Diary entry 19 December 1939.

47. Sadoul (1977), p. 108. Diary entry 18 December 1939.

48. Sadoul (1977), p. 111. Diary entry 22 December 1939.

49. Sartre (1995), p. 430. Diary entry 17 February 1940.

50. Sadoul (1977), p. 110. Diary entry 19 December 1939.

51. Sadoul (1977), p. 121. Diary entry end of January 1940.

52. Sadoul (1997), p. 141. Diary entry 27 February 1940.

53. Crémieux-Brilhac (1990), p. 321.

54. Article reproduced in Crémieux-Brilhac (1990), p. 322.

55. See Amouroux (1997), p. 137.

56. See Amouroux (1997), p. 139.

57. See Amouroux (1997), p. 138.

58. A predecessor of *Paris-Match* that was founded in 1949.

59. Junot (1998), p. 16.

60. Sadoul (1997), p. 146. Diary entry 4 March 1940.

61. Giraudoux (1987), p. 116: "Maison de la propagande," 24 December 1939.

62. Giraudoux (1987), pp. 76–77: "Le Front de la démocratie," 27 October 1939. Broadcast to a forum of American intellectuals organised by the *New York Herald-Tribune*. Reproduced in the Paris edition of that newspaper.

63. Giraudoux (1987), p. 76: "Le Front de la démocratie," 27 October 1939.

64. Giraudoux (1987), pp. 79–80: "Le Front de la démocratie," 27 October 1939.

65. Quoted in Michel (1971), p. 205.

66. Monzie, quoted in Maurice Barthélemy, "En Guise d'Introduction," in Giraudoux (1987), p. 14.

67. De Polnay (1957), p. 17.

68. He replaced Daladier on 20 March 1940. Daladier resigned following France's nonintervention against the Soviet Union in Finland.

2. Blitzkrieg and Exodus

1. Junot (1998), p. 51.

2. Ernest May, *Strange Victory* (New York: Will and Wang, 2000), quoted in Jackson (2003), p. 39.

3. Werth (1940), p. 28. Diary entry 12 May 1940.

4. Werth (1940), pp. 29–30. Diary entry 12 May 1940.

5. André Beaufre, *The Fall of France* (London: Cassell, 1967), p. 189, quoted in Jackson (2003), p. 47.

6. Groult and Groult (1962), p. 17. Diary entry 13 May 1940.

7. Werth (1940), p. 39. Diary entry 14 May 1940.

8. Groult and Groult (1962), p. 17. Diary entry 14 May 1940.

9. Groult and Groult (1962), p. 17. Diary entry 15 May 1940.

10. Werth (1940), p. 43. Diary entry 16 May 1940.

11. Quoted in Jackson (2003), p. 10.

12. Quoted in Tombs and Tombs (2007), p. 549.

13. Quoted in Cobb (2009), p. 13.

14. Crémieux-Brilhac (1990), p. 551.

15. Bourget and Lacretelle (1959), p. 9.

16. Quoted in Junot (1998), p. 66.

17. Quoted in Junot (1998), p. 67.

18. Werth (1940), p. 53. Diary entry 18 May 1940.

19. See Junot (1998), p. 68.

20. Werth (1940), p. 51. Diary entry 18 May 1940. "On fout le camp" ("People are clearing off") in French in the text.

21. Crémieux-Brilhac (1990), p. 556.

22. Michel (1981), p. 26.

23. Diamond (2007), p. 35, gives the figure of two million, about a third of the total population. No source is cited.

24. Werth (1940), p. 65. Diary entry 21 May 1940.

25. A large department store on the *grands boulevards*.

26. Werth (1940), p. 70. Diary entry 22 May 1940.

27. Groult and Groult (1962), p. 26. Diary entry 1 June 1940.

28. A total of 338,226 soldiers in all—198,315 British and 139,911 Allied (mostly French). See Jackson (2003), p. 95.

29. Diamond (2007), p. 42.

30. See de Foville (1965), pp. 95–96.

31. De Foville (1965), p. 85.

32. In the rue François-Millet.

33. De Schotten (n.d.).

34. Today, most of the factories have disappeared from the 15th arrondissement, which has become considerably more chic than it was during the 1930s with its concentration of factory workers living around the place Saint-Charles. In May 1936 this constituency was represented by Charles Michel, a Communist *député*.

35. De Foville (1965), p. 57.

36. Groussard, quoted in Walter (1960), p. 20.

37. Bood (1974), p. 21. Diary entry 12 June 1940.

38. Vidalenc (1957), p. 251.

39. Dubois (1946), p. 58.

40. Dubois (1946), pp. 58–59.

41. De Polnay (1957), pp. 33–34.

42. Diamond confirms that "the majority of Parisians who left home were women" and adds "it has been estimated that between a third and a quarter of those on the road were children." Diamond (2007), p. 5.

43. *La Gerbe*, 11 July 1940, quoted in Walter (1960), p. 32.

44. Pierre Mendès France, quoted in Amouroux (1997), p. 327.

45. Ilya Ehrenbourg, *La Chute de Paris* (Paris: Éditions Hier et Aujourd'hui, 1944, p. 432), quoted in Rajsfus (1997), pp. 42–43.

46. Eyewitness account reported in Sadoul (1977), p. 319. Diary entry 13 June 1940.

47. Sadoul (1977), p. 319. Diary entry 13 June 1940. Orléans is almost 70 miles from Paris.

48. Maurois (1940), p. 201. In the end, Maurois managed to fly to London and then went on to the United States. He arrived in New York in the autumn and spent the rest of the war there. Because he was Jewish (born Émile Salomon Herzog) and because he had left France, he was frequently the object of ferocious attacks in the collaborationist Paris press during the Occupation. See Loyer (2005), esp. pp. 112–115.

49. Buisson (2008), p. 50.

50. At Concarneau.

51. Groult and Groult (1962), pp. 32–33. Diary entry 9 June 1940.

52. Werth (1992), p. 14.

53. Werth (1992), p. 17.

54. Werth (1992), p. 30.

55. Werth (1992), p. 38.

56. Werth (1992), p. 48.

57. Bianca Bienenfeld was a student of de Beauvoir's who was involved in a triangular relationship with Sartre and de Beauvoir. She appears in their writings as Louise Védrine. When the posthumously published Sartre/Beauvoir correspondence revealed how Sartre and de Beauvoir actually perceived her, Bienenfeld had a nervous breakdown. For Bienenfeld's own account, see Lamblin (1993).

58. De Beauvoir (1990a), p. 307. Diary entry 11 June 1940.

59. Sadoul (1977), p. 363. Diary entry 16 June 1940.

60. The first elections in which women had the right to vote were held in 1945.

61. See Ollier (1970), p. 169.

62. Anne Jacques, *Journal d'une française* (Paris: Seuil, 1946, p. 38), quoted in Buisson (2008), p. 54.

63. This case is reported in Diamond (2007), p. 77.

64. Werth (1992), p. 40.

65. See Diamond (2007), p. 56.

66. Sadoul (1977), p. 320. Diary entry 13 June 1940.

67. Buisson (2008), p. 60. Buisson gives no source for this figure.

68. Diamond (2007), p. 63.

69. Gabriel Danjou, *Exode 1940* (Paris: Alternance, 1960, pp. 111–112), quoted in Rajsfus (1997), pp. 41–42.

70. Arved Arenstam, quoted in Lottman (1992), p. 239.

71. Bourget (1970), p. 39.

72. Ollier (1970), p. 156.

73. Ollier (1970), p. 156.

74. Guidez (1989), pp. 25–26.

75. Amouroux (1997), pp. 335–337.

76. Amouroux (1997), pp. 354–355.

77. Quoted in Langeron (1946), p. 17. Diary entry 11 June 1940.

78. Langeron (1946), p. 18. Diary entry 11 June 1940.

79. Michel (1981), p. 18. Reynaud later denied that he said *in* Paris.

80. Léon Blum, quoted in Bourget (1970), p. 38.

81. See Bourget and Lacretelle (1980), p. 20; p. 14 in 1959 edition.

82. Langeron (1946), p. 18. Diary entry 11 June 1940.

83. J. J. Hiappe, G. Contenot, R. Fiquet, M. de Fontenay, M. Héraud, N. Pinelli, and A. le Troquer.

84. See Bourget (1970), p. 44.

85. Bourget (1970), p. 41.

86. Poster reproduced in Bourget and Lacretelle (1980), p. 21; p. 17 in 1959 edition.

87. An outer suburb of Paris, lying about eight miles to the north of the suburb of Saint-Denis.

88. The confusion stemmed from a mistranslation by a French police officer of *beschossen*, which means fired at, not killed.

89. Lottman (1992), p. 338.

3. Parisians and Germans, Germans and Parisians

1. Goglin and Roux (2004), p. 22.
2. Langeron (1946), p. 40. Diary entry 14 June 1940.
3. Langeron (1946), p. 41. Diary entry 14 June 1940.
4. Archives de la Préfecture de Police de Paris, B/a 1792, Dossier 1. Report of 17 June 1940 from the keeper of the flame at the Arc de Triomphe to the Directeur Général de la Police Municipale on events in Paris on 10–14 June 1940, quoted in Lallam (1999–2000), p. 22.
5. Ehmer (1943), p. 154.
6. Later in the day, at the insistence of some local Paris councillors, the flag was removed.
7. Quoted in Kageneck (2012), pp. 56–57.
8. No force existed that was capable of leading a resistance effort: the army was in disarray and on the run and the government had declared Paris an open city, packed its bags, and gone as had most of its civil servants. The only other force that *might* have been capable of mounting resistance was the French Communist Party (PCF). Paris was one of the party's traditional strongholds. The PCF had its headquarters there and an estimated third of its members lived and worked in the city or its suburbs. But the party leaders' enthusiastic support for the Nazi-Soviet Non-Aggression Pact had severely weakened it: the abrupt switch from being in the vanguard of the anti-fascist struggle to proclaiming that France and Britain's conflict with Germany was an "inter-imperialist war" had caused huge dissention and dislocation in its ranks. Moreover, the PCF had been banned by the French government, its leaders had gone underground, and thousands of its members were being hunted down by the French police and imprisoned.
9. Personal account supplied by Police Commissioner Gaubiac to Pierre Bourget in Bourget (1970), pp. 59–62.
10. Langeron (1946), p. 46. Diary entry 14 June 1940.
11. In the event, neither was punished and both men were later given posts by the French government after it established itself in Vichy. Dentz became high commissioner for French colonies in the Middle East while Groussard was given overall responsibility for the Vichy government's national security services.
12. Quoted in Kageneck (2012), p. 59.
13. Its official title is the Church of Sainte Marie-Madeleine. Meant to be a church, construction began in 1763 but was halted around 1790. In 1806 Napoleon decreed it should be a temple to honour his army, but Louis XVIII later ruled that it should become a church once again and it was finally consecrated in 1845.
14. It was initially built during Louis XIV's reign to house some 4,000 wounded and disabled soldiers. In 1840, the body of Napoleon who had died nineteen years earlier was returned by the British. Napoleon was interred in a specially built tomb in Les Invalides in 1861.
15. Quoted in Kageneck (2012), p. 69.
16. Léautaud, vol. 13 (1962), pp. 82–83. Diary entry 14 June 1940. Léautaud lived at 24, rue Guérard in Fontenay-aux-Roses about five miles from the centre of the city.
17. De Beauvoir (1990a), p. 330. Diary entry 2 July 1940.
18. De Polnay (1957), p. 49.
19. Lottman (1992), p. 349.

20. Léautaud vol. 13 (1962), p. 82. Diary entry 14 June 1940.

21. Dupuy (1940), p. 12.

22. De Polnay (1957), p. 51.

23. Dupuy (1940), p. 17.

24. Lottman (1992), p. 351.

25. De Polnay (1957), p. 50.

26. Lottman (1992), p. 351.

27. Joseph Meister, who, as a child, had been the first patient vaccinated against rabies and who had later worked at the Pasteur Institute, is often cited as another who committed suicide that day, but recent research has revealed this to be incorrect. Carroll and Dufour's research reveals that Meister died not on 14 or 16 June as is frequently asserted but on 24 June; he did not shoot himself but gassed himself and it seems the motivation was guilt arising from the mistaken belief that his wife and family, whom he had sent away from Paris, had died in enemy bombing. See Carroll and Dufour (2013), pp. 32–33. Thanks to Matthew Cobb for drawing this article to my attention.

28. Le Boterf (1974), p. 31.

29. Langeron (1946), p. 62. Diary entry 15 June 1940.

30. Les Halles market dates back to the beginning of the twelfth century. Renovated in the nineteenth century it closed in 1969 and was relocated to Rungis, near Orly airport. The nineteenth-century Les Halles is the setting for Emile Zola's *Le Ventre de Paris* and also features in Orwell's classic reportage, *Down and Out in Paris and London.*

31. Langeron (1946), pp. 69–70. Diary entry 17 June 1940.

32. While in the first one-page issue on 17 June editor Gustave Hervé denounced the "factional parliamentary regime" of the Third Republic, attacked the Versailles Treaty of 1919, and declared that he backed Hitler's claims, the German authorities were less impressed with his romantic call to follow the road that leads to "fraternity between people" and the international community of nations. In the 19 June issue Hervé was more explicit: it was stated that *La Victoire* advocates "the federation of all European nations, large and small, and refuses to accept the subjugation of a single one," a rather different perspective from that of Germany. The next issue (20 June) was *La Victoire*'s last. See Quéval (1945), pp. 13–15.

33. Deutsches Nachrichten Bureau.

34. See Walter (1960), p. 64.

35. Benoît-Guyod (1962), p. 33. Diary entry 17 June 1940.

36. De Beauvoir (1990a), p. 312. Diary entry 30 June 1940.

37. Reynaud was frustrated that his colleagues had refused to accept an offer from Churchill that, as a way of continuing the fight, Britain and France should become a single national entity. Churchill noted in his memoirs that rarely had such a generous proposal encountered such a hostile reception. When President Albert Lebrun invited Pétain to replace Reynaud, the wily octogenarian calmly produced from his pocket a list of people he wanted in his government that he had already prepared having anticipating this eventuality.

38. Poster reproduced in Bourget and Lacretelle (1980), p. 23; 1959 edition p. 24.

39. "C'est le coeur serré que je vous dis aujourd'hui *qu'il faut cesser le combat,*" see Pétain (1989), p. 57.

40. Langeron (1946), pp. 66–67. Diary entry 17 June 1940.

41. Shirer (2002), pp. 412–413.

42. Rist (1983), p. 73. Diary entry 19 June 1940.

43. Humbert (2004), p. 91. Diary entry 20 June 1940.

44. Humbert (2004), p. 92. Diary entry 20 June 1940.

45. Langeron (1946), p. 75. Diary entry 18 June 1940.

46. Audiat (1946), pp. 16–17.

47. Running from the rue Guynemer to the rue de Médicis.

48. Langeron (1946), p. 86. Diary entry 21 June 1940.

49. See Langeron (1946), p. 88. Diary entry 21 June 1940.

50. Langeron (1946), p. 90. Diary entry 21 June 1940.

51. An examination taken at the end of secondary school. Those who pass have an automatic right to proceed to university.

52. Langeron (1946), p. 82. Diary entry 20 June.

53. In a clearing in the Forest of Compiègne, some thirty miles to the north of Paris.

54. This area encompassed the Aisne, the Ardennes, the Meuse, the Meurthe-et-Moselle, and the Vosges.

55. Guéhenno (2002), p. 17. Diary entry 25 June 1940.

56. Groult and Groult (1962), p. 37. Diary entry 18 June 1940. There is a confusion here between Pétain's call for hostilities to cease and the signing of the armistice.

57. Langeron (1946), p. 93. Diary entry 23 June 1940.

58. La Jeunesse étudiante chrétienne.

59. Pierquin (1983), p. 29. Diary entry 11 August 1940.

60. Quoted in Burrin (1995), p. 30.

61. Paul Claudel, *Journal II, 1933–1955* (Paris: Gallimard, 1969, p. 317 [Entry 25 June 1940]), quoted in Burrin (1995), p. 25.

62. Sadoul (1977), p. 378. Diary entry 23 June 1940.

63. Historians and witnesses disagree about the date of Hitler's visit: see Gruat (2010), pp. 40–44. French politician Pierre Mendès France says it was on 15 June; in his diaries, Cardinal Baudrillart, a future advocate of collaboration, gives 16 June; Breker, who accompanied Hitler, asserts it was 23 June as does Herbert Lottman in *The Fall of France*. Albert Speer who was also in Paris with Hitler states it was 28 June, a date put forward by British historian Ian Kershaw in his biography of Hitler. In the 1990 edition of *1940, l'année terrible* leading French historian of the Second World War, Jean-Pierre Azéma opts for 23 June, but in a revised edition *(1940, l'Année noire)* published in 2010 he gives 28 June. To complicate things further, in *Paris juin 1940* Paris prefect of police Roger Langeron claims Hitler made two visits to Paris (18 June and 23 June).

64. Arno Breker, *Paris, Hitler et moi* (Paris: Presses de la Cité, 1970, p. 96), quoted in Cointet (2001), p. 35.

65. Lifar (1965), p. 180.

66. Langeron (1946), p. 101. Diary entry 26 June 1940.

67. Langeron (1946), p. 108. Diary entry 4 July 1940.

68. Quoted in Le Boterf (1974), p. 163.

69. De Châteaubriant had been awarded the prestigious Goncourt literary prize in 1911. Following a visit to Germany in 1935 when he met Hitler, he embraced a cranky quasi-religious vision of Nazism that inspired one of his descrip-

tions of Hitler reaching out to the masses with one hand while clutching God's hand with the other. *La Gerbe*, whose offices were at 23, rue Chauchat (9th arrondissement), was launched on 11 July, the same day that the Œuvre Theatre reopened.

70. Le Boterf (1974), pp. 163–164.

71. Albert Speer, *Inside the Third Reich* (New York: Simon and Schuster, 1970, p. 184), quoted in Riding (2011), pp. 50–51.

72. Legally, they could be increased by 30 percent from 20 December 1941 but theatres were quite slow to introduce the increase. See Serge Added, "L'Euphorie théâtrale dans Paris occupé," in Rioux (1990), p. 326.

73. The four publicly owned stations were Le Poste National, Radio-Paris, Paris-Tour Eiffel, and Paris-PTT. See Karine Le Bal, "Réseaux et méditations culturelles," in Taliano-des-Garets (2012), p. 178, n. 5.

74. Quoted in Cointet (2001), p. 80.

75. Groult and Groult (1962), p. 101. Diary entry 1 October 1940.

76. The owner, Jean Prouvost, had left Paris for Lyons before the Germans arrived with all his staff—except one, a one-eyed Alsatian named Schisselé. It was he who gathered together printers and journalists and relaunched the paper, which by August was selling over 800,000 copies. The relaunch of *Paris-Soir* scuppered Bunau-Varilla's plans of publishing an evening edition of *Le Matin*.

77. Quoted in Amouroux (1998a), p. 361.

78. Quéval (1945), p. 47. This echoed, perhaps deliberately, Maurice Chevalier's hit of the autumn of 1939 "Paris sera toujours Paris" ("Paris will always be Paris").

79. Feyel (1999), p. 175.

80. *Le Matin, Paris-Soir, Les Dernières Nouvelles de Paris*, and *La France au Travail*. See Langeron (1946), p. 108. Diary entry 3 July 1940.

81. Walter (1960), p. 76.

82. Bourget and Lacretelle (1980), p. 27.

83. *Le Matin* (Paris edition), 6 July 1940, p. 1.

84. The air force (Luftwaffe) usually performed in the Luxembourg Gardens near their headquarters in the requisitioned Luxembourg Palace.

85. Langeron refers to a concert on 21 July in front of Notre-Dame attended by about 1,000 people and another three days later on the place de la République in front of a crowd of about 2,000. Langeron (1946), p. 130. Diary entry 24 July 1940. De Folville writes of a concert staged on the place de la Concorde on 12 July in front of a crowd of some 30,000 people, de Folville (1965), p. 286.

86. Dupuy (1940), p. 44.

87. He established himself in the former offices of the French Ministry of Labour in the rue de Grenelle.

88. Noël quoted in Bourget (1970), p. 173.

89. Langeron (1946), p. 116. Diary entry 11 July 1940.

90. Michel (1981), p. 257, gives a figure of 2,278,633 for the twenty arrondissements of Paris when the last census before the war was held in 1936 and 4,138,614 for the Seine department.

The last census before the war (1936) gives the population of Paris as 2,278,633 and of the Seine department as 4,138,614. Michel (1981), p. 257. For population figures 1941–1944, see p. 258.

91. De Beauvoir (1990a), p. 314ff.

92. Mme. D, in *Paris Jour*, 24 June 1940, quoted in Buisson (2008), p. 81.

93. *Le Matin*, 30 July 1940, p. 2.

94. At the Gare de Lyon, 4,000 passengers arrived daily between 22 and 29 July; a week later it rose to between 5,000 and 6,000 a day. The Gare Montparnasse was even busier: on average, 21,000 passengers arrived daily between 29 July and 4 August. Trains arriving at the Gare d'Austerlitz brought back refugees mainly from the centre and southwest of the country of whom about 60 percent were civil servants: on 22 July 6,000 passengers arrived; a day later, 14,000 on eleven trains, including 5,000 demobbed soldiers; and for the next four days, more than 20,000 people arrived daily. Figures quoted in Alary (2010), p. 365.

95. Langeron (1946), p. 121. Diary entry 16 July 1940.

96. Auroy (2008), p. 87. Diary entry 6 July 1940.

97. Bood (1974), p. 36. Diary entry 30 July 1940. "Boche" was a pejorative term for a German, common in France during the First World War.

98. Groult and Groult (1962), p. 56. Diary entry 26 July 1940.

99. De Beauvoir (1990a), p. 311. Diary entry 30 June 1940.

100. De Beauvoir (1990a), p. 312. Diary entry 30 June 1940.

101. Maurice Sachs (1906–1945), an observer of the prewar Paris scene (*le tout Paris*) who was friendly with André Gide, Jean Cocteau, and others. After a brief flirtation with communism he turned to playing the black market, living in a homosexual brothel, and collaborating (despite being Jewish). In 1942, he was sent to Germany to spy on French workers. He formed a relationship with a young Jesuit resister and was arrested and imprisoned. In April 1945, the prisoners were moved out on a forced march. Those who could not keep up were shot on the spot. It is believed this was how Sachs met his end. See Venner (2000), p. 644, and Jackson (2001), pp. 190–191.

102. Quoted in Amouroux (1997), p. 576.

103. Quoted in Amouroux (1997), p. 576.

104. Auroy (2008), p. 95. Diary entry July 1940. She later left the city for the summer and returned again in the autumn.

105. Groult and Groult (1962), p. 52. Diary entry 19 July 1940.

106. Bood (1974), p. 35. Diary entry 30 July 1940.

107. Gex le Verrier (1942), p. 32.

108. Groult and Groult (1962), p. 60. Diary entry 5 August 1940.

109. Groult and Groult (1962), p. 78. Diary entry 22 August 1940.

110. Groult and Groult (1962), p. 78. Diary entry 22 August 1940.

111. See Alary et al. (2006), pp. 150–151.

112. For more on transport during the Occupation, see Borgé and Viasnoff (1975).

113. Groult and Groult (1962), p. 78. Diary entry 22 August 1940.

114. Auroy (2008), pp. 105–106. Diary entry August 1940. Luchon, also known as Bagnères-de-Luchon, is a spa town in the French Pyrenees on the border between France and Spain.

115. Dubois (1946), p. 70.

116. Report from the prefect of the Seine-et-Oise department to the minister of the interior, 9 September 1940, quoted in Junot (1998), p. 225.

117. Léautaud, vol. 13 (1962), p. 73. Diary entry 11 June 1940.

118. De la Hire (1940), p. 85.

119. Amouroux (1997), p. 585.
120. De Beauvoir (1990a), p. 329. Diary entry 2 July 1940.
121. De Beauvoir (1990a), p. 331. Diary entry 2 July 1940.

4. Paris, German Capital of France

1. Einsatzgruppen.
2. Wehrmacht troops also committed atrocities but senior commanders liked to refer to the honour of the German army and to disassociate themselves from the activities of the Einsatzgruppen.
3. Oberkommando der Wehrmacht (OKW).
4. The most comprehensive analysis of the MBF is Eismann (2010). For a detailed review of the structure, see especially pp. 97–137.
5. General Bogislav von Studnitz and General Kurt von Briesen.
6. The Propaganda-Abteilung (Propaganda Section) and its subsidiaries the Propaganda-Staffeln (Propaganda Units).
7. Abetz's associates included Ernst Achenbach, former adviser at the German embassy, who maintained extensive contacts among French and German industrialists; Friedrich Sieburg, prewar Paris correspondent of the *Frankfurter Zeitung* and author of the best-seller, *Dieu, est-il français?* (1929); Friedrich Grimm, vice president of the prewar Franco-German Society.
8. The police was divided into two sections: the Order Police, which dealt with minor offences, and the Reich Security Police (Sicherheitspolizei or Sipo). The Sipo comprised the state political and criminal investigation security agencies, namely the Gestapo (secret state police) and the Kripo (criminal police). In September 1939 the secret police force of the SS and the Nazi Party, the Sicherheitsdienst (or SD), was brought together with the Sicherheitspolizei within the RSHA, thus merging the state agencies and party agencies. The RSHA was headed by Reinhard Heydrich, who answered to Heinrich Himmler, who in turn answered to Hitler.
9. The Geheime Feldpolizei (GFP). Until June 1942, the GFP and the Feldgendarmerie (FG) were commanded and coordinated by the Kommandostab and were responsible for maintaining order. The FG's main duties were carrying out traffic control, ensuring German directives were respected, patrolling the streets, checking identity papers, and liaising with French police. The GFP, whose members were allowed to work in plainclothes, was the executive arm of the Abwehr, and it focused its attention on anti-Reich activities, in particular Resistance efforts. Most of its members were professional police officers. See Eismann (2010), p. 106.
10. The unit then moved into the Hôtel Scribe, later 57 boulevard Lannes, and finally 72, avenue Foch. Once the first bridgehead was established, a second Sonderkommando of about the same size under Hauptsturmführer Kieffer was sent as reinforcements and a third contingent arrived in August under Untersturmführer Nosek with a brief to concentrate on collecting political information. See Delarue (1962), pp. 250ff.
11. The Geheime Staatspolizei. For a short, clear historical overview of the German security forces see Auda (2002), especially pp. 29–39.

12. Langeron (1946), p. 55. Diary entry 15 June 1940.

13. Some had been sent by special train to Montauban as soon as war was declared; others were taken by truck, while yet more were taken out of Paris on steam-powered barges along with 25kg of dynamite so the barges could, if necessary, be blown up rather than have the documents fall into German hands. See Langeron (1946), pp. 55–59. Diary entry 15 June 1940.

14. Langeron (1946), p. 71. Diary entry 17 June 1940.

15. In the rue Cadet (19th arrondissement) and the rue Puteaux (17th arrondissement), respectively.

16. See Rossignol (1981), p. 97.

17. The raiders were assisted in their task by two documents. A 300-page inventory drawn up before the war by German specialists in Paris working under the supervision of Otto Kummel, head of the Berlin museums. They also had an *Inventory of the Archives of French Libraries.* It ran to over 3,000 pages, giving details and locations of the most significant historical documents from Germany's point of view held in the most important archives and libraries in France. See Poulain (2008), p. 20.

18. See also José Corti, *Souvenirs désordonnés* (Paris: Librarie José Corti, 1983, p. 190), quoted in Biélinky (1992), p. 40, n. 9.

19. Léautaud, vol. 13 (1962), p. 138. Diary entry 25 July 1940.

20. Langeron (1946), pp. 103–104. Diary entry 29 June 1940. Charles Mangin, nicknamed "the Butcher," was a strong advocate of the deployment of troops from France's colonies and was alleged by the Germans to have handed over German women to assuage the rapacious sexual appetites of black soldiers. A new statue of Mangin was erected on the avenue de Breteuil in 1957.

21. Edith Cavell was found guilty of treason by a military tribunal and executed by a German firing squad on 12 October 1915. She had been helping hundreds of British, French, and Belgian soldiers escape from German-occupied Belgium. After the war, she was given a state funeral in Westminster Abbey and a memorial to her stands in St. Martin's Place near Trafalgar Square, London. She will soon be featured on a new British £2 coin.

22. Bourget (1979), p. 31.

23. This relatively late enrolment could have been because inscriptions to the Nazi Party were suspended from May 1933. It should not be forgotten that, with Ribbentrop's encouragement, Abetz joined the SS in 1935 and rose to the grade of Brigadeführer. See Burrin (1995), p. 100.

24. Quoted in Bourget (1970), p. 137.

25. For more details on people whose release Abetz secured, see Burrin (1995), pp. 378–379.

26. Denise Ginollin played an active role in the Resistance after June 1941. She was arrested and deported first to the concentration camp at Ravensbruck before being transferred to Mauthausen. After the Liberation she served as a Communist Party député from 1945 to 1951.

27. The Propaganda Abteilung.

28. Jeanne Schrodt.

29. They also included exploring the relaunch of the Communist evening paper *Ce Soir.*

30. It is no coincidence that Abetz took one of the party's slogans *La France au travail* (France at Work) as the name for his paper. See Rossi (1954), pp. 78–81.

31. See Lambauer (2001), p. 152.

32. Rayssac (2007), pp. 149–150.

33. Rayssac (2007), p. 150.

34. Such cinemas were called *Soldatenkinos;* theatres became *Deutsches Soldatentheater.*

35. The previous exchange rate was 1:12.

36. Audiat (1946), p. 20.

37. Auroy (2008), p. 96. Diary entry July 1940.

38. Audiat (1946), p. 20.

39. Audiat (1946), p. 28; Bourget (1970), p. 151.

40. Audiat (1946), p. 28.

41. Officially known as *Nachrichtenhelferinnen.*

42. Audiat (1946), p. 29.

43. *Der deutsche Wegleiter für Paris* (The German Guide for Paris). A selection of articles from this publication are to be found in Anonymous (2013).

44. The Arc de Triomphe, place de la Concorde, the Madeleine, the Opéra, place Vendôme, the Louvre, Notre-Dame, the Palais de Justice, the Luxembourg Palace, the Panthéon, and Les Invalides; the Eiffel Tower, Trocadéro (where Hitler had posed for the camera during his visit), the Sacré-Coeur basilica, and the zoo at Vincennes were listed separately.

45. The information in this paragraph is derived from Gordon (1996), p. 290.

46. Bourget and Lacretelle (1980), p. 37.

47. Léautaud, vol. 13 (1962), p. 128. Diary entry 11 July 1940.

48. Meinen (2006), pp. 88–89.

49. Quoted in Kageneck (2012), p. 71.

50. The only two German cities to have underground transport systems before the Second World War were Berlin (opened in 1902) and Hamburg (opened in 1912).

51. Quoted in Kageneck (2012), p. 70.

52. See Le Marec and Zwang (1995), p. 40. A letter to the German High Command in Paris reproduced in Bourget (1970), p. 106, provides more details. The soldier forced his way into a private home and attacked the woman. He threw her to the ground and beat her repeatedly so hard with a pistol that she had to be taken to hospital, covered in blood with serious injuries to the head and hands. The same letter identifies three German soldiers who had deserted.

53. Buisson (2009), p. 174.

54. See Le Boterf (1975), pp. 151–162.

55. Buisson (2008), p. 291.

56. See Fishman (1991), p 47. Much of what follows is taken from this excellent study.

57. See Fishman (1991), p. 47.

58. See Fishman (1991), p. 49.

59. See Fishman (1991), p. 59.

60. Buisson (2008), pp. 294–295.

61. De Beauvoir (1990a), p. 327. Diary entry 1 July 1940.

62. See Fishman (1991), p. 28.

63. See Fishman (1991), p. 29.

64. See Fishman (1991), p. 64. Sarah Fishman changed the names of her witnesses to protect their anonymity. I am grateful to her confirmation that those

from whose testimonies I have quoted were indeed living in Paris or, in one case, the suburb of Nanterre during the war.

65. Quoted in Deroy and Pineau (1985), p. 28. Many thanks to Hanna Diamond for lending me this document.

66. See Fishman (1991), p. 64.

67. See Fishman (1991), pp. 69–70.

68. See Fishman (1991), p. 71.

69. See Fishman (1991), p. 73.

70. Galtier-Boissière (1944), p. 11. Diary entry 16 August 1940.

71. Mitchell (2008), p. 7.

72. Jean Texcier, *Conseils à l'occupé*, reproduced in Bourget (1979), pp. 54–55.

73. Bourget (1979), p. 55.

74. See Cobb (2009), p. 41.

75. Langeron (1946), p. 64. Diary entry 16 June 1940.

76. Groult and Groult (1962), p. 56. Diary entry 26 July 1940.

77. Pierquin (1983), p. 30. Diary entry 11 August 1940.

78. Guéhenno (2002), p. 41. Diary entry 7 September 1940.

79. Audiat (1946), p. 30.

80. Gex le Verrier (1942), p. 42.

81. Gex le Verrier (1942), p. 42.

82. Biélinky (1992), p. 40. Diary entry 31 July 1940.

83. Claude Aveline, *Le Temps mort* (Paris: Mercure de France, 1962, p. 160), quoted in Cobb (2009), p. 50.

84. Jean Cassou, *Une Vie pour la liberté* (Paris: Robert Laffont, 1981, p. 138), quoted in Blanc (2004), p. 23.

85. Humbert (2004), p. 97. Diary entry 6 August 1940.

86. Humbert (2004), p. 100. Diary entry 18 August 1940.

87. Bourget (1970), pp. 81–83.

88. Langeron (1946), pp. 147–148. Diary entry 13 August 1940.

89. See Bourget (1970), p. 83.

90. See Mitchell (2008), p. 19.

91. On 20 August, Pétain appointed General Fornel de la Laurencie to replace Noël as Vichy's official representative in Paris in the hope that a soldier would be more acceptable to the German military authorities than a civilian.

92. See Atkin (2000), p. 187. See also Atkin (2001), esp. p. 62.

93. De Beauvoir (1990b), p. 155. Letter dated 11 July 1940 in the afternoon.

94. Groult and Groult (1962), p. 52. Diary entry 19 July 1940.

95. Auroy (2008), p. 95. Diary entry July 1940.

96. See Biélinky (1992), pp. 12–32; and Friedländer (2009), pp. 196–197.

97. Biélinky (1992), pp. 39–40. Diary entries 26 July and 29 July 1940.

98. Bood (1974), p. 36. Diary entry 30 July 1940.

99. Pétain (1989), p. 73.

100. Paris Prefecture of Police, *La Situation à Paris: Rapports de la quinzaine*, 19 August 1940.

101. Paris Prefecture of Police, *La Situation à Paris: Rapports de la quinzaine*, 9 September 1940; 16 September 1940.

102. Quoted in Grenard (2008), p. 40.

103. Groult and Groult (1962), p. 64. Diary entry 6 August 1940.

104. Groult and Groult (1962), pp. 77–78. Diary entry 22 August 1940.

105. Léautaud, vol. 13 (1962), pp. 161–162. Diary entry 30 August 1940.

106. See, for example, Jackson (2001), especially pp. 142–165. For an analysis of the Révolution nationale, see Cointet (2011), esp. pp. 211–345.

107. See Paxton (1982), p. 171.

108. Lambauer (2001), p. 155.

109. Hitler had been taken aback by the speed and ease with which France was conquered and remained remarkably coy about his intentions concerning the country's future. In *Mein Kampf* (1925–1927), he had rejected France's "unacceptable desire to impose its hegemony on Europe" and referred to France as the enemy that hates Germany; but aside from wishing to crush France no details were given as to what should happen should France be defeated. Some clarification came with a directive issued by the government of the Third Reich on 9 July 1940: "In the future, France will play the role of a 'bigger Switzerland' and will become a tourist destination as well as undertaking some production for the fashion industry. Supporting any attempt by the French government to establish an authoritarian regime would therefore make no sense at all. Any form of government which appeared to want to make France powerful again would be opposed by Germany" (quoted in Thalmann [1991], p. 15).

110. Memorandum from Abetz, 30 July 1940, on "Political Work in France"; extracts reproduced in Cointet and Cointet (2000), p. 11. My emphasis.

111. Otto Abetz, *Histoire d'une politique franco-allemande*, quoted in Assouline (2006), p. 367.

112. See Lambauer (2001), p. 160.

113. Wolff-Metternich, who was finally dismissed in the summer of 1942, was decorated after the war by the French state for his attempts to protect its art treasures during the Occupation.

114. Communication dated 17 September 1940 from Field Marshal Wilhelm Keitel, head of the Supreme High Command of German Armed Forces to the MBF, reproduced in Valland (2014), pp. 235–236.

115. Nicholas (1994), pp. 125–126.

116. Quoted in Rossignol (1981), p. 105.

117. André Combes, *La Franc-maçonnerie sous l'Occupation* (Paris: Éditions du Rocher, 2001), see Amouroux (2005), pp. 481–482.

118. Guéhenno (2002), p. 45. Diary entry 19 September 1940.

119. R. de Beauplan, *L'Illustration*, 12 October 1940, quoted in Rossignol (1981), p. 94.

120. Amouroux (1997), p. 687.

121. Faÿ had been active in circles of the Far Right in the 1930s, and in 1937 he was one of the co-founders of the Comité du rassemblement national pour la reconstruction de la France (Committee for a National Movement for the Reconstruction of France) whose principles anticipated those of Pétain's National Revolution.

122. See Delarue (1993), p. 25.

123. The co-called Marchandeau Law of 21 April 1939 amended an 1881 law on the press.

124. See, for example, Winock (2004), esp. pp. 105–215; Benbassa (1997), esp. pp. 215–249; Hyman (1998), esp. pp. 91–159.

125. Langeron (1946), p. 134. Diary entry 29 July 1940.
126. Poznanski (1997), p. 49.
127. Biélinky (2011), pp. 41–42. Diary entry 8 August 1940.
128. Biélinky (2011), p. 45. Diary entry 20 August 1940.
129. See Biélinky (2011), p. 47. Diary entry 29 August 1940.
130. Biélinky (2011), p. 40. Diary entry 1 August 1940.
131. Biélinky (2011), p. 45. Diary entry 22 August 1940.
132. Biélinky (1992), p. 46. Diary entry 25 August 1940.
133. Langeron (1946), p. 124. Diary entry 18 July 1940.
134. Langeron (1946), p. 140. Diary entry 3 August 1940; p. 144. Diary entry 7 August 1944.
135. Langeron (1946), p. 155. Diary entry 26 August 1940.
136. Today part of the northern suburbs of Paris.
137. Biélinky (1992), p. 50. Diary entry 6 September 1940.
138. Wieviorka (1986), p. 62.

5. Unemployment, Rationing, Vichy against Jews, Montoire

1. Langeron (1946), pp. 158–161. Diary entry 1 September 1940.
2. Figures quoted in Milward (1970), p. 292.
3. Renault, for example had only 2,000 workers compared with 25,000 before the war; Citroën had 1,550 instead of 21,000. See Michel (1981), p. 180.
4. Of more than one million POWs "as winter approached," an estimated 537,000 POWs came from the Paris region, a figure that fell to about 300,000 by April 1941, according to figures quoted in Courtois (1980), p. 170.
5. Michel (1981), pp. 180–181.
6. Michel (1981), p. 180–181.
7. Michel (1981), p. 181.
8. See Chapter 7 for more details.
9. Michel (1981), p. 200.
10. Langeron (1946), p. 167. Diary entry 16 September 1940.
11. *Aujourd'hui,* 13 September 1940, quoted in Walter (1960), p. 94.
12. Assouline (2006), p. 359.
13. The Bernhard List.
14. See Galtier-Boissière (1944), p. 16. Diary entry end of September 1940.
15. The German hostility to psychoanalysis meant that Karl Jung was also on the proscribed list.
16. Jacob was Jewish by birth but was baptised as a Catholic during the First World War.
17. Assouline (2006), pp. 374–375. As part of the anti-Semitic cultural offensive, the Sarah Bernhardt Theatre (named in memory of a famous French actress) was renamed the Théâtre de la Cité, although it continued to be advertised, even in the German press, as the ex-Théâtre Sarah Bernhardt; the standard school history textbook known as Mallet and Isaac became "Mallet" alone, even though Jules Isaac had done most of the writing of it.
18. Mitchell (2008), p. 30.
19. See Simonin (2008), p. 14.

20. Biélinky (2011), p. 51. Diary entry 16 September 1940.

21. Guéhenno (2002), p. 45. Diary entry 19 September 1940.

22. Benoît-Guyod (1962), p. 121. Diary entry 30 October 1940.

23. Veillon (1995), p. 116.

24. Biélinky (1992), p. 55. Diary entry 25 September 1940.

25. Pierquin (1983), p. 31. Diary entry 15 September 1940.

26. Besson (n.d.), p. 40.

27. Langeron (1946), p. 168. Diary entry 21 September 1940.

28. Bobkowski (1991), pp. 180–181. Diary entry 19 December 1940.

29. In the 6th arrondissement near Odéon between the boulevard Saint-Germain and the Seine.

30. Benoît-Guyod (1962), p. 113. Diary entry 10 October 1940.

31. Paris Prefecture of Police, *La Situation à Paris: Rapports de la quinzaine*, 30 September 1940. My emphasis.

32. Veillon (1995), pp. 101–102.

33. For more on "Otto" Brandl, see Delarue (1993), esp. pp. 27–61.

34. For a reproduction of a blank card, see, for example, Paxton et al. (2009), p. 67.

35. Guéhenno (2002), p. 68. Diary entry 20 November 1940.

36. Auroy (2008), p. 116. Diary entry not specified, probably October 1940.

37. They were concentrated in five arrondissements, the 11th around La Bastille, the 20th farther to the east around Belleville, the 18th in the north of the city, the 3rd and the adjacent 4th, which included the Marais.

38. Kaspi (1997), pp. 28–29.

39. For the breakdown of the Jewish population in Paris, see Poznanski (1992), p. 27.

40. Langeron (1946), p. 131. Diary entry 25 July 1940.

41. See Josephs (1989), p. 28. Josephs does not give a reference for this quotation.

42. Robert Debré, *L'Honneur de vivre* (Paris: Stock, 1974, p. 214), quoted in Kaspi (1997), p. 95.

43. Wieviorka (1986), p. 59.

44. Jean Giraudoux, *Pleins pouvoirs* (Paris: Julliard, 1994, p. 66 [First published, 1939]), quoted in Badinter (1997), p. 26.

45. See Marrus and Paxton (1995), p. 36.

46. Lambauer (2001), pp. 199–200.

47. Eismann (2010), p. 181.

48. Thus, when considering how to calibrate their response to any sabotage or assassination attempts it was decided to drop the term "reprisals" *(Vergeltungsmassnahmen)* which was a controversial term, and replace it with "repressive measures" *(Strafmassnahmen)* or "expiatory measures" *(Sühnemassnahmen)*, both of which were implicitly recognised under Article 50 of the Hague Convention. See Eismann (2010), p. 125: for more on the legal/political dynamic, see Eismann (2010), pp. 123–134.

49. Representatives of both the justice and police units of the MBF agreed on this. Bargatzy (Justice): "Given that all the measures taken against the Jews as such and taken *only* against the Jews are targeting a group which is not only racial but religious, these are justified under Article 46 of the Hague Convention in so far as

they are motivated by concerns about security." Bardenhauer (Police): "There is no doubt at all about the hostile attitude adopted towards the Third Reich by Jews in the Occupied Zone. It follows that the Jewish population in the Occupied Zone constitutes a continuing threat for the occupying troops." Eismann (2010), p. 180.

50. A Jew was defined using a religious criterion, namely anyone practising the Jewish religion who had two or more Jewish grandparents (again defined by religious practice).

51. The posters bore the phrases *Entreprise juive* and *Jüdisches Geschäft*.

52. A total of 113,462 Jewish males and females over fifteen years of age from Paris and the suburbs registered: about 28,989 were born in France, some 28,502 were naturalised French citizens, and nearly 55,849 were foreign nationals, almost half of whom (26,158) were Poles. See Rayski (1992), p. 23. Personal details were filed on a multicoloured card index system known as the "Tulard File," named after the French police official who devised it.

53. A street in the 11th arrondissement near the place de la Nation inhabited by a large number of mainly Jewish families from Poland.

54. Edgar Morin, *Vidal et les siens* (Paris: Éditions du Seuil, 1989, p. 264), quoted in Semelin (2013), p. 195.

55. Poznanski (1997), p. 60.

56. Foss and Steinberg (1996), p. 49.

57. An anonymous, thirty-six page typewritten document, covering the period from September 1940 to spring 1941 probably written by a left-wing Zionist. See Rayski (1992), p. 23.

58. The number of small shops displaying a yellow poster in the poor areas was as follows: 740 (3rd arrt), 717 (10th arrt), 746 (11th arrt), 517 (18th arrt), 496 (20th arrt); those in well-off areas in the west of the city: 69 (16th arrt), 192 (17th arrt). Figures relating to small shops displaying yellow posters taken from Poznanski (1997), pp. 62–63.

59. Biélinky (2011), p. 57. Diary entry 4 October 1940.

60. Biélinky (2011), p. 57. Diary entry 5 October 1940.

61. An area in the Marais district with a high concentration of small Jewish-owned shops.

62. Biélinky (2011), pp. 63–64. Diary entry 25 October.

63. Biélinky (2011), p. 61. Diary entry 14 October 1940.

64. Biélinky (2011), p. 64. Diary entry 25 October 1940.

65. Auroy (2008), p. 147. Diary entry February 1941.

66. See Rochebrune and Hazera (1995), p. 540.

67. Auroy (2008), p. 147. Diary entry 1941.

68. Auroy (2008), p. 147. Diary entry 1941.

69. The first Statut des Juifs was passed on 4 October 1940 and published on 18 October 1940. When Raphaël Alibert, Vichy's minister of justice in 1940 and architect of the law, was tried in 1947 no evidence was found of any official or unofficial contact with the German authorities over this law, let alone any pressure on Vichy from the Germans to introduce it. See Marrus and Paxton (1995), p. 5.

70. Under the French legislation, a Jew was defined as "anyone who has three grandparents of the Jewish race or two grandparents of the same race if his/her spouse is Jewish." See Rémy (1992), p. 87.

71. *Le Matin*, 18 October 1940, quoted in Poznanski (1997), p. 61.

72. Guéhenno (2002), p. 57. Diary entry 19 October 1942.

73. Rist (1983), p. 99. Diary entry 20 October 1940.

74. Groult and Groult (1962), p. 114. Diary entry 17 October 1940.

75. Close to the Champs-Elysées, just west of the place de la Concorde.

76. Quoted in Rossignol (1981), p. 121.

77. Thérive (1948), pp. 36–37.

78. See Amouroux (2005), p. 494.

79. Letter received by Faÿ on 22 November 1940, quoted in Rossignol (1981), p. 118. The officer delegated to supervise Faÿ's work was an SS police lieutenant, August Moritz (real name Rodolph Noterman), who in 1943, after his transfer to Lyons, took part in the assassination of human rights activist Victor Basch and his wife. See Poulain (2008), p. 111.

80. Léautaud, vol. 13 (1962), p. 192. Diary entry 13 October 1940.

81. Schroeder (2000), p. 55. Diary entry 19 October 1940.

82. Auroy (2008), p. 117. No precise date given, probably October 1940.

83. Badia (1995), p. 12.

84. Badia (1995), p. 12.

85. E—babies and children under three; minors aged 3–21 were divided into two categories J1, J2; adults aged 21–70 were classified as A; those over 70 as V with extra allocations supposedly reflecting need; a J3 category was subsequently added as were subcategories for pregnant women and workers with especially demanding jobs.

86. Auroy (2008), p. 119. No date given, probably end of October or beginning of November 1940.

87. Bood (1974), p. 41. Diary entry 10 October 1940.

88. Badia (1995), p. 12.

89. 26 October 1940, quoted in Cotta (1964), p. 90.

90. 26 October 1940, quoted in Cotta (1964), p. 91.

91. "Monsieur le Maréchal, merci," *Le Petit Parisien*, 24 October 1940, p. 1.

92. Letter reproduced in Junot (1998), pp. 229–233. See esp. pp. 229–230.

93. Langeron (1946), pp. 183–184. Diary entry 29 October 1940.

94. Guéhenno (2002), p. 60. Diary entry 26 October 1940.

95. Rist (1983), p. 100. Diary entry 26 October 1940.

96. Benoît-Guyod (1962), pp. 119–120. Diary entry 26 October 1940.

97. Groult and Groult (1962), p. 119. Diary entry 27 October 1940.

98. See Pétain (1989), pp. 94–96.

99. Bourget (1970), p. 207.

100. Pétain (1989), p. 95.

101. *Aujourd'hui*, 15 and 16 November 1940, quoted in Ory (1995), pp. 63–64.

102. Langeron (1946), p. 185. Diary entry 30 October 1940.

6. From Mass Street Protest to the "Führer's Generous Gesture"

1. Letter from de la Laurencie to Pétain, 27 October 1940, reproduced in Junot (1998), pp. 232–233.

2. See Buisson (2008), p. 107.

3. Luneau (2005), p. 93.

4. Langeron (1946), p. 181. Diary entry 28 October 1940.

5. Lallam (1999–2000), p. 88.

6. Bood (1974), p. 83. Diary entry 18 February 1941.

7. Lallam (1999–2000), p. 87.

8. Schroeder (2000), p. 68. Diary entry 13 February 1941.

9. Lallam (1999–2000), p. 93.

10. Thérive (1948), pp. 24–25. Diary entry October 1940.

11. Thérive (1948), pp. 25–26. Diary entry October 1940.

12. Thérive (1948), p. 27. Diary entry October 1940.

13. Mitchell (2008), p. 15.

14. At the 11th hour on the 11th day of the 11th month.

15. This symbolic site lies under the Arc de Triomphe on the place de l'Étoile (today the place Charles de Gaulle) at the top of the Champs-Élysées.

16. Quoted in Tandonnet (2009), p. 97.

17. Bood (1974), p. 42. Diary entry 6 November 1940.

18. Tandonnet (2009), p. 67.

19. Before the war, Paul Langevin had been a fellow-traveller, a leading member of the League of Human Rights, and a member of the famous anti-fascist committee of intellectuals (Comité de vigilance des intellectuels antifascistes). He was arrested on 30 October 1940.

20. However, Claude Lalet, one of the organisers, was stopped a fortnight later and found to be in possession of the names of nineteen comrades. All the people on the list were arrested, and three months later sentenced to between three months and one year in prison.

21. Amouroux gives the name both as Baudoin [Amouroux (1998a) and Baudouin [Amouroux (2005), p. 621].

22. Tandonnet (2009), p. 112.

23. See Tandonnet (2009), p. 250.

24. Guéhenno (2002), p. 66. Diary entry 15 November 1940.

25. Bood (1974), pp. 45–46. Diary entry 11 November 1940.

26. See Tandonnet (2009), p. 131ff.

27. Monchablon (2011) puts the number of demonstrators at 3,000, but Pierre Daix, a Communist militant who was present, thinks this number is too high and points out that as it was dark at 6 p.m. making an accurate estimate of numbers was almost impossible. See Daix (2013), pp. 24–25. A police report estimated that by 6 p.m. about 24,500 people had walked past the Arc de Triomphe, and although the report records more than 1,500 bunches of flowers and fifty-eight wreathes being left there is apparently no mention of the huge cross of Lorraine in flowers carried by de Schotten and Dubost (or Dufort as Amouroux refers to him). See Amouroux (2005), p. 621.

28. Bood (1974), p. 46. Diary entry 11 November 1940.

29. Bood (1974), p. 49. Diary entry 23 November 1940.

30. David Schoenbrun, *Soldiers of the Night: The Story of the French Resistance* (London: Hale, 1981, p. 94), quoted in Cobb (2009), p. 47.

31. Léautaud, vol. 13 (1962), p. 216. Diary entry 15 November 1940.

32. This was with the connivance of Paul Rivet, the head of the museum and the friend of Cassou.

33. Letter from Humbert to Georges Friedman, 23 November 1940, quoted in Blanc (2010), p. 145.

34. Friends of René Creston, a sociologist at the Musée de l'Homme, living in Brittany passed on drawings of the submarine pens and the huge dry dock at

Saint-Nazaire. The plans were forwarded to London and used in a British assault on the Saint-Nazaire shipyards in March 1942 when a British destroyer packed with explosives crashed into the dock gates. Railway workers in the Resistance network headed by Robert Fawtier, professor of medieval history at the Sorbonne, provided information about troop movements. See Cobb (2009), pp. 53–54.

35. Lambauer (2001), p. 192.
36. Quoted in Chadwick (2002), p. 150.
37. See Chadwick (2002), pp. 150–151.
38. For more on the NRF in June 1940–June 1941, see Hebey (1992).
39. See Simeone (2006), pp. 27–28. My thanks to Renée Stewart for bringing this article to my attention.
40. Mitchell (2008), pp. 27–28.
41. Lambauer (2001), p. 240.
42. Burrin (1995), p. 305.
43. Bobkowski (1991), p. 178, quoted in Burrin (1995), p. 305.
44. Alfred Fabre-Luce, quoted in Burrin (1995), p. 305.
45. Bood (1974), p. 49. Diary entry 21 November 1940.
46. Bood (1974), p. 70. Diary entry 17 January 1941.
47. Badia (1995), p. 12.
48. In his diary entry for 16 November 1941, Charles Rist reflected on how tobacco had become a form of currency, "a means of acquiring other things." See Rist (1983), pp. 208–209.
49. One of the earliest references to the black market was in *Le Petit Parisien* on 21 September 1940.
50. "Comment lutter contre le marché noir" ("How to Fight the Black Market") in *L'Œuvre*, 24 October 1940, quoted in Grenard (2008), p. 18.
51. Paris Prefecture of Police, *La Situation à Paris: Rapports de la quinzaine*, 27 January 1941.
52. Paris Prefecture of Police, *La Situation à Paris: Rapports de la quinzaine*, 20 January 1941.
53. Grenard (2008), p. 47.
54. Grenard (2008), p. 49.
55. Paris Prefecture of Police, *La Situation à Paris: Rapports de la quinzaine*, 27 January 1941.
56. See Grenard (2008), p. 32.
57. Prefecture of Police, *La Situation à Paris: Rapports de la quinzaine*, 27 January 1941.
58. See Grenard (2008), pp. 37–39.
59. Le Boterf (1975), p. 121.
60. Jamet et al. (1975), p. 135.
61. Jamet et al. (1975), p. 125.
62. Auroy (2008), p. 117. Undated entry, probably October 1940.
63. Guéhenno (2002), p. 56. Diary entry 16 October 1940.
64. Amouroux (1997), p. 603.
65. Auroy (2008), p. 120. Undated diary entry.
66. Auroy (2008), p. 123. Diary entry, probably December 1940.
67. Schroeder (2000), p. 57. Diary entry 28 November 1940.
68. Georges Duhamel, *Chronique des saisons amères*, quoted in Veillon (1995), p. 135.

69. In the nearby rue d'Anjou (8th arrondissement) between the Madeleine and Gare Saint-Lazare railway station.

70. Omnès (1991), pp. 22–23.

71. Declaration by Hitler to high-ranking members of the German military, 4 November, quoted in Jäckel (1968), p. 178.

72. Pierquin (1983), p. 37. Diary entry 27 December 1940.

73. Pétain did this by inviting all his ministers to tender their resignations but only accepted those of Laval and of the minister for state education (instruction publique), Georges Ripert, who really did want to resign.

74. Marcel Déat, *L'Œuvre*, 2 November 1940, quoted in Veillon (1984), p. 83.

75. Quoted in Bourget (1970), pp. 252–253.

76. Quoted in Lambauer (2001), pp. 266–267.

77. Guéhenno (2002), pp. 79–80. Diary entry 15 December 1940.

78. Rist (1983), p. 117. Diary entry 15 December 1940.

79. Diary entry by General Laure, quoted in Bourget (1970), p. 263.

80. Guéhenno (2002), p. 80. Diary entry 15 December 1940.

81. Guéhenno (2002), p. 80. Diary entry 15 December 1940.

82. Pierquin (1983), p. 38. Diary entry 27 December 1940.

83. Pierquin (1983), p. 38. Diary entry 27 December 1940.

84. Langeron (1946), p. 212. Diary entry 15 December 1940.

85. Galtier-Boissière (1944), p. 25. Diary entry 15 December 1940.

86. Fabre-Luce (1946), p. 316.

87. Pierquin (1983), p. 38. Diary entry 27 December 1940.

88. Abetz and de Brinon had known each other when frequenting Franco-German circles between the wars. De Brinon shot to fame in 1933 when he published the first of his interviews with Hitler. He was a man much more to Abetz's ideological liking than de la Laurencie and, like Abetz, he had been accused before the war of being a German spy.

89. Singer (1992), p. 159.

90. Carcopino, a personal friend of Pétain's, had replaced Gustave Roussy as *recteur* after the 11 November demonstration.

91. Singer (1994), pp. 193–194.

92. Veillon (1984), pp. 236–237.

93. It had taken place in Herblay, a small town about twelve miles northwest from the centre of Paris, today part of the suburbs.

94. For eyewitness accounts, see Bourget (1970), pp. 278–279.

95. Bonsergent, the youngest of nine children, was born in Brittany in September 1912. He had studied at the École des Arts et Métiers in Angers. After the June defeat he had found work in a factory in the northern suburbs of Saint-Denis.

96. Schroeder (2000), p. 62. Diary entry 21 December 1940.

97. Guéhenno (2002), p. 85. Diary entry 25 December 1940.

98. Biélinky (2011), p. 84. Diary entry 25 December 1940.

99. Biélinky (2011), p. 84. Diary entry 26 December 1940.

100. Schroeder (2000), p. 63. Diary entry 31 December 1940.

101. Bood (1974), p. 62. Diary entry 31 December 1940.

7. Protests, Pillaging, "V" for Victory, the First Roundup of Jews

1. Luneau (2005), p. 119.

2. Cardinal Baudrillart, *Les Carnets du cardinal* (Paris: Le Cerf, 1998, p. 774), quoted in Luneau (2005), p. 119.

3. Auroy (2008), pp. 134–135. Diary entry January 1941.

4. Bood (1974), p. 63. Diary entry 1 January 1941.

5. Léautaud, vol. 13 (1962), p. 258. Diary entry 2 January 1941.

6. Guéhenno (2002), p. 89. Diary entry 3 January 1941.

7. Groult and Groult (1962), p. 151. Diary entry 3 January 1941.

8. Léautaud, vol. 13 (1962), p. 263. Diary entry 5 January 1941.

9. Levert (1994), pp. 121–125.

10. Mathieu (2011), p. 95.

11. Auroy (2008), p. 136. Diary entry January 1941.

12. Auroy (2008), p. 136. Diary entry January 1941.

13. Bood (1974), p. 65. Diary entry 5 January 1941.

14. Auroy (2008), p. 143. Diary entry February 1941.

15. Auroy (2008), p. 145. Diary entry February 1941.

16. Schroeder (2000), pp. 64–65. Diary entry 10 January 1941.

17. Brasillach (1955), p. 163.

18. Auroy (2008), p. 140. Diary entry January 1941.

19. Léautaud, vol. 13 (1962), p. 301. Diary entry 4 March 1941.

20. Galtier-Boissière (1944), p. 37. Diary entry 13 February 1941. The ubiquitous rutabaga (swede) came to epitomise the dreadful state of food provisions. Before the war it was considered suitable only for cattle. Jacques Biélinky wrote on 6 February 1941, "Everyone has ended up disgusted by rutabaga: you can find it everywhere, you don't need tickets to buy it nor to queue, but its nutritional value is mediocre" [Biélinky (1992), p. 96]. From February 1942 it could be bought only using tickets.

21. Quoted in Halami (1976), p. 43. The Lido opened in March 1941.

22. Groult and Groult (1962), pp. 163–164. Diary entries 28 and 29 January 1941.

23. Schroeder (2000), p. 66. Diary entry 17 January 1941.

24. Groult and Groult (1962), p. 154. Diary entry 11 January 1941.

25. Groult and Groult (1962), p. 190. Diary entry 5 April 1941.

26. Veillon (1990), p. 83.

27. Bood (1974), p. 203. Diary entry 9 July 1943. Micheline was travelling free on the Métro using a German *Ausweis* that she had forged. The German policeman who took her away took pity on her and did not charge her.

28. See Delarue (1993), p. 68.

29. See Aziz (1984), pp. 53–62, esp. p. 54; Delarue (1993), pp. 17–140.

30. Grenard (2008), p. 46.

31. Desprairies (2009), p. 35.

32. Quoted in Sanders (2001), p. 175.

33. Directive signed by Göring, 5 November 1940. Reproduced in Valland (2014), p. 72.

34. Wolff-Metternich, quoted in Rayssac (2007), p. 240.

35. Nicholas (1994), p. 131.

36. See Nicholas (1994), p. 132.

37. Nicholas (1994), p. 133.
38. Whenever he was in Paris, Göring would stay in a spacious apartment at the Ritz that was permanently at his disposal. He also had a sumptuous office at the quai d'Orsay, which had previously been used by President Poincaré. On his desk stood an inkstand that had belonged to the famous French diplomat Talleyrand.
39. Valland (2014), p. 95.
40. Valland (2014), p. 187.
41. Valland (2014), p. 105.
42. See Luneau (2005), p. 104.
43. MBF report quoted in Mitchell (2008), p. 30.
44. Bourget and Lacretelle (1959), p. 49.
45. Léautaud, vol. 13 (1962), p. 277. Diary entry 30 January 1941.
46. Quoted in Veillon (1995), p. 129.
47. In April, Nordmann was sentenced to two years imprisonment.
48. Humbert (2004), p. 121. Diary entry 5 February 1941.
49. See Humbert (2004), pp. 127–128. Diary entry March 1941.
50. In the rue Geoffroy-Saint-Hilaire.
51. Blanc (2010), p. 391. For more on the Musée de l'Homme network, see also Humbert (2004); Blanc (2000), 89–103; Cobb (2009), esp. pp. 50–57; Blumenson (1977).
52. See Jackson (2001), p. 405.
53. Thorval (2007), pp. 26–27.
54. Information given by Dominique Desanti and Simone Devouassoux-Debout, the two surviving members of Socialisme et Liberté at a meeting at the Gimpel and Müller gallery, rue Guénégaud, Paris, on 27 April 2008.
55. For more on Socialisme et Liberté, see Cohen-Solal (1985), pp. 224–244.
56. Desanti et al. (2004), p. 77.
57. Amouroux (1998a), p. 589.
58. See Lambauer (2001), p. 295.
59. See Lambauer (2001), p. 280.
60. See Lambauer (2001), p. 272.
61. See Lambauer (2001), p. 296.
62. Quoted in Le Marec and Zwang (1995), p. 61.
63. Claude Varennes, *Le Destin de Marcel Déat* (Paris: Éditions Jeanmaray), quoted in Tournoux (1982), p. 90.
64. Jackson (2001), p. 193.
65. Auroy (2000), p. 151. Diary entry March 1941.
66. See Luneau (2005), p. 132.
67. Guéhenno (2002), p. 120. Diary entry 24 March 1941.
68. Schroeder (2000), p. 86. Diary entry 30 May 1941.
69. Bood (1974), pp. 92–93. Diary entry 28 March 1941.
70. Bourget and Lacretelle (1959), p. 55.
71. Auroy (2008), p. 151. Diary entry March 1941.
72. Pierquin (1983), p. 45. Diary entry 21 March 1941.
73. Pierquin (1983), p. 45. Diary entry 21 March 1941.
74. Pierquin (1983), p. 46. Diary entry 21 March 1941.
75. Bood (1974), p. 98. Diary entry 12 April 1941.

76. Bood (1974), p. 102. Diary entry 27 April 1941.

77. Bood (1974), p. 106. Diary entry 9 June 1941.

78. Bood (1974), pp. 106–107. Diary entry 9 June 1941.

79. Xavier Vallat, quoted in Delarue (1962), p. 276. Vallat was appointed by Pétain as the first head of the CGQJ (Commissariat général aux questions juives).

80. "The CGQJ was responsible for the preparation of all laws relating to the removal of Jews from the French body politic, for the implementation of all the government decrees concerning Jews, for the encouragement of other government ministries to do likewise, for the liquidation of Jewish property, for the appointment of trustees to do this, for the supervision of these trustees, and for the initiation of police measures against Jews as dictated by the general interest." Billig, *Le Commissariat général aux questions juives*, 3 vols. (Paris: Éditions du Centre, 1955–1960), p. 76, quoted in Callil (2006), p. 231.

81. See Callil (2006), p. 230.

82. Sézille was directly answerable to Baron von Behr, who headed Rosenberg's ERR in Paris.

83. For more on Montandon, see Chevassus-au-Louis (2004), pp. 185–198.

84. By March 1940, the camps held over 3,000 Communists arrested and held after the crackdown on the party. They were then expanded in size and number to accommodate some 350,000 foreigners, including Republican refugees who had crossed the Pyrenees into France after the victory of Franco's forces in the Spanish Civil War as well as anti-fascist refugees from Germany and Austria. Arthur Koestler was at Le Vernet camp, which he described in his account, *Scum of the Earth*, as "below the level of Nazi concentration camps"; at the camp at Gurs, in the Pyrenees, thirty people had died every day during the 1940–1941 winter. For more on the French camps, see Peschanski (2002).

85. Rayski (1992), pp. 60–62.

86. My thanks to Alan Riding and Jacques Toros for this letter.

87. His father was deported to Auschwitz in June 1942. Adler (1987), p. ix.

88. Minc (2006), p. 115.

89. BBC scripts quoted in Luneau (2005), pp. 152–153.

90. *Paris-Soir*, 11 May 1941, p. 2, quoted in Luneau (2005), p. 154.

91. Luneau (2005), pp. 156–157.

8. Resistance and Repression

1. Montefiore (2004), p. 317.

2. The Barbarossa offensive was named in tribute to Frederick I of Barbarossa, head of the Holy Roman Empire in the thirteenth century, who set off to recapture Jerusalem from Saladin.

3. By the second week in July, over 600,000 Russians had been taken prisoner. See Evans (2009), p. 179.

4. General Gotthard Heinrici, quoted in Evans (2009), p. 179.

5. Guidelines issued on 19 May ordered troops to take "ruthless and energetic action against Bolshevik agitators, irregulars, saboteurs, Jews and the total elimination of all active and passive resistance." Quoted in Evans (2009), p. 175. In practice, this served as a justification for killing anybody.

6. Lukacs (2006), p. 7. In February 1941 Hitler had told General Bock that a German defeat of Russia would convince Britain it was hopeless to fight on. See Bock (1996), p. 197. He reiterated his intention to invade Russia to senior army commanders a month later. See Bock (1996), p. 206.

7. At a meeting on 2 May to discuss the invasion and Occupation, the German army's planning secretariat recorded, "1. The war can only be continued if the entire Wehrmacht is fed from Russia in the third year. 2. If we take what we need out of the country, there can be no doubt that many millions will die of starvation." See Hastings (2011), pp. 141–142. For more on the background to Germany's invasion of Russia, see Kershaw (2008), pp. 54–90; Evans (2009), pp. 160–178; Mazower (2009), pp. 140–157.

8. See Montefiore (2004), p. 323.

9. See Ferro (2012), pp. 326–329. Russia agreed to establish links with the Free French but emphasised that this did not imply recognition.

10. Rist (1983), p. 172. Diary entry 22 June 1941.

11. See Mitchell (2008), p. 47.

12. See Rossi (1954), p. 189.

13. Auroy (2008), p. 168. Diary entry June 1941.

14. Bood (1974), p. 108. Diary entry 22 June 1944.

15. Schroeder (2000), p. 89. Diary entry 9 August 1941.

16. Humbert (2004), p. 173.

17. Thurman (1999), p. 454.

18. Groult and Groult (1962), p. 203. Diary entry 25 June 1941.

19. Thomas (1995), p. 138. Diary entry 22 June 1941.

20. Maurice Baudot, "L'Opinon publique devant l'invasion de la Russie," *Revue d'histoire de la deuxième guerre mondiale* 64 (October 1966), quoted in Bourget (1970), pp. 292–293.

21. Guéhenno (2002), pp. 155–156. Diary entry 23 June 1941.

22. Rist (1983), p. 172. Diary entry 25 June 1941.

23. Pierquin (1983), p. 60. Diary entry 23 June 1941.

24. Bobkowski (1991), p. 205. Diary entry 22 June 1941.

25. Fauxbras (2012), p. 40. Diary entries 22 June 1941 and 5 July 1941.

26. Léautaud, vol. 14 (1963), p. 18. Diary entry 21 July 1941.

27. Delarue (1993), p. 147.

28. Rebatet (1976), p. 20.

29. On 22 June at the PPF conference in Villeurbanne in the outskirts of Lyons in the Unoccupied Zone Doriot called for the creation of such a force and promised he would be among the first volunteers to leave; on 23 June, Eugène Deloncle, leader of the Mouvement social révolutionnaire, wrote to Pétain advocating the creation of a Legion of Volunteers.

30. Costantini (n.d.), p. 1.

31. Darlan gave his approval in August. Although Pétain was at that time equivocal, in November he endorsed the LVF in a letter prepared by de Brinon which was used for LVF propaganda and publicity purposes. See Ferro (2012), p. 331.

32. At this point the former grudgingly tolerated it and the second did not try to ban it.

33. Bourget and Lacretelle (1980), pp. 56–57.

34. In January 1942 the LVF central committee moved its headquarters to 19, rue Saint-Georges in the 9th arrondissement.

35. See Giolitto (2007), pp. 40–44.

36. Report of the Renseignements généraux (21 August 1941), quoted in Bourget (1970), pp. 301–304.

37. Doriot's active commitment boosted his position within the PPF and in the intense in-fighting that raged among the collaborationists behind the façade of unity built around the LVF. In addition, Doriot's enhanced status would act as protection, if needed, against Pierre Pucheu, a die-hard opponent of Doriot and the PPF who was appointed minister of the interior in the Vichy government in mid-July. See Wolf (1969), p. 349.

38. Entry for 21 August, quoted in Brunet (1986), p. 367.

39. Abetz took these men at their word and told Hitler the LVF was capable of supplying between 80,000 and 100,000 men. See Giolitto (2007), p. 47.

40. Bourget (1970), p. 305. There are a number of reasons for the low number of volunteers. The thought of setting off in a German uniform to fight in Russia might have had more appeal to some if it was clear that the plan was enthusiastically backed by Germany or the French government. However, despite claims by LVF organisers that Hitler and Pétain approved the initiative, it was obvious that neither Vichy nor Berlin was offering much active support for the LVF. The continuing presence of the Germans on the streets of Paris was a constant reminder of France's defeat: few men were willing to risk their lives for the country that had been the root cause of food and fuel shortages for the past year or so and which still held hundreds of thousands of POWs. Even if someone was tempted, there was the fear of opprobrium from friends and family and the risk of being assaulted if they were spotted in a German uniform.

41. See Langeron (1946), pp. 216–218. Diary entries 3 January 1941–20 January 1941.

42. Letter intercepted between 15 April and 15 May 1944, quoted in Giolitto (2007), pp. 71–72.

43. Christian de la Mazière, former member of the LVF and the French Waffen SS, quoted in Ophuls (1980), p. 173.

44. Kageneck (2012), p. 166.

45. Figures quoted in Burrin (1995), p. 439.

46. "Souvenirs d'un volontaire de la légion antibolchevique" (New Delhi: Bureau d'information de la France combattante, 1943), p. 1, quoted in Giolitto (2007), p. 77.

47. A single man received 1,800 francs a month if he was in France; 2,400 if he was on active service. The rate for married soldiers was 2,400 and 3,000, respectively. There were daily bonuses for those volunteers involved in combat and for those with children. See Giolitto (2007), p. 46.

48. Giolitto (2007), p. 51.

49. See Evans (2009), p. 187.

50. They need not have worried. Although the first detachment did not leave until September the battle on the Eastern Front had a good while yet to run.

51. Thomas (1995), pp. 141–142. Diary entry 23 July 1941.

52. Auroy (2008), p. 173. Diary entry August 1941.

53. Rist (1983), p. 176. Diary entry 23 July 1941.

54. Guéhenno (2002), p. 167. Diary entry 25 July 1941.

55. Guéhenno (2002), p. 167. Diary entry 25 July 1941.

56. Auroy (2008), p. 173. Diary entry August 1941.

57. The Bataillons de la jeunesse were formally part of the Communist Party's Organisation spéciale (Special Organisation), which provided protection for leaflet distributors and oversaw sabotage actions. However, the Bataillons de la jeunesse enjoyed a high degree of autonomy. For more on the Bataillons de la jeunesse from an orthodox PCF view, see Ouzoulias (1967). For a view that is critical of the PCF leadership's role see Daix (2013). This text, written by a leader of the OS, draws on Daix's personal experience reviewed in the light of material published in Berlière and Liaigre (2004).

58. Communist involvement in resistance activities before June 1941 remains an extremely controversial issue. While individual Communists carried out acts of sabotage against German installations, the *official* party line was to assert that the war was an anti-imperialist conflict, to attack Vichy as reactionary and conservative and denounce de Gaulle as a tool of British capital. However, in the months before the German invasion of Russia the clandestine *L'Humanité* became increasingly anti-German, calling for united action to secure the independence of France. For more on this, see, for example, Courtois (1980); Azéma (1986); Avakoumovitch (1980); Avakoumovitch (1981); Avakoumovitch (1983); Bourderon and Willard (1983); Pike (1993); Rossi (1954); Imlay (2005).

59. Guy Môquet was the son of Prosper Môquet, Communist deputy for the 17th arrondissement, who was interned by the French authorities in March 1940. Guy Môquet was arrested in October 1940, was released briefly in January 1941, was detained again under an administrative order, and was eventually transferred to Choisel in May 1941. He was chosen for execution as a hostage on the morning of 22 October 1941 and shot later that day along with twenty-seven others from the same camp. He is often seen as the symbol of the anti-Nazi resistance by French youth although Communist leaflets produced and distributed at the time of his arrest targeted de Gaulle, the British, and the Vichy government rather than the Nazi occupiers. Like Jacques Bonsergent, Guy Môquet has a Paris Métro station named after him. For more on Môquet, see Berlière and Liaigre (2009).

60. Lévy-Osbert (1992), p. 37.

61. See Lévy-Osbert (1992), pp. 37–38.

62. Lévy-Osbert (1992), pp. 39–40.

63. Berlière and Liaigre (2004), p. 52.

64. Amouroux (1998a), pp. 657–658.

65. Bourget and Lacretelle (1980), p. 62.

66. Le Comité de coordination des oeuvres de bienfaisance juives du Grand Paris was created in January 1941 following pressure from Dannecker. See Laffitte (2003), pp. 27–39.

67. Quoted in Rayski (1992), p. 62.

68. See Laffitte (2003), pp. 32–34.

69. Rayski (1992), p. 63.

70. Biélinky (1992), pp. 135–136.

71. Jean Guéhenno asserts there were demonstrations and clashes at both points. See Guéhenno (2002), p. 177. Diary entry 17 August 1941.

72. Other accounts specify German motorcycles with side cars, which is more likely. See, for example, Ouzoulias (1967), p. 98.

73. Lévy-Osbert (1992), p. 48.

74. A hospital on the Île de la Cité between Notre-Dame Cathedral and the Prefecture of Police.

75. Paris Prefecture of Police, *La Situation à Paris: Rapports de la quinzaine*, 18 August 1941.

76. Information on all three incidents taken from Paris Prefecture of Police, *La Situation à Paris: Rapports de la quinzaine*, 18 August 1941.

77. Maurice Le Berre, Jacques d'Andurain, and Marcel Bourdarias. See Berlière and Liaigre (2004), pp. 100–101 and p. 284.

78. His mother, the wealthy Marquise d'Andurain with whom he lived in a sumptuous villa in the well-heeled suburb of Neuilly-sur-Seine, was a familiar figure on the Paris social circuit. She was also a cocaine addict, an opium smuggler, involved in the murky world of spying, and possibly a triple agent working for the British, French, and Germans. She was murdered in 1948 and her body was recovered from the Bay of Tangiers. See Berlière and Liaigre (2004), p. 99.

79. Berlière and Liaigre (2004), pp. 100–101.

80. Paris Prefecture of Police, *La Situation à Paris: Rapports de la quinzaine*, 18 August 1941.

81. Bobkowski (1991), p. 212. Diary entry 18 August 1941.

82. Brustlein (1989), pp. 102–103.

83. Rizo attributed by Brustlein (1989), p. 96. Besides fundamental differences with Communists over issues of revolutionary organisation and the role of the state, many anarchists believed that violent acts by individuals could hasten a revolution whereas Communist orthodoxy held such actions, divorced from workers' struggles, would only alienate the working class, who were, they believed, destined by history to be the revolutionary vanguard.

84. See Brustlein (1989), p. 96.

85. Gautherot was born in Paris in 1920 and worked as a metal worker in Gentilly. "Titi" Tyszelman was born in Poland in 1921. He and his mother had come to Paris in 1924 to join Titi's father, who had arrived the year before; the family was naturalised in 1939. See Ouzoulias (1967), pp. 100–101.

86. Lévy-Osbert (1992), p. 50.

87. Vichy was simply informed the day before the roundup began, see Wieviorka and Laffitte (2012), p. 25.

88. In the second half of August, the police recorded 502 political slogans and leaflets there compared with 193 in the 19th arrondissement, 129 in the 12th, 78 in the 20th, and 48 in the 9th. The same pattern continued through September, October, and November 1941, thus "conferring on the 11th arrondissement the privilege of being the most active in the capital from the point of view of Communist propaganda." Berlière and Liaigre (2004), p. 106.

89. Charonne, Voltaire, Saint-Ambroise, and Oberkampf.

90. Except American Jews. See Wieviorka (1986), p. 106. Hitler was keen not to antagonise the United States, but the number of American Jews living in the 11th arrondissement would have been tiny. In May 1941, only foreign and stateless Jews had been arrested after being summoned to report to the police; this time about 1,000 French citizens were among those detained, including some 150 veterans from both world wars and about forty lawyers.

91. For example, a Dr. Samuel Steinberg was picked up by two French police officers during an identity check outside the railway station in Neuilly. See Rajsfus (2004), p. 31.

92. The Société des transports en commun de la région parisienne.

93. Wieviorka and Laffitte (2012), p. 31; Epelbaum (2009), p. 103.

94. Israel (1975), pp. 111–112.

95. The Prefecture of the Seine Department had only been told at the last minute about Drancy being used as a holding camp for Jews but managed nevertheless to provide about 1,000 bunk-beds. See Anon. (2010), p. 4.

96. Israel (1975), p. 113.

97. Epelbaum (2009), p. 117.

98. Christian Lazare, quoted in Rajsfus (2004), p. 84.

99. See Rajsfus (2004), p. 85.

100. See Rajsfus (2004), p. 85.

101. Epelbaum (2009), p. 109.

102. Wieviorka and Laffitte (2012), pp. 66–67.

103. See Rajsfus (2004), p. 84.

104. Epelbaum (2009), pp. 112–114.

105. Witness statement, quoted in Epelbaum (2009), p. 117.

106. "Gabriel Ramet to his mother and sister, 1 September 1941," in Sabbagh (2002), p. 23.

107. For more on the early days at Drancy, see Wellers (1973), p. 126ff; Wieviorka and Laffitte (2012), esp. pp. 21–32; Rajsfus (2004), esp. pp. 29–76.

108. Brustlein (1989), p. 113.

109. Some writings refer to an earlier assassination of a German officer as he left a brothel near the Porte d'Orléans (see, for example, Amouroux [1998a], p. 668). In their extensive research, Berlière and Liaigre found no contemporaneous mention of this attack and conclude it is probably a legend. See Berlière and Liaigre (2004), pp. 101–102.

110. In a letter to the military command in Fontainebleau, Schaumburg specified that the number of hostages executed should be "in accordance with the severity of the deed," which might lead to the death sentences of "several Jewish-Communist leaders." For details, see Mitchell (2008), pp. 48–49.

111. André Bréchet, Emile Bastard, and Abraham Trzebucki. See Ouzoulias (1967), p. 133.

112. The proposal was put forward by Jean-Maris Ingrand, the French Ministry of Interior's representative in Paris and Fernand de Brinon, the government's representative in Paris. See Jäckel (1968), pp. 269–271.

113. The Gaullists were Honoré d'Estienne d'Orves, Berlier and Yan Doornik; the Communists were Nogarède, Ottino, Sigonney, Rapinat, and Justice. See · Ouzoulias (1967), p. 134.

114. Although Laval had no direct involvement in the LVF, he was contacted by a close friend of Eugène Deloncle, the leader of the MSR, who insisted that he attend the passing-out parade. Laval found this idea ridiculous but was present nonetheless.

115. The Germans had banned the playing of the Marseillaise by the military band. See Giolitto (2007), p. 58.

116. LVF meetings were among the very rare public events when the French flag was allowed to be flown and when people were permitted to sing the Marseillaise.

117. The authorities were quick to blame "the Communists" while rumours proliferated alleging a settling of scores among the collaborationists. However, it would seem most likely that Collette was acting alone. He was sentenced to death

commuted to a life sentence of hard labour. He was deported in 1943 and, after the war, returned to his native Normandy. In 1984 he was awarded the *Légion d'honneur*. See Giolitto (2007), pp. 58–69.

118. Kupferman (1987), p. 307.

119. Quoted in Kupferman (1987), p. 308.

120. Guéhenno (2002), p. 182. Guéhenno appears to have got the date wrong. The diary entry is for 26 August and he says the newspapers carried the story of the attempted assassination "yesterday morning."

121. Paris Prefecture of Police, *La Situation à Paris: Rapports de la quinzaine*, 1 September 1941.

122. Ernest Hoffmann was hit in the left shoulder outside the Hôtel Terminus-Est, 5, boulevard de Strasbourg, in the 10th arrondissement on 3 September 1941 See Berlière and Liaigre (2004), p. 285.

123. Cardon-Hamet (2005), p. 34.

124. See Mitchell (2008), p. 49.

125. *Le Matin*, 17 September 1941, p. 1.

126. Arrested for taking part in 14 July demonstration. See Biélinky (2011), p. 149, n. 90.

127. Groult and Groult (1962), p. 218. Diary entry 17 September 1941.

128. Fauxbras (2012), p. 71. Diary entry 22 September 1941.

129. Fauxbras (2012), p. 75. Diary entry 28 September 1941.

130. Fauxbras (2012), p. 75. Diary entry 29 September 1941.

131. Mitchell (2008), p. 50.

132. Thomas (1995), p. 151. Diary entry 28 September 1941.

133. Mitchell (2008), p. 55.

134. The structure of the police organisations in Paris was extremely complex. At the forefront of the anticommunist offensive were the Brigades spéciales (Special Brigades). The BS1 were created in September 1939 by the Daladier government and they kept an up-to-date database of known and suspected Communists, which had been started with the formation of the PCF in 1920; the BS1 were placed under the Renseignements généraux (which dealt with matters pertaining to political security). The Brigades spéciales 2 (created in January 1942) concentrated on identifying, arresting, and brutally interrogating people they suspected of carrying out or planning "terrorist attacks."

135. See note 59.

136. See Ferro (2012), pp. 344–345; Amouroux (1998), pp. 705–709, esp. p. 707, for the text of a letter from the subprefect to the German military commander in Châteaubriant explicitly citing Pucheu's involvement.

137. Amouroux (1998a), p. 704.

138. Bood (1974), p. 118. Diary entry 19 September 1941.

139. Lévy-Osbert (1992), p. 52. Albert Ouzoulias, leading cadre of the Bataillons de la jeunesse alongside Pierre Georges, echoes this point of view. "To go out one evening onto the streets of Paris, to wait for an officer or a Nazi soldier and execute him—you have to understand what that means for an eighteen-year-old, or for any other man. This struggle was made even more difficult given that the majority of the population did not yet understand it and the vast majority, at this particular time, condemned the actions of the guerrillas." Ouzoulias (1967), pp. 119–120.

140. Naïtchenko (2003), p. 247.

141. On his return from the Nantes mission, a leading cadre of the PCF told Brustlein, "On behalf of the leadership of the Party. I say this to you: 'Well done guys. Now let's get Stülpnagel.'" Brustlein (1989), p. 156.

142. For example, see *L'Humanité* (25 September): "Now the German soldiers are starting to kill their own officers. There have been mutinies but now Stülpnagel is using anything as an excuse to execute hostages." Two days later another clandestine Communist paper claimed the Barbès killing of Moser in August was a settling of scores between officers over a sexual matter. Towards the end of the year (5 December) after a bomb attack on a German hotel in the rue Championnet on 26 November *L'Humanité* trumpeted: "The famous restaurant which was blown up in the 18th arrondissement was nothing but a brothel for the exclusive use of Germans. It could only have been a Nazi who blew up this building." See Courtois (1980), p. 225.

143. Brustlein (2011).

144. Guéhenno (2002), p. 202. Diary entry 26 October 1941.

145. Badia (1995), pp. 17–18. This testimony needs to be treated with caution for, as Badia admits "it is difficult today for me to recall exactly what I felt then about these questions."

146. Radio broadcast, 21 September 1941, reproduced in Pétain (1989), pp. 184–185.

147. Guéhenno (2002), p. 187. Diary entry 22 September 1941.

148. Radio broadcast, 22 October 1941, reproduced in Pétain (1989), pp. 203–204.

149. See Luneau (2005), pp. 170–171.

150. Bood (1974), p. 118. Diary entry 19 September 1941.

151. Audiat (1946), p. 137.

152. Guéhenno (2002), p. 187. Diary entry 20 September 1941.

153. Biélinky (2011), pp. 144–145. Diary entry 2 September 1941.

154. Auroy (2008), p. 169. Diary entry July 1941.

155. Poster reproduced in Bourget and Lacretelle (1980), p. 77.

156. Auroy (2008), pp. 170–171. Diary entry July 1941.

157. An early 1930s building set between the boulevard des Italiens, the rue Louis-le-Grand, the rue de la Michodière, and the rue de Hanovre. It was inaugurated as the Palais de Hanovre but took the name Palais Berlitz shortly afterwards when the Berlitz language school established itself there.

158. See Kaspi (1975); Kaspi (1997), pp. 104–110.

159. See Desprairies (2008), p. 57.

160. Roger Berg, "Les Attentats contre les synagogues en 1941," quoted in Klarsfeld (1987), p. 38.

161. Those on the rue de la Victoire, rue Notre-Dame-de-Nazareth, rue Sainte-Isaure, rue Copernic, rue Chasseloup-Laubat, rue des Tournelles, and rue Pavée.

162. At the synagogue in the rue Pavée (4th arrondissement).

163. Biélinky (2011), p. 155. Diary entry 10 October 1941.

164. Roger Berg, "Les Attentats contre les synagogues en 1941," quoted in Klarsfeld (1987), p. 40.

9. Resistance, Punishment, Allied Bombs, and Deportation

1. Paris Prefecture of Police, *La Situation à Paris: Rapports de la quinzaine*, 18 August 1941.

2. Paris Prefecture of Police, *La Situation à Paris: Rapports de la quinzaine*, 25 August 1941.

3. The sending of potatoes was outlawed. As was meat, except for poultry and game weighing up to 3kg. People were allowed to send 5kg of asparagus, 2kg of mushrooms, 10kg of fresh fruit and citrus fruits, 1kg of tripe and offal, 5kg of tinned vegetables, 1kg of tinned fish, and two dozen eggs. See Veillon (1995), p. 174, n. 29.

4. Veillon (1995), p. 176.

5. Sauvy (1978), p. 134. Sauvy identifies the wealthy areas as the 7th, 8th, 9th, and 16th arrondissements.

6. Dubois (1946), p. 130. Also quoted in Veillon (1995), p. 176, n. 34.

7. See Veillon (1995), p. 176.

8. Auroy (2008), pp. 184–185. Diary entry end of October 1941.

9. Auroy (2008), p. 185. Diary entry end of October 1941.

10. Auroy (2008), p. 184. Diary entry end of October 1941.

11. Schroeder (2000), p. 110. Diary entry 19 November 1941.

12. Galtier-Boissière (1944), p. 103. Diary entry 26 November 1941.

13. Schroeder (2000), p. 110. Diary entry 19 November 1941.

14. Fauxbras (2012), p. 84. Diary entry 21 November 1941.

15. Schroeder (2000), p. 108. Diary entry 12 November 1941.

16. Schroeder (2000), p. 109. Diary entry 12 November.

17. Bood (1974), p. 121. Diary entry 11 November 1941.

18. Bobkowski (1991), p. 244. Diary entry 16 December 1941.

19. Bobkowski (1991), p. 244. Diary entry 16 December 1941.

20. Bobkowski (1991), p. 249. Diary entry 23 December 1941.

21. Bobkowski (1991), p. 295. Diary entry 5 February 1942.

22. For an extensive list, see Le Marec and Zwang (1995), pp. 90–91. The authorisation had originally been decreed by the Vichy government in October 1941; they were allegedly removed in order to recycle the metal. See Perrault (1987), p. 27. For more on this, see Poisson (2006).

23. Guéhenno (2002), p. 231. Diary entry 7 January 1942.

24. Auroy (2008), p. 207. Diary entry January 1942. The Square Vintimille has been renamed the Square Berlioz.

25. Biélinky (2011), p. 180. Diary entry 3 January 1942.

26. Biélinky (2011), p. 173. Diary entry 22 December 1941.

27. Auroy (2008), p. 199. Diary entry December 1941.

28. Bood (1974), p. 128. Diary entry 25 January 1942.

29. Wieviorka and Laffitte (2012), p. 37.

30. For conditions in Drancy, see Wieviorka and Laffitte (2012), pp. 33ff; report by André Baur, in Biélinky (2011), pp. 287–290; Poznanski (1997), pp. 266 ff.

31. Wieviorka and Laffitte (2012), pp. 44–45; Renée Poznanski gives the figure of "about 30 deaths" between 20 October and 5 November, see Biélinky (2011), p. 162, n. 108.

32. Noël Calef, *Camp de représailles* (Paris: Éditions de l'Olivier, 1997), p. 335 and p. 369, quoted in Wieviorka and Laffitte (2012), p. 44.

33. Biélinky (2011), p. 163. Diary entry 12 November 1941.

34. Biélinky (2011), p. 164. Diary entry 14 November 1941.

35. See Daix (2013), esp. chapter 9.

36. In September, there were twenty-five anti-German attacks; in November the number had fallen to thirteen. See Berlière and Liaigre (2004), p. 245.

37. Berlière and Liaigre (2004), p. 141.

38. Berlière and Liaigre (2004), p. 246.

39. Pierre Tourette, Georges Tondelier, Louis Coquillet, Maurice Le Berre, Pierre Georges (Colonel Fabien), Marcel Bourdarias, and Maurice Feferman. See Berlière and Liaigre (2004), p. 288.

40. Galtier-Boissière (1944), p. 106. Diary entry 8 December 1941.

41. This was a joint exercise carried out by members of the Bataillons de la jeunesse and the OS.

42. Auroy (2008), p. 189. Diary entry 2 December 1941.

43. Auroy (2008), pp. 189–190. Diary entry 2 December 1941.

44. Joseph Kerscher was shot and wounded in an attack on the boulevard de Magenta in the 10th arrondissement. The attack took place around 11:30 P.M.

45. The LVF recruitment station was based in local offices of the RNP. The attack took place late in the afternoon but caused little damage.

46. Major Friese was attacked at about 8:30 P.M. at the junction of the rue de Seine and the rue Clément (6th arrondissement). He was shot twice in the hip.

47. Fauxbras (2012), p. 87. Diary entry 5 December 1941.

48. Lieutenant Paul Rahl was shot in the stomach and seriously injured. The attack took place at the junction of the rue Rennequin and the boulevard Pereire.

49. At 171, rue de la Convention in the 15th arrondissement.

50. Text reproduced in Bood (1974), pp. 123–124. Diary entry 8 December 1941.

51. Guéhenno (2002), p. 221. Diary entry 8 December 1941.

52. Biélinky (2011), p. 169. Diary entry 9 December 1941.

53. Auroy (2008), pp. 194–195. Diary entry 9 December 1941.

54. Bood (1974), p. 124. Diary entry 8 December 1941. In the event, on 14 December the 6 o'clock curfew was lifted. "What a shame," wrote Micheline Bood. See Bood (1974), p. 125.

55. The Germans ordered the Union générale des israélites de France (General Union of the Israelites of France, UGIF) to collect the billion francs as reparation for the attacks on German soldiers although no evidence existed that any of the perpetrators were Jewish. The UGIF had recently been created by Vichy (29 November 1941) and replaced all other Jewish organisations. The creation of such an organisation made it easier for both the German occupiers and Vichy to control and coordinate anti-Jewish policy. The Germans anticipated four payments of 250 million francs each, the first of which was due on 15 January. To raise the money for the fine, the UGIF appealed to the French authorities for a loan based on the value of Jewish goods that had been confiscated and Jewish bank accounts that had been frozen. A consortium of twenty-nine banks and the Bank of France advanced the loan and paid themselves back by raiding the accounts of the more

wealthy Jews. See Poznanski (1997), pp. 281–282. According to Biélinky, individual Jews with a monthly income of more than 13,000 francs a month would be "fined," but there appears to be no evidence that this happened. Biélinky noted wryly that he did not even earn 13,000 francs a year. See Biélinky (2011), p. 174.

56. It was widely believed at the time that this was a result of Germany's declaration of war on the United States, which occurred the previous day. However, the rafle had been planned before the Japanese attack on Pearl Harbor (7 December) and was part of the reprisal policy in France as announced by Stülpnagel. Most of those arrested were deported to Auschwitz in March 1942.

57. Eismann (2010), p. 271.

58. Jean-Jacques Bernard, *Le Camp de la mort lente: Compiègne, 1941–1942* (Paris: Albin Michel, 1944), quoted in Kaspi (1997), p. 216.

59. Michel (2012), p. 203 and p. 218.

60. Wieviorka and Laffitte (2012), pp. 107–108. According to Gaël Eismann, the hostages included sixty-seven "anarchists" and "Communists" held by the French authorities of whom fifty-one were Jews; nineteen Communists who had been condemned by French courts and at least two Communists condemned by German courts. See Eismann (2010), p. 562.

61. Galtier-Boissière (1944), pp. 108–109. Diary entry 15 December 1941.

62. Bobkowski (1991), p. 240. Diary entry 8 December 1941.

63. Paris Prefecture of Police Report, 27 December 1941, quoted in Peschanski (1997), pp. 131–132.

64. Pétain (1989), p. 216.

65. For the transcript of the whole speech, see Pétain (1989), pp. 211–216.

66. Guéhenno (2002), pp. 230–231. Diary entry 3 January 1942.

67. Bood (1974), p. 126. "However much you might love a Boche—and at our age it's never very serious (especially in my case)—but he's still a Boche. I'd have too many regrets if I gave my first kiss to a man I didn't know and who is an enemy." Diary entry 21 December 1941.

68. Auroy (2008), p. 200. Diary entry 15 December 1941.

69. Biélinky (2011), p. 181. Diary entry 10 January 1942.

70. Groult and Groult (1962), pp. 245–246. Diary entry 4 January 1942.

71. Guéhenno (2002), p. 216. Diary entry 28 November 1941.

72. Bobkowski (1991), p. 259. Diary entry 1 January 1942.

73. Guéhenno (2002), p. 229. Diary entry 1 January 1942.

74. Guéhenno (2002), p. 232. Diary entry 24 January 1942.

75. Schroeder's father was born in the United States in 1897. He fought in France during the First World War and met and married a French woman. Liliane was born in France in October 1920. Her father left her mother and returned to the United States in 1935 but the divorce was finalized only later, hence the arrest of Liliane's mother by the Germans.

76. Schroeder (2000), p. 119. Diary entry 17 December 1941.

77. Groult and Groult (1962), p. 244. Diary entry 31 December 1941.

78. This should not be taken as an endorsement of the view that before June 1941 the German authorities had always acted leniently when dealing with resisters and opponents of the Occupation. Within the Occupied Zone from June 1940 those accused of anti-German activities were hauled before German military tribunals where they were tried in camera in German before three military judges.

Evidence gathered against the accused was not made available to him/her and there was no right of appeal. Between June 1940 and July 1941 there were 162 calls for the death sentence, of which forty-two were carried out. Between June 1941 and May 1942, 80 percent of the 493 death sentences were carried out. See Blanc (2010), pp. 425–426, drawing heavily, as he acknowledges, on Gaël Eismann, "La Politique de 'maintien de l'ordre et de la sécurité' conduit par le Militärbefehlshaber in Frankreich et ses services, 1940–1944," doctoral dissertation presented at the Institut d'études politiques de Paris, 2005.

79. Close to Orly airport.

80. Humbert (2004), pp. 189–190. Diary entry Fresnes prison, 8 January 1942.

81. Humbert (2004), p. 191. Diary entry Fresnes prison, 8 January 1942.

82. Humbert (2004), p. 191. Diary entry Fresnes prison, 8 January 1942.

83. The account of the trial is drawn essentially from Blumenson (1977), esp. pp. 227ff.

84. Agnès Humbert was so impressed with Roskothen's conduct that she sent him a signed copy of her diary after its publication in 1946.

85. Guéhenno (2002), p. 242. Diary entry 24 February 1942. Guéhenno knew or knew of those who had been executed as they all worked in education (although Guéhenno initially thought that three women had been executed as well as the seven men). Paulhan, one of the pioneers of the intellectual resistance and a co-editor of the clandestine Resistance publication *Les Lettres françaises,* had close links with the Musée de l'Homme network and in May 1941, two months after Vildé's arrest, he was quizzed about a duplicator he had hidden for the group. When Vildé and Lewitsky were arrested, he had dismantled the machine and dropped the pieces into the Seine. Paulhan was released without charge following the intercession of the collaborationist writer Drieu La Rochelle, whom Abetz had brought in to replace Paulhan as editor of the NRF.

86. See Eismann (2010), pp. 294–297.

87. Quoted in Eismann (2010), p. 290.

88. Junger arrived in Paris in April 1941 and two months later was living in the Hôtel Raphaël. This establishment was close to the MBF headquarters in the Hotel Majestic, where he maintained an office until 1944.

89. Jünger (2008), p. 288. Diary entry 3 March 1942.

90. Hatry (1974), p. 2. My thanks to Michel Rapoport who obtained a copy of this document for me.

91. The first commissioner was Carl Schippert, who had headed the Mercedes offices in Paris. After six months he was replaced by his deputy Prince von Urach, also from Mercedes (Paris), who remained in the post until the Liberation. See Hatry (1974), p. 8, n. 37.

92. Overy (2013), p. 556.

93. In the early months of the war, Britain had launched daytime "precision bombing raids" on Germany but these soon proved too costly in terms of personnel and material and the tactic was abandoned in March 1940. They were replaced by a tactic of using nighttime "precision raids," but a report in August 1941 found these to be largely ineffective since most bombs missed their target. The Gee technique, as set out in a document in February 1942, envisaged using flares to make the targets visible. See d'Abzac-Epezy (1993), pp. 74–75. See also Overy (2013), pp. 273–274 and 290–291.

94. Biélinky (2011), p. 192. Diary entry 3 March 1942.

95. Bobkowski (1991), p. 302. Diary entry 3 March 1942 (23h.20).

96. Auroy (2008), p. 209. Diary entry 3 March 1942. She later learned that they were "balls of light attached to parachutes dropped by the planes and which were held hanging in clusters." Auroy (2008), p. 210. Diary entry 3 March 1942.

97. Galtier-Boissière (1944), p. 123. Diary entry 3 March 1942.

98. Oberlé (1942), p. 477.

99. Quoted in Evans (2013).

100. Overy (2013), p. 556.

101. Quoted in Hatry (1974), p. 4.

102. See Hatry (1974), p. 12.

103. Quoted in Hatry (1974), p. 5.

104. Auroy (2008), p. 212. Diary entry 3 March 1942.

105. Guy Zuccarelli in *Les Nouveaux Temps*, 5 March 1942, quoted in Hatry (1974), p. 4.

106. *Les Nouveaux Temps*, 6 March 1942, quoted in Hatry (1974), p. 4.

107. *L'Œuvre*, 4 March 1942, quoted in Hatry (1974), p. 4.

108. Pétain (1989), pp. 239–240. Barthélemy delivered the message on the steps of the town hall in Boulogne-Billancourt; Jérôme Carcopino read out the message in front of the church in Sèvres.

109. Hatry (1974), p. 6.

110. Bobkowski (1991), p. 304. Diary entry 5 March 1942.

111. Leaflets reproduced in Bourget (1979), pp. 128–129.

112. Leaflets reproduced in Bourget (1979), pp. 130–131.

113. Hatry (1974), p. 7. The open letter was entitled "You need to make a distinction between occupation and extermination"; see Florentin (2008), p. 73. The letter was signed by all the usual suspects, including Abel Bonnard, Robert Brasillach, Drieu La Rochelle, Alphonse de Châteaubriant, and Céline. It was quoted by Guéhenno (2002), p. 245. Diary entry 16 March 1942.

114. Quoted in Florentin (2008), p. 73.

115. Brunet (1986), p. 334.

116. Pierquin (1983), p. 76. Diary entry 3 March 1942. Pierquin probably means the rue de Sèvres. Pierquin may have been mistaken about the tanks here. Despite claims in the British press and indeed in one leaflet dropped over Paris by the RAF, the Renault works were not producing tanks for the Wehrmacht, although they had produced tanks for the French army. It is possible that Pierquin saw the wreckage of tanks that had been stationed outside the factories.

117. Pierquin (1983), p. 76. Diary entry 3 March 1942.

118. Schroeder (2000), p. 130. Diary entry 13 March 1942.

119. Schroeder (2000), p. 130. Diary entry 13 March 1942.

120. Bobkowski (1991), p. 303. Diary entry 4 March 1942.

121. Auroy (2008), pp. 212–213. Diary entry 3 March 1942.

122. Other sources cite 9,000 casualties for the bombing raid on Rotterdam. Maybe Galtier-Boissière is plucking a figure out of the air or confusing casualties and the number of people made homeless. Galtier-Boissière (1944), p. 124. Diary entry 4 March 1942.

123. The plan was to bomb a requisitioned school housing German soldiers at 41, rue de Tanger (19th arrondissement). The attack was planned by Pierre Georges,

who was present but the bomb failed to go off. See Berlière and Liaigre (2004), p. 293.

124. For further details of this trial, see Alary (2000) from which much of the information that follows has been taken.

125. The ruling dated 19 September 1941 stated: "all French males arrested for Communist or anarchist activity by the French authorities shall be considered to be prisoners of the MBF." See Alary (2000), p. 72.

126. The other defendants were Roger Hanlet (19), Pierre Milan (17), Robert Peltier (20), Fernand Zalkinov (19), and Acher Semahya (27). All lived in the 11th arrondissement except Zalkinov, who lived in the 20th arrondissement. See Alary (2000), pp. 65–67.

127. After the trial, a German report on the situation February–March 1942 noted: "The trial of seven Communist terrorists who were part of the Brustlein gang has ended. For the first time the press was allowed to attend the sessions. The conduct of the trial and the seven death sentences have been used for propaganda purposes in the press in the Occupied and Unoccupied Zones." See Alary (2000), p. 70.

128. See Alary (2000), p. 75; for texts of the letters, see pp. 117–123.

129. See Wieviorka and Laffitte (2012), p. 119.

130. The actresses were Junie Astor, Suzy Delair, Danielle Darrieux, and Viviane Romance. Their twelve-day trip followed three cultural goodwill tours—all in October 1941—that left France for Nazi Germany. The first two trips included writers and journalists attending the First European Writers' Congress in Weimar: Jacques Chardonne, Marcel Jouhandeau, and Ramon Fernandez left on 4 October and undertook an extended tour of Germany and Austria before arriving at Weimar. The second and larger contingent, which included Pierre Drieu La Rochelle and Robert Brasillach, left later and headed straight for Weimar. (See Dufay [2000]; Riding [2011], pp. 247–249.) The artists in a third group, which left on 30 October, included sculptor Charles Despiau, Auguste Rodin's former collaborator the painter/sculptor Aristide Maillol, and André Derain.

131. Raymond Bruckberger, *Tu finiras sur l'échafaud* (Paris: Flammarion, 1972, p. 342), quoted in Grenard (2008), p. 99.

132. Fabre-Luce (1946), p. 401.

133. Quoted in Grenard (2008), p. 125.

134. Quoted in Grenard (2008), p. 129.

135. *Paris-Midi*, 29 January 1942, quoted in Grenard (2008), p. 129.

136. Editorial in *Le Temps*, 5 February 1942, quoted in Grenard (2008), p. 129.

10. SS Seizure of Security, the Yellow Star, the Vél'd'Hiv' Roundup, La Relève

1. Guéhenno (2002), p. 249. Diary entry 9 April 1942.

2. Air Vice-Marshall Alan Lee believed the modern Matford factory at Poissy was turning out twenty trucks a day for the Wehrmacht. According to a leaflet dropped by the RAF, Ford had the most modern equipment in Europe. Its production of trucks at its new factories at Poissy (now its only centre of production in France) was almost as high as that at the Renault plant. See Florentin (2008), p. 78 and pp. 80–81.

3. A raid on Poissy in early April, for example, resulted in one death, twenty injured; forty houses were destroyed and 400 damaged. See Florentin (2008), p. 80. Allied bombs also landed in the suburbs of Cormeilles, Sannois, and Argenteuil.

4. During the 5–6 April raid, a private house, a shared dwelling, and a hotel-restaurant in Gennevilliers, home to thirteen families were hit; in Colombes, there were five dead, thirty-three injured, more than 400 displaced persons, and ten apartment blocks destroyed. After a second raid at the end of the month, thousands of windows and tiles at the Gnome and Rhône factory at Gennevilliers had to be replaced although the factory did not sustain a direct hit. Nearby Colombes once again bore the brunt of the raid, even though it was not officially a target: five factories hit, thirty-one buildings destroyed, twenty dead, forty injured, and more than 720 displaced persons. See Florentin (2008), pp. 81–83.

5. Bood (1974), pp. 135–136. Diary entry 27 April 1942.

6. *Le brevet sportif.*

7. Bood (1974), p. 137. Diary entry 30 April 1942.

8. Guéhenno (2002), p. 249. Diary entry 9 April 1942.

9. Auroy (2008), p. 215. Diary entry April 1942.

10. It stands in the rue Saint-Dominique in the 7th arrondissement and is one of the many centres of learning on the Left Bank.

11. Among them was Spartaco Guisco who had been with Brustlein in Nantes when Kommandant Hotz was assassinated.

12. Those deported were two women Marie-Thérèse Lefebvre and Simone Schloss, whose sentences had been commuted; Pierre Lefebvre, judged to have been unaware of his wife's activities, received a five-year sentence; André Kirschen was sentenced to ten years' imprisonment because of his young age. The Lefebvre couple and Kirschen returned: Schloss was decapitated in Cologne in July 1942.

13. See Rossel-Kirschen (2002), p. 35.

14. Rossel-Kirschen (2002), pp. 81–82.

15. On the boulevard Pasteur in the 15th arrondissement.

16. Burgard was later deported to Germany and executed in Cologne in June 1944.

17. Four of the pupils—Pierre Benoît, Jean-Marie Arthus, Jacques Baudry, Pierre Grelot—were from the Lycée Buffon. They were joined by Lucien Legros, a school student from another *lycée*. In France, they are usually referred to as the Five Martyrs of the Lycée Buffon.

18. These included an attack on a German officer in the rue de Vaugirard on 10 May and another on a colonel in the German air force on the quai Malaquais on 19 May.

19. Another account claims that what was envisaged was "a pillage of a large shop which was part of the Eco chain and which was reserved for German customers." Yvonne Dumont, quoted in Mezzasalma (2005). Available on line at http://www.cahiers dugerme.info/index.php?id=152 [Consulted 22/03/2013].

20. Benoît, Legros, Arthus, and Grelot.

21. In 2009, a year after her death, a street in the 20th arrondissement was named after Madeleine Marzin.

22. He was arrested in the square Louis XVI, near the Saint-Lazare railway station.

23. Constitutional Act No. 11, see Rémy (1992), pp. 177–178.

24. Laval, Laval, Laval. Qui aime tant les Allemands. Laval, Laval, Laval. Qui aime tant l'argent.

25. Auroy (2008), p. 221. Diary entry May 1942.

26. Höherer SS -und Polizeiführer, or HSSuPF. A decree issued in November had authorised Himmler to appoint an HSSuPF in each military district of the Reich. An HSSuPF was also appointed in Norway, the Netherlands, Poland, and Russia.

27. For more on Heydrich, see Gerwarth (2011). Binet (2013) tells the story of the attack on Heydrich and is interwoven with his thoughts on historiography.

28. On 6 May 1941 the *Journal official* published a law, which had been passed on 23 April, stating: "The services of the police are placed under the authority of the Minister of the Interior and led by the Secretary of State for the Police." See Delarue (1980), p. 9.

29. Peschanski (2003), p. 4.

30. Vallat was an anti-Semitic Catholic nationalist who found the idea and the practice of working with the Germans difficult. His anti-Semitism was rooted in his reading of Christian texts; his nationalism led him to try to protect French Jews, although he was willing to sacrifice foreign Jews.

31. For a chilling reconstruction of the Wannsee meeting, see the television film *Conspiracy* (BBC/HBO films 2001), directed by Frank Pierson. It is now available on YouTube and on DVD. My thanks to John Doggart for lending me a copy of this.

32. On 30 January 1942, for example, in his annual speech marking his appointment as chancellor, Hitler reminded his audience in the Sports Palace in Berlin of his warning in 1939 that if the Jews started a world war they would be annihilated. It had been part of his rhetoric since 1939 that the Jews *had* started the war. "We are clear," he told his audience, "that the war can only end either by the Aryan peoples being exterminated or by Jewry disappearing from Europe." See Evans (2009), p. 267.

33. The directive *(ordonnance)* was announced on 29 May; for the text of the *ordonnance*, see Poliakov (1999), p. 43. The star had to be "the size of a hand and bordered in black" bearing the word *Juif* in mock Hebrew black lettering. Each Jew had the right to three stars, which could be collected from their local police station—in exchange for a one-point ration ticket from their clothing allowance.

34. The prefect complied but insisted that no poster to this effect should be posted and that the public should not be officially told about this. See Berr (2008), p. 59, n 1.

35. A total of 78,655 Jews applied for their stars before the deadline expired out of the 100,455 Jews calculated to be living in the Occupied Zone. In total, 92,600 Jews reported to police stations to receive their three stars. See Laffitte (2006), pp. 129–130.

36. Quoted in Poliakov (1999), p. 52.

37. Quoted in Poliakov (1999), p. 53.

38. Poliakov (1999), p. 48. Unfortunately, Poliakov does not give the date or more details of this survey.

39. Biélinky (2011), pp. 213–214. Diary entry 1 June 1942.

40. Her father had been vice chairman of the Kuhlmann group of chemical companies until he was removed from his post as part of the "economic Aryanisation" measures. In 1971 Kuhlmann merged with Pechiney to form Pechiney-Ugine-Kuhlmann. My thanks to Jean-Marc Benammar for this information.

41. Berr (2008), p. 54. Diary entry 4 June 1942.

42. Poznanski (1997), p. 293.

43. Report by the Renseignements généraux, quoted in Rajsfus (2002a), p. 66.

44. On 13 February 1943. See Burinovici-Herbornel (2001), p. 58. Thanks to Simon Kitson for this reference.

45. Auroy (2008), pp. 229–238; p. 424.

46. Quoted in Poliakov (1999), p. 114.

47. Quoted in Poliakov (1999), pp. 113–114.

48. Unnamed witness, quoted in Poznanski (1997), p. 297.

49. Henri Szwarc, "Souvenirs: L'étoile jaune," *Annales. Économies, Sociétés, Civilisations* 48, no. 3 (1993): 630, quoted in Semelin (2013), p. 316.

50. Berr (2008), p. 60. Diary entry 9 June 1942.

51. Biélinky (2011), p. 217. Diary entry 8 June 1942.

52. *L'Avant-Garde*, newspaper of the Féderation des jeunesses communistes distributed in July 1942. See Poznanski (1997), p. 360.

53. Galtier-Boissière (1944), p. 133. Diary entry 6 June 1942.

54. Bobkowski (1991), p. 334. Diary entry 9 June 1942.

55. Groult and Groult (1962), p. 264. Diary entry 7 June 1942.

56. Auroy (2008), p. 227. Diary entry 7 June 1942.

57. Jünger (2008), p. 310. Diary entry 7 June 1942.

58. Szwarc (1993), quoted in Semelin (2013), p. 316.

59. Biélinky (2011), p. 217. Diary entry 8 June 1942.

60. Biélinky (2011), p. 222. Diary entry 14 June 1942.

61. Facsimile of the police report displayed with a couple of "alternative" yellow stars in the Museum of the Prefecture of Police, 4, rue de la Montagne-Sainte-Geneviève, in the 5th arrondissement.

62. See Walter (1960), pp. 185–186.

63. Marrus and Paxton (1995), p. 239.

64. Groult and Groult (1962), p. 264. Diary entries 7 June and 9 June 1942.

65. Auroy (2008), p. 227. Diary entry 5 June 1942.

66. Bood (1974), p. 142. Diary entry 1 June 1942.

67. Quoted in Foss and Steinberg (1996), p. 150.

68. For more details, see Siefridt (2010), pp. 97ff. A report dated 10 June from the anti-Jewish Section of the Gestapo referred to "some 40 cases" of non-Jews wearing mock yellow stars; see Rajsfus (2002a), p. 91. For more on Parisians wearing mock yellow stars, see Rajsfus (2002a), pp. 81ff.

69. On the rue Santerre.

70. See Lévy and Tillard (1967), p. 117.

71. List taken from Poliakov (1999), pp. 56–57.

72. Biélinky (2011), p. 233. Diary entry 15 July 1942.

73. Before taking their prisoners away, the police had to check that gas, water, and electricity were turned off and to give any animals and keys to the concierge, who was deemed responsible for everything left in the flat. If there was no concierge, the keys were to be handed over to a neighbour.

74. Vincenot (2012), pp. 123–125.

75. Jean Laloum, *Les Juifs dans la banlieue parisienne* (Paris: CNRS Éditions, 1998), p. 220, quoted in Rajsfus (2002b), p. 43.

76. Annette Muller, *La Petite Fille du Vél' d'Hiv'* (Paris: Denoël, 1991), p. 85, quoted in Rajsfus (2002b), p. 44.

77. See Rajsfus (2002b), p. 45.

78. Lévy and Tillard (1967), p. 51.

79. Lévy and Tillard (1967), p. 45.

80. Rajsfus (2002b), p. 49.

81. Cardon-Hamet (2005), p. 46.

82. Cardon-Hamet (2005), p. 49.

83. Wieviorka and Laffitte (2012), p. 158.

84. Lévy and Tillard (1967), p. 117.

85. Wieviorka and Laffitte (2012), pp. 131 and 147.

86. J. M. Matthey-Jonais, quoted in Taieb (2011), pp. 192–193.

87. Rosette Shalit in William Karek and Blanche Finger, *Vent printanier* (Paris: La Découverte, 1992), pp. 37 and 39, quoted in Rajsfus (2002b), p. 70.

88. See Josephs (1989), p. 63.

89. Hélène Zytnicki, in William Karel and Blanche Finger, *Vent printanier* (Paris: La Découverte, 1992), pp. 154–155, quoted in Rajsfus (2002b), p. 69.

90. For example, Gabriel Wachman who was aged fourteen at the time. See Wachman and Goldenberg (2006).

91. She lived in the rue de Lancry in the 10th arrondissement.

92. Traube (2005), pp. 28–34; see Semelin (2013), pp. 362–363.

93. Fernand Baudvin, a fireman *(sapeur-pompier)* at the station in the rue des Entrepreneurs; see Taieb (2011), pp. 186–192.

94. Auroy (2008), p. 253. Diary entry 15 July 1942.

95. Rist (1983), p. 262. Diary entry 24 July 1942.

96. Bobkowski (1991), p. 344. Diary entry 4 August 1942. The St. Bartholomew's Day Massacre refers to the slaughter of thousands of Huguenots (French Protestants) in Paris during the night of 23–24 August 1572; the killings subsequently spread to other towns and cities.

97. Quoted in Duquesne (1996), p. 274.

98. Cointet (1998), p. 225.

99. The total number arrested was 12,884 (3,031 men, 5,802 women, 4,051 children).

100. For details, see Ménager (2007), pp. 20–21.

101. Photograph of letter in Anon, *La Rafle du Vélodrome d'Hiver* (n.d.).

102. Convoys sent from Pithiviers on 31 July, 3 August, and 7 August; from Beaune-la-Rolande on 5 and 7 August. See Wellers (1973), p. 104.

103. See Lévy and Tillard (1967), p. 107.

104. Wellers (1973), p. 141.

105. Georges Wellers's testimony at the Eichmann trial, 9 May 1961. See http://www.holocaustresearchproject.org/trials/wellers.html, esp. p. 6. See also Wellers (1973), pp. 140–142.

106. Quoted in Josephs (1989), p. 71.

107. Taken from two Polish words *pić* (to drink) and *poić* (to water cattle).

108. Wellers (1973), p. 142.

109. Thomas (1995), p. 188. Diary entry 31 August 1942. This diary entry inspired a front-page article entitled "Crier la vérité" ("Shout out the Truth"), which appeared in October 1942 in the second issue of the underground Resistance paper *Les Lettres françaises*. In her impassioned cry for truth, Thomas emphasised that being a writer meant "telling the truth. The truth is all or it is nothing. The truth: people having to wear stars on their chests, children snatched away from their mothers, men who are executed every day, the degradation of an entire people—the truth is forbidden." See Eychart and Aillaud (2008), p. 27.

110. One of the more extreme examples occurred in December 1940 in Lille, a northern industrial city then in the Forbidden Zone, when some 300 men were stopped coming out of the cinema. Threatened with reprisals against their families if they refused, they were given a date on which they were to report to Lille railway station and were packed off to work in Germany. See Evrard (1972), p. 26.

111. Arnaud (2014), p. 22.

112. According to German sources, between September 1941 and March 1942, only 14,000 volunteers left France, making a total of only 62,600 French workers in all compared with 134,000 Dutch workers, 122,000 Belgian workers, and 63,000 Danish workers. French sources quote 82,000 departures up until 1 June 1942, but more than half of these (45,000) failed to return to Germany after a period of leave in France. See Evrard (1972), p. 34.

113. See Kupferman (1987), pp. 333–334.

114. Quoted in Bourget and Lacretelle (1980), p. 94.

115. Auroy (2008), p. 223. Diary entry May 1942.

116. Reproduced in Bourget and Lacretelle (1980), p. 97.

117. Evrard (1972), p. 47.

118. Kupferman (1987), p. 341.

119. Paris Prefecture of Police, *La Situation à Paris: Rapports de la quinzaine*, 13 July 1942.

120. See poster reproduced in Bourget and Lacretelle (1980), p. 91.

121. Quoted in Bourget and Lacretelle (1980), p. 108.

122. Marcel Cretagne and Fosco Focardi. For more details, see Berlière and Liaigre (2007), pp. 85–93.

123. See Berlière and Liaigre (2007), p. 383.

124. Outcome of attacks as given by Berlière and Liaigre (2007), pp. 384–385; Bourget and Lacretelle (1980), p. 108, give the following figures: Garenne-Palace (8 September): one German soldier killed, several wounded; attack on a patrol in the rue d'Hautpoul (10 September): one soldier dead, nine injured; Rex Cinema (16 September): two dead and nineteen injured.

125. A total of forty-six were selected from prisoners held at Romainville; seventy others were executed in Bordeaux.

126. Bourget and Lacretelle (1980), p. 108.

11. Denunciations, Distractions, Deprivations

1. See Wieviorka and Laffitte (2012), p. 151.

2. Adler (1987), p. 43. Adler notes: "The precise number of Jews who left Paris in the aftermath of the July events is impossible to establish, although evidence

indicates a significant shift of population." Various offices of the UGIF in the Unoccupied Zone, especially those near the demarcation line, reported large numbers of Jewish arrivals in August 1942.

3. Berr (2008), p. 93. Diary entry 3 July 1942.

4. Semelin (2013), p. 331.

5. De Beauvoir (1960a), p. 587.

6. On 14 September, more than 200 Jews from the Baltic states, Bulgaria, the Netherlands, and Yugoslavia were arrested, followed a week later (23 September) by more than 1,500 Romanian Jews. Five days later it was the turn of Jews from Luxembourg, Belgium, and Danzig, and on 4–5 November more than 1,000 Greek Jews on the official register of some 1,400 were arrested. (See Poznanski 1997, p. 366).

7. See Grunberg (2001).

8. In April 1944 Grunberg wrote that Monsieur L., whom he described as a fascist, was paid 7,000 francs a month for following people he knew and denouncing them to the authorities. See Grunberg (2001), p. 299. Diary entry 21 April 1944.

9. Joly (2007), p. 142.

10. Joly (2007), p. 142.

11. See Laurent Joly, "La Dénonciation dans la traque des communistes et les Juifs, 1940–1944," in Joly (2012b), p. 120.

12. Halimi (1998), p. 23.

13. Joly (2013). My thanks to Laurent Joly for sending me this article prior to its publication.

14. See Joly (2013).

15. *Le Dépôt de la Préfecture de police.*

16. Siefridt (2010), p. 101. Diary entry 18 June 1942.

17. De Beauvoir (1960a), p. 611.

18. See Joly (2013), p. 40.

19. Denunciators had a choice of writing to many bodies, including the German security agencies, the Commissariat général aux questions juives (CGQJ), the German military, the French police, or their local *mairie*. Few records of these letters have survived, to which, in any case, an unknown number of denunciations made by telephone or in person would need to be added.

20. See Joly (2012b).

21. See Joly (2007), pp. 140, 144–146.

22. The German, or German-backed, organisations included the SS, which prioritised deportation of foreign Jews; the CGQJ with its own police officers, the Service spécial des affaires juives (SSAJ) and its own armed branch, the Section d'enquête et de contrôle (SEC). The Paris police also had its own section, the Service juif, devoted to tracking down Jews.

23. Joly (2007), p. 141.

24. See Berlière and Liaigre (2004), p. 158, referred to in Joly (2012a), p. 124.

25. See Berlière and Liaigre (2004), p. 135.

26. See Berlière and Liaigre (2004), pp. 158–159.

27. The main Zazou meeting places in the Latin Quarter were two cafés on the boulevard Saint-Michel—the Capoulade and the Dupont-Latin, while those Zazous, on the whole a little older, who congregated around the Champs-Élysées used to meet up at the local Pam-Pam or the Colisée.

28. See Siefridt (2010), photographs between p. 120 and p. 121.

29. These recordings are available as part of a four CD collection *Swing Tanzen Verboten: Swing Music and Nazi Propaganda; Swing Music during World War II*, Properbox Records, Properbox 56, Proper Records Ltd, Gateway Business Centre, Kangley Bridge Road, London SE26 5AN, England. For a selection of jazz that Parisians listened to during the "dark years," see the CD *Jazz sous l'Occupation*, Universal Music (2002), issued on the Gitanes label.

30. Régnier (2009), p. 58.

31. The programme for two concerts in the Salle Gaveau on 16 and 18 January 1941 included Count Basie's "Blue and Sentimental" (advertised as Bleu et sentimental), Jean Kruppa's "My Grandfather's Clock" (L'Horloge de grand'père), and Bix Beiderbecke's "In a Mist" (En souvenir). All composers are listed but no Jews are included.

32. *Vedettes*, 11 January 1942; see Tournès (1999), pp. 318–319.

33. The Folies Belleville, the Alhambra (in the show *Rythmes 42*), Bobino, the European.

34. Hess and Trenet formed a double act when they started out in show business and there are suggestions that they may have been sexual partners as well. See Buisson (2008), pp. 220–221.

35. With the exception of the sunglasses and the umbrella they bore more than a passing resemblance to the Teddy Boys in 1950s Britain.

36. See Régnier (2009), pp. 132–133.

37. Marcel Bucard, leader of the Franciste movement, speaking at a meeting in November 1942, quoted in Buisson (2008), p. 218.

38. De Beauvoir (1960a), p. 588.

39. The PPF had its own youth organisation, the Union populaire de la jeunesse française (UPJF), since November 1936. At the end of May 1942, the UPJF joined forces with another eight groups, all strongly influenced by the PPF, to form the JPF.

40. See Buisson (2008), p. 219.

41. See Loiseau (1977), p. 157.

42. Members of the JPF (and Doriot's PPF) joined the French police in the huge roundups of Jews that took place shortly afterwards.

43. See Halls (1981), p. 176.

44. Loiseau (1977), p. 162. According to Loiseau there were a hundred or so "dancing classes." Loiseau does not give a date or a source for his figure. In addition he cites Sunday dances in the suburbs, dances held in premises when they were officially closed, and private parties.

45. In addition, a register had to be kept, no one but the students and their parents were to be admitted, no drinks could be consumed, and no advertising was allowed. See Régnier (2009), p. 163.

46. He went on to become a successful music producer working with singers such as Jacques Brel and Charles Aznavour.

47. See Régnier (2009), p. 164.

48. Quoted in Loiseau (1977), p. 163.

49. Quoted in Buisson (2008), p. 460.

50. "Boris Vian gently mocked the Zazous' lack of musical sophistication in 'Swing-Concert II'" in *Cent sonnets*, a collection of 112 poems written between 1940

and 1944. See Boris Vian, "Swing-Concert II," in *Cent Sonnets* (Héritiers Vian et Christian Bourgeois, 1984), p. 52. An extract from "Swing-Concert II" is quoted in Régnier (2009), p. 135.

51. They married in September 1942 and remained married until 1947.

52. See Régnier (2009), p. 165.

53. Paris Prefecture of Police, *La Situation à Paris: Rapports de la quinzaine*, 10 August 1942.

54. *L'Illustration*, 15 August 1942, quoted in Kupferman (1987), p. 356.

55. See Vinen (2006), p. 197.

56. Guéhenno (2002), p. 283. Diary entry 23 August 1942.

57. Quoted in Tournoux (1982), pp. 164–165.

58. See Mitchell (2008), p. 65. This book is the source of much of the material in the next few paragraphs.

59. Mitchell (2008), p. 66.

60. Mitchell (2008), p. 66.

61. See Arnaud (2014), p. 30.

62. Speech reproduced in *Le Matin*, 21 October 1942, p. 1, under the heading "Cette épreuve est décisive" ("This test is decisive").

63. "Comment seront recrutés pour la relève les 133,000 spécialistes" ("How 133,000 specialists will be recruited for *la relève*"), *Le Matin*, 6 October 1942, p. 1.

64. Paris Prefecture of Police, *La Situation à Paris: Rapports de la quinzaine*, 21 September 1942.

65. Paris Prefecture of Police, *La Situation à Paris: Rapports de la quinzaine*, 5 October 1942.

66. Auroy (2008), p. 261. Diary entry Autumn 1942.

67. Vittori (1982), pp. 65–66.

68. *Le Matin*, 18 September 1942, p. 1.

69. "We are worried that not all French people have understood," *Le Matin*, 3–4 October 1942, p. 1.

70. "France will look after the families properly," *Le Matin*, 3–4 October 1942, p. 1.

71. In May 1942 Sauckel had told Laval he wanted 350,000 French workers of whom 150,000 should be skilled workers. See Arnaud (2013), p. 19.

72. Paris Prefecture of Police, *La Situation à Paris: Rapports de la quinzaine*, 5 October 1942.

73. Toasted bread sold in packets and often eaten at breakfast.

74. Article in *Documents français*, 15 February 1943, quoted in Veillon (1995), p. 220.

75. See Veillon (1995), p. 220.

76. Paris Prefecture of Police, *La Situation à Paris: Rapports de la quinzaine*, 21 September 1942.

77. Paris Prefecture of Police, *La Situation à Paris: Rapports de la quinzaine*, 21 September 1942.

78. Fabre-Luce (1946), p. 450.

79. Groult and Groult (1962), p. 300. Diary entry 12 November 1942.

80. Berr (2008), p. 161. Diary entry 8 November 1942.

81. Galtier-Boissière (1944), p. 153. Diary entry 8 November 1942.

82. Benoît-Guyod (1962), p. 227. Diary entry 8 November 1942.

83. Bood (1974), p. 166. Diary entry 9 November 1942.

84. Bood (1974), p. 166. Diary entry 8 November 1942.

85. Adolf Hitler, 23 December 1942, quoted in Jäckel (1968), p. 371.

86. Laborde had learned of Hitler's orders to seize the French fleet and, rather than let it fall into German hands or into the hands of the British—the traditional enemy of the French navy—he gave orders for the fleet to be sunk. More than fifty modern ships representing 90 percent of the French fleet were permanently put out of action.

87. Benoît-Guyod (1962), p. 228. Diary entry 27 November 1942.

88. Groult and Groult (1962), p. 301. Diary entry 12 November 1942.

89. Guéhenno (2002), p. 300. Diary entry 14 November 1942.

90. See Mitchell (2008), pp. 94–95.

91. News of this had reached Berlin and Hitler had to intervene to tell Abetz that such a scenario was out of the question and instructed him to quash all such rumours.

92. Burrin (2003), p. 479.

93. Quoted in Lambauer (2001), p. 582.

94. See Lambauer (2001), p. 583. Abetz also added that they were definitively responsible for his dismissal as ambassador in 1944.

95. In July 1942 the BCRA (Free French Intelligence Service) told the Communist Party it would receive three million francs, and Colonel Rémy, a key figure in the Resistance who was one of the first Frenchmen to join de Gaulle, later gave the PCF another two million from his own funds. See Cobb (2009), p. 118.

96. Auroy (2008), p. 264. Diary entry based on notes made in December 1942 but written up in November 1944.

12. Labour Conscription, Resistance, the French Gestapo

1. The sum was initially set at 400 million francs a day but was reduced to 300 million francs a day in April 1941.

2. *Le Matin*, 2 January 1943, p. 1.

3. Guéhenno (2002), p. 308. Diary entry 27 December 1942; Bobkowski (1991), p. 402. Diary entry 19 January 1943.

4. Guéhenno (2002), p. 311. Diary entry 18 January 1943.

5. Rist (1983), p. 315. Diary entry 29 January 1943.

6. Bobkowski (1991), p. 401. Diary entry 14 January 1943.

7. Bobkowski (1991), p. 401. Diary entry 15 January 1943.

8. Rist (1983), p. 314. Diary entry 25 January 1943.

9. Rist (1983), p. 318. Diary entry 1 February 1943.

10. Figures given in Mitchell (2008), p. 119.

11. Arnaud (2013), p. 20.

12. Guéhenno (2002), p. 320. Diary entry 22 February 1943.

13. *L'Humanité*, 12 March 1943, quoted in Amouroux (1998b), p. 469.

14. Braibant (1945), p. 188. Diary entry 2 May 1943.

15. Guéhenno (2002), p. 320. Diary entry 22 February 1943.

16. Luneau (2005), p. 236.

17. Pierquin (1983), p. 95. Diary entry 6 March 1943.

18. Figures in this paragraph taken from Mitchell (2008), p. 119.

19. See Cobb (2009), p. 161.

20. Pierquin (1983), p. 94. Diary entry 25 February 1943. However, in the summer, students of the 1942 class became eligible for STO call-up and in September it was the turn of those, like Pierquin, who were in the Class 40 and were finishing their studies (see Pierquin [1983], p. 101 and p. 104).

21. Das Nationalsozialistische Kraftfahrkorps.

22. D'Hoop (1971), p. 80.

23. Guéhenno (2002), pp. 367–368. Diary entry 17 November 1943.

24. Pierquin (1983), pp. 101–102. Diary entry 30 June 1943.

25. Auroy (2008), p. 289. Diary entry "End of the summer 1943."

26. See Vinen (2006), p. 253.

27. Braibant (1945), p. 132. Diary entry 18 February 1943.

28. Evrard (1972), p. 115.

29. Arnaud (2013), p. 21.

30. Located in the rue de Mogador in the 9th arrondissement.

31. See Evrard (1972), pp. 128–139.

32. See Evrard (1972), p. 141.

33. Aron (1979), p. 1158.

34. See Cobb (2009), p. 161.

35. See Arnaud (2013), p. 22.

36. Mitchell (2008), p. 96.

37. Arnaud (2013), p. 21.

38. See Arnaud (2013), p. 21.

39. Christian Pineau, *La Simple Vérité* (Julliard, 1960), quoted in Cobb (2009), p. 66.

40. See Matthew Cobb's brilliant disentangling of the background to the creation of the CNR, in Cobb (2009), esp. pp. 88ff.

41. See Simonin (2008), p. 43ff.

42. 15, rue Pierre-Nicole.

43. "Oreste et la Cité," *Les Lettres françaises*, 12 December 1943, p. 1, in Eychart and Aillaud (2008), p. 103.

44. *Les Lettres françaises*, January–February 1943, reproduced in Eychart and Aillaud (2008), p. 52.

45. Marcel Déat, *Journal de guerre*, Diary entry 23 November 1942, quoted in Tournoux (1982), p. 233.

46. Quoted in Giolitto (2002), p. 127.

47. Pétain (1989), p. 304.

48. See Mitchell (2008), pp. 97–98.

49. See Delarue (1985), p. 65.

50. The German Currency Office in France, the Devisenschutzkommando Frankreich (DSK), sometimes called the Devisendeutschkommando (DDK), was in the former premises of the Lazard Frères Bank in the rue Pillet-Will in the 9th arrondissement.

51. On 25 March 1942, Operation Möbel (Operation Furniture), a pillaging operation run by the ERR, was handed over to the Dienstelle des Westens, headed by Kurt von Behr. It was responsible for pillaging from that date more than 4,000 Jewish homes in Paris and removing more than 40,000 tons of furniture and furnishings. See Desprairies (2009), p. 491.

52. In November 1944, *Défense de la France* became *France-Soir*.

53. Thorval (2007), pp. 76–77.

54. Auda (2002), pp. 157–159.

55. See Aziz (1970), pp. 133–137.

56. See Auda (2002), pp. 123–128.

57. Lormier (2013), pp. 75–76. See also Buisson (2008), pp. 425–428.

58. See Auda (2002), pp. 135–136.

59. For more on torture, see Auda (2002), pp. 159–166.

60. The Romanian Detachment, the Jewish Detachment, the Italian Detachment, a detachment composed mostly of Spaniards and some Armenians that from July 1943 devoted itself exclusively to train derailments. In an addition, there was a Bulgarian "team" deemed too small to be called a detachment. See Courtois et al. (1989), pp. 146–149.

61. In September FTP-MOI units carried out twenty attacks, including one in which a three-man Italian FTP-MOI group shot and lobbed grenades at members of Doriot's PPF, killing two and injuring a number of others. One member of the FTP-MOI group was caught almost immediately afterwards at the nearby Jasmin Métro station. In October the FTP-MOI was responsible for eleven armed actions, including a grenade attack by a Romanian FTP-MOI group on German soldiers exercising in the Jean-Bouin stadium at Montrouge. Two members of this FTP-MOI unit were picked up almost immediately and two more a few days later. All were executed at Mont-Valérien the following March. In November FTP-MOI units carried out another ten attacks and a further twelve in December. See Courtois et al. (1989), p. 164 and p. 171.

62. Lucienne Goldfarb (real name Kajla Goldfarb) was born in 1924 in Poland and arrived in Paris with her parents in 1931. She resurfaced after the Liberation as a prostitute and then as a brothel madam living under police protection. See Courtois et al. (1989), pp. 208–209.

63. Letter reproduced in Courtois et al. (1989), p. 217.

64. www.crrl.fr/Ressources/concours_resistance/Concours 2008/cacheJuifs /htm#.Anna Neustadt; www.crrl.fr/Ressources/concours_resistance/Concours 2006/noirvaut.htm. Consulted 23 February 2014.

65. The convoys left on 9 February, 11 February, and 13 February. See Wellers (1973), p. 247.

66. A total of 689, including Biélinky, aged sixty-two, were in their sixties, 447 were in their seventies, fifty-four were in their eighties, and four were ninety-year-olds. See Renée Poznanski, "Introduction," in Biélinky (2011), p. 11.

67. Courtois et al. (1989), p. 218.

68. On the rue Saint-Charles in the 15th arrondissement.

69. Courtois et al. (1989), pp. 164–169.

70. Courtois (1985).

13. Anti-Bolshevism, Black Market, More Bombs, Drancy

1. Number given by Courtois (1985), p. 3.

2. The two occupants were Lieutenant-Colonel Moritz von Ralibor and staff officer Corvey. Neither was hurt despite FTP-MOI claims that the occupants of the car had been blown to pieces. See Courtois et al. (1989), p. 319.

3. The Maison de la Chimie was where one of the big Resistance trials had been held in March 1942.

4. According to Boris Holban, an FTP-MOI leader, the FTP-MOI units carried out ninety-two actions during the first six months of 1943—fourteen derailments and acts of sabotage, thirty-four attacks on premises, and forty-three attacks against members of the German army and a failed assassination of a traitor. This figure did not include innumerable individual bomb and grenade attacks carried out by individual FTP-MOI members. See Boris Holban, *Testament* (Paris: Calmann-Lévy, 1989), p. 157, quoted in Berlière and Peschanski (1997), pp. 146–147.

5. Figures given in Courtois (1985), p. 3.

6. Peschanski (2014), p. 14.

7. Interview, Mélinée Manouchian, in Boucault (2013).

8. Adam Rayski, quoted in Courtois (1985), p. 5.

9. "Missak Manouchian to his wife." Letter written in Fresnes prison and dated 21 February 1944, reproduced in Krivopissko (2013), p. 203. My emphasis.

10. Interview, Philippe Ganier-Raymond, in Boucault (2013). Ganier-Raymond set out his arguments in *L'Affiche rouge* (Paris: Fayard, 2001). For a critique of Ganier-Raymond's position, see Wieviorka (1986), pp. 224–226.

11. Bobkowski (1991), p. 402. Diary entry 23 January 1943.

12. Bood (1974), p. 183. Diary entry 4 February 1943.

13. Pierquin (1983), p. 93. Diary entry 9 February 1943.

14. Bood (1974), p. 183. Diary entry 4 February 1943.

15. See Audiat (1946), p. 231.

16. A film with this title, directed by Roger Guédiguian, based on the activities of Manouchian and his comrades, was released in 2009 and is now available on DVD.

17. Law No. 95 of 11 February 1943. See Rémy (1992), p. 209.

18. Quoted in Giolitto (2007), p. 243.

19. Since 1977 place Malesherbes has been called place Géneral-Catroux.

20. See Delarue (1993), pp. 226–227; Giolitto (2007), pp. 244–245.

21. Quoted in Giolitto (2007), p. 255.

22. Braibant (1945), p. 275. Diary entry 7 September 1943.

23. See Giolitto (2007), p. 390. A tiny number of Frenchmen working for the National Socialist Drivers Corps (NSKK) had already managed to get themselves transferred to the Waffen-SS or had gone straight to the Waffen-SS recruitment bureaus in Brussels or Antwerp.

24. Französich SS Freiwilligen Sturmbrigade. See Ory (1976), p. 265; Giolitto (2007), p. 422.

25. Quoted in Giolitto (2007), pp. 399–400.

26. See Bourget and Lacretelle (1980), p. 138.

27. See Bourget and Lacretelle (1980), pp. 140–141.

28. Quoted in Giolitto (2007), pp. 401–402.

29. Burrin (1995), p. 441.

30. Quoted in Giolitto (2007), p. 414.

31. Forbes (2010), p. 44.

32. See Giolitto (2007), pp. 409–415.

33. Ory gives the figure of 2,480. See Ory (1976), p. 266.

34. Reproduced in Bourget and Lacretelle (1980), pp. 118–119.
35. Pierquin (1983), p. 93. Diary entry 9 February 1943.
36. Bood (1974), p. 195. Diary entry 20 April 1943.
37. In 1943, Paris needed 900 tons of meat a day to feed its inhabitants on a (theoretical) ration of 120g a week; it was only officially receiving 500 tons. In order to honour the milk ration tickets for young children, 470,000 litres of milk a day were required; the official delivery had fallen to 415,000. See Meyer (1979), pp. 1672–1673.
38. Braibant (1945), p. 107. Diary entry 23 January 1943.
39. Grenard (2008), p. 189. According to figures quoted by Grenard, the German demand for cereals had risen from 485,000 tons (12 percent total production) in 1941–1942 to 714,000 tons (17 percent total production) in 1942–1943. Supplies of meat to Germany had risen from 140,000 tons (15 percent total production) to 227,000 tons (23 percent total production) over the same period.
40. Braibant (1945), p. 179. Diary entry 18 April 1943.
41. Braibant quotes a colleague from Normandy who reported that German soldiers paid between 800 and 900 francs a kilo for butter, which cost about half that amount on the black market in Paris. (The official price was 64 francs a kilo.) See Braibant (1945), p. 87. Diary entry 12 January 1943.
42. The film *La Traversée de Paris* is a Franco-Italian production, directed by Claude Autant-Lara and starring Bourvil, Jean Gabin, and Louis de Funès. It was released in 1956 and is based on *Traversée de Paris*, a short story by Marcel Aymé. See Marcel Aymé, *Le Vin de Paris* (Paris: Gallimard, 1947), pp. 27–82.
43. Braibant (1945), p. 87. Diary entry 12 January 1943.
44. Braibant (1945), p. 87. Diary entry 12 January 1943.
45. Grenard (2008), pp. 176–178.
46. *Les Nouveaux Temps*, 29 November 1940, quoted in Grenard (2008), p. 160.
47. Grenard (2008), p. 160.
48. Braibant (1945), p. 85. Diary entry 8 January 1943.
49. Braibant (1945), p. 177. Diary entry 16 April 1943.
50. Meyer (1979), p. 1673.
51. *L'Assommoir*, the title of a novel by Émile Zola, refers to a dive that sold rotgut, which "slammed" *(assommé)* those who drank it.
52. Meyer (1979), p. 1675.
53. Interview in Pryce-Jones (1981), p. 244.
54. Beltran and Carré (1991), p. 280.
55. Beltran and Carré (1991), p. 285.
56. Bobkowski (1991), p. 449. Diary entry 4 April 1943.
57. Jünger (2008), p. 490. Diary entry 5 April 1943.
58. Bood (1974), p. 191. Diary entry 11 April 1943 (Micheline's seventeenth birthday). Bood gives Marcel-Sembat as the Métro station and writes of "over 300 fatalities." Figure of eighty deaths taken from Florentin (2008), p. 161.
59. Guéhenno (2002), p. 333. Diary entry 5 April 1943.
60. Bood (1974), p. 191. Diary entry 11 April 1943.
61. *Le Matin*, 5 April 1943, p. 1.
62. Schroeder (2000), p. 185. Diary entry 29 April 1943.
63. Braibant (1945), pp. 165–166. Diary entry 5 April 1943.
64. Incident cited in Florentin (2008), pp. 164–165.

65. Bobkowski (1991), p. 520. Diary entry 3 September 1943.
66. Galtier-Boissière (1944), p. 203. Diary entry 3 September 1943.
67. Bobkowski (1991), p. 521. Diary entry 3 September 1943.
68. Braibant (1945), p. 270. Diary entry 3 September 1943.
69. Florentin (2008), p. 238.
70. Florentin (2008), p. 238.
71. Bobkowski (1991), p. 521. Diary entry 3 September 1943.
72. Florentin (2008), p. 242.
73. Florentin (2008), p. 242.
74. See photograph reproduced in Fonkenell (2009), p. 135.
75. See Florentin (2008), p. 260; Fonkenell (2009), p. 134; Benoît-Guyod (1962), p. 248. Diary entry 25 September 1943; Audiat (1946), pp. 250–251.
76. Wellers (1973), p. 188.
77. See Wieviorka and Laffitte (2012), p. 227.
78. Quoted in Wieviorka and Laffitte (2012), p. 250.
79. See Wellers (1973), p. 191.
80. See Wellers (1973), p. 194.
81. The Italian troops had withdrawn as part of an armistice agreement signed between the Allies and the Italian government headed by Marshal Badoglio on 3 September following the fall of Mussolini.
82. It was Brunner's decision to switch the station from which the deportation trains left from Le Bourget to Bobigny, where the buses taking the deportees from Drancy to the trains had direct access to the railway tracks.
83. See Wieviorka and Laffitte (2012), pp. 283–290; Wellers (1973), pp. 216–218.
84. Between 16 July 1942 and 2 July 1943, fifty convoys of deportees left Drancy. Those of 18 and 31 July departed after Brunner's arrival but included prisoners who had been arrested before he arrived. Between 2 July 1943 and 17 August 1944 (excluding those of 18 and 31 July) there were twenty convoys. The monthly average for the first period was 4.52 convoys a month; 1.54 a month for the second period when Brunner and the SS had taken over running the camp. See Wellers (1973), pp. 249–250.
85. Serge Klarsfeld, *Le Calendrier de la pérsecution des Juifs en France, 1940–1944* (Paris: Les Fils et filles des déportés juifs en France, 1993), p. 74, quoted in Callil (2006), p. 357.
86. On the evolution of attitudes within the French police, see Kitson (2002).
87. See Mitchell (2008), p. 134.
88. Of the 75,721 Jews deported from France, 24,500 were French; the remainder were foreign, stateless, or of unknown nationality. Serge Klarsfeld, *Le Mémorial de la déportation des Juifs de France* (Paris: Self-published, 1978), quoted in Wieviorka (1992), p. 142.
89. After the end of the war, many of *Les Justes* refused any official recognition for their bravery. Nevertheless by 2007, 2,740 people in France had been honoured, including 270 from Paris. See Ménager (2007), p. 1.
90. See Ménager (2007), p. 45.
91. Bood (1974), p. 193. Diary entry 16 April 1943.
92. These examples are taken from Ménager (2007), pp. 16–18.

93. Wolff Lévitan had fled to the south of France. After the war, Lévitan was reinstalled in his premises, which remained a household furniture shop until the 1980s. It still exists but is located in Montigny-lès-Cormeilles, northwest of Paris. Thanks to Jean-Marc Benammar for this information.

94. Dreyfus and Gensburger (2003), p. 113.

95. Dreyfus and Gensburger (2003), p. 129.

96. Dreyfus and Gensburger (2003), p. 145.

97. Dreyfus and Gensburger (2003), p. 133.

98. Dreyfus and Gensburger (2003), p. 118.

99. See Dreyfus and Gensburger (2003), p. 138. The property was in Warthegau, a territory that Germany established in October 1939 in the part of Poland which was incorporated into the Reich.

100. Dreyfus and Gensburger (2003), p. 139.

101. Georges Geissman, quoted in Dreyfus and Gensburger (2003), p. 157.

102. Georges Geissman, quoted in Dreyfus and Gensburger (2003), p. 159.

103. Déat (1989), p. 838.

104. See Déat (1989), p. 836.

105. For the text of the letter, see Ferro (2012), pp. 506–510.

106. Other bodies under his control included all special police forces, fire brigades, and the prison service. See Cointet (2011), p. 655.

107. Pierquin (1983), p. 92. Diary entry 5 January 1943.

108. Bobkowski (1991), p. 402. Diary entry 20 January 1943.

109. Braibant (1945), p. 110. Diary entry 27 January 1943.

110. Braibant (1945), p. 116. Diary entry 1 February 1943.

111. Bobkowski (1991), p. 407. Diary entry 16 February 1943. He also noted that the Red Army had retaken Kharkov, and that Rostov and Vorochilograd had been retaken two days earlier.

112. Schroeder (2000), p. 181. Diary entry 25 March 1943.

113. Rist (1983), p. 325. Diary entry 8 March 1943.

114. Pierquin (1983), p. 95. Diary entry 6 March 1943.

115. Pierquin (1983), p. 98. Diary entry 28 March 1943.

116. Pierquin (1983), p. 104. Diary entry 7 September 1943.

117. Pierquin (1983), pp. 104–105. Diary entry 16 September 1943.

118. Leaflet reproduced in Bourget and Lacretelle (1980), p. 144.

119. Audiat (1946), p. 233.

14. A Serial Killer on the Run, Pétain in Paris, the Milice on the Rampage, the Allies on Their Way

1. King (2012), pp. 94–99.

2. See King (2012), pp. 130–133.

3. See King (2012), p. 331.

4. On 19 September 1944 a journalist and Resistance fighter named Jacques Yonnet published an article entitled "Petiot, Soldier of the Reich" in *Résistance*, a former underground paper now openly on sale. The newspaper received a long rebuttal in what was authenticated as Petiot's handwriting. The rebuttal was

published in full in *Résistance* on 18 October. It not only proved that Petiot was still alive, but also gave some clues as to his whereabouts. He was arrested on the platform of Saint-Mandé-Tourelle railway station on the morning of 31 October. He was calling himself Henri-Jean Valeri, the leader of an FFI counterespionage unit tasked with tracking down traitors and collaborators, the members of which were actively searching for Petiot. See King (2012), pp. 194–198.

5. Florentin (2008), p. 390.

6. Quoted in Florentin (2008), p. 397.

7. Quoted in Florentin (2008), p. 398.

8. Figures given in Florentin (2008), p. 399.

9. See Florentin (2008), pp. 400–401.

10. Braibant (1945), pp. 441–442. Diary entry 20 April 1944.

11. Quoted in Florentin (2008), p. 407.

12. Guéhenno (2002), p. 405. Diary entry 20 April 1944.

13. Alfred Fabre-Luce, quoted in Florentin (2008), p. 409.

14. Auroy (2008), pp. 296–297. Diary entry 20 April 1944.

15. Quoted in Florentin (2008), p. 410.

16. Figures given in Florentin (2008), p. 410.

17. Fabre-Luce (1947), p. 607, quoted in Florentin (2008), p. 411.

18. Auroy (2008), pp. 298–300. Diary entry "The day after the bombing."

19. Auroy (2008), p. 300. Diary entry "The day after the bombing."

20. Figures given in Ferro (2012), p. 542.

21. Audiat (1946), p. 252.

22. Fauxbras (2012), p. 177. Diary entry 21 April 1944.

23. Rist (1983), p. 399. Diary entry 23 April 1944.

24. See Cointet (2001), p. 271.

25. See Ferro (2012), p. 543.

26. André Brissaud, quoted in Amouroux (1999a), p. 333.

27. Quoted in Amouroux (1999a), p. 336.

28. Claude Mauriac, *La Terrasse de Malagar: Le temps immobile* (Paris: Grasset, 1977), quoted in Jackson (2001), p. 536.

29. Claude Mauriac, *La Terrasse de Malagar: Le temps immobile* (Paris: Grasset, 1977), quoted in Cointet (2001), p. 270.

30. Ferro (2012), pp. 545–546.

31. Pétain (1989), p. 325–326.

32. See Beevor (2009), p. 17.

33. Braibant (1945), p. 489. Diary entry 6 June 1944.

34. Bobkowski (1991), p. 555. Diary entries 8 June 1944 and 10 June 1944.

35. Groult and Groult (1962), p. 423. Diary entry 10 June 1944.

36. Schroeder (2000), p. 222. Diary entry 6 June 1944.

37. Auroy (2008), p. 306. Diary entry 8 June 1944.

38. Auroy (2008), p. 307. Diary entry 8 June 1944.

39. Auroy (2008), p. 308. Diary entry 8 June 1944.

40. See Mitchell (2008), pp. 140–141.

41. Figures taken from Mitchell (2008), p. 141.

42. See Mitchell (2008), p. 142.

43. Quoted in Azéma (1990), p. 94.

44. Cointet (2011), pp. 665–666.

45. See Giolitto (2002), p. 289.

46. See Cobb (2009), pp. 239–241; Guérin (2000), pp. 1138–1148.

47. See Giolitto (2002), pp. 303–314, esp. pp. 310–314.

48. Radio broadcast by Laval, quoted in Giolitto (2002), p. 315.

49. Poster reproduced in Bourget and Lacretelle (1980), p. 177.

50. Quoted in Jackson (2001), p. 531.

51. Braibant (1945), p. 501. Diary entry 28 June 1944. Also quoted in Giolitto (2002), p. 318.

52. Quoted in Giolitto (2002), p. 319.

53. Guéhenno (2002), p. 421. Diary entry 28 June 1944. Also quoted in Giolitto (2002), p. 318.

54. Quoted in Giolitto (2002), p. 319.

55. Benoît-Guyod (1962), p. 275. Diary entry 28 June 1944.

56. Giolitto (2002), p. 315; see also Ferro (2012), pp. 574–575.

57. For more detail on Mandel and Mandel's murder, see Giolitto (2002), pp. 338–359, and Delpierré de Bayac (1969), pp. 505–515.

58. It would seem that Oradour was chosen at random and the purpose of the massacre was to intimidate the *maquis*, which was active in the area. The SS wanted to terrorise them into passivity by showing what sort of reprisals against civilians could be expected.

59. See Cobb (2013), p. 20; Kitson (1995), pp. 43–44.

60. Quoted in Ouzoulias (1967), p. 398.

61. Auroy (2008), p. 312. Diary entry 14 July 1944.

62. Auroy (2008), p. 314. Diary entry 14 July 1944.

63. Auroy (2008), p. 315. Diary entry 14 July 1944.

64. Quoted in Giolitto (2002), p. 416.

65. For this episode, see also Delpierré de Bayac (1969), pp. 493–495.

66. For the background to Stauffenberg's attempt to kill Hitler, see Kershaw (2000), pp. 655–671.

67. Bood (1974), p. 306. Diary entry 22 July 1944.

68. Manvell and Fraenkel (1964), p. 155.

69. Kershaw (2000), p. 684.

70. See Wieviorka and Laffitte (2012), pp. 300–302.

15. The Liberation of Paris

For this chapter I am much indebted to Matthew Cobb's lively and detailed study *Eleven Days in August* (New York: Simon and Schuster, 2013), which is, in my view, the best and most comprehensive account in English of the Liberation of Paris.

1. Boegner (1992), p. 276.

2. Ousby (1999), p. 277.

3. André Enfière, one of Laval's close associates, claimed to have received assurances from Allen Dulles, the U.S. spy chief and future head of the CIA, that Roosevelt would support Laval's plan. See Cobb (2013), p. 53.

4. Pierquin (1983), p. 130. Diary entry 13 August 1944. For more on the railway strike, see Cobb (2013), pp. 46–49.

5. Dupuy (1945), p. 5.

6. Quoted in Amouroux (1999a), pp. 891–892.

7. Choltitz, quoted in Cobb (2013), p. 75.

8. For more details see Cobb (2013), pp. 99–104.

9. Darnand had left on 15 August, de Brinon followed the next day, and Déat left at daybreak on the 17th. Members of Doriot's PPF left the capital on 17 August and members of the Milice were not far behind. Georges Benoît-Guyod saw trucks parked outside one of their bases—the Lycée Saint-Louis on the boulevard Saint-Michel—ready to drive them away from the capital. Doriot left on 19 August and headed straight for Germany to stay with Josef Bürckel, an old German friend and an enemy of Abetz who had previously been in charge of the annexed French province of Lorraine.

10. Quoted in Amouroux (1999a), p. 871.

11. Audiat (1946), p. 268.

12. Kent (1947), p. 201.

13. Audiat (1946), p. 268.

14. In Pierre Truffaut's film *Le Dernier Métro (The Last Metro)* Raymond Boursier (played by Maurice Risch) pedals in this way to help produce electricity for the theatre where he works as a technician.

15. Quoted in Amouroux (1999a), p. 873.

16. Galtier-Boissière (1944), p. 252. Diary entry 15 August 1944.

17. Groult and Groult (1962), p. 432. Diary entry 17 August 1944.

18. See Michel (1982), pp. 287–288.

19. Galtier-Boissière (1944), p. 253. Diary entry 17 August 1944.

20. Galtier-Boissière (1944), pp. 253–255. Diary entry 17 August 1944.

21. Galtier-Boissière (1944), p. 255. Diary entry 18 August 1944.

22. Seine-et-Oise, Seine-et-Marne, Oise.

23. Moulin was arrested in June 1943. He was horribly tortured, first in Lyons and then Paris, before being transferred to Germany. He died on or around 8 July somewhere between Metz and Frankfurt without giving away any information.

24. The Comité d'action militaire.

25. For an analysis of the various strands of the Paris Resistance during the Liberation of Paris, see Wieviorka (1994).

26. Olivier Wieviorka, quoted in Lévisse-Touzé (1994b), pp. 137–138. On 23 October 1941, after the Communists had started assassinating German soldiers in Paris, de Gaulle made a broadcast from London in which he already envisaged armed Resistance from within the country, rising up, albeit on his orders, and helping drive the Germans out of France. See Luneau (2005), p. 171.

27. Chaban-Delmas, quoted in Francis Crémieux, *La Vérité sur la Libération de Paris* (Paris: Pierre Belfond, 1971), p. 187. Quoted in Kaspi (2004), p. 110.

28. "It has to be short," Emmanuel d'Astier, de Gaulle's minister of the interior telegrammed Parodi at the end of May 1944. "It should not last longer than three of four days, 48 hours if possible." See Wievorka (1994), p. 138.

29. General Omar Bradley, quoted in Cobb (2009), p. 259.

30. Poster reproduced in Lévisse-Touzé (1994b), opposite p. 264.

31. Léo Hamon, quoted in Cobb (2013), p. 145.

32. See Footitt and Simmonds (1988), p. 125.

33. For the full text of this appeal, see Dansette (1966), pp. 373–374.

34. See Footitt and Simmonds (1988), p. 125.

35. Parodi in *Le Figaro,* 19 August 1964. Quoted in Footitt and Simmonds (1988), p. 125.

36. Auroy (2008), p. 324. Diary entry 19 August.

37. Dubois (1944), p. 72; see Cobb (2013), p. 452.

38. Poster reproduced in Bourget and Lacretelle (1980), p. 202.

39. Bobkowski (1991), p. 608. Diary entry 19 August 1944.

40. See Footitt and Simmonds (1988), pp. 128–129.

41. Auroy (2008), p. 319. Diary entry 19 August 1944.

42. Boegner (1992), p. 283. Diary entry 19 August 1944.

43. De Beauvoir (1960a), p. 677.

44. Groult and Groult (1962), pp. 433–434. Diary entry 19 August 1944.

45. Bobkowski (1991), p. 608. Diary entry 19 August 1944.

46. Sartre (1944), p. 1. De Beauvoir later admitted that she had written parts of the seven articles that appeared in *Combat.*

47. Sartre (1944), p. 1.

48. Bobkowski (1991), p. 608. Diary entry 19 August 1944.

49. Groult and Groult (1962), p. 434. Diary entry 19 August 1944.

50. He had been told by some passersby that if he did not tear it off at once they would do it themselves.

51. Auroy (2008), p. 318. Diary entry 19 August 1944.

52. Bood (1974), p. 316. Diary entry 19 August 1944.

53. Benoît-Guyod (1962), p. 285. Diary entry 19 August 1944.

54. Bood (1974), p. 317. Diary entry 19 August 1944.

55. Bourget (1994), pp. 243–244.

56. See Cobb (2013), p. 162.

57. Choltitz tried to portray himself to the Allies as an anti-Nazi but after the war in British custody he told General Wilhelm Ritter von Thoma, "The worse job I ever carried out—which however I carried out with great consistency—was the liquidation of the Jews [in southern Russia]. I carried out this order down to the very last detail." He never faced a war crimes tribunal for these atrocities. See Beevor (2009), p. 482.

58. Boegner (1992), p. 285. Diary entry 20 August 1944; Galtier-Boissière (1944), p. 264. Diary entry 20 August 1944.

59. Auroy (2008), pp. 321–322. Diary entry 20 August 1944.

60. Galtier-Boissière (1944), p. 264. Diary entry 20 August 1944.

61. Auroy (2008), p. 322. Diary entry 20 August 1944.

62. Bobkowski (1991), p. 610. Diary entry 20 August 1944.

63. Groult and Groult (1962), p. 435. Diary entry 20 August 1944.

64. Benoît-Guyod (1962), p. 292. Diary entry 20 August 1944.

65. Benoît-Guyod (1962), p. 292. Diary entry 20 August 1944.

66. For a detailed account of the 20 August meetings and discussions about the cease-fire, see Cobb (2013), chapter 9, pp. 165–185.

67. Rol-Tanguy, quoted in Crémieux, *La Vérité sur la Libération de Paris,* p. 91 in Bourget (1994), p. 250.

68. Galtier-Boissière (1944), p. 261. Diary entry 20 August 1944.

69. Galtier-Boissière (1944), p. 261. Diary entry 20 August 1944.

70. Bood (1974), p. 317. Diary entry 19 August 1944.

71. Bood (1974), p. 323. Diary entry 21 August 1944.

72. Benoît-Guyod (1962), p. 289. Diary entry 20 August 1944.

73. Groult and Groult (1962), p. 435. Diary entry 20 August 1944.

74. See de Gaulle (1956), p. 347.

75. De Gaulle (1956), p. 491.

76. Erwen Bergot, *La 2ème D.B.* (Paris: Presses de la Cité, 1980), p. 107, quoted in Cobb (2013), p. 223.

77. Text reproduced in Dansette (1966), p. 393.

78. Text reproduced in Dansette (1966), pp. 393–394.

79. Beevor and Cooper (1995), p. 41.

80. Galtier-Boissière (1944), p. 265. Diary entry 21 August 1944.

81. Galtier-Boissière (1944), p. 273. Diary entry 24 August 1944.

82. Pierquin (1983), p. 131. Diary entry 22 August 1944.

83. See Audiat (1946), pp. 294–295.

84. Bood (1974), p. 329. Diary entry 23 August 1944.

85. See d'Astier (1965), pp. 203–205.

86. See Cobb (2013), pp. 231–232.

87. See Cobb (2013), p. 233.

88. Quoted in Dansette (1966), p. 254.

89. Bood (1974), p. 331. Diary entry 23 August 1944.

90. Galtier-Boissière (1944), p. 272. Diary entry 23 August 1944.

91. Guéhenno (2002), p. 437. Diary entry 24 August 1944.

92. Auroy (2008), p. 329. Diary entry 24 August 1944.

93. Audiat (1946), pp. 318–319.

94. Galtier-Boissière (1944), p. 272. Diary entry 23 August 1944.

95. Bood (1974), p. 331. Diary entry 23 August 1944.

96. See Amouroux (1999a), p. 947.

97. Braibant (1945), p. 554. Diary entry 24 August 1944 (midnight).

98. Interview with author in Paris. Bedel was a member of a Free French Resistance group comprising former journalists from *Le Matin* newspaper, which fed information back to London. Today a plaque on the corner of the rue Saint-Séverin and the rue de Condé marks the spot where Rastello fell.

99. Raymond Dronne, *La Libération de Paris* (Paris: Presses de la Cité, 1970), p. 82, quoted in Cobb (2013), p. 269.

100. The bunker, 26 metres below ground, had been built by the French government before the war to serve as a command centre if the city were bombarded. It had more than twenty rooms, including dormitories, generators, an air-conditioning system and, crucially, a telephone switchboard that allowed Rol-Tanguy to maintain contact with the Prefecture of Police and the Hôtel de Ville. See Cobb (2009), p. 262, and Cobb (2013), p. 195.

101. Cited by Amouroux (1999a), p. 950.

102. Galtier-Boissière (1944), pp. 275–276. Diary entry 25 August 1944.

103. Ernie Pyle, quoted in Cobb (2013), p. 286.

104. Pierquin (1983), p. 134. Diary entry 27 August 1944.

105. Galtier-Boissière (1944), p. 277. Diary entry 25 August 1944.

106. De Gaulle (1956), p. 496. "Paris, Paris outragé, Paris brisé, Paris martyrisé mais Paris libéré ! Libéré par lui-même, libéré par son peuple avec le concours des armées de la France, avec l'appui et le concours de la France tout entière: c'est-à-

dire de la France qui se bat. C'est-à-dire de la seule France, de la vraie France, de la France éternelle."

107. Quoted in Kaspi (2004), pp. 130–131.

108. On 29 August de Gaulle and General Bradley took the salute as the 28th U.S. Infantry Division and the 5th Armoured Division marching twenty abreast, followed by American tanks and field artillery, marched through Paris on their way to engage with the units of the German army to the north and east of the city. See Cobb (2013), pp. 340–341.

109. De Gaulle (1956), p. 364.

110. Quoted in d'Astier (1965), p. 216.

111. Bood (1974), p. 338. Diary entry 26 August 1944.

112. See Amouroux (1999a), p. 976, n. 2.

113. Auvinet (2012), p. 15. My thanks to Simon Kitson for bringing this document to my attention.

114. Lévisse-Touzé (1994a), pp. 76–77.

115. La Rochelle, Saint-Nazaire, and Lorient remained in German hands until 9 May 1945.

116. Beevor (2009), p. 513.

117. De Gaulle (1956), p. 371.

Conclusion

1. See Sauvy (1978), p. 221.

2. It was not until October 1944, for example, that the first main-line rail link opened with just one twelve-hour train journey a day in each direction between Paris and Marseilles.

3. Steven Philip Kramer, in *Revue d'histoire de la Seconde Guerre mondiale* 3 (July 1978): 26ff., quoted in Bourget and Lacretelle (1980), p. 205.

4. Auroy (2008), pp. 342–343.

5. Fernand Picard, *Carnets de guerre et d'occupation, 1939–1945: Usines Renault*, quoted in Veillon (1995), p. 291, n. 5.

6. Fernand Picard quoted in Veillon (1995), p. 293, n. 12.

7. Janet Flanner, *Paris Journal, 1944–1965* (New York: Atheneum, 1965), quoted in Giles (1991), p. 16.

8. See Grenard (2008), p. 259.

9. Quoted in Grenard (2008), p. 258.

10. Prefecture of Police report, quoted in Grenard (2008), p. 260.

11. Lafont was executed on 26 December 1944; Bonny on 27 December 1944.

12. See Wieviorka and Laffitte (2012), p. 310.

13. Muggeridge (1973), p. 217.

14. Beevor and Cooper (1995), p. 92.

15. See Cobb (2013), p. 352.

16. For an analysis of the debates in the world of culture, see Assouline (1990).

17. In September 1944, the northern coalmines were nationalised, followed, in January 1945, by Louis Renault's car plant. Louis Renault was arrested and charged with collaboration. In May 1945, Gnome & Rhône, which had contributed to the

German war effort, was also nationalised, followed a month later by the creation of a state airline Air France.

18. The Communists argued that their popular support merited their being awarded at least one key ministry (Interior, Defence, or Foreign Affairs). De Gaulle refused and they accepted four ministries: National Economy, Economy, Labour, and Industrial Production and Armaments.

19. A total of 400,000 cases of collaboration were heard in Belgium, 110,000 in the Netherlands, and 90,000 in Norway, all of which had smaller populations than France. See Giles (1991), p. 14.

20. See Dank (1974), p. 323.

21. Pierre Pucheu, the Vichy minister of the interior, was executed in Algiers on 20 March 1944.

22. See Dank (1974), p. 277.

23. For more on Doriot's death, see Brunet (1986), pp. 487ff.

24. For a detailed account of Darquier's life, see Callil (2006).

25. This was not an isolated case. The CIA employed Klaus Barbie, "the Butcher of Lyons," to train the Bolivian security forces in interrogation techniques, including the use of torture.

26. See Josephs (1989), pp. 180–186.

27. Amouroux (1999b), p. 725.

28. See Arnaud (2014), p. 546.

29. Jean-Louis Quereillahc, quoted in Arnaud (2014), p. 549.

30. See Arnaud (2014), p. 550.

31. Vinen (2006), p. 364.

32. See Arnaud (2014), p. 550.

33. There were eight deportees for every 100 STO workers and POWs; this figure falls to 4 per 100 if Jews are excluded. See Wieviorka (1992), pp. 47–48.

34. See Kaspi (2004), p. 287, n. 41.

35. Pierre Assouline provides a fictional account (underpinned by serious research) of interviews with returnees from the camps in Assouline (2005), p. 325ff.

36. Daix (1976), p. 144.

37. Simone Veil, quoted in Wieviorka (1992), p. 170.

38. Quoted in Poznanski (1997), p. 552.

39. Jean-Marc Benammar in an email to the author.

40. Clark and Costelle (2011).

41. For more details, see Rayssac (2008) and Riding (2011), pp. 165–167.

42. Place-des-Cinq-Martyrs-du-Lycée-Buffon.

43. "Allocution de M. Jacques Chirac, Président de la République, prononcé lors des cérémonies commémorant la grande rafle des 16 et 17 juillet 1942" (Speech delivered 16 July 1995). Accessed on the official website of the Elysée Palace (http://elysee.fr), 2 July 2014.

Bibliography

All publications in French are published in Paris unless otherwise indicated; all those in English are published in London unless otherwise indicated. All translations in the text from French works are mine unless otherwise indicated.

Adler, Jacques. *The Jews of Paris and the Final Solution.* Oxford: Oxford University Press, 1987.

Alary, Eric. *Un Procès sous l'Occupation au Palais Bourbon, mars 1942.* Éditions Assemblée Nationale, 2000.

———. *L'Exode.* Perrin, 2010.

Alary, Eric, Bénédicte Vergez-Chaignon, and Gilles Gauvin. *Les Français au quotidien, 1939–1949.* Perrin, 2006.

Amouroux, Henri. *Les Français sous l'Occupation.* Audiocassette K1052, "La LVF/Les Premières mesures anti-sémites," Cassettes Radio France/France Inter, n.d.

———. *La Grande Histoire des Français sous l'Occupation.* Vol. 1, *Le Peuple du désastre/Quarante millions de Pétainistes 1939–1941.* Collection Bouquins. Robert Laffont, 1997.

———. *La Grande Histoire des Français sous l'Occupation.* Vol. 2, *Les Beaux Jours des collabos/Le peuple réveillé juin 1940–juin 1942.* Collection Bouquins. Robert Laffont, 1998a.

———. *La Grande Histoire des Français sous l'Occupation.* Vol. 3, *Les Passions et les haines/L'impitoyable guerre civile: avril 1942–décembre 1943.* Collection Bouquins. Robert Laffont, 1998b.

———. *La Grande Histoire des Français sous l'Occupation.* Vol. 4, *Un printemps de mort et d'espoir/Joies et douleurs du peuple libéré septembre 1943–août 1944.* Collection Bouquins. Robert Laffont, 1999a.

———. *La Grande Histoire des Français après l'Occupation.* Vol. 5, *Les Règlements de comptes/La page n'est pas encore tournée.* Collection Bouquins. Robert Laffont, 1999b.

———. *Pour en finir avec Vichy.* Vol. 2, *Les Racines des passions, 1940–1941.* Robert Laffont, 2005.

Anonymous. *La Rafle du Vélodrome d'Hiver: Les archives de la police.* Préfecture de Police (Paris), Service de la mémoire et des affaires culturelles, n.d.

———. *Ce que le public doit savoir en matière de défense passive.* Préfecture de Police (Paris), 1938.

———. "Le Camp de la cité de la Muette à Drancy 1941–1944." *Patrimoine,* no. 37, Conseil général de la Seine-Saint-Denis, 2010.

———. *Wohin Paris? Où sortir à Paris.* Alma, 2013.

Arnaud, Patrice. "Le STO: Cadeau inespéré à la Résistance." In "Résistants et collabos, 1943: La France déchirée." *Le Nouvel Observateur,* Hors Série 84 (November–December 2013): 19–23.

———. *Les STO: Histoire des Français requis en Allemagne nazie, 1942–1945.* Collection Biblis. CNRS Éditions, 2014.

Aron, Robert. "De la Relève au S.T.O." *Les Années 40,* no. 42. Tallandier/Hachette, 1979, 1149–1158.

Assouline, Pierre. *Gaston Gallimard: Un demi-siècle d'édition française.* Collection Folio. Gallimard, 2006. First published Éditions Balland 1984.

———. *L'Épuration des intellectuels.* Éditions Complexe, 1990.

———. *Lutetia.* Collection Folio. Gallimard, 2005.

Atkin, Nicholas. "Seduction and Sedition: Otto Abetz and the French, 1918–1940." In *Problems in French History: Essays in Honour of Douglas Johnson.* Edited by Martyn Cornick and Ceri Crossley, 180–196. Palgrave, 2000.

———. *The French at War, 1934–1944.* Seminar Studies in History. Pearson, 2001.

Auda, Grégory. *Les Belles Années du "milieu," 1940–1944.* Éditions Michalon, 2002.

Audiat, Pierre. *Paris pendant la guerre.* Hachette, 1946.

Auroy, Berthe. *Jours de guerre: Ma vie sous l'Occupation.* Bayard, 2008.

Auvinet, André. *Journal de la Libération de Paris, 18 au 28 août 1944.* http://liberation-de-paris.gilles-primout.fr/mon-journal-de-la-liberation-de-paris-2. Accessed 12 June 2014.

Avakoumovitch, Ivan. "Le PCF vu par le commandement des troupes d'occupation allemandes, août 1940–mai 1941." *Le Mouvement social* 113 (October–December 1980): 91–99.

———. "La Résistance du PCF vu par la Wehrmacht." *Cahiers d'Histoire de l'Institut de recherches marxistes* (6 July–September 1981): 16–36.

———. "La Résistance du PCF vue par l'occupant, juillet 1940–juin 1941." *Cahiers d'Histoire de l'Institut de recherches marxistes* 14 (numéro spécial) (September 1983): 47–110.

Azéma, Jean-Pierre. "La Milice." *Vingtième Siècle: Revue d'histoire* 28 (October–December 1990): 83–105.

Azéma, Jean-Pierre, Antoine Prost, and Jean-Pierre Rioux. *Le Parti Communiste Français des années sombres, 1938–1941.* Seuil, 1986.

Aziz, Philippe. *Tu trahiras sans vergogne.* Fayard, 1970.

———. *Le Livre noir de la trahison: Histoires de la Gestapo en France.* Éditions Ramsay, 1984.

Badia, Gilbert. "Vivre à Paris, 1939–1944: Impressions d'un témoin." In *Paris sous l'Occupation/Paris unter deutscher Besatzung: Actes du 3ème colloque des Universités d'Orléans et de Siegen,* 11–22. Heidelberg: Universitätsverlag, 1995.

Badinter, Robert. *Un Antisémitisme ordinaire*. Livre de Poche, 1997.

Bair, Deirdre. *Simone de Beauvoir: A Biography*. Jonathan Cape, 1990.

Bardoux, Jacques. *Journal d'un témoin de la IIIe République*. Fayard, 1957.

Beauvoir, Simone de. *La Force de l'âge*. Folio. Gallimard, 1960a.

———. *La Force des choses*. Gallimard, 1960b.

———. *Journal de guerre*. Gallimard, 1990a.

———. *Lettres à Sartre*. Gallimard, 1990b.

Beevor, Anthony. *D-Day: The Battle for Normandy*. Viking, 2009.

Beevor, Anthony, and Artemis Cooper. *Paris after the Liberation*. Penguin, 1995.

Beltran Alain, and Patrice A. Carré. *La Fée et la servante*. Belin, 1991.

Benbassa, Esther. *Histoire des Juifs de France*. Éditions du Seuil, 1997.

Benoist-Méchin, Jacques. *De la Défaite au désastre*. Vol. 1, *Les Occasions manquées, juillet 1940–avril 1942*. Julliard, 1984.

Benoît-Guyod, Georges. *L'Invasion de Paris*. Les Éditions du Scorpion, 1962.

Berg, Roger. "Les Attentats contre les synagogues en 1941." In *Mémoire du génocide: recueil de 80 articles du "Monde juif," 1946–1986*. Edited by Serge Klarsfeld, 38–40. Revue du Centre de la Documentation juive, 1987.

Berlière Jean-Marc, and Franck Liaigre. *Le Sang des communistes*. Fayard, 2004.

———. *Liquider les traîtres: La face cachée du PCF, 1941–1943*. Robert Laffont, 2007.

———. *L'Affaire Guy Môquet: enquête sur une mystification officielle*. Larousse, 2009.

Berlière, Jean-Marc, and Denis Peschanski. "Police et policiers parisiens face à la lutte armée, 1941–1944." In *Pouvoirs et polices au XXème siècle*. Edited by Jean-Marc Berlière and Denis Peschanski, 137–176. Brussels: Éditions Complexe, 1997.

Berr, Hélène. *Journal*. Tallandier, 2008.

Besson, Jean-Louis. *Paris rutabaga: souvenirs d'enfance, 1939–1945*. Gallimard, n.d.

Biélinky, Jacques. *Un Journaliste juif à Paris sous l'Occupation*. Le Cerf/CNRS, 2011.

Binet, Laurent. *HHhH*. Vintage Books, 2013.

Blanc, Julien. "Le Réseau du Musée de l'Homme." *Esprit* 261 (February 2000): 89–103.

———. "Introduction." In *Notre guerre*. By Agnès Humbert, 9–80. Tallandier, 2004.

———. *Au commencement de la Résistance: Du côté du Musée de l'Homme, 1940–1941*. Éditions du Seuil, 2010.

Blumenson, Martin. *The Vildé Affair*. Boston: Houghton Mifflin, 1977.

Bobkowski, Andrzej. *En Guerre et en paix*. Montricher, Switzerland: Les Éditions noir sur blanc, 1991.

Bock, Fedor von. *The War Diary, 1939–1945*. Translated by David Johnston. Schiffer Military History. Atglen, PA: Schiffer, 1996.

Boegner, Philippe. *Carnets du Pasteur Boegner, 1940–1945*. Fayard, 1992.

Bood, Micheline. *Les Années doubles*. Robert Laffont, 1974.

Borgé, Jacques, and Nicolas Viasnoff. *Les Véhicules de l'Occupation*. Balland, 1975.

Boucault, Mosco Levi. *Des "Terroristes" à la retraite*, 1985. Released on DVD as *Les FTP-MOI: Paris-Toulouse 1942–1944*. Arte France, 2013. This DVD includes another film directed by Boucault entitled *Ni Travail, ni famille, ni patrie*.

Bourderon Roger, and Germaine Willard. "Documents communistes (mai 1939–novembre 1941)." *Cahiers d'Histoire de l'Institut de recherches marxistes* 14 (numéro spécial) (1983): 159–193.

Bourget, Pierre. *Histoires secrètes de l'Occupation de Paris.* Vol. 1, *Le joug.* Hachette, 1970.

———. *Paris, 1940–1944.* Plon, 1979.

———. "La Trève." In *Paris 1944: Les enjeux de la libération.* Edited by Christine Lévisse-Touzé, 243–257. Albin Michel, 1994.

Bourget, Pierre, and Charles Lacretelle. *Sur les Murs de Paris, 1940–1944.* Bibliothèque des Guides Bleus. Librairie Hachette, 1959.

———. *Sur les Murs de Paris.* Hachette, 1980.

Braibant, Charles. *Lumière bleue.* Fayard, 1940.

———. *La Guerre à Paris.* Éditions Corrêa, 1945.

Brasillach, Robert. *Journal d'un homme occupé.* Les Sept Couleurs, 1955.

Brunet, Jean-Paul. *Jacques Doriot: Du communisme au fascisme.* Balland, 1986.

Brustlein, Gilbert. *Le Chant d'amour d'un "terroriste à la retraite."* Société européenne des arts graphiques, 1989.

———. *Agir.* In the series *Le Choix des hommes.* DVD. La Documentation française, 2011.

Buisson, Patrick. *1940–1945: Années érotiques.* Vol. 1, *Vichy, ou les infortunes de la vertu.* Albin Michel, 2008.

———. *1940–1945: Années érotiques.* Vol. 2, *De la grande prostituée à la revanche des mâles.* Albin Michel, 2009.

Burinovici-Herbornel, Claudine. *Une Enfance traquée.* L'Improviste, 2001.

Burrin, Philippe. *La France à l'heure allemande, 1940–1944.* Collection Points Histoire. Seuil, 1995.

———. *La Dérive fasciste.* Seuil, 2003.

Callil, Carmen. *Bad Faith: A Story of Faith and Fatherland.* Vintage, 2006.

Cardon-Hamet, Claudine. *Triangles rouges à Auschwitz: Le convoi politique du 6 juillet 1942.* Collection Mémoires 115. Éditions Autrement, 2005.

Carroll, Sean, and Héloïse Dufour. "Great Myths Die Hard." *Nature* 502 (October 2013): 32–33.

Chadwick, Kay. *Alphonse de Châteaubriant: Catholic Collaborator.* Bern: Peter Lang, 2002.

Chapsal, Jacques. *La Vie politique en France depuis 1940.* Presses universitaires de France, 1966.

Charpentier, Pierre-Frédéric. *La Drôle de guerre des intellectuels français, 1939–1940.* Lavauzelle, 2008.

Chevassus-au-Louis, Nicolas. *Savants sous l'Occupation.* Perrin, 2004.

Clarke, Isabelle, and Daniel Costelle. *L'Occupation intime.* DVD. TF1-Vidéo, 2011.

Cobb, Matthew. *Resistance.* Simon & Schuster, 2009.

———. *Eleven Days in August.* Simon & Schuster, 2013.

Cohen-Solal, Annie. *Sartre.* Gallimard, 1985.

Cointet, Jean-Paul. *Paris 40–44.* Perrin, 2001.

Cointet, Michèle. *L'Église sous Vichy.* Perrin, 1998.

———. *Nouvelle Histoire de Vichy.* Fayard, 2011.

———. "La Milice: L'état meurtrier." In "Résistants et collabos: 1943, La France déchirée." *Le Nouvel Observateur,* Hors Série 84 (November–December 2013): 28–30.

Cointet, Michèle, and Jean-Paul Cointet, eds. *Dictionnaire historique de la France sous l'Occupation.* Tallandier, 2000.

Cornick, Martyn, ed. *Paulhan-Armand Petitjean: Correspondance 1934–1948.* Gallimard, 2010.

Costantini, Pierre. *La Haute Signification de la Légion.* Imprimerie spécial de la LVF, no. 185, n.d.

Cotta, Michèle, *La Collaboration, 1940–1944.* Collection Kiosque. Armand Colin, 1964.

Courtois, Stéphane. *Le PCF dans la guerre.* Éditions Ramsay, 1980.

———. "Le 'Groupe Manouchian' sacrifié ou trahi?" *Le Monde,* 2–3 June 1985. http://www.lemonde.fr/archives/article/1985/06/03/le-groupe-manouchian-sacrifie-ou-trahi_2754119_1819218.html.

Courtois, Stéphane, Denis Peschanski, and Adam Rayski. *Le Sang de l'étranger: Les immigrés de la MOI dans la Résistance.* Fayard, 1989.

Crémieux-Brilhac, Jean-Louis. *Les Français de l'an 40.* Vol. 1, *La guerre oui ou non?* Gallimard, 1990.

d'Abzac-Epezy, Claude. "Les Premiers Bombardements alliés sur la France et leur utilisation politique." *Revue historique des armées,* no. 191 (June 1993): 73–84.

Daix, Pierre. *J'ai cru au matin.* Robert Laffont, 1976.

———. *Les Combattants de l'impossible.* Robert Laffont, 2013.

Dank, Milton. *The French against the French.* Cassell, 1974.

Dansette, Adrien. *Histoire de la Libération de Paris.* Fayard, 1966. First published 1946.

D'Astier, Emmanuel. *De la Chute à la Liberation de Paris.* Gallimard, 1965.

Déat, Marcel. "Mourir pour Dantzig?" *L'Œuvre,* 4 May 1939.

———. *Mémoires politiques.* Denoël, 1989.

Delarue, Jacques. *Histoire de la Gestapo.* Fayard, 1962.

———. "La Police sous l'Occupation." *L'Histoire* 29 (December 1980): 6–15.

———. "La Bande Bonny-Lafont." *L'Histoire* 80 (July–August 1985): 62–69.

———. *Trafics et crimes sous l'Occupation.* Fayard, 1993.

Delatour, François. "SS et Français: Pourquoi?" *Historia,* Hors Série 32 (1973).

Delpierré de Bayac, Jacques. *Histoire de la Milice, 1918–1945.* Fayard, 1969.

Deroy, Jacqueline, and Françoise-Renée Pineau. *Celles qui attendaient . . . témoignent aujourd'hui.* Melun, France: ANRPAPG, 1985.

Desanti, Dominique, Jean-Toussaint Desanti, and Roger-Pol Droit. *La Liberté nous aime encore.* Odile Jacob, 2004.

Desprairies, Cécile. *Ville lumière-années noires: Les Lieux du Paris de la collaboration.* Éditions Denoël, 2008.

———. *Paris dans la collaboration.* Éditions du Seuil, 2009.

D'Hoop, Jean-Marie. "La main-d'oeuvre française au service de l'Allemagne." *Revue d'histoire de la Deuxième Guerre mondiale* 81 (January 1971): 73–88.

Diamond, Hanna. *Fleeing Hitler: France 1940.* Oxford: Oxford University Press, 2007.

Drake, David. *Intellectuals and Politics in France from the Dreyfus Affair to the Occupation*. Palgrave Macmillan, 2005.

Dreyfus, Jean-Marc, and Sarah Gensburger. *Des Camps dans Paris: Austerlitz, Lévitan, Bassano, juillet 1943–août 1944*. Fayard, 2003.

Dubois, Edmond. *Vu pendant la libération de Paris: Journal d'un témoin*. Lausanne, Switzerland: Librairie Payot, 1944.

———. *Paris sans lumière*. Lausanne, Switzerland: Librairie Payot, 1946.

Duchatelet, Bernard. *Romain Rolland tel que lui-même*. Albin Michel, 2002.

Dufay, François, *Le Voyage d'automne*. Plon, 2000.

Dupays, Paul. *Paris: Chronique historique, septembre 1939–juin 1940*. Éditions de la critique, Hachette, n.d.

Dupuy, Ferdinand. *Quand "ils" entrèrent à Paris*. Librairie-Imprimeries réunies, 1940.

———. *La Libération de Paris vue d'un commissariat de police*. Librairie-Imprimeries reunites, 1945.

Duquesne, Jacques. *Les Catholiques français sous l'occupation*. Points Histoire. Bernard Grasset, 1996.

Ehmer, Wilhelm. *La Nuit devant Paris: 13 juin 1944*. Trois Épis, 1943. Translation by J. Berthelle of *Die Nacht vor Paris*. Stuttgart: Verlag J. Engelhorns Nachf., Adolf Spemann, n.d.

Eismann, Gaël. *Hotel Majestic: ordre et sécurité en France occupée, 1940–1944*. Tallandier, 2010.

Epelbaum, Didier. *Obéir. Les déshonneurs du capitaine Vieux, Drancy, 1941–1944*. Stock, 2009.

Evans, Richard J. *The Third Reich at War*. Penguin, 2009.

———. "The Staggering Inaccuracy of Bombs." Review of Richard Overy, *The Bombing War: Europe 1939–1945* (London: Allen Lane, 2013). *The Guardian* (Review Section), 28 September 2013, p. 9.

Evrard, Jacques. *La Déportation des travailleurs français dans le IIIe Reich*. Fayard, 1972.

Eychart, François, and Georges Aillaud, eds. *Les Lettres françaises et les Étoiles dans la clandestinité, 1942–1944*. Le Cherche Midi, 2008.

Fabre-Luce, Alfred. *Journal de la France, 1939–1944*, Éditions Amiot-Dumont (La Diffusion du Livre), 1947.

Fauxbras, César. *Le Théâtre de l'Occupation*. Éditions Allia, 2012.

Ferro, Marc. *Pétain*. Collection Pluriel. Fayard, 2012.

Feyel, Gilles. *La Presse en France des origines à 1944*. Ellipses, 1999.

Fishman, Sarah. *We Will Wait: Wives of French Prisoners of War, 1940–1945*. New Haven, CT: Yale University Press, 1991.

Florentin, Eddy. *Quand les Alliés bombardaient la France, 1940–1945*. Collection Tempus. Perrin, 2008.

Fonkenell, Guillaume. *Le Louvre pendant la guerre*. Éditions Musée du Louvre, 2009.

Footitt, Hilary, and John Simmonds. *France, 1943–1945*. Leicester University Press, 1988.

Forbes, Robert. *For Europe: The French Volunteers of the Waffen-SS*. Mechanicsburg, PA: Stackpole, 2010.

Foss, Myriam, and Lucien Steinberg. *Vie et mort des Juifs sous l'Occupation*. Plon, 1996.

Foville, Jean-Marc de. *L'Éntrée des Allemands à Paris*. Calmann-Lévy, 1965.

Friedländer, Saul. *Nazi Germany and the Jews*. Phoenix, 2009.

Galtier-Boissière, Jean. *Mon Journal pendant l'Occupation*. La Jeune Parque, 1944.

Gaulle, Charles de. *Mémoires de guerre: L'unité, 1942–1944*. Collection Pocket. Plon, 1956.

Gerwarth, Robert. *Hitler's Hangman: The Life of Heydrich*. New Haven, CT: Yale University Press, 2011.

Gex le Verrier, Madeleine. *Une Française dans la tourmente*. Hamish Hamilton, 1942.

Giles, Frank. *The Locust Years: The Story of the Fourth Republic, 1946–1958*. Secker & Warburg, 1991.

Giolitto, Pierre. *Histoire de la Milice*. Collection Tempus. Perrin, 2002.

———. *Volontaires français sous l'uniforme allemand*. Collection Tempus. Perrin, 2007.

Giraudoux, Jean. *Messages du Continental: Allocutions radiodiffusées du Commissaire à l'information*. Cahiers Jean Giraudoux 16. Grasset, 1987.

Goglin, Jean-Louis, and Pierre Roux, eds. *Souffrance et liberté: Une géographie parisienne des années noires*. Paris-Musées, 2004.

Gordon, Bertram. "*Ist Gott Französisch?* Germans, Tourism, and Occupied France." *Modern and Contemporary France* NS 4, no. 3 (1996): 287–298.

Grenard, Fabrice. *La France du marché noir, 1940–1949*. Payot, 2008.

Groult, Benoîte, and Flora Groult. *Journal à quatre mains*. Livre de Poche, 1962.

Gruat, Cédric. *Hitler à Paris, juin 1940*. Éditions Tirésais, 2010.

Grunberg, Albert. *Journal d'un coiffeur juif à Paris sous l'Occupation*. Éditions de l'Atelier, 2001.

Guéhenno, Jean. *Journal des années noires, 1940–1944*. Collection Folio. Gallimard, 2002.

Guérin, Alain. *Chronique de la Résistance*. Éditions France Loisirs, 2000.

Guidez, Guylaine. *Femmes dans la guerre*. Collection Terres des Femmes. Perrin, 1989.

Halami, André. *Chantons sous l'Occupation*. L'Harmattan, 1976.

———. *La délation sous l'Occupation*. Edition 1, 1998.

Halls, Wilfred D. *The Youth of Vichy France*. Oxford: Clarendon, 1981.

Hastings, Max. *All Hell Let Loose: The World at War, 1939–1945*. Harper Press, 2011.

Hatry, Gilbert. "Objectif Renault: Le bombardement du 3 mars 1942." In the bi-annual review of the Section d'histoire des Usines Renault: *De Renault Frères à Renault Régie Nationale*, June 1974, 1–24.

Hebey, Pierre. *La Nouvelle Revue française des années sombres, 1940–1941*. Gallimard, 1992.

Hire, Jean de la. *Le Crime des évacuations: Les horreurs que nous avons vues*. Éditions Tallandier, 1940.

Hoare, Quintin. Translator's Introduction to Jean-Paul Sartre, *War Diaries: Notebooks from a Phoney War 1939–1940*, vii–xviii. Verso Editions, 1984.

Humbert, Agnès. *Notre guerre: Souvenirs de Résistance*. Tallandier, 2004. First published in 1946 by Éditions Émile-Paul.

Hyman, Paula. *The Jews of Modern France.* Berkeley: University of California Press, 1998.

Imlay, Talbot. "Mind the Gap: The Perception and Reality of Communist Sabotage during the Phoney War." *Past and Present* 189, no. 1 (November 2005): 179–223.

Israel, Gérard. *Heureux comme Dieu en France.* Laffont, 1975.

Jäckel, Eberhard. *La France dans l'Europe de Hitler.* Fayard, 1968.

Jackson, Julian. *France: The Dark Years 1940–1944.* Oxford: Oxford University Press, 2001.

———. *The Fall of France.* Oxford: Oxford University Press, 2003.

Jamet, Fabienne, Albert Kantof, and René Havard. *One Two Two.* Olivier Orban, 1975.

Jarreau, Patrick, and Edwy Plenel. "Les ombres de 1943." *Le Monde,* 2 July 1985. www.lemonde.fr/archives/article/1985/07/02/les-ombres-de-1943_2739476 _1819218. html?xtmc=les_ombres_1943&xtcr=9. Accessed 15 May 2015.

Joly, Laurent. "La Délation anti-sémite sous l'Occupation." *Vingtième Siècle: Revue d'Histoire* 96 (October–December 2007): 137–149.

———. "La Dénonciation dans la traque des communistes et des Juifs 1940– 1944." In Laurent Joly, ed. *La Délation dans la France des années noires.* Perrin, 2012a.

———. "Quand la délation empoisonnait la France." Interview with Laurent Joly. Fribourg, Switzerland. *La Liberté,* 3 February 2012b. http://www.laliberte .ch/sites/default/files/article_pdf/histoirevivante_veo30212.pdf. Accessed 15 May 2015.

———. "Le Cas Annette Zelman et les débuts de la 'solution finale' en France (mai–juin 1942)." *Vingtième Siècle: Revue d'Histoire* 119 (2013): 29–41.

Josephs, Jeremy. *Swastika over Paris.* Bloomsbury, 1989.

Jünger, Ernst. *Journaux de guerre.* Vol. 2, *1939–1948.* Bibliothèque de la Pléiade. Gallimard, 2008.

Junot, Michel. *1940, tel que je l'ai vécu.* France-Empire, 1998.

Kageneck, August von. *La France occupée.* Perrin, 2012.

Kaspi, André. " 'Le Juif en France': Une exposition à Paris en 1941." In *Mémoire du génocide: recueil de 80 articles du "Monde juif," 1946–1986.* Edited by Serge Klarsfeld, 60–72. Revue du Centre de la Documentation juive, 1987. First published in *Le Monde juif,* 1975.

———. *Les Juifs pendant l'Occupation.* Éditions du Seuil, 1997.

———. *La Libération de la France, juin 1944–janvier 1946.* Collection Tempus. Perrin, 2004.

Kedward, H. R. *Occupied France: Collaboration and Resistance, 1940–1944.* Basil Blackwell, 1987.

Kent, Victoria, *Quatre ans à Paris,* Le Livre du Jour, 1947.

Kershaw, Ian. *Hitler, 1939–1946: Nemesis.* Allen Lane, 2000.

———. *Fateful Choices: Ten Decisions That Changed the World, 1940–1941.* Penguin, 2008.

King, David. *Death in the City of Light.* Sphere, 2012.

Kitson, Simon. "The Police in the Liberation of Paris." In *The Liberation of France: Image and Event.* Edited by H. R. Kedward and Nancy Wood, 43–56. Oxford: Berg, 1995.

———. "From Enthusiasm to Disenchantment: The French Police and the Vichy Regime." *Contemporary European History* 11, no. 3 (August 2002): 371–390.

Knowles, Elisabeth, ed. *The Oxford Dictionary of Quotations.* Oxford: Oxford University Press, 1999.

Koestler, Arthur. *Scum of the Earth.* Jonathan Cape, 1941.

Krivopissko, Guy, ed. *À vous la vie: Lettres de fusillés du Mont-Valérien, 1940–1944.* Tallandier, 2013.

Kupferman, Fred. *Laval, 1883–1945.* Balland, 1987.

Laffitte, Michel. *Un Engrenage fatal.* Liana Levi, 2003.

———. *Juifs dans la France allemande.* Tallendrier, 2006.

Lallam, Sandra. *La Population de la Seine et les forces d'occupation allemandes, 14 juin 1940–25 août 1944.* Master's thesis, Paris IV Sorbonne, 1999–2000.

Lambauer, Barbara. *Otto Abetz et les Français.* Fayard, 2001.

Lamblin, Bianca. *Mémoires d'une jeune fille dérangée.* Éditions Balland, 1993.

Langeron, Roger. *Paris, juin 40.* Flammarion, 1946.

Léautaud, Paul. *Journal littéraire.* Vol. 12, *mai 1937–février 1940.* Mercure de France, 1962.

———. *Journal littéraire.* Vol. 13, *février 1940–juin 1941.* Mercure de Paris 1962.

———. *Journal littéraire.* Vol. 14, *juillet 1941–novembre 1942.* Mercure de France, 1963.

Le Boterf, Hervé. *La Vie parisienne sous l'Occupation.* Vol. 1. Éditions France Empire, 1974.

———. *La Vie parisienne sous l'Occupation,* Vol. 2. Éditions France-Empire, 1975.

Le Marec, Gérard, and Suzanne Zwang. *Paris, 1939–1945.* Martelle Éditions, 1995.

Levert, Jean-Pierre. *Un Lycée dans la tourmente.* Calmann-Lévy, 1994.

Lévisse-Touzé, Christine. *Paris libéré, Paris retrouvé.* Collection Découvertes. Gallimard, 1994a.

———, ed. *Paris 1944: Les Enjeux de la Libération.* Albin Michel, 1994b.

Lévy, Claude, and Paul Tillard. *La Grande Rafle du Vél' d'Hiv'.* Robert Laffont, 1967.

Lévy-Osbert, Liliane. *La Jeunesse vers l'abîme.* Études et documentation internationales, 1992.

Lifar, Serge. *Ma Vie.* Hutchinson, 1965.

Loiseau, Jean-Claude. *Les Zazous.* Le Sagittaire, 1977.

Lormier, Dominique. *La Gestapo et les Français.* Pygmalion, 2013.

Lottman, Herbert. *The Fall of Paris.* Sinclair-Stevenson, 1992.

Loyer, Emmanuelle. *Paris à New York: Intellectuels et artistes français en exil, 1940–1947.* Collection Pluriel. Hachette, 2005.

Lukacs, John. *June 1941: Hitler and Stalin.* New Haven, CT: Yale University Press, 2006.

Luneau, Aurélie. *Radio Londres: Les voix de la liberté, 1940–1944.* Collection Tempus. Perrin, 2005.

Manvell, Roger, and Heinrich Fraenkel. *The July Plot.* Pan, 1964.

Marchand, Bernard. *Paris: Histoire d'une ville, XIXe–XXe siècle.* Seuil, 1993.

Marrus, Michael, and Robert Paxton. *Vichy France and the Jews.* Stanford, CA: University of Stanford Press, 1995.

Mathieu, Georges. *La Sorbonne en guerre, 1940–1944.* L'Harmattan, 2011.

Maurois, André. *The Battle of France.* Translated by J. Ludman. John Lane/The Bodley Head, 1940.

Mazower, Mark. *Hitler's Empire.* Penguin, 2009.

Meinen, Isna. *Wehrmacht et prostitution sous l'Occupation, 1940–1944.* Payot, 2006.

Ménager, Camille. *Le Sauvetage des Juifs à Paris, 1940–1944.* Mairie de Paris, 2007.

Meyer, Charles. "Obsession du ravitallement." *Les Années 40* 60 (19 December 1979): 1672–1676.

Mezzasalma, Philippe. "De la Défense du parti de la Résistance: Itinéraires de jeunes militantes communistes." *Les Cahiers de la GERME* 25 (2005): 84–96. Available as a PDF at www.germe-inform.fr/wp-content/uploads/2013/10dossier-cahiers25.pdf. Accessed 14 May 2015.

Michel, Alain. *Vichy et la Shoah.* CLD Éditions, 2012.

Michel, Henri. *La Drôle de guerre.* Hachette, 1971.

———. *Paris allemand.* Albin Michel, 1981.

———. *Paris résistant.* Albin Michel, 1982.

———. *La Libération de Paris.* Brussels: Éditions Complexe, 1990.

Milward, Alan S. *The New Order and the French Economy.* Oxford: Clarendon, 1970.

Minc, Joseph. *L'Extraordinaire Histoire de ma vie ordinaire.* Éditions du Seuil, 2006.

Missika, Dominique. *La Guerre sépare ceux qui s'aiment, 1939–1945.* Grasset, 2001.

Mitchell, Allan. *Nazi Paris.* Oxford: Berghahn, 2008.

Monchablon, Alain. "La Manifestation à l'Étoile du 11 novembre 1940," *Vingtième Siècle: Revue d'Histoire* 110 (April–June 2011): 67–81.

Montefiore, Simon Sebag. *Stalin: The Court of the Red Tsar.* Weidenfeld & Nicolson, 2004.

Mousset, Paul. *Quand le temps travaillait pour nous.* Grasset, 1941.

Muggeridge, Malcolm. *Chronicles of Wasted Time.* Vol. 2, *The Infernal Grove.* Collins, 1973.

Naïtchenko, Maroussia. *Une Jeune Fille en guerre.* Imago, 2003.

Nicholas, Lynn H. *The Rape of Europa.* Macmillan, 1994.

Noth, Erich Ernst. *La Guerre pourrie.* Montreal: Valiguette, n.d.

Oberlé, Jean. "Images anglaises," *La France libre* 3, no. 18, 17 (April 1942): 475–478.

Ollier, Nicole. *L'Éxode: Sur les routes de l'an 40.* Robert Laffont, 1970.

Omnès, René. *Pourquoi as-tu fait cela mon fils?* Les Éditions La Musse, 1991.

Ophuls, Marcel. *Le Chagrin et la pitié.* Éditions Alain Moreau, 1980.

Ory, Pascal. *Les Collaborateurs.* Collection Points Histoire. Seuil, 1976.

———. *La France allemande.* Gallimard, 1995.

Ousby, Ian. *Occupation: The Ordeal of France, 1940–1944.* Pimlico, 1999.

Ouzoulias, Albert. *Les Bataillons de la jeunesse.* Éditions Sociales, 1967.

Overy, Richard. *The Bombing War: Europe, 1939–1945.* Allen Lane, 2013.

Paris Prefecture of Police. *La Situation à Paris: Rapports de la quinzaine.* Prefecture de Police, 1939–1944.

Paxton, Robert. *Vichy France.* New York: Columbia University Press, 1982.

Paxton, Robert, Olivier Corpet, and Claire Paulhan. *Archives de la vie littéraire sous l'Occupation.* Tallandier/IMEC, 2009.

Perrault, Gilles. *Paris sous l'Occupation.* Belfond, 1987.

Peschanski, Denis. *Vichy, 1940–1944: Contrôle et exclusion.* Brussels: Éditions Complexe, 1997.

———. *La France des camps: L'internement, 1938–1946.* Gallimard, 2002.

———. "La Confrontation radicale. Résistants communists parisiens vs Brigades spéciales." http://hal.archives-ouvertes.fr/hal-00363336/fr/, 2003. The text later appeared in François Marcot and Didier Musiedlak, eds., *Les Résistances, miroir des régimes d'oppression. Allemagne, France, Italie*, 335–349. Besançon: Presses Universitaires de Franche-Comté, série historiques, 2006.

———. "Des Étrangers engagés dans la libération de la France, filés et arrêtés par des policiers français oeuvrant au service de l'occupant." In *Vingt et trois étrangers et nos frères pourtant, L'Humanité* hors série, February 2014, 14–15.

Pétain, Philippe. *Discours aux Français, 17 juin 1940–20 août 1944.* Albin Michel, 1989.

Pierquin, Bernard. *Journal d'un étudiant parisien sous l'Occupation.* chez l'auteur, 1983.

Pike, David Wingate. "The French Communists from the Collapse of France to the Invasion of Russia." *Journal of Contemporary History* 8, no. 3 (July 1993): 465–485.

Poisson, Georges. "La Guerre des statues." *Magazine 39–45*, January 2006, pp. 9–13.

Poliakov, Léon. *L'Étoile jaune.* Editions Grancher, 1999.

Polnay, Peter de. *Death and Tomorrow.* Panther, 1957 (First published by Secker & Warburg, 1942).

Poulain, Martine. *Livres pillés, lectures surveillées.* Gallimard, 2008.

Poznanski, Renée. "Avant les premières grandes rafles: Les Juifs à Paris sous l'Occupation, juin 1940–avril 1941." *Les Cahiers de l'IHTP (Institut d'Histoire du Temps Présent)* 22 (December 1992): 25–66.

———. *Les Juifs en France pendant la Seconde Guerre mondiale.* Pluriel. Hachette, 1997.

Pryce-Jones, David. *Paris in the Third Reich: A History of the German Occupation, 1940–1944.* Collins, 1981.

Quéval, Jean. *Première page, cinquième colonne.* Librairie Anthème Fayard, 1945.

Ragache, Gilles. *Les Enfants et la guerre.* Perrin, 1997.

Rajsfus, Maurice. *Les Français de la débâcle.* La Cherche-Midi, 1997.

———. *Opération étoile jaune.* Le Cherche Midi, 2002a.

———. *La Rafle du Vél' d'Hiv'.* Collection Que Sais-Je? Presses universitaires de France, 2002b.

———. *Drancy: Un camp de concentration très ordinaire, 1941–1944.* J'ai Lu, 2004.

Rayski, Adam. *Le Choix des Juifs sous Vichy.* Éditions de la Découverte, 1992.

Rayski, Benoît. *L'Affiche rouge.* Denoël, 2009.

Rayssac, Michel. *L'Éxode des musées.* Payot, 2007.

———. "Août 1944: Le train d'Aulnay-sous-Bois." *Historail*, January 2008, pp. 30–33.

Rebatet, Lucien. *Les Mémoires d'un fasciste.* Pauvert, 1976.

Régnier, Gérard. *Jazz et société sous l'Occupation.* L'Harmattan, 2009.

Rémy, Dominique, ed. *Les Lois de Vichy.* Éditions Romillat, 1992.

Richer, Philippe. *La Drôle de guerre des Français.* Olivier Orban, 1990.

Riding, Alan. *And the Show Went On.* Duckworth, 2011.

Rioux, Jean-Pierre. *La Vie culturelle sous Vichy.* Brussels: Éditions Complexe, 1990.

Rist, Charles. *Une Saison gâtée.* Fayard, 1983.

Rochebrune, Renaud de, and Jan-Claude Hazera. *Les Patrons sous l'Occupation.* Éditions Odile Jacob, 1995.

Rol-Tanguy, Henri, and Roger Bourderon. *Libération de Paris: Les cent documents.* Pluriel. Hachette, 1994.

Rossel-Kirschen, André. *Le Procès de la Maison de la Chimie.* L'Harmattan, 2002.

Rossi, A(ngelo?). *La Guerre des papillons: Quatre ans de politique communiste, 1940–1944.* Les Îles d'Or, 1954.

Rossignol, Dominique. *Vichy et les Francs-Maçons: La liquidation des sociétés secrètes, 1940–1944.* J-C Lattès, 1981.

Sabbagh, Antoine. *Lettres de Drancy.* Tallandier, 2002.

Sadoul, Georges. *Journal de guerre 39–40.* Éditeurs français réunis, 1977.

Sanders, Paul. *Histoire du marché noir, 1940–1946.* Perrin, 2001.

Sartre, Jean-Paul. "Un Pomeneur dans Paris insurgé: I., L'insurrection," *Combat,* 22 August 1944, 1–2.

———. *Situations X.* Gallimard, 1976.

———. *Lettres au Castor.* 2 Vols. Gallimard, 1983.

———. *War Diaries.* Verso, 1984.

———. *Les Carnets de la drôle de guerre.* Gallimard, 1995.

Sauvy, Alfred. *La Vie économique des Français de 1939 à 1945.* Flammarion, 1978.

Schotten, Igor de. "Juin 1940: Le bac d'un lycéen." Archives of the Paris Prefecture of Police (PPP), B^A2361 (n.d.).

Schroeder, Liliane. *Journal d'Occupation: Paris, 1940–1944.* Guibert, 2000.

Semelin, Jacques. *Persécutions et entraides dans la France occupée: Comment 75% des Juifs en France ont échappé à la mort.* Les Arènes-Seuil, 2013.

Shirer, William. *The Collapse of the Third Republic.* William Heinemann/Secker & Warburg, 1970.

———. *Berlin Diary.* Baltimore, MD: The John Hopkins University Press, 2002.

Siefridt, Françoise. *J'ai voulu porter l'étoile jaune.* Robert Laffont, 2010.

Simeone, Nigel. "Making Music in Occupied Paris." *Music Times,* Spring 2006, 23–50.

Simonin, Anne. *Les Éditions de Minuit 1942–1955.* Institut Mémoires de l'édition contemporaine, 2008.

Singer, Claude. *Vichy, l'université et les Juifs.* Collection Pluriel. Les Belles Lettres, 1992.

———. "L'Exclusion des Juifs de l'université en 1940–1941: Les Réactions." In *Les Facs sous Vichy.* Edited and presented by André Gueslin, 189–204. Clermont-Ferrand, France: Publications de l'Institut d'Études du Massif Central Université Blaise-Pascal (Clermont II), 1994.

Stéphane, Roger. *Chaque homme est lié au monde.* Éditions du Sagittaire, 1946.

Taieb, Karen. *Je vous écris du Vél' d'Hiv'.* Collection J'ai Lu. Robert Laffont, 2011.

Taliano-des-Garets, Françoise, ed. *Villes et culture sous l'Occupation.* Armand Colin, 2012.

Tandonnet, Maxime. *1940, un autre 11 novembre.* Tallandier, 2009.

Thalmann, Rita. *Mise au pas.* Fayard, 1991.

Thérive, André. *L'Envers du décor.* Éditions de la Clé d'Or, 1948.

Thomas, Edith. *Pages de journal, 1939–1944.* Viviane Hamy, 1995.

Thorval, Anne. *Paris: Les Lieux de la Résistance.* Parigramme, 2007.

Thurman, Judith. *Secrets of the Flesh: A Life of Colette.* Bloomsbury, 1999.

Tiersky, Ronald. *French Communism, 1920–1972.* New York: Columbia University Press, 1974.

Tombs, Robert, and Isabelle Tombs. *That Sweet Enemy.* Pimlico, 2007.

Tournès, Ludovic. *New Orleans sur Seine.* Fayard, 1999.

Tournoux, Raymond. *Le Royaume d'Otto: France, 1939–1945.* Flammarion, 1982.

Traube, Anna. *Evadée du Vél' d'Hiv'.* Éditions du Manuscrit, 2005.

Valland, Rose. *Le Front de l'art: Défense des collections françaises, 1939–1945.* Réunion des musées nationaux–Grand Palais, 2014.

Veillon, Dominique, ed. *La Collaboration: Textes et débats.* Livre de Poche, 1984.

———. *La Mode sous l'Occupation.* Éditions Payot, 1990.

———. *Vivre et survivre en France, 1939–1947.* Payot, 1995.

Venner, Dominique. *Histoire de la collaboration.* Éditions Pygmalion/Gérard Watelet, 2000.

Vidalenc, Jean. *L'Exode de mai–juin 1940.* PUF, 1957.

Vincenot, Alain. *Vél' d'Hiv', 16 juillet 1942: Des survivants de la rafle témoignent.* L'Archipel, 2012.

Vinen, Richard. *The Unfree French.* Allen Lane, 2006.

Vittori, Jean-Pierre. *Eux, les S.T.O.* Éditions Ramsay, 1982.

Wachman, Gabriel, and Daniel Goldenberg. *Évadé du Vél' d'Hiv'.* Calmann-Lévy, 2006.

Walter, Gérard. *La Vie à Paris sous l'Occupation.* A. Colin, 1960.

Weber, Eugen. *The Hollow Years: France in the 1930s.* Sinclair-Stevenson, 1995.

Wellers, Georges. *L'Étoile jaune à l'heure de Vichy: De Drancy à Auschwitz.* Fayard, 1973.

Werth, Alexander. *The Last Days of Paris.* Hamish Hamilton, 1940.

Werth, Léon. *33 jours.* Viviane Hamy, 1992.

Wieviorka, Annette. *Ils étaient Juifs, résistants, communistes.* Denoël, 1986.

———. *Déportation et génocide.* Hachette Pluriel, 1992.

Wieviorka, Annette, and Michel Laffitte. *À l'intérieur du camp de Drancy.* Perrin, 2012.

Wieviorka, Olivier. "La Résistance intérieure et la Libération de Paris." In *Paris 1944: Les enjeux de la libération.* Edited by Christine Lévisse-Touzé, 137–151. Albin Michel, 1994.

Winock, Michel. *La France et les Juifs.* Éditions du Seuil, 2004.

Wolf, Dieter. *Doriot: Du communisme à la collaboration.* Translated by Georgette Chatenet. Fayard, 1969.

Chronology

Entries in **bold** have a particular relevance for Paris.

1938

29 September   Signing of Munich Agreement, which ceded the northern and western parts of Czechoslovakia (Sudetenland) to Germany.

30 September   **Edouard Daladier's triumphal return to Paris.**

1939

15 March   German dismemberment of Czechoslovakia continues as German troops march into rump of Czechoslovakia; Slovakia becomes a German protectorate (16 March) and German troops occupy Bohemia and Moravia (the present Czech Republic).

4 May   Marcel Déat's article "Mourir pour Dantzig?" ("Is Danzig Worth Dying For?") published in *L'Œuvre*

23 August   Germany and the Soviet Union sign mutual non-aggression pact.

25 August   French government seizes Communist papers *L'Humanité* and *Ce Soir*.

1 September   Germany invades Poland.

1 September	French government announces general mobilisation.
2 September	French parliament votes in favour of military credits.
3 September	Germany refuses to withdraw from Poland.
3 September	France and Britain at war with Germany.
3 September	**Start of "first exodus" from Paris**.
26 September	Dissolution of the French Communist Party and its organisations.

1940

20 March	Paul Reynaud replaces Daladier as head of French government.
10 May	Germany invades Belgium, the Netherlands, and Luxembourg.
13 May	German army enters France crossing the Meuse at Dinant and Sedan.
15 May	First World War hero Marshal Philippe Pétain recalled to Paris from Madrid.
17 May	**Reynaud publicly denies French government will leave Paris**.
18 May	Reynaud appoints Pétain as deputy head of government (*vice-président du conseil*).
19 May	Reynaud dismisses General Gamelin as commander-in-chief of French armed forces; Gamelin replaced by General Weygand; **"second exodus" from Paris begins**.
3 June	**German planes bomb Renault and Citroën factories in southwestern suburbs of Paris**.
10 June	**French government announces it is leaving Paris**.
13 June	**Paris declared an "open city."**
14 June	**Germans enter Paris**.
16 June	Reynaud resigns as head of government; replaced by Pétain.
17 June	Pétain broadcasts a call for an end to the fighting.
18 June	Charles de Gaulle broadcasts an appeal from London to keep the flame of resistance alive.
22 June	Armistice agreement signed by France and Germany at Compiègne.

28 June	**Hitler visits Paris (some historians give the date as 23 June 1940).**
1 July	French government establishes itself at Vichy.
3 July	British sink French fleet at Mers-el-Kebir.
9 July	**Léon Noël appointed Vichy's official representative to Paris.**
10 July	Pétain accorded full constitutional powers by 569 out of the 649 members of the National Assembly who had managed to reach Vichy.
11 July	Pétain becomes head of the new État français, which replaces the Third Republic.
12 July	Pierre Laval appointed prime minister (*vice-président du Conseil*) and Pétain's heir apparent.
19 July	**First meeting between Otto Abetz and Pierre Laval; Noël resigns as Vichy government's representative in Paris.**
22 July	Vichy announces review of all naturalisations since 1927.
2 August	De Gaulle sentenced to death in absentia.
13 August	Vichy announces dissolution of all secret societies (targeting the Freemasons).
23 August	**General Benoît-Léon Fornel de la Laurencie appointed Vichy government's representative in Paris.**
27 August	Vichy abrogates Marchandeau law, which banned the incitement of hatred on basis of ethnicity or religion.
17 September	Rationing introduced for cheese, bread, meat.
27 September	MBF publishes definition of a Jew. Jews ordered to register at their local police station by 30 October; Jewish businesses ordered to display yellow posters declaring Jewish ownership.
28 September	Circulation of Otto List of banned books.
3 October	Vichy publishes its own definition of a Jew and bans Jews from working in the media, education, or as senior civil servants.
13 October	**Anti-Freemasonry exhibition opens in Paris; Guy Môquet arrested while distributing Communist leaflets outside the Gare de l'Est.**

20 October	German directive: all Jewish business to be placed in non-Jewish hands.
20 October	Rationing system modified to take account of age and need.
24 October	Hitler and Pétain meet at Montoire.
25 October	General Otto von Stülpnagel appointed MBF (head of the German military forces in France).
28 October	Laval appointed Vichy's foreign minister.
30 October	Pétain declares on radio that he has chosen the path of collaboration.
11 November	**Mass street demonstration against the Occupation by lycée pupils and university students.**
13 December	Pétain dismisses Laval.
14 December	**Marcel Déat arrested on Vichy's orders, then released under pressure from Germans.**
14–15 December	**Ashes of Duc de Reichstadt (*l'Aiglon*) interred in Les Invalides.**
18 December	**Fernand de Brinon replaces de la Laurencie as Vichy's representative in Paris.**
23 December	**Jacques Bonsergent executed for "an act of violence towards a member of the German army."**

1941

1 January	De Gaulle's radio appeal from London for "stay indoors protest."
1 February	Marcel Déat founds the Rassemblement national populaire (RNP).
22 March	Free French (London) launches "V" campaign.
29 March	Xavier Vallat appointed head of French Commissariat-General for Jewish Affairs (CGQJ), created six days earlier.
11 May	Inaugural meeting of the anti-Semitic Institute for the Study of Jewish Questions (IEQJ).
11 May	De Gaulle calls for day of silent protest to mark Joan of Arc's birthday.
14 May	**First *rafle* (roundup) by French police of just over 3,700 (mostly Polish) Jews in Paris.**

22 June	Germany invades the Soviet Union (Operation Barbarossa).
8 July	Public announcement of creation of a Legion of French Volunteers against Bolshevism (LVF), officially founded 8 August.
July	**German "V" campaign begins.**
19 August	**Two young Communists executed for having participated in street protest six days earlier.**
20 August	**4,232 Paris Jews, mostly from 11th arrondissement, rounded up and interned at Drancy just outside Paris.**
21 August	**Pierre Georges (Colonel Fabien) assassinates a German at Barbès-Rochechouart Métro station.**
27 August	**Paul Collette shoots and wounds Déat and Laval at LVF passing-out parade in Versailles.**
5 September	**Opening of anti-Semitic exhibition "The Jew and France."**
2–3 October	**Seven Paris synagogues bombed.**
11 October	**MBF announces the removal of statues from public squares in Paris.**
13 October	Vichy government allows "family food parcels" to be sent to cities from the countryside.
20 October	Feldkommandant Hotz gunned down in Nantes.
22 October	Twenty-seven hostages (including Guy Môquet) executed at Châteaubriant, sixteen in Nantes, and five at Fort Romainville, near Paris.
23 October	Fifty hostages executed in Bordeaux (in reprisal for shooting of German military adviser on 21 October).
21 November	**Attack on collaborationist Rive Gauche bookshop on boulevard Saint-Michel.**
28 November	**Three German soldiers killed in attack on Hôtel du Midi (18th arrondissement); curfew imposed on the whole 18th arrondissement.**
29 November	Union générale des israélites de France (UGIF) founded.
7 December	Japan attacks Pearl Harbor; United States enters the war.
8–14 December	**As punishment for anti-German attacks, MBF imposes 6 P.M.–5 A.M. curfew for whole of Seine department.**

12 December	743 Jews rounded up and interned in camp at Compiègne-Royallieu, along with 300 transferred from Drancy.
15 December	Ninety-five hostages executed at Mont-Valérien (western suburbs of Paris).
17 December	As part of reprisals, a billion franc fine is imposed on Jews of Paris.

1942

8 January–17 February	Trial of members of Musée de l'Homme Resistance group.
13 February	Carl-Heinrich von Stülpnagel replaces his cousin Otto von Stülpnagel as MBF.
23 February	Execution of seven members of Musée de l'Homme Resistance group.
1 March	Opening of exhibition denouncing Bolshevism.
3 March	Allied bombing raid on Renault factories in southwestern suburbs.
4 March	Trial opens in former Chamber of Deputies of seven members of the Communist Bataillons de la jeunesse.
15 March	Vichy passes law permitting small-scale black-market transactions.
27 March	First deportation train leaves Drancy for Auschwitz: 1,112 Jews arrested in the 20 August and 12 December *rafles* are deported; only twenty-three returned.
April	More Allied bombing raids on industrial suburbs.
7 April	Trial opens at the Maison de la Chimie of twenty-seven members of the armed Resistance.
16 April	Anti-German protest at Lycée Buffon.
18 April	Laval installed as head of the French government with responsibility for domestic and foreign policy.
6 May	Darquier (de Pellepoix) replaces Vallat as Commissariat-General for Jewish Affairs (CGQJ).
31 May	Street demonstration outside Eco food store in the rue de Buci; two French policemen shot dead.

1 June	Responsibility for security and policing officially passes from the German army to the secret police under SS General Carl Oberg.
7 June	**Jews in Occupied Zone over age of six required to wear yellow star.**
22 June	Laval's radio broadcast announcing La Relève in which he declared that he hoped for a German victory.
8 July	**Jews in Occupied Zone banned from public places and only allowed to shop between 3 P.M. and 4 P.M.**
10 July	Germans threaten severe punishment for relatives of those suspected of being involved in anti-German activities.
16–17 July	**Vél'd'Hiv' *rafle*: 13,500 Jews arrested (45 percent women, 31 percent children).**
11 August	Laval at Compiègne to greet first contingent of French POWs returning under La Relève scheme.
4 September	Laval signs new labour law empowering Vichy to send French men to work in Germany.
7–8 November	Operation Torch: Allied landings in North Africa.
11 November	Germans occupy the southern (hitherto unoccupied) zone.

1943

30 January	Founding meeting of La Milice, far-right militia headed by Joseph Darnand.
2 February	General Paulus surrenders at Stalingrad.
8 February	**Five schoolboy resisters from the Lycée Buffon are executed.**
9 February	**Deportations from Drancy to Auschwitz resume.**
16 February	Laval introduces compulsory labour conscription (Service du travail obligatoire, or STO).
4 April	**Allied bombing raid on factories in southwestern suburbs of Paris; Longchamp racecourse hit.**
27 May	**Inaugural meeting of the National Resistance Council (Conseil national de la Résistance, or CNR) uniting the main resistance movements, whose leaders unanimously recognised de Gaulle as head of the Resistance.**

3 June	Creation in Algiers of de Gaulle's Comité Français de Libération Nationale (CFLN), the French National Liberation Committee.
2 July	**Germans under Alois Brunner take over the running of Drancy camp.**
22 July	Laval signs decree allowing French citizens to join German army units "to fight against Bolshevism" (i.e., join the Waffen-SS).
July	**Drancy annexe opens within Paris, in former Lévitan furniture store in 10th arrondissment.**
August	Darnand joins Waffen-SS and swears oath of loyalty to Hitler.
August	**Formation of Paris Liberation Committee (Comité parisien de la Libération; or CPL).**
3 September	**Allied bombs hit southern districts of Paris (Montparnasse, 15th and 16th arrondissements).**
9 September	**Allied bombing raids on northwestern suburbs of Paris.**
15 September	**Another Allied bombing raid, targeting Renault.**
23–24 September	**Allied plane crashes into a department store near the Louvre.**
28 September	**FTP-MOI unit assassinates Julius Ritter, Sauckel's representative in Paris.**
November	**Second Drancy annexe opens near the Gare d'Austerlitz.**
30 December	Darnand placed in charge of law and order in French government, effective from 1 January 1944.

1944

January	**Ten-day photographic exhibition in Paris honouring the French Waffen-SS.**
6 January	Philippe Henriot appointed French minister of information and propaganda.
27 January	**Milice allowed to operate in Paris and the rest of the former "Occupied Zone."**
19 February	**Trial opens of twenty-three members of the Manouchian resistance group, dubbed "The Army of Crime" by the Germans; all executed on 21 February.**

11 March	**Discovery of piles of charred human remains at 21, rue Le Sueur, 16th arrondissement.**
March	**Third, smaller Drancy annexe opens on the rue de Bassano in the 8th and 16th arrondissements (it links avenue d'Iéna and Champs-Élysées).**
16 March	Déat becomes minister of labour in French government.
20 April	**Massive Allied bombing raid on La Chapelle area in the north of Paris, with more than 650 civilian fatalities.**
26 April	**Pétain pays his first visit to Paris since the Occupation began.**
June	Fighters from different Resistance groups across the country, including Paris, brought together under the banner of the Forces françaises de l'intérieur (FFI), whose commander-in-chief (based in London) was General Pierre Koenig.
3 June	In Algiers de Gaulle's French Committee for National Liberation (CFLN) renamed Provisional Government of the French Republic (GPRF).
6 June	Allied D-Day landings on Normandy beaches of northern France.
7 June	Darnand issues call to Milice to save France.
9 June	German SS atrocities in Tulle; ninety-nine inhabitants hanged, 150 deported.
10 June	German SS massacre of 642 villagers in Oradour-sur-Glane.
14 June	De Gaulle pays brief visit to Bayeux, first French town to be liberated.
28 June	**Philippe Henriot, Vichy minister of news and propaganda, assassinated by the Resistance.**
7 July	The Milice murder Georges Mandel, former minister of the interior in Reynaud's government.
14 July	**Bastille Day street celebrations.**
14 July	**Mass breakout attempt at La Santé prison put down by the Milice.**
20 July	German army officers' failed attempt to assassinate Hitler.
21 July	**Stülpnagel orders the arrest of all German security personnel.**

21–22 July	Brunner organises roundup of some 250 Jewish children.
31 July	Most of the children rounded up on 21–22 July deported in Convoy 77, one of the biggest to leave Drancy (1,300 deportees).
1 August	French second tank division (2e DB), led by General Leclerc, lands at Utah Beach in Normandy.
5 August	Hitler summons General Dietrich von Choltitz to Poland and appoints him as head of all the German military and police forces in Paris.
9 August	**General von Choltitz arrives in Paris.**
10 August	**Railway workers in Paris suburb of Noisy-le-Sec go on strike.**
12 August	**Métro stops running.**
14 August	**Alexandre Parodi, in Paris since 1940, appointed by de Gaulle as minister in territories not yet liberated.**
15 August	**Last deportation train leaves Drancy for Auschwitz; Paris police go on strike; 1,500 civil servants demonstrate outside Hôtel de Ville; Allied landings in the south of France.**
16 August	**Germans trap and gun down some forty young resisters in the Bois de Boulogne and 16th arrondissement.**
17 August	**Laval and other French government ministers in Paris forced to leave for Belfort under armed German escort; last day collaborationist press in Paris appears.**
18 August	**SS Oberg and SS Knochen leave Paris; CGT and CFTC trade unions call for a general strike; Rol-Tanguy prepares poster calling on Parisians to join FFI units; Radio-Paris stops broadcasting.**
19 August	**Police occupy the Prefecture of Police; armed clashes across the city; German tank fires on Prefecture of Police.**
20 August	**Cease-fire announced, but ignored by too many resisters to hold; Hôtel de Ville occupied by Resistance; René Bouffet, prefect of the Seine, arrested;** in Vichy, Pétain taken prisoner by Germans and driven to Belfort.

22 August	Allied command gives Leclerc the go-ahead to advance on Paris; **Rol-Tanguy announces the cease-fire is officially over; Rol-Tanguy issues call "Everyone to the Barricades."**
23 August	**Grand Palais on fire; BBC broadcasts news that Paris has been liberated.**
24 August	**In the evening, tanks from Leclerc's 2e DB enter Paris.**
25 August	**Remainder of 2e DB enters Paris, as does General Barton's U.S. 4th Infantry Division; Choltitz surrenders; de Gaulle arrives in Paris, delivers speech at Hôtel de Ville, and is acclaimed by crowds gathered outside.**
26 August	**De Gaulle leads triumphal march down the Champs-Élysées; de Gaulle attends mass at Notre-Dame; shooting incident at the cathedral and many others reported across the city; punitive air attack by German planes in the evening.**
28 August	De Gaulle tells Resistance leaders their job is done; members of the Resistance will be absorbed into French army.
31 August	**French government moves from Algiers to Paris.**

1945

2 April	**De Gaulle bestows upon the city of Paris the Cross of Companion of the Liberation for its role in the liberation of France.**
8 May	Germany capitulates.

Dramatis Personae

Otto Abetz   German ambassador to Paris.

Pierre Audiat   Journalist and author resident in Paris.

Berthe Auroy   Retired schoolmistress who lived in the rue Lepic (18th arrondissement). Diarist.

François Bard   Admiral and prefect of Paris police (15 May 1941–21 May 1942).

Simone de Beauvoir   Schoolteacher and aspiring philosopher/writer. Diarist.

Kurt von Behr   Head of the ERR in Paris.

Georges Benoît-Guyod   Officer recently retired in the French Republican Guard who lived in the rue de Grenelle. Diarist.

Hélène Berr   Jewish student at the Sorbonne studying English. Diarist.

Jacques Biélinky   Born in Vitebsk, Russia (present-day Belarus); naturalised French Jew; art critic, journalist, and diarist. Deported 23 March 1943.

Andrzej Bobkowski   Polish refugee employed as social worker in Paris factory. Diarist.

Karl Boemelburg   Paris head of the Gestapo, which was based in the rue des Saussaies and the avenue Foch.

Pierre Bonny   Side-kick of Henri Lafont in the "French Gestapo."

Jacques Bonsergent   Engineer who, on 23 December 1940, became the first Parisian executed by the Germans.

Micheline Bood   Paris schoolgirl living with her parents in the rue du Faubourg Saint-Honoré, near the Champs-Élysées. Diarist.

René Bouffet   Prefect of Seine department (21 September 1942–19 August 1944).

René Bousquet   Civil servant appointed by Laval in April 1942 to head French police force.

Charles Braibant   Archivist living on the boulevard Murat (16th arrondissement). Diarist.

Hermann "Otto" Brandl   Abwehr officer who made a fortune running "purchasing offices."

Alois Brunner   Sadistic Austrian SS captain placed in charge of Drancy in July 1943.

Gilbert Brustlein   Leading member of Communist Youth Battalions. Assassinated Hotz in Nantes.

Amédée Bussière   Prefect of Paris police (21 May 1942–19 August 1944).

Jacques Chaban-Delmas   Charles de Gaulle's national military delegate in Paris.

Dietrich von Choltitz   General and head of German military and police in Paris in August 1944.

Édouard Daladier   French head of government (10 April 1938–20 March 1940). Replaced by Paul Reynaud.

Theodor Dannecker   Protégé of Adolf Eichmann, head of Department of Jewish Affairs from summer 1941 to March 1942.

Joseph Darnand   French First World War hero turned pro-Nazi. Head of the Milice and appointed Vichy minister of the interior on 30 December 1943.

Louis Darquier (de Pellepoix)   Rabid anti-Semite; replaced Xavier Vallat as head of Commissariat-General for Jewish Affairs (CGQJ) in May 1942.

Marcel Déat   Former government minister and socialist who moved to the Far Right. Founder of the Rassemblement national populaire (RNP). Appointed Vichy minister of labour 16 March 1944.

Eugène Deloncle   Leader of the Mouvement social révolutionnaire (MSR) and founder of prewar Far Right terrorist group La Cagoule.

Henri Dentz   French general and commander of the Paris region (appointed 4 June 1940).

Jacques Doriot   Former Communist turned collaborationist. Founder of the Parti populaire français who served in the LVF.

Pierre Drieu La Rochelle   Collaborationist appointed editor of *La Nouvelle Revue française*.

Edmond Dubois   Paris-based Swiss journalist. Diarist.

Ferdinand Dupuy   Chief administrative officer in Paris *commissariat* (police station) in the 6th arrondissement.

Ilya Ehrenbourg   Russian author, journalist, and veteran of the Spanish Civil War.

Karl Epting   Director of the German Institute.

César Fauxbras   Author and diarist.

Jean Galtier-Boissière   Journalist, essayist, and diarist.

Maurice Gamelin   General and commander-in-chief of French army, sacked by Reynaud on 19 May 1940 and replaced by General Weygand.

Charles de Gaulle   Leader of the Free French based in London and then in Algiers. Head of Provisional Government of the French Republic.

Pierre Georges (Colonel Fabien)   Veteran of the Spanish Civil War, assassinated the first German in Paris.

Josef Goebbels   German minister of propaganda.

Hermann Göring   Hitler's deputy and head of the Luftwaffe.

Benoîte Groult and Flora Groult   Two sisters aged nineteen and fifteen, respectively, in 1940, living in the 7th arrondissement.

Albert Grunberg   A Jewish Romanian hairdresser who remained in hiding above his salon from autumn 1942 until August 1944.

Jean Guéhenno   Secondary schoolteacher and essayist living in the rue des Lilas (19th arrondissement). Diarist.

Philippe Henriot   Member of the Milice and Vichy minister of news and propaganda assassinated by the Resistance in Paris in June 1944.

Pierre Héring   General and military governor of Paris (appointed 4 June 1940).

Agnès Humbert   Member of the Musée de l'Homme Resistance group, deported into slave labour in Germany in 1942. Diarist.

Liliane Jameson   Supporter of the Free French who had a French mother and an American father. Diarist.

Joseph Joinovici   Millionaire rag-and-bone man born in Bessarabia, Romania; black-market dealer.

Ernst Jünger   Author and German army captain.

Wilhelm Keitel   German field marshal; head of the Supreme Command of the German armed forces.

Helmut Knochen   Deputy head of German security forces in Paris.

Pierre Koenig   General and commander-in-chief (based in London) of the Forces françaises de l'intérieur (FFI).

Henri Lafont (real name Henri Chamberlin)   Small-time crook who became head of the "French Gestapo of the rue Lauriston."

Roger Langeron   Paris prefect of police (17 March 1934–26 February 1941). Diarist.

Benoît-Léon Fornel de la Laurencie   French general and Vichy's official representative in Paris (23 August 1940–December 1940).

Pierre Laval   Prime minister *(vice-président du Conseil)* in the Vichy government (June 1940–13 December 1940; head of French government 18 April 1942–August 1944).

Paul Léautaud   Eccentric writer and literary critic. Diarist.

Philippe Leclerc (real name Philippe de Hauteclocque)   General and commanding officer of the Second (French) Tank Division, the first Allied contingent to enter Paris in August 1944.

Liliane Lévy-Osbert   Member of the Communist Youth Battalions.

Charles Paul Magny   Prefect of the Seine department (4 November 1940–10 September 1942).

Missak Manouchian Jewish Armenian émigré and leader of the most famous FTP-MOI group.

Camille Marchand Interim prefect of Paris police (26 February 1941–14 March 1941).

Guy Môquet Sixteen-year-old arrested distributing Communist leaflets outside the Gare de l'Est station in October 1940. Youngest of twenty-seven hostages shot on 22 October 1941 at Châteaubriant as a reprisal for the killing by the Resistance of a senior German officer at Nantes.

Léon Noël Vichy's first official representative in Paris (9–19 July 1940).

Carl Oberg Head of German security forces in Paris.

Alexandre Parodi General de Gaulle's minister in territories not yet liberated.

Philippe Pétain French marshal who replaced Reynaud as head of government 16 June 1940 and became head of the French state based in Vichy.

Marcel Petiot Doctor and serial killer who lured Parisians to their death by promising to help them leave Paris.

Fernand Picard Engineer at the Renault car works at Boulogne-Billancourt in the southwestern suburbs of Paris.

Bernard Pierquin Medical student, active member of a Catholic student organisation who took part in the liberation of Paris. Diarist.

Peter de Polnay Anglophile Hungarian living in Paris when the Germans arrived.

Paul Reynaud Succeeded Daladier as prime minister 22 March 1940. Resigned 16 June 1940 and was replaced by Philippe Pétain.

Joachim von Ribbentrop German foreign minister (1938–1945).

Charles Rist Banker and economist. Diarist.

Colonel Henri Rol-Tanguy Communist veteran of the Spanish Civil War and regional commander of the Forces françaises de l'intérieur (FFI) for the Seine and three adjacent departments.

Ernst Roskothen Presiding judge at the trial of the Musée de l'Homme Resistance group.

Heinrich Röthke Replaced Dannecker as head of the Department of Jewish Affairs in Paris in November 1942.

Georges Sadoul   Surrealist turned Communist conscript. Diarist.

Jean-Paul Sartre   Schoolteacher and writer. Diarist.

Fritz Sauckel   Appointed by Hitler to oversee labour recruitment to German factories from occupied countries.

Carl-Heinrich von Stülpnagel   Replaced his cousin Otto as MBF; implicated in July 1944 plot to kill Hitler.

Otto von Stülpnagel   Head of German armed forces in France (MBF) (25 October 1940–13 February 1942).

Edith Thomas   Writer who joined the French Communist Party in 1942. Member of the Comité national des écrivains (CNE). Diarist.

Rose Valland   Worked at the Jeu de Paume museum where she secretly tracked pillaged works of art.

Xavier Vallat   Appointed by Pétain as the first head of the Commissariat-General for Jewish Affairs on 29 March 1941.

Boris Vildé   Ethnographer and de facto leader of the Musée de l'Homme Resistance group.

Achille Villey (full name Villey-Desmeserets)   Prefect of the Seine department (5 February 1934–13 October 1940).

Alexander Werth   Paris correspondent of the *Manchester Guardian* newspaper. Diarist.

Léon Werth   author and essayist.

Maxime Weygand   French general brought out of retirement to replace General Gamelin as commander-in-chief of French armed forces on 19 May 1940. Became advocate of armistice with Germany and supporter of Pétain's National Revolution.

Count Franz Wolff-Metternich   Head of the Art Treasures Protection Unit of the MBF.

Glossary

Abwehr German military intelligence, based in the Hôtel Lutetia.

AMGOT Allied Military Government of Occupied Territories. The organisation the Allies envisaged would administer liberated France until elections could be held. De Gaulle successfully prevented the implementation of this plan.

Arrondissement An administrative district of Paris, of which there are twenty.

BS Brigades spéciales. Units within the Paris Prefecture of Police linked to the Renseignements géneraux, specialising in compiling information about Communists, tracking them down, and interrogating and torturing them before usually handing them over to the Germans.

CFLN Comité français de libération nationale. The French Committee for National Liberation, headed by de Gaulle and based in Algiers, was the precursor of the French Provisional Government (see GPRF).

CFTC Confédération française des travailleurs chrétiens. Christian trade union confederation.

CGQJ Commisariat général aux questions juives. The Commissariat-General for Jewish Affairs was created by the Vichy government on 23 March 1941 to coordinate its anti-Semitic policies in the Unoccupied and Occupied Zones.

CGT Confédération générale du travail. Communist trade union confederation.

CI Commissariat général à l'information. News and information censorship service created by the Daladier government and based in the Hôtel Continental.

523

CNR Conseil national de la Résistance. The National Resistance Council, founded in Paris on 27 May 1943 to coordinate Resistance movements within France.

COMAC Comité d'action militaire. Military leadership of the CNR.

Comintern Communist International (1919–1943), also known as the Third International.

Comité de coordination des oeuvres de bienfaisance juives du Grand Paris The Jewish Co-ordinating Committee for Charitable Works in Greater Paris was created in January 1941 following pressure from Dannecker and subsumed all Jewish welfare organisations. It in turn was absorbed into the UGIF.

Comité national des écrivains Clandestine national organisation of writers and intellectuals opposed to Nazism and the Occupation. Linked to the **Front national**.

commissariat (de police) police station.

Commissariat général à l'information French government news and propaganda service established by Daladier and based in the Hôtel Continental. See also **CI**.

CPL Comité parisien de la Libération. The Paris Liberation Committee—leadership of the Paris Resistance—founded August 1943.

2e DB Deuxième Division blindée. The Second Tank Division of the French army, led by General Philippe Leclerc.

department In 1939, France was divided into ninety departments (*départements*), with Paris in the Seine department. In 1968, the Seine department was replaced by four new departments.

Défense passive Civil defence organisation.

ERR Einsatzstab Reichsleiter Rosenberg. German group, headed in Paris by Kurt von Behr, that played a central role in pillaging artefacts owned by Jews and Freemasons.

FFI Forces françaises de l'intérieur. A national organisation formed in June 1944, bringing together in a single body the fighting units of the main Resistance groups in France. Henri Rol-Tanguy was FFI commander for Paris and the surrounding area (Île de France).

Free French Generic term for supporters of General de Gaulle.

Front national The National Front, a broad-based Resistance movement launched by the Communist Party on 15 May 1941. Not to be confused with the Far Right movement founded by Jean-Marie Le Pen in 1972.

FTP Franc-Tireurs et partisans français (French Sharp-Shooters and Partisans). An armed Communist organisation.

FTP-MOI Armed Communist organisation comprising immigrant workers.

GFP Geheime Feldpolizei. German military secret police.

GPRF Gouvernement provisoire de la République française. The Provisional Government of the French Republic, founded 3 June 1944, replacing the CFLN.

HSSuPF Höherer SS und Polizeiführer. Supreme SS and Head of Police responsible for policing and security. Post occupied by Carl Oberg.

IEQJ Institut d'étude des questions juives (Institute for the Study of Jewish Questions). A German-funded anti-Semitic meeting place and propaganda centre in Paris.

La Nueve A unit in Leclerc's 2e DB comprising Republicans from the Spanish Civil War.

LVF Légion des volontaires français contre le bolchevisme. Founded August 1941 and comprising Frenchmen who volunteered to fight alongside German soldiers on the Eastern Front.

lycée Secondary school.

mairie Town hall.

le maquis Collective term for bands of rural French Resistance fighters, or *maquisards*.

MBF Militärbefehlshaber in Frankreich. Commander of the German military forces in France, based in the Hôtel Majestic. Title refers to both the organization and to the general who headed it.

Milice Pro-Nazi paramilitary organisation founded 30 January 1943 and headed by Joseph Darnand. Specialised in tracking down Jews and STO refusers, and fighting the Resistance.

MOI Main d'oeuvre immigrée. French Communist Party organisation comprising foreign workers.

MSR   Mouvement social révolutionnaire. A collaborationist movement led by Eugène Deloncle.

NAP   Noyautage des administrations publiques. A Resistance movement operating within the French state bureaucracy.

NSDAP   Nationalsozialistische Deutsche Arbeiterpartei. The Nazi Party.

NSKK   Transport Division of the Nazi Party, known in English as the National-Socialist Motor Corps, or the National-Socialist Drivers' Corps.

PCF   Parti communiste français. French Communist Party, founded in 1920.

POW   Prisoner of war.

PPF   Parti populaire français (French People's Party), founded in June 1936 by Jacques Doriot; became one of the main collaborationist organisations.

Prefecture of Police   Paris police headquarters on the Île de la Cité.

Prefecture of the Seine Department   Based in the Hôtel de Ville and responsible for the administration of the Seine department.

RSHA   Reichssicherheitshauptamt. The Reich Security Main Office, headed by Heinrich Himmler, an umbrella secret-police organisation that included the Gestapo, devoted to fighting Germany's enemies at home and abroad.

RNP   Rassemblement national populaire. French collaborationist movement launched by Marcel Déat on 1 February 1941.

SFIO   Section française de l'Internationale ouvrière. French Socialist Party.

SNCF   Société nationale des chemins de fer français. French state-owned railway company.

SOL   Service d'ordre légionnaire. Far-right paramilitary organisation, precursor of the *Milice*.

SS   Schutzstaffel (defence corps). Originally responsible for protecting Hitler, but under Heinrich Himmler it became the most powerful security force of the Third Reich.

STCRP   Société des transports en commun de la région parisienne. Company providing public transport in and around Paris. Absorbed into the Compagnie du chemin de fer métropolitain de Paris in 1942.

STO   Service du travail obligatoire. Compulsory conscription programme supplying French workers for German factories.

TSF   French radio set.

UGIF   Union générale des israélites de France, created 29 November 1941 and subsuming all existing Jewish organisations. It was charged with "representing Jews to the public authorities," but in practice it was cynically manipulated by Germans in pursuit of their own anti-Semitic policies.

Wehrmacht   German army.

Acknowledgements

I am very grateful to the following individuals who helped me by answering my queries, passing on references, and lending or sending me books, articles, and, in one case, a DVD: Patrice Arnaud, Jean Bedel, Ian Birchall, Jean-Pierre Boulé, Marc Bouyer, Tony Bunyan, Martyn Cornick, Hanna Diamond, John Doggart, Andy Edwards, Sarah Fishman, Nigel Fountain, Alain Geismar, Fabrice Grenard, Laurent Joly, Jonathan Judaken, Andy Leak, Barbara Mellor, Jean-Claude Meunier, Guillaume Piketty, Ian Pindar, Pierre Ramel, Michel Rapoport, Keith Reader, John Reid, Renée Stewart, Rosemary Sullivan, Jacques Toros, and Olivier Wieviorka. My thanks also to the following students at the Université Inter-Ages de Créteil et du Val-de-Marne for sharing their memories of Paris during the war with me: Anne-Marie Barreau, Andrée Buvat, Denise Camdana, Gaetane Jeanine Chauvet, Robert Coutant, Guy Lamy, Jeanine Pascoe, and Anne-Marie Vivango. Many thanks to Jeffery Pike for rescuing material from my PC, which I was told was irretrievable, and for his expert help with maps and photos.

Thanks also to the staff at the British Library, the Senate House Library, and the Institute of Historical Research in London. In Paris, thanks to the staff at the Bibliothèque Sainte-Geneviève, the Bibliothèque de Documentation Internationale Contemporaine (BDIC) in Nanterre, and the Préfecture de Police—to those employed in the archives and Emmanuelle Broux-Foucaud and Françoise Gricquel in the Service de la Mémoire des Affaires Culturelles. I also wish to thank the curators at the Musée de la Résistance nationale at Champigny and the staff at the Musée du Général Leclerc de Hauteclocque et de la Libération de Paris–Musée Jean Moulin for their valuable help.

In addition, I would like to thank two others for their kindness and generosity: Antoine Sabbagh, for giving me his permission to publish the photo of Agnès Humbert, his grandmother, and Jean-Baptiste Ordas, for allowing me to reproduce images from his wonderful collection of ephemera relating to the Occupa-

tion of Paris, some of which can be seen on his website www.occupation-de-paris
.com.

Writing a book can be a lonely business, and I have been enormously helped by
the following who read and commented on parts or all of the text: Sue Gee cast a
novelist's eye over the early chapters; Simon Kitson applied his expertise to review the content; John Reid kindly read the text through the eyes of "the general
reader." Jean-Marc Benammar checked the text against his extensive knowledge
of French politics, culture, and history and pointed out where I had inadvertently
reconfigured the topography of Paris. When starting work on the book I had the
good fortune to meet Matthew Cobb, author of *Resistance*, when he was working
on another excellent book on the Liberation of Paris, which has since been published as *Eleven Days in August*. As well as sending me many, many reference materials and articles, discussing issues, and answering queries, Matthew read the
manuscript, rigorously commenting on the style as well as on what I had (and had
not) included.

Two very good friends, Monique Prunet and Marc Bouyer, lent me their apartments when I was in Paris on research trips. I am very pleased to be able to thank
them publicly for their kindness and generosity. In London, my thanks go to
Camilla Palmer and Andrew Nicol, who made a workroom available in their house
before I found space somewhere else to establish a more permanent base. That
"somewhere else" was in Jan Elson's house, where she kindly and generously allowed one room to be taken over, piled high for years with books and articles on
Paris and the Occupation, thus providing me with an oasis of calm where I
could work without interruption or distraction. Thank you, Jan.

Thanks also to John Kulka at Harvard University Press, who gave encouragement throughout the project and useful feedback on the early chapters as well as
much-valued support and guidance in the later stages.

My biggest vote of thanks is reserved for Sarah Harrison, who has supported
me practically and emotionally from the time when this book was just an idea to
its completion—even during the later stages, when she was severely incapacitated.
Her support, interest in the project, suggestions, challenging questions, and encouragement have been invaluable.

I am, of course, responsible for the final outcome and for any infelicities that
may have found their way into the text.

Index